DATE DUE

MY 27 99			
DE 18 99			
MY 2 4 00			

DEMCO 38-296

The Symphony

THE SYMPHONY
A Listener's Guide

MICHAEL STEINBERG

New York   Oxford
OXFORD UNIVERSITY PRESS
1995

Oxford   New York
Athens   Auckland   Bangkok   Bombay
Calcutta   Cape Town   Dar es Salaam   Delhi
Florence   Hong Kong   Istanbul   Karachi
Kuala Lumpur   Madras   Madrid   Melbourne
Mexico City   Nairobi   Paris   Singapore
Taipei   Tokyo   Toronto

and associated companies in
Berlin   Ibadan

Published by Oxford University Press, Inc.,
198 Madison Avenue, New York, New York 10016

Oxford is a registered trademark of Oxford University Press

Library of Congress Cataloging-in-Publication Data
Steinberg, Michael, 1928–
The symphony : a listener's guide / Michael Steinberg.
p. cm.   Includes bibliographical references
ISBN 0-19-506177-2
1. Symphonies—Analysis, appreciation.
MT125.S79   1995   784.2′184′015—dc20   95-5568

9 8 7 6 5 4

Printed in the United States of America
on acid-free paper

To my three musicians—
Jorja, Sebastian, and Adam

Introduction

When the Oxford University Press invited me to put together a collection of my program notes for publication in book form, we decided to organize it by musical genres, beginning with symphonies. This follows the plan used in the 1930s, when the Press began to publish, as *Essays in Musical Analysis,* the notes that D. F. Tovey had written over a period of many years for his concerts with the Reid Orchestra at the University of Edinburgh. (Ever since, Tovey has been the patron saint of all us program note writers.) Here, then, is a volume of essays on symphonies; another, on concertos, is forthcoming. After that, who knows?

In the early stages of planning this book, I sometimes said that deciding on the contents would be the hardest part. I was wrong, but not entirely. Of course, some decisions were hardly decisions at all: the nine Beethoven symphonies had to be included, so did the four Brahms, certain Haydns, Mozarts, Schuberts, and so on. These necessaries by themselves take a lot of room and left much less space than I should have liked for the electives. (The sensation was familiar from my years of planning programs, first for the San Francisco Symphony, later for the Minnesota Orchestra.) The absences—from the sons of Bach to Knussen and Kernis—pain me, and hope there will be a chance to make amends later. Here I must mention John Harbison, who was most helpful in the early stages of sorting out the question of what to include.

Most of these essays began life as program notes for symphony concerts. All have been revised and rewritten, sometimes slightly, often thoroughly. The following notes originally appeared in some form in the program book of the Boston Symphony Orchestra, whose program annotator I was from 1976 to 1979: Beethoven Symphonies Nos. 2, 4, 5, 7, and 9; Brahms Symphonies Nos. 1–4; Bruckner Symphonies Nos. 5, 7, and 9; Dvořák Symphony No. 8; Haydn Symphonies Nos. 64, 100, and 102; Mahler Symphonies Nos. 1–4, 9, and 10; Mendelssohn Symphony No. 4; Mozart Symphonies Nos. 35, 36, and 38; Prokofiev Symphony No. 5; Rachmaninoff Symphony No. 2; Schubert *Unfinished* Symphony; Schumann Symphony No. 4; Shostakovich Symphonies Nos. 1, 4, 5, and 8; Sibelius Symphonies Nos. 3 and 4; Tchaikovsky Symphonies Nos. 4 and 5; and Walton Symphony No. 1.

The following notes originally appeared in some form in the program book of the San Francisco Symphony, whose program annotator I have been since 1979: Beethoven Symphonies Nos. 1, 3, 6, and 8; Berlioz *Symphonie fantastique*; Bruckner Symphonies Nos. 4, 6, and 8; Copland Short Symphony (No. 2); Dvořák Symphony Nos. 6, 7, and 9; Elgar Symphonies Nos. 1 and 2; Harbison Symphony No. 2; Haydn Symphonies Nos. 86, 88, 93, 94, 97, 98, 103, and 104; Hindemith *Mathis der Maler* Symphony; Honegger *Symphonie liturgique* (No. 3) and Symphony No. 5; Ives Symphony No. 4; Mahler Symphonies Nos. 5, 7, and 8; Mendelssohn Symphony No. 3; Nielsen Symphonies Nos. 4–6; Prokofiev Symphony No. 6; Rachmaninoff Symphony No. 3; Schuman Symphony No. 6; Schumann Symphony No. 3; Sessions Symphony No. 2; Shostakovich Symphonies Nos. 7, 10, and 15; Sibelius Symphonies Nos. 5 and 6; Stravinsky Symphony in Three Movements; Tchaikovsky Symphony No. 6; and Vaughan Williams Symphony No. 5. I am most grateful to both orchestras for their permission to use this material, copyright by them in its original form. In addition, the note on Shostakovich Symphony No. 6 originally appeared in different form in the program of the Minnesota Orchestra, that on Stravinsky Symphony in C in the program of the Saint Louis Symphony. The musical excerpts from Franz Schmidt's Fourth Symphony and Stravinsky's Symphony in C are used by permission of European American Music Distributors Corporation, sole U.S. and Canadian agent for Universal Edition, A.G., Vienna, and B. Schott's Söhne, Mainz, and Schott & Co. Ltd., London.

Not least, I am forever grateful to the Boston Symphony Orchestra and to the San Francisco Symphony for having given me the opportunity to write about this music—and much else—in the first place. I want to direct these thanks more personally: to Thomas W. Morris, Executive Director of the Cleveland Orchestra but General Manager of the Boston Symphony when I worked for that orchestra, and especially to Peter Pastreich, Executive Director of the San Francisco Symphony. I first wrote program notes for Peter in 1958 when he was the Manager of the Greenwich Village Symphony and later contributed some to the program book of the Saint Louis Symphony while he was Executive Director there. He is properly demanding, generous in praise, and almost always on target in his forthright criticisms. It has also been a privilege to work for Herbert Blomstedt, the San Francisco Symphony's Music Director from 1984 to 1995, and, like Peter, a keen—and keenly critical—reader.

At both orchestras, I have been blessed with wonderful collaborators: Marc Mandel and Jean Miller Mackenzie at the Boston Symphony, and in San Francisco, Susan Feder, David Bowman, and since 1984, Laurence Rothe as program editors, and, since 1980, Katherine Cummins as Publications Managing Editor. Whatever is good in the contents of this book owes much to these remarkable people. Working with Larry and Katherine for more than a decade has been a special joy. To Katherine I am especially indebted, not only for her support, loyalty, and friendship at every turn over the years, but because she undertook to read the book in proof. Debra Podjed is another San Francisco Symphony friend, and I warmly thank her for preparing the musical examples with such care.

I have always enjoyed reading the thank-yous at the beginnings of books; it gives me even greater delight now to write some of my own. I begin by expressing my gratitude—and inevitably the expression is inadequate to the occasion—to the three people who read the book in manuscript—my wife, Jorja Fleezanis, and two dear friends, Robert P. Guter and Anne Hadley Montague. They were sharply observant, veritable founts of helpful suggestions, and always kind in cushioning their criticism in cheering comments. It is a cliché to say at this point that the problems that remain are entirely my fault because I did not unfailingly take their advice, but it is true. I am also deeply grateful to two friends and outstanding Berlioz scholars, David Cairns and Katherine Reeve, for going over my *Symphonie fantastique* essay with fine-toothed combs.

A complete list of thanks would have to be a whole intellectual and musical autobiography. That is self-evidently impossible; nonetheless, I want to begin by thanking Kenneth Hardacre, my English teacher and housemaster when I was a schoolboy in England fifty-two years ago, for first putting a volume of Tovey into my hands. I am grateful to the many people who have been encouraging and helpful about my writing over the years. Chief among these, along with friends I have already mentioned, are John Adams, Deborah Borda, David Cairns, Mary Ann Feldman, the late Malcolm Frager, John and Patricia Gidwitz, Richard Goode, David Hamilton, Garrick Ohlsson, Klaus George Roy, Patrick Smith, and Jane Steinberg. Orchestra librarians are essential components of a well-functioning orchestra, although they remain nearly invisible except to players and conductors (concertgoers get an occasional glimpse as they put out or remove music at the beginnings and ends of concerts). Program annotators constantly need their knowledge and experience, and Victor Alpert at the Boston Symphony, John Van Winkle, Donald Ontiveros, Margo Kieser, and John Campbell at the San Francisco Symphony, as well as Paul Gunther, Eric Sjostrom, and Carole Keller at the Minnesota Orchestra have been unstinting in their helpfulness.

Many others have been generous in countless ways. Arthur Cohn of Carl Fischer, Inc. provided a score of Hanson's Symphony No. 4; Susan Filler has shared the results of her research into Mahler's last illness and death; Andrew Massey, Music Director of the Toledo (Ohio) Symphony, put scores and recordings of the symphonies of Franz Schmidt at my disposal; Elisabeth Rebman and Judy Tsou of the Music Library at the University of California at Berkeley helped with the gathering of composers' signatures. Others who quickly responded to pleas for help in various matters—or in some instances helped without being aware of it—are Marshall Burlingame, Marc Mandel, and Eleanor McGourty (Boston Symphony Orchestra); James Goldsworthy (University of St. Thomas, Saint Paul, Minnesota); Jack Diether; Angela Hewitt; Donna Hewitt; Sara Honstein; Philip Huscher (Chicago Symphony); Tony Kelley (*Stagebill*); Charles Kemper; Ernst Krenek; Jim Lee; Louise Litterick (Mount Holyoke College); Paul Moor; Asadour Santourian, Francis Thevenin, and Emily Basinger (Minnesota Orchestra); Robert Winter (University of California at Los Angeles); and Harry Zohn (Brandeis University). This summary listing does not do justice to the warmth of my gratitude to them all. It saddens me that Jack Diether and Ernst Krenek are no longer here to read these words.

In the book, I occasionally take off after conductors, but, as I hope I also make clear, I have much to thank them for as well, for it often seems to me that I have learned most of what I know about the symphonic repertory at concerts and rehearsals. Many of them have also been stimulating and exciting teachers in conversation. I record with special gratitude the names of Leonard Bernstein, Herbert Blomstedt, Sir Adrian Boult, Sir Colin Davis, James Dixon, Antal Dorati, Christopher Hogwood, Erich Leinsdorf, Kurt Masur, Roger Norrington, Seiji Ozawa, Libor Pesek, Frederik Prausnitz, Kurt Sanderling, Stanislaw Skrowaczewski, Jeffrey Tate, Michael Tilson Thomas, Edo de Waart, Benjamin Zander, and David Zinman. I especially treasure the memory of a conversation with Bernstein at a party at Tanglewood in the summer of 1977. He had known me only as a critic, and as one who had not always liked his work. He had just read my program notes for the first time and, wheeling over to me, he said: "You—you have always been such a bitch to me, but now it turns out you love music." I hope that love comes across.

Bruce Phillips at the Oxford University Press in Oxford introduced me to Sheldon Meyer, his counterpart in New York, and I owe and hereby give him warmest thanks for that. As for Sheldon, I cannot say enough about what his faith in this project and his saintly patience in waiting for the delivery of the manuscript, and our friendship have meant to me. At the Press, I was fortunate to have the demanding and vigilant Leona Capeless as my editor. I also thank Andrew Albanese, who oversaw the mechanical aspects of production, Joellyn Ausanka, who has been helpful from the beginning in countless ways, and everyone else at OUP who has contributed to turning a pile of paper into a book.

The putting together of this book was also an occasion finally to understand what it *really* means when writers, in this part of a book, thank their spouses for their encouragement and forbearance. Without Jorja, it would and could not have happened. And more, through her vibrant and participating interest, she turned this labor into joy.

Edina, Minnesota   Michael Steinberg
March 1995

Contents

The Symphony

Ludwig van Beethoven

Ludwig van Beethoven was born in Bonn, twenty or so miles up the Rhine from Cologne and then an independent electorate, probably on 16 December 1770 (his baptismal certificate is dated the 17th). He died in Vienna on 26 March 1827.

A mass of images, remembrances, and ideals comes instantly to mind when we hear the word *symphony*. This mass, our idea of "symphony," has been shaped for us overwhelmingly by the nine symphonies that Beethoven composed across a quarter of a century—eight of them in thirteen years.

Beethoven's grandfather and father were musicians at the Electoral Court at Bonn, the former being the more accomplished by far. Like many a musical child in his generation, young Ludwig suffered because Mozart, his senior by fifteen years, had set alarming standards for prodigies. Beethoven was not that kind of child: he lacked the quickness, the pliability, the seductive charm. In a house that jangled with the tensions between a domineering grandfather whom he idolized, an alcoholic father, and an embittered mother, himself subjected to a brutal and uncomprehending education, he was a withdrawn, uncommunicative boy desperately hungry for love.

Nonetheless, he composed, made impressive progress at the piano, and became a competent string player. At twelve, he was deputy to his teacher, the court organist Neefe, and was part of Bonn's professional community. At sixteen, he visited Vienna and played for Mozart, who said, "Keep an eye on him, he'll make a big noise in the world some day." Five years later, Beethoven had an opportunity to show some of his music to Haydn, who had stopped at Bonn on his way to London. Haydn was impressed. The Elector was in turn impressed by Haydn's approval and decided to send his assistant organist and theater violist to study in Vienna. Beethoven set out early in November 1792. He never saw his birthplace again.

He arrived in Vienna with a stack of music he had composed in Bonn, some letters of introduction, and a plan to study with Haydn. At first, he was cautious about presenting himself to the public of the musical capital of Europe, a public in part knowing, in part merely inordinately opinionated, but, either way, demanding—in other words, a lot like the Viennese public today. Beethoven learned much from Haydn's scores and would continue to do so all his life, but the actual lessons with the master, then entering his sixties, were not a success. When it came to formal instruction, he did better with Johann Schenk, an experienced theater composer, with the famous Antonio Salieri, and with that excellent pedagogue Johann Georg Albrechtsberger, all of them more attentive than Haydn and less apt to be put off by the lackadaisical religious views, the left-wing politics, and the rough manners of the young Rhinelander.

Haydn was an uneasy presence in Beethoven's life, and it is surely no coincidence that it was during the senior master's absence in London that Beethoven signed his first contract with a publisher. In May 1795, he offered Artaria & Co. three trios for piano, violin, and cello, which duly came out that October as his Opus 1. Five months later, Artaria announced Opus 2, three piano sonatas. To keep up with demand, Beethoven published two works from his Bonn stash, but he was soon writing new works with amazing energy and industry. By the time he completed his Symphony No. 1 early in 1800, he had amassed an imposing catalogue that included ten piano sonatas, two sonatas for cello and three for violin, five string trios, and, as his most ambitious venture to that point, a set of six string quartets. He was consolidating his fame as a pianist, playing connoisseurs' music such as the preludes and fugues of Johann Sebastian Bach as well as more current repertory like Mozart's D-minor Concerto (his cadenzas for that are still played today). He raised goosebumps with his fantastic improvisations. All in all, with Mozart dead and Haydn moving gradually but surely into retirement, Beethoven had quickly established himself as the excitement center in Viennese musical life.

Symphony No. 1 in C major, Opus 21

Adagio molto—Allegro con brio
Andante cantabile con moto
Menuetto: Allegro molto e vivace
Finale: Adagio—Allegro molto e vivace

Beethoven completed his Symphony No. 1 early in 1800, having begun it the year before, and conducted the first performance at the Hofburgtheater in Vienna on 2 April 1800. He had intended to dedicate the work to his former patron and employer, the Elector of Bonn, but Maximilian Franz died in July 1801, five months before the publication of the orchestral parts. The dedication then went to Baron Gottfried van Swieten—aptly, not only because the elderly Court Librarian had been kind and helpful to the young newcomer to Vienna, but because, by introducing Haydn and Mozart to the music of Bach and Handel, he had so powerfully affected the classical style, one of whose most remarkable chapters begins with Beethoven's debut as a symphonist.

Two flutes, two oboes, two clarinets, two bassoons, two horns, two trumpets, timpani, and strings.

Woodwinds and horns, accented by plucked strings, slowly play a question-and-answer pair of chords. This is a formula that ought to end a piece, and using it to begin one is a good Haydn joke. Haydn had in fact used it a couple of times in string quartets: it is an example of what Beethoven could learn from Haydn's scores, but something one cannot imagine Haydn teaching in a lesson.

   The "answer" part of the first two chords seems not to be the answer after all, and it is only when Beethoven has given us three such cadences at different pitches that the strings, now playing non-pizzicato for the first time, allow this pleasingly mysterious introduction to emerge into clear daylight. Even then, Beethoven keeps the music exploring and moving forward with great skill until he reaches his main, quick tempo. Critics objected to Beethoven's beginning on a dissonance, which does not mean "discord"; it is simply a technical term for a chord that wants resolution to another, more stable chord. He did not care and began his next orchestral piece, the overture to the ballet *The Creatures of Prometheus*, with a more pungent version of the same harmonic ploy.

Strings alone start the perky Allegro, and when the winds enter, it is with cadences much like those at the beginning of the introduction. A new theme in a new key, the dominant, is flavorfully scored for solo wood-winds, the accompaniment being derived from the first theme. Haydn must have approved of that economy. This seems like an innocent sort of move-ment, but a minor-key dialogue of low strings and oboe quickly dispels that notion. There is a taut and adventurous development; a special feature of the recapitulation is the way those woodwind cadences that were reminis-cent of the introduction are expanded when they reappear. Rising trumpet fanfares give an appealing brightness to the coda, and the wind-biased so-nority of the whole movement is most handsome. This is not aggressively "new" music like, for example, the famous *Pathétique* Piano Sonata of 1799, but even in Beethoven's most mannerly works of the first Viennese decade, detail after detail, strategy after strategy, attest to the presence of a personality not at all like Haydn's or Mozart's, and, for that matter, to a technical command ever more equal to the task of providing that personal-ity with a voice.

The second movement is cousin, a slightly less learned cousin, to the corresponding movement in the C-minor Quartet, Opus 18, no.4, written around the same time. Beethoven clearly enjoys the fact that, unlike a string quartet, an orchestra provides drums. In that first drum passage it also gives him pleasure to accompany the 3/8 tune for flute and violins with chords in 2/8. The exposition has ended quite normally in C major. The development begins in C minor, but this is only a feint, the first real station being a quite remote D-flat major, and *fortissimo,* no less. Upon its return, the first theme gets a bouncy new counterpoint in staccato sixteenth-notes.

Beethoven calls his next movement a minuet, but apart from being the third movement of a symphony and in 3/4 time, the connection with the old French court dance is nil. Following the example of the 1790s quartets—but not symphonies—of Haydn, who also kept calling such movements minuets, Beethoven is writing a really fast one-in-a-bar scherzo: your tongue would cramp, your arm would fall off if you tried to count or beat one-two-three in each measure. The harmonic range here is wide: like the previous movement, this one demonstrates a remarkable fondness for the exotic territory of D-flat. The brief trio—a play of wind chords and string scales—is sweetly witty.

Beethoven surprises—and amuses—us by setting a slow introduction at the beginning of the Finale. In the first movement he had used a scale to make his way from adagio to allegro. Here he does the same thing, except that now he makes a joke out of it, a simple but good one that is better heard than described. Nor has he, at this point, had the last of his fun with scales in this movement. The comic beginning nicely sets the mood for a high-spirited conclusion.

Symphony No. 2 in D major, Opus 36

> *Adagio molto—Allegro con brio*
> *Larghetto*
> *Scherzo: Allegro*
> *Allegro molto*

Beethoven began his Symphony No. 2 in 1801, but did most of the work on it in the summer and early fall of 1802, completing it that October. He led the first performance at a concert in the Theater an der Wien in Vienna on 5 April 1803. His Piano Concerto No. 3 and his oratorio *Christ on the Mount of Olives* had their first outings on the same occasion, and the program also included the Symphony No. 1. The dedication is to Prince Carl von Lichnowsky, one of Beethoven's most devoted friends and patrons, to whom the composer had already dedicated his piano trios, Opus 1.

Two flutes, two oboes, two clarinets, two bassoons, two horns, two trumpets, and strings.

The year of the Second Symphony, 1802, was the beginning of a period of unparalleled fertility for Beethoven. Aware of having entered a special time, he wrote: "For a while now I have been gaining more than ever in physical strength and in mental strength, too. Every day I come closer to my goal, which I can sense but don't know how to describe." To another friend he wrote: "I live only in my notes, and with one work barely finished, the other is already started; the way I write now I often find myself working on three, four things at the same time."

Energy for work and for life was limitless. If, inescapably aware of his advancing deafness, Beethoven knew the despair that speaks in the will he wrote at Heiligenstadt in October 1802—"as the leaves of autumn fall and are withered—so likewise has my hope been blighted. . . . Even the high courage—which has so often inspired me in the beautiful days of summer—has disappeared"—he also knew the state of mind in which he could say that he would "seize fate by the throat." And the composer who commanded the tragic accents of the Third Piano Concerto and who would soon begin to sketch the wild new music of the Fifth Symphony could also turn from such visions to the lyricism, the wit, the easy and playful energy of the Symphony No. 2 in D.

Beethoven introduced his new symphony on 5 April 1803, Tuesday of Holy Week. The rehearsal that day—it was the only rehearsal for that long and demanding program—had gone nonstop from 8:00 a.m. until 3:00 p.m.; Beethoven himself had been awake since before five, when his pupil, Ferdinand Ries, had discovered him sitting up in bed copying trombone parts. Mid-afternoon, Beethoven's patron, Prince Lichnowsky, sent out for cold-cuts and wine, stoked up the exhausted players and singers, and asked them to run through the oratorio "just one more time."

Ignaz von Seyfried, the young conductor at the Theater an der Wien who had been recruited to turn pages for Beethoven in the concerto and who had sweated bullets trying to decipher the composer's impossible manuscript, reported that all retired afterwards to "a jovial supper." Well might it have been jovial. The box office, at double and triple normal prices, had been terrific, and the reviews, which would be mixed, were not in yet. When they did come, the Second Symphony was compared, not to its advantage, to the already popular First. (But now watch for the reviews of the Third!) One critic commented that "the First Symphony is better than the more recent one because it is developed with lightness and is less forced, while in the Second the striving for the new and surprising is more apparent." Whatever he thought of the new symphony, the reviewer was right in noting a world of difference between it and No. 1. We always think of the *Eroica* of 1803–04 as Beethoven's great breakthrough symphony, which in many ways it is; nonetheless, the distance between the Second and the *Eroica* is not a lot bigger than that between the First and Second. At the time of the Second Symphony, Beethoven spoke of setting out on a fresh path. Artists often say such things for purposes of propaganda or even to cheer themselves along, but this declaration of Beethoven's is one to take seriously.

Beethoven begins with a slow introduction, one without precedent in sheer size. In the opening Adagio of the First Symphony, Beethoven had followed Haydn's practice of compressing much dramatic event into few notes. Now, seeking to create something spacious and varied, he turned to Mozart for a model, specifically to the *Prague* Symphony, which is in the same key of D major. Not just the festive grandeur of the two introductions and the amazing richness and range of material, but many details of gesture and harmonic strategy reveal their kinship. Both begin with a loud affirmation of the keynote and later include a lyric melody which is interrupted and then resumed; extended play with a figure based on a turn; surprising emphasis on B-flat major; a dramatic arrival on D minor; and finally a dominant pedal against which the upper voices create considerable harmonic tension. Changing both order and proportion, Beethoven of course does not follow Mozart slavishly. I do not know a better pair of examples from which to see how one great composer learns from the work of another. Beethoven's introduction to the Second Symphony encompasses large and bold harmonic excursions, as well as comprehending a wide range of musical characters, from pliant lyricism to the stern D-minor unison *fortissimo* that so startlingly anticipates the Ninth Symphony.

After mounting suspense—that big unison proclamation is followed by ten measures anchored to the dominant, A—the introduction spills into a quick movement of extraordinary verve. There is even something fierce in its high spirits. We get fair warning when the opening theme, heard first in an excited *piano,* is repeated *forte* by the full orchestra and at once rushes up to a sharply accented C-natural, a note as contradictory as possible to the prevailing D major. Beethoven being Beethoven—that is, an artist always bent on making even the most implausible events organic—this C-natural turns out to be not just an ornery detail but a purposeful disruption bearing the seed of remarkable possibilities. What happens in this instance is that Beethoven revisits two of the most attention-grabbing features of the introduction, his surprise landings on B-flat major and D minor. Another hint for the future is the strong and unexpected emphasis on F-sharp in the second, march-like theme: more of that in a moment. The music proceeds in a mixture of innocence and unpredictability. The movement is spaciously laid out, something we might not immediately notice because of the very quick tempo; repeating the exposition, as Beethoven asks, also helps our perception of scale.

The development starts with further exploration of D minor, and you hear plenty of B-flats and C-naturals. The other big harmonic destination is F-sharp minor, a follow-up to that emphasis on F-sharp in the march theme. This F-sharp also provides the door—one we never spotted in the wall—through which Beethoven plunges into the recapitulation. Haydn, had he known this piece and were he not still too consumed by jealous irritation, would have been proud of his former pupil for that stroke.

That earlier disruptive element, the C-natural, has its day when Beethoven uses it to precipitate an astonishingly extended, harmonically active, fiery coda. With its fifty-six measures, this coda is two-thirds the length of the development (eighty-one measures) and of the recapitulation (eighty-seven measures) and it has the force and the harmonic tension of a second development. It is full of implications of D minor—full, in other words, of B-flats and C-naturals—and reaches a crest in an extraordinary passage in which the bass rises by chromatic steps through more than an octave.

Ex. 1

This provides the momentum for the final affirmation of D major. Almost to the end, Beethoven whips up excitement with fierce off-beat accents.

The Larghetto brings a sweetness that is new in Beethoven's language. The music unfolds in a leisurely way that seems far from the worlds of both Haydn and Mozart. It does point to the future, though: what would Schubert have done without this music to lean on? With respect to interpretation I have often thought that this must be one of the most difficult movements in the nine Beethoven symphonies, something I measure not by how much it makes the conductor and the orchestra sweat, but by the likelihood of hearing a convincing performance. It seems at first blush to be all A-major smiles, but there is more variety here, even an element of gently humorous capriccio, that most conductors either do not find or dare not play with.[1]

In the First Symphony, Beethoven still called his very fast one-in-a-bar third movement a minuet; here he admits that he is writing a scherzo, actually using that word in his tempo/character designation. We should note that it flirts with D minor and makes a delightfully surprising and quite extended excursion to B-flat major. The trio is oboe-tinged and pastoral. This sonority and the melody's smooth contour have often evoked comparisons to the corresponding page in the Ninth Symphony; the tempi, however, are very different, that in the Ninth being much faster. The most striking feature of this trio is the huge and boldly bizarre emphasis on F-sharp. It is as though a speaker had suddenly gone mad and got ever more frantically stuck on a single word: "When to the sessions of sweet silent thought/I summon up remembrance *remembrance* **remembrance** REMEMBRANCE *REMEMBRANCE* **REMEMBRANCE REMEMBRANCE.**"

---

[1] Erich Kleiber's boldly flexible recording from the early 1930s gets it exquisitely right and is worth seeking out.

It takes a very loud call to order from the timpani and all the winds to get things back on track.

The finale begins with a gesture of captivating impudence, a two-note flick up high, followed by a dismissive growl down below. This has splendid comic possibilities, and Beethoven neglects none of them. There are two contrasting themes, one dolce and richly scored, the other elegant and playful. Again, Beethoven does not let us forget either D minor or F-sharp.

In the first and second movements we have watched Beethoven work on an unabashedly broad scale. The Scherzo is compact by comparison, and our first impression of the finale is also that its procedures are highly compressed. In contrast to the first movement, for example, there is no repeat of exposition (another good reason to be sure to observe the one in the first movement). We would probably be quite satisfied if the finale met our initial expectation of coming quickly to a bright close after the recapitulation. We would then have heard a symphony with proportions rather like those of one of Haydn's late ones for London, with third and fourth movements far briefer than the first and second.

But Beethoven has something quite different in mind. Propelled at first by the little dolce theme that, slyly, he had been careful to keep out of much prominence earlier, a coda gets under way and grows like a genie let out of a bottle. We have heard in the first movement how bold Beethoven can be with a coda. Now he goes still further, for this one grows to the point of accounting for more than a third of the movement. That C-natural and F-sharp have a lot to do in the coda goes almost without saying. The *Eroica* is open revolution; the Second is revolution within the conventions of eighteenth-century high comedy.

Ten years later, in his Eighth Symphony, the greatest symphonic comedy not by Haydn, Beethoven will give us an even wilder show of the tail wagging the dog. That finale, and this one, are the two most wonderful Beethoven invented in his nine symphonies.

Symphony No. 3 in E-flat major, Opus 55, *Sinfonia eroica*

Allegro con brio
Marcia funebre: Adagio assai
Scherzo: Allegro vivace
Finale: Allegro molto—Poco Andante—Presto

The earliest sketches were probably written in the summer or fall of 1802, but Beethoven did most of the work on this symphony in the second half of 1803, completing the score early in 1804. Private performances were given at the palace of Prince Franz Joseph von Lobkowitz, beginning in the second half of 1804. Early in 1805, the symphony was heard in a semi-public Sunday morning concert series presented by the bankers Würth and Fellner; the conductor was Franz Clement, who would later be the first soloist to play Beethoven's Violin Concerto. Beethoven himself conducted the first public performance, which was given on 7 April 1805 in the Theater an der Wien, Vienna. The dedication, after much turmoil, was to Prince Lobkowitz, a generous patron of Beethoven's and the recipient of a great series of dedications, including the Opus 18 and Opus 74 string quartets, the Fifth and Sixth symphonies, the Triple Concerto, and the song cycle *An die ferne Geliebte* (To the Distant Beloved).

Two flutes, two oboes, two clarinets, two bassoons, three horns, two trumpets, timpani, and strings.

In May 1804, Napoleon had himself crowned Emperor. He had been acceptable to Beethoven as a military dictator as long as he called himself First Consul, but now the disappointed and angry composer scratched out the words "intitolata Bonaparte" on the title page of his newly completed Third Symphony. The erasure, accomplished with a knife, was so violent that it left a hole in the paper.

Actually, Beethoven blew hot and cold on the issue of Napoleon. Three months after he had taken the knife to the title page, he told the publisher Breitkopf & Härtel in Leipzig that this symphony, which he was offering them along with the oratorio *Christ on the Mount of Olives*, the Triple Concerto for piano, violin, and cello, and three piano sonatas (including the *Waldstein* and *Appassionata*), "is really called 'Ponaparte' [sic]." In 1810 he considered dedicating his Mass in C to the Emperor, then at the zenith of his power. At some point, too, Beethoven penciled the words "Geschrieben auf Bonaparte" (Written on Bonaparte) on the mutilated title page of the Symphony No. 3. But the first printing in October 1806 tells us only that this is a "sinfonia eroica," a "heroic symphony . . . composed to celebrate the memory of a great man."

"I'll pay another kreuzer if the thing will only stop," a gallery wit called out at the public premiere of the *Eroica*. (The offer was not generous: it is about one-fourth what the man would have paid for his ticket.) One critic conceded that in this "tremendously expanded, daring, and wild fantasia" there was no lack of "startling and beautiful passages in which the energetic and talented composer must be recognized," but felt that the work "lost itself in lawlessness. . . . This reviewer belongs to Herr Bee-thoven's most sincere admirers, but he must confess that in this composi-tion he finds too much that is glaring and bizarre, hindering greatly one's grasp of the whole, and a sense of unity is completely lost." (Happily this champion of law and order found that satisfaction in another E-flat sym-phony on the same program, one by Anton Eberl, a Viennese composer and pianist who may have studied with Mozart.)

Another critic, deploring the composer's ways of achieving "a certain undesirable originality," pointing out that "genius proclaims itself not in the unusual and fantastic, but in the beautiful and sublime," declaring the new symphony with its "inordinate length" to be "unendurable to the mere music-lover," expressed the wish that

> Herr van B. would employ his admittedly great talents in giving us works like his symphonies in C and D, his ingratiating Septet in E flat, the inge-nious Quintet in C, and others of his early works that have placed him for ever in the ranks of the foremost instrumental composers. . . . The public and Herr van Beethoven, who conducted, were not satisfied with each other on this evening. The public thought the symphony too heavy, too long, and himself too discourteous because he did not nod his head in recognition of the applause which came from a portion of the audience. For his part, Bee-thoven found that the applause was not strong enough.[2]

Having no difficulty ourselves finding the *Eroica* "beautiful and sub-lime," we slip easily into a position of feeling superior to this critic. We would do well at this point to remember that we are not likely to find it "unusual and fantastic" either—which, if so, is very much our loss. When it comes to maintaining a sense of the "unusual and fantastic" or just of freshness, we are not much helped by conductors, particularly the ones whose attitude of reverence and awe before A Great Classic leads them into "monumental" tempi at which the length of the work easily becomes "inordinate," if not "unendurable." Of course the rare conductor of genius like Furtwängler or Klemperer can make a convincing case for a "monu-mental" *Eroica*. More valuable by far is the fiery performance—at Beetho-ven's tempi or something close to them—that can give us an experience like the one the audience in the Theater an der Wien in 1805 must have had, that of an electrifying, frightening encounter with revolution, with a force sufficient to blast doors and windows out of the room. Once in a while that happens, but it is rare. Too rare.

In any event, Beethoven had given his public, lay and professional,

[2] From *Der Freymüthige*, quoted in *Thayer's Life of Beethoven*, edited and revised by Elliot Forbes (Princeton: Princeton University Press, 1964).

plenty to be upset about: a symphony half again as long (even at the right tempi) as any the audience would have ever heard before; one unprecedented in its demands on orchestral virtuosity, demands that were almost certainly inadequately met; unprecedented as well in the complexity of its polyphony, in the unbridled force of its rhetoric, in the weirdness of details like the famous "wrong" horn entrance in the first movement (of which more later).

The *Eroica* begins with two forceful chords of E-flat major (but only *forte*, not *fortissimo*). They set key and tempo as well as giving us an idea of the character of the music. When the cellos start the "real music," what they play is nothing more than an E-flat chord tipped on its side, as it were—made horizontal and turned into a melody. The agitated syncopations in the first violins suggest the possibility of trouble, and indeed this anchored security of E-flat major does not last. Less than ten seconds into the work, the cello line is derailed, slipping to a totally alien C-sharp, upon which Beethoven builds a diminished-seventh chord, whose special usefulness resides in its open-endedness. In other words, it can be a junction to many destinations. In this instance, since this is after all the beginning of the piece, Beethoven returns swiftly to E-flat, but something has happened: our sense of consonance and home is no longer sure, and this dramatic (though quiet) intrusion of dissonance and ambiguity so early in the game is a clue that the horizons will be broad and that complex events lie ahead.

For a few moments everything proceeds calmly as the cello melody spreads through the orchestra and is beautifully expanded. But almost immediately, having already disturbed melodic regularity and harmony, Beethoven even more radically disturbs the rhythm with explosive off-beat accents that superimpose a two-beat pattern onto the 3/4 measures.

As we continue to listen, we sense another seeming contradiction: the music moves with exciting concentration and at high speed, yet it is amazingly filled with unhurried event. Many and diverse musical characters pass before us. The move to a new key—B-flat major, the dominant—is safely accomplished and triumphantly affirmed. The symphony's first theme was literally down to earth in its steady downbeats. The new one heard now presents a completely different sort of rhythmic pattern: a long series of upbeats lead to a crest on what would normally be a weak third beat. When the phrase is repeated, the accompaniment adds new complications of its own, and all that dissolves in a series of ever weaker afterbeats.

The music gathers new energy, but again Beethoven introduces his off-beat accents and finally disrupts the gait completely with a fierce sequence of sharply emphatic chords, separated by silences, and dissonant enough to make even more telling the effect of their metrical displacement. This disruption nicely undoes our sure feeling that we know where we are going, and so the exposition ends in a mix of firmness and uncertainty, the former produced by the emphatic rhetoric, the latter by everything else.

The beginning of the development is hushed but hardly quiet. Harmonically, the music is in a state of unrest, and a growing density of counterpoint adds to our sense of agitation. Familiar ideas are so transformed as to seem like new themes. The dissident syncopations from the end of the exposition are picked up and heightened with harmonic clashes that still shock.

This development has enormous sweep. It is also more than half again as long as the exposition, which is a good reason to observe the repeat of the exposition that Beethoven asks for. Worth noting as well is the way instrumental sonorities themselves become a means of building tension— for example, the series of woodwind chords so precariously suspended in the air as Beethoven enters the final phase of preparation for entrance into the recapitulation.

Three things now happen at the same time: the rate of harmonic change becomes very slow, the surface action speeds up, and the dynamic level drops by degrees from *fortissimo* to *pianissimo*. Violins, alternating with woodwinds and horns, first approach, then actually play, at least part of the dominant-seventh chord. The procedure is agonizingly slow, the music on the edge of the inaudible. All this generates an uncanny feeling of suspense. We are on the very doorstep of home. While the violins, now *pianississimo*, tremble on B-flat and A-flat, a horn, as though unable to bear the waiting any longer, sounds the first notes of the principal theme. What has happened is that the horn has begun the recapitulation while the strings are still preparing for it. Tonic and dominant collide. At the rehearsal, one of Beethoven's brightest students, sitting with the composer, exclaimed in anger at the hornist's "mistake." The clash arouses the orchestra, which gives us two strong measures of the dominant seventh, after which the recapitulation really begins.

Now we can also learn something more about the wonderful possibilities of the diminished-seventh chord. As at the beginning of the movement, the cellos play the melody that is really a chord of E-flat major. In the exposition, the chord produced by the cellos' derailment to C-sharp led immediately back to E-flat so that the music could continue almost as though nothing had happened. Now that same diminished-seventh chord reappears on schedule, but this time the C-sharp descends one more step to C-natural. This opens a door to F major, a key that Beethoven has miraculously managed to save for this moment, and it is there that a solo horn sings a wonderfully poetic variant of the first melody. But Beethoven goes farther. One more unexpected harmonic turn sends the music to an even more remote key, D-flat major, where the flute echoes what the horn just played, but in an aura still more Romantically magical. It is a fantastic idea, to *destabilize* the harmony at the very point where you expect every move to be focused on *restabilizing* it after the wide-ranging adventures of the development. No less extraordinary is Beethoven's fancy of making this moment, where usually everything says "Enough of roaming, now we get on with it," one of musing and dream. The effect, furthermore, is the more stunning in the context of such fiery and forward-thrusting music. Only after these excursions—brief by the clock, but immense in their expressive effect—does Beethoven really settle in E-flat and proceed with the recapitulation.

The coda brings a last series of major surprises. In the first and last movements of the Second Symphony, Beethoven had discovered how to come close to making the tail wag the dog. Here, not surprisingly, given the huge scale on which the music has unfolded, the coda, only a few measures shorter than the exposition and the recapitulation, is again a major part of the design. The structural purpose of a coda is to finally affirm the harmonic center and, so to speak, settle the music. The coda here accomplishes this magnificently; at the same time, it proffers so much action that we almost hear it as a second development. This is settling and unsettling at the same time, adding one more ingredient to the *Eroica*'s many and bold contradictions.

Beethoven's entrance into this coda is an amazing moment within an amazing symphony. The recapitulation has done its job of re-establishing E-flat major, and the coda begins with a quietly confident statement of the opening phrase in that key. At this point Beethoven hushes the music down to *pianissimo* and then simply picks the phrase up and sets it down in another key: this is D-flat major, which played so special a role at the beginning of the recapitulation but is quite remote from E-flat. There, in D-flat, he repeats the opening phrase, this time in a richly scored *forte*. But this is not enough. Once more Beethoven picks the phrase up bodily, this time setting it down in C major and *fortissimo*. Thus, in two gestures and about eight seconds, he undoes all the structural work of the recapitulation.[3] Now the task of the coda is to undo the damage it itself has wrought, to get back to E-flat and really salt it down, and this is something Beethoven of course accomplishes with immense élan and consummate sense of timing.

Next, in C minor, comes a Funeral March for the hero (whom we

---

[3] The effect here of making a drastic harmonic move at a most unexpected moment and then topping it with another parallels that of the poetic horn and flute solos at the beginning of the recapitulation.

have probably forgotten in the musical excitement of the first movement). It begins in strings, *pianissimo* and sotto voce, but the instrumental color most dramatized in this movement is that of the oboe, a good instrument for mourning. Its first solo is accompanied by a symbolic drumming figure in the strings.

Beethoven lays this music out on the grandest possible scale and in doing so provides bold departures and shifts of tone. The first of these consists of a section in C major that contains within itself the contrast between its gentle beginning and a heroic trumpets-and-drums climax. When the original march music resumes, it is diverted almost immediately into a fugal section. Once again, as he does in the first movement's development, Beethoven uses counterpoint to produce exceptional intensity.

Eventually the music comes to rest in G minor, and there, again sotto voce, the violins attempt to start the first theme. Faltering, they find themselves stranded and isolated on a high A-flat. At that point the cellos and basses fiercely seize A-flat with an air of "*we* know where to go with this note." Persistent quick triplets agitate the air, and it is in this restless atmosphere that the last full statement of the opening theme is embedded. Beethoven carries the march to one more climax. Again he seems to run aground on A-flat. This time it turns out to be the dominant of D-flat, and there, with a new lyric idea, he moves into the coda.

Now comes the most radical touch of all, one probably incomprehensible to most people at the first performance. The stay in D-flat was brief, and the music is soon back in C minor. For a moment Beethoven returns to the phrase he had used at the beginning of the movement to prepare the first return to the theme of the march. This seems to be the idea here as well, only now the line breaks apart, sobbing, stammering, disintegrating. We can make out the theme, sotto voce though it is, but we hear it a few notes at a time, sundered by pauses. At the end, over a final drumming in the cellos and basses, the woodwinds utter a last despairing cry.[4]

The Scherzo has a mad coiled-spring energy, an impression that owes

---

[4] Hector Berlioz was a wonderful writer about music as well as a great composer, and his essay on Beethoven's symphonies, published in a collection called *A travers chants*, makes stirring reading. For Berlioz the premature horn entrance in the first movement is a caprice, a bizarrerie, and he comes to the conclusion that "ce caprice est une absurdité." He writes that in general the public tends to resist the first movement, which he himself admires greatly (except for the puzzling caprice). On the other hand, audiences share his own emotion upon hearing the Funeral March, which for him is the counterpart of the funeral procession of Pallas in Book X of *The Aeneid*. Its strange close he finds "profoundly moving. The theme of the march reappears, but in fragments separated by silences and with no accompaniment except for three pizzicato notes of the basses. And when the tattered fragments of the mournful melody, alone, naked, shattered, erased, have collapsed, one after one, on the tonic chord, the wind instruments emit a cry, the last farewell of warriors to their comrade in arms."

much to the prevalence of *piano* and *pianissimo*. The trio is a virtuoso turn
for the horn section. When the Scherzo itself returns, Beethoven introduces another of his violent metrical twists, cutting across the quick three-
in-one gait with a series of slashing one-twos. The coda, though brief,
is powerful.

A final and startling newness in the *Eroica* is the way the center of
gravity is shifted from the first movement to the last. Or almost. This is a
structural and psychological innovation of Beethoven's to be more fully
developed in the Fifth and Ninth symphonies. It becomes an essential feature of symphonic design for most of his successors from Schubert to Shostakovich. To put matters into perspective, it should be noted that the
Eroica is not an absolutely radical departure in this respect. As we have
seen, Beethoven had already made a powerful move in this direction in his
Second Symphony, and for that matter the possibilities of such a shift are
adumbrated in Mozart's *Jupiter* (1788). But even to the most history-
minded listener, the *Eroica*, with its Finale that is not just an ending but
a culmination and a place of resolution for an enormous range of accumulated tensions and questions, comes across as a new sort of symphony.

Facing a new challenge, Beethoven turned to old music; that is, he
made for this Finale a set of variations on a theme he had used three times
before: in a group of contradances in 1800–1801, soon afterward in the
finale of his ballet *The Creatures of Prometheus*, and in 1802 in Fifteen
Variations and a Fugue for Piano, Opus 35 (often called the *Eroica* Variations).

The bass of Beethoven's contradance/*Prometheus* theme is simple,
sturdy, easily grasped, remembered, and identified. The melody up above
shares these characteristics.

Ex. 1

It is also readily subject to transformation and decoration, though it has a
sufficiently clear profile to keep it recognizable no matter what happens to
it. Beethoven's first and perhaps most remarkable discovery in his 1802
Piano Variations was that the bass all by itself, in spite of its neutrality,
has attractive possibilities. In that work he presents us first with the bass

and three variations upon it; only then does he reveal it for what it is, the accompaniment to the "real" theme.

In the symphony, Beethoven follows his own example, but since this is a work on a much larger scale than the Piano Variations, he provides a grander, more rhetorical introduction or "frame." After the witty exploration of the possibilities of the bass alone comes a powerful set of variations on the combined melody and bass.

In the Piano Variations he had wrapped it all up with a fugue. Now he does something subtler. Instead of making a separate chapter of his excursion into polyphonic style, he infuses his variations with polyphony throughout their course. The vitality of texture this gives him is one of the chief sources of propulsive energy in this finale. Among the non-fugal variations are a D-major virtuoso number for violins and flute, and a gypsy dance in G minor.

True to classical tradition for variations, Beethoven slows the tempo near the end, but where in the piano work his largo episode is a lovely lyric outpouring, the slow variations here are an apotheosis, a climax of towering force. (This kind of climax is new, and the whole nineteenth century lived on it.) Carefully, Beethoven dismantles this structure: the music is almost an echo of the "disintegration" of the Funeral March. Then he resumes speed—returns in fact to a quasi-variation of the initial "frame"—to close, to fulfill his "heroic symphony" in triumphantly affirmative noise.

Symphony No. 4 in B-flat major, Opus 60

Adagio—Allegro vivace
Adagio
Allegro vivace
Allegro ma non troppo

Beethoven composed his Symphony No. 4 in the summer and early fall of 1806. It was first performed in March 1807 at a private concert at the Vienna town house of Prince Franz Joseph von Lobkowitz, the *Coriolan Overture* and the Piano Concerto No. 4 receiving their premieres on the same occasion. The dedication is to Count Franz von Oppersdorff, a Silesian nobleman and occasional patron with whom Beethoven was on friendly terms.

Flute, two oboes, two clarinets, two bassoons, two horns, two trumpets, timpani, and strings.

To Robert Schumann, the Fourth Symphony was "a slender Grecian
maiden between two Nordic giants," but if we can accept that image at all
we must add that this maiden is an Atalanta in her springy athleticism. It
is true that Beethoven's even-numbered symphonies are generally more lyrical, less aggressive than their odd-numbered neighbors. People who plan
orchestra programs also know that, except for the *Pastoral,* the even-
numbered ones do less well at the box office. It is dead wrong, though, to
play down or to hear past the strength of these pieces, particularly the
Fourth and Eighth symphonies, just as it is a form of deafness not to hear
the strength in Haydn and Mozart, and to treat their symphonies as charming curtain-raisers.

The Fourth Symphony is contemporaneous with the Fifth; more precisely, Beethoven's work on the Fifth brackets that on the Fourth. The
English composer Robert Simpson writes illuminatingly about the relationship between the two works:

> [The B-flat-major Symphony] is highly compact, as the C-minor was
> going to be, yet lighter in character, as if Beethoven, unsure how to release
> the thing that roared in his head like a caged tiger, turned his attention to
> less obstreperous inhabitants of his extraordinary domain. If the *Eroica* is like
> a noble stallion, the C-minor and B-flat symphonies might be thought of as
> belonging to the cat family, the one fierce, the other lovable, but both shar-
> ing compact suppleness of movement, a dangerous lithe economy that makes
> them akin and, together, different from their predecessor. The Fourth be-
> longs to the Fifth—and never so much as in the Stygian darkness of its
> introduction, abruptly obliterated by vivid light.[5]

It is also interesting to compare the very different openings of the
Fourth and Fifth symphonies and to discover that they are close cousins.
Each is a sequence of descending thirds.

Ex. 1

---

[5] Robert Simpson, *Beethoven Symphonies* (Seattle: University of Washington Press, 1970).

Ex. 2

The key signature says B-flat major, but the music is really in B-flat minor. The most musical of the guests at the Lobkowitz Palais in 1807 would have been more aware than most of us today of just how slowly this music moves—not so much in terms of notes per minute (which most conductors today ration out more slowly than Beethoven's time signature and metronome mark indicate) as in the passage of events. The harmony nearly stands still, and the effect of suspended motion is underlined by the *pianissimo* that lasts—as Beethoven reminds us four times—unbroken through the first twelve measures.

These twelve measures lead us, with exquisitely wrought suspense, back to the beginning. This time the five octaves of B-flat that were the symphony's first sound are played just a bit more emphatically than before, but the continuation is the same, a *pianissimo* expansion outward from G-flat. The effect of this G-flat as a point of arrival is delicately dissonant and unstable. The first time, Beethoven resolves it quite normally by going a half-step down to F, the note that exerts the most powerful homeward pull to B-flat. Thus, in spite of its strange wanderings, the music is brought back into the orbit of the home key.

Ex. 3

The second time, however, Beethoven treats the G-flat as though it were in no need of resolution, and the music continues by surrendering to the magnetic pull of G-flat, which is in the direction of C-flat.[6]

---

[6] Because C-flat major entails so many accidentals and is such a nuisance to read, Beethoven writes this passage in B major rather than in C-flat. Later in the movement, and for the same reason of convenience, he also treats C-flat and B (likewise G-flat and F-sharp) as though they were the same note. On the piano they are the same note, but in theory they are different and string players can make that subtle distinction.

Ex. 4

This, in the context of a universe whose center has been defined as B-flat, comes across as an absolutely reckless excursion.

Beethoven finds his way back to the threshold of his proper harmonic home—not, of course, without adventure and suspense—and the first entrance of trumpets and drums helps push the music into a quick tempo.[7]

One other detail in the introduction is worth pointing out. Beethoven often likes to go to the harmony you expect him to go to, but to get there just a bit sooner than you think he will. Here, after his surprise exploration of G-flat, you clearly sense that he is feeling his way back to B-flat; however, when the chord of B-flat finally arrives, it does so not on the downbeat, which is where you expect a major harmonic change to occur, but on the preceding upbeat. The effect is that of a syncopation, and for a moment you almost feel that you should change step:

Ex. 5

The material in the Allegro vivace is of almost studied neutrality. (The same could be said of the introduction.) The life of this ebullient music resides in the contrast between those passages where the harmonies change slowly (as they mostly do) and others where harmonic territory is traversed at a great rate, in the syncopations, in the sudden *fortissimo* outbursts, and in such colorful details as the stalking *pianissimo* half-notes. The development ventures a few moments of lyric song, but most of the

[7]Michael Tilson Thomas has suggested that this introduction is a prime example of a kind of "groping" music that reflects the disorientation of deafness and of which, he believes, there are many instances in Beethoven's work. It is a provocative thought.

orchestra is impatient with that sort of thing, impatient to get on and to get back.

The task of steering the music back to the home key and the first theme sends Beethoven into a wonderful passage that deliciously combines wit and mystery. Still infected by the indiscretions of the slow introduction, the strings, slyly abetted by a sotto voce kettledrum, so far forget themselves as to prepare not B-flat, but B-natural. A pun comes to the rescue. The way to prepare B-natural is with the dominant chord of that key, which would be F-sharp/A-sharp/C-sharp, possibly with E-natural added. That is what the strings play, *pianissimo* and even *pianississimo*, the timpani linking these chords with *pianissimo* rolls on A-sharp. But A-sharp is the same as B-flat, and so it turns out that those reiterated soft drumrolls do not just show us how to get home, but reveal that we have in fact been home for quite some time without realizing it.

This return is another instance of Beethoven's arrival at a harmonic destination sooner than expected; only this time the effect is writ large. This marvelous passage also recapitulates the harmonic scenario of the introduction: the straying into B and the recovery (earlier than expected) into B-flat. To make sure that the effect of the B-major aberration is quite undone, Beethoven concludes the movement with an exceptionally long and emphatic assertion of the tonic.

The Adagio is an expansive, rapt song; rarely does Beethoven insist so often on the direction "cantabile." Before the song begins we hear a measure of ticking accompaniment in the second violins. It is characteristic of Beethoven that this accompaniment refuses to disappear, but remains an insistent presence and a fascinating foil to the flowing melodies. Few listeners today might agree, but Schumann perceived it as humorous, and in an article "On the Comic Spirit in Music" he calls it "a veritable Falstaff, especially when it occurs in the bass or the timpani." Not until the Ninth would Beethoven again write a symphony with a really slow "slow movement."

Concerned with bringing his scherzos in line with the expanding scale of his symphonies, quartets, and trios, Beethoven at about this time sometimes arranged a double trip through the scherzo-trio-scherzo cycle. Here is an example. The ferociously energetic scherzo is fired by cross-rhythms that cut athwart the 3/4 measures with two-beat phrases. The trio is based on a dialogue in which the violins give distinctly impertinent answers— flicking grace notes and pointed sforzandi—to the dolce propositions of the woodwinds and horns.

In the finale, a comedy worthy of Haydn, certain characters from the first movement reappear, newly costumed, but this Allegro ma non troppo is a more relaxed kind of movement than the first Allegro vivace.[8] In the

development, Beethoven also reminds us that he, at least, has not forgotten the B-natural/B-flat games of the first movement. I have said elsewhere
that Beethoven learned more from Haydn's scores than from Haydn's lessons: the Symphony No. 4, for which Haydn's Symphony No. 102 clearly
served as model, is a case in point.

Having begun with Schumann, we can end with some good words
of his:

> Yes, love [Beethoven], love him well, but never forget that he reached
> poetic freedom only through long years of study, and revere his never-ceasing
> moral force. Do not search for the abnormal in him, but return to the source
> of his creativeness. Do not illustrate his genius with the Ninth Symphony
> alone, no matter how great its audacity and scope, never uttered in any
> tongue. You can do as much with his First Symphony, or with the Greek-
> like slender one in B-flat major! And do not grow arrogant over rules that
> you have never thoroughly worked out. Nothing is more dangerous; even a
> man with less talent could, after a moment's hesitation, draw the mask from
> your reddening face.[9]

Symphony No. 5 in C minor, Opus 67

Allegro con brio
Andante con moto
Allegro
Allegro

Beethoven began to sketch the Symphony No. 5 early in 1804, immediately after completing the *Eroica*, continued to work on it sporadically until
1806, but interrupted the project to complete the *Rasumovsky* quartets,
Opus 59, and to write the Piano Concerto No. 4, the Symphony No. 4,
and the Violin Concerto. The main work on the Fifth Symphony was done

---

[8] At least it is more relaxed in character if not in speed. Tempo in Beethoven is a vexing question.
Part of what makes it so in this instance is that sometimes Beethoven's metronome marks (which
he only added in 1817, five years after the completion of the Eighth Symphony) and his verbal
tempo and character indications seem to contradict one another. The meaning of Allegro ma non
troppo ought to be clear enough; however, the metronome mark of 80 to the measure gives a
tempo so fast that one could hardly play this finale any faster even if Beethoven had marked it
just plain allegro.
[9] Robert Schumann, *On Music and Musicians*, edited by Konrad Wolff, translated by Paul Rosen-
feld (New York: Pantheon, 1946).

in 1807, and the score was completed early in 1808. Some revisions followed the first performance at a concert at the Theater an der Wien, Vienna, on 22 December 1808. On this occasion, desperately underrehearsed, the *Pastoral* Symphony and the Choral Fantasy also had their premieres, the Fourth Piano Concerto had its first public performance, and several movements of the Mass in C and the concert aria *Ah! perfido* had their first hearings in Vienna. Beethoven also offered one of his famous solo improvisations at the piano. What those who attended might have remembered most vividly is that the heating apparatus had broken down. The dedication is to Count Andreas von Rasumovsky and Prince Franz Joseph von Lobkowitz.

Two flutes and piccolo, two oboes, two clarinets, two bassoons and contrabassoon, two horns, two trumpets, three trombones, timpani, and strings.

How wild the driving Fifth Symphony must have sounded to an audience that did not meet it as the most familiar of classical masterpieces and that encountered its aggressive mien after the spaciousness and warmth of the Fourth Piano Concerto and the *Pastoral* Symphony as those people in the freezing Theater an der Wien did. The Fifth and the *Pastoral* are opposites in harmony, pace, and mood. But they are also twins, in gestation at the same time and born very nearly together. Each sheds light on the other.

The first movement of the *Pastoral* portrays "the awakening of joyful feelings upon arriving in the country"; of its counterpart in the Fifth, Beethoven said, "Thus Fate knocks at the door." In the *Pastoral,* he evoked serenity, the enveloping of the harried city dweller in the peace of the countryside, by a slowness of motion that was new to music. Again, as in the introduction to the Fourth Symphony, it is not that the actual tempo is slow, but the procedures are. Sometimes the harmony does not change for twenty-eight measures at a time, and the melodic patterns with which Beethoven fills those spaces are almost as static and unchanging.

All this creates an extraordinary sense that the music is saturated by certain chords and figurations. But saturation is also the very word one wants in order to describe what happens in the first movement of the Fifth, where the famous ta-ta-ta-TA pattern is hardly ever absent (and where its rare absences always create tremendous tensions). The difference is that where the saturations in the *Pastoral* produce an infinitely spacious feeling, those in the Fifth generate music that seems faster, more impacted and compressed, than any ever heard before.

About the ta-ta-ta-TA: Beethoven begins with eight notes. They rhyme, four plus four, and each group of four consists of three quick notes plus one that is lower and much longer, in fact unmeasured. The space between the two rhyming groups is minimal (about one-seventh of a second if we go by Beethoven's metronome mark); moreover, Beethoven clarifies the shape by lengthening the second of the long notes. This lengthening, which was an afterthought, is tantamount to writing a stronger punctuation mark. As the music progresses we can hear in the melody of the second theme, for example, or, later in the pairs of antiphonal chords of woodwinds and strings, that the connection between the two four-note units is crucial to the movement and constantly invoked.

It has often been said that the first movement of the Fifth Symphony is all "built up" from its first four notes. But, as Donald Tovey pointed out long ago, if that were so we would have, instead of a Beethoven allegro, one by Schumann, a composer who really does put movements together by that kind of additive process. The source of Beethoven's unparalleled energy here is in his writing long sentences and broad paragraphs whose surfaces are articulated with exciting activity. Indeed, we discover soon enough that the double ta-ta-ta-TA is an open-ended beginning, not a closed and self-sufficient unit.[10]

What makes this opening so dramatic is the violence of the contrast between the urgency in the eighth-notes and the ominous freezing of motion in the unmeasured long notes. The music starts with a wild outburst of energy, but immediately crashes into a wall. Seconds later, Beethoven jolts us with another such sudden halt. The music draws up to a half-cadence on a G-major chord, short and crisp in the whole orchestra, except for the first violins, who hang on to their high G for an unmeasured length of time. Forward motion resumes with a relentless pounding of eighth-notes. The music modulates to a new key, E-flat, the relative major, and only now do we get a change of atmosphere.

Ex. 1

[10] Misunderstanding of this opening was nurtured by a nineteenth-century performance tradition in which the first five measures were read as a slow, portentous exordium, the main tempo being attacked only after the second hold. In World War II, when the Allies co-opted Beethoven by declaring that ta-ta-ta-TA represented V for Victory in Morse code, that tradition was occasionally revived.

Ex. 2

The horns introduce this new chapter with a fanfare that is a variant of the symphony's opening. The initial rhythm, the ta-ta-ta-TA, is the same. Beyond that, what Beethoven has done is to stretch the intervals: the thirds (G/E-flat, F/D) have been opened up into fifths (B-flat/E-flat, F/B-flat). The middle two notes, F/E-flat, are the same as before, even though other essentials such as manner of presentation, key, orchestration, and context are different. Another difference is that this time there is no space between the two pairs of notes: you go from E-flat to F without a break. This suggests that at the opening it is important for the conductor not to lengthen the silence on the first beat of measure 3: the fermata applies to the E-flat, not to the rest right after.

Another interesting detail about the horn call in Ex. 2 is that the fourth note, B-flat, is held for thirteen measures so that it serves as a bass to the dolce violin melody that follows. This corresponds to the extra length of the D at the beginning of the symphony (measures 4-5), and no doubt when Beethoven had the afterthought of lengthening that D it was to clarify this relationship. As for the violin melody, the first two measures outline B-flat/E-flat (though in reverse order), and the third and fourth outline F and B-flat. In other words, it uses the same pitch vocabulary as the opening and the horn call, and again the link in the middle is E-flat/F. So with horns and upper strings retaining the pitches of the opening motif, the cellos and basses meanwhile make sure that the ta-ta-ta-TA rhythm stays in our consciousness. All this is an amazing tour de force of concentration and saturation.

For a long time the development is totally occupied with ta-ta-ta-TA. This rhythm becomes so much a norm for us that when it is lengthened to

Ex. 3

or

Ex. 4

the effect is of something crazed.

Next, Beethoven re-examines the horn call, and this begins his transition toward the recapitulation. Winds and strings play antiphonal chords, first by pairs, then as single chords. As in the corresponding passage in the first movement of the *Eroica*, the greater the harmonic tension, the softer the dynamic level. These are patches of illusory calm before violent storms. Once, a five-measure outburst of furious *fortissimo* interrupts the *pianissimo*. Three things come together at that point: the shape of the opening, with the thirds and the five-measure length, the rhythm of the horn call, and a harmonization that is derived from the antiphonal chords in the development.

A great thunder of eighth-notes sends us flying into the recapitulation.[11] When first we heard the famous opening notes of this symphony they were played by strings and clarinets; this time Beethoven hurls them at us with his full orchestra.[12] What follows is also rescored in that to the agitated eighth-notes in the strings Beethoven adds more sustained lines for oboe and bassoons as well as supporting chords from flutes and clarinets. And now, when he arrives at the cadence where in the exposition the first violins stopped time by clinging to their high G, it is the oboe that detaches itself from the rest of the orchestra, not just to play that high G but to use it as the start of a pathos-filled cadenza. The cadenza both disrupts and integrates. It totally halts forward motion, but at the same time its melody is a perfectly organic continuation of what the oboe itself and the first violins have been playing in the preceding fourteen measures. This paradoxical multiplicity of function is completely characteristic of Beethoven.

---

[11] Many conductors slightly (or not so slightly) broaden the tempo as they approach that moment. It is an understandable impulse. Richard Strauss, bringing his composer's intuition and empathy into play in his work on the podium, increases the speed of that last barrage of preparatory eighth-notes, a gesture that illuminates the urgent character of this passage much more vividly.

[12] This means "full orchestra" as defined for the first three movements. Piccolo, contrabassoon, and trombones enter only in the finale.

Ex. 5

That cadenza looks forward as well as back, for it sets up the pathos that the wind instruments, the oboe in particular, inject into the movement just before its close.[13]

The coda is forceful and big. The proportions of this movement yield interesting numbers: exposition 124 measures (meant of course to be repeated), development 122 measures, recapitulation 126 measures, coda 127 measures. Beethoven puts a big silence, articulative as well as dramatic, between the end of the exposition and the beginning of the development, but when he gets to the corresponding joint between the recapitulation and the coda, he tears from one into the other without a break and in wild abandon. The rhythmic disruptions and distentions are even more violent than those in the development.

It is softness that is pursued in the second movement. In one sketch it is marked "Andante quasi Menuetto," and Beethoven worked hard and long before he found the right shape for the melody and the right expressive tone. Upon that melody he writes a series of variations. The first two break the theme down into faster notes. The third variation is in minor, and Tovey aptly characterizes it as "smiling through tears." These variations are, however, separated by interludes that begin softly in A-flat major, like the theme itself, but move on to C major, with drums and blazing trumpets and horns. (In the sketch referred to earlier, this contrasting idea was to serve as trio to the quasi-minuet.) What makes this movement different from the variations sets by Haydn that it in some ways resembles is the absence of full closures after the martial interludes. Furthermore, some of these transitions are so leisurely that they suspend forward motion as surely and—at least to Haydn- and Mozart-trained ears in 1808—as startlingly as the fermatas in the first movement.

The ecstatic transformation at its last appearance of the little cadential tag at the end of the main theme is a wonderful, proto-Romantic touch. Three times we have heard it, *piano,* descending gently from E-flat

[13] The Peter Schickele/P.D.Q. Bach sportscaster report on the progress of the Fifth Symphony's first movement is not just funny but offers acutely responsive commentary on the music, especially the oboe cadenza (on *The Wurst of P.D.Q. Bach,* recorded on Vanguard).

through C to the keynote, A-flat; this last time, the C swells in crescendo and the melody soars up to the high G.

After the storms of the first movement, the second is an oasis of pure and lovely music-making. With the grotesque and creeping and threatening scherzo, the drama is resumed. E. T. A. Hoffmann, that vital and original writer, musician, and artist, in his review of the Fifth, for him a quintessentially Romantic symphony, points out how unexpected extensions of phrases—again, interferences with "normal" rhythm—are responsible for the "mounting effect" of the scherzo, "its restless yearning . . . heightened to a fear which tightly constricts the breast, permitting only fragmentary, disconnected sounds to escape."

The scherzo is a ghostly affair that is back in C minor, much of it in *pianissimo*, but with forceful reminders of the first movement's ta-ta-ta-TA rhythm. The trio is in C major, fierce and jocular at the same time, and also a real virtuoso turn for the cellos and basses.[14] It has no formal close, but leads directly into the reappearance of the scherzo. When the scherzo returns, it is much altered. The opening phrase is stretched into a more sinister variant, while the whole design is compressed from 160 measures (to be repeated) to 88. It is, all of it, in relentless *pianissimo*, even the reminders of the ta-ta-ta-TA motif.

Beethoven's original plan was to make the scherzo-trio-scherzo circuit twice, as in the Fourth Symphony (and later in the Sixth and Seventh). The first repetition of the scherzo was to be identical with the original statement, the second was to introduce the spooky, attenuated variant that leads to the finale, thus:

scherzo/trio/scherzo/trio/spooky variant of scherzo/transition
          [———x———]

Beethoven soon had second thoughts about the rightness of such an expansive design for this forward-thrusting symphony. A set of orchestra parts issued by the Leipzig publisher Breitkopf & Härtel in April 1809, just four months after the first performance, already omits the extra repeat (marked **x,** above), and in subsequent correspondence with Breitkopf about those parts, Beethoven does not touch on this question. Presumably he made his revision for the sake of tighter dramatic progress. Most conductors choose Beethoven's final version; surely, though, it is a good idea from time to time to examine, in public performance, the original de-

---

[14] Berlioz tells us that in his day the basses in Parisian orchestras maintained discreet silence here. Nowadays it is a passage that is assigned at every bass audition for a major orchestra.

sign.[15] The latter really demands taking the repeat of the exposition in the finale as well—a good idea in any case—and these decisions then yield a symphony that is more grand than taut.

The victory symphony was a new kind of symphony, and Beethoven's invention here of a path from strife to triumph became a model for symphonic writing to the present day. This seems to us so central to the whole idea of the Fifth Symphony that it is surprising to learn that it was not part of Beethoven's original plan at all. An early sketch for the finale shows a theme in C minor and in 6/8 time, a nervously impassioned variant of another C-minor piece Beethoven admired vastly—the finale of Mozart's Piano Concerto, K.491. But once it was clear to him how the symphony wanted to end, other changes followed. For one, the martial C-major interludes in the Andante lost their formal closes; thus they ceased to be quasi-independent episodes but became adumbrations of both a mood and a key to be explored more fully later.

Likewise, certain ideas Beethoven had about the scherzo came into focus. Two sounds had already occurred to him: the diversion of the harmony from C minor to A-flat major by way of a deceptive cadence, and the persistent beating of a drum on C. At some point he saw that these were not separate ideas but belonged together, and with that, one of the most amazing passages in all music came into being.

The scherzo is never completed, for Beethoven steers what we expect to be its final cadence into a murky tunnel of thudding drums and groping bits of melody. This is an extraordinary joining of Fifth Symphony tension to *Pastoral* Symphony stasis. At last we emerge into the sureness and daylight of C major, marked by the new sounds of trombones (heard here for the first time in any symphony), piccolo, and contrabassoon.[16]

Beethoven asserts his C-major triumph with all the force he can muster. Not only trombones but shrilling piccolo and thunderous contrabassoon add their voices to the orchestra. We are accustomed to those sounds, but in 1808 the shock and the expressive effect must have been tremendous.

"Look out for the part where you think you have done with the goblins and they come back," says Helen Schlegel in E. M. Forster's *Howards End*. Beethoven does bring them back before his affirmation is final: more technically put, their return constitutes the transition to the recapitula-

---

[15] Perhaps "choose" is too charitable. Many conductors are not aware of the alternative.

[16] Any other composer would have built suspense by having the drum beat persistently on the dominant, G. But Beethoven's drum is on C, so here is another instance of his anticipating his harmonic destination.

tion. "But the goblins were there," Forster adds. "They could return. He had said so bravely, and that is why one can trust Beethoven when he says other things."[17]

The goblins do indeed return, and Beethoven has to make his C major return a second time. (Mahler powerfully annexed the psychology and the design of this plan in the finale of his Symphony No. 1.) Many people have made fun of Beethoven's concluding forty-one measures of tonic and dominant (twenty-nine of them just tonic C-major chords)—Dudley Moore even did it wittily in *Beyond the Fringe*—but after such a hurricane, nothing less would do to properly ground this music.

As a boy, Mendelssohn had tried hard and not entirely successfully to convert the elderly Goethe to a belief in the Fifth Symphony, or at least to an understanding of it. As a young man, Berlioz tried no less hard to persuade an older man who was almost as determined to resist that impact as Goethe had been. Now let Berlioz have the last word. He was addressing his former teacher, Jean-François Lesueur,

an honest man without envy in his nature, and devoted to art. François-Antoine Habeneck's carefully prepared performances of Beethoven's symphonies were causing an immense stir in the music world of Paris, but Lesueur took no notice. Confronted with the immense enthusiasm of musicians in general and me in particular, he shut his ears and carefully avoided the Conservatoire concerts. To have gone would have meant committing himself to a personal opinion of Beethoven; it would have meant being physically involved in the tremendous excitement which Beethoven aroused. This was just what Lesueur . . . did not wish to happen. However, I kept on at him, solemnly pointing out that when something as important as this occurred in our art—a completely new style on an unprecedented scale—it was his duty to find out about it and to judge for himself; and in the end he yielded and let himself be dragged to the Conservatoire one day when the C-minor Symphony was being performed. . . .

When it was over . . . I found him in the corridor, striding along with a flushed face. "Well, master?"

"Ouf! Let me get out. I must have some air. It's amazing! Wonderful! I was so moved and so disturbed that when I emerged from the box and attempted to put on my hat, I couldn't find my head. Now please leave me be. We'll meet tomorrow."

. . . The next day I hurried round to see him. . . . Lesueur let me

---

[17] The description of a performance of the Fifth Symphony in *Howards End* is something not to miss, but in the movie, with the event changed for financial reasons from a concert to a lecture, the scene goes for nothing. For more on the matter of goblins and on the different ways the various members of the Schlegel family hear this music, see Peter Kivy's *Music Alone* (Ithaca: Cornell University Press, 1990).

talk on for some time, assenting in a rather constrained manner to my exclamations of enthusiasm. But it was easy to see that my companion was no longer the man who had spoken to me the day before, and that he found the subject painful. I persisted, however, and dragged from him a further acknowledgement of how deeply Beethoven's symphony had moved him; at which he suddenly shook his head and smiled in a curious way and said, "All the same, music like that ought not to be written."

"Don't worry, master," I replied, "there is not much danger."[18]

Symphony No. 6 in F major, Opus 68, *Pastoral*

Awakening of Cheerful Feelings upon Arriving in the Country (Allegro ma non troppo)
Scene by the Brook (Andante molto moto)
Merry Gathering of Country Folk (Allegro)
Thunderstorm (Allegro)
Shepherd's Song—Happy and Thankful Feelings After the Storm (Allegretto)

A few of the sketches for the *Pastoral* Symphony go back as far as 1803, but Beethoven did most of the work on the piece in the fall of 1807 and the early months of 1808. By September 1808 he had sold the work to the Leipzig publisher Breitkopf & Härtel, who issued it the following April together with the Fifth Symphony. The *Pastoral* and the Fifth were also introduced at the same concert at the Theater an der Wien, Vienna, on 22 December 1808 (for details see my essay on the Fifth). The dedication is to Count Andreas von Rasumovsky and Prince Franz Joseph von Lobkowitz.

Two flutes and piccolo, two oboes, two clarinets, two bassoons, two horns, two trumpets, two trombones, timpani, and strings.

The most famous opening bars of any symphony, indeed of any piece of "classical" music, are without doubt those of Beethoven's Fifth; those of the *Pastoral*, which had its premiere about two hours earlier—mistakenly

[18] Hector Berlioz, *Memoirs*, edited and translated by David Cairns (New York: Norton, 1969).

listed as No. 5—are, if less universally recognizable, no less remarkable. The Fifth begins as violently as possible, and there is nothing that even comes close to rivaling it until the Mahler Second more than eighty years later. In the *Pastoral,* Beethoven's aim is to begin as gently as possible. We hear a soft drone, F and C, in cellos and violas, and over that an ambling bit of melody for the first violins, with the seconds joining in for some harmony. In a matter of four or five seconds the music stops, coming to rest on a softly suspenseful chord of C major: some conductors even play the whole phrase from the beginning as a retard into that unmeasured halt on the dominant.

Having the music stop almost as soon as it has begun is something the *Pastoral* has in common with the Fifth, though in expression the two beginnings are each other's opposite. The ideal—unattainably ideal—performance of the *Pastoral* Symphony is one in which you don't hear the music start at all, you are simply aware that it has begun. It is as though it had been going on all along but the listener has only just come within earshot. The imperceptible beginning—or, for that matter, the imperceptible close, as in Tchaikovsky's *Pathétique*—is a typically Romantic device. Beethoven invents it here, so to speak, because his subject is "the awakening of cheerful feelings upon arriving in the country." Music and country are ever there, ready to welcome us, and the awakening of feelings—Beethoven's, and through the power of his vision, ours as well—is soft and sweet.

The great outdoor composers, the ones for whom contact with nature was essential, are Beethoven and Mahler (whose Symphony No. 1 has one of the most dangerous of inaudible beginnings, with an instruction to the conductor to make it "like a sound of nature"), Schubert and Bartók. Each day that he was in Vienna, Beethoven took a long walk around the ramparts, and he spent his summers in the country, out of doors more than in, doing a lot of composing in his head on his energetic stomps through the countryside. In 1803, the *Eroica* year, he had sketched a theme that he marked "murmur of the brook," adding, "the more water the deeper the note." What he jotted down is in fact ancestor to the Scene by the Brook in the *Pastoral* Symphony, a score fed by many ideas that occurred to him over the next three years.

Beethoven himself gave the five movements their titles:

Awakening of Cheerful Feelings upon Arriving in the Country
Scene by the Brook
Merry Gathering of Country Folk
Thunderstorm
Shepherd's Song—Happy and Thankful Feelings After the Storm

all but borrowing them from *Le Portrait musical de la nature,* a symphony for fifteen instruments by a then much-admired Rhenish composer, Justin Heinrich Knecht.[19] Sir George Grove, not only the father of the most important music reference work in English but also the author in 1896 of the valuable book *Beethoven and His Nine Symphonies,* pointed out that Knecht's *Portrait* was advertised on the same page of a 1783 issue of *Cramer's Music Magazine* as the twelve-year-old Beethoven's three piano sonatas, WoO47.[20] Lest anyone misunderstand his intentions, Beethoven added a cautionary note to the program at the premiere of the *Pastoral:* "more an expression of feeling than painting."

The *Pastoral* is a beautifully gauged mix of the explicit and the suggestive. Among the explicit elements are the birdcalls that close the Scene by the Brook and which Beethoven actually marks "nightingale" (flute), "quail" (oboe), and "cuckoo" (two clarinets in unison); the sometimes disarrayed village band to which the country folk dance; the thunderstorm; and the yodeling shepherd's song, which is rather like the one Rossini quotes in the *William Tell* Overture and which Beethoven himself may have taken over from the piano fantasia *A Spring Morning, Noon, and Night* by Mozart's pupil and friend Franz Jakob Freystädtler. But all these things make sense simply as music (even the birds sing in the form of a classical cadenza) so that you never need a key to understand what is going on. As Beethoven himself noted in his sketches for the *Pastoral,* "Even without description one will recognize the whole. . . . Anyone who has ever had an idea of country life can imagine for himself what the author [intends]."

I have already described the symphony's beginning, the bagpipe drone, set as fundament to the ambling melody that detaches itself from it. There is something wonderfully leisurely to all this, and it is altogether characteristic of the *Pastoral*—and not at all characteristic of Beethoven in general—that in this movement the harmonies tend to lie still for amazingly long periods. The development is most extraordinary in this way.

---

[19] Here, translated from the French, are the descriptions of the movements of Knecht's *Portrait:*

1. A lovely region where the sun shines, gentle zephyrs flutter, brooks cross the valley, birds warble, a waterfall descends from high, a shepherd sounds his pipe, lambs leap about, and a shepherdess sings in her sweet voice.

2. The sky begins to darken, people can scarcely breathe and become frightened, black clouds rise, winds commence to howl, thunder rumbles from afar, and the storm draws near, step by step.

3. The storm, accompanied by rushing winds and battering rains, rages with all its strength, there is a roaring in the treetops, and the falls spill their water with a terrifying sound.

4. The storm becomes gradually milder, the clouds disperse, and the sky becomes clear.

5. All Nature, in a transport of joy, raises her voice toward heaven and in sweet and lovely songs renders heartfelt thanks to the Creator.

[20] WoO, a designation used in Georg Kinsky's thematic catalogue of Beethoven's works, stands for *Werk ohne Opus* (work without opus number). Pronounce it "woo."

Seventy-two of its first ninety-four measures are given over to the contemplation of a single figure

Ex. 1

derived from the symphony's second bar

Ex. 2

Beethoven lays it before us, twelve times in B-flat, twenty-four times in D (how wondrously refreshing that shift of perspective is!), then, after ten transitional measures, twelve more times in G and twenty-four in E. Basil Lam writes that "this is perhaps the broadest expanse of harmony in all of the classics, wonderfully scored (every detail contributes to the effect) and in its motion as unhurried as the sky-drift of summer clouds, yet as rapid as their shadows crossing a field." Robert Simpson speaks of the "sublime monotony" of these pages, suggesting that these figures repeat themselves like "leaves on trees." Again, the saturation of the Fifth Symphony's first movement with the ta-ta-ta-TA rhythm of its first four notes comes to mind as an instance parallel in technique but reversed in expressive effect.

Another feature that accounts for the beatific serenity of this movement is Beethoven's absolute avoidance of diminished chords and near-total eschewal of minor triads (and how touching are the few of these that he introduces about halfway through). There is as well an unusual prevalence of chords in root position, their most stable distribution. Of course a dearth of dissonance can be cloying, and Beethoven cannily uses triplets that cut across the prevailing duple meter to create rhythmic dissonance in place of the harmonic kind.

The Scene by the Brook is more spacious still. Having thus far moved generally toward the brighter side of the harmonic spectrum—namely, those patches of D major, G major, and E major in the first movement's development—Beethoven now explores those softer, more cushioned regions of the flat keys. In no work does Beethoven's orchestral fantasy run so untrammeled as in the *Pastoral,* and of course his fantasy is deeply informed by his skill and experience. You sense this particularly in the first movement, so economical in melody, harmony, and rhythm; there Beethoven articulates his material by sorting out textures through orchestration, that most subtle form of polyphony. Without Beethoven's wonderful sense of the actual, physical sound of music, a sense not at all disturbed by his worsening deafness, we would not have "sublime monotony," just monotony.[21]

The orchestral sound of the brook music is itself a sensuous thrill. The gently rolling water is portrayed in the flowing eighth-notes of second violins and violas in thirds, the same music being duplicated an octave lower by two solo cellos, muted. Plucked cellos and basses strike the bass notes, which are caught by the sustaining pedal of a pair of horns. Against this background, the first violins sigh their fragments of melody in lazy, sun-drenched ecstasy. It is from the close and loving study of these pages that Berlioz learned how to write the Scene in the Fields in the *Symphonie fantastique.* It is at the peaceful close of this movement that Beethoven introduces his inspired cadenza for nightingale, quail, and cuckoo.

The dance scene introduces a new element of humor as the members of the village band try hard to keep their place. It is also part of Beethoven's strategy that the rhythmic dislocations in this piece of affectionate genre painting have a delightfully spiky effect after the tranquillity of motion in the two preceding movements. Beethoven redresses the harmonic balance after the brook scene by moving again toward brighter sharp keys, even designing the first theme so that it leaps abruptly from F major to D major when it is only two or three seconds under way. The earthy trio is clearly one of those dances in which the participants slap their thighs.

The festivities are interrupted in a thrillingly operatic way by a summer storm. For this depiction of pelting rain, blinding bolts of lightning, and terrifying thunder, Beethoven holds in reserve part of his orchestral arsenal, the piercing piccolo, a pair of trombones, and the kettledrums, as well as some of his most potent harmonic resources, the long-withheld

---

[21] Much of this wonder resides in Beethoven's choice of instrumental colors, but it depends no less on his decisions about spacing, about how much air to let into the chords. Even in Liszt's loving and scrupulous piano transcription the monotony remains sublime.

diminished chords and, even more stunningly, that most obvious item in an F-major symphony, the chord of F minor. The storm is immensely powerful, but its power comes from its classical precision and economy. Using far more lavish physical resources, not even Wagner, Verdi, or Strauss evoked nature's unconcerned ruthlessness with such force; the musical storm that is the worthy successor of this one as nature poetry is the delicately limned one—it touches *forte* just once—in the *Fantastique*.

The storm dies down. We hear a phrase of a hymn, and then we enter the finale with another of Beethoven's unexpectedly early arrivals on the expected harmony. The "thankful feelings" are directed to God. We know this both from the sketchbooks, where Beethoven actually writes words from the Mass, "gratias agimus tibi," and from a note he sent his concertmaster at the 1808 concert. This music returns to the ease of the first movement, but an ease which, in the final minutes, takes on a new and magical radiance.

Symphony No. 7 in A major, Opus 92

> *Poco sostenuto—Vivace*
> *Allegretto*
> *Presto*
> *Allegro con brio*

The sketches for this symphony began to take shape in the latter part of 1811 in what is now called the Petter sketchbook after one of its nineteenth-century owners. The work was completed on 13 April 1812 and first performed under the composer's direction on 8 December 1813 in the auditorium of the University of Vienna. The dedication is to Count Moritz von Fries.

Two flutes, two oboes, two clarinets, two bassoons, two horns, two trumpets, timpani, and strings.

The concert at the University of Vienna on 8 December 1813 at which the Seventh Symphony had its premiere—a benefit for Austrian and Bavarian soldiers wounded in the recent battle of Hanau—was probably the most wildly successful of Beethoven's career. What caused the excitement was not, however, Opus 92, the new symphony, but Opus 91, *Wellington's*

Victory, or The Battle of Vitoria, often called the *Battle* Symphony.[22] Beethoven wrote *Wellington's Victory* for a mechanical instrument called the panharmonicon, an invention of the ingenious Johann Nepomuk Maelzel, who had organized this concert and whom we shall encounter again in connection with the Eighth Symphony. Even at its first performance, however, the *Battle* Symphony was presented in the now familiar version for full orchestra. Between the Seventh Symphony and *Wellington's Victory,* another gadget of Maelzel's, a mechanical trumpeter, played marches written for the occasion by Dušek and Pleyel. So great was the success that the entire program was repeated later in the month, again in January 1814, and once more in February.

Perhaps *Wellington's Victory* does not legitimately belong in a discussion of Beethoven's symphonies. It is not, after all, really a symphony; nonetheless, I want to say a word in defense of a piece much sneered at. None of it merits anyone's sneering. Much of it is naive descriptive music, with fanfares, challenges, calls to arms, agitated battle music, and the disintegration of the defeated forces' theme song (here "Malbrouck s'en va-t-en guerre," a tune we know as "The Bear Went Over the Mountain" or "For He's a Jolly Good Fellow"). There is nothing original about that; the musical literature abounds in portrayals of largely forgotten battles of Trenton, Prague, and so forth, though it must be said that Beethoven does his job with address and a master's sense of timing. When the battle is over and the guns are still, he writes a victory finale. It lasts only two minutes or so, but it is a concentrated, superbly composed page that is absolutely vintage 1813 Beethoven and worth waiting for.

Beethoven must have been glad to do something for the enemies of Napoleon, not just because of any lingering ambivalence about the *Eroica* episode but because he, like all the Viennese, had suffered in the war. "Nothing but drums, cannons, human misery of every sort!," he had written to his Leipzig publisher, Gottfried Christoph Härtel, in 1809, when Austria was at war with France for the fourth time in eighteen years. Each peace, furthermore, brought Austria new humiliations, new territorial losses, new economic chaos.

---

[22] Vitoria is a city in northeastern Spain. There, on 21 June 1813, an army of English, Spanish, and Portuguese troops under the Duke of Wellington met a French army under Joseph Bonaparte, for whom his younger brother Napoleon had found useful employment as King of Spain. After about twelve hours of heavy fighting, the French left in full retreat. It was a decisive battle. Napoleon lost his power on the Iberian peninsula and Joseph lost his job. The battle of Hanau, which is just a few miles east of Frankfurt, was fought four months later. The Grande Armée had been savaged at the Battle of Nations at Leipzig earlier that month, and a typhus epidemic was making its way through the French forces; nevertheless, Napoleon managed to thrash the mostly Bavarian army that attempted to block his retreat toward the southwest.

Amid this crescendo of public wretchedness, Beethoven worked with phenomenal concentration: between 1802 and 1808 he wrote the five symphonies from the Second through the *Pastoral;* the three *Rasumovsky* string quartets and the two piano trios of Opus 70; four sonatas for violin, including the *Kreutzer,* and the Cello Sonata, Opus 69; six piano sonatas, among them the *Waldstein* and *Appassionata;* the Third and Fourth piano concertos, the Violin Concerto, and the Triple Concerto; *Fidelio* in its original form and in its first revision; the oratorio *Christ on the Mount of Olives,* the C-major Mass, and the Choral Fantasy—to mention only the large-scale works. Even so, one can understand that he was seriously tempted late in 1808 to accept the offer of a post as court composer to Jerôme Bonaparte, the puppet king of Westphalia. That gave the Viennese another cause for alarm, in response to which three wealthy patrons, the Archduke Rudolph and the princes Lobkowitz and Kinsky, banded together to guarantee Beethoven an income for life provided that he stay in Vienna or some other city within the Austrian Empire. In 1809, the worst year for the Viennese, Beethoven completed the Piano Concerto No. 5 (whose Anglo-American nickname of *Emperor* ironically commemorates Napoleon), the Opus 74 String Quartet, the *Farewell* Sonata for piano and two smaller ones, the wonderfully lyric F-sharp major, Opus 78, and its snappy companion in G, Opus 79.

Excellence is undiminished, but in quantity, 1809 is a slender year compared with the previous seven. Perhaps the contract with the princes was a symbol of acceptance and arrival that allowed Beethoven not to push himself as hard, though in fact, because of the prevailing fiscal chaos, the promised monies did not always arrive punctually and dependably. Whatever the reasons, Beethoven never again composed as prolifically as he had between 1802 and 1808. His biographer Maynard Solomon calls that period Beethoven's "heroic decade." The *Sinfonia eroica* of 1803 most forcefully defined the new manner; the *Emperor* Concerto represents its summit and, in effect, its termination. The Seventh Symphony is a brilliant postscript.

To Beethoven's annoyance, the critic of the *Wiener Zeitung* referred to the Seventh as having been composed "as a companion piece" to *Wellington's Victory.* But the public liked the "companion piece" too, and the composer Louis Spohr, who sat assistant concertmaster for the whole series of concerts, reports that the second movement was encored each time.

Other famous musicians in this orchestra were the Italian composer and guitarist Mauro Giuliani, who played cello, Giacomo Meyerbeer, Johann Nepomuk Hummel, and the celebrated pianist Ignaz Moscheles, all of whom helped out with the extra percussion in *Wellington's Victory;* Antonio Salieri, who functioned as sub-conductor for the percussion and artillery; Ignaz Schuppanzigh, the most famous quartet leader of his time (he played premieres of Haydn, Beethoven, Schubert, all prepared under the composers' supervision), usually addressed by Beethoven as "Milord Falstaff" and praised by him on this occasion for the way he, as concertmaster, had "swept the orchestra along with his fiery and expressive playing"; and Joseph Mayseder, second violin of the Schuppanzigh Quartet, who led the seconds in the orchestra.

Spohr described Beethoven's conducting:

> [He] had accustomed himself to indicate expression to the orchestra by all manner of singular body movements. Whenever a *sforzando* occurred, he tore his arms, previously crossed upon his breast, asunder with great vehemence. At *piano* he crouched down lower and lower according to the degree of softness he desired. If a crescendo then entered he gradually rose again and at the entrance of the *forte* he jumped into the air. Sometimes, too, he unconsciously shouted to strengthen the *forte*. . . . It was obvious that the poor man could no longer hear the *piano* in his music. This was strikingly illustrated in the second portion of the first Allegro of the [Seventh] Symphony. In one place there are two holds, one immediately after the other, the second of which is *pianissimo*. This Beethoven had probably overlooked, because he began again to beat time before the orchestra had begun to play the second hold. Without being aware of it, therefore, he had hurried ten or twelve measures ahead of the orchestra when it began again, and indeed *pianissimo*. Beethoven, to indicate *pianissimo*, had in his wonted manner crouched clean under the desk. At the succeeding crescendo he became visible, straightened up once more, and jumped into the air at the point where according to his calculations the *forte* ought to begin. When this did not happen he looked about in a startled way, stared at the orchestra to see it still playing *pianissimo*, and found his bearings only when the long-expected *forte* came in and was visible to him. Fortunately this comical incident did not take place at the performance.[23]

Spohr is talking about the passage beginning at measure 299 in the first movement. Obviously Schuppanzigh contributed more than just fire and expression.

A semi-slow introduction, the largest ever heard in any symphony until then, and still one of the largest, defines great harmonic spaces: first A major, then C major (with a gently lyric oboe tune), then F major (the same tune on the flute). The excursions to C and F are entered upon with

---

[23] Quoted in *Thayer's Life of Beethoven*, revised and edited by Elliot Forbes (Princeton: Princeton University Press, 1964).

startling bluntness. Beethoven means to draw attention not only to the startling shifts themselves but to these new harmonic areas, both distant from the home key of A major. Every one of the symphony's important journeys is foreshadowed here.

The material—scales, and melodies that either outline common chords or move along scales—is of reckless simplicity. Gradually, with delicious feeling for suspense, Beethoven draws the Vivace from the last flickers of the introduction. Having done so, he propels us with fierce energy and speed through one of those movements of his that are dominated by a single rhythm, in this instance that of an ebullient dance. The coda, as so often in Beethoven, is virtually another development, and Beethoven heaves it to a tremendous climax by making a crescendo across a tenfold repetition of an obsessive, harmonically off-balance bass.

There is no slow movement. The Allegretto that was so wildly popular with audiences throughout the nineteenth century was often played very slowly and used on occasions of mourning, but it is in fact leisurely only by comparison with what comes before and after.[24] A subtly unstable wind chord begins and ends the movement. It is a chord of A minor, but with the "wrong" note—E instead of A—in the bass and thus deliberately made unstable.[25] The effect is curious and piquant, and it must have been startling in 1813. Beethoven had originally planned a theme much like the first one of this movement for the not-so-slow "slow movement" of the C-major String Quartet, Opus 59, no. 3. The movement that Beethoven finally put in the Quartet (it is marked "Andante con moto quasi Allegretto") is also in A minor, and its first four measures are poised over a persistent E in the bass: I imagine that some connection in Beethoven's mind between the idea of beginning with an A-minor six-four chord and the theme that ended up in the symphony may account for his curious beginning here.

The first time we hear this chord, it sets up the walking music of the lower strings; when it reappears to end the movement (an effect still more startling), it is not so much a conclusion as a slightly eccentric preparation for the F-major explosion of the Scherzo.

This is Beethoven's most ebullient scherzo. Its speed alone would make it exciting; its rhythmic vagaries, sparing but cunningly placed, make

[24]The German composer Friedrich Silcher (1789–1860) turned many themes from Beethoven's instrumental works into songs. The text by Heinrich Stieglitz he attached to the second movement of the Seventh Symphony is called *Gesang der Peris* (Song of the Peris) and begins: "Cradle him, wrap him in slumber, loving and mild."

[25]This is called a six-four chord because in a chord of, for example, A minor, with E in the bass, the other two notes, C and A, are respectively a sixth and a fourth higher than the E. It is the chord with which the orchestra announces the cadenza in a classical concerto.

it an intoxicating adventure. For the most part the theme itself moves in nicely regular four-bar periods, but from time to time Beethoven throws you with a two-bar unit, for example, the eruption right at the beginning and the tumbling cadence at the end of the first paragraph. Here is another work in which Beethoven goes round the scherzo-trio-scherzo cycle twice. He takes special care to vary these repetitions by reducing the dynamics of the second trip through the scherzo to Lilliputian scale. The internal repeats yield delightful surprises and explosions, though most conductors ignore them. The movement ends with a joke that Beethoven had first tried in the Fourth Symphony and that he must have liked, because this is not the last time it turns up.

The trio itself, with its rich wind-band sonorities, may or may not be a quotation of a pilgrims' hymn. It is marked to go "very much less fast" (Assai meno presto)—Beethoven says 132 measures per minute for the scherzo and 84 for the trio—but there is a long performance tradition for taking the trio a lot slower than that. Ever since Toscanini took it not just strikingly faster than his colleagues but faster than Beethoven directs, conductors, critics, and others have not ceased to argue about just what Beethoven meant. How much less is "very much less"? Even if one can fault Toscanini for going "meno presto" but not "*assai* meno presto"—100 in his marvelous 1936 recording with the New York Philharmonic-Symphony—he comes very much closer to the character that Beethoven was obviously after than does, say, Furtwängler at 60.[26] Schumann cited the burps of the second horn in the draft of an essay on humor in music.

The finale is fast, too, but the sense of pace is quite different. The scherzo, sharply defined, moves like a superbly controlled machine; the finale carries to an extreme point, unimagined before Beethoven's day and rarely reached since, the sense of a truly wild and swirling motion adumbrated in the first movement. Here, too, Beethoven builds the coda upon an obsessively repeated bass—just a pair of notes grinding away, G-sharp/A at first, then working its way down through chromatic degrees until the dominant, E, and its neighbor, D-sharp, are reached. The whole inspired and mad process is spread across fifty-nine measures.

Of course, to sound wild it must be orderly. Here, as in the notoriously difficult first movement, rhythmic definition is everything. Felix Weingartner remarked in his book on conducting Beethoven's symphonies that whenever he got compliments about the vertiginous speed of his performance of the finale, it was when he had taken it particularly slowly.

---

[26] It was also Toscanini who was responsible for the now current but long-resisted, quicker tempo for the second movement.

Symphony No. 8 in F major, Opus 93

Allegro vivace e con brio
Allegretto scherzando
Tempo di Menuetto
Allegro vivace

Beethoven wrote the Symphony No. 8 in 1811–12, doing most of the work on it in the summer of 1812 at the Bohemian spas of Teplitz, Carlsbad, and Eger, immediately after the completion of the Seventh Symphony. The fair copy is dated October 1812. Beethoven conducted the first performance on 27 February 1814 in Vienna.

Two flutes, two oboes, two clarinets, two bassoons, two horns, two trumpets, timpani, and strings.

Just as in 1807–08 Beethoven had worked on his Fifth and *Pastoral* symphonies together and as a study in contrast, so in 1811–12 did he compose the Seventh and Eighth symphonies more or less simultaneously. It would be twelve years before Beethoven completed another symphony and, given the obviously special nature of the Ninth, with its unprecedented length and the invasion of the orchestra by the human voice, we might well say that the Eighth represents the end of the run of Beethoven's "normal" symphonies.

The Seventh is Beethoven's (for the time being) last and vibrant word on the big style he had cultivated in the preceding decade. In the Eighth he does something new by seeming to return to something old. He writes, that is, a symphony shorter than any since his First. It is almost as though he wanted to call his entire development throughout that decade into question. Indeed, over the remaining years of his life he would confidently explore in opposite directions, writing bigger pieces than before and ones more compressed, his most rhetorical music and his most inward, his most public and his most esoteric, compositions that proclaim the inexhaustible possibilities of the sonata style and those that propose utterly new ways of organizing material, music reaching extremes of the centered and the bizarre.

If, however, we think of the Eighth as a nostalgic return to the good old days, we misunderstand it. To say that it is 1795 revisited from the vantage point of 1812 is not right either. What interests Beethoven is not so much brevity for its own sake—and certainly not something called "classicism"—as concentration. It is as though he were picking up where he had left off in the densely saturated first movement of the Fifth Symphony to produce another tour de force of tight packing. He had already done something like this two years earlier in one of his most uncompromising works, the F-minor String Quartet, Opus 95. But a symphony is not "private" connoisseurs' music like a string quartet; by comparison, the Symphony No. 8 is Opus 95's friendly, open-featured cousin, even though its first and last movements bring us some of the most violent moments in Beethoven. Taking the tempo and character indications seriously makes all the difference: Allegro vivace e con brio, that is, quick, lively, and fiery, with the bars going by sixty-nine a minute for the first movement; Allegro vivace at eighty-four bars to the minute for the finale.[27]

The music takes off like a house afire. The first movement is fast not only in tempo, but at the rate at which it roars from event to event. It is also rambunctious. Its melodies are of amazing brevity; yet, what would seem to be neutral accompaniment or cadential figures sometimes claim enormous amounts of real and psychological room. Beethoven doesn't even care that in sheer, reckless exuberance he drowns out the theme at the start of the recapitulation. (Gustav Mahler did care and reorchestrated the passage, giving the opening six-note motif to the timpani.) But who laughs last laughs best, and it is that drowned theme that has the nose-thumbing last word.

The great adagio composer gives us no slow movement at all. In its place he puts a joke, a witty adaptation of music he had written at about the same time, the spring of 1812, as a salute to Johann Nepomuk Maelzel, the inventor of the first practical metronome.[28] The first words of the canon that Beethoven had written for Maelzel are "ta ta ta ta ta ta ta ta-ta ta ta-ta ta ta-ta ta," and that amiable ticking dominates the Eighth Symphony's delicious second movement.

Then comes a minuet, a standard feature in the symphonies of Haydn and in most of Mozart's, but hitherto in Beethoven's music always replaced by a quicker, less courtly scherzo. Beethoven had in fact not written a

---

[27] "Seriously" is not the same as "literally" when it comes to the metronome marks. If, for example, a conductor decides that in a particular hall the first movement can be more clearly articulated at $\text{♩.} = 63$ rather than $\text{♩.} = 69$ and keeps the "vivace e con brio" clearly in mind, that is fine. On the other hand, $\text{♩.} = 56$ and a character of "gioviale" or even "maestoso" definitely will not do.

[28] About 1820, Maelzel came to the United States, where, according to Beethoven's great nineteenth-century biographer, Alexander Wheelock Thayer, "he passed the rest of his life (except for a voyage or two to the West Indies), exhibiting [Kempelen's Mechanical] Chessplayer, the Conflagration of Moscow, and his other curious inventions. [On 21 July 1838] he was found dead in his berth on board the American brig Otis." As well as inventing the panharmonicon for which Beethoven originally wrote *Wellington's Victory*, Maelzel also designed some of the ear-trumpets the composer used.

minuet since the String Quartet, Opus 59, no. 3, of 1806, and after the Eighth Symphony he would not again include one in a large work. This one is grandly bewigged at first; then, in a famous horn solo, it turns out to be full of romance and mysterious stirrings.

In his wonder of a finale Beethoven returns to the speed, the wild good humor, and the astonishing density and original invention of the first movement—plus a rude jolt or two. He begins with *pianissimo* buzzings in violins, the tiny melodic turn, such as it is, subtly underlined first by violas, then by flute and oboe. Something more like a melody grows in the violins, but still everything feels suspenseful, preparatory. The music becomes even softer, going all the way down to *ppp*, and is interrupted by breaths of silence. What happens next is not in the least what has been prepared. It is an explosion on C-sharp, a note that has nothing to do with F major, the prevailing key. Beethoven even pretends it didn't happen; ignoring this unmannerly interruption, he offers us the most "normal" continuation imaginable, a big statement, *fortissimo tutti,* of the opening music. If you left out the C-sharp, the music would make perfect sense; it would even be captivating and amusing. But the C-sharp makes the big F-major tutti something other than innocent. We ourselves are not so innocent as to believe that something this explosive could happen without further consequences.

The strange thing is that no consequences appear to be forthcoming: there are silences, unexpected accents, and other surprises, but nothing that seems a likely offspring of that explosion of violent humor (so like what we read of Beethoven's verbal humor). One special and flavorful surprise is that the contrasting second theme occurs not where we expect it, in C major, the dominant, but in a somehow softer A-flat major. Has C-sharp put C-natural out of court? Another oddity: suddenly there is a motion to recapitulate the opening theme in A major (subversion from the C-sharp underworld?—it does mean that the tune now begins on C-sharp). However, bassoon and timpani organize a *pianissimo* counterrevolution, and the music is swung back into F major.[29] Again the C-sharp interrupts and is ignored. The contrasting theme, when it reappears, is in D-flat major, which is a sneaky alternative way of spelling C-sharp major, but this is only an episode, quickly rediverted to F major.

[29] The normal tuning for timpani in the classical style is for one drum to be on the keynote, the other on the dominant. Beethoven first departs from this in the introduction to Act 2 of *Fidelio,* where he tunes the drums to the odd interval of a diminished fifth (A-natural/E-flat), an effect copied by Wagner in *Siegfried.* The first and third movements of the Eighth Symphony use normal tuning to F and C (the second has no timpani), but for the finale he uses F's in octaves instead. It makes for an amusing instrumental effect when timpani and bassoon bop up and down together on the two F's. He will use octave tuning again in the scherzo of the Ninth Symphony.

All this has passed very swiftly; this would seem to be a quick, light finale on the scale of one of Haydn's. But not the least of the jolts here is one of Beethoven's most outrageously outsize and adventurous codas. It is artfully prepared, and when it begins after due suspense, it is unexpectedly serious. It moves, to begin with, in fairly sedate half-notes, though the triplets of the opening measures still buzz through the air and maintain an atmosphere of comedy. The music shows astonishing harmonic enterprise, including an attempt to slip into D major. This is again foiled by the quietly watchful bassoon and timpani so that once more the music can return to its F-major beginning, though in slightly expanded form.

But this time when the C-sharp returns, it will not be ignored. It insists five times, which is enough for the orchestra to take it seriously and accept it as the dominant of a hitherto untouched key, F-sharp minor. This is hopelessly remote from F major. Again the timpani save the day, this time with a bold pun. E-sharp is a perfectly good note in F-sharp minor, being the important leading tone of the scale. But E-sharp is, to all intents and purposes, the same as F, and when the drums, seconded by horns and trumpets, keep banging away at E-sharp/F, they soon succeed in rechanneling the music into the paths of righteousness, which is to say, F major. After which we hear no more of C-sharp. And if Beethoven then needs fifty-three bars of tonic and dominant to reassure us that F major is what he really means, no wonder.[30]

He was proud of what he had achieved here. Someone asked him why the Seventh Symphony was more popular than the Eighth. "Because the Eighth is so much better," he growled.

Symphony No. 9 in D minor

> *Allegro ma non troppo, un poco maestoso*
> *Molto vivace—Presto—Tempo I*
> *Adagio molto e cantabile—Andante moderato*
> *Finale:* Ode To Joy

Although some of the ideas eventually used in the Ninth Symphony appear in sketches of 1817–18, Beethoven only began concentrated work on the

---

[30] Had Beethoven ever seen or heard Haydn's delicious Symphony No. 67, also in F major? The last measures of its quicksilver finale might have given Beethoven the idea for those F-major wind chords that swing up and down like gibbons on a jungle gym.

score in 1822. It occupied him throughout 1823, and he completed it in February 1824. The first performance took place at the Kärntnerthor Theater in Vienna on 7 May 1824, the new symphony being preceded by the *Consecration of the House* Overture and the first hearing in Vienna of the *Kyrie, Credo,* and *Agnus Dei* of the *Missa solemnis.* The deaf composer stood on stage beating time and turning the pages of his score, but the real conducting was done by Michael Umlauf. The vocal soloists were Henriette Sontag, Karoline Unger, Anton Haitzinger, and Joseph Seipelt. The dedication is to King Frederick William III of Prussia.

Two flutes and piccolo, two oboes, two clarinets, two bassoons and contrabassoon, four horns, two trumpets, three trombones, timpani, triangle, cymbals, bass drum, and strings, plus soprano, alto, tenor, and bass solos, and four-part mixed chorus.

Few musicians would assert that the Ninth is the greatest of all symphonies, that it is the summit of Beethoven's achievement, perhaps not even that it is his finest symphony or, in any altogether personal way, their own favorite. Yet we treat it as though we did in fact believe all those things. It claims a special place, not only in the history of the symphony and in Beethoven's growth as an artist, mensch, and public figure, but also in our own hearts and heads, in what we remember in our lives and what we look forward to. A performance of it can never be an ordinary event, just another concert, and not even the phonograph record—whose democratic way of making all things indiscriminately accessible is certainly a mixed blessing—has been able to kill that. Insistently, its shadow falls across the music of the nineteenth century and the early years of our own. Everywhere, we hear the echoes of its mysterious opening, of its bizarreries, its recitatives and hymns, its publicly waged struggle for coherence and resolution.

More, by carrying to new heights the concept of the victory symphony as worked out in the *Eroica* and the Fifth, it redefines the nature of symphonic ambition. Explicitly, it seeks to make an ethical statement as much as a musical one. It stands as roadblock, model—often a dangerous model—and inspiration. It demands that we come to terms with it. Adrian Leverkühn, the composer hero of Thomas Mann's *Doctor Faustus,* must "revoke" it, and Michael Tippett began his Third Symphony, an eloquent report in music on the human condition in the year 1972, from the urge to respond to its affirmation with some questions of his own. Quite simply, it is "the Ninth Symphony"—or even just "the Ninth"—and when Leverkühn gives voice to his need to "revoke the Ninth Symphony," we do not stop to wonder whether he means Haydn's or Dvořák's or Mahler's.

The Ninth is the confluence of many currents and forces in Beethoven's life: of an involvement since boyhood with the work of Friedrich von Schiller and a plan cherished over thirty years to set his ode *An die Freude* (To Joy); of a fugue subject jotted down in a notebook about 1815 and again in somewhat altered form two or three years later (this became the main theme of the scherzo); of an invitation from the Philharmonic Society of London to visit England in the winter of 1817–18 and to bring two new symphonies with him; of plans actually made around 1818 for two symphonies, one in D minor, the other to include a choral "Adagio Cantique . . . in ancient modes"; of Beethoven's acceptance in 1822 of the London Philharmonic Society's commission of a symphony, this being the outcome finally of the negotiations begun in 1817.[31]

Since 1812, the year of the great and frustrated passion between himself and Antonie Brentano, "the Immortal Beloved," Beethoven's life had been in a continuous state of crisis, the most draining elements of which were those tied to the drawn-out litigation over the guardianship of his nephew Karl. Since 1812, the year of the Seventh and Eighth symphonies and of his last violin sonata, Opus 96, he had written little, at least measured by his standards of inspiration and industry. The other major works of the decade were the final revision of *Fidelio* and the E-minor Piano Sonata, Opus 90 (both in 1814); the two cello sonatas, Opus 102 (1815); the song cycle *An die ferne Geliebte* (To the Distant Beloved) and the A-major Piano Sonata, Opus 101 (both in 1816); and the *Hammerklavier* Sonata, Opus 106 (1819). Beethoven's legal battle with his sister-in-law came to an end in April 1820 with a ruling in his favor—technically, anyway, though in fact Beethoven's assumption of guardianship over Karl precipitated new miseries for uncle and nephew alike.

In any event, Beethoven, as Maynard Solomon puts it, "set about reconstructing his life and completing his life's work." The process was slow. In what was left of 1820, he completed the E-major Piano Sonata, Opus 109, and the following year he was able to do most of the work on its two successors, the A-flat Sonata, Opus 110, and the C-minor, Opus 111. By 1822 he was again possessed by a rage of energy, putting the final touches on the last two sonatas, composing the *Consecration of the House* Overture, finishing the *Missa solemnis* (for which the deadline had been March 1820), and achieving most of the shockingly inventive *Diabelli* Variations.

---

[31] Re-examining the evidence, such as it is, Nicholas Cook suggests in his monograph on the Beethoven Ninth in the Cambridge Music Handbooks that the alleged two symphonies, the one in D minor and the one with the Adagio Cantique, may in fact have been one and the same.

As part of this regeneration, the various projects and ideas connected with the Ninth Symphony began to sort themselves out. In the summer of 1822, Beethoven was possibly still thinking of a pair of symphonies analogous to the Fifth/*Pastoral* and Seventh/Eighth pairs of 1808 and 1812. But by 1823, with his other projects completed, he was ready to focus on a single work, though he was not yet sure whether the finale would be vocal or instrumental (the material he sketched for a "finale instrumentale" grew in 1825 into the last movement of the A-minor String Quartet, Opus 132). The first movement was ready fairly early in 1823; most of the remainder was complete at least in outline in Beethoven's head by the end of that year. Not surprisingly, what gave Beethoven the most trouble was the question of how to get into the finale; how, that is, to write a passage whose task it would be to "justify" the unprecedented intervention of the human voice in a symphony. The "Eureka!" moment seems to have occurred around November 1823. Anton Schindler, Beethoven's amanuensis of those years, tells us that "one day [Beethoven] entered the room exclaiming 'I've got it! I've got it!' and showed me the sketchbook with the words, 'Let us sing the song of the immortal Schiller—Freude,' whereupon a solo voice immediately begins the hymn to joy."

Once the score was finished, a performance had to be organized. Beethoven, annoyed with the Viennese and their passion for Rossini, flirted with Berlin, and only the energetic and flattering intervention of his friends saved the premiere for the city that had been his home for the previous thirty-one years. Endless difficulties attended the choice of theater, conductor, and soloists, not to mention questions of budget and the price of tickets. The program itself occasioned more argument; it was definitely good that the original plan of preceding the new symphony with the *Missa solemnis* in its entirety was scrapped. (The three movements of the Mass that were, in the event, sung had to be billed as Three Grand Hymns to get around the ecclesiastical interdict against the performance of liturgical music in a theater.)

Beethoven was especially pleased with his astonishing young women soloists: Henriette Sontag, only eighteen, had already created the title role in Weber's *Euryanthe* and was to go on to a career of high distinction; the twenty-year-old Karoline Unger later earned the considerable regard of Donizetti and Bellini. The tenor, Anton Haitzinger, then twenty-eight, also had an impressive career ahead of him; little is known of Joseph Seipelt, the bass, other than that he was a compromise third-choice candidate and that at the concert his high F-sharp gave out.

Not least of the touchy questions that had to be dealt with was that of Beethoven's own participation. Although by then as good as totally deaf, he had nonetheless tried to conduct the dress rehearsal of the November 1822 *Fidelio* revival and suffered a dreadful and humiliating disaster. (For that matter, remember Spohr's account of the preparations for the Seventh Symphony's premiere in 1813.) Even so, the possibility was discussed of having Beethoven conduct the exceedingly difficult *Consecration of the House* Overture. That did not happen, but he did stand on the stage during the Ninth Symphony before an orchestra and chorus who had been instructed by the "real" conductor, Michael Umlauf, to pay no attention to him.

Though a financial catastrophe for Beethoven, the concert evoked intense enthusiasm. The scherzo was actually interrupted by applause—probably at the surprise timpani entrance in the second section—and an encore was demanded. When the performance ended, Beethoven was still hunched over, turning the leaves of his score, and Karoline Unger gently turned his head around so that he might see the applause he could not hear.

Schott of Mainz published the symphony in the summer of 1826. Beethoven agonized long over the dedication, rejecting in turn his pupil Ferdinand Ries (the one who had been so startled by the "wrong" horn entrance in the *Eroica*), Emperor Francis I of Austria, Tsar Alexander I of Russia, the London Philharmonic Society, and Louis XVIII of France. He settled at last on Frederick William III of Prussia, son of the cellist-king, Frederick William II, for whom Mozart had written his last three string quartets. Beethoven's choice of this drably cautious monarch seems odd, but Maynard Solomon suggests a haunting explanation. Since 1810, rumors had circulated in print that Beethoven was the illegitimate son of Frederick William II (or in some versions Frederick the Great), and no appeals to concern for his mother's honor or just common sense moved the composer to deny these stories. "One wonders," Solomon writes, "if it is altogether accidental that Beethoven chose to dedicate his symphony on the brotherhood of man to the son of the man rumored to be his own father."

The Ninth Symphony traces a path from darkness to light, and of this process and of the struggle for clarification, the famous opening, imitated over and over in the nineteenth century, offers a microcosmic view. We hear at first just two very soft notes, E and A, sustained in the horns, vibrating in violins and cellos. As at the beginning of the *Eroica*, where the initial E-flat chords were made horizontal and turned into a melody, two-note figures—sometimes E/A, sometimes A/E—detach themselves as melodic fragments. Their appearances come to be more closely spaced, and they cease to be so surely and regularly downbeating. The two notes even become three. The effect is of crescendo, but it is a crescendo achieved by rhythmic and harmonic tension and by the gradual expansion of range as well as by actual increase in volume.

At a certain point in the crescendo the E's drop away, to be instantly replaced by D's in bassoons and horns that cloud the texture more than they penetrate it; the new note in fact sounds strangely dissonant against the prevailing A's. The D turns out to be the "answer" the whole orchestra agrees on at the great *fortissimo* summit of that first crescendo; the tense anticipation of that note is Beethoven's utterly personal mark. The same could be said of the powerful perversity that has Beethoven finally arrive in D minor with a great downward-plunging theme that begins by emphasizing A.

This is the only first movement in a Beethoven symphony in which no repeat is marked for the exposition. Even so, this is, as the scale of the initial arrival at D minor suggests it will be, a huge structure. The material itself is diverse, ranging from the sternly angular to the softly lyric, from the calmly scored to the intensely intertwined. The most songful of Beethoven's ideas, a sweetly euphonious melody for woodwinds, has about it a haunting sense of something familiar, but the speed of events is such that we scarcely have time to trace this.

The entrance into the development is striking. Beethoven has taken the music to B-flat major, and that is where he concludes the exposition with a series of emphatic cadences. At this point, instead of modulating to another harmonic area, he picks the music up and puts it down somewhere else (as he had at the start of the *Eroica*'s first-movement coda). To be specific, he goes the smallest possible step from B-flat to A (with a wonderful orchestral detail: a *pianissimo* A on trumpets and timpani half a measure after the shift, as though to ratify it). And we are back to the A/ E open fifths of measure 1. Beethoven, in other words, sets us up to believe that he is going to repeat the exposition in the conventional way, and it is the startling intrusion of F-sharp to produce the chord of D major—the more startling because still *pianissimo*—that alerts us to the fact that we are on a new patch of road.

D major turns out to be a mirage. Of course Beethoven is never casual about placing anything so noticeable, but for the moment we must wait to discover what else he has in mind. He presents the development in two large chapters. The first is concerned with stirring the elements of the first theme around in various ways: here the moods and sonority shift quickly and often. The second chapter is also based on the first theme, but now Beethoven treats it in a fugued texture.

As the temperature rises, we come to realize that the F-sharp in the D-major chords at the start of the development was the seed of the most dramatic event in the movement. This is the recapitulation. Beethoven approaches it with a superlative sense of drama and suspense, and when the long buildup on the dominant has reached the bursting point, the resolution is not the D-minor arrival that we expect, but a cataclysm in D major. The sense of pressure is tremendous because the chord is not given with the stabilizing D in the bass but, rather, is tensely poised over the critical F-sharp. At the same time, the D-ness, so to speak, is affirmed by a thirty-eight-measure timpani roll on D.

After this volcanic entry, the rest of the recapitulation seems more normal, but *seems* must be stressed. Everything is recognizable as a revisiting of something from the exposition, but at the same time, Beethoven sheds new light on every element and every event, by placing it in a new harmonic context, by scoring it differently, and, most subtly and beautifully, by his constant contractions and expansions. For example, ideas that occurred two measures apart earlier on are now separated by four measures; on the other hand, a fifty-measure process is now compressed into twelve.

The coda is astonishing. First of all, it is exceptionally long. In thematic manipulation it partakes of the character of a second development, though the steady harmonic orientation to D minor makes it very different from a development. D major makes a touching return in a dolce horn solo, but here again Beethoven withholds something by setting the episode over an A in the bass rather than the firm D. In a wonderfully imaginative passage, single woodwinds add their chatter to the serene horn solo, only to find themselves gradually drowned by the growing assertiveness of the strings as they stalk up and down broken chord figures. Then the strings recede, to reveal that the woodwinds' chatter has never ceased. For the final section of this chapter, Beethoven introduces one of his ostinato basses to initiate a crescendo to the final *fortissimo* statement of the first D-minor theme. Franck and Bruckner are two composers who were much taken with this device.

The scherzo is a huge structure, as obsessive in its driving and exuberant play with few ideas as the first movement was generous in its richness of material. Much as the tiny scherzo in the *Hammerklavier* Sonata is a satiric variant of the ferocious first movement, so does this scherzo continue—bizarrely—what came before. Here Beethoven starts right off with his descending D-minor chord, but was a chord ever laid out more oddly than this one with its irrepressible kettledrums? When first we heard D major it was amid the roaring flames of the first movement's recapitulation. When it returns in the trio, it is rustic, comfortable, more in the manner of the pastoral horn solo in the first movement's coda. There is also something about it of hymnic or communal music. It reaches forward toward the world of the Ode to Joy, and bit by bit we begin to get the idea that

the conquest of D major is at the center of the Ninth Symphony's scenario.

Two bars of upbeat—clarinets, bassoons, middle and lower strings—
ease us into the Adagio. Beethoven at first alternates two themes of contrasting gait (Adagio molto e cantabile in 4/4 and Andante moderato in 3/
4), key (B-flat major and D major), and temperature. He varies both
themes, drops the second altogether after a single return (in G major—D
must still be held in reserve), but envelops the first in ever more fanciful
decoration. It is carried to a double climax with noble fanfares and a magnificent striding into new harmonic regions. The effect is one of exaltation
and, at the end, profound peace.

The metronome mark in the score of 60 to the beat for the Adagio is
worth observing; however, conductors are so much in thrall to tradition,
one based on a language of solemnity from much later in the nineteenth
century, that the tempo we most often hear is likely to be something like
two-thirds of the one Beethoven indicates. At the traditional slow pace,
the music must move with four, or even eight, impulses per measure. If
you transfer the habit of four or eight impulses per measure to Beethoven's
tempo, the effect will be of scramble and haste. If, on the other hand, you
pay attention to how the harmony moves and let that determine your
breathing and pulse rate, you will discover that with only two impulses
per measure you can, at exactly the tempo Beethoven prescribes, have a
wonderfully spacious sense of forward motion, a true adagio molto. In one
of the later variations, the violins take wing in fantastical flights of
sixteenth-notes and sixteenth-note triplets. At Beethoven's tempo we can
hear that he does not intend an espressivo, much-leaned-into violin melody with some vague wind chords behind; rather, the winds play the
theme, clearly and intelligibly, and the violins add an ecstatic—and brilliantly virtuosic—counterpoint, comparable to the rapturous obbligato
with which the solo violin accompanies the *Benedictus* in the *Missa solemnis*.

The most horrendous noise Beethoven could devise shatters the peace
in which this great Adagio concludes, and now an extraordinary drama is
played before us. Cellos and basses protest what Wagner called the
"Schreckensfanfare" (fanfare of terror) in the gestures of operatic recitative.
Instrumental recitatives are not in themselves new: examples so specific
one could set words to them occur in such familiar works as Mozart's great
Piano Concerto in E-flat, K.271, and Haydn's Concertante in B-flat, and
one scholar has pointed out close and particular resemblances of the Beethoven Ninth recitatives to those in a piano concerto by Ludwig Böhner.[32]

---

[32] Böhner (1787–1860), celebrated both as pianist and composer, is believed to have been the
model for E.T.A. Hoffmann's eccentric, Romantically overwrought capellmeister Johannes
Kreisler.

But these recitatives of Beethoven's are not just stylized allusion to opera; they are part of a real scenario. At stake is a problem that Beethoven turned into a mighty headache for generations of composers to follow: what are we going to do for a finale?

The suggestion the orchestra makes initially is to return to the first movement. As silly as it is unlikely, this proposal is turned down by the low strings in an angry recitative. Suggestions to go back to the second and third movements meet the same scornful, furious response. Finally, after three tries and three rejections, the woodwinds offer something apparently new and different. It is the mere adumbration of a theme, but even so, those hectoring cellos and basses change their tone: with some emphatic cheering along by winds and drums, they lose no time in expressing their enthusiasm. Now we might in retrospect understand why the lyric melody near the beginning of the first movement sounded somehow familiar: it foreshadowed the fresh idea that the woodwinds have just offered.

Are there listeners left who, when they hear that foreshadowing, do not hear beyond it to the melody to come? But what must this moment have been like for Franz Schubert and the others who heard it in the Kärntnerthor Theater on 7 May 1824 and for whom the tune just around the corner was not yet a fact of life? Those four bars of quiet melody, poised on a dominant harmony, all eagerness and anticipation, what did they sound like, what did they suggest?

The orchestra rounds off the strings recitative with a firm cadence, and without a second's pause for breath—a wonderful and characteristic detail wiped out by generation after generation of mindless conductors— one of the world's great songs begins. It was J. W. N. Sullivan, in his beautiful book *Beethoven: His Spiritual Development,* who tied to the music of the composer's last years Wordsworth's phrase about "a mind forever/ Voyaging through strange seas of thought, alone." But we also find in late Beethoven a quest for simplicity, for immediacy, and here, his "großer Wurf," his great gamble, to invent *the* quintessentially popular tune succeeds miraculously. (It includes that one anticipation, the shift that comes one beat before we expect it—the note to which the word *alle* will eventually be set—to remind us that this is, after all, by Beethoven.) This song Beethoven spreads before us in a series of simple and compelling orchestral variations, interrupted by a return of the horrendous fanfare that began the movement. What earlier was matter for our imaginations now becomes explicit. The recitative is really sung now, and to words that Beethoven himself invented as preface to Schiller's Ode (and not quite the ones he had blurted out to Schindler): "O friends, not these tones; Rather, let us tune our voices In more pleasant and more joyful song."

Having begun with variations, Beethoven continues on that path. It is a free set that begins simply, much like the orchestral variations that followed the first statement of the theme. The chorus seconds the solo bass, but Beethoven reserves the sound of the soprano voice, solo and chorus, for a line that must have pierced the ever lorn and lonely composer deeply: "Wer ein holdes Weib errungen,/Mische seinen Jubel ein!" (He who has found a goodly woman,/Let him add his jubilation too!). The vision of the Cherub standing before God is set before us by a harmonic diversion of great simplicity and stunning power. Then, with a boldness of contrast that no other composer except perhaps Mahler would have dared, he brings us the sound of a distant and approaching marching band as men are bidden to follow their courses "gladly, like a hero to the conquest." The orchestra continues the discourse in a double fugue, whose complexities are effectively spelled by a return of the Ode in grandly plain form.

Classical variations traditionally had a slow variation near the end. Here this becomes what is in effect an entire slow movement. The command, "Seid umschlungen, Millionen!" (Be embraced, ye Millions!), is given at first by men's voices, trombones, and low strings in unison, in a manner meant to evoke church chant—a remnant of the old plan for an "Adagio Cantique . . . in ancient modes." For Schiller's verses about the Creator, the loving Father who surely dwells "above the canopy of the stars," Beethoven invents the most mysterious, anti-gravitational, unearthly music in the symphony. While he does not want the Adagio to be too slow, he does want the singing and playing to be *divoto*. After the vision of the Creator, all is pure joy, and the music, pausing only for an ecstatically virtuosic cadenza for the solo quartets, rushes headlong to its intoxicated finish.

Schiller himself did not think much of his ode *To Joy*—and who, reading it away from Beethoven's setting, would disagree with him? He had been dead eighteen years when Beethoven set it to music, and it is impossible, though intriguing, to guess how he might have reacted to Beethoven's symphony. But Beethoven read into it what he needed. What is sure is that he transformed it, not only in spirit, but literally, by selecting, omitting (above all, omitting), transposing, reordering. And once the words have entered, they, and of course even more, Beethoven's transcendent responses to them, sweep us along

> As joyously as His suns fly
> Across the glorious landscape of the heavens
> . . . Gladly, like a hero to the conquest.

O Freunde, nicht diese Töne!	O friends, not these tones!
Sondern laßt uns angenehmere anstimmen, und freudenvollere.	Rather, let us tune our voices in more pleasant and more joyful song.
—Ludwig van Beethoven	

Freude, schöner Götterfunken,
Tochter aus Elysium,
Wir betreten feuertrunken,
Himmlische, dein Heiligtum!
Deine Zauber binden wieder,
Was die Mode streng geteilt;
Alle Menschen werden Brüder,
Wo dein sanfter Flügel weilt.

Wem der große Wurf gelungen,
Eines Freundes Freund zu sein,
Wer ein holdes Weib errungen,
Mische seinen Jubel ein!
Ja—wer auch nur *eine* Seele
Sein nennt auf dem Erdenrund!
Und wer's nie gekonnt, der stehle
Weinend sich aus diesem Bund.

Freude trinken alle Wesen
An den Brüsten der Natur;
Alle Guten, alle Bösen
Folgen ihrer Rosenspur.
Küsse gab sie uns und Reben,
Einen Freund, geprüft im Tod,

Wollust war dem Wurm gegeben,
Und der Cherub steht vor Gott.

Froh wie seine Sonnen fliegen
Durch des Himmels prächt'gen Plan,
Laufet, Brüder, eure Bahn,
Freudig wie ein Held zum Siegen.

Freude, schöner Götterfunken,
Tochter aus Elysium,
Wir betreten feuertrunken,
Himmlische, dein Heiligtum!
Deine Zauber binden wieder,
Was die Mode streng geteilt;
Alle Menschen werden Brüder,
Wo dein sanfter Flügel weilt.

Seid umschlungen, Millionen!
Diesen Kuß der ganzen Welt!
Brüder—überm Sternenzelt
Muß ein lieber Vater wohnen.

Ihr stürzt nieder, Millionen?
Ahnest du den Schöpfer, Welt?
Such ihn überm Sternenzelt!
Über Sternen muß er wohnen.

Joy, beauteous, godly spark,
Daughter of Elysium,
Drunk with fire, O Heavenly One,
We come unto your sacred shrine.
Your magic once again unites
That which Fashion sternly parted.
All men are made brothers
Where your gentle wings abide.

He who has won in that great gamble
Of being friend unto a friend,
He who has found a goodly woman,
Let him add his jubilation too!
Yes—he who can call even one soul
On earth his own!
And he who never has, let him steal
Weeping from this company.

All creatures drink of Joy
At Nature's breasts.
All good, all evil souls
Follow in her rose-strewn wake.
She gave us kisses and vines,
And a friend who has proved faithful even in
death.
Lust was given to the Serpent,
And the Cherub stands before God.

As joyously as His suns fly
Across the glorious landscape of the heavens,
Brothers, follow your appointed course,
Gladly, like a hero to the conquest.

Joy, beauteous, godly spark,
Daughter of Elysium,
Drunk with fire, O Heavenly One,
We come unto your sacred shrine.
Your magic once again unites
That which Fashion sternly parted.
All men are made brothers
Where your gentle wings abide.

Be embraced, ye Millions!
This kiss to the whole world!
Brothers—beyond the canopy of the stars
Surely a loving Father dwells.

Do you fall headlong, ye Millions?
Have you any sense of the Creator, World?
Seek Him above the canopy of the stars!
Surely he dwells beyond the stars.

Freude, schöner Götterfunken,
Tochter aus Elysium,
Wir betreten feuertrunken,
Himmlische, dein Heiligtum.

Seid umschlungen, Millionen!
Diesen Kuß der ganzen Welt!

Ihr stürzt nieder, Millionen?
Ahnest du den Schöpfer, Welt?
Such ihn überm Sternenzelt!
Brüder—überm Sternenzelt
Muß ein lieber Vater wohnen.
Freude, Tochter aus Elysium!
Deine Zauber binden wieder,
Was die Mode streng geteilt;
Alle Menschen werden Brüder,
Wo dein sanfter Flügel weilt.

Seid umschlungen, Millionen!
Diesen Kuß der ganzen Welt!
Brüder—überm Sternenzelt
Muß ein lieber Vater wohnen.
Freude, schöner Götterfunken,
Tochter aus Elysium!
Freude, schöner Götterfunken!

—Friedrich von Schiller, adapted by
    Ludwig van Beethoven

Joy, beauteous, godly spark,
Daughter of Elysium,
Drunk with fire, O Heavenly One,
We come unto your sacred shrine.

Be embraced, ye Millions!
This kiss to the whole world!

Do you fall headlong, ye Millions?
Have you any sense of the Creator, World?
Seek Him above the canopy of the stars!
Brothers—beyond the canopy of the stars
Surely a loving Father dwells.
Joy, Daughter of Elysium!
Your magic once again unites
That which Fashion sternly parted.
All men are made brothers
Where your gentle wings abide.

Be embraced, ye Millions!
This kiss to the whole world!
Brothers—beyond the canopy of the stars
Surely a loving Father dwells.
Joy, beauteous, godly spark,
Daughter of Elysium!
Joy, beauteous, godly spark!

—transl. Donna Hewitt

Donna Hewitt's translation was commissioned by the Boston Symphony Orchestra with a grant from The First National Bank of Boston and Bank of Boston International–New York © 1979 Boston Symphony Orchestra.

/Hector Berlioz

Hector Berlioz

Louis-Hector Berlioz was born on 11 December 1803 in La Côte-Saint-André, Department of Isère, France, and died in Paris on 8 March 1869.

Episode in the Life of an Artist, Fantastic Symphony in Five Parts, Opus 14

Dreams, Passions: Largo—Allegro agitato e appassionato assai—Religiosamente
A Ball: Valse: Allegro non troppo
Scene in the Fields: Adagio
March to the Scaffold: Allegretto non troppo
Dream of a Witches' Sabbath: Larghetto—Allegro

Berlioz composed his *Fantastic* Symphony in 1830, though some of the material goes back as far perhaps as 1819. François-Antoine Habeneck conducted the first performance on 5 December 1830 in Paris. Again with Habeneck on the podium (and with Berlioz as one of the drummers), a considerably revised version was presented in Paris on 9 December 1832, together with a newly composed sequel, the lyric mono-drama *Lélio, ou Le Retour à la vie* (The Return to Life).

Two flutes (second doubling piccolo), two oboes (second doubling English horn), two clarinets (first doubling E-flat clarinet), four bassoons, four

horns, two cornets, two trumpets, three trombones, two ophicleides (generally replaced nowadays by boomier and fatter-sounding bass tubas), timpani, bass drum, snare drum, cymbals, bells (in whose absence "one or more pianos" may be substituted), two harps, and strings.

No disrespect to Mahler or Shostakovich, but this is the most remarkable First Symphony ever written. And right away I want to note that it is the first of four symphonies by Berlioz, the others—*Harold en Italie*, after Byron, with solo viola (1834), *Roméo et Juliette*, after Shakespeare, with chorus and solo singers (1839), and *Grande Symphonie funèbre et triomphale*, with military band (1840; later with strings and chorus added)—being equally ambitious. *Roméo et Juliette* is indeed the summit of Berlioz's achievement as a maker of musical poetry.

Not the least of the many amazing things about the *Symphonie fantastique* is its date. Of course, much that was new and forward-looking was in the air in 1830, particularly in the social, political, and scientific spheres. The Parisians had torn up their cobblestones and gotten rid of a king who believed in Divine Right; a new word, socialism, was added to the language; the Poles made one of their periodic and doomed bids for freedom; Mazzini was about to found his Young Italy movement; the British parliament had just passed the Catholic Emancipation Act and would soon enact the first in a series of reform bills designed to enfranchise the middle class; suttee was abolished in British India; and America experienced the Nat Turner revolts and the first effective moves toward abolition. Faraday and Maxwell made revolutionary discoveries in the field of electromagnetism; chloroform came into use, as did the screw propeller for steamships; the first regular railway service began on a forty-mile stretch between Manchester and Liverpool; London got its first steam-driven trams; and geese breathed easier when a Midlands engineer called Perry patented a wonderfully efficient steel nib for writing, slit and with a center hole. Some of this knocking down of old walls was reflected in art and books—in, for example, Delacroix's *Liberty Leading the People*; in the work of Daumier, who drew his first caricatures in 1830; in the vast forty-novel panorama, *La Comédie humaine*, which Daumier's friend Balzac began that year; in Victor Hugo's *Hernani* and Stendhal's *Le Rouge et le noir*; and in the *Poems, Chiefly Lyrical* by Alfred Tennyson, just one year down from Cambridge.

It would be surprising if music had not exploded as well. When the 1830s were over, Chopin had written his Etudes and Preludes, Schumann had done most of his important work for solo piano, and Liszt's transcriptions (which included Berlioz's *Fantastique* and *Harold en Italie* as well as two of his overtures) and original compositions practically constituted a reinvention of the piano. Paganini vastly expanded the possibilities of the violin, and important technical advances were achieved in the design of wind instruments.

From the vantage point of the end of the twentieth century, we can see fairly easily that the beginnings of a new music were to be found in two places where not every observer in 1830 would have thought to look: in the works of Beethoven and Bach. And the better we know the *Fantastique,* the more clearly we can sense in it the presence of Beethoven and of that classical tradition Beethoven brought to so remarkable a pass. At the same time, however deeply he was in debt to Beethoven, Berlioz strove to write "new music." He succeeded. The *Fantastic* Symphony sounds and behaves like nothing ever heard before. Berlioz's orchestra is as new as Paganini's violin and Liszt's piano; his expressive intentions and his willingness to stop at nothing in their realization are unheard-of departures. Of course Beethoven had written some stunning new music of his own in the 1820s: his last quartets, particularly Opus 131, and the Ninth Symphony and the *Missa solemnis* are masterpieces in some ways even more radical than the *Fantastique* and casting yet longer shadows into the future. Still, the *Fantastique* takes off on paths Beethoven could never have imagined; that it was written just three years after the death of Beethoven is a fact to stagger the historical imagination.

On 11 September 1827 Berlioz had gone to the Paris Odéon for a performance of *Hamlet* by a company from London. It was a distinguished group, whose leading men were Edmund Kean and Charles Kemble, two of the most renowned actors on the English stage. The younger female roles were taken by Harriet Smithson, a twenty-seven-year-old actress who had been brought up in Ireland. Her accent kept her from success of the first order in London, but it did not disturb the Parisians. Berlioz fell instantly and wildly in love with her. He spoke next to no English then (later he made considerable and quite successful efforts to learn it), so the violent effect upon him of that evening's *Hamlet* was a combination of verbal music, his vivid and detailed recollection of the play from his reading of it in the Letourneur-Guizot translation, and, as far as Ophelia was concerned, sheer Eros. He wrote to Smithson repeatedly, but they did not meet. He heard gossip about an affair between her and her manager. This hurt him, but it also provided, for a moment, enough distance to enable him to plan and to begin work on the symphony whose design he described in detail to his friend the poet Humbert Ferrand.

In brief, "an artist, gifted with a vivid imagination [falls in love with] a woman who embodies the ideal of beauty and fascination that he has long been seeking. . . . He imagines that there is some hope; he believes himself loved." Later, in a sudden fit of despair, "he poisons himself with opium, but the narcotic, instead of killing him, induces a horrible vision" in which he believes that, having murdered his beloved, he is condemned to death and witnesses his own execution.[1] After death "he sees himself surrounded by a foul assembly of sorcerers and devils. . . . [His beloved] is now only a prostitute, fit to take part in such an orgy."

The premiere of the *Fantastique* took place on 5 December 1830. At this point, Harriet—or Henriette, as Berlioz always called her—had been replaced in his affections by Camille Moke for a time.[2] Two years later, when Berlioz returned from a lengthy stay in Rome as a stipendiary at the French Academy, he was ready to present a newly sharpened and improved version of his symphony. It now had a sequel, *Lélio,* in which the actor Pierre-Touzé Bocage played a Berlioz-like figure and whose script was full of unmistakable allusions to his passion for Miss Smithson. She was in fact in Paris again, this time overseeing a much less successful season; further-more, Berlioz discovered that upon his return from Rome he had taken the apartment vacated by her the day before. Probably through the connivance of Maurice Schlesinger, the publisher who would issue the first edition of the *Fantastique* in 1845, she was persuaded to attend Berlioz's concert on 9 December 1832, though it seems she went without realizing beforehand the nature of the event or the identity of the composer.

On the morrow of the *Fantastique*'s second premiere, Berlioz and Smithson finally met. Before long, she had pronounced the fatal "Berlioz, je t'aime," and on 3 October 1833 they were married. Her French was roughly on the level of his English. The whole business was a disaster. They separated in the summer of 1844 and should have done so much sooner. By then, Smithson had lost her looks, and an accident had put an end to her career. She died in 1854, an alcoholic and paralyzed. Berlioz, who had meanwhile entered into a second unhappy liaison with the singer Marie Recio, supported Smithson financially until her death. From the wreckage he drew two more musical memorials to their passion, the great *Roméo et Juliette* Symphony and the heart-rending song *La Mort d'Ophélie,*

---

[1] As Leonard Bernstein put it at one of his New York Philharmonic Young People's Concerts, "Berlioz tells it like it is. . . . You take a trip, you wind up screaming at your own funeral."

[2] Camille Moke, a superbly gifted pianist and an immensely beautiful woman, was nineteen when Berlioz fell in love with her and they exchanged rings. While he was in Italy and after a disturbing period without news from her, he received a letter from her mother announcing Camille's engage-ment to the pianist and piano manufacturer Camille Pleyel. Determined to kill both Camilles, Mme. Moke, and himself, he acquired disguise as a lady's maid, scribbled some instructions about the *Fantastique* to the conductor Habeneck, and set out on the next mail coach to Paris. En route, his rage cooled. From Nice he wrote a letter asking to be readmitted to the Academy at Rome, received a "friendly, sympathetic, paternal" reply from Horace Vernet, the director, spent three more happy weeks at Nice composing his splendid *King Lear* Overture, and returned to Rome and to his labors on the revised *Fantastique* and its sequel.

which, arranged for two-part female chorus with orchestra, he later incorporated in the collection he called *Tristia*.

In 1831, Carlyle remarked on "these Autobiographical times of ours" (*autobiography* was another new word of the time). Berlioz wrote several programs for this autobiographical—indeed Autobiographical with a capital A—and in every way fantastic symphony of his, and it has been remarked that the differences between them serve as a barometer of his changing feelings for Harriet Smithson. What follows in italics, sudden explosions of CAPITAL LETTERS and all, is the note he published with the score in 1845 and described as "indispensable for a complete understanding of the dramatic outline of the work." The commentary in brackets is mine.

The composer's aim has been to develop, to the extent that they have musical possibilities, various situations in the life of an artist. The plan of the instrumental drama, which is deprived of the help of words, needs to be outlined in advance. The following program should therefore be thought of like the spoken text of an opera, serving to introduce the musical movements, whose character and expression it calls into being.

Part One: Dreams, Passions—The author imagines that a young musician, afflicted with that moral disease that a celebrated writer [Chateaubriand] calls "the surge of passions," sees for the first time a woman who embodies all the charms of the ideal being of whom he has dreamed, and he falls hopelessly in love with her. Through a bizarre trick of fancy, the beloved image always appears in the mind's eye of the artist linked to a musical thought whose character, passionate but also noble and reticent, he finds similar to the one he attributes to his beloved.

The melodic image and its human model pursue him incessantly like a double idée fixe. [3] *This is the reason for the constant appearance, in every movement of the symphony, of the melody that begins the first Allegro. The passage from this state of melancholic reverie, interrupted by a few fits of unmotivated joy, to one of delirious passion, with its movements of fury and jealousy, its return of tenderness, its tears, its religious consolation—all this is the subject of the first movement.*

[Even the first two preparatory measures for a few wind instruments are so unconventionally voiced—though without ostentation—that their authorship is unmistakable. But more remarkable still is what follows: the sound of the muted strings, the unmeasured pauses between phrases, the single pizzicato chord for violas and cellos, the two strange interventions (also pizzicato) for the basses, the mysterious cello triplets rocking back and forth at the first climax, the one appearance of flutes and clarinets

---

[3] Berlioz took the phrase *idée fixe* from Victor Hugo's brand-new *Le Dernier jour d'un condamné*.

with horns. The plaintive violin melody with which the symphony begins is that of a song, *Je vais donc quitter pour jamais*, that Berlioz, still in his teens, had written for Jean-Pierre Florian's pastoral *Estelle et Némorin*. This, as the American Berlioz scholar Katherine Reeve pointed out to me, is important because it so specifically brings Estelle Dubeuf, Berlioz's child-hood love (nineteen to his twelve), "into the backlog of inspiration that went into this *summa* of his early life." Finally, what an amazing effect it is at the end of the slow introduction when the chord of winds with tremo-lando strings is hushed from *mezzo-forte* to *pianissimo*, to swell again to *fortissimo*, like music carried on the whim of capricious winds.

What is classical is Berlioz's concern with proportions and relations. He specifies, for example, that each measure of the Allegro should equal one beat of the Largo introduction. The Allegro itself is agitato e appassio-nato assai, but it also begins as a sonata form, repeated exposition and all. In the recapitulation (which begins with the return of the *idée fixe* in the dominant) and his *coda religiosa*, Berlioz is more inclined to go his own way; even so, the sense of continuous evolving is not more radical than what we hear in many a recapitulation/coda in late Haydn. The subtly shaped *idée fixe* itself—the melody that violins and flute play to an accom-paniment of nervous interjections by the strings when the Allegro begins—goes back to 1828 and a cantata called *Herminie*, composed as part of an unsuccessful application for the Prix de Rome. Berlioz found the perfect place for it here.]

Part Two: A Ball—The artist finds himself in the most varied situations—in the midst of THE TUMULT OF A FESTIVITY, in the peaceful contempla-tion of the beauties of nature; but wherever he is, in the city, in the country, the beloved image appears before him and troubles his soul.

[The first three dozen measures of the waltz are a magical transition into the relatively remote key of A major (remote, that is, from the pre-ceding C major), and they paint for us the ballroom with its glitter and flicker, its swirling couples, the yards and yards of whispering silk. All this becomes gradually visible, like a new scene in the theater. This softly scintillating waltz is exquisitely scored. At some late stage, Berlioz added a part for a single cornet at the bottom of the autograph, but it was only published posthumously. Few conductors include it.]

Part Three: Scene in the Fields—Finding himself in the country at evening, he hears in the distance two shepherds piping a ranz des vaches in dialogue.[4] *This pastoral duet, the scenery, the quiet rustling of the trees gently disturbed by the wind, certain hopes he has recently found reason to entertain—all these come*

---

[4] A *ranz des vaches* is a tune sung or played by Swiss cattle herders. The most familiar example of it is the English-horn solo in Rossini's *William Tell* Overture. —M.S.

*together in giving his heart an unaccustomed calm, and in giving a brighter color
to his ideas. He reflects upon his isolation; he hopes that soon he will no longer
be alone. . . . But what if she were deceiving him! . . . This mixture of hope
and fear, these ideas of happiness disturbed by black presentiments, form the
subject of the ADAGIO. At the end, one of the shepherds again takes up the
ranz des vaches; the other no longer replies. . . . The distant sound of thunder
. . . solitude . . . silence.*

[The Scene in the Fields speaks very much from a new sensibility, yet
it is also here that we most feel the presence of Beethoven, particularly
the Beethoven of the Fifth and *Pastoral* symphonies.[5] It is also from the
Pastoral that Berlioz takes at least something of the design of his five-
movement symphony. Berlioz's piping shepherds are mutations of Beethoven's nightingale, quail, and cuckoo, but there is nothing in music before
this, or since, like the pathos of the recapitulated conversation with one
voice missing. As a picture of despairing loneliness it is without equal.
And the thunder—mostly in *piano* and *pianissimo*—of chords for four kettledrums is the voice of a new orchestral imagination. The principal theme
of the movement—that is, the almost unaccompanied melody for flute and
violins played immediately after the first conversation between English
horn and oboe—is one that Berlioz salvaged from the *Messe solennelle* he
composed in 1824 and that was believed lost until its rediscovery in 1991.]

*Part Four: March to the Scaffold—Having become certain that his love
goes unrecognized, the artist poisons himself with opium. The dose of the narcotic, too weak to kill him, plunges him into a sleep accompanied by the most
horrible visions. He dreams that he has killed the woman he had loved, that he
is condemned, led to the scaffold, and that he is witnessing HIS OWN EXECU-
TION. The procession moves forward to the sounds of a march that is now
somber and fierce, now brilliant and solemn, in which the muffled noise of heavy
steps gives way without mediation to the most noisy clangor. At the end of the
march, the first four measures of the IDÉE FIXE reappear like a last thought of
love interrupted by the fatal blow.*

[The March to the Scaffold, which Berlioz said he composed in a
single night, is another instance of finding the right destiny for an idea too
good to vanish in an abandoned project. Here the source is the opera *Les
Francs-juges* (The Judges of the Secret Court) written in 1826-27 but for
the most part destroyed by the composer. The Overture survives as one of
his strongest. In this stunning march, an instant knockout, Berlioz's orchestral imagination—the hand-stopped horn sounds, the use of the bas-

[5] While those are the Beethoven works most relevant to the *Fantastique*, Berlioz carefully studied
the Ninth Symphony (without which it is hard to imagine *Roméo et Juliette*) as well as the late
quartets and piano sonatas.

chestral imagination—the hand-stopped horn sounds, the use of the bassoon quartet, the timpani writing (again in chords as at the end of the slow movement)—is astonishing in every way.]

Part Five: Dream of a Witches' Sabbath—He sees himself at the sabbath, in the midst of a frightful assembly of ghosts, sorcerers, monsters of every kind, all come together for his funeral. Strange noises, groans, outbursts of laughter, distant cries which other cries seem to answer. The beloved melody appears again, but it has lost its character of nobility and reticence; now it is no more than the tune of an ignoble dance, trivial and grotesque: it is she, come to join the sabbath. . . . A roar of joy at her arrival. . . . She takes part in the devilish orgy. . . . Funeral knell, burlesque parody of the DIES IRAE,[6] SABBATH ROUND-DANCE. The sabbath round and the Dies irae combined.

[As we enter the final scene, with its trim thematic transformations, its bizarre sonorities—deep bells (or one or more pianos if you can't get the right bells), squawking E-flat clarinet, the beating of violin and viola strings with the wooden stick of the bow, glissandos for wind instruments, violent alternations of *ff* with *pp*—its grotesque imagery, its wild and coruscating brilliance, we have left the Old World for good.]

---

[6] Hymn sung in the funeral rites of the Catholic Church. —H.B.

Liszt wrote a powerful set of variations on this chant (*Totentanz*, 1849), and Tchaikovsky, Saint-Saëns, Rachmaninoff, Respighi, Shostakovich, and Dallapiccola are among the many composers who have followed Berlioz's example in quoting it. —M.S.

Johannes Brahms

Johannes Brahms was born in the Free City of Hamburg on 7 May 1833 and died in Vienna on 3 April 1897.

Symphony No. 1 in C minor, Opus 68   ·

Un poco sostenuto—Allegro—Meno allegro
Andante sostenuto
Un poco allegretto e grazioso
Adagio—Più andante—Allegro non troppo ma con brio—Più allegro

The first signs of the Symphony No. 1 date from 1862 in the form of a sketch for the main theme of the first movement copied by Clara Schumann in a letter to the violinist, conductor, and composer Joseph Joachim. Another sketch survives from 1868. Brahms does not seem to have begun to put the entire work together in earnest until about 1874; he finished it in the summer of 1876 at the resort of Sassnitz in the North German Baltic islands. Otto Dessoff conducted the premiere at Karlsruhe, Baden, on 4 November 1876. Numerous performances that season led to further revisions, particularly in the second and third movements, before the score finally appeared in print in 1877.

Two flutes, two oboes, two clarinets, two bassoons and contrabassoon, four horns, two trumpets, three trombones, timpani, and strings.

On 1 July 1862, Clara Schumann wrote to Joseph Joachim:

> The other day Johannes sent me—imagine my surprise!—the first move-
> ment of a symphony with the following bold opening:

Ex. 1

> That is rather strong, but I have become used to it. The movement is
> full of wonderful beauties, and the themes are treated with a mastery that is
> becoming more and more characteristic of him. It is all interwoven in a most
> interesting fashion and at the same time it bursts forth absolutely spontane-
> ously. One enjoys it in great drafts without being reminded of all the work
> there is in it.[1]

The Allegro of the First Symphony still began that way when Brahms
completed the piece fourteen years later—"rather strong" and, as the composer put it to Carl Reinecke, then the conductor at the Leipzig Gewandhaus, "not exactly lovable." By then the symphony had acquired an introduction and had undergone who knows what other changes. Brahms
disliked having the unauthorized peek into his workshop, and he fore-
stalled posthumous trespasses by destroying the sketches and preliminary
versions of virtually all his major works. What we know about the often
long and troubled compositional process of Brahms's works we must learn
or infer from his correspondence (and occasionally the letters that friends
like Clara Schumann and Joachim wrote to each other).

Brahms had begun to write a symphony in 1854, but that work eventually turned into his First Piano Concerto. The years passed. He composed two string sextets, two piano quartets, a piano quintet, a horn trio,
a cello sonata, piano variations on themes by Handel and Paganini, variations on a theme by Schumann and a book of waltzes for piano duet, A
German Requiem, the Alto Rhapsody, the Song of Destiny, motets, part

[1] Berthold Litzmann, Clara Schumann, an Artist's Life, translated by Grace E. Hadow (London:
Macmillan, 1913), Vol. 2.

songs, duets, the *Liebeslieder* Waltzes for vocal quartet with piano duet accompaniment, many albums of lieder . . .

On 22 February 1873, his publisher, Fritz Simrock, asked: "Aren't you doing anything any more? Am I not to have a symphony from you in '73 either? Not to mention the quartets and so many other things with which you are so stingy?" Quartets, yes. That year Simrock received the two that make up Opus 51. There was even an orchestral work, his first in fourteen years, the Variations on a Theme by Haydn, which was introduced that November in Vienna, and with unequivocal success. But only the year before, Brahms, haunted by the ghost of Beethoven, as were so many nineteenth-century composers, had said: "I shall never write a symphony! You can't have any idea what it's like always to hear such a giant marching behind you!"

The next three years brought some glorious songs, including *Dämmerung senkte sich von oben, Auf dem See, Regenlied,* and *Dein blaues Auge;* then another set of *Liebeslieder,* a third string quartet, and the great C-minor Piano Quartet, Opus 60, which we may well see as the last act of preparation before facing down the giant.

Brahms was forty-three when he finished putting himself through the torment of first-symphony birth pangs. Mozart had managed it at nine, and among other teenage and subteen debutants we can find Prokofiev (eleven), Mendelssohn (twelve), and Schubert and Glazunov (both fifteen). Typically composers take that step in their twenties—from Schumann and Rachmaninoff, who were twenty-two, through Dvořák, Franz Schmidt, Ives, Copland, Stravinsky, William Schuman, Berlioz, Tchaikovsky, Haydn, Nielsen, Mahler, and Tippett, on to Beethoven, who was twenty-nine. Sessions, Havergal Brian, Sibelius, Harris, Vaughan Williams, Bruckner, and Kancheli were in their thirties. Walter Piston was forty-three, like Brahms, and so was John Harbison. Two major symphonists waited even longer, Elgar and Martinů, who were both fifty-one.

It is hard to know what conclusions to draw from such a list. Martinů, for example, came to the genre late partly because his interests had lain in other directions, but when he came to America at fifty, conductors began asking him for symphonies. Piston waited because he was skeptical about opportunities to get such pieces performed. Also, some composers face life with more nerve than others. Mozart, Mendelssohn, and Schubert were not boys given to fretting, but Bruckner, Brahms, and Elgar were worriers in excelsis. Besides, for the history-minded Brahms, symphony was not just another genre among many, but rather *the* genre in which a composer had to prove himself if he wanted to be taken seriously as a claimant to a place in the great tradition (or The Great Tradition).

One of the forms Brahms's worrying took was that even in his forties, long after it was practical or in any way appropriate, he still entertained the idea from time to time that he ought to have a regular job as a conductor somewhere. In 1876 he was offered the post of music director in Düsseldorf. He did not go, but the thought was on his mind (or he pretended it was) enough for him to write to his friend the surgeon Theodor Billroth that at least one good thing had come out of the plan, "namely that I have arrived at the decision to come out with a symphony. . . . I just think I ought to offer the Viennese something presentable by way of farewell."

It was a characteristically roundabout way of admitting to himself that he was ready to deal with that giant and write a symphony. The giant had died six years before Brahms was born, but his shadow fell the length of the nineteenth century and some way beyond. Schubert already had a sense of that when, hardly into his twenties and after six symphonies, he made up his mind to break a path "zur großen Sinfonie," meaning a symphony in the Beethoven manner. What he began in the *Unfinished* and achieved, boldly and completely, in the Great C-major added mightily to the challenge for the next generation.

Beethoven is all over Brahms's First Piano Concerto, the score into which Brahms channeled the energies he had hoped to devote to his first essay in symphony: the choice of the Ninth Symphony key of D minor, the rhetorical stance, the wild *Hammerklavier* Sonata trills, the modeling (as Donald Tovey points out) of the finale on the one in the C-minor Piano Concerto. For that matter, Brahms's real First Symphony is still within earshot of the giant's echoing footsteps, and it was not for nothing that Hans von Bülow called it the Beethoven Tenth. To write a C-minor symphony with a triumphant C-major conclusion was anything other than a trivial decision, and Brahms knew just what he was about when, at the great arrival in C major, he evoked the *Ode to Joy*.

Beethoven's fist-shaking C-minor gestures and sheer physical energy are vividly present in the Allegro that Brahms sent—in some form or other—to Clara Schumann in 1862. So much in the introduction speaks in a new voice: the hardness that results from the way the lines move in contrary motion (composed retrospectively, as it were, from the similar "hard" beginning of the Allegro); the way the strings, swinging up and down on G's and E-flats, insist on this strangely ambiguous C-minor chord that has no C in it; even the "medium" tempo.[2] What a wonderful stroke of expressive and structural imagination it was that made Brahms sense

---

[2] About the tempo: this introduction is, more often than not, taken quite slowly, and commentaries on the symphony usually refer to a "slow introduction." In fact, Brahms marks it un poco sostenuto, which means "somewhat sustained." In other words, while obviously slower than the Allegro that follows, it is by no means "slow."

that the "beginning" he had sent to Clara was no beginning at all but a release, a resolution, the articulation with untrammeled energy of an idea darkly forming itself during the introduction.[3]

The music reaches a point of high tension; then the oboe and the cellos, in more lyric mood, coax the music forward to a moment of expectant hush. This is harshly broken by a firmly rapped out C, the keynote. The introduction is over, the Allegro has begun. In the introduction, Brahms set phrases covering a broad gamut against tight chromatic lines; as we have already seen, he continues that contrast in the Allegro. Something else he carries over from the introduction—and I refer to the way we hear the piece, not the order in which Brahms composed it—is the series of wide-ranging arpeggios on G and E-flat. Almost immediately he arrives at an arresting feature of marked profile, a sequence of plunging sevenths and sixths in *fortissimo*. These set abrupt punctuation marks to many sentences, and even the second theme, begun by the oboe and somewhat—only somewhat—calmer in mood, is permeated by them. Three descending notes introduced by the violas, marcato against pizzicato chords, generate a firestorm of energy that brings the exposition to its close.

In one respect this excited close is highly original. Usually when a sonata-form movement is in minor, the exposition will end in the relative major. Here, for a movement in C minor, that would be E-flat major: however, Brahms rings a change on this convention by going to E-flat *minor*. Brahms asks for the exposition to be repeated. The turn back entails what may be the most startling harmonic progression in all of his music. A few conductors revel in this *coup de théâtre*; many dislike what they hear as a disagreeably jarring change of key and move straight into the development.

The move forward into the development is also managed by a dramatic turn of harmony, but one not so "strong," to borrow Frau Schumann's adjective. The emphatic E-flats and G-flats at the close of the exposition are suddenly reinterpreted as D-sharps and F-sharps. This allows the music to plunge into B major, thus opening a harmonic window whose existence we had not suspected at all.

As the strings sweep up and down what have now become the familiar arpeggios we first heard in the introduction, the energy continues unabated. Suddenly, though, the music sinks to *pianissimo*, initiating a long

---

[3] It is interesting that, deeply as he felt drawn to classical devices, Brahms rarely composed "slow" introductions. There are only four: the Sostenuto that begins the finale of the Piano Sonata No. 2 in F-sharp minor, Opus 2 (1852); the Poco sostenuto that introduces the finale of the F-minor Piano Quintet, Opus 34 (1862—also, as Opus 34bis, in an 1864 version for two pianos); and the two in the Symphony No. 1. The Adagio at the beginning of the First Symphony's finale is the only one of the four in a true slow tempo.

voyage through dense thickets. A couple of times there is clarity, as when mists part to reveal, for a moment, a sought-for landmark. More of the time, this is music of searching, of struggle. Once in rehearsal, I heard Herbert Blomstedt ask the musicians to think of flowers straining to break through concrete. The bass tends more and more to settle on or near the dominant, G: the moment of homecoming is being prepared. The forward motion is powerful, but so is the harmonic resistance. Tension builds to enormous heights; Brahms's sense of timing is consummate. Finally the breakthrough: the home key and the main theme make a triumphant re-entry.

The events of the recapitulation correspond clearly to those of the exposition. Toward the end, the music builds to one final great cresting, which subsides into the brief but spacious, perfectly timed coda. How did this movement end when Clara Schumann first saw it? Were the seventeen measures of coda an afterthought that came along with the introduction? As it now stands, the coda is a wonderful recapitulation by suggestion. We tend to think of it as music that returns us to the introduction, but in fact just a few touches suffice to create that impression: the return to a slower tempo (just meno allegro, not necessarily the poco sostenuto of the beginning, though you would not guess this from what most conductors do here), the pulsing drum, the first notes of the passage in contrary motion, and finally the incomplete broken chord. We first hear the woodwinds play this arpeggio; then it is gloriously resolved as the strings climb up a sonorous and complete chord of C major.

The first chord of the Andante sounds miraculously fresh: E major is a long way from the C-minor/major world we have just left. Brahms learned that from Beethoven (whose Third Piano Concerto presents the same relationship between its first and second movements), and they had both learned it from Haydn. Everything else is equally fresh: the triple meter, the clear, diatonic harmony, above all the serene mood. It is characteristic of Brahms to arrange matters so that the beginning of his first melody can serve as bass to accompany the new theme in the oboe. This leads to a blazingly impassioned music for the first violins, into which they draw the seconds and violas. From this grows another oboe melody, like music from a Bach cantata but from the perspective of 150 years later.

In her letter to Joachim about the Allegro, Clara Schumann commented on how skillfully Brahms had managed the transition from the development into the recapitulation. Assuming that it was then the way it is now, one can only agree: Brahms sweeps you home and into C minor excitingly and with splendid élan. But how much more special is the veiled entrance into the recapitulation of the Andante: ambiguous harmonies blur the moment, as do the *pianissimo* drumroll and the unexpected off-beat entrance of the woodwinds. We listen more to the lovely curve of the violins' and violas' slow arabesque than to the flutes and oboes and clarinets who carry the melody, and we seem to become aware of the moment of recapitulation only in retrospect.[4] This is Brahms "at his Brahms-most," as the Boston music critic and Boston Symphony program annotator William Foster Apthorp liked to say. The second theme makes a final appearance in a magical scoring for solo violin, oboe, and horn, but it is the violin alone, with a faraway remembrance of pulsing drums, that sings the movement to its tranquil close. The perfection of form is the result of a severe reworking after the first performance.

Beethoven's scherzos were quite a bit faster than the minuets from which they had evolved, though it is undoubtedly true that symphonic minuets were played more quickly in the eighteenth century than through most of the twentieth. Brahms, on the other hand—perhaps with Schumann's *Rhenish* Symphony as a model—slowed these movements down again. His Allegretto here, neither slow nor fast, is in the gentle, lightly sentimental mood we encounter often in his intermezzi for piano. The pulse for the middle section continues the same, but it seems faster because the rhythmic subdivisions are smaller. The way the middle section softly haunts the coda is a lovely Brahmsian touch.

Harmonically, the third movement was the same distance from the second as the second from the first. Now another step of the same size carries us from the third movement's key of A-flat to C, the key of the finale, of the first movement, and of the whole symphony. It is C *minor* at first, and there is a darkness, a strangeness, a mood of mystery we have not encountered since the symphony's introduction. Marked adagio, it is also the first truly slow music in the symphony. In part, the minor harmonies and the character of the gestures are what make this music mysterious, but what also contributes powerfully to this effect is the way Brahms juxtaposes highly disparate elements in quick succession.

The movement begins with an outcry similar in character to the music with which the symphony begins. This is followed by an accelerating passage for plucked strings. Both these ideas are immediately repeated in dramatically condensed form. Next, a swirling, syncopated music rises to an urgent climax. A sudden parting of the storm clouds reveals, in major, a horn call that is luminously continued in the flute.[5] Bassoons and trombones declaim a solemn phrase that could come from a hymn. The horn

---

[4] I would guess that Mahler, writing the first movement of his Fourth Symphony, must have studied this page carefully.

[5] The horn call was an old idea too. Brahms had put it on a birthday card to Clara Schumann many years earlier with the words: "Hoch auf'm Berg, tief im Tal, grüß' ich Dich viel tausendmal" (High on the mountain, deep in the valley, I send you many thousands of greetings).

call is heard again, half as long as before, but more elaborate because another horn, flute, oboe, and clarinet add a series of overlapping imitations.
It will be the task of the finale to integrate this diversity of material into
a cohesive movement, something Brahms will accomplish with sovereign
command and stunning originality.

Now comes the Allegro and, with it, *the* tune, in Brahmsian under-
stated *poco forte*. This melody, both deeply personal and greatly in debt to
the Beethoven Ninth, is an expansion and clarification of the outcry that
began the movement. Brahms's response when people offered to point out
the Beethoven resemblance was entirely appropriate: "Any ass can hear
that."[6]

A contrasting melody, dolce and animato, leads to a rise in temperature and to music that approaches the first movement in agitation. A return of the grand melody starts the development. As before, the dynamic
marking is only *poco forte*, but this time Brahms asks to have it played with
breadth (largamente). He also gives it a wonderful new sound. Earlier it
was played by the first violins accompanied by the other strings with two
horns and bassoons; now cellos along with horns and bassoons in alternation join the violins, and the full orchestra (except the trombones) accompanies. Enjoy the melody now: it will not return, at least not whole.

Brahms actually continues as though he meant to give us the melody
once more, in a new key, E-flat, but he abandons it almost immediately.
The pizzicatos from the introduction appear in ghost form and insist on
attention. Fragments of the great melody—specifically, its second, third,
fourth, and fifth notes—stay in the air. The mood becomes ever more
restless and excited. The surprising vehicle for this heightening is a musical
idea that we first met in an atmosphere of sovereign calm, the luminous
horn call from the introduction. With violent rhythmic dislocations, this
theme propels the music into the recapitulation. Nothing is more exciting
than the one beat of silence—it is a downbeat at that—just before the
horn call returns, *fortissimo* and with the passionato quality that was always
latent in it now fully realized.

The recapitulation itself is fiercely compressed, the most notable point
of compaction being the omission of the great "Beethoven Ninth" theme.
First, the tensions generated in the preceding couple of minutes of the
development are released in a passage of spacious broadening and calming.
From this, Brahms moves directly into the graceful dolce-and-animato

---

[6] Schoenberg in his essay "Brahms the Progressive" ties this famous response to the even more
blatant similarity between the opening of Brahms's Piano Sonata No. 1 and Beethoven's *Hammerklavier* Sonata.

theme. Shimmering string tremolandos remind us of the introduction, and we hear the first few notes, but only the first few notes, of the "Beethoven" melody. Then Brahms accelerates into a driving coda, at whose high point the solemn hymnal phrase from the introduction blazes its way across the stage in a final and triumphant transformation.

For his successors, Beethoven was a presence both scary and inspiring. Schubert responded with self-confidence. Brahms was neurotic, but when at last he brought himself to move, he moved surely. Joachim, writing to him in March 1877 from Cambridge, England, where he had just introduced the First Symphony, refers to it as a piece that "really gets to people." That has not changed.

Symphony No. 2 in D major, Opus 73

> *Allegro non troppo*
> *Adagio non troppo*
> *Allegretto grazioso (quasi andantino)—Presto ma non assai—*
> *Tempo I—Presto ma non assai—Tempo I*
> *Allegro con spirito*

Brahms composed the Symphony No. 2 in the summer of 1877, and Hans Richter conducted the first performance at a Vienna Philharmonic concert on 30 December that year.

Two flutes, two oboes, two clarinets, two bassoons, four horns, two trumpets, three trombones, tuba, timpani, and strings.

Each spring in his later years, Brahms had to resolve the crisis of deciding where to spend the summer. Those summers were crucial. That was when he got his composing done, the really concentrated and demanding part of it. The rest of the year was devoted to sketching scores to be dealt with the following summer, to polishing what had been accomplished the summer before, to the tedious and seemingly endless labor of proofreading, and to whatever performing as conductor or pianist he cared to take on. Each of these summer hideouts was "used up" after a couple of years, and so the problem constantly had to be addressed anew. Three summers his choice fell on Pörtschach on Lake Wörth in southern Austria, a region, he once said, where melodies were so abundant that one had to be careful not to step on them. He wrote the Second Symphony in the first of his Pörtschach summers, then did most of the work on his Violin Concerto there in 1878.[7] He would return for one more summer, when the soil yielded the loveliest and most original of his violin sonatas, the G major, Opus 78.

Brahms had hesitated a long time before taking the big step of writing a symphony. That story is told in the essay on the Symphony No. 1. But once he had overcome his inhibitions and completed his First Symphony in 1876 he was so elated both by his hard-won spiritual victory and by the success the new piece enjoyed at its early performances that he set to work on another symphony as soon as he could.

The First is a heroic *per ardua ad astra* symphony in the vein (and the key) of the Beethoven Fifth.[8] Brahms's Second, by comparison, is all relaxation and expansiveness, and critics were quick to point out the parallel with Beethoven's Fifth/*Pastoral* pair of 1807–08. Not that Brahms himself was eager to let on what the character of his new symphony was. "You have only to sit down at the piano," he advised his friend Elisabet von Herzogenberg on 22 November 1877, "placing your little feet on the two pedals in turn and striking the chord of F minor several times in succession, first in the treble, then in the bass (*ff* and *pp*)." (Brahms will have enjoyed the prospect of his friend's eventual discovery that there is not a single F-minor chord in the entire symphony.) Three weeks later he was still referring to his "latest" as "the F minor," and writing to Frau von Herzogenberg on the day of the dress rehearsal for the premiere he reported that "the orchestra here plays my new '*Sinfonie*' with crepe bands on their sleeves because of its dirge-like effect, and it is to be printed with a black border too."[9]

Brahms played no such flirtatious games with the critic Eduard Hanslick, to whom he wrote, "In the course of the winter I shall let you a hear a symphony that sounds so cheerful and delightful you will think I wrote it especially for you, or rather for your young wife." The work went bril-

---

[7] Fifty-seven years later, Alban Berg was delighted and proud to be writing his Violin Concerto, the most Austrian of them all, on the opposite shore of the same lake.

[8] *Ad astra per aspera* (To the stars over rough roads) is a well-known Latin motto of unknown origin. Perhaps for no better reason than that I grew up in wartime England, I like the variant *Per ardua ad astra* (Through struggle to the stars), the motto of the RAF.

[9] Frau von Herzogenberg had complained about Brahms's modern spelling—"How can you write an elegant word like 'symphony' with an f?"—but Brahms had replied that the work was indeed "merely a *Sinfonie.*"

liantly in Vienna, and within the year there were performances, many of them under Brahms's own direction, in Leipzig, Bremen, Amsterdam, The Hague, Hamburg, Dresden, Düsseldorf, and Breslau.

The Dresden concert precipitated a crisis that Brahms enjoyed immensely. Clara Schumann was to be the pianist in Beethoven's Choral Fantasy, but Franz Wüllner, newly appointed court conductor in Dresden, had put the Magic Fire Music from *Die Walküre* on the program too (he had led the first performances of *Rheingold* and *Walküre*), and Frau Schumann shuddered at the thought of sharing a program with the detested Wagner. "Imagine our poor friend's torture," wrote Brahms to Heinrich von Herzogenberg. "I shall of course write and urge her to come, though the whole thing is so comic that I shall find it hard to be serious about it." Brahms actually expected Frau Schumann to cancel, but her professionalism and her curiosity about the new symphony overcame her musico-political principles and she kept the date. Elisabet von Herzogenberg, an intelligent but priggish and humorless woman, was very much on Clara Schumann's side and thought Brahms's attitude frivolous: "There really is a want of delicacy to the arrangement of the program. How can any audience be expected to appreciate really artistic work and a piece like the Magic Fire Music on one and the same evening? O Wüllner, Wüllner! I always thought you a gentleman, but this program betrays the impresario."

Much as Beethoven's *Pastoral*, for all its "harmless" surface, is one of his most tightly composed works, so is the Brahms Second a singularly integrated, concentrated symphony. It begins with a double idea, a fairly neutral four-note motif in cellos and basses, upon which horns, joined almost at once by bassoons, superimpose a romantically atmospheric melody. But it is the bass component of this double theme

Ex. 1

that turns out to be crucial. Variants of that phrase appear five times in the next dozen or so measures. Brahms wants us to have it clearly in our ears, and for good reason: it is germinal to the entire symphony, many of whose ideas share the pattern of those first three notes (note, neighbor, return to the initial note).

This first movement is uncommonly rich and varied in its material, the salient ideas being a three-chord growl for low brass with cellos, bracketed between a soft drumroll and an isolation of the three-note motto; a soaring melody presented as a conversation between violins and flute and beginning with the three-note motto; a glowing tune for cellos and violas in thirds, with the cellos on top; and a buoyantly leaping theme—to be played quasi ritenente (as if held back) for just a little extra emphasis— with which Brahms celebrates his long-delayed arrival in the dominant, A major. There is much to listen to and to absorb, and that is a good reason for taking the repeat: from the Herzogenberg correspondence it emerges clearly that Brahms himself always did.

The development reaches the extreme points, for this movement, both of dusky harmony and radiant physical energy. Brahms takes particular pains over the actual moment of recapitulation. He sends unmistakable signals by referring to the three-note motto (first at half speed and in softly shimmering tremolando), to the romantic horn phrase, and to the soaring violin-and-flute tune, but he manages the pacing of all this so subtly and is at the same time so canny about withholding a clear-cut D-major harmony that he seems magically to move straight from anticipation and expectation to a point where we realize the recapitulation is already under way. This is one of the exceedingly rare moments at which Brahms permits himself the marking "espressivo." The coda brings another such moment, combined with a characteristically Brahmsian challenge—muffed outright by most conductors—to be at the same time sempre tranquillo and in tempo.

Reviewing a Brahms concert by the Philadelphia Orchestra, Virgil Thomson wrote that he had heard a lady say on her way out of Carnegie Hall, "Brahms is so dependable." We do rather think of him that way, not least because his music is so familiar, particularly the four symphonies. When it was new, though, his music was thought abstruse and excessively intellectual—in a word, "difficult." Listening to the slow movement of the Second Symphony—really listening, that is, not just switching to automatic pilot the moment we've made sure they haven't slipped in the Andante from the Fourth—we can perhaps recapture what made Brahms a difficult composer. Or, rather, what *makes* him a difficult composer, because some of his music is so tightly packed and densely argued that it still cuts the inattentive no slack.

Nowhere is Brahms's desire for concentration more evident than in this Adagio. The cello theme with which it begins, accompanied by the bassoons in contrary motion, is one of his most amazing inspirations. It is also a melody whose subtle internal repetitions and delicate rhythmic displacements make it, even with familiarity, anything other than easy for the conductor to shape and the listener to grasp. It was his intense study of Mozart and his knowledge of Renaissance and Baroque music that gave him his liking for and ease with rhythm other than the four-square.

The first movement of the Second Symphony is sunny, but the sunshine is shadowed. Now, in the Adagio, which is in B major, the shadows and the moments of agitation that are background in the first movement come to the fore. The horn picks up a fragment of the cello melody and uses it to begin a fugue, though this is not developed far. A new theme, grazioso and given an element of caprice by its persistent syncopations, divides the measures differently so as to create the illusion of faster motion. A third idea in flowing, conjunct motion continues in this vein. Against this, various instruments in turn set agitated waves of sixteenth-notes so that the effect is one of ever faster motion.

This is the background against which Brahms introduces the slowest music we have yet heard, the first movement's three-note motto, now sounded as solemn warning by trombone and bassoon, answered by tuba and basses. Brahms does not choose to inject quicker notes here; he does, however, stir the blood by accelerating the rate at which the harmonies change, and it is with almost disorienting speed that in just one and a half quiet measures he travels across vast harmonic spaces to B major, so that the recapitulation can begin. Every detail, every relationship is reconsidered, and right up to those last melancholy descents of violins and clarinet that so beautifully set off the peaceful closing chords, the movement continues as it began—something always beyond our power to predict yet, at every turn, perfectly convincing.

The third movement is one of those leisurely quasi-scherzos that are a Brahms specialty. The oboe starts it with an ambling dance tune. Mahler might have marked it "altväterisch"—old-fashioned. The first trio arrives very soon, scurrying, quicker, and a variation of the oboe tune, which is itself yet another expansion of the three-note motto. A second trio combines the light-footed gait of the first with the triple meter of the oboe theme and adds some witty off-beat accents of its own. The close is sweetly wistful.

There follows a swift finale. The sotto voce opening is a variation of the first bars of the whole symphony. Later themes move more broadly across the measures, though not with less energy. A touch of gypsy music enlivens the scene, and this exuberant movement culminates in a blazing affirmation of D major (and, by the way, a wonderful demonstration of how exciting Brahms makes every trombone entrance by using those instruments sparingly and knowingly).

Symphony No. 3 in F major, Opus 90

Allegro con brio
Andante
Poco Allegretto
Allegro—Un poco sostenuto

Brahms began his Third Symphony in 1882 and completed it at Wiesbaden the following summer, though it may be that some of the music goes back to an abandoned *Faust* project of 1880–81. With Ignaz Brüll, Brahms gave a two-piano performance for a small group of friends at Ehrbar's Piano Emporium in Vienna on 9 November 1883. This was followed by another such reading, presumably for the benefit of the critic Eduard Hanslick on 22 November. Hans Richter conducted the first orchestral performance at a Vienna Philharmonic concert on 2 December that year.

Two flutes, two oboes, two clarinets, two bassoons and contrabassoon, four horns, two trumpets, three trombones, timpani, and strings.

The Brahms symphonies come as two pairs. The First and Second were finished in 1876 and 1877 respectively; the Fourth was begun in the summer of 1884, as soon as possible after the completion of the Third. Each pair embodies a powerful internal contrast. The First Symphony is heroic, the Second pastoral and cheerful; while the Fourth inhabits a tragic world, the Third leads neither to victory nor to tragedy, but ends in resignation and hard-won calm.

There were Wagnerians on hand to hiss the premiere of the Third, but their demonstration only reinforced the larger part of the audience in its enthusiasm. The history of music is full of occasions that make us wonder at the failure, at first, of works that ought to have been successes. Here we may be surprised in another direction—not, to be sure, at the success of a work that ought to have failed, but at the extraordinary success of one so subtle in its discourse, so reticent in its tone of voice, and, moreover, so difficult to perform.

That concert, at any rate, was one of the greatest triumphs Brahms was ever to experience. He found success difficult to deal with, though. He thought the praise for the new work extravagant and unjustified, and it left him uneasy about his probable inability to live up to new and higher expectations. Almost six weeks later, this mood persisted, leading him to write to his friend Heinrich von Herzogenberg, "The reputation [the famous F-major] has acquired makes me want to cancel all my engagements."

The opening of the Third Symphony is assertive and fiery, though too few conductors remember that the allegro is con brio. It is also a rich broth of ambiguities. Right away, F major and F minor contradict each other with collision force. The first measure—that bold sound of woodwinds with horns and trumpets itself a surprise—is clear F major, but the second, with A-flat placed so prominently as the top note of the chord, suggests the darker mode. The entry of the violins with their passionato melody seems to settle that F *major* is what is meant, but even before the phrase is over, the A-flat in the bass argues minor.

Ex. 1

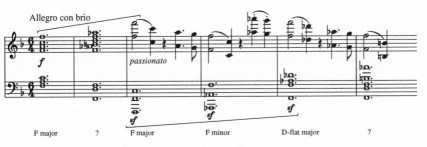

And are we meant to hear the six beats in each measure as three times two or as twice three? Or both, in unresolved tension?

At the same time, we might notice something else: the rising sequence of F/A-flat/F with which the winds begin returns exactly and forcefully (cellos, basses, trombone, contrabassoon) as the bass line that supports the headlong descent of the violins' first phrase. Clearly, this is going to be a taut, closely argued work as well as one full of ambiguities. It will turn out to be Brahms's shortest symphony and the one with the most intricate and richly implicative network of internal reference.[10]

The opening, then, is a strange and profoundly Brahmsian mixture of the fiery, perhaps even the heroic, with the ambiguous, with something uncertain. In less than half a minute all traces of the assertive are gone. Gentler themes take over, a sighing one for violins and cellos, and, in measures that have suddenly become half again as long, a fluently lyric

---

[10]The F/A(-flat)/F is external reference, continuing a lifelong conversation with the violinist, conductor, and composer Joseph Joachim, Brahms's friend by now of thirty years. Joachim had chosen for himself the motto F/A/E, "frei aber einsam" (free but lonely) and Brahms, the lifelong bachelor, had countered with F/A/F for "frei aber froh" (free but glad).

one, marked grazioso, for clarinet. Nor is the F/A/F shape forgotten. Brahms has also moved into unexpected harmonic territory, A major. This key sounds wonderfully luminous in this context, something we can especially relish because the harmony lies still for many measures on end.[11] And so the exposition comes to a close, not with textbook propriety in the dominant, C major, but in A, though the A has by now been darkened by storm clouds and is A *minor*.

I have sometimes enjoyed performances that have rushed headlong into the development, ignoring Brahms's request that the exposition be repeated; on the whole, though, it is good to take the repeat. For one thing, the exposition is short and packed. (Short though it is, the exposition, even unrepeated, is the longest section of this amazingly concise movement.) For another, the measure that swings the music back to the beginning—just stark octaves on A and C—is so arresting that it is a pity to miss it. Still more important, the plunge into the development is itself wonderfully exciting, and its effect is even greater if its arrival has been deferred.

Finally, there is a reason whose force struck me not in a session of score study but while listening to an especially revelatory performance by Valery Gergiev: each important harmonic juncture so far has involved a descent by a major third. The movement begins in F, the sighing theme for violins and cellos starts in D-flat (a third below F), and the grazioso one for clarinet is in A (a third below D-flat). One more descent by the same interval takes us back to F. This completes the cycle, but in order to achieve that completion we have to go back to the beginning—in other words, to observe the repeat. Once that cycle has been traversed we can, the next time, take the other road and charge ahead.[12]

The development begins with exhilarating impetuosity as the cellos turn the clarinet theme into an impassioned, agitated aria in C-sharp minor. It progresses swiftly and purposefully, but with the appearance of a romantic horn solo (on the F/A/F idea), underlined by the contrabassoon's unearthly rumble, it turns melancholy. The world has grown dark.[13]

---

[11] The A-major clarinet theme is introduced by a phrase that is virtually a quotation from Beethoven's Symphony No. 3, the *Eroica*. Was Brahms punning on the number? He was quite capable of it.

[12] Brahms also uses the cycle of major thirds as a structural element in his Symphony No. 1, but in the opposite direction and on a broader scale. There each movement is a major third higher than the previous one (C minor/E major/A-flat major/C minor and major).

[13] I mentioned that the contrabassoon is part of the bass group that sounds the rising F/A-flat/F against the descending violin melody at the beginning of the movement. That thunderous double-reed is the only woodwind not to play in the first two measures; while it has a crucial role in defining the characteristic sonority of the Third Symphony, it plays in only one-fourth of all the measures (more than one-half of them in the dramatic, compressed finale). This kind of economy and precision of thought is as Brahmsian as can be.

Moving more slowly and very softly, the music returns to the descending melody with which the symphony began—and which we have not heard since then. But now the tempo is slower, the dynamic level is held to *pianissimo,* major alternates uneasily with minor, and of brio there is not a trace. The suspense is tremendous: an event of immense importance is being prepared. At the same time, something is wrong: the harmonic placement is off. This portentous preparation is happening in E-flat, a place quite remote from any the symphony has explored thus far. Is this unexpected emphasis on E-flat part of Brahms's allusion to Beethoven's *Eroica?*

The harmony grows still darker and more mysterious. A slow reawakening releases the music from this tension. The bass line has found its way down to F, the keynote, and on top of that F there is an F-major chord for wind instruments, much like the one that began the movement. Technically, legally, the recapitulation has begun. But Brahms does not let us *feel* it yet. Ambiguity again: as in the first three measures of the movement, the top notes are F, A-flat, and F; this time, however, Brahms gives us chords that veer swiftly and forcefully away from F major, all the way over to D-flat. Only then does he take the great harmonic strides that carry the music firmly and unambiguously back into F major.

Ex. 2

This expansion is a matter of no more than two measures, but this stretching of the harmonic horizon makes a difference far vaster than one would expect from only three or four seconds of real time. The effect of the expansion is twofold. It adds to the suspense before the final reconquest of the home key; at the same time, this luxurious stretching enhances the sense of triumph inherent in that arrival. And here is another wonderful touch of Brahmsian ambiguity. Fresh, startling, dramatic as this excursion to D-flat is, it is not new, for the harmony here moves by exactly the same steps as those Brahms used to get into the exposition's second (D-flat-major) theme. You can, indeed, go still further back, to measure 5, where the seed of D-flat as an important entity was first planted.

Harmonic perspectives are shifted, but otherwise the recapitulation, after its astonishing beginning, proceeds without major surprise. There is a splendid and expansive coda, a double coda, if you like, the first part impassioned, the second meditative. At the close we learn for the first time the potential for lyric poetry of the grand opening melody. That potential will find sublime realization in the symphony's final bars.

Here is the U-turn in the symphony. So far, the music has been forceful, passionate, concentrated. Now, in the Andante, it becomes gentle and pastoral. So at least it begins. The first sounds are soft: clarinets and bassoons, with a few notes by horns and flutes, and the lovely echoes of divided violas and cellos. Even this idea contains the F/A/F shape. Then, in complete contrast, Brahms offers a wistful song for clarinet and bassoon. It begins with two notes, short-long. That sigh is echoed again and again in the accompaniment, and it comes to be harmonized with chords of Schubertian magic. Of the melody's triplet figure we shall hear much more.

At the beginning of this Andante, Brahms made us wait a while for the sound of violins. Their real moment of glory arrives toward the end of the movement when, on a new melody, they lead the orchestra into a glorious crescendo. The music subsides in deep calm over a long tonic pedal with solemn chords that pronounce a minor-mode Amen. (Closing "amen" cadences are more frequent in Brahms than the assertive "normal" ones that approach the tonic from the dominant.)

The first movement's harmonic doubts resolved themselves in F major after all. The Andante is clear, sunlit major, wistful sometimes, but with only a few clouds of the minor mode. On the last page, though, the woodwinds play darker harmonies, and their gentle insistence prepares the sweetly melancholy intermezzo that follows. In this third movement, Brahms gives us one of his most wonderful melodies, one that sounds as natural and unstudied as possible even while it is full of rhythmic subtleties and surprises. First taken by the cellos, it is musing and inward rather than full-throated song. (Brahms wants it both "mezza voce" and "espressivo.") Later we hear the melody in a flavorful combination of flute, oboe, and horn; as a horn solo; and finally in violins and cellos, three octaves deep. Between its second and third appearances there is an interlude ever so slightly more dance-like in character.

All of this is confident indulgence in sentiment and glorious orchestral euphony; even the minor mode is part of the movement's character as a softly colorful genre piece. That the finale is also in minor comes as a shock, one reinforced by the sinuous lines, the stark octaves, the sotto voce delivery. Brahms's art of transformation, variation, and expansion is operating at the highest pitch of intensity here. The gliding eighths and quarters of the opening are realigned in new rhythmic shapes, now with strange delays on certain notes, now with mysteriously choked-off silences.

Ex. 3

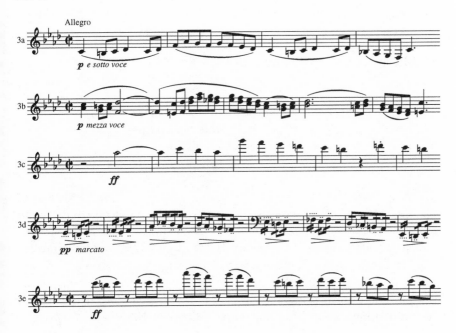

The theme from the second movement with the two-note sigh and the triplets returns, changed now into matter of tragic solemnity. Storm clouds first darken, then dominate the sky. Passages incredibly packed alternate with others spectrally spare, scarcely breathing. Suddenly, muted violas cut across the music with yet another transformation of the first theme, laid before us now in placid and even triplets.

Ex. 4

The pace becomes slower. Oboe and horn remind us of the F/A-flat/F motto. They play it obliquely, on the "wrong" pitches, but its identity is in its shape, and so it is always recognizable. At last, just when the bass settles on the keynote F, the flute, hesitant, playing the first two notes twice, gives us the true F/A-flat/F.[14] We are home. As the flute reaches the high F, the violins, *pianissimo* and in shimmering broken chords, play a transfigured remembrance of the symphony's first phrase, the descending melody. They pass it down to violas and cellos while the wind instruments sustain their serene and glowing chords. The garden is softly lit in the glow of sunset.

Symphony No. 4 in E minor, Opus 98

> *Allegro non troppo*
> *Andante moderato*
> *Allegro giocoso*
> *Allegro energico e passionato—Più allegro*

The first mention of the Fourth Symphony is in a letter dated 19 August 1884 from Brahms to his publisher, Fritz Simrock; the work was completed about a year later at Mürzzuschlag in Styria. In October 1885 Brahms and Ignaz Brüll gave a two-piano reading of it for a small group of friends including the critic Eduard Hanslick, the surgeon Theodor Billroth, and the historian and Haydn scholar C. F. Pohl. Brahms conducted the first orchestral performance at Meiningen on 25 October 1885.

Two flutes and piccolo, two oboes, two clarinets, two bassoons and contrabassoon, four horns, two trumpets, three trombones, timpani, triangle, and strings. Piccolo and triangle appear only in the third movement, contrabassoon only in the third and fourth movements, and trombones only in the finale.

Just as Brahms's First and Second symphonies appeared in rapid succession as a contrasting pair, so did the Third and Fourth. The Third was finished in the summer of 1883 and the Fourth was begun the following summer. That year Brahms had chosen Mürzzuschlag in Styria for his annual holiday, that is to say, for one of those hardworking summer retreats when he got most of his composing done. "The cherries don't ever get to be sweet and edible in this part of the world," he wrote to several of his friends, adding that he feared his new piece had taken on something of their flavor.

---

[14]This extra F/A-flat/F pair is a beautiful counterpart to the two "extra" measures—also F/A-flat—that so wonderfully stretch the moment of recapitulation in the first movement.

As always, he was cautious about announcing work in progress. To his publisher he made some vague noise about a need for manuscript paper with more staves. To Hans von Bülow he reported in September 1885: "Unfortunately nothing came of the piano concerto I should have liked to write. I don't know, the two earlier ones are too good or maybe too bad, but at any rate they are obstructive to me. But I do have a couple of entr'actes; put together they make what is commonly called a symphony. On tour with the Meiningen Orchestra [playing the Concerto No. 2] I often imagined with pleasure what it would be like to rehearse it with you, nicely and at leisure, and I'm still imagining that now, wondering by the way whether the piece would ever have much of an audience."

Bülow, fifty when he began his five-year stint as conductor of the superb orchestra in the duchy of Meiningen in 1880, was one of the most imposing and brilliant musical personalities of the nineteenth century. A remarkable pianist, conductor, and polemicist, he was a prominent Wagnerian and led the first performances of *Tristan und Isolde* and *Die Meistersinger*. He was caught in a wretched personal situation when his wife, the daughter of Franz Liszt, left him for Wagner. He continued to conduct Wagner's music, but became one of the most fervent admirers and effective champions of Brahms, and thus one of the few to bridge what then seemed a vast gulf between musical ideologies.[15]

He was delighted to have Brahms come to Meiningen with his new symphony. "Difficult, very difficult," Bülow reported after rehearsals had begun. "No. 4 gigantic, altogether a law unto itself, quite new, steely individuality. Exudes unparalleled energy from first note to last." The premiere went well, and the audience tried hard but unsuccessfully to get an encore of the scherzo. Bülow conducted a repeat performance a week later, after which the orchestra set off on tour, with Brahms conducting the new symphony in Frankfurt, Essen, Elberfeld, Utrecht, Amsterdam, The Hague, Krefeld, Cologne, and Wiesbaden. It was liked and admired everywhere, though Vienna rather resisted the presentation by the Philharmonic under Hans Richter two months later, a performance unfortunately prepared nowhere near as well as those by the Meiningen Orchestra.

While the public took to the Fourth, Brahms's friends, including professionals and near-professionals like Eduard Hanslick and Elisabet von Herzogenberg, had trouble with it. That can be explained. The public, except in Vienna, heard superbly realized performances, while Hanslick knew it first from a two-piano reading (he remarked that it was like being beaten up by two tremendously intelligent, witty people) and Frau von

---

[15] Bülow was also the first pianist to play Tchaikovsky's Piano Concerto No. 1 (in Boston in 1875). There was music to give the Brahmsians and the Wagnerians something to agree on in haughty disapproval.

Herzogenberg, cursing the difficult horn and trumpet transpositions, had to decipher it at the piano from the manuscript of Brahms's full score. Where the public would chiefly have been aware of and carried away by the sweep of the whole, the professionals, with their special kind of connoisseurship and perception of detail, would have been more struck by what was—and is—genuinely difficult in the score.

Take the opening. The violins play a melody that starts as a series of two-note sighs, each sigh consisting either of a descending third (for example, B to G) or of the same interval inverted into an ascending sixth (for example, E to C, but going *up* to the next-highest C rather than down). Woodwinds echo these figures, but as chords, with the two notes played simultaneously.

It is hard for us to think of a lovelier, more inviting opening to a symphony—of course, its familiarity helps—but Joseph Joachim, who knew Brahms's music as well as anyone, found it disconcerting. Something preparatory, he suggested, even if it were only two measures of unison B, would help listeners find their way in. (Brahms's correspondence with Joachim shows that originally there were preparatory measures of just that kind and Brahms had struck them out.) This opening is immediately followed by a second statement of the melody, this time in broken octaves and in dialogue between first and second violins, with elaborate decorative material in violas and cellos. This was thought exceedingly difficult to unravel.[16]

The next big landmark in the exposition is a jagged figure in triplets for woodwinds and horns. In its immediate context it serves to introduce a broadly swinging, memorable melody for cellos and horns; long-range we shall discover that the triplet figure is second in importance only to the opening theme. The rhythmic dissonance created by the collision of threes and twos is typical Brahms and exciting to us, but his fondness for cross-rhythms was thought by many a terrible irritant when his music was new. Woodwinds and pizzicato strings play a vigorous variant of the first theme, after which the violins sing out in a new, soaring melody. For a moment everything dissolves in a strange mist (Brahms looking out into the world without his glasses?), and then the orchestra rallies to bring the exposition to an exultant close.

Brahms's friends were upset by what we think of as one of the most wonderful strokes in the work, and that is the way he gets into the development. He seems to start on a conventional, classical repeat of the exposition, but eight measures into it he changes one chord. That chord opens

---

[16] Here is another passage that makes full acoustical sense only with the orchestral seating that Brahms knew and wrote for, that is, with the first and second violins on opposite sides of the stage.

undreamed-of harmonic horizons, and we realize that he has not gone back, he is going on. Brahms found inspired precedent for this feint in the first of Beethoven's *Rasumovsky* string quartets, the F major, Opus 59, no. 1, and in the first movement of the Ninth Symphony. Only after this leisurely start does he move into his dense, harmonically far-reaching, closely argued development. He begins with the opening theme, which is first ruminative, then forceful. In the second phase, after reminding us of his myopic mist, he concentrates on the idea of triplets.

Then it is time to prepare the recapitulation, and all the early listeners admired the dreamily mysterious way Brahms leads us home. A long sequence of sighing one-measure phrases subsides into one of only four places marked *ppp* in all of Brahms's orchestral music. Oboes, clarinets, and bassoons emerge in their severe yet gentle reediness to sound the first four notes of the opening melody in immense magnification, while strings, using the sounds and figures of the myopic mist, weave an enigmatic garland about the last note. The next four notes of the theme are stretched in the same way. Then the music's melancholy flow resumes in the expected way, and we realize we have crossed the border into the recapitulation.

This itself brings no dramatic surprises: the development and the retransition have been sufficiently packed with event. Brahms does, however, gives us a dramatic coda. He begins by playing the first theme in close canon, low strings and horns leading, high strings and woodwinds following. This generates tremendous tension, which seduces many conductors, even some of the best, into wild speeding up. That is redundant: the acceleration is already composed into the music, and the double underlining is just not necessary. The ending, on a kind of Amen cadence in minor and with powerful drum strokes, is magnificent.

For Brahms to build a slow movement on the same keynote as the first movement is rare; yet he does it here and finds an inspired way of simultaneously celebrating the continuity and the contrast of E minor (the first movement) and E major (the second). The first movement comes to an emphatic, even grim close, with timpani powerfully asserting the keynote E. Then, after a pause—and surely applause as well in the 1880s and for some time after—the horns play something beginning on E, a note well established in our ears. It begins on E, sounds like C major, and turns out to be something more like the old Phrygian mode.[17] It is in any case fresh enough and ambiguous enough to accommodate the clarinets' hushed suggestion that one might put a G-sharp over the E, thus inaugurating an idyllic E major.

---

[17] If you have a piano handy, playing the white keys from E to E will give you a Phrygian scale.

Before long, the idyllic gives way to the impassioned, and finally a storm of triplet sixteenth-notes opens the way to a glorious cello melody which the other strings and the bassoons accompany with shameless wallowing in whipped cream. It is difficult, in fact, to think of another movement in Brahms's orchestral music that is scored with so much uninhibited pleasure in the sheerly sensuous side of music. It would also be hard to think of pieces orchestrated with more skill. The cello melody makes a glorious comeback, now on strings alone, but with second violins, violas, and cellos divided into two sections each, and this time Brahms divulges that the first phrase makes a handsome accompaniment to the second. The end of the movement sinks into a darkness to which the softly beating drums add a touch of something ominous.

The Andante began with a suggestion of C major, a false trail, as it turned out; however, the notion of a C-major beginning is not forgotten and is fully pursued in the massively rambunctious scherzo. For this movement Brahms introduces the giddy sounds of the piccolo and the triangle. The material is simple, but the harmonic strides are huge and adventurous.

For the finale, Brahms goes back to the E minor where the symphony began, but he does so with a theme whose first chord is A minor and thus very close to the C-major world of the scherzo. Not only that: this theme explains, so to speak, a strange moment half a minute before the end of the scherzo when the generally rowdy mood is broken by a sequence of broad and forceful chords. In retrospect we understand that this alien apparition was a preview of the finale.

The eight chords with which the finale begins are the theme of a set of thirty-two variations (plus coda). Brahms's knowledge of Renaissance and Baroque music was extensive and profound. When, as he does here, he writes a chaconne or passacaglia, a set of variations on a repeated bass or reiterated harmonic progression—and to do so at all must have seemed like sheer madness to the up-to-date Wagnerians—he does it like a man composing living music with not a speck of antiquarian dust about it. He had been impressed by a cantata, then believed to be by Bach (listed as No. 150, *Nach dir, Herr, verlanget mich*), whose closing chorus is a set of variations over a repeated bass, and he maintained that something could still be done with such a bass, though the harmonies would probably have to be made richer. Of course he knew well Bach's great Chaconne for solo violin; in fact, he had made a transcription of it for piano left-hand about eight years earlier.

Woodwinds and brasses, joined at the last by rolling drums, proclaim the sequence of eight chords. Brahms has saved the trombones for this moment, and even now it is characteristic that the statement is *forte* rather than *fortissimo*. The finale falls into four large sections. First Brahms gives us twelve statements of the eight-bar set, with bold variations of texture, harmonic detail, and rhetoric. This phase subsides to inaugurate a contrasting section—first still in minor, but soon to move into major—in which the measures are twice as long, the motion thus twice as slow. (Brahms is explicit about wishing the beats of the quarter-notes to move at the same speed as before, though there are now twice as many of them per measure. In other words, the double length of the measures is enough to make this the "slow movement" of the finale, and the conductor should not impose a further slowing down.) Four of these double-size variations make up this second section.

The original pace is resumed with what sounds like a recapitulation. But the strings intervene passionately midway through the eight-chord sequence, and the ensuing sixteen variations bring music more urgently dramatic than any yet heard in the symphony. The passion and energy are released in an extensive, still developing, still experiencing coda at a faster speed. Tying one more set of threads together, Brahms brings in the tumbling chords in thirds that echoed the melody at the beginning of the first movement. Thus the symphony drives to its conclusion, forward-thrusting yet measured, always new in its details yet organically unified, stern, noble, and with that sense of inevitability that marks the greatest music.

Anton Bruckner

Joseph Anton Bruckner was born in Ansfelden, Upper Austria, on 4 September 1824 and died in Vienna on 11 October 1896.

B ruckner's father, like his father before him, was schoolmaster in the village of Ansfelden. Before that, and as far back as the fourteenth century, the Bruckners had been farmers and laborers. Anton sang in the choir, was allowed to play the organ, and learned the rudiments of music from a cousin. In 1837, the year his father died, he was taken as a choirboy into the Augustinian monastery of Saint Florian, whose buildings, Austrian Baroque at its most splendid, dominate the countryside southeast of Linz. There the musician and the man gradually emerged.

He was unconfident and slow to decide to make music his vocation, preferring for safety's sake to follow in his father's and grandfather's footsteps as an elementary school teacher. When he did settle on a career in music, he found it impossible to give up student status, needing the constant reassurance of examinations successfully passed, of diplomas and certificates. As Wilhelm Furtwängler once remarked, "Schubert and Mozart had already completed their life's work when Bruckner was still writing counterpoint exercises." Later in life, his professorial appointment and his honorary doctorate (the first ever conferred on a musician in Vienna) were of enormous importance to him: he insisted on being addressed as "Herr Doktor" and even made attempts to have doctorates awarded by Cambridge and the University of Pennsylvania (which he thought was in Cincinnati).

In 1840 he heard orchestral music by Beethoven and Weber for the first time. He studied Bach's *Art of Fugue* and *Well-Tempered Clavier*, became acquainted with the works of Schubert and Mendelssohn, played dance music for a living, and equipped himself to teach school. In 1848 he was appointed organist at Saint Florian. All his life he would never feel so sure anywhere as on an organ bench. As organist he enjoyed the success that was denied him as a composer. In Paris he played in a crowded Notre Dame before an audience that included Franck, Saint-Saëns, Auber, and Gounod; the Vienna Chamber of Commerce sponsored a series of recitals in London, one every day for a week in the Royal Albert Hall and five more in the Crystal Palace; and when the sixty-seven-year-old master stood as a newly created Doctor of Philosophy before the Rector magnificus of Vienna's university and his attempt at a formal reply had been several times derailed, he said, "I cannot find the words to thank you as I would wish, but if there were an organ here I could tell you."

At Saint Florian, he composed whatever the surrounding community needed, from sacred motets to dances for piano four-hands to part songs for men's choral societies. In 1855 he began to travel regularly to Vienna for lessons with Simon Sechter, the tsar of Austria's music-theory world. (Twenty-seven years earlier, at the same age but, as it turned out, just two weeks before his death, Schubert had taken the same step.) Sechter was a curious figure who, to clear his head, wrote a fugue first thing in the morning every day of his adult life. His compositions included polyphonic fantasias for piano duet on operatic airs as well as settings from chapters of a geography textbook and, once, of an entire issue of a Vienna newspaper.

In Bruckner he met his match when it came to compulsive counterpointing. On one occasion, when his pupil delivered seventeen filled exercise books at one time, Sechter felt obliged to caution the young man about the possible peril to his health of overdoing it. In person and by correspondence, Bruckner worked with Sechter for six years, during which time he was forbidden to do any free composition. He emerged with a Meisterbrief (a certificate of mastery like those issued by the old craft guilds), a sovereign command of contrapuntal technique, and a nervous breakdown. But his hunger for learning was not yet sated, and he went on to study with Otto Kitzler, principal cellist in the theater orchestra at Linz. Whereas Sechter was oriented to the past, Kitzler taught from modern scores by Beethoven, Mendelssohn, and even Wagner, whose *Tannhäuser* he was determined to perform at Linz and which he analyzed with his eager student.

At the end of his time with Kitzler, Bruckner was in his fortieth year and ready at last to heed his calling as a composer. He began work on a symphony he would later call "die Nullte"—No. 0—and, over the next decade, followed that with three Masses and the first versions of his symphonies 1 through 4. Like many nineteenth-century composers, he became a specialist: with just one significant exception, the String Quintet of 1879, whose Adagio is as great a slow movement as chamber music has to show after Schubert, his lifework, once he attained his late maturity as a composer, consisted of choral music, almost all of it on sacred texts in Latin, and of symphonies. The Fifth Symphony, of 1876, the craggiest of Bruckner's mountains, is the summit of the first long stage of his growth, of his gradual discovery of a new and extraordinary idea of "symphony." The subtle Sixth, which Bruckner himself thought his boldest, was completed in 1881. The Seventh, which brought him his most immediate and unqualified success, and the Eighth came along, respectively, in 1883 and 1887.

Other momentous events in the (comparatively) earlier part of his life were seeing *Tristan und Isolde* and meeting its composer, both in 1865, and the success of his First and Second symphonies in Linz and Vienna in 1868 and 1873 respectively. In 1868, Bruckner moved to Vienna with his favorite sister, Maria Anna—"Nani" to her family—and before long he wondered why. He had left the pleasures of life in Upper Austria, the country's northwest corner, where he felt at home and where his dialect mingled with that of his neighbors; he had given up the security of his post as Cathedral Organist at Linz and with it the promise of a pension. Friends, however, had urged him to move to the capital to teach organ, counterpoint, and figured bass at the Conservatory for less money than he had earned at the Cathedral, and to assume the unpaid, indeed essentially imaginary, position of Court Organist *in exspectans*.

He was drawn into the musico-political war between the Wagnerians and the Brahmsians, a conflict for which he was temperamentally unsuited and which did not really interest him anyway. His relations with Eduard Hanslick, the critic of the *Neue freie Presse* and originally a warm supporter, soured, and Hanslick, influential and feared, was a bad man to have for an enemy. Bruckner failed in repeated attempts to get government grants and a teaching appointment at the University of Vienna. "It is all too late," he wrote to a friend in 1874. "To work hard at piling up debts and to enjoy the fruits of my labors in debtors' prison where I can also consider the idiocy of having moved to Vienna—that's likely to be my lot. They've taken 1,000 florins a year from me, and this year there's no replacement for that, no stipend or anything. I can't afford to have my Fourth Symphony copied."

He did not go to prison, and in the summer of 1875 the university did create a lectureship in harmony and counterpoint for him, unpaid to begin with, but properly compensated from 1877 on. Truly though, with his peasant speech, his social clumsiness, those trousers of which it was said that they looked as though a carpenter had built them, his disastrous inclination to fall in love with girls of sixteen, his distracting compulsions, his piety (he knelt to pray in the middle of a counterpoint class when he heard the angelus sound from the church next door), his powerful intelligence that functioned only when channeled into musical composition or teaching, a Neanderthal male chauvinism that even his contemporaries found remarkable, his unawareness of intellectual or political currents of his or any other day, Bruckner was not a likely candidate for success in that compost heap of gossip and intrigue that was Vienna, nor indeed anywhere in a world where a composer's success in the sense of making a living and getting performances and publications depends on so much other than skill at inventing music.

And of public success, Bruckner knew little. The Symphony No. 2, in a Vienna Philharmonic performance arranged by stubborn supporters over more or less everyone's dead body, made a powerful impact in 1873. In the winter of 1884–85, the Symphony No. 7 excited audiences to tremendous ovations in Leipzig under Arthur Nikisch and in Munich under Hermann Levi, and had rapidly continued its triumphant conquest in Dresden, Frankfurt, Karlsruhe, Hamburg, Cologne, Vienna, Graz, Amsterdam, The Hague, and Utrecht. (London, Chicago, New York, and Boston heard it too, but resisted.) Bruckner was a respected teacher; he continued to make a sensation wherever he appeared as an organist; he even received an Imperial decoration, the Order of Francis Joseph, as well as a grant from the privy purse; and his last residence was something like a gatekeeper's cottage at the Belvedere, an Imperial property to which he moved in 1895 at the invitation of Emperor Francis Joseph.[1] Whatever else, an apartment at the Belvedere was a long way from the schoolmaster's house at Ansfelden.

But against this, one must set a history of rejection by the public, savage attacks in the press, and humiliations by orchestras. Bruckner never heard his Fifth or Sixth symphonies. No. 5 had two performances in his lifetime, in Graz in 1894 and in Budapest in 1895; both times it was the falsification of the score by his pupil Franz Schalk that was presented, and the composer was in any case too ill to attend. Of No. 6, the Adagio and Scherzo only were played by the Vienna Philharmonic in 1883. The whole work was performed for the first time, though in mutilated form, under Gustav Mahler in 1899. Bruckner must have felt that the reception of the Seventh Symphony in Leipzig and Munich was a turning point in his fortunes, yet nothing describes his state of mind more poignantly than the

---

[1] Bruckner's neighbor at the Belvedere was the heir presumptive to the Austro-Hungarian throne, that Archduke Francis Ferdinand whose assassination at Sarajevo on 28 June 1914 became the proximate cause of World War I.

story of how, when the Vienna Philharmonic wanted to get on the band-wagon and play No. 7, Bruckner begged them not to lest the expected bad (in both senses) review by Dr. Hanslick in the *Neue freie Presse* "obstruct the course of my dawning fame in Germany." (The Philharmonic ignored his plea: the public success of the performance under Hans Richter was unequivocal, the composer having to take four or five bows after each movement, but if the Hanslick review was as expected, it had no effect on Bruckner's reputation.)

Once Bruckner began his real life as a composer, he found he was offering the world music that it really did not know what to do with. Furtwängler, addressing the German Bruckner Society in 1939, put it aptly and characteristically:

> The relevance of [Bruckner's great art] today is perhaps due to the fact that it directs our awareness towards the sphere of the absolute, forcing us to abandon the usual historical methods which, in the fullest sense of the word, "encumber" modern man's direct communion with the art of the past. This is not meant to imply that Bruckner did not emerge as a product of his age, although he did stand to one side while his contemporaries Wagner and Brahms were, to a great extent, active in forming and moulding their era, becoming . . . the real architects of their time. Bruckner did not work for the present; in his art he thought only of eternity and he created for eternity. In this way he became the most misunderstood of the great musicians. . . .
>
> Bruckner is one of those geniuses who have appeared but seldom in the course of European history, whose destiny it was to render the transcendent real and to attract, even to compel, the element of the divine into our human world. Whether it found expression in the battle of demons or in the sounds of blissful ecstasy in his music, this man's whole meditation and his aspirations were basically directed towards this element of the divine that he perceived in himself and beyond himself. He was not a musician at all, but really a descendent of those German mystics like Eckhart and Jakob Böhme.[2]

Yet, though he could be wounded, bewildered, and momentarily distracted from his path, Bruckner found himself firm in his vocation as a symphonist. He made music like no other, naive and complex together, homely and sublime. From Beethoven he had learned about scale, prepara-

---

[2] Furtwängler, *Ton und Wort* (Wiesbaden: Brockhaus, 1954). Eckhart von Hochheim, known as Meister Eckhart, a thirteenth-century Dominican, was a speculative mystic whose Latin and German writings dealt chiefly with the soul's union with God. Jakob Böhme was a shoemaker whose religious crisis in 1600 precipitated a life of writing; his nature mysticism in particular made him a figure much beloved by the Romantics. Furtwängler does not say but would have expected his listeners to know that both Meister Eckhart and Jakob Böhme were rejected by most of their contemporaries, that like Bruckner they were not working "for the present." —M.S.

tion and suspense, mystery, and the ethical content of music; from Schubert something about a specifically Austrian tone and much about harmony; from Wagner, along with a few mannerisms, everything about a sense of slow tempo and a breadth of unfolding hitherto unknown in instrumental music. The vision, in the largest sense, was his own. So was the simple magnificence of sound, achieved with an astonishing and magisterial economy. Wagner tubas and a second quartet of horns enter Bruckner's orchestra only from the Seventh Symphony forward, only the Seventh and Eighth use percussion other than timpani (and just for a single moment each), and only the Eighth calls for harps. The splendors of the Fifth Symphony, for example, are achieved with an orchestra that, except for a third trumpet, is no bigger than Brahms's (and Bruckner does without Brahms's contrabassoon).

In response to the perplexity, not to say dismay, that Bruckner's new music provoked at so many of its performances, three of his pupils—Josef and Franz Schalk and Ferdinand Löwe—decided that if, with some cosmetic magic, Bruckner's symphonies could be brought closer to what people expected, all would be well. They cut and restitched, they imposed a Wagnerian ebb and flow on Bruckner's sense of pace, and they changed the orchestration from the unfussy magnificence of the originals to—again—a Wagnerian impasto. Always with some difficulty, they persuaded Bruckner to accept their changes as well as to make some cuts of his own. With no participation whatever on Bruckner's part, Franz Schalk issued a totally spurious score of the Fifth Symphony and Löwe one of the Ninth.

In the 1920s, however, scholars and conductors began to take an interest in the question of authenticity in Bruckner's scores, and the full extent of the Schalk-Löwe vandalism was disclosed dramatically in Munich in 1932 when Siegmund von Hausegger conducted both versions of the Ninth at the same concert: the familiar Löwe edition to begin with; then, for the first time, the original, with cut passages restored and Löwe's added measures removed, with the inspired plainness of Bruckner's massive orchestral registration in place of the Wagnerian mixed palette, and with the music organized in clearly defined blocks of tempi rather than *Nibelungen* ebb and flow. The legend of the non-viability of Bruckner's originals was disposed of in one evening. Later in the 1930s, the other symphonies were reintroduced in unretouched versions, and the corrupt editions began to disappear from the active repertory.[3]

The devotion of Löwe and the Schalk brothers and their sincere desire

---

[3] This last phrase is too smooth and optimistic. For a clear account of this complicated issue—and the problems that remain—see Deryck Cooke's essay "The Bruckner Problem Simplified" in his collection *Vindications* (Cambridge: Cambridge University Press, 1982).

to help their master and to promote recognition of his genius cannot be doubted any more than their spitefulness, their paranoia (like much of the Bruckner circle, though not including Bruckner himself, they believed that a Jewish conspiracy was holding Bruckner down), and, most crucially, their failure to understand what the specific nature of that genius was. Deafened by their hatred of Brahms and his chief supporters in the Viennese press, Eduard Hanslick and Max Kalbeck, their understanding of the differences between Brahms and Wagner was fatally crude. They wished to present Bruckner as a kind of Wagnerian symphonist in opposition to Brahms and felt that the only thing wrong with Bruckner's symphonies was that they were not Wagnerian enough.

The Schalks and Löwe had made a mistake about Bruckner's intelligence, which was formidable when he was composing or teaching. Bruckner could be depressed, frightened, confused, and pushed around, but he knew his own music. Ultimately he was not convinced by his students' efforts on his behalf. He was inclined to be resistant to their proposed changes; he refused to sign the printer's copy of the Franz Schalk/Löwe edition of the Fourth Symphony; he insisted frequently that their recensions were provisional makeshifts and that only his own versions, whether they represented the works in their original form or in revisions for which he himself was responsible, should be valid in some future time. One might wish that Bruckner had stood up absolutely to these well-meaning, unscrupulous, and not impressively talented students of his, but that would mean entirely remodeling his personality—and thus, surely, his music. In any event, it is a matter now of spilt milk.

Symphony No. 4 in E-flat major, *Romantic*

> *Moving, not too fast*
> *Andante quasi Allegretto*
> *Scherzo and Trio: Moving—Not too fast, on no account dragging*
> *Finale: Moving, but not too fast*

Bruckner began the Symphony No. 4 on 2 January 1874 and completed it on 22 November that year. That version, however, remained unperformed until 1979. Bruckner made what he regarded as the definitive version between 18 January 1878 and 5 June 1880, and this was introduced by Hans Richter and the Vienna Philharmonic on 20 February 1881. In 1886, Bruckner made some further and fairly slight revisions for the Hungarian conductor Anton Seidl, who led the first performance of this version in New York on 16 March 1888. A word on editions: the International Bruckner Society score edited in 1936 by Robert Haas gives the 1880 version, as does the 1975 International Bruckner Society score edited by Leopold Nowak. Nowak's 1953 score for the Society is of the 1886 edition. This essay is based on the 1880 score. The Kalmus score reprints Haas; the other conducting and miniature scores published under the imprints of Gutmann, Eulenburg, Peters, Philharmonia, and Universal are of a spurious version made in 1886–87 by Bruckner's pupils Franz Schalk and Ferdinand Löwe.

Two flutes, two oboes, two clarinets, two bassoons, four horns, three trumpets, three trombones, bass tuba, timpani, and strings.

Bruckner begins with a chord of E-flat major played by the strings, tremolando, and as softly as possible: "no crescendo" is an additional and emphatic instruction. Ideally you do not hear the music begin; rather, you become aware that it has begun. Upon this screen, a French horn projects a series of simple and brief calls, simple to the point that only one note in the first sixteen is something other than E-flat or B-flat. The errant note, the first one of the second phrase, is a C-flat, which is not part of the normal vocabulary of E-flat major: it opens—with the symphony's second chord—a vista onto the minor mode, introducing thereby a touch of mystery.

The artful blurring of the borderline between silence and music, the use of the French horn with its singular evocative powers, and the touch of expressive mystery are typically Romantic devices. This brings us to the question of the symphony's title. Bruckner had private pet names for several of his symphonies, for example "das kecke Beserl" (the fresh brat) for No. 1 and "die Fantastische" for No. 5, but the Fourth is the only one he set into the world with an official and public title, "die Romantische." Long after writing the music, he offered his friends this scenario for the first movement: "Medieval city—dawn—morning calls sound from the towers—the gates open—on proud steeds, knights ride into the open— woodland magic embraces them—forest murmurs—bird song—and thus the Romantic picture unfolds." It is hard to take this seriously except as documentation of a feeble—because unconvinced—attempt on Bruckner's part to ally himself with the "progressive" programmatic side of the musical *Zeitgeist.*

While the horn sounds its four calls, the harmony in the strings becomes more active (though no louder). Woodwinds pick up the call, the horn answers them, and the strings tremolando takes on a new coloring as it is now scored for violins divided into four sections and for violas, with cellos and basses silent. The harmony ranges more widely. Bruckner now allows some crescendo and introduces, as a rhythmic energizer, his favorite division of a measure into two plus three; in this way he builds rapidly up to his first *fortissimo* for full orchestra. For a moment he halts his mighty stride and resumes the music quietly in an unexpected mellow and Schubertian D-flat major.

The violins' perky comments, Bruckner once explained, represent the call of the titmouse, while the viola melody expresses his own happiness at being allowed to hear these "familiar sounds of nature" in the woods. As though remembering the C-flat at the beginning of the movement, the second violins delicately darken the harmony with a couple of F-flats. There we have the material for this movement. Bruckner, with total command of form and pace, plays brilliantly upon the contrasts of musical character and the harmonic implications of what has happened so far. The issue of B-flat versus D-flat, the "normal" key for a second thematic group in an E-flat movement as against the more exotic key in which that group was actually presented, is paramount.

The exposition having quietly and calmly run its course, development, as the English composer Robert Simpson puts it, "commences in reflective mystery." Bruckner covers territory that is enormous and wide-ranging with respect both to harmony and expressive character. He even introduces a new and wonderful theme, a chorale, splendidly scored for trumpets, trombones, and tuba (with horn accents), accompanied by shimmering violins and majestic broken chords in the violas and woodwinds. The afterglow of this episode prepares the recapitulation, whose horn calls are subtly echoed on drums and with the flute adding a "holy ghost" counterpoint. Here, too, Bruckner's economy and sense of structure are magnificent. He is, for example, more than nine-tenths through the movement before he enters C minor, which, as the relative minor of E-flat, one would expect to be one of the most obvious—even inevitable—way stations for this piece, and it is not until sixteen measures from the end that he allows the horn call to be projected in open *fortissimo*.

Many commentators on the Fourth Symphony have called its Andante a funeral march.[4] True, we hear the harmonies of C minor, the sound of muted violins and violas, and the measured tread we know so

---

[4]Bruckner heads the movement "Andante" as a generic title, just as he puts the word "Scherzo" on the first page of the third movement, but his actual tempo mark is the somewhat faster Andante quasi Allegretto.

well from Schubert's "walking" songs like *Gute Nacht* at the beginning of *Winterreise*, but surely the atmosphere is not so much tragic as wistfully melancholic. Probably the nearest Schubertian correlative is the C-minor Andante con moto in the E-flat major Piano Trio, D.929. This music is, in any event, much less "present" than most of Schubert's movements of this type or indeed than most of Bruckner's work altogether. Its elusive atmosphere—and it is a piece that easily miscarries in performance, becoming either logy or frivolous—resides in a certain sense of distance between the musical events and ourselves. The sounds are articulate and clearly defined; nevertheless, we perceive the music as though through a scrim.

From his "walking" tune, Bruckner proceeds to a soft string chorale, then to an expansive viola melody (with pizzicatos to mark the continuation of the forward tread), and so to faraway echoes of a somber march. With the opening tune sounding in the horns and (upside down) in the trumpet, violins and violas glow in a pair of melodies of wonderful and smiling radiance. After a climax, the recapitulation, subtly and freshly arranged, leads to an even broader and more sonorous pinnacle, with a brief, tristful, penseroso close.

The Scherzo brings another instance of Bruckner's two-plus-three rhythm. This is active music, vigorously forward-moving, masterfully scored both in its full-blooded *fortissimos* and in its far more frequent passages of enchanting delicacy. Bruckner has occasion to refer to the principal idea as a "hunting theme," and in the autograph of the symphony's first version the sweetly simple trio is marked "dance tune at mealtime on the hunt."

Bruckner lays out the finale on the grand scale of his first movement, although—and it is better to be candid about something that will be obvious to the listener anyway—with a less certain sense of design.[5] The music begins with a rapid pulsation in the strings—three simultaneous pulsations actually, all *pianissimo*, a rapid thudding of repeated notes in cellos and

---

[5] The symphonic finale presented a problem to several nineteenth-century composers, bent, as many of them were, upon imitating Beethoven at shifting the focal point of the symphony to a climactic, summing-up last movement. Schubert, for example, found himself stymied to the point of abandoning a symphony after two movements of extraordinary greatness. Brahms had no problems, but a whole run of excellent composers from Mendelssohn and Schumann to Franck, Dvořák, and Mahler show signs of strain in their finales. Tchaikovsky conquered the problem only when he dared the boldly original solution he put forward in his *Pathétique*. Nor was the challenge beyond Bruckner, who was exceptionally ambitious with respect both to grandeur and originality. In his Second, Fifth, and Eighth symphonies he confidently achieved finales commensurate with his ambition, symphonic summations that can stand with any in the repertory. Robert Simpson's discussion of this problem with respect to Bruckner in his book *The Essence of Bruckner* (Chilton, 1968) is profoundly perceptive.

basses, a tremolando in the first violins and violas, and a spinning figure in the second violins. All this is set upon B-flat (B-flat minor to begin with), and only as the crescendo builds, with echoes of the Scherzo's hunting horns not yet dispersed, does the music turn toward the symphony's home key of E-flat. This is also in the minor mode at first, an expanded and explicit variation of the E-flat quasi-minor of the symphony's first page, just as the succession of brief phrases for horns and clarinets against string accompaniment recalls the gestures of the opening. The relatively dark coloration of the finale was one of the results of Bruckner's massive 1878–80 revision of the score.

Bruckner is lavish with the amount of material he presents and uses. Many of his abruptions are powerfully eloquent, and the themes themselves are full of variety and character. And he certainly achieves here one of his greatest codas, a journey in grandly confident strides across huge territories of the harmonic universe, surely paced, magnificently scored, and attaining a proud sense of arrival and affirmation that is altogether Bruckner's own.

Symphony No. 5 in B-flat major

> *Adagio—Allegro*
> *Adagio*
> *Scherzo: Molto vivace*
> *Finale: Allegro moderato*

Bruckner began work on his Fifth Symphony on 14 February 1875 and completed it on 16 May 1876. That summer he went to Bayreuth for the opening of Wagner's Festspielhaus and the first *Ring* cycle, later worked on revisions of his Third and First symphonies, then returned to the Fifth, which occupied him off and on until 4 January 1878. Bruckner himself heard the Fifth only in a two-piano reading in Vienna in 1887. The first orchestral performance was given on 8 April 1894 in Graz under the direction of Franz Schalk. Bruckner was already too ill to attend; in any event, Schalk, without his knowledge, gave the piece in a much cut and completely reorchestrated version of his own. Moreover, it was in Schalk's edition that the Fifth was first published in 1896, Bruckner's original score not being performed until 1935 or published until 1936. The dedication is to Karl Ritter von Stremayr, then Minister of Education in the Austro-Hungarian Empire.

Two flutes, two oboes, two clarinets, two bassoons, four horns, three trumpets, three trombones, bass tuba, timpani, and strings.

The Fifth is alone among Bruckner's symphonies in beginning with a slow introduction. Plucked cellos and basses, *pianissimo*, stalk up and down a scale segment, while above, violas and violins spread a tissue of softly dissonant suspensions, disturbed three times by sighing accents. I imagine Bruckner was remembering the touching music for basset horns that begins the *Recordare* in Mozart's Requiem. The full orchestra, kettledrums excepted, makes a peremptory, sharply rhythmic announcement in stark octaves. Another silence, and brasses powerfully intone a hymn. Silence again. The octaves come back, and so does the hymn fragment. Then a new and quicker tempo leads with great urgency to a fuller statement of the hymn. A sudden hush and, with yet another idea, the Allegro proper is on its way.

"No symphony ever opened like this," writes Robert Simpson in his exciting study *The Essence of Bruckner.* I have described the opening of what Bruckner liked sometimes to call his "Fantastic" Symphony in detail because it is so special, so strange—fantastic indeed—so disjunct, all those qualities being underlined by the way each new event flings us in a different harmonic direction. By the time the Allegro is under way, we have already been offered an immense variety of musical characters. Bruckner's task now is to establish the unity of all these musics, and the first movement unfolds as a great and dramatic struggle to bring everything safely and justly into port in its home key of B-flat major.

The Adagio opens with the same sound as the first movement, *pianissimo* plucked strings, but with different notes. It is both adumbration of and then accompaniment in cross-rhythm to a melancholy oboe solo. This oboe melody was the first idea Bruckner got down onto paper in February 1875. The contrasting theme, for strings alone, at once sumptuous and noble, he wants played "markig," meaning powerful, vigorous, pithy, and in fact derived from *Mark,* marrow. The Adagio rises to a high level of tension, though not to one of those heaven-opening climaxes we know from the Seventh and Eighth symphonies. At its close, it collapses into fragments and in pathos.

The Scherzo now begins with the same notes as the Adagio, still *pianissimo* and again in strings, but four or five times as fast as before, and bowed rather than plucked. This, too, turns out to be an accompaniment to a woodwind melody, cousin in shape though not in mood to what the oboe sang so poignantly in the slow movement. The trio proceeds with a sense of caprice that occurs only once more in Bruckner's music, in the corresponding section of the Ninth Symphony. The first notes the cellos and basses play outline the same shape as those scale segments with which they began the symphony.

Each movement, then, begins like some other, either in sonority or in the actual choice of notes. The Finale in fact begins exactly as the first movement did, except that a clarinet twice very softly drops a falling octave into the texture. When the strings come to the end of their opening music, more compressed here than in the first movement, they turn to the clarinet to ask, "What was that you said?" The clarinet tells them, and in surprisingly impertinent tones. Bits of the first Allegro and of the Adagio pass by, but the clarinet, getting his number-two player to help, insists. "All right," say the strings, offering to turn the idea into a ferocious fugue.

By now we have some idea of Bruckner's sense of movement and space. This fugued music and what quickly follows it, up to a glorious brass chorale (with soft string echoes), is all preparatory. Looking back, we perceive that even the first three movements have, in a sense, been preparatory. After the chorale, the music subsides into hesitations, silence, suspense. The violas begin a fugue on the chorale tune. They begin it quietly, but before long the current is irresistible and fierce. Beethoven has provided Bruckner with two models in the same key, the finale of the *Hammerklavier* Sonata and the Great Fugue for string quartet, and you do have to reach as far back as those to find a parallel for what Bruckner unpacks here. At the last, a final, stunning appearance of the chorale resolves the friction-charged dialectic.

Symphony No. 6 in A major

> *Majestoso*
> *Adagio: Very solemn*
> *Scherzo and Trio: Not fast—Slow*
> *Finale: Moving, but not too fast*

Bruckner began work on the Symphony No. 6 on 24 September 1879, but interrupted it while he wrote a new finale for the Symphony No. 4. He completed the first movement on 27 September 1880, the second by 22 November, the third by 17 January 1881, and the finale on 3 September that year. Wilhelm Jahn led the Vienna Philharmonic in a reading rehearsal in February 1883, but at a concert on the 11th of that month only the second and third movements were played. That was the nearest thing to a performance in Bruckner's lifetime. On 26 February 1899, Gustav Mahler conducted all four movements in Vienna, also with the Philharmonic, but in a performance disfigured by many cuts. The first complete performance was given in Stuttgart under the direction of Karl Pohlig on 14 March 1901.

Two flutes, two oboes, two clarinets, two bassoons, four horns, three trumpets, three trombones, bass tuba, timpani, and strings.

Bruckner's Fourth and Seventh symphonies are repertory works; the Eighth and Ninth, though more "special occasion" works than these, are regularly unveiled for contemplation; even the grand and problematic Fifth, the still more problematic but attractive Third, and the fresh and confident Second get their outings. No. 6 tends to be left on the shelf, though audiences enjoy it when given a chance and wonder why they haven't heard it before or don't hear it more often. Writing this essay brought me back to the work after a fifteen-year separation, but the feeling of being amazed by its beauties, particularly those of the Adagio, which is unsurpassed in Bruckner's symphonies, was familiar.

The Beethoven symphony that the sixteen-year-old Bruckner heard at his first orchestral concert in Linz was the Fourth. Starting a symphony that way, in mystery, was a concept that was always to fascinate him. Six of Bruckner's symphonies begin with a hum from which thematic fragments detach themselves or against which he projects a spacious melody. The opening of Beethoven's Ninth Symphony came to provide him—and many other nineteenth-century composers—with a model still more striking. Other Bruckner symphonies commence with a rhythmic accompaniment figure, the tromp-tromp of Nos. 0 and 1 or the nervous chirrup of high violins in No. 6.

Often the first sound establishes the key as well: in No. 7, for example, the violins play an E-major chord (two-thirds of one anyway, enough for identification), and when the cellos come in, they tip it on its side from vertical to horizontal, turning it into a glorious melody that starts as a stretched-out chord of E major. In No. 6, the accompaniment consists of a single note, C-sharp. By itself, this is not enough for harmonic identification, but the E-A opening of the melody in the low strings "places" this C-sharp as part of a chord of A major. (This is not at all what we most expect: if a piece begins with a single note, we are likely to assume either that it is the keynote or that it will turn out to be the fifth of the chord, as in *The Star-Spangled Banner* or the *Marseillaise*.)

The beginning is mysterious. Where are we, harmonically? This opening, however, is not that hush of penumbral cathedral and dusky forest, that sense of slowly getting our bearings as our eyes become accustomed to the half-light, which Bruckner's symphonies so often suggest. Rather, the jumpy, complex rhythm in the violins creates an atmosphere of suppressed excitement. If Bruckner's opening melodies usually begin by outlining the tonic chord, they quickly move to expand the harmonic horizon. The striding theme that begins the Symphony No. 6 is in an uncommon hurry to leave home: already with its third note it begins to travel.

Ex. 1

After that, no fully settled chord of A major returns until measure 25, when the orchestra rings out in restatement of the melody in a grandly sonorous Bruckner *fortissimo*. Then you can wait a good ten minutes for the recapitulation to bring another such chord.

With its individual atmosphere and speed of harmonic change, this is not ordinary Bruckner. The composer himself thought it his boldest work. From his Third Symphony forward, Bruckner leaned more and more toward the monumental, but in that progression No. 6 is a step off the main road, an intermezzo almost; it is even by a few minutes his shortest symphony after the First. Its departure from the most obvious Bruckner norm may even be a reason for its comparative neglect. Another reason occasionally suggested for that neglect is the first movement's rhythmic complexity, difficult to sort out and make transparent in performance. The second theme presents a typical example. The eloquent beginning is fairly simple,

Ex. 2

but as the paragraph unfolds, it involves the simultaneous overlay of rhythmic patterns like this

Ex. 3

or this

Ex. 4

The exposition will eventually settle in E major, toward which this E-minor theme is a somewhat vague promissory note, but before that destination is safely reached, several harmonic crises must be weathered. The settling in E major, when it comes, is a moment of lovely calm.

Early in its course, the development brings what one might take to be a new theme, but which is in fact a free inversion of the opening one.

Ex. 5

Enjoy the sound of the orchestra here. Donald Tovey remarks on Bruckner's "curious and effective" device of accompanying such melodies with "echoes, which are always imperfect, and always scored for weaker instruments just on the border-line of audibility."

Something happens that sounds and behaves like a recapitulation, but there is also something about this thunderous reappearance of the opening theme that feels wrong. It should, for it is in E-flat, as remote and as irrelevant as anything could be in an A-major context. But a good pun is in the making here. The bass rises to G-flat, to G-natural, to A-flat. At this point Bruckner suddenly claims that his A-flat really means G-sharp. The timpani playing an E, in fact playing for the first time since the development began, support this view, for their entrance unmistakably turns the note in question into the third of an E-major chord, and there, when we had least expected it, we are on the very doorstep of A major and home. This is one of the most dramatic and astonishing entries into the recapitulation in any classical or Romantic symphony.

Ex. 6

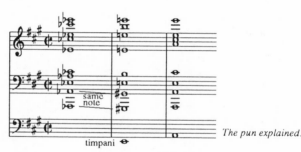

The pun explained.

The coda is one of Bruckner's most splendid. It begins with a version of the opening heard simultaneously right side up (horn) and inverted (oboe). Then, if I may quote Tovey again, it passes "from key to key beneath a tumultuous surface sparkling like the Homeric seas." The closing pages are a blazing combination of fanfare and Amen.

The first movement was in A major, constantly imperiled by invasions from the flat side of the harmonic spectrum. Now, in the "very solemn" Adagio, that invasion comes to pass, but not at all as fiercely as the explosions in the first movement of C major, E-flat major, and other keys from the flat side had threatened. This new music is in F major and leans toward still darker harmonies, but it is music of the utmost nobility of spirit. The key of A major in the first movement was defined more by suggestion than by assertion. Here the establishing of F major is subtler still. The first note is F, and F alone, but the descent to E-flat in the bass on the second note already hints that F is not the keynote but part of the world of B-flat minor.[6]

There is a most tentative cadence on F at the beginning of the fifth measure, but the B-flat-minor suggestion is immediately and powerfully reinforced by the lament the oboe superimposes on the violin melody. As the music rises to a crest, its F-major orientation becomes clear, but by the time a cadence is achieved all is adrift again. Unambiguous A-major chords were rare in the first movement; it will be a long time before Bruckner gives us an unambiguous statement of F major in this Adagio.

A new paragraph—the main melody in the violins, an ecstatic countertheme in the cellos—begins in the remote, mysterious region of E major:

Ex. 7

[6] Bruckner's notation is revealing. He puts a natural sign before the violins' A in the first measure. Technically there is no need for this: the key signature indicates A-natural, and there has been no A-flat or A-sharp to contradict this. Bruckner assumes, however, that the violinists, hearing the cellos and basses descend from F to E-flat to D-flat, would hear the music as being perhaps in D-flat major (the relative major of B-flat minor) and, trusting their ears more than their eyes, would play A-flat. So, while incorrect or, at the very least, eccentric, Bruckner's notation shows singular psychological delicacy.

The effect of mystery is enhanced by the stillness—on E—of the bass. One of Bruckner's most inspired inventions, especially in its harmonies, it rises to a great climax before subsiding to a *pianissimo* melody that suggests the passing of a cortège. The development is brief. Toward its end, the keening lament of the oboe is heard again, and this, in a most touching way, becomes the bridge into the recapitulation. The horns have the melody now, and the surrounding texture is gorgeously rich. The wonderful theme that was formerly in E major now reappears in F, and this is the first undisturbed settling in that key. And in the coda, even the opening melody is heard in a serene and unclouded F major. Again the bass is absolutely still—this time of course on F—and remains so for the last twenty-one measures of this sublime movement by the greatest composer of adagios after Beethoven.

The tempo of the A-minor Scherzo is, as Bruckner's indication tells us, "not fast," but the beats are busily filled in. The harmonies are both extraordinarily simple and extraordinarily subtle. For quite a stretch, the bass consists only of E's and A's, yet Bruckner, with wonderful effect, evades—for an amazingly long time, in fact until nine measures before the end—the resolution of a clear tonic chord in its most stable position. The atmosphere is a little exotic, perhaps Bohemian. Like most of Bruckner's trios, this one is in duple meter and at a much slower tempo. Three elements are juxtaposed: a strange, upward-leaping figure for pizzicato strings, an imperturbable response from the horns (whose major triads are in strong contrast to the strings' diminished chords), and, from the woodwinds, a quotation from Bruckner's own Fifth Symphony. The strings, who ask the most puzzling question here, also function as peacemakers, rounding off each episode with the smoothest of cadences. The Scherzo is repeated in full.

The Finale continues the Scherzo's A minor, beginning with a darkly impassioned theme. As in the first movement, harmonic stability is constantly threatened by invasions from the flat side. The F's and B-flats that played so important a role in the symphony's opening theme are built powerfully into the first theme of the finale as well and, though the music soon wants to swing into the brightness of A major, the brass are quick to contradict with intimations of B-flat minor (the key that so ominously darkened the F-major calm of the Adagio). A new and sweetly naive theme brings contrast; it is in C major, a key that is something like a halfway house between A minor and F major.

The quest for firm possession of A major becomes the central drama of this movement, surely Bruckner's most confidently argued finale next to that of the Eighth Symphony, and the drama is the more intense because the threats from the worlds of F and B-flat continue almost to the end. As the coda begins, the music is suspended uncertainly at the edge of B-flat minor, and the assertion, finally, of A major is, if anything, even more sudden and dramatic than the re-establishment of that key in the recapitulation of the first movement. Once there, it cleans up swiftly. Even the rhythm of the B-flat-minor brass contradictions from the beginning of the movement is pressed into service. If we have some experience with Bruckner's music, we wait for the symphony's opening theme to enter and pull everything together, and so it does, its contours reshaped to make a fanfare for the trombones to proclaim across the final A-major blaze.

Symphony No. 7 in E Major

Allegro moderato
Adagio: Very solemn and slow—Moderato
Scherzo and Trio: Very fast—A little slower
Finale: Moving, but not fast

Bruckner began work on his Symphony No. 7 on 23 September 1881, completing the first movement on 29 December 1882. The Adagio was ready in sketch on 22 January 1883 and in score three months later, on 21 April. The Scherzo was sketched by 14 July 1882 and finished on 16 October that year. The Finale, and with it the entire symphony, was completed on 5 September 1883. Bruckner's pupils Josef Schalk and Franz Zottmann had already played the first and third movements on two pianos in Vienna in February 1883; Schalk and another Bruckner pupil, Ferdinand Löwe, gave the whole symphony in that form in Vienna a year later. Bruckner undertook a few revisions after the formal premiere, which Arthur Nikisch conducted with the Leipzig Gewandhaus Orchestra on 30 December 1884. The dedication, which Bruckner decided upon after the first performance of the work in Munich, is "to H.M., King Ludwig II of Bavaria, in deepest reverence."

Two flutes, two oboes, two clarinets, two bassoons, four horns, four Wagner tubas (two tenor and two bass), three trumpets, three trombones, bass tuba (alternating with contrabass tuba), timpani, and strings. The question of the cymbal and triangle parts in the Adagio is discussed below.

The Seventh Symphony, uniquely, enjoyed immediate and warm success in Bruckner's lifetime, success that came as a happy and restorative surprise to this much-battered composer. Speaking to today's audiences with singular directness, it remains the most loved of the nine—or ten, or eleven, depending on whether you count the symphonies before the official No. 1.

Bruckner begins with an unmistakable assertion of E major. This takes the form of a soft, non-articulated hum, a background for an event rather than an event in its own right. This is also a declaration that E is the tonal center, just as the E-flat chords that begin Beethoven's *Eroica* are, among other things, a declaration that this is going to be a symphony in E-flat major. The task of the next hour's music is to affirm that tonal center.[7]

As Robert Simpson so aptly puts it in his beautiful study *The Essence of Bruckner*, this "entrance . . . leads to a very lofty and light interior," a vastly arching melody in which the cellos are subtly supported, now by a horn, now by the violas, now by a clarinet. To the extent that Bruckner conveys the feeling of an immense arch, he is giving us in microcosm the sense of the entire movement, with its grand pull away from the opening E major into the regions of B minor and B major, and its sovereign reconquest of the original tonality.

This is the first of three vividly contrasted themes, and it expands to become a paragraph of immense breadth. The second theme is slower and calmer. The melody rises, embellished by a graceful turn in its first phrase, but it is full of hesitations that make it sound touchingly vulnerable. Against soft brass chords, oboe and clarinet set it on its course. This too fills space grandly, and Bruckner does not fail to show us how beautiful the melody is when it is inverted. The music swells to an assertive *fortissimo* on suspenseful harmonies. What emerges from here is a theme, unharmonized and gray, that dances in a mysterious *pianissimo*. It gathers momentum and volume, arrives at a series of taut and loud brass chords like those that introduced it, then falls back into a suspenseful hush.

Thus the development begins in darkness. Its journey is varied, with a range from densely active paragraphs to wonderful moments in contemplative stasis. The entrance into the recapitulation is sly, a serious counterpart to those unexpected, seemingly unprepared slippings into the home key that Haydn was so good at in humorous contexts. The coda, as almost always in Bruckner, is extraordinary. Its fifty-three measures are set over an unchanging E in the bass. For almost half of them, bass and superstruc-

---

[7]This is Bruckner's procedure in all his symphonies up to the Seventh and again in the unfinished Ninth. In the Eighth, however, he plays a different game, approaching his tonal center, C, obliquely and withholding unambiguous affirmation of it as long as possible.

ture are quietly at odds; then suddenly the orchestra gets the point, and the last thirty-one measures expand the bass-note upward into the great E-major affirmation we have been waiting for.

Until the solemn Adagio actually begins, we do not even notice that Bruckner has so far stayed away from one of the most obvious harmonies a movement in E major would naturally travel toward, that of its relative minor, C sharp.[8] With this harmony that is at once so close and so new, he introduces a new sound, that of a quartet of Wagner tubas, an instrument designed by Wagner for *Der Ring des Nibelungen* and intended to combine the mellowness of French horns with something of the weight of tuba tone. Here there is, however, a deeper association with Wagner. In January 1883 Bruckner wrote to the conductor Felix Mottl: "One day I came home and felt very sad. The thought had crossed my mind that before long the Master would die, and just then the C-sharp-minor theme of the Adagio came to me." Wagner did in fact die on 13 February, and the quiet closing music that begins with the quartet of Wagner tubas plus contrabass tuba became Bruckner's memorial to the man he worshiped above all living musicians. What would one not give to have been present when, at one of his improvisations at Saint Florian's, Bruckner wove together his own Adagio with the music for Siegfried's funeral?[9]

Taking the slow movement of Beethoven's Ninth as a model, Bruckner builds his Adagio on two contrasting ideas, the initial solemn one in minor, in 4/4 time, and a more pastoral, Schubertian one in major and in triple meter. The second of these is abandoned after two statements, both scored with striking richness and loveliness. What the strings play immediately after the movement begins, a firm sequence of rising steps, is an allusion to Bruckner's own *Te Deum*, his last large-scale choral work, in progress at the same time as the Seventh Symphony and completed in March 1884. The words at that point of the *Te Deum* are "non confundar in aeternum" (let me not be confounded for ever), and Bruckner uses the momentum of those upward steps to build a great climax in the first variation. Later he achieves another, one as stupendous as we can find in any symphony, and reached at a place—C major—almost unimaginably far from the harmonic origins of the movement. From that summit the music

[8] The relative minor is that minor key whose scale uses the same notes as that of its relative major. In general, when two keys share a large number of notes we speak of them as closely related; conversely, when two keys share relatively few notes we speak of them as distant or remote. The more distant two keys are, the more striking, or dramatic, or out-and-out startling, a shift from one to the other is likely to be. Sometimes, as in this transition from the first movement to the second, a composer can, paradoxically, make a closely related key feel like fresh territory.

[9] The concert at which Bruckner's Symphony No. 7 had its premiere was a benefit to raise funds for a Wagner monument.

descends into the grief-stricken, then profoundly peaceful, threnody for Wagner.

In most performances, the thrilling arrival at the great C-major climax in the Adagio is marked by a clash of cymbals with a roll of drums and triangle. This has been controversial almost from the beginning. It is clear that the cymbals and triangle were an afterthought of Bruckner's, for their entry appears on an insert to the autograph score. To this insert Bruckner added six question marks! These have been crossed out and the words "gilt nicht" (not valid) added above the measure in question; not all scholars, however, are convinced that this notation is in Bruckner's hand.

From a letter written by Josef Schalk to his brother Franz, we know that the cymbal clash in the Adagio of the Seventh was their idea and that the twenty-nine-year-old Arthur Nikisch, who conducted the premiere, talked Bruckner into accepting it—"which delights us wildly." The structurally similar climax of the Adagio of the Symphony No. 8 has two cymbal clashes of undisputed authenticity; citing this parallel case, some measure of doubt about who added the "gilt nicht," and the undeniable effectiveness of this spectacular punctuation, most conductors use the cymbals and triangle in the Seventh.

The third movement is a Scherzo dominated by the restless ostinato of strings and the cheerily trumpeting cock-crow with which it begins. As is Bruckner's custom, the Trio is somewhat slower, lightly scored, and pastoral in character. One of the features that define its pastoral nature is the prevalence of bagpipe-like long-held notes in the bass much as one might find them in musette movements in Baroque music.

The Finale, to quote Simpson again, "blends solemnity and humor in festive grandeur." It presents highly diversified ideas that run the gamut from the capricious and even the magnificently grotesque to the sublimely simple. At the end, all is gathered into a blaze of E major as we hear intimations of the symphony's beginning and as the heavens open.

Symphony No. 8 in C minor (1887/90, ed. Haas)

Allegro moderato
Scherzo and Trio: Allegro moderato—Slow—Tempo I
Adagio: Solemnly slow, but not dragging
Finale: Solemn, not fast

Bruckner finished sketching the first movement of the Symphony No. 8 on his sixtieth birthday, 4 September 1884, completing the sketch of the

Adagio on 16 February 1886, and those of the Scherzo and Finale on 26 July and 16 August respectively. He marked this arrival in his sketchbook with a big "Hallelujah!" He immediately began work on the full orchestral score, but, progressing slowly because of constant revisions, he only completed this on 10 August 1887. The first time any of the music was heard in public was on 28 August 1886, when some of its themes, interwoven with others from Wagner's *Götterdämmerung*, provided the material for an organ improvisation by Bruckner at the Abbey of Saint Florian. Because this score was rejected by the conductor Hermann Levi, hitherto a great supporter of Bruckner's, the composer, working together with his student Josef Schalk, revised and cut the symphony, most of this task being accomplished between April 1889 and March 1890. This version was performed on 18 December 1892 by the Vienna Philharmonic under Hans Richter. (The 1887 version was not performed in its entirety until September 1973, when Hans-Hubert Schönzeler conducted the Bournemouth Symphony for a BBC broadcast, although Eugen Jochum had conducted the first movement alone at the International Bruckner Festival in Munich on 2 May 1954.) This essay is based on the edition by Robert Haas, which is of the 1890 version, but with the cuts reopened. This controversial question is discussed below. No dedication appears in the score, but Bruckner sent a dedicatory letter to Emperor Franz Joseph of Austria.

Three flutes, three oboes, three clarinets, three bassoons, eight horns (four doubling Wagner tubas—two tenor and two bass), three trombones, contrabass tuba, timpani, triangle, cymbals, harp (three, if possible), and strings.

Bruckner was shattered when his student Josef Schalk brought him the news that Hermann Levi had rejected the Eighth Symphony. He had sent the score on his sixty-third birthday with a note: "Hallelujah! At long last, the Eighth is finished, and my artistic father must be the first to know. . . . May it find grace!" Levi, Court Conductor in Munich and famous for leading the first performances of *Parsifal*, had become Bruckner's "artistic father" by virtue of his outstandingly successful presentations of the Seventh Symphony and *Te Deum*, in addition to which he had raised money for the publication of the Fourth and Seventh symphonies.

No one's rejection could, at that moment, have hurt more. Its immediate effect was to plunge Bruckner into a deep depression—by no means his first, nor was this the first time this devout Catholic was tormented by the temptation of suicide. The long-range consequence was that Bruckner entered a phase of what one of his biographers has called "revision mania": between the end of 1887 and 1891, he rewrote five of his symphonies—

Nos. 1, 2, 3, 4, and 8. This is a complicated issue because much of the rewriting was done not by Bruckner alone, but by and with some of his students. Certain of these second thoughts, especially when they are Bruckner's own, are clear improvements, nowhere more so than in the Eighth Symphony; many of them, especially when they are not Bruckner's own, are disasters, and the Eighth includes several of these as well.

This revision mania had consequences of its own. Some believe it took so much time and energy that Bruckner had none left to crown his life's work by completing his Ninth Symphony. That is to some extent speculative. What is certain is that the revisions, whose pedigrees are in some cases obscure and which include much that is spurious, hampered clear perception of Bruckner's work for more than thirty years after his death. In the case of the Eighth Symphony, some confusion persists to this day.

Bruckner had a hand in two versions of No. 8. The first was the one sent to and rejected by Levi in 1887 and, as I noted earlier, unpublished and, except for a single movement on two occasions, unperformed until 1973. The second, a revision undertaken with Josef Schalk, was completed in 1890, performed that year by Hans Richter with great success, and published in 1892. In 1934, the International Bruckner Society began a project of publishing all of Bruckner's works in authentic editions, the man in charge of the project being Robert Haas, an Austrian scholar born in Prague. In 1935, when Haas came to the Eighth Symphony, he made a bold, dangerous, inspired decision. He chose to issue neither Bruckner's 1887 score nor the Bruckner-Schalk score of 1890; rather, recognizing that the 1890 revision hugely improved the work as a whole even while it spoiled some crucial features of the third and fourth movements, he offered the 1890 score but with Schalk's contributions removed, that is, with the cuts reopened and with a couple of clumsy transitions replaced by their superior 1887 counterparts.

In purely musical terms, the Haas edition thus offers the best of both worlds. The trouble is that it offers the work in a form in which Bruckner did not write it. This became an issue after World War II, and not only because of dissension on this important musicological point within the community of Bruckner scholars. Haas, though not an enthusiastic Nazi like some of his colleagues, had prefaced some of his Bruckner scores with politically compromising, boot-licking introductions. It was enough, after 1945, to get him fired from the academic and other posts he had held, and for the opposition party among the Brucknerites to begin a complete edition all over again, this time under the general editorship of Leopold Nowak, a Viennese scholar.

When Nowak got to the Eighth Symphony in 1955, he issued it in the 1890 version, though with some blatant Schalkisms such as an interpolated cymbal clash in the finale eliminated. It was also Nowak who issued the 1887 score in 1973. In his 1955 score, Nowak was quick to draw attention to the illegitimacy, from the scholarly point of view, of Haas's procedure, saying that the materials from separate sources could not be mixed, that the only proper course would be to publish 1887, 1890, or both, but not to concoct a composite of the two. This, unquestionably, is kosher scholarly practice. The matter is immensely complicated and far beyond the scope of this essay, though it is of interest to point out—not in defense of one view or the other but to show that this is not exclusively a Brucknerian problem—that *Messiah* and *Don Giovanni* are two exceedingly famous works that are almost always heard in comparably hybrid versions.

Strictly speaking, Nowak was right, and the political taint that clings to Haas no doubt contributes to a widespread pro-Nowak bias. Ideally, scholarship and musicianship work in harmony. Most of the time, they even do so in reality. The cleanest text gives the performer the best chance to function as mountain guide, to take us to the top and show us the view (to borrow Artur Schnabel's metaphor). Here is an exception. Haas's compositional insight weighs more than Nowak's scholarly rectitude. Try it at your leisure. Listen to a recording of the Adagio in the Nowak edition, paying particular attention to the approach to the climax a little more than three-quarters of the way through the movement (for score readers, rehearsal letters X-Y); then listen to it again with Rudolf Kempe or Herbert von Karajan using Haas. I am talking about thirty-five seconds of music, but the difference is stunning. The test is in the listening. After that, the defense rests.

Bruckner begins his Eighth Symphony with a long-held F, below which we hear a serious questioning phrase, *pianissimo* in low strings:

Ex. 1

violas, cellos, basses (three octaves deep)
Allegro moderato

pp

Not the least interesting thing about this phrase is the rest between the second and third notes. (It is not quite a silence, because two horns and the violins, all *pianissimo*, sustain their F the whole time.) A second phrase that makes a kind of rhyme to the first follows an even longer rest, though here the gap is partially bridged by a mysterious two-note call of the clarinet. Giving us a melody that obviously intends to be of immense breadth, but presenting it phrase by widely separated phrase, Bruckner is combining his thematic-fragments and spacious-melody techniques. He also continues to insert little bridging comments by woodwind instruments.

Where is this music going as it gathers power? In isolation, the mysterious opening phrase would appear to be in B-flat minor, but neither the "rhyme" nor anything else that follows supports that impression. The harmony is on the move, rapidly and energetically. When the violins and basses exchange roles, the former becoming melody instruments and the latter accompanists, the music seems finally to want to land in C minor, only to be frustrated at the very last moment by the irruption of a *fortissimo* F. To be back on F is, in effect, to be back on square one. What happens now is a counterstatement of the opening paragraph—loud and declamatory this time, with the silences filled in, and leading (again by a startling deceptive cadence) to a different harmonic outcome.

I have described this in detail because to hear and understand what happens in the first minute and a half is to have a sense of Bruckner's strategy for the whole symphony. He thinks in large blocks, which, measured by the standards of refined masters of transition like Wagner and Brahms, are very roughly, even crudely, juxtaposed. One of the most persistent misunderstandings of Bruckner has been the assumption that he *could* not do what he simply *chose* not to do. This applies equally to his deliberately non-Wagnerian orchestration, which perfectly corresponds to and illuminates his compositional vision.

Bruckner is patient, and he expects patience from his listeners as well as a capacity for attention across a long range. He makes it clear that C is the center of this particular world (even if you don't know it is called C, you feel the magnetic pull nonetheless), but he does not give you a firm landing on C. This music sounds nothing like *Tristan*, but when Bruckner saw that opera in 1865, he had obviously paid close attention to the evasion of a clear tonic chord in the Prelude. The Bruckner Eighth is, among other things, a great study in long-range harmonic evasion.

Here Bruckner arrives at his tonic obliquely (B-flat minor is a strange place from which to approach C minor), and the harmonic ambiguity of his mysterious opening melody, one that seems to wander so strangely yet is so certain of its goal, is an extraordinarily powerful resource. Bruckner in fact did not even realize its full potential until he came to make his revision in 1889–90.

From here on, my map for you is, for the most part, comparatively crude, locating only the largest landmarks. After the big counterstatement of the opening paragraph, Bruckner introduces two more themes, a lyric violin melody in the duplet-plus-triplet pattern of which he is so fond, and a sinister proto-Mahlerian march in minor.

The exposition ends with hushed reminders of the opening melody. The development deals both with that theme and with the lyric two-plus-three melody; most of its concern, though, is with finding the way to the recapitulation. Bruckner seems, quite properly, to be preparing C minor when, by a sudden slewing about of the harmony that sounds as wonderfully mad today as it must have in 1892, he suddenly diverts the thrust so that the opening reappears on the old B-flat-minor slant, but this time with stupendous physical and emotional force. A sudden *pianissimo* cuts into this climax and, without quite knowing how we got there, we are at last in the home key. The *pianissimo* flute and drum are the still, small voice after the wind and the fire and the earthquake. This arrival was something to wait for.

A word, finally, about the coda. Bruckner's first movements usually end with a climactic restatement of the opening theme, the coda also being a preview of the coda in the Finale. This is how it worked in the 1887 version of this movement. While he was revising, Bruckner realized that he had already set up a scenario in which suspense about the opening theme and suspense about the home key were integral parts. When will we hear the opening phrase, not aslant on B-flat minor, but set squarely on C? When will there be an arrival on the home key in grand style rather than in *pianissimo*? Will these two goals eventually be combined in a climactic arrival at the opening melody in the tonic?

Then—obviously I do not know this, I infer it from the difference between the 1887 and 1890 scores—it must have occurred to Bruckner that he could make a more powerful structure by delaying this consummation until the end of the Finale. Accordingly, he scrapped his grand coda and, in a moment of profound inspiration, invented the one we hear now. Death Watch is what he called it. It is a last meditation on the opening phrase with its clarinet pendant, and in another of those characteristically Brucknerian reaches across a great space, the composer seems to say: "That opening phrase always sounded harmonically strange, at an angle. But listen again. Its last three notes are D/D-flat/C, and so, though I have concealed it from you until now, it makes a beautiful cadence in C minor after all."

Hitherto in his symphonies, Bruckner had placed the slow movement second and the scherzo third. Here, following the Beethoven Ninth model, he reversed that order, as he would again in his own Ninth Symphony. His Scherzo is of ferocious energy, pounding, as Robert Simpson says, "like some colossal Celestial Engine of Milton's imagining." The sound is amazing, especially the serpent tongues of string chords. Once more the harmonic strategy, with its visits to keys carefully avoided in the first movement, is masterly. Again I stress that these are things you feel even if you cannot name or diagnose them. The Trio, a very short slow movement, is a much-revised version of the original one from 1887. Earlier in his life, Bruckner had declared that the harp does not belong in a symphony. Now, happily, he changed his mind.

The Adagio is the heart of the Eighth Symphony. Its key is D-flat major. This is a new area, untouched so far, though the note D-flat has been prominent in the first two movements. The result is that the opening, with its throbbing chords from the *Tristan* love music and its yearning violin phrases, sounds both fresh and familiar. Like the first movement, the Adagio begins with a spacious paragraph that is immediately restated but made to lead to a different destination. After this double traversal, the cellos are given an impassioned melody of contrasting character. When we hear the opening music for the third time, it builds to a considerable climax, followed by further contemplation of the cello melody.

The fourth time the opening theme begins (in second violins), the violas hang garlands of sixteenth-notes on it and the violins add commentary of deep pathos. Now Bruckner builds patiently, with many fresh starts from *piano* or *pianissimo*, to the high crest of the movement, that arrival being marked by the only appearance (in just two measures) of cymbals and triangle. Here is another place where Bruckner rethought his design. In the 1887 score, this climax is in C major; now, in order to hold the effect of C in reserve for something more important later on, he goes instead to E-flat and then immediately, by another of his violent deceptive cadences, to C-flat.

Again, Bruckner ends with a transcendent coda. The syncopated string chords still throb, but with less agitation than before; the yearning violin melody has become a horn solo, accompanied by two more horns; the violins sing an elegy. For thirty-three slow measures the harmony does not change. As in the first movement, this is music of disintegration, of crumbling into ever smaller components, but the *Eroica* and *Coriolan* tragedy and pain are tempered by acceptance and serenity.

Inevitably, the last movement concerns itself further—and finally—with the connected questions of the "centering" of the opening melody and the unambiguous establishing of C. Again I gratefully quote Simpson, whose writing on Bruckner is the best I know: "This is the greatest specimen of Bruckner's characteristic new kind of finale, which one should not expect to 'go' like a classical finale. The best way to appreciate its grandeur, perhaps, is to imagine some great architect wandering in and about his own cathedral, sometimes stirred and even exhilarated, sometimes stock-still in rapt thought."

Making another of his broad-spanned connections, Bruckner begins in D-flat, the key of the Adagio, but approaching it sideways with a galloping repeated F-sharp.[10] Concerning this connection, Simpson remarks: "It is as if Bruckner is acknowledging that the peace of mind achieved at the end of the Adagio has made it possible to see clearly the way ahead." This movement, too, is rich in material, and its unfolding is the most complex in the symphony.

Very surely, traversing great harmonic spaces, revisiting the familiar, exploring the new, Bruckner, who has kept the symphony's opening theme in our minds by often reminding us of its rhythm (which is that of the opening theme of Beethoven's Ninth), finally boils up a quick and intense crescendo at whose culmination the brass proclaim

Ex. 2

It is the opening phrase in the form so carefully withheld until now, set on C minor over a G pedal in basses and timpani.[11] The answer to the symphony's great questions is now within reach. Once more the music subsides, still with its suspenseful dominant pedal. After a silence it resumes, *pianissimo,* horns softly repeating the jubilant fanfare with which the Finale had begun, and, to quote Simpson once more, violins playing "smoky figurations that burst into flame as the burning sun touches them." The burning sun is the great release into the radiance of C major, the horns' recollection of the Celestial Engine of the scherzo, and finally the combined procession of the main themes of the first three movements.

No, not finally, for what Bruckner boots us into heaven with in the very last bar is a musical figure pulled from the symphony's first phrase, proclaimed now by the whole orchestra in unison.

---

[10] Here the ear may well catch on more quickly than the score-reading eye. The F-sharps on the page suggest no connection with the key of D-flat, but the innocent ear has no difficulty in hearing them as G-flats, whose connection with D-flat major is obvious and close. Bruckner chose the F-sharp notation because it makes more sense in his C-minor context.

[11] This form actually appears once before, in the first movement's recapitulation, but set with deliberate non-prominence in the oboe against swirling flute and violins, with every suggestion of arrival or resolution denied. It is a "What is this?" question for whose answer we must wait an hour.

Symphony No. 9 in D minor

Solemn, mysterious
Scherzo: Moving, lively
Adagio: Very slow, solemn

Bruckner began concentrated work on this unfinished Ninth Symphony in April 1891, though some of the material goes back to sketches made in August or September 1887 and in 1889. He completed the first movement on 23 December 1893, the Scherzo on 15 February 1894, and the Adagio on 30 November that year. He began sketches for a finale on 24 May 1895. Bruckner said that, having dedicated his Seventh Symphony to the great sovereign in the world of art, "poor King Ludwig II of Bavaria," and the Eighth to the greatest sovereign he recognized on earth, "our dear, exalted" Emperor Francis Joseph of Austria, he would dedicate the Ninth to the Supreme Sovereign of all, and the score does indeed bear the dedication "An den lieben Gott." The Ninth Symphony was first performed in a posthumous falsification by Ferdinand Löwe under Löwe's direction in Vienna on 11 February 1903. Löwe had simply made what he regarded as necessary changes after Bruckner's death, compounding his dishonesty by failing to reveal that what the Viennese firm of Doblinger published in 1903 and what he and such eminent colleagues as Richard Strauss, Arthur Nikisch, Theodore Thomas, Fritz Steinbach, Ernst von Schuch, Karl Muck, Eugène Ysaÿe, and Hans Richter conducted in the next half-dozen years was anything other than the genuine article. Löwe had died (in 1925) by the time what Bruckner actually wrote was first heard. This occurred at a special concert for an invited audience in Munich on 2 April 1932 when Siegmund von Hausegger conducted two performances of the Ninth, first in Löwe's version, then in Bruckner's own. The first public performance of Bruckner's original was given by Clemens Krauss and the Vienna Philharmonic on 23 October 1932.

Three flutes, three oboes, three clarinets, three bassoons, eight horns (four doubling Wagner tubas—two tenor and two bass—in the Adagio), three trumpets, three trombones, contrabass tuba, timpani, and strings.

Bruckner died a long and hard death. In 1892, his health took a decisive turn for the worse. The excitement of the long-delayed premiere of the

Eighth Symphony with Hans Richter and the Vienna Philharmonic on 18 December that year seriously exhausted him, and from the first days of January 1893 on, burdened with a heart condition, progressive liver failure, and dropsy, he struggled through growing discomfort. In the last two years, his mind began to disintegrate along with his body. The uncertainties, the depressions he had suffered all his life plagued him more frequently and more severely. He grew suspicious, confused, incoherent. That he would be unable to complete his Ninth Symphony, which he already realized would be his last and which he also hoped would be his best, became a source of unquenchable torment.

The persistent trembling of his hands made the physical act of writing difficult, and many of the minutes at his desk were invested in laborious cleaning up in the wake of blots and smudges. The effort of composition was beyond his summoning much of the time, and from what witnesses and even the ruled, numbered, but often blank pages tell us, it is evident that ideas would no longer come. Yet he persisted, and persisted to the end. The very last day, one of the easier ones, was a Sunday, bright but windy. He spent the morning at his old Bösendorfer piano working on the sketches for the finale, allowed himself to be talked out of his daily fifteen-minute walk because of the wind, had no appetite for lunch, complained suddenly of feeling cold, and asked for tea. He heeded his housekeeper's counsel and returned to bed, sipped three times from the bowl she brought him, turned to face the wall, sighed deeply twice, and gave up the ghost.

"It will be my last symphony," Bruckner told a visitor in 1892, and to another he said, "The Ninth will be my masterpiece. I just ask God that he'll let me live until it's done." The number itself was an issue, for no major composer since Beethoven had gone beyond nine symphonies. A Ninth Symphony was something special practically by definition. Bruckner, moreover, knew that he was asking for trouble by casting his new work in D minor, the key of Beethoven's Ninth. To August Göllerich, his chosen biographer, he said: "Come on, I'm not about to compete with Beethoven. Sure, it's in D minor because it's such a beautiful key, but with a chorus, like Beethoven—nah, Bruckner isn't that dumb. I can't help it that the main theme came to me in D minor; it just happens to be my favorite key." Hans von Bülow, a brilliant musician and a bitter man, was quick off the mark with a witticism (not, except for its malice, up to his usual standards) to the effect that Bruckner's D-minor Ninth would end with an "Ode to Schadenfreude."

Six of Bruckner's symphonies begin with a hum from which thematic fragments detach themselves or against which a spacious melody is projected. The Ninth is of the former type, and the debt, up to a point, to

Beethoven's Ninth is clear. The difference, however, is greater and more interesting than the resemblance. Beethoven's mystery resides to a large extent in the harmony, and that aspect of it is dispelled the moment the crescendo culminates in *fortissimo* and unambiguous D minor. But Bruckner actually begins in unambiguous D minor. The strings, with punctuations first by woodwinds, then by trumpets and drums, hold D, while all eight horns, with deep breaths between phrases, play fragments of the chord of D minor (and once of the D-minor scale): D-F-D, D-A-D, F-D, A-D, E-D. Under the last pair of notes a slight crescendo begins, but it leads not to clarification—nothing, after all, could be more stubbornly and statically clear than what we have thus far heard—but to disruption, as the horns leap upward into altogether foreign territory. Only after a considerable ex-cursion is D minor dramatically reaffirmed in a huge outburst by the entire orchestra, after which a slow subsidence—descending scales in plucked strings and odd flickers in woodwinds—brings the vast opening paragraph to a close.

Bruckner's favorite method of getting from one thing to the next, and one that earned him much derision on the part of the Brahmsians, is sim-ply to stop, take a breath, and move on. This is what he does when he introduces a lyric theme in A major, whose scoring, with lovely figurations in the second violins, he was particularly proud of. This paragraph builds, digresses, returns, builds again, and subsides. It leads, astonishingly, back to D minor and to a new, stark sort of music that settles finally in F major, almost as an afterthought. With some shift of harmonic perspective, these three paragraphs are restated, after which the music moves into one of Bruckner's characteristic suspense-to-glory codas.

Emphatic though this close may be, it is less than conclusive. That is on purpose. In his Fifth Symphony, Bruckner had learned how to extend a symphonic argument across an entire four-movement span, and in the Eighth he had again realized that ambition with special magnificence. The unresolved tensions, the unanswered questions of the Ninth's first move-ment were to have been worked out, "explained" in the finale that Bruck-ner was unable to compose. Nothing in his music is more moving than the last pages of the Adagio with which the Ninth now ends, but we must not lose sight of the fact that the symphony is a fragment and, as Robert Simp-son points out in *The Essence of Bruckner*, that by the criterion of the composer's normal procedures, even the three completed movements are, in effect, first drafts.

The Scherzo is a new kind of music for Bruckner. His earlier scherzos are energetic and of varying degrees of jolliness and rambunctiousness. Here, the harmonic piquancy of the opening, with its endlessly sustained, menacing, skewed dominant, gives us fair warning. Piquancy turns to a brutality of dissonance that has not lost its power to shock, and the savage tone and gesture are unprecedented. The oboe's offer to act innocent only sets the hellish atmosphere into greater relief. The usual Bruckner trio is slower than the scherzo and in a leisurely 3/4 meter. Bruckner in fact sketched two such trios for this symphony, both in F and both with viola solo. He rejected both in favor of something in triple meter (though about twice as fast as the scherzo proper) and in the exotic key of F-sharp major. It is an uncannily ghostly, weightless music, whose beginning, especially, one would hardly be likely to identify as Bruckner no matter how well one knew the rest of his work.

It may be that one reason for Bruckner's choice of a key so far to the sharp side was to prepare for the E major—not quite so far over as F-sharp—of the Adagio, and the idea seems the more plausible given his treatment of the new tonic. In the first movement, the point is that the music can barely wrench itself away from its home key of D minor. In the Adagio, the problem is how to reach E major in the first place. In the strings' and woodwinds' rapturous ascent in the sixth and seventh measures, Bruckner alludes to *Parsifal*, but he has in mind more than the specific Grail motif, a variant of which we hear. The Prelude to Act 3 of Wagner's last drama represents the wanderings of Parsifal in his search for the Castle of the Grail and for Amfortas, whom he must heal. Or, if you will, this page of *Parsifal*, even more than *Tristan*, is a piece of music in search of its tonic.

This search is the idea upon which Bruckner builds. The opening swing up and down for violins alone is clearly—or, at the very least, plausibly—an upbeat to a cadence on E major. And E major does indeed come at the end of the *Parsifal* ascent, but only after diversions so powerful that, as a resolution to the opening proposition, it has almost no reality at all. That sense of adventure, of wholly potent fantasy, that we feel so strongly in the scherzo now possesses Bruckner more strongly than ever. In response, he writes music of the boldest design, the most intense expression, the most refulgent sound. E major is at last affirmed about two-thirds of the way through the movement, but the conquest is virtually undone by a climax on a wildly tearing dissonance in eight slow measures of sustained *fortissimo*.[12] The coda is another of Bruckner's spacious and solemn subsidences, and I shall return to it.

Bruckner intended to follow the Adagio with an instrumental finale in D minor, one with a fugued recapitulation and, among its themes, a chorale that would serve as a great gathering-in climax, much as in the

---

[12] Löwe puts an agreeable, harmless chord in its place.

Fifth Symphony.[13] A couple of musicians with whom he discussed his plans report that, rather than inventing a chorale of his own, he thought of using the melody of *Christ lag in Todesbanden*, but the sketches do not bear this out.

We have seen how, from the beginning of his labors on the Ninth, Bruckner reckoned with the possibility of being unable to finish it and how, with growing despondency, he watched that possibility turn into certainty. The question of what to do "in case" occupied him from 1894 on, and on 12 November that year, after remarking that, given his age and failing health, he ought not to have taken on so taxing a project at all, he told his students at the university: "If I should die before the completion of the symphony, then my *Te Deum* must be used as the fourth movement. I have already decreed and disposed matters that way."

We do not know whether he had this idea on his own or whether Hans Richter or someone else suggested it to him, but in any event he stuck by the plan, which evidently gave him comfort as at least some sort of solution. One student recalled that Bruckner had played for him a proposed transition from some point in the finale into the *Te Deum*, and the ostinato string figures that churn the opening of the *Te Deum* along also occur, appropriately labeled, in the sketches. But, to judge by the context, this seems more in accord with Bruckner's habit of self-quotation than with any intent to introduce the *Te Deum* as finale. The two works are stylistically so far apart, and the notion of a C-major finale to a D-minor symphony is so preposterous for a work by Bruckner, that the whole idea of the *Te Deum* as fourth movement is terrible. Simply to perform the two pieces at the same concert, as Löwe did in 1903 and as many conductors have since, is of course an entirely different matter.

But to return to the Ninth Symphony as it now ends: Bruckner spoke repeatedly of the need to provide the work with a proper close. I believe, however, that unconsciously he had become reconciled to the idea that the Ninth would end with its Adagio, whose last pages he therefore made as "final" as he could, and more final than he would have if there had been a true finale to follow. Indeed, given Bruckner's difficulties with finales, given also how beautiful the close to his Adagio is, I would go so far as to say thank God he was not able to finish the fourth movement.

---

[13] Though the sketches penetrate some way into the recapitulation, they do not suggest, as for example the sketches for the unfinished movements of Mahler's Tenth Symphony do, that the composer had a clear vision of the whole design. Nonetheless, some attempts at "completion" have been made. In an article published as part of the proceedings of a 1986 international symposium on the Mahler Tenth, the Dutch musicologist Cornelis van Zwol lists twelve of these, the first one, by Else Krüger, dating to 1934.

As almost always, Bruckner ends with an expansive affirmation of the tonic. Here we have six very slow measures on E, exquisitely scored, and then, after a two-bar interruption, sixteen more such measures. When the basses at last join in and the motion in the violins has become very gentle, Bruckner turns to look back. His quartet of Wagner tubas plays the first notes of the Adagio of the Eighth Symphony, at the original pitch, but harmonized with a newfound serenity. After a flute wafts the music heavenward, the quartet of horns quietly recollects the majestically soaring phrase that begins the Seventh Symphony. "So ends Bruckner's uncompleted life work," writes Robert Simpson. "Though we may regret the absence of the vast background to all this that might have been disclosed by an achieved finale, we may be grateful that this last Adagio, though it is not his most perfect, is his most profound."

Aaron Copland

Aaron Copland was born in Brooklyn, New York, on 14 November 1900 and died in Peekskill, New York, on 2 December 1990.

On 11 January 1925, when the sixty-three-year-old German-born Walter Damrosch had finished conducting the New York Symphony in the premiere of Aaron Copland's Symphony for Organ and Orchestra, he turned to his Carnegie Hall audience and said, "If a young man at the age of twenty-three can write a symphony like that, in five years he'll be ready to commit murder." Damrosch lived until 1950, but no further utterance of his about Copland is recorded. Very likely he would have regarded the Piano Variations, composed about five years after the symphony, as a reasonable fulfillment of his prophecy. Next to the Variations, the Organ Symphony is rather sweet.

At seventeen, Copland, who had begun by trying to learn harmony from a correspondence course, became a pupil of Rubin Goldmark, nephew of the Viennese composer Karl Goldmark. Himself a student of Robert Fuchs in Vienna and Dvořák in New York, Goldmark had a lot to teach by way of traditional theory and form.[1] But while Copland was producing sonatas, rondos, and counterpoint exercises for Goldmark, he was also writing Copland to please himself. When he showed his teacher a "scherzo humoristique" called The Cat and the Mouse, Goldmark said, "I can't tell you anything about this. I don't understand how you go about it or what

---

[1] Goldmark's most famous student was another young man from Brooklyn, George Gershwin.

the harmonies are all about."[2] It occurred to Copland that he needed to move on.

"In those days," Copland recalled in 1967 in a conversation with Edward T. Cone, "it was clear that you had to be 'finished' in Europe. Remember that I was an adolescent during the First World War, when Germany and German music were very unpopular. The new thing in music was Debussy and Ravel—also Scriabin. . . . It seemed obvious that if you went to Europe you would want to study in France. . . . All the new things seemed to be coming from Paris—even before I knew the name of Stravinsky."

So to Paris he went and landed, ironically, in the composition course of Paul Vidal, "the Goldmark of the Paris Conservatory," as Copland called him. But he kept hearing about another teacher, a woman in her thirties by the name of Nadia Boulanger, who was active at the Conservatory, the École Normale, and the newly founded American College at Fontainebleau. With Melville Smith, Marion Bauer, and Herbert Elwell, Copland was in the first wave of Americans to go to the "boulangerie." Roy Harris, Walter Piston, Marc Blitzstein, Virgil Thomson, Douglas Moore, Elliott Carter, David Diamond, Irving Fine, Arthur Berger, Harold Shapero, Easley Blackwood, and Philip Glass were among those who followed, many of them inspired by Copland's example.

Boulanger did more for Copland than help him to develop the technique that freed him to be himself. Serge Koussevitzky, who had come to Paris from Russia in 1920, had invited her to appear as organ soloist in his first season (1924–25) as conductor of the Boston Symphony, and she was also engaged to perform with Damrosch in New York; she asked Copland for a concerto for these concerts. He was nervous, but Boulanger insisted, and the Organ Symphony was the outcome.

Koussevitzky was a good friend to acquire. He believed passionately in the cause of new music and in his obligation as head of one of America's most important musical institutions to support American musicians. He presented the Organ Symphony soon after Damrosch and went on to give the first performances of Copland's *Music for the Theatre* in 1925, the Piano Concerto in 1927, and the Symphonic Ode in 1932. Although, with the exception of the Third Symphony, Copland's premieres after that went elsewhere, Koussevitzky continued to play his music, which meant significant exposure on the radio and eventually on recordings as well.

---

[2] Copland described *The Cat and the Mouse* as "rather like Debussy." His first piece to be published, it came out under the imprint of Durand, "and the exciting thing to me was that it was Debussy's publisher who had accepted it. I still remember the thrill of that . . . seeing the familiar Durand cover on my first published piece!" It still sells about 1000 copies a year.

Much of Copland's music in the 1920s was touched by the rhythms and gestures of jazz. The music historian Alfred Einstein spoke for many when he called jazz "the most abominable treason against all the music of Western civilization," and these people deeply resented its invasion of Boston's Symphony Hall or Carnegie. Others were delighted by the emergence of a distinctively American style.

In 1932, Copland retreated to Mexico, a country for which he had an abiding love, in order to think his way through a stylistic crisis. He felt he needed to move away from what he called "a—shall we say—Hebraic idea of the grandiose, of the dramatic and the tragic, which was expressed to a certain extent in the Organ Symphony [1924] and very much in the Symphonic Ode [1929]. . . . The Ode was a major effort, on which I worked for several years. It really seemed like a culminating work, so that I had do to something different after that." A more severe style emerged in the spare and tough Piano Variations of 1930, though Copland came to think in retrospect that the Variations represented "another version of the grandiose, except that it had changed to a very dry and bare grandiosity, instead of the fat grandiosity of a big orchestral work." Out of the Mexican retreat came the Short Symphony. It and the Variations are the twin summits of Copland's achievement in his young years.

Copland went on to explore many musical worlds during his long life. He composed for Carnegie Hall and Hollywood, conducted, played the piano, wrote, taught, did television shows, encouraged the young, symbolized the possibility of being a serious composer in this country and this century. He never wrote inattentively nor without huge signs declaring "made in America" and "only by Aaron Copland." He was also the author of two books of blessedly demystifying clarity, *What to Listen For in Music* and *The New Music*.

It was a delight and a privilege to be one of Copland's contemporaries. We could meet some now indispensable classics as brand-new music, we saw him conduct and heard him play the piano, watched him on television, listened to him speak. With his powerfully sculpted head, exuberant stride, and that smile composed in equal parts of benevolence and mischief, he was a vibrant presence. The sound he created is so much part of American listeners that when, for example, we hear the first moments of *Appalachian Spring* with their magical conjunction of the plain and the sublime, we can hardly imagine a world without that music in it.

He wrote three symphonies, the early Organ Symphony, the Short Symphony, and the Third. The Third is by far the best known of the three, and its Shostakovich Fifth ending brings audiences to their feet. It also shows that Copland never completely lost his taste for the grandiose. Perhaps the most illuminating comment he himself made about his Third Symphony is that it was important to remember it was written for Koussevitzky, with *his* penchant for hyper-utterance. It has beautiful quiet moments—even the dread *Fanfare for the Common Man* becomes tolerable in Copland's poetic transformation of it at the beginning of the finale—but all in all, I cannot believe the piece. Virgil Thomson sensed "something false" in it, and even the intensely devoted Leonard Bernstein, who was a marvelous interpreter of it, had considerable reservations. (They are spelled out in a letter reprinted in full in Copland's and Vivian Perlis's *Since 1943.*) If you want a Copland symphony, you do much better with the Short Symphony; if you want Copland in the rhetorical manner of the Third Symphony, you do better with the splendid and almost unknown Symphonic Ode.

Short Symphony (Symphony No. 2)

Tempo: [quarter] 144 (preciso)
Tempo: [half] c. 44
Tempo: [quarter] 144 (preciso e ritmico)

Copland composed his Short Symphony in 1932–33. Carlos Chávez, to whom it is dedicated, conducted the Orquesta Sinfónica de México in the first performance on 23 November 1934 in Mexico City.

Two flutes (one doubling alto flute) and piccolo, two oboes and heckelphone (doubling English horn), two clarinets and bass clarinet, two bassoons and contrabassoon, four horns, two trumpets, piano, and strings. Copland indicates that English horn may be substituted for the heckelphone throughout. The heckelphone is a baritone oboe pitched an octave below the regular oboe. It is named for Wilhelm Heckel, who designed the instrument in 1904, twenty-five years after a conversation with Wagner in which the composer complained of the lack of a powerful double-reed instrument in the baritone range.

The jazz-influenced dislocations of meter that are so characteristic of Copland's music in the 1920s are more prevalent than ever in the Short Symphony, but the "fat" orchestral sound of the Symphonic Ode, completed in 1929, has given way to one that is hard and lean, and the compositional procedures are fiercely concentrated.

Carlos Chávez, himself a distinguished composer, braved the score with his orchestra in Mexico City; his North American colleagues with their virtuoso ensembles did not. Copland was bitterly disappointed:

> Although the performance time is only fifteen minutes, it took me, on and off, almost two years to complete it. On other occasions I've written fifteen minutes of music in two weeks: if I expended so much time and effort on the Short Symphony it was because I wanted to write as perfect a piece as I could. So you can imagine my feelings when, shortly after its first performance, the American premiere [by Leopold Stokowski in Philadelphia] was canceled. Serge Koussevitzky [in Boston] followed suit. Both conductors told me that they had not had enough time to prepare the piece.[3]

Copland's practical response, which he termed "an act of desperation," was to transcribe the Short Symphony as a Sextet for string quartet with clarinet and piano, in which form it is often played. Stokowski did finally give the U.S. premiere of the Short Symphony, but only in 1944; there was no other performance in the United States until 1954. It is a rarity still.[4]

Copland gave this description of it:

> The work is in three movements (fast, slow, fast) played without pause. The first movement is scherzo-like in character. Once, I toyed with the idea of naming the piece *The Bounding Line* because of the nature of the first section. The second movement is in three brief sections—the first rises to a dissonant climax, is sharply contrasted with a song-like middle part, and returns to the beginning. The finale is once again bright in color and rhythmically intricate.[5]

In 1954, Arthur Berger, Copland's first biographer, composed a set of brilliant and witty One-Part Inventions for piano; surely he found the model in the kind of writing that dominates the first movement of the Short Symphony. The instruments of Copland's orchestra—and note the absence of heavy brass and the use of the piano as the sole percussion instrument—dart in and out of the texture; the look of the page is busy. For the most part, though, we hear only one pitch at a time, and rarely more than two. When there are two notes, they are often a semitone apart, and the second, dissonant note comes across less as an independent harmonic or melodic entity than as a dynamic accent. Most of the move-

---

[3] Aaron Copland, liner note to Columbia recording MS7223 (1967).
[4] In 1989, the New York–based chamber orchestra Orpheus performed and recorded the Short Symphony without conductor.
[5] Copland, liner note to Columbia recording MS7223 (1967).

ment is indeed a single "bounding line." The time signature changes continually—6/8, 7/8, 5/8, 6/8, 7/8 on a single page is typical—but even within any one measure the groupings are hardly ever "normal." In a 4/4 bar, for example, the principal accents might well fall on the second half of "one" and on "four."

The slow movement provides strong contrast to what Berger called the both "playful and frantic" athletic exuberance of the first. It also displays contrast within itself, when the intense opening music gives way to the touching and simply harmonized song of the middle section. The finale synthesizes what has gone before, bringing back the "bounding line" and the delightful rhythmic shocks of the first movement, but having also learned something from the slow movement about harmony and the possibilities of denser textures.

It is a critical cliché that there are two Coplands, one being the composer of popular essays in Americana—both urban like *Music for the Theatre* and *El salón México,* and pastoral like *Billy the Kid* and *Appalachian Spring*—and the other the composer of more severe, certainly more abstract, less referential works such as the Piano Variations, the Piano Quartet, the Piano Fantasy, and his late orchestral scores, *Connotations* and *Inscape.* The two Coplands are of course one, and the two styles are connected, each drawing strength and substance from the other. The Short Symphony is a remarkable synthesis of the learned and the vernacular, and thus, in all its brevity, a singularly "complete" representation of its composer.

Antonín Dvořák

Antonín Leopold Dvořák was born at Mühlhausen (Nelahozeves), Bohemia, on 8 September 1841 and died in Prague on 1 May 1904. The D at the beginning of his name is silent.

When the Oxford University Press published Volume 2 of Donald Francis Tovey's *Essays in Musical Analysis* in 1935, very few of Tovey's readers and browsers would have ever heard three of the four Dvořák symphonies discussed in that book, the three then known as Nos. 1, 2, and 3, and now more accurately as Nos. 6, 5, and 7. (The other one that Tovey included was the super-familiar *From the New World.*) And how startling to come across this sentence: "I have no hesitation in setting Dvořák's [Seventh] Symphony along with the C major Symphony of Schubert and the four symphonies of Brahms, as among the greatest and purest examples of this art-form since Beethoven."[1]

To be sure, in those days of fewer but more-educated listeners, some people would have read these pieces at home as piano duets. Tovey had conducted them with the Reid Orchestra at the University of Edinburgh (the *Essays* were his program notes), but performances of any Dvořák sym-

---

[1] What Tovey actually wrote was "Second Symphony," which is how the D-minor Symphony was known until 1955, when the complete critical edition of Dvořák's works began to come out in Prague. Only five of Dvořák's nine symphonies were published during his lifetime, and only after the appearance of the critical edition did people adopt the present numbering that takes all nine symphonies into account and places them in their correct chronological order. The old numbering reflects the order of publication.

phonies other than the *New World* were rare, at least outside Czechoslovakia. For most people the "other" Dvořák symphonies were a discovery of the years after the war.

If a reader sixty years ago found Tovey's exceedingly high valuation of the Sixth and Seventh symphonies surprising, that was also because neither professional musicians nor listeners—again, outside Czechoslovakia—were inclined to take Dvořák terribly seriously. He was the amiable composer of the Symphony *From the New World,* the *Carnival* Overture, and the Slavonic Dances. Except for the *American* Quartet, Opus 96, the chamber music was unknown. The appearance in 1937 of the great recording by Casals with George Szell of the Cello Concerto was the first step in establishing the present popularity of that wonderful work.

Dvořák's fame at home had begun with the performance in 1873 of a patriotic cantata called *The Heirs of the White Mountains.*[2] In 1878, at Brahms's urging, the Berlin publishing house of Simrock added Dvořák to its list. Simrock began by issuing the Moravian Duets for soprano and mezzo-soprano that had so impressed Brahms in the first place, following that in 1878 with the first set of Slavonic Dances for piano four-hands. This achieved huge success, enough to convert Dvořák's reputation from local to international. The first performance of the *Stabat Mater* in Prague in 1880 made an immense impression; meanwhile, Joseph Joachim, who had heard about Dvořák from Brahms, began to champion his chamber music. His work was also coming to be known in America, especially in New York, as well as in Cincinnati and Saint Louis, with their big settlements of music-loving Germans. The first performance of the Symphony *From the New World,* in New York in 1893, was the high-water mark of his reputation during his lifetime.

Estimation of Dvořák changed after his death. He continued to be loved but seemed ever more narrowly known. He was seen as a composer for popular concerts, a genre- and landscape-artist, friendly, colorful, but not a plausible person to have written one of "the greatest and purest" symphonies since Beethoven (Tovey on No. 7), not one whose work evoked the word *sublime* (Tovey on No. 6), certainly not one to be mentioned in the same breath as so secure a tenant in the pantheon as Johannes Brahms. The first to disagree with that prejudicial judgment would have been the redoubtable Dr. Brahms himself, he who had used his prestige to set up his younger colleague with an important publisher, helped him to get a series of government grants, was ever available to him with

---

[2] It was the defeat of the Bohemians by the Austrians at the battle of the White Mountain just outside Prague in 1620 that led to the absorption of Bohemia into the Habsburg Empire, a condition that obtained until 28 October 1918.

kindness and advice, and said of the Cello Concerto that, had he known it could be done so beautifully, he would have written one of his own.

Symphony No. 6 in D major, Opus 60

> *Allegro non tanto*
> *Adagio*
> *Scherzo: Presto (Furiant)*
> *Finale: Allegro con spirito*

Dvořák sketched this symphony between 27 August and 20 September 1880, writing the full score between 27 September and 15 October that year. The score is dedicated to Hans Richter, who was supposed to conduct the Vienna Philharmonic in the first performance; more of that below. In the event, the first performance was given by the Prague Philharmonic under Adolf Čech on 25 March 1881.

Two flutes (second doubling piccolo), two oboes, two clarinets, two bassoons, four horns, two trumpets, three trombones, tuba, timpani, and strings.

In November 1879, Hans Richter programmed Dvořák's Slavonic Rhapsody No. 3 at one of his Vienna Philharmonic concerts. This meant a lot: though only thirty-six, as the conductor of the first Bayreuth Festival and principal conductor at the Vienna Court Opera and of the Vienna Philharmonic, Richter was very much an eminence in Europe's musical life, Dvořák, who had been sitting on the organ bench with Brahms, was called to the front of the stage, where he was stunned both to be embraced by Richter and by the splendid ovation that greeted him. The next day, Richter gave a dinner for Dvořák and made him promise to write a symphony for the Philharmonic's next season. It was just a year later, November 1880, that Dvořák took his new score—the one of this symphony—to Vienna to play it to Richter. Together with the Gypsy Songs and the revision of the Violin Concerto, it had been his chief project for that year. Richter was delighted by the work and, as Dvořák recounted to his friend Alois Göbl, kissed the composer after each movement.

Then things fell to pieces. Richter announced the premiere of the symphony for the end of December, but pleading overwork, not on his own behalf but that of the orchestra, postponed the performance until March. As the new date neared, he begged for a further extension: his wife was about to have a child, the older children had diphtheria, his mother had just died, and along with all that he was terribly over-extended. Dvořák was not heartless in the face of these circumstances; nonetheless, he began to suspect that there might be other problems. He was right. Anti-Czech elements existed in the Philharmonic, and some of these players were influential and successful in making their case that too much music by this, to them, insignificant young Czech composer was being programmed. Dvořák retained the dedication to Richter, but gave the first performance to Prague and to Adolf Čech, an old friend and his stand-partner in the days when both had played viola in the pit of the Prague Opera House. Vienna heard the D-major Symphony in 1883, though not under Richter. Over the long haul, though, the friendship between Dvořák and Richter held firm, the conductor continuing to play many of Dvořák's works in Vienna, London, and elsewhere.[3]

The opening is wonderful. Horns and divided violas softly play synco-pated chords of D major. Woodwinds diffidently suggest that two notes of this chord might make a fine beginning, a thought seconded by the bas-soons, cellos, and basses. Taking courage, they expand the idea ever so slightly, playing the second note twice. At this point the violins join in, still in *pianissimo*, now playing the last note four times and moving the phrase forward, even swelling to *forte* for its highest note, and turning it into a beautiful lyric sentence. This goes to an unexpected destination, and the continuation is no less surprising, a vehement outburst begun by the second violins, building up considerable tension, and leading to a *for-tissimo* reappearance—Dvořák marks it grandioso—of the opening melody. And what lovely scoring it is: effortlessly ample, not aggressive, neither blaring nor thick.

Dvořák has a dark side, which dominates the Symphony No. 7 and, to a surprising degree, the *New World.* The Symphony No. 6, by contrast, seems to promise to be sunny, and indeed it does not enter the tragic territory occupied by the Seventh and Ninth symphonies. Sudden out-bursts, on the other hand, are by no means uncommon in it, and while there is plenty of sunshine, the needle hovers much of the time over that part of the barometer dial marked "changeable."

---

[3] The success of Richter's performance of the Symphony No. 6 in London in May 1882 led the Royal Philharmonic Society to invite Dvořák to conduct concerts two years later and to commis-sion the Symphony No. 7.

The transition to a new key and a new theme is itself full of event and full of charm. The new theme is a glorious cello-and-horn melody, deliciously accompanied, and followed by yet another tune, this one introduced by the oboe. It is this oboe tune, translated into grandly sonorous *fortissimo*, that rounds off the exposition. Dvořák asks for the exposition to be repeated and takes exceptional pains to make the transition back to the beginning beautiful.

Just before this return—or, when you arrive here the second time, the transition into the development—the music quiets down to *pianissimo*. This of course prepares the reappearance of that beguilingly shy opening; even more, it makes possible the most magical pages of this movement. Symphonic developments are usually more active than expositions: more material is processed in a greater variety of ways, the rate of change is faster, more ground is covered. Even though the tempo does not change, the music feels faster. Here Dvořák, in a moment of touching and mysterious poetry, chooses to do the opposite. The tempo does not change here either, but suddenly, after the exuberance and variety of the exposition, the music feels slow. The harmonies change less frequently—G, the last bass note of the development's initial paragraph, stays put for nineteen measures—and everything is held in *pianissimo*, even *ppp*, with Dvořák adding a cautionary "sempre molto tranquillo."

The first theme provides plenty to work with and, as at the beginning of the movement, its lyricism is broken into by an outburst of vehemence. At one point Dvořák's sense of orchestral color leads him to an effect most unusual for its time, having the second violins and violas play an accompaniment sul ponticello, that is, with the bow practically at the bridge, which produces a strangely glassy and rasping sound. This section rises to high drama, and the transition into the recapitulation is managed with splendid panache and a gloriously wrenching harmonic surprise. After the recapitulation, Dvořák gives us an expansive and inventive coda—a sweet dream and another brusque awakening.

Dvořák's is surely one of the delightfully individual and instantly recognizable voices in Romantic music. At the same time, he never chooses to conceal from us which music by his elders he likes, loves, admires.[4] Schubert and Brahms, particularly Brahms, often come to mind in this connection. That inspired harmonic jolt that leads into the recapitulation of the first movement could almost bear a notation of "(c)Johannes Brahms 1877." Brahms himself said what one wishes could have been the last word on the matter of similarities when someone pointed out the resemblance

[4] And sometimes, one should in frankness add, music he feels he ought to be emulating.

between the big tune in the finale of his First Symphony and the one in the Beethoven Ninth: "Das hört ja jeder Esel" (Any ass can hear that). So, if you think you hear a bit of a Schubert Trio here or a touch of the Brahms Second there, well, yes, exactly. Restudying this symphony, I get a strong sense of Dvořák's ambition, comparable to Schubert's in the 1820s and Brahms's from somewhere in the 1850s into the 1870s, to write a Beethoven symphony. To compose "Beethoven" was perhaps no more basic to Dvořák's genes and temperament than it was to Schubert's, but this extraordinary first movement of the Sixth Symphony, with its powerful and imaginative grasp of the sonata style, shows that he certainly did have it in him.

Having admitted the possibility of honorable indebtedness, I have no compunction about pointing out the obvious, namely that the four bars of wind-instrument upbeat that introduce the violin melody at the beginning of the Adagio come from the corresponding place in the Beethoven Ninth. The violin melody itself is tender, inspired, subtle. It lends itself in Dvořák's hands to many kinds of meditation and variation. The whole movement is a feast of delicate orchestral invention. The coda is one of Dvořák's most poetic dreams.

From it we are roused by a whirling Scherzo, a furiant: a Bohemian folk dance whose principal characteristic is the alternation and cross-cutting of triple and duple meters. *Grove's Dictionary* states that "the Czech name has no etymological connection with 'fury.'" On the other hand, Paul Nettl, himself Czech, writes in *Die Musik in Geschichte und Gegenwart,* the German counterpart of *Grove,* that "the Czech word 'furiant,' a loan-word from the Latin, carries the colloquial meaning of a wild and frivolous person." However that all may be, Dvořák's music is, if not frivolous, certainly wild in its driving energy. The trio, by contrast, is another page of sweet musing. It is here that the piccolo gets its single outing in this symphony.

The Finale starts with an unabashed bow to the recent D-major Symphony by the friend who had shared the organ bench at that memorable performance of the Third Slavonic Rhapsody. At least the sound is the sound of the finale of the Brahms Second; the opening theme itself, though in *pianissimo,* is "definite" and march-like in character. As is typical in Dvořák's symphonies, the movement is lavishly provided with engaging themes. The coda is of captivating brilliance, Dvořák achieving a rousing effect by breaking the first theme up into a new rhythm of note-note/rest-rest/note-note. To the very last chord, Dvořák's sense of pace is totally commanding and secure.

Symphony No. 7 in D minor, Opus 70

Allegro maestoso
Poco adagio
Vivace—Poco meno mosso
Allegro

Dvořák began to sketch this symphony on 13 December 1884 and completed the score on 17 March 1885. He conducted the premiere at a concert of the Royal Philharmonic Society at St. James's Hall, London, on 22 April 1885. The score as we now know it incorporates a few revisions made in June 1885.

Two flutes and piccolo, two oboes, two clarinets, two bassoons, four horns, two trumpets, three trombones, timpani, and strings.

In my introductory note on Dvořák I quoted Tovey's praise of this great symphony. His words go back to a time when performances of any of Dvořák's symphonies other than the *New World* were extremely rare, at least outside Czechoslovakia. Václav Talich's wonderful recording of No. 7 with the Czech Philharmonic came out in 1938, but record buyers in those days were also relatively few and had smaller collections, to say nothing of the fact that during the war, with the ingredients of shellac needed for a more urgent cause, there was a huge and frustrating discrepancy between what manufacturers listed in their catalogues and what one could actually find in stores. In sum, for most people the "other" Dvořák symphonies were a discovery of the years after the war. Even today one can too easily think of Dvořák as a composer of three symphonies to which he gave the numbers 7, 8, and 9.

The success of Dvořák's *Stabat Mater* was nothing less than sensational when Joseph Barnby introduced it in London in 1883, and particularly in that peculiarly English world of choir festivals Dvořák became beloved and revered like no composer since Mendelssohn. (For a dissent on this side of Dvořák's music, go to G.B. Shaw's reviews.) The Royal Philharmonic Society invited him to conduct concerts in London in 1884. These were his first appearances as a conductor outside his own country and the occasion of the most excited welcome he had yet received anywhere. It was in response to the success of the Symphony No. 6 in D major, then known

as No. 1, that he was at once invited to write a new symphony for performance the following year. (Hans Richter had already introduced that work
to grand effect in 1882.) Dvořák's response to the Society's invitation was
the Symphony No. 7 in D minor.

The opportunity set him afire with ambition. "Just now," he wrote to
his friend Judge Antonín Rus on 22 December 1884, "a new symphony
(for London) occupies me, and wherever I go I think of nothing but my
work, which must be capable of stirring the world, and God grant me that
it will!" Dvořák had been excited by Brahms's newest symphony, the
Third, which he had gone to Berlin to hear in January 1884 and which
gave him a new standard to shoot for. Moreover, as a letter to Simrock in
February 1885 tells us, he was spurred by Brahms's verbal exhortations as
well as by his direct musical example: "I have been engaged on a new
symphony for a long, long time; after all it must be something really worth-
while, for I don't want Brahms's words to me, 'I imagine your symphony
quite different from this one [No. 6 in D major]' to remain unfulfilled."

A scan of the Brahms correspondence has failed to uncover any comment on the Seventh Symphony, but it is impossible to believe that
Brahms was disappointed: the new work could hardly have been more different from its sunshine-and-blue-skies predecessor. Where Dvořák began
the D-major Symphony by floating a soft horn melody across simple though
colorful harmonies (not without some debt to the Brahms Second, then in
circulation for just three years), he makes his way into the new D-minor
Symphony with a theme that is as dark and under cover as it is determined. And before the violas and cellos even articulate that idea, a low D
pedal (horns, drums, and basses) has already done its work in defining
the atmosphere.

The theme, at least its beginning, came to Dvořák at the Prague railway station, where he had gone to see the arrival of a train bringing several
hundred anti-Habsburg Hungarians to the National Theater Festival. The
theme's subject, so to speak, is not the train itself but the political reasons
for its journey.[5] Even that puts it too strongly, for in no sense is the Seventh Symphony program music. But in the early 1880s, Dvořák was at a
point of crisis. His mother, to whom he was close, had died in December
1882, and he was in distress over the steadily deteriorating mental health

---

[5] Next to his country, his family, and music, Dvořák loved trains better than anything in the
world, and watching trains, more than anything else, kept him going during his later lonely times
in New York. Like Hindemith, he had an uncanny aptitude for memorizing international timetables, but he never composed a railway piece. That genre does exist and was invented, so far as
I know, by Rossini, whose *Album for Over-Achievers* (a fair rendering of *Album des enfants dé-
gourdis*) includes a graphic and bloody miniature tone poem called "Un petit train de plaisir."

of Bedřich Smetana, the founding father of modern Czech music. (Smetana was released by death in May 1884.)

Not least, Dvořák was perplexed about his own life. Being swept along on waves of success also meant being put under growing pressure, internal and external, to consolidate his position and turn from a provincial composer into an international one. But "international" really meant Austro-German; the idea was for him to move to Vienna, to write operas on German texts, and to quit pestering his German publisher about having his name appear as Ant., if not actually Antonín, rather than the German Anton. It was hard for him to say no to the well-meaning advice of people like Brahms and the critic Eduard Hanslick; on the other hand, to deny his own ethnic and linguistic heritage was impossible for someone who identified himself so closely with the rising tide of Bohemian nationalism. It added up to a troubled time for him: for a while even the phrase "Bohu diky!" (Thanks to God) ceased to appear on the final pages of his manuscripts. It was during this period and in this mood that he wrote his two masterpieces in tragedy—the F-minor Trio, Opus 65, whose slow movement is imbued with an all but unbearably poignant sense of parting and farewell, and this D-minor Symphony.

To get back, then, to Dvořák at the station witnessing the arrival of the Hungarian patriots, we might say that the experience gave focus to latent thought and stimulated the birth of a specific musical embodiment for that thought. Dvořák's biographer John Clapham studied the sketches of the D-minor Symphony and published a fascinating account of them (in *Music and Letters* XLII, 1961), in which he pointed out that it took Dvořák several attempts before he arrived at the details that contribute so powerfully to the oppressive atmosphere, sharpening the rhythm of the upbeats, for example, and adding the shuddering halt on the diminished-seventh chord in the theme's sixth measure.

The clarinets continue the thought plaintively. The harmony is as unyielding as in the first phrase, but the tough tonic pedal has given way to the question mark of the ever ambiguous diminished seventh. Characteristically, Dvořák includes a wealth of thematic ideas. Quickly he builds to a climax, withdraws for a moment into a pastoral conversation of horn and oboe, then works up to an even more intense crisis (always with the new, sharper version of the upbeat as motor) before settling into a new key, B-flat major, and delighting us with a wonderfully spacious melody. It is one from the house of Brahms: specifically, it reminds us of the cello solo in the Piano Concerto No. 2, first performed in 1881 and published in 1882, and of the song *Immer leiser wird mein Schlummer*, yet to come.

This is expanded magnificently until the rich exposition comes to a close poised on the dominant of D minor, just as though there were going to be a formal repeat.[6] Instead, however, the music plunges—*pianissimo* but with great intensity—into the development. This moves swiftly and masterfully, and it covers much territory. The recapitulation is tautly condensed—it even begins in mid-paragraph—and only in the dying-away coda does the music draw more leisurely breaths. (Tchaikovsky liked and admired Dvořák, whom he met in Prague in 1888, and it could be that in some matters of proportion and form, this movement was a model for the first movement of the *Pathétique*.) D minor is a key that has a special sound, partly because all the string instruments have open strings tuned to D and A. It also has a special set of sonorous and expressive associations, defined by a whole series of works including Mozart's D-minor Piano Concerto and *Don Giovanni*, Beethoven's and Bruckner's Ninth symphonies, and Brahms's Piano Concerto No. 1 and *Tragic* Overture. Before leaving this first movement I should point out that it is very much and very consciously part of this D-minor tradition.

The Adagio is, with those in his F-minor Trio and G-major String Quartet, Opus 106, one of Dvořák's most searching. Here, too, is an astonishing richness and variety of material, presented lucidly, with a profoundly original sense of order, and gloriously scored. The most personal paragraph is one in which a reiterated phrase with a melancholy falling seventh in *pianissimo* strings is punctuated by pairs of soft chords for woodwinds and pizzicato strings. This I take to be an obeisance to a similar moment in the Brahms Third Symphony, a piece that, as I mentioned earlier, was a significant inspiration to Dvořák.[7]

The scherzo moves in flavorful cross-rhythms, the swinging theme in violins and violas falling into three broad beats per measure, while the cello-and-bassoon tune is in two. It is all force and energy, after which the trio brings contrast in every aspect, by being in a major key, by its gentleness, and by the skillful and evocative blurring of outlines and textures. The trios in Dvořák's scherzos are usually picturesque in a folksy sort of way; this one is out of the ordinary not merely for its cunningly clouded sound but also in being so richly developed and extended. In most ways, this scherzo is a moment of relaxation after the densely composed,

---

[6]This in fact is what Dvořák had originally planned, and only in the final stages of composition did he decide to eliminate the repeat. The first movements of his next two symphonies, No. 8 and the *New World*, do repeat their expositions; in other words, Dvořák's decision to eliminate the repeat here is not so much the expression of a modernist stance as a response to the nature of this particular movement.

[7]Brahms himself had been writing in loving emulation of the famous page in the second movement of Schubert's *Great* C-major Symphony, a piece Dvořák also loved deeply, that Schumann described so beautifully as a moment "where a horn calls as though from afar—this seems to me to have come down from another sphere. Here everyone is hushed and listening, as though some heavenly visitant were quietly stealing through the orchestra."

attention-demanding two movements that precede it, but the coda reminds us that the setting is one of tragedy.

The finale also presents a wealth of themes, from the first impassioned gesture, through the dark chorale that follows immediately, to the confidently striding A-major tune for the cellos. The development is ample and rises to a tempestuous climax. The taut recapitulation leads to a solemn peroration in D major, the remarkable harmonies at the end suggesting that Dvořák was invoking the close of Schubert's great F-minor Fantasy for Piano Four-Hands.

Symphony No. 8 in G major, Opus 88

Allegro con brio
Adagio
Allegretto grazioso
Allegro ma non troppo

Dvořák wrote his Symphony No. 8 between 26 August and 8 November 1889 and conducted the first performance in Prague on 2 February 1890.

Two flutes and piccolo, two oboes (second oboe doubling English horn for three measures only), two clarinets, two bassoons, four horns, two trumpets, three trombones, tuba, timpani, and strings.

I have been reading this symphony in a handsomely printed full-size score published by Novello, Ewer, and Co. of London and New York, copyright 1892, and priced at thirty shillings. The Novello imprint represents an act not only of disloyalty but of clear breach of contract on Dvořák's part. No less a colleague than Johannes Brahms, who had earlier helped him get a series of government grants that provided something like financial independence, had also persuaded his own publisher, Simrock, to take him on. Next to talent, nothing matters so much to a young composer as having a responsible and energetic publisher to get the music into circulation, a subject many a composer today could address eloquently.

Unlike Haydn and Beethoven, Dvořák never sold the same work to two different publishers, but there were these occasions when he fled the Simrock stable, succumbing to the willingness of the London firm of Novello to outbid the competition in Berlin. The other Novello publications were vocal works, including his great dramatic cantata *The Specter's Bride*, the oratorio *Saint Ludmilla*, the Mass in D, and the Requiem. Given the English passion for Dvořák engendered by his *Stabat Mater* in 1883, it is no wonder that Novello was willing to bid high.

Simrock primarily wanted piano pieces, songs, chamber music, and, above all, more and more Slavonic Dances—in other words, quick sellers—while Dvořák, for his part, accused Simrock of not wanting to pay the high fees that large works like symphonies merited. (Simrock, having paid 3000 marks for the Symphony No. 7, offered a mere and insulting 1000 for No. 8.) But Dvořák was not just interested in money, though as someone who had grown up in poverty he was not indifferent to comfort. He had grand goals as a composer of symphony and opera—not just to do those things, but to do them, especially symphony, in as original a way as he was capable. Understandably, therefore, and in full awareness of the value of Simrock's initial support, he resented a publisher who showed some reserve about endorsing his most ambitious undertakings. I also suspect that another factor in these occasional infidelities of Dvořák's was his unabated irritation with Simrock for his insistence on printing his name as German Anton rather than Czech Antonín; they eventually compromised on "Ant." Novello was willing to go with Antonín.

It had been four years since Dvořák's last symphony, the magnificent—and very Brahmsian—No. 7 in D minor. During those four years, Dvořák had made yet another attempt at opera (this time with a political-romantic work called *The Jacobin*, full of superb music), revised the Violin Concerto into its present form, written a second and even finer series of Slavonic Dances, and composed two of his most loved and admired pieces of chamber music, the A-major Piano Quintet and the Piano Quartet in E-flat major. He felt thoroughly ready to tackle another symphony, and as he got to work in the seclusion of his country house, each page of freshly covered manuscript paper bore witness to how well founded was his faith in himself and his ability to write something that, as he said, would be "different from other symphonies, with individual thoughts worked out in a new way."

The Symphony No. 7 is a famously somber work, but we tend to forget how much darkness there is in this G-major Symphony and especially in the great No. 9, *From the New World*. The very key signature belies the mood. Its single sharp says G major, but the in-tempo introduction is clearly in G minor.[8] This melody, which sounds gloriously rich on

---

[8] Schumann's *Manfred* Overture is another instance of a work whose key signature, E-flat major, is a curious denial of the actual key, E-flat minor.

cellos, clarinets, bassoons, and horns, was actually an afterthought of Dvořák's, and having been visited by this wonderful inspiration, he also figured out how to bring it back most tellingly at crucial points in the first movement.

This melody comes to rest on a luminous chord of G major, a launching pad from which the flute can begin the Allegro proper (there is no actual tempo change). Energy runs high, and a more emphatic affirmation of the key occurs with the arrival of a theme sonorously scored for much-divided violas and cellos. The second group of themes, instead of being in the expected dominant, D major, is set in B minor, the relative minor of D major, which then moves to B major. Going into minor provides another touch of darkness; the extension to B major, though a logical outcome of B minor, is exceedingly adventurous in the harmonic context of the whole movement and creates a sudden sense of wide opening of harmonic horizons.

The music quiets down and we find ourselves back with the opening melody for cellos and winds. It sounds as though Dvořák were repeating the exposition in classical style, but this time the G-major chord is subtly different—a *pianissimo* tremolando instead of just three still notes—and an F-natural slipped under the flute melody sends everything off into a new direction. In other words, the development has begun by pretending to be a repeat of the exposition, a device, witty, mysterious, or dramatic, familiar from such works as Beethoven's first *Rasumovsky* quartet, the Brahms Fourth Symphony, and the Prokofiev Fifth.

Once under way, the development becomes increasingly impassioned, and it arrives at a huge climax when the opening melody makes a third appearance, this time on brilliant trumpets with an accompaniment of strings swirling about in chromatic scales. It is just after this, for the reappearance of the flute theme, that the English horn has its brief moment: Dvořák wants to present this theme in a new light, with a certain sense of distance and nostalgia, and he wants oboe tone in a register lower than the oboe can reach. The recapitulation is full of delightful detail, and even at the jubilant close, the G major is darkened by suggestions of the minor mode.

The Adagio also begins on a harmonic slant. Those first rapturous phrases for strings are—or seem to be—in E-flat major, and it is only in the eighth measure that the music settles into its real key, C minor. Now we sense the long shadow cast by Beethoven's *Eroica*, because the moment C minor is established, the music concentrates on gestures that are unmistakably those of a funeral march. The allusion to the great model is subtle. Beethoven begins in stern C minor, then answers that with a more lyric, expansive music in E-flat; Dvořák has simply reversed the order. A radiant C-major middle section, introduced by a characteristic triplet upbeat, makes the *Eroica* reference even more unmistakable. This maggiore interlude rises to a magnificently sonorous climax, and here we are reminded for a moment how moved Dvořák was playing in the orchestra when Wagner came to Prague in 1863 to conduct some of his own music as well as a Beethoven symphony. After some moments of calm, the music becomes more impassioned than ever (the analogous place in the *Eroica* is the fugue) and finally subsides into a coda that is both elegiac and tender. It is also, like most of this symphony, a marvel of imaginative scoring.

By way of a schěrzo, Dvořák gives us a leisurely dance in G minor, full of melancholy chromatic droops. The trio is in G major. This is one of Dvořák's most enchanting pages, made so not only by the lovely melody but also by the beguiling breezes created by the pervasive, but always soft, cross-rhythms in the accompaniment. Listen to the strings at the beginning, to the drums throughout. The main section of the movement returns in the usual way, after which Dvořák gives us a quick coda which is the trio transformed, music he actually borrowed from his own comic opera of 1874, *The Stubborn Lovers*.

Having proffered a strong and delightful taste of national flavor in the third movement, Dvořák becomes more Czech than ever in the finale, a movement one might describe as footloose variations. This movement, too, is replete with delightful orchestral effects, some subtle, like the scoring of the cello melody right after the opening trumpet summons, or spectacular, like the virtuosic flute variations or the recurrent whooping of high horns that looks forward to the happy point of arrival in Octavian's and the Marschallin's lovemaking in *Der Rosencǎvalier*. A friend has described Dvořák's closes as resembling the slow progress of reluctantly departing guests from front door down the driveway to the car. He seems always to be loath to let go, and sentiment grows intense, but then there is sudden resolution, a return of good cheer, and a joyous rush to the final barline.

Symphony No. 9 in E minor, Opus 95, *From the New World*

Adagio—Allegro molto
Largo
Molto vivace
Allegro con fuoco

Dvořák made the first sketches for this symphony on 19 December 1892 and completed the four movements on 28 January, 14 March, 10 April, and 24 May 1893. Anton Seidl conducted the New York Philharmonic in a "public rehearsal" on 15 December 1893 and in the official premiere the following evening.

Two flutes and piccolo, two oboes and English horn, two clarinets, two bassoons, four horns, two trumpets, three trombones, timpani, triangle, cymbals (for a single stroke), and strings.

It would not have seemed to be in the cards that the eldest son of František Dvořák, butcher and publican in a village just north of Prague, would find himself director of a music school in New York City when he was fifty-one. Still, on 27 September 1892, Antonín Dvořák, with his wife, their eldest daughter, and eldest son, disembarked from the SS *Saale* in Hoboken, New Jersey. Within a few days the Dvořáks were installed in an apartment on East 17th Street. Three weeks later, the composer conducted his three concert overtures, *In Nature's Realm, Carnival,* and *Othello,* in Mr. Carnegie's seventeen-month-old Music Hall.

The person responsible for bringing Dvořák to America was Jeannette M. Thurber, whose husband had made millions, many of them, in the wholesale grocery business. She had failed with a National Opera Company, set up in 1884 as competition for the new Metropolitan Opera and dedicated to the proposition of opera in English. In 1885, she threw her resources into the founding of a National Conservatory of Music, appointing as director the Belgian baritone Jacques Bouhy, who had been Escamillo in the first production of *Carmen.* When Bouhy returned to Europe in 1889, Mrs. Thurber knew that she wanted to replace him with a composer. Having asked advice from many musicians at home and abroad, by April 1891 she had set her sights on Dvořák. He had just assumed a professorship in Prague and was not interested in making the move; that Mrs. Thurber had him hooked six months later is testimony to the imaginative generosity of the terms she offered and to her persistence.

Dvořák generally enjoyed his first American visit. He had no objection to being lionized, he liked conducting his music with excellent orchestras in Chicago and New York, he found places in the city where he could watch trains, figured out what spot in Central Park afforded the most pigeons (trains and pigeons were always important to him), and discovered a new pleasure in going to the docks to see the big liners come in and depart. There was also the refreshing, emotional, and musically productive experience of a long summer visit with his family to the Bohemian colony at Spillville in Winneshiek County, northeast Iowa (even though Spillville offered neither pigeons nor ocean liners, and the nearest trains were at Calmar, nine miles away).

At the National Conservatory, Dvořák found composition pupils who were at least serious, but the playing of the student orchestra, which he had to conduct, was torment. With some difficulty he was talked into returning in 1894. This time he was more persistently homesick, and the pleasures of New York had paled. When he sailed back to Europe in April 1895, on the same *Saale* that had brought him the first time, it was for good and without regret, though as late as August 1897 Mrs. Thurber was still trying to get him back. Her Conservatory survived some years into the new century.

The principal works of Dvořák's first sojourn in America were the Symphony *From the New World,* the once immensely popular Violin Sonatina in G, and the Biblical Songs, Opus 99, all written in New York, and two masterpieces of chamber music, the *American* String Quartet in F major, Opus 96, and the String Quintet in E-flat, Opus 97, both achieved in Spillville.

The symphony was the first of these, and its swift progress was helped by two joyous prospects, the escape to Spillville and the arrival for the summer of the other four Dvořák children, accompanied by their Aunt Terezie and a nanny. The closing page of the score carries the notation: "Praise God! Finished on 24 May 1893. The children have arrived at Southampton. Antonín Dvořák. A cable arrived at 1:33 this afternoon." Dvořák's biographer John Clapham comments that "the exciting news of his four children's progress on their way to the United States . . . was too much for the composer: when the work was first rehearsed he discovered that he had forgotten to add parts for the trombones in the last bars."

The *New World* could not have been in better hands. Anton Seidl, a Hungarian, was one of the great conductors of his time, associated with the Metropolitan Opera since 1885 and the New York Philharmonic after 1891, and especially admired for the flexibility and delicacy of his Wagner performances. For all that Seidl's atheism made the devout Dvořák uneasy, the two men were good friends.

The introduction of the new symphony gave Dvořák the greatest public triumph of his life. "I had to show my gratitude like a king from the box in which I sat," he reported to Fritz Simrock. "It made me think of Mascagni in Vienna (don't laugh!)."[9] Henry T. Finck, writing in the *New York Evening Post,* summed up critical consensus: "Any one who heard it could not deny that it is the greatest symphonic work ever composed in this country. . . . A masterwork has been added to the symphonic literature."

[9] *Cavalleria rusticana* had enjoyed a stunning triumph in Vienna the year before.

Finck also asked the question, "But is it American?" The program note, written by Arthur Mees but completely representing Dvořák's ideas, stated that

> on his arrival in America, the composer was deeply impressed by the conditions peculiar to this country and the spirit of which they were the outward manifestation. In continuing his activity he found that the works which he created here were essentially different from those which had sprung into existence in his native country. They were clearly influenced by the new surroundings and by the new life of which they were the material evidence.[10]

While the symphony was still work-in-progress, Dvořák had written to his friend Dr. Emil Kozánek, a lawyer and fine amateur musician, that "[it] pleases me very much and will differ very substantially from my early compositions. The *influence* of America can readily be felt by anyone with 'a nose.' " As for the title, which he had added shortly before delivering the score to Seidl, Dvořák later explained that he meant "impressions and greetings from the New World."

American music definitely fascinated Dvořák. He tried to acquaint himself with American Indian music, though his sources were as scarce as they were dubious—Buffalo Bill's Wild West Show, for example. Harry T. Burleigh, whose concert arrangements of spirituals were to become an essential part of the recital repertory, was a student at the National Conservatory and often sang for Dvořák. Stephen Foster's songs also made a strong impression on the visitor. As a Bohemian citizen of the Austro-Hungarian Empire, a member therefore of a linguistically and culturally oppressed minority, Dvořák was deeply in sympathy with Mrs. Thurber's ideal, one virtually unheard of then, of opening her school to African-American and Native American students.

Himself a composer whose musical language was saturated with the songs and dances of his native land, Dvořák was eager to encourage American composers to find inspiration in their national music, a view he propagated in a widely read article in *Harper's*. Quite consistently he disavowed "that nonsense" of his having made actual use of Native American or African-American themes, though he had, he said, tried to reproduce their spirit: "I have simply written original themes embodying the peculiarities of Indian music, and using these themes as subjects, have developed them with all the resources of modern rhythms, harmony, counterpoint, and orchestral color."

Every American who has heard the *New World* Symphony has noticed

---

[10]New York Philharmonic program, 15–16 December 1893.

that the flute theme in the first movement is a near quotation of *Swing Low, Sweet Chariot*. Clapham points out additional resemblances to a couple of less familiar songs, Hattie Starr's *The Little Alabama Coon* (in the continuation of the *Swing Low* theme) and A. Johnson's *Massa Dear* (in the famous English-horn melody of the Largo, which one of Dvořák's white students in New York, William Arms Fisher, turned into a pseudo-spiritual called *Goin' Home*).

Henry Wadsworth Longfellow enters the picture as well. As a young man, Dvořák had read *The Song of Hiawatha* in a Czech translation by his friend Josef Sládek. When he came to New York, Mrs. Thurber repeatedly pestered him about a *Hiawatha* opera, a project for which he even made a few sketches before foundering on the inept libretto she had handed him. But Dvořák did reread Longfellow's epic, and, as is clear from contemporary press interviews and articles, it left its mark on the second and third movements of the *New World* Symphony. The Dvořák scholar Michael Beckerman goes so far as to call these "at least in part, tone poems based on . . . *The Song of Hiawatha*." More of this later.

Back home in Europe, Dvořák was less eager to stress the American associations of his last symphony than he had been as an enthusiastic and courteous visitor. And certain it is that the *New World* Symphony contains music as Czech as any he ever wrote, something equally true of the Iowan quartet and quintet. Had it been presented as an "old world" symphony written in Prague, it might well have aroused no suspicion of alien influence. The music Dvořák found in America enriched his palette by a few shades, but confirmed more than altered who he was.[11]

Through much of the twentieth century, Dvořák was greatly loved, if too narrowly known by the large public, and his popularity made him, like Tchaikovsky, rather suspect with the professionals. Even at the end of the century, with something of a Dvořák rehabilitation under way, plenty of people still condescend to the *New World* Symphony. You will hear the work more rewardingly if you keep in mind Kurt Masur's contention that, imbued with the pain of homesickness, it is one of the great tragic nineteenth-century symphonies.

Dvořák begins with very slow music for low strings alone, somber and, as very few conductors remember, *pianissimo*. This deeply shadowed introduction adumbrates the thrusting horn theme with which the Allegro bursts into being. As always, Dvořák is prodigal in his spread of melodies,

---

[11] First prize for the most bizarre commentary on the subject goes to Leopold Stokowski. In the "outline of themes" offered as the last side of his sometimes lurid but mostly glorious 1927 Philadelphia Orchestra recording of the *New World*, he says of the *fortissimo* G-major theme after the clarinet solo in the finale that it is "influenced by Negro jazz."

marvelously inventive and colorful in his scoring, and boldly resourceful and original in his harmonic strategy. The first of the new themes, played by flute and oboe together, is a melancholy dance with dark modal harmonies; the other is the one that resembles *Swing Low, Sweet Chariot.* Because it is packed and very brief, Dvořák's request that the exposition be repeated is very much worth taking seriously, though few conductors share this belief.

The development starts with extended and energetic play with the *Swing Low* theme. The thrusting horn theme stages a dramatic and *fortissimo* reappearance, but in a totally wrong key, E-flat minor. This is hastily corrected to the right key, E minor. It seems as though the recapitulation has begun even though the development was awfully short. Too short, indeed, and Dvořák backs off, giving himself another half-minute of suspense-building, before bringing the thrusting horn theme back in unassuming *mezzo-forte.* This now is the real thing. The order of events in the recapitulation is what we expect; on the other hand, the harmonic perspectives are surprising and miraculous. The coda is clenched-fist fierce.

Now comes the famous Largo. It took Dvořák a while to realize how slow this movement really needs to be. In his sketches it is andante. Then it became larghetto, and it was only after he heard Seidl rehearse it at a tempo far slower than the one he had imagined, but which proved to fit perfectly, that he changed it to largo. He casts this music in a remote key, D-flat major, to which he finds his way by an inspired series of seven chords for low woodwinds and brass. Beckerman suggests persuasively that these chords, whose spell seems never to wear thin, represent the transition into the world of legend, the world of *Hiawatha.*[12]

Even if all concur that this movement has *something* to do with *Hiawatha,* there has never been agreement as to just what that connection is. Henry Krehbiel, critic of the *New York Tribune,* who was on excellent terms with Dvořák, maintained that the music portrayed Hiawatha's wooing of Minnehaha; another tradition of long standing, one that seems more plausible in view of the music's darkness, associates this music with Minnehaha's funeral. Still more persuasively, Beckerman proposes that it has to do with Hiawatha's and Minnehaha's long and slow journey home after their wedding, but less with the journey itself than, as the pastoral tone of the music suggests, the landscape through which the couple pass.

The English-horn melody is itself a marvel, and so is the harmonic

---

[12] Longfellow is as unjustly condescended to as Dvořák used to be. No question, though, George A. Strong's deft *Hiawatha* parody—"When he killed the Mudjokivis/Of the skin he made him mittens,/Made them with the fur side inside,/Made them with the skin side outside . . . "— hits home.

and orchestral setting that Dvořák contrives for this jewel. After a muted French horn plays a last echo, the melody gives way to an episode in minor, agitated at first, then taking on the manner and gait of a grieving funeral music. Here perhaps we have an evocation of the poignant scene of Minnehaha's forest burial. This is also landscape music, and the American landscape—imagined by Dvořák, who at this point had seen only New York City—is full of bird song.[13] Inevitably, the funeral-march language is based on the great march in Beethoven's *Eroica*.

A beautiful transition takes us back to the song for the English horn. Dvořák was one of the few musicians of his time who knew and loved Schubert's piano sonatas; with Henry Finck functioning as his scribe, he wrote what is still one of the most perceptive essays we have on Schubert. The heart-stopping silences that interrupt the last recital of *the* melody when it is heard on just a few muted strings were surely borrowed, lovingly, from the final page of Schubert's great Sonata in A major, D.959.

Now Beethoven returns, for the witty start of Dvořák's scherzo is a leaf from the Beethoven Ninth. In this movement we are on sure ground in the matter of the *Hiawatha* connection: this, Dvořák told an interviewer from the *New York Herald*, was inspired by the description of the dance of Pau-Puk-Keewis in Longfellow's poem. The music is now rambunctious, now glowingly lyrical. The energetic dance is spelled by a warm and song-ful interlude; the trio, introduced, as Tovey says, by the summoning of The Ghost of the first movement, is a cheerful dance.

The finale is a feast of inspired tunes, and as though there were not enough of these, Dvořák lards it with recollections of earlier movements. The drama becomes dark and intense; the chords that introduced the Largo return, now evoking the *Siegfried* Wanderer in their new *fortissimo* scoring. In tragic mode, the music becomes ever more fragmented. Just as it seems on the point of vanishing, the finale's first theme rallies the forces and leads the music to a tight and decisive conclusion. The last chord is a surprise.

In September 1893, on their way back from Iowa to New York, the Dvořáks stopped at Niagara Falls. "Damn," exclaimed the admiring composer, "that will be a symphony in B minor!" On his next American visit he composed what is still the greatest cello concerto we have, and in B minor! At home he wrote, among other things, two more superb string quartets and a couple of impressive operas, *Kate and the Devil* and *Rusalka*.

---

[13] When Dvořák finally experienced the Iowa countryside, he found all the empty space "strange. . . . Especially in the *prairies* there are endless acres of field and meadow and that is all you see (I call it the Sahara). . . . It is very 'wild' here, and sometimes very sad—sad to the point of despair."

As for orchestral music, in 1896 he composed four fascinating symphonic poems, all based on ballads by Karel Jaromír Erben, but he seems to have lost faith in the possibilities of the symphony.[14] His fervently inspired greeting from the New World, a greeting at once exuberant and melancholy, was his last essay in a genre he had learned to command with seldom surpassed mastery.

[14]Coming as a postscript to a series of extraordinary symphonies, these bewitching tone poems can suggest that Dvořák was suddenly caught in some strange Lisztian-Wagnerian draft. There is a lot of Brahms in Dvořák's music, but long before he entered that orbit, he had been a committed Wagnerian. As a twenty-one-year-old violist he had even had the intoxicating experience of playing a Beethoven-Wagner concert under the Meister's baton. Wagner could be a haunting presence even at the height of what we might call Dvořák's symphonic period, for example in the great F-minor Piano Trio. When Dvořák turned to the tone poem in 1896, it was a return to the musical passions of his youth.

Edward Elgar

Edward William Elgar—Sir Edward after being knighted by King Edward VII on 4 July 1904—was born at Broadheath, Worcestershire, England, on 2 June 1857 and died in Worcester on 23 February 1934.

Whose is the voice that speaks in these symphonies? Reviewing Michael Kennedy's *Portrait of Elgar*, David Cairns sketches a hypersensitive, touchy, moody, at times almost suicidally unhappy genius with small, nervous hands: an English eccentric who loved fishing, Bradshaw,[1] dogs, recondite information, and bonfires, who practised chemistry and patented the Elgar Sulphuretted Hydrogen Apparatus, and who nursed within him a wound that never healed.[2]

What must we add? He was poor, he was self-taught, he was Catholic. At forty, he was capable of refusing at the last minute an invitation previously accepted, writing to his hostess that she "would not wish to have [her] board disgraced by the presence of a piano-tuner's son." Many years after that, as a baronet and Master of the King's Musick, a similar fit of resentment and misery suddenly made him decide that he and his family could not attend the coronation of George V. Poverty was a presence far into his life. In the midst of his work on the First Symphony, he wrote to his friend Frank Schuster: "Yes: I am trying to write music, but the bitterness

---

[1] Bradshaw, as Sherlock Holmes readers know, was the publisher of railway timetables for the British Isles. —M.S.
[2] David Cairns *Responses* (New York: Knopf, 1973).

is that it pays me not at all & I must write & arrange what my soul loathes to permit me to write what you like & I like." He felt, and probably exaggerated, the disapproval of his Worcestershire neighbors because he had married, as one said in those days, above his station (and a woman eight years older than himself). Being Catholic in a land of often uninhibited anti-Roman sentiment further nourished his sense of isolation.

William Elgar did tune pianos, but he also owned a music shop whose collection of scores together with the books at home and the concerts at the Three Choirs Festivals provided his son with a rich if unconventional education. Edward played violin, also some bassoon, cello, and piano, and he conducted amateur bands and orchestras, including that of the County and City of Worcester Pauper Lunatic Asylum. He became, and no wonder, an immensely resourceful and practical musician.

Only once did he venture into the academy (other than to accept honorary degrees, of which he received eight in as many years after the blazing success of the *Enigma* Variations). In 1905–06 he gave eight lectures ("A Future for English Music") at the University of Birmingham, and he told his listeners exactly what he thought of the scene in his and their country. He had a keen sense of just how much he offended the academics and the critics: Leaving the hall at the end of his last lecture, he muttered, "I must go and buy some strychnine. This is the end of me."

One famous passage from the inaugural lecture tells us much about Elgar's temper of mind:

> Critics frequently say of a man that it is to his credit that he is never vulgar. Good. But it is possible for him—in an artistic sense only, be it understood—to be much worse; he can be commonplace. . . . The commonplace mind can never be anything but commonplace, and no amount of education, no polish of a University, can eradicate the stain from the low type of mind which is the English commonplace. . . . An Englishman will take you into a large room, beautifully proportioned, and will point out to you that it is white—all over white—and somebody will say what exquisite taste. You know in your own mind, in your own soul, that it is not taste at all—that it is the want of taste—that it is mere evasion. English music is white, and evades everything.[3]

[3] Edward Elgar, "A Future for English Music" and Other Lectures, edited by Percy Young (London: Dennis Dobson, 1966). Elgar had been anticipated—less aggressively—in these thoughts by Ralph Vaughan Williams in a 1902 article "Good Taste": "If a composer is naturally vulgar, let him be frank and write vulgar music instead of hedging himself about with an artificial barrier of good taste." And here is another great composer, Arnold Schoenberg, on the same subject: "In my vocabulary [taste] stands for 'arrogance and superiority-complex of mediocrity,' and: Taste is sterile—it can not produce. And: Taste is applicable only to the lower zones of human feeling, to the material ones. It is no yardstick in spiritual matters. And: Taste functions mainly as a restricting factor, as a negation of every problem, as a minus to every number."—M.S.

One hesitates before a phrase like "Elgar is the English Mahler." It is too pat as a "placing" of Elgar; besides, to provide such a pigeonhole is always to invite a reader to stop thinking. Still, an affinity exists between these two great symphonists of our century's first decade. Gloom-pleased (Keats's wonderful adjective), life-loving, incorruptible, tactless, they were pursued by similar demons, they relished their sense of exile even as they suffered under it, they had religious feelings at once intense and ambivalent, they were exceedingly dependent husbands, they were intellectual musicians who reveled in the popular touch. Both detested white rooms, both took what their censorious contemporaries saw as an unholy delight in orchestral virtuosity, and Elgar's injunction to conductors that he wanted his music to be played "elastically and mystically" applies equally to Mahler. Elgar has not Mahler's wildness; Mahler does not command what Yeats called Elgar's "heroic melancholy" (and which Elgar himself referred to as "my stately sorrow"). Mahler looked and behaved like an exasperated genius; Elgar had correct English manners, an unabashed sense of humor, and he took pains to disguise himself as Colonel Blimp. Elgar and his music fooled a lot of people with that disguise, among them such intelligent observers as Edward J. Dent, Constant Lambert, Osbert Sitwell, and W.J. Turner, and between the wars his reputation sank as startlingly as it had risen just after 1900.[4]

Mrs. Richard Powell, the Dorabella of the *Enigma* Variations, tells us that to go to a concert with Elgar was to come home with a bruised arm, so fiercely was he apt to clutch his neighbor when he was in the grip of emotion. Michael Kennedy, citing Compton Mackenzie, describes Elgar as "he trembled all over and veins and beads of sweat stood out alarmingly on his head with the excitement of listening to the March to the Scaffold from Berlioz's *Symphonie fantastique.*" This is clearly the same man about whom Bernard Shaw, writing to Virginia Woolf, tells the story of lunch with Roger Fry, the art critic. Fry had remarked that there was after all "only one art, all the arts are the same." Shaw continues:

> I heard no more. My attention was taken by a growl from the other side of the table. It was Elgar, with his fangs bared and all his hackles bristling, in an appalling rage. "Music," he sputtered, "is written on the skies for you to note down. And you compare that to a DAMNED imitation!"[5]

---

[4] I don't know whether Elgar knew Mahler's music, though Henry J. Wood conducted the First and Fourth symphonies in London in 1903 and 1905 respectively and *Das Lied von der Erde* in 1914. Mahler's works were then, and long thereafter, regarded in England as the tasteless aberrations of a famous but eccentric conductor. I recall no comments by Mahler about Elgar, but he did conduct the *Enigma* Variations and *Sea Pictures* during his directorship of the New York Philharmonic.

[5] Quoted in Michael Kennedy, *Portrait of Elgar* (Oxford: Oxford University Press, 1968), 136.

Symphony No. 1 in A-flat major, Opus 55

Andante. Nobilmente e semplice—Allegro
Allegro molto
Adagio
Lento—Allegro

Elgar played the great opening melody of this symphony to his family on 27 June 1907 but began concentrated work on the piece only in November of that year. In part using material from earlier sketches, he completed the score at Plâs Gwyn, his house at Hereford, on 25 September 1908. It is dedicated to "Hans Richter, Mus. Doc., True Artist and True Friend," and it was Dr. Richter who gave the first performance with the Hallé Orchestra at the Free Trade Hall, Manchester, on 3 December 1908.

Three flutes and piccolo, three oboes and English horn, two clarinets and bass clarinet, two bassoons and contrabassoon, four horns, three trumpets, three trombones, bass tuba, timpani, bass drum, cymbals, snare drum, two harps, and strings.

> *"There is no programme beyond a wide experience of human life with a great charity (love) and a massive hope in the future."*
>
> *—Elgar, 13 November 1908*

"Here it was!" and the first three bars of this symphony's opening melody— that was Elgar's message on a picture postcard of the Appian Way sent to W. G. McNaught at the offices of his publisher. He had spent most of the winter of 1907–08 in Rome with his wife and their seventeen-year-old daughter Carice, delighted by the flavorful food and the wine, the sunsets, the weather, sight-seeing, French lessons at Berlitz, the opera, the display of temperament all around, the low cost of living.

To write a symphony was that season's goal. Elgar was fifty, which makes Brahms, who had waited till forty-three, seem downright impulsive. In 1898, Elgar had declared himself "possessed" by the idea of a symphony on the life and character of General Gordon, who, virtually abandoned by the British government, had been killed in 1885 in the defense of Khartoum in the Sudan. Possessed, "but," said Elgar, "I can't write it down yet." No *Gordon* Symphony ever materialized, though it is possible that some of the material Elgar sketched for it made its way into the Second Symphony (1910).

Between the impact that even a *Gordon* Symphony (and the eccentric general had posthumously become very much a national hero) by Elgar might have made in 1898 and the impact the Symphony in A-flat did in fact make a decade later there is a world of difference. In 1898 Elgar had just begun the breakthrough from a provincial reputation to a cosmopolitan, thanks chiefly to the Imperial March written for Queen Victoria's Diamond Jubilee. In 1908 he was the renowned composer of the *Enigma* Variations, *Sea Pictures*, *The Dream of Gerontius*, the first four *Pomp and Circumstance* marches (the famous No. 1 got a double encore at its premiere in 1901 and as *Land of Hope and Glory* had become a second, unofficial national anthem), the *Cockaigne* Overture, *The Apostles*, *The Kingdom*, the Introduction and Allegro for Strings, *The Wand of Youth*. After a spell as Dr. Elgar (*honoris causa* at Cambridge, 1900) he was Sir Edward and, with the exception only of the soprano to whom he referred in a letter as that "battered old w——e . . . Melba" he was the most prominent, the most popular musician in the British Empire and he looked it, every inch.

The testy Hans von Bülow had called England "das Land ohne Musik." Bülow was no more ignorant about Byrd and Purcell than any other musician of his generation; he was, in any event, thinking of his own day, in which British musical life was dominated by a professors' mutual admiration society whose principal members were Sir Alexander Mackenzie, Sir Hubert Parry, and Sir Charles Villiers Stanford.[6] Elgar changed that. G. B. Shaw, who used to take off after that trio with relish in his music critic days, recalled his first hearing of the *Enigma* Variations: "I sat up and said 'Whew!' I knew we had got it at last."

By 1908, the public had the highest expectations of Elgar; indeed, it had been quicker to catch on than most of the professionals. For that matter, foreigners were often quicker than the English. Arthur Johnstone, the sharp critic of the *Manchester Guardian*, wrote after one of the early performances of the *Enigma* Variations that "the audience seemed rather astonished that a work by a British composer would have had other than a petrifying effect upon them." But Elgar's encompassing professionalism, especially his brilliant command of the orchestra, rendered him suspect in

---

[6]None of these was an Elgar or anywhere near it, but in justice one should say that Stanford could be a very engaging composer and Parry an extremely impressive one.

a society that, in season and out, admired the amateur spirit. "Ah, music and cricket," as Sir Peter Ustinov sighs in one of the most delicious-malicious of his skits.

In any event, it is striking how many of the most ardent and effective of the first generation of Elgarians were not British, though a few of them had become very much part of British musical life: foremost Hans Richter, trumpeter in the first performance of the *Siegfried Idyll*, first conductor of *The Ring of the Nibelung*, immensely popular in England between 1880 and his retirement in 1911, the first conductor of the *Enigma* Variations and *The Dream of Gerontius*; August Jaeger, Elgar's editor at Novello and one of his most beloved friends, the Nimrod of the Variations (*Jäger* is the German for hunter); Julius Buths, the Düsseldorf conductor who introduced *Gerontius* on the Continent; Richard Strauss, who hailed Elgar as "the first English progressive"; Fritz Steinbach, Bülow's successor at the Meiningen Orchestra, who programmed the *Enigma* Variations when he brought that famous group to London (and didn't that ever impress the English!); Arthur Nikisch, though Elgar thought his *Enigmas* "rum"; Felix Weingartner; Alexander Siloti, whose *Enigma* performances delighted Rimsky-Korsakov and Glazunov; Wilhelm Backhaus, who could play *Gerontius* by heart; Fritz Kreisler, for whom Elgar wrote his Violin Concerto; and Adolph Brodsky, who as a young man had introduced Tchaikovsky's Violin Concerto and who came out of retirement for a last performance of Elgar's Concerto on the composer's seventieth birthday. And when Elgar wrote to Jaeger from Chicago in 1907 he could report, "A fine orchestra (100) & they knew (via dear old Theodore Thomas) *everything* of mine backwards." On the English side you find only Henry J. Wood, a vigorous pioneer in the Theodore Thomas mold, and a bit later, Landon Ronald.

It was an intensely emotional evening when Elgar's First Symphony was heard for the first time. Richter was one of the first of the modern conductors who discouraged applause between movements, and after eleven years he had his Manchester public well trained. But the Adagio—about which Jaeger was not wrong when he wrote to Elgar that it was "not only one of the very greatest slow movements since Beethoven but . . . *worthy of that master*"—broke down the audience's reserve, and Richter at that point called the composer to the stage to acknowledge the storms of cheers and handclapping.

The next day, Richter traveled to London to prepare the work with the London Symphony. "Let us now rehearse the greatest symphony of modern times," he said to the musicians, "*and not only in this country.*" The reception in the capital surpassed the one in Manchester, an extra performance had to be scheduled within the week, and Elgar's biographer

Percy M. Young tells us that "during 1909 the symphony was played on eighty-two occasions, including seventeen performances in London, ten in America, others in Vienna, Berlin, Leipzig, Bonn, Saint Petersburg, Toronto, and Sydney," Munich, Budapest, and Rome being added in 1910.

The theme Elgar copied onto his postcard to McNaught is the emblem of the symphony. There is no need for an injunction to remember it well, so impressive is it in its nobility and breadth. Also, for nearly three minutes, it is the only musical matter for us to attend to. Elgar gives it to us twice, first quietly in a spare texture consisting, save for a few horn notes that add delicate coloristic and harmonic accent, only of the tune and its staccato bass (thrusting and urgent in his own recording), then in a large and effortless *fortissimo*. The tune, with its internal repetitions, unfolds naturally and at the same time unpredictably; the relationship of the accents and releases of the harmony to its rise and fall is similarly "right" and subtle.

Abruptly Elgar plunges into an impassioned Allegro in a distant key, D minor. This is music as restless, changeable, nervous as the opening was stable and consistent. At crucial moments, that opening intervenes, a reminder of another world, another life, another way, almost always quietly, in muted horns, in single woodwinds with half the cellos, or from the last desks of strings. Once it rises to *fortissimo*, but against ruthless interference from most of the orchestra. The movement ends *pianissimo*, with ghost music, creeping shadows, and darting flecks of light. Of the great tune just a shred remains, but its A-flat major has prevailed over the D-minor demons.

The second movement, a whipping scherzo (not so named by Elgar), makes another bold harmonic leap, this time into F-sharp minor. Elgar took pains to remind Jaeger that "the widest *looking* divergencies are often closest relationships," and indeed this movement, as it goes along, "explains" the key connection in a way that parallels Elgar's skill at gradually making manifest the connections between at first apparently unrelated themes. The delicately scored trio, which comes twice, he wanted played "like something you hear down by the river." As a small boy he was once found at the riverside with pencil and paper, trying "to write down what the reeds were saying."

Gradually the momentum of this brilliant music runs down: when Elgar slips a D under the violins' and violas' F-sharp, the great Adagio has begun.[7]

---

[7] This is exactly how he manages the magical key change from "W.N." to "Nimrod" in the *Enigma* Variations.

The notes are the same as those of the scherzo, but now, in Michael Kennedy's words, "becalmed into a melody of limitless consolatory powers."

Ex. 1

Ex. 2

Jaeger, as we have seen, invoked Beethoven in thanking Elgar for these pages; about a new melody with gently upward thrusting sevenths that appears so surprisingly near the end, he says that there "we are brought near to Heaven." It is one of the rare moments since Beethoven of a music altogether beatific. How rare it also is for Elgar to be so at peace, but here he did recapture what he had once found for the singing of "Softly and gently, dearly-ransomed soul,/In my most loving arms I now enfold thee," the Angel's Farewell that brings *The Dream of Gerontius* to a close.[8]

But the music that begins the finale is music of "shuddering dread . . . cold dismay—pang of heart" (to borrow words from Cardinal Newman's *Gerontius* poem). The sounds are as dark as those of the Adagio were radiant. The symphony's opening melody is faintly heard behind the gusts and the footsteps: again it is ruthlessly swept aside by a restless yet forceful Allegro in D minor. This is a movement full of event and contrast, visited by specters. At last the grand melody steps forward, not as a ghost, but in a blaze. The orchestra tries to crush it, furious waves break upon it. The tune prevails, but only just. It is perhaps the most ambiguous peroration to any symphony, and one of the most moving.

---

[8] The Adagio of the First Symphony is used most affectingly at Ralph Richardson's death in the movie *Greystoke*.

Symphony No. 2 in E-flat major, Opus 63

> *Allegro vivace e nobilmente*
> *Larghetto*
> *Rondo: Presto*
> *Moderato e maestoso*

Elgar dated the Symphony No. 2 "Venice-Tintagel (1910–11)." More specifically, sketches for some of the material go back to 1903 and 1904, when he wanted to write a symphony for Hans Richter, but he did not return to this material until October 1909, a year after he had completed his Symphony No. 1. Concentrated work on the Symphony No. 2 began a year after that, in October 1910, when he described the process of composing it as "weaving strange and wonderful memories into very poor music." He completed the four movements at the end of January, 6 February, 21 February, and 28 February 1911 respectively. Elgar himself conducted the first performance with the Queen's Hall Orchestra at the London Festival on 24 May 1911.

Elgar dedicated the work "to the Memory of His Late Majesty King Edward VII," who had died on 6 May 1910. He appended the following note, dated 16 March 1911: "This Symphony designed early in 1910 to be a loyal tribute, bears its present dedication with the gracious approval of His Majesty the King [George V]." At the end of the score, Elgar placed the first two lines of Shelley's Invocation: "Rarely, rarely comest thou,/ Spirit of Delight!" He wrote about that to Ernest Newman: "My attitude toward the poem, or rather to the 'Spirit of Delight' was an attempt to give the reticent Spirit a hint (with sad enough retrospections) as to what we should like to have!"

Three flutes (third doubling piccolo), two oboes and English horn, two B-flat clarinets as well as E-flat and bass clarinet, two bassoons and contrabassoon, four horns, three trumpets, three trombones, tuba, timpani, bass drum, snare drum, cymbals, two harps, and strings. Several years after the publication of the score, Elgar suggested to Adrian Boult the use of a thirty-two-foot (or if available, sixty-four-foot) organ pedal stop to reinforce the bass for sixteen measures in the finale.

I do but hide
Under these words, like embers, every spark
Of that which has consumed me.

—from Shelley's *Julian and Maddalo*

Elgar's Symphony No. 1 was emotionally, joyously received as England's First Symphony when Hans Richter introduced it in Manchester at the end of 1908.[9] Eighty-two performances in six countries during the following year confirmed that triumph. The Violin Concerto, introduced by Kreisler in November 1910, stirred almost as fervent an outpouring of admiration and love. Six months later, the Second Symphony failed. The hall was not filled. "What's the matter with them, Billy?" Elgar asked W. H. Reed, his concertmaster. "They sit there like a lot of stuffed pigs." What *had* happened?

Elgar's First Symphony ends in ambiguity. One can miss this strangeness; at least I have heard musicians—and others—speak of this finale as though it were one of the *Pomp and Circumstance* marches. But no one could mistake the mood of the last pages of the Second Symphony. I do not think the "stuffed pigs" in Queen's Hall did. Most urgently on the minds of Londoners in May 1911 was the coronation that was due to take place in a few weeks after a year of Court mourning. Longing for *Jubilate* and *Te Deum*, perhaps they heard all too well something that told them the glory years were not for ever.[10]

"I have worked at fever heat and the thing is tremendous in energy," Elgar wrote. The volcanic gesture with which the symphony begins, vivace

[9] Sir Neville Cardus, the English writer on cricket and music, who heard that concert as a young man of nineteen, remembered many years later how "those of us who were students were excited to hear at last an English composer addressing us in a spacious way, speaking a language which was European and not provincial. No English symphony existed then, at least not big enough to make a show of comparison with a symphony by Beethoven or Brahms and go in the programme of a concert side by side with the acknowledged masterpieces, and not be dwarfed at once into insignificance."

[10] The crowded pre-coronation social calendar and the equally crowded concert calendar of the London Festival, which included such box office draws as a Brahms Double Concerto with Kreisler and Casals, would in part account for the disappointing attendance at the premiere of the Elgar Second. Looking at this "failure," Michael Kennedy also "wonders how well or badly [the Symphony No. 2] was played in 1911–14 and suspects the worst." Frank Bridge heard a performance in 1916 at which the Philharmonic "scrambled through the Symphony as though they had never before seen it. . . . Performances of this kind do far more harm than good." It is a difficult, subtle score, not the kind that readily survives inadequate performance. It seems that the first time it made a strong impression in concert was in 1920 when the then unknown, thirty-one-year-old Adrian C. Boult conducted it.

and (Elgar's special adverb) nobilmente, is "tremendous in energy" indeed. I imagine that first audience smiling: this is just what they would have hoped to hear. The energy is not just in the tempo and in the upward-thrusting intervals, but resides even more in the way the music unfolds, in its metabolism. Short themes, distinct yet related, succeed each other rapidly, so that the sweep of events gathers enormous force. The rhythm is supple, Elgar specifying six different speeds, not counting "en route" tempi as he moves from one area to another and a constant series of local modifications. A tenderly lyric, wistful music succeeds the initial storms, but so restless are the harmonies and the passings of shadows in the flux of the dynamics that we get no sense of repose. This uneasy quiet is soon over, as the music recaptures its former pace.

Darkness falls. Against slowly oscillating horn chords, muted violins trace strange descending lines. Flute scales snake upward. Drums and plucked basses rumble. All this is as hushed as possible. "I have written the most extraordinary passage," he said in a letter to his friend Alice Stuart-Wortley, " . . . a sort of malign influence wandering thro' the summer night in the garden." The Spirit of Delight theme, if we may so name the symphony's first phrase, seeks to dispel what Michael Kennedy aptly calls this "sinister nocturne," but the oppressive shadows persist. What ever happened to King Edward VII, in tribute or in memoriam? Kennedy suggests persuasively that the dedication is a royal red herring designed "to divert public attention from the intimate personal character of the music." We cannot say what personal experiences, what "strange and wonderful memories" Elgar was here transmuting into a symphony, nor need we know, but that these are private pains we need not doubt. "I have written out my soul in the [violin] concerto, Sym II, and the Ode [*The Music Makers*] and you know it . . . in these three works I have shewn myself," he told Mrs. Stuart-Wortley. When he sent a progress report on what he called "the 'Spirit of Delight' symphony" to another friend, Frances Colvin, he quoted the lines that stand at the head of this essay (changing Shelley's "words" to "notes"). If he had never written a letter in his life, the music would tell us.

Energy at last supplants brooding, and Elgar moves toward the recapitulation of the opening. Having prepared the moment with gripping tension, he thunders the return with demonic force, splitting the Spirit of Delight phrase in two with a rhetorical pause.[11] The recapitulation proceeds much as we expect. There are no further allusions to the sinister

---

[11] Here is an astonishing similarity to a famous moment in Mahler, the blazing E-major climax at the end of the Fourth Symphony's slow movement. The elements in common are the upward thrust of the major sixth and the *Luftpause* in mid-phrase.

nocturne, and the final gesture, based on the Spirit of Delight phrase, is brilliant and surprising.

I do not know to what extent Elgar, composing his E-flat Symphony, was thinking of its great predecessor in that key, Beethoven's *Eroica*. What happens now, a great orchestral dirge, certainly brings the connection to mind, and so, more remotely, does a certain feature of the finale. Elgar does not call his second movement a *marcia funebre*, but the vocabulary is unmistakable and once again his letters confirm our musical response. The public associated this music with the death of Edward VII, and that was quite all right with Elgar. He had, however, sketched the music in 1904 upon the death of his friend Alfred E. Rodewald, a wealthy textile merchant and the able conductor of the amateur Liverpool Orchestral Society. (That group had the honor of giving the premieres of the first two *Pomp and Circumstance* marches.) Rodewald's death affected Elgar more painfully than any before Alice Elgar's in 1920. It was Alice who identified the sketch that became the Second Symphony's Larghetto as a "lament for dear Rodey and all human feeling."

The orchestral writing is wonderfully imaginative; for example, the top line takes on a quasi-muted effect simply by virtue of being given to the second violins, who in a 1911 orchestra would have sat to the conductor's right and thus had their instruments facing the back of the stage. But such ingenuities are merely the means of making Elgar's grief articulate. This movement, too, is rich in themes of vivid profile and attains stirring climaxes. At the close, we sense again the presence of the Spirit of Delight, now in quiet, fragmented phrases (a reminiscence, surely, of the disintegration at the end of the *Eroica*'s funeral march). "May [this] not be," asked Elgar, "like a woman dropping a flower on the man's grave?"

The scherzo, in C major, moves at high speed and is full of harmonic and rhythmic mystery. Woodwinds propose a more genial, countrified music, something that seems to look forward to Justice Shallow's orchard as Elgar would evoke it in *Falstaff* a couple of years later. But again the skies darken, shifting harmonies are glued to an unyielding E-flat in the bass, the drums are softly but inescapably insistent, and the "malign influence" that crept through the garden of the first movement is among us once more. Bernard Shore, principal violist of the BBC Symphony at the time, recalled Elgar saying at a rehearsal of this passage: "I want you to imagine that this hammering is like that horrible throbbing in the head during some fever. It seems gradually to blot out every atom of thought in your brain and nearly drives you mad." To his friend W. H. T. Gairdner, a canon at Worcester Cathedral who never had any doubt that this symphony embodied a "passionate pilgrimage" of the soul, Elgar quoted lines from Tennyson's *Maud* that were associated in his mind with this madness:

> Dead, long dead,
>   Long dead!
> And my heart is a handful of dust
> And the wheels go over my head,
> And my bones are shaken with pain,
> For into a shallow grave they are thrust,
> Only a yard beneath the street,
> And the hoofs of the horses beat, beat,
> The hoofs of the horses beat,
> Beat into my scalp and brain
> With never an end to the stream of passing feet . . .

A violent cymbal clash rends the air, and after it the nightmare recedes. We pass again through the first part of the movement in rather shortened form and head into a brilliant and swift C-major coda.

The scherzo's C major—with C-minor fever—effectively provides both contrast and connection with the dirge that comes before it. Now the exciting C-major close nicely sets up the finale's return to E-flat major, which sounds mellow and comfortable in this context. Low woodwinds, horns, and cellos softly sing a melody whose serene expansiveness does not admit even the possibility of madness. Two grander, more rhetorical themes come next, one of ever widening upward leaps, the other a handsome and sure melody marked nobilmente. One of the two is a portrait of Richter, that is, it was marked in the sketch, "Hans himself!" Here Elgar's two most authoritative recent biographers are in disagreement, Michael Kennedy identifying the latter as the "Hans himself" theme and Jerrold Northrop Moore the former; I do not know who is right.

Ex. 1

Ex. 2

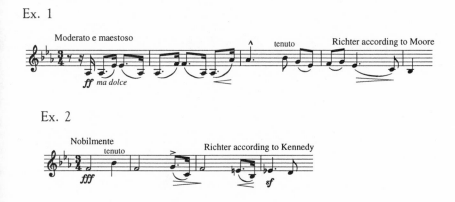

After a busy but brief development comes a regular recapitulation. Now the movement flows into its unexpected and sublime coda. The climax after the return of candidate no. 2 for the Hans Richter theme suggests that Elgar is aiming at a grandly triumphal close, something perhaps on the order of the *Enigma* finale. Instead, the direction is "più tranquillo." The serene opening theme returns, over an E-flat pedal, which is now reassuring rather than threatening, and with a lovely descant for the violins. The principal theme fades from our hearing, and as the descanters step forward, we recognize what they are singing. It is the upbeat to the Spirit of Delight theme. The woodwinds understand. Slowly, sweetly, they lay the melody across the orchestra like a quiet blessing. There is something here of the sublime close of the Brahms Third, which, with the Mozart G-minor, was the symphony Elgar loved most. But the benison here, infinitely poetic and lovely music, seems to lose itself in allusions, recollections, regrets. What we hear is always just beyond our grasp.

The music rallies, rises for a moment to a richly sonorous *forte,* then sinks away into the distance. Here Elgar must have recalled the ending of that bold, self-declared heir of the *Eroica,* also in E-flat, *Ein Heldenleben* by the German colleague who had befriended, admired, and reassured him when he badly needed it. Strauss's close, with its quick rise to *fortissimo* after long pages of calm and equally quick descent to *pianissimo,* is surprising, original, beautiful, and always affecting. Elgar's close, coming out of greater uncertainty and deeper ambiguities, is surprising, original, beautiful, and—ultimately—disturbing. At the end of his score (though the publisher has moved it to the beginning), Elgar wrote

> Rarely, rarely comest thou,
> Spirit of Delight!

But, devoted poetry reader that he was, he knew not just those famous lines but all of Shelley's Invocation. It ends:

> But above all other things,
>   Spirit, I love thee—
> Thou art love and life! Oh, come,
> Make once more my heart thy home.

Górecki

Henryk Górecki

Henryk Mikołaj Górecki was born on 6 December 1933 in
Czernika, Poland, a few miles from what was then the
Polish-German border. The name is pronounced Goretski.

Symphony No. 3, *Symphony of Sorrowful Songs*

Lento (sostenuto tranquillo ma cantabile)
Lento e largo (tranquillissimo, cantabilissimo, dolcissimo, legatissimo)
   —Molto lento
*Lento (cantabile, semplice)—Lento e largo—Molto lento—Largo ben
   tenuto*

Górecki composed his Symphony No. 3 in the last three months of
1976 on commission from the Southwest German Radio, Baden-
Baden. The texts are taken from a fifteenth-century Lamentation
of the Holy Cross Monastery at Łysa Gora; a prayer inscribed
on the wall of a prison cell at Gestapo headquarters in Zakopane, Poland,
by the eighteen-year-old Helena Wanda Błażusiakówna; and a folk song
in the dialect of the Opole region of Upper Silesia. It was first performed
on 4 April 1977 at Royan, France, by the orchestra of the Southwest German Radio under Ernest Bour with Stefania Woytowicz, soprano. The
score is dedicated to the composer's wife.

The Boosey & Hawkes score of the Symphony No. 3 carries this unsigned comment about the symphony's title:

The subtitle "Śymfonia pieśni żałosnych" has suffered much in translation. "Piesni" is simply "songs," but the qualifying "Żałosnych" is archaic, and more comprehensive than its modern English, German, or French equivalents. It comprises not only the sense of both the wordless "song" of the opening double basses and the monastic lament which follows, but also the prayer and exhortation ("Do not weep") of the Zakopane graffito, and the lullaby, both elegiac and redemptive, of the final folk song. Renderings such as "Lamentation Songs" or "Klagelieder" (with their overtones of Jeremiah or Gustav Mahler) are thus even more misleading than the alternative of "Sorrowful Songs."

Four flutes (third and fourth doubling piccolo), four clarinets, two bassoons and two contrabassoons, four horns, four trombones, harp, piano, and strings (minimum 16–16–12–12–8), plus solo soprano.

In April 1992, Elektra-Nonesuch released a recording of Górecki's fifteen-year-old Symphony No. 3 conducted by David Zinman and with Dawn Upshaw as the soprano soloist. Within a few weeks it was at the top of the classical charts in the United States and Great Britain, and in Britain it rode high on the pop charts as well. In two years more than 700,000 copies were sold, which is at least 400 times the expected lifetime sales of a recording of a symphony by a relatively unknown twentieth-century composer. No one cared about the other two available recordings of the Third Symphony, nor did the success of that work arouse interest in other music by the composer. Record companies tried their best, and all of us who are curious to hear more Górecki have been the beneficiaries of their efforts: virtually all of his major compositions became available in excellent recordings.[1] The phenomenon was not a creation of media hype. Like the surge of interest in Gregorian chant in 1994—and this, too, was overwhelmingly focused on a single recording—it took off by itself, in part through word of mouth, to some extent through repeated exposure on the radio. The daughters of Ernest Bloch, noting how the popularity of *Shelomo* was turning their father into a one-piece composer, proposed that a Society for Bloch's Other Works be organized. Górecki is ready for similar attention.

The Górecki Third frenzy came out of nowhere. The music had gone

---

[1] I am sorry to say that when I saw a CD of sacred choral music by Gorczycki, a Polish contemporary of Bach, in a record store, I wondered whether some record-company executive had entertained the hope that it might be bought in a moment of mistaken identity. It was in fact in the Górecki bin.

unnoticed when some of it was used in a Gerard Depardieu film, *The Police*. Ninety-nine percent or more of the people who bought the Third Symphony can't ever have heard of Górecki before. New-music buffs knew his name as that of one of the composers who had sparked the postwar Polish music renascence, but opportunities actually to get to know his work were few.

It is primarily a CD phenomenon. The symphony has had some concert performances, but, while it is not a turn-off at the box office, it does not guarantee sold-out houses either. (There is less overlap than one might think between the record audience and the concert audience.) In some ways, this *is* more a piece for the living room than for the concert hall. If you really want to sink into the music, you can do that more easily at home—no coughing, no dropped programs, no distractions from the stage.

Questions arise. Are people really listening to this symphony? How many CD buyers discover that fifty-four minutes of very slow music with a little singing in a language they don't understand is more than they want? Is it being played as background music to Chardonnay and brie?[2]

Górecki, as stunned as anybody by what has happened, said in a conversation with Vladimir Levitski, the Minnesota Orchestra's pianist: "Perhaps people find something they need in this piece of music. . . . Somehow I hit the right note, something they were missing. Something, somewhere had been lost to them. I feel that I instinctively knew what they needed." Taking the most optimistic view of the response to the Third Symphony, it does indeed seem that the music speaks to a real need. It is a need that has also been addressed by two of Górecki's contemporaries who, although musically quite different personalities, have made similarly "mystical" discoveries and statements, the Estonian, Arvo Pärt, and the Georgian, Giya Kancheli. Both these composers are also better known to CD buyers than to symphony audiences.

Górecki's Symphony No. 3 is also motivated by an urgent need to bear witness, and he described this to Levitski: "I can tell you that what I write is my commentary on what is happening around me. I don't live in an ivory tower. I participate in life—the war that went through here, and then that damned Communism, and now all this social upheaval and the changes that are bombarding us. I am not a person who can be indifferent. I absorb these things. My music is my commentary."

Górecki's musical journey began with piano lessons at the music

---

[2] It brings to mind the *Doctor Zhivago* phenomenon of 1958. Everybody rushed to buy the book; few managed actually to read it. The appearance of the movie in 1965 rescued us all from the necessity.

school in Rybnik, the nearest middle-size town to Czernika, the village where he was born and grew up. He was twenty-one before he moved on to serious instruction in composition: this he got at the State Conservatory in the much bigger city of Katowice, where his teacher was Bolesław Szabelski, a highly regarded composer, then of neoclassic inclinations, who later became a serialist. Later, Górecki made Katowice his home and joined the faculty of the Conservatory.

With Witold Lutosławski, Górecki's senior by twenty years, providing spiritual, moral, and artistic leadership, the late 1950s and the 1960s were an exciting time for music in Poland—really the most exciting ever, inasmuch as the country's greatest composer, Chopin, left home at twenty and did virtually all his most significant work in Paris and on Majorca. Lutosławski himself, Tadeusz Baird (whose relatively early death robbed the world of a composer of music of remarkable expressive and sensuous beauty), Krzysztof Penderecki, and Górecki emerged quickly as the leading figures in this adventurous and exciting Polish rebirth.

It is interesting to take a tour through some of Górecki's music, from the 1957 Sonata for Two Violins to the String Quartet No. 2, *Quasi una fantasia*, of 1991. In the Sonata, we meet an immensely gifted young composer writing lively, brilliantly effective music that, like Lutosławski's work of that time, is under the spell of Bartók. Shostakovich is a presence as well.

The next year, 1958, was critical. In February, the Silesian State Philharmonic in Katowice gave a concert devoted entirely to his music, a remarkable opportunity for a twenty-four-year-old composer. As a result of this event, Górecki was asked to write something for that year's Warsaw Autumn Festival. His response to that invitation introduces a new Górecki who has joined the advance guard. *Epitafium* for chorus and small, mixed instrumental ensemble is, all five minutes of it, an exquisite composition. It was written for what was otherwise an all-Webern program and evokes beautifully the disjunct *pianissimo* magic of that master's songs and cantatas.

Over the next few years, Górecki's music becomes tougher, more aggressive. In *Scontri* (Collisions) for large orchestra and in the three pieces that make up the cycle called *Genesis* (*Elementi* for string trio, *Canti strumentali* for fifteen players, and *Monodramma* for soprano and orchestra), the dissonance factor is high—Górecki has no fear of "scontri," of collisions of the most ferocious sort—and the sheer physical energy is tremendous. Górecki also uses the tone clusters, slides, and special instrumental effects so characteristic of the Polish avant-garde of that time. The *Canti strumentali* are clearly inspired by Penderecki's *Threnody for the Victims of Hiroshima*

(1960), a work that made enough of a splash to attract wide notice outside the new-music community.

Górecki's fascination with what the musicologist Bohdan Pociej has described as a sense of a "slow, almost stubborn dragging from the depths"—something profoundly of the essence of the Third Symphony—is first manifest in the opening section of *Refrain*, an orchestral work from 1965. Here is the first hint of the "new" Górecki. It was in that year that the critic Stefan Jarocinski, summing up the Polish scene for an American journal, *The Musical Quarterly*, wrote about Górecki that "enormous power is latent in this unusually vital and sensitive composer. It is with great spiritual tension that we listen to his music, which is imbued with profound emotion and 'metaphysical' unrest."

It is hard to imagine a setting more wrong for the introduction of Górecki's Third Symphony than the Royan Festival. Royan was a place where one went to hear the spikiest new music by Barraqué, Kagel, Ligeti, Maderna, Penderecki, Stockhausen, Xenakis. The admirers of *Epitafium*, *Scontri, Genesis, Refrain*, and Górecki's first two symphonies were scandalized. To most of that audience, the Third Symphony, with its predominantly consonant modal harmonies, avoidance of violent contrast (to say nothing of collisions), eschewal of orchestral pointillism and anything else "colorful," was undisguised apostasy.

To many, this music, with its slow, patient unfolding, represents sublime metaphysical calm; others experience only maddening stasis. The dismay at Royan was fueled in considerable part by musical politics: the new work was perceived as a betrayal of the avant-garde. Some of the hostile criticism of Górecki in the aftermath of the astounding circulation of the Third Symphony has been "political" too. But we need to separate musical questions from musico-political ones; furthermore, we need to get rid of the idea that using major triads—or avoiding them—is a moral issue. Just as, for example, the densely packed music of Roger Sessions is not for everyone, neither is the Górecki Third. It is, among other things, a question of the listener's temperament and musical metabolism. Not everyone can slow down to Górecki's pace. Stravinsky once said that whenever he tried to listen to a Bruckner symphony he found himself mentally turning pages ahead of the conductor.

It is a reasonably reliable general rule that good composers remain good composers even when their aesthetic and expressive aims change. (It also works the other way, and composers who were dull serialists don't become interesting born-again tonalists either.) Górecki, who composed so well in his twenties and thirties, was still a very good composer when he wrote the Third Symphony and the works that followed it, such as the

Lerchenmusik for clarinet, cello, and piano (1984), and his two string quartets, *Already It Is Dusk* (1988) and *Quasi una fantasia* (1991).[3] Górecki's command of large musical spaces is imposing. The music sounds—and should sound—like free flow, but as Górecki said about the ten-voice canon in the Third Symphony's first movement, "Can you imagine how I had to use my brain?" His sense of span is equally remarkable in the thirty-minute String Quartet No. 2 and especially in the extraordinarily impressive forty-minute *Lerchenmusik*.

The musical language of the Third Symphony unites ancient and modern, a harmonic vocabulary that is based on the church modes of Renaissance music and an unmistakably twentieth-century sensibility and tone. In *The New Grove Dictionary of Music and Musicians*, Bohdan Pociej writes about Górecki's attraction to the past and cites "simple peasant devotion, liturgical organ music, the polyphony of Palestrina, the dynamism of Beethoven, and the force of the late Romantic orchestra" as among the most important elements to have nourished his music. It is worth noting that there is nothing "antiqued" about Górecki's modal music: he uses the modes for their musical strength and never for their associations or as atmosphere.

All three movements of the Third Symphony are hung on texts about mothers and the tragic deaths of their children.[4] The first is a lamentation from the collection of sacred songs at the Holy Cross Monastery at Łysa Góra. The words in which Mary mourns Jesus are embedded in the middle of the movement. Half the double basses begin the music with a song founded on E. When the melody has run its slow course, the other basses begin it a fifth higher, on B. With the successive entrances by other groups of strings, the melody slowly rises through the orchestra. Each new entrance is a fifth higher than the previous one; the imitations are not exact, however, because Górecki is using the Aeolian scale and avoids introducing accidentals outside that mode.

When all the strings are in and playing in eight separate parts, Górecki proceeds slowly to unwind the music until all the instruments except the now silent basses are united on E. Now we hear a new sound, piano and harp. Woodwinds enter, first flutes, then bassoons, horns, and trom-

---

[3] *Lerchenmusik* can be translated as "lark music," but it was named for Louise Lerche-Lerchenborg, who commissioned the work, and for Lerchenborg, the Danish castle where she runs a music festival.

[4] The symphony makes a very different sort of impact on the recording conducted by Wlodzimierz Kamirski with the soprano Stefania Woytowicz, the latter singing in her own language, and passionately focused on vivid declamation of the words and not at all on "beautiful singing." Zinman and Upshaw offer the comfort listeners long for; Górecki's compatriots make us feel the pain.

bones. (The more biting oboes and trumpets are absent from this orchestra.) Against a backcloth of softly dissonant orchestral sound, the soprano sings the simple lament. The strings break into her last note to resume the eight-part canon at its *quasi fortissimo* summit, just as though the slow winding-down and Mary's plaint had never occurred. This time the texture consists of ten strands. Again, voices drop out one by one, until only cellos, basses, and piano are left, sounding the low E that was the birthplace of this twenty-seven-minute arch.[5]

The Holy Cross Lamentation comes from the fifteenth century; the words Górecki sets in the second movement were written in his own lifetime. He has long been vitally interested in the Podhale, a mountainous area where Poland borders Slovakia. He has studied its history and collects artifacts from there. On one visit he found a book titled *The Slaughterhouse of Podhale*, a documentary history of the "Palace," the Gestapo headquarters in the town of Zakopane during the war. In it there was a photograph of a poem, a farewell to her mother, scratched into the wall of cell no. 3 by the eighteen-year-old Helena Wanda Błażusiakówna. Górecki thinks of this find as the moment when his vision of the Third Symphony began. Whereas the first movement is an orchestral piece with a brief but emotionally concentrated vocal center, the second is entirely a song, one whose simplicity perfectly matches the words.

To end his symphony, Górecki turns to folk poetry from the province of Opole, not many miles northwest of his home territory. Again it is a mother mourning her son, this time a soldier fallen in battle. Górecki originally wanted to use a folk melody, but in the end, he said, "I composed one of my own, in the style of folk song and using part of a church hymn." The flavor is authentic, the melody itself poignant. Górecki introduces another national element in alluding to one of Chopin's most haunting mazurkas, Opus 17, no. 4, whose strangely unsettled opening and closing harmonies slowly seesaw through much of this movement. Finally, when the mother prays that the birds may sing for her son and the flowers blossom about his grave, the song finds its way into the soft glow of A major.

I return to Jarocinski's assessment in 1965 "that enormous power is latent in this unusually vital and sensitive composer. It is with great spiritual tension that we listen to his music, which is imbued with profound emotion and 'metaphysical' unrest."

---

[5] Bartók is still in Górecki's life here. The model for the design of this movement—the building up and unwinding of a polyphonic texture with imitative entrances by fifths and the interruption by a contrasting middle section—is to be found in the first movement of Bartók's *Music for Strings, Percussion, and Celesta.*

Synku miły i wybrany
Rozdziel z matką swoje rany
A wszakom cię, synku miły, w swem
   sercu nosiła,
A takież tobie wiernie służyła,
Bo już jidziesz ode mnie, moja nadzieja
   miła.

My son, my chosen and beloved,
Share your wounds with your mother,
And because, dear son, I have always
   carried you in my heart
And always served you faithfully,
Speak to your mother to make her
   happy,
Although you are already leaving me,
   my cherished hope.
                     —Lamentation of the
                        Holy Cross Monastery

Mamo, nie płacz, nie.
Niebos Przeczysta Królowo,
Ty zawsze wspieraj mnie.
Zdrowaś Mario Łaskiś Pełna.

No, mother, do not weep,
Most chaste Queen of Heaven.
Support me always.
Hail, Mary, dear and glorious.
                     —Helena Wanda Błażusiakówna

Kajze mi sie podzioł
mój synocek miły?
Pewnie go w powstaniu
złe wrogi zabiły.

Where has he gone,
My dearest son?
Perhaps the cruel enemy
Killed him during the uprising.

Wy niedobrzy ludzie,
dlo Boga świętego,
cemuście zabili
synocka mojego?

Ah, you wicked people,
In the name of God the most Holy,
Tell me, why did you kill
My son?

Zodnej jo podpory
juz nie byda miała,
choćbych moje stare
ocy wypłakała.

Never again
Will I have his support.
Even if I cry
My old eyes out,

Choćby z mych łez gorzkich,
drugo Odra była,
jesce by synocka
mi nie ozywiła.

Not even if my bitter tears
Were to create another River Oder,
Would they restore to life
My son.

Lezy on tam w grobie,
a jo nie wiem kandy,
choć sie opytuja
między ludźmi wsandy.

He lies in his grave,
And I do not know where
Although I keep asking people
Everywhere.

Moze nieborocek
lezy kaj w dołecku,
a mógłby se lygać
na swoim przypiecku.

Perhaps the poor child
Lies in a rough ditch,
And instead, he could have been
Lying in his warm bed.

Ej, ćwierkejcie mu tam,
wy ptosecki boze,
kiedy mamulicka
znaleźć go nie moze.

A ty, boze kwiecie,
kwitnjize w około,
niech sie synockowi
choć lezy wesoło.

Oh, sing for him,
God's little song-birds,
Since his mother
Cannot find him.

And you, God's little flowers,
May you blossom all around
So that my son
May sleep a happy sleep.

—Opole folk song, transl.
Krystyna Carter

Howard Hanson

Howard Hanson

Howard Harold Hanson was born in Wahoo, Nebraska, on 28 October 1896 and died in Rochester, New York, on 26 February 1981.

Symphony No. 4, Opus 34, *Requiem*

Kyrie (Andante inquieto)
Requiescat (Largo)
Dies irae (Presto)
Lux aeterna (Largo pastorale)

Hanson composed his Symphony No. 4 in 1943 and led the Boston Symphony Orchestra in its first performance on 3 December that year. Before that, Hanson had conducted the orchestra of the Eastman School of Music in Rochester, New York, in an informal reading. The dedication reads "In memory of my Beloved Father." The work was awarded the Pulitzer Prize.

Two flutes and piccolo, two oboes, two clarinets and bass clarinet, two bassoons and contrabassoon, four horns, three trumpets, three trombones, tuba, timpani, snare drum, xylophone, and strings.

Along with Copland, Piston, and Sessions, Howard Hanson was one of the strong personalities that emerged on the American scene in the 1920s.

Reviewing a Boston Symphony concert in the January-February 1940 issue of *Modern Music*, Elliott Carter wrote: "Among the reactionary pieces played by the Boston orchestra, Howard Hanson's Third Symphony proved once again how skillful, fine, and ambitious a composer he is." For Carter, himself nurtured on Ives, Schoenberg, Bartók, and Stravinsky, "reactionary" is a disapproving adjective, and "ambitious" could be double-edged. On the other hand, "skillful" and "fine" are clear enough. In his 1971 survey *American Music Since 1910*, Hanson's exact contemporary, Virgil Thomson, is generous ("composer of a wide variety of excellent music . . . a Romantic composer of warm heart"), but when he wrote about the Symphony No. 2, the *Romantic*, twenty-four years earlier, he had not held back. Admitting that audiences enjoy Hanson's music, Thomson goes on to say: "I have never yet found in any work of his a single phrase or turn of harmony that did not sound familiar. His *Romantic* Symphony is no exception; it is as standardized in expression as it is eclectic in style. Not a surprise from beginning to end, nor any adventure."

I think I am finally too grown up to be offended by Hanson's entrenched conservatism per se, but I still find him a frustrating figure. For although each of his symphonies contains richly inspired passages of great beauty, each, with the exception of the Fourth, is disfigured by some appalling banality or blush-inducing claptrap. The first piece of his I ever heard—and hugely enjoyed—was one of his earliest works, *The Lament for Beowulf* (1925), and fifty years later I still find it appealing. I have come to wonder, though, whether the ambition Carter refers to, which I take to be ambition in the direction of grand symphonic utterance, was sometimes in Hanson's way. With the exception again of the Fourth Symphony, I most enjoy such works as the Concerto for Organ, Harp, and Strings (1941), the Serenade for Flute, Harp, and Strings (written to celebrate his own wedding to Margaret Elizabeth Nelson in 1946), and the exquisite Elegy in Memory of Serge Koussevitzky (1956), in which he speaks quietly, seems content to be a musician and skilled craftsman, and in which weight of utterance is not an issue.

Hanson's parents, Hans and Hilma Hanson, were Swedish immigrants. He learned piano from his mother, became an able cellist, studied at the University of Nebraska, the Institute of Musical Art (now the Juilliard School), and Northwestern University; while he was a senior at Northwestern, Frederick Stock and the Chicago Symphony performed his Symphonic Prelude. A lifetime of teaching began with an appointment to the faculty of the College of the Pacific at San Jose, California. He spent three years at the American Academy in Rome, where he wrote his Symphony No. 1, *Nordic*. On a visit to Rochester, he met and mightily impressed George Eastman of Kodak fame, who was looking for a director for the music school that had just been founded with his money and his name as an adjunct to the University of Rochester. And so it came about that Hanson, not quite twenty-eight, became director of that school; there he remained for forty years, until 1964.

Hanson's career prospered: his music was widely performed, and even the Metropolitan Opera, in one of its rare acknowledgments of American music, staged the premiere of *The Merry Mount* in 1934. He was also a good colleague to his fellow-composers, organizing an important annual festival of American music at Eastman and, as an expert and lively conductor, making valuable recordings of American music. His last act at Eastman was to found an Institute of American Music at the school. Convinced that with eminence came responsibility, he was tireless in service on committees, juries, and the like. In Rochester he served several times as intermediary between the management of the Rochester Philharmonic and the American Federation of Musicians during contract negotiations.

Hanson was as much a conservative in life as in music. He was retired by the time things were heating up in American universities and schools; however, he had by then begun to write an uninhibited weekly column for the Rochester *Times-Union,* and from that platform, aside from addressing a wide range of musical issues with vigorous common sense, he complained indefatigably about student protests against the Vietnam war, anarchy in public-school classrooms, and the beginnings of what we had not yet learned to call p.c.—all this of course the fault of "liberals."

I can attest to Hanson's sense of humor. Early in my time as a music critic, I once referred to his *Romantic* Symphony as "Sibelian slush." Some five or six years later I met Hanson for the first time at an international music critics' symposium at Eastman. Hanson, who spoke at the opening session, had something individual and appropriate to say to each of the dozen and a half participants. When he came to me, he told the "Sibelian slush" story. Then, after a beautifully timed silence, he added: "Of course Mr. Steinberg was quite wrong. [Applause]. It is my *Nordic* Symphony that is 'Sibelian slush.' "

As one of the American composers who were beneficiaries of Serge Koussevitzky's enthusiastic devotion to the cause of American music, Hanson had a long history with the Boston Symphony. In 1930, Koussevitzky himself conducted the premiere of Hanson's *Romantic* Symphony (No. 2), a Boston Symphony commission to celebrate the orchestra's fiftieth anniversary, and he invited Hanson to come to Boston to conduct the *Nordic* Symphony in 1929 as well as the first performances of the Third and Fourth symphonies (1939 and 1943 respectively). Appropriately enough, the touching *Elegy in Memory of Serge Koussevitzky* was also the fulfillment of a Boston commission, this one tendered by Charles Munch for the orchestra's seventy-fifth anniversary.

Each of the four movements of the Symphony No. 4 has a liturgical title drawn from the Roman Catholic Mass for the Dead.[1] The first is headed *Kyrie*, from *Kyrie eleison* (Lord, have mercy upon us). It begins with an upward leap in the French horn, a low grace note followed by a long, accented note an octave higher. While the horn sustains this long D, the lower strings begin a pattern of triplets in contrary motion, first pizzicato, then bowed. To this, the bassoons add a sustained line that corresponds roughly to what is happening in the strings but is just independent enough to create considerable dissonance and tension. All of this prepares the entrance of the four horns in unison, whose powerful chant represents the singing of the *Kyrie eleison* while the turbulent triplets in the strings continue.

The tempo slows down for a supple cello melody (also in three-note groups), actually a variant of the *Kyrie* chant. Then comes a new episode in the form of a pastoral dance, predominantly for woodwinds. The strings return to develop an impassioned melody, underneath which the trombones introduce a sturdy chorale. The music gathers momentum and force. Where it crests, another point of forceful dissonance, Hanson has written the words "Christe eleison" into the score. This is a departure from tradition: traditionally, the *Christe eleison* is softer, more lyric than the *Kyrie*, but Hanson makes the direct appeal to Christ the most intense point of his orchestral prayer. All the wind instruments cry "Christe" three times; then the music comes to an abrupt stop with two repetitions of the octave leap with which it began, the first loud for horns, the second soft with a solo bassoon.

The second movement is headed *Requiescat* in the score, but the program at the first performance gave it as *Elegy*. The tempo is very slow. Again, the first sound is that of a horn with the characteristic octave leap, and here, too, it introduces pizzicato cellos and basses. They move along a walking bass line, over which a bassoon plays a tender melody that is related both to this bass as well as to the impassioned string melody in the *Kyrie*. The chorale appears unobtrusively in the trombones and for a brief moment the oboe sings out an anguished phrase, but aside from that, the bassoon melody, which passes through the orchestra, serves as the thematic

---

[1] If he had not become a musician, Hanson would probably have become a Lutheran pastor. His Symphony No. 5, introduced in 1955 by Eugene Ormandy and the Philadelphia Orchestra, is a symphonic triptych inspired by the account of the Resurrection in the Gospel According to Saint John.

material for this movement. At the close, the strings in unison state the oboe phrase; its character, plaintive and tormented before, is now ominous. After a silence, a single bassoon quietly plays the octave leap. It is a poignantly sad and forlorn ending.

The third movement, the *Dies irae* (Day of Wrath), also begins with this leap; here, however, Hanson gives it to a group of brass instruments and diminishes the upward motion to a fifth in the horns and to a second in the trumpets. This is a fiery scherzo in which both the *Kyrie* theme and the upward leap are prominent.

Hanson heads the final slow movement *Lux aeterna* (Everlasting Light). The rising octave is again present, but here it is stretched and subtly embedded in a rich string texture: the first measure begins on G and the third on the G one octave higher. Here we relive much of what we experienced in the earlier movements: the *Kyrie*'s turbulent triplets, now whirling up even greater storms, the *Kyrie* theme itself, the chorale, the ominous theme that came at the end of the *Requiescat*. This movement is the most intense of the four as well as the one that is harmonically most complex. The chorale rings out grandly in the brass, while various instruments recall the supple cello theme from the first movement. It is a brief, gentle, fantastical dream. Then, three times we hear a low E in timpani and low strings, and three times the violins, very high, set on it the aureole of a C-major chord. It is loving and beatific, this farewell from son to father.

John Harbison

John Harbison was born in Orange, New Jersey, on 20 December 1938.

Symphony No. 2

Dawn (Luminoso)
Daylight (Con brio, non pesante)
Dusk (Poco largo, lambente)
Darkness (Inesorabile)

The San Francisco Symphony commissioned Harbison's Symphony No. 2 in celebration of the orchestra's seventy-fifth anniversary season. Harbison began the composition in the summer of 1985 and completed it the following summer, but then completely rewrote the end, which took until 8 September 1986. He reached what he calls "the legitimate double bar," finishing his last revisions, on 23 January 1987. Herbert Blomstedt conducted the San Francisco Symphony in the first performance on 13 May 1987. The work is "dedicated, in friendship, to Michael Steinberg."

Two flutes and piccolo (doubling third flute), two oboes and English horn, two clarinets with E-flat clarinet and bass clarinet, two bassoons and contrabassoon (doubling third bassoon), four horns, four trumpets, three trombones, tuba, timpani, glockenspiel, vibraphone, crotales, triangle, snare drum, suspended cymbals, sizzle cymbal, crash cymbals, tam-tam, gong (low), three tom-toms, side drum (lower than tom-toms), bass drum, temple blocks, castanets, thunder sheet, lion's roar, harp, piano, celesta, and strings.

In fear and trembling, I think I would fulfill my life
Only if I brought myself to make a public confession
Revealing a sham, my own and of my epoch:
We were permitted to shriek in the tongue of dwarfs and demons
But pure and generous words were forbidden
Under so stiff a penalty that whoever dared to pronounce one
Considered himself a lost man. . . .

—Czesław Miłosz[1]

Miłosz's poem, John Harbison has said, was his "theme song" during the composition of the Symphony No. 2. Language is an issue here, as it has been for many American composers in recent years. Early in 1987, when I was preparing to write a program note for the first performance of this work, Harbison gave me tapes. One was *Remembering Gatsby*, an overture he wrote for Robert Shaw and the Atlanta Symphony that used material for a *Great Gatsby* opera he had once hoped to write; the other was *Flight into Egypt*, a work composed for the Cantata Singers, a group in Cambridge, Massachusetts, devoted primarily to Baroque music, whose music director Harbison was at one time. *Remembering Gatsby* is a delectable entertainment, 1920s elegant; the austere *Flight into Egypt*, for which Harbison was awarded the 1986 Pulitzer Prize, comes from his Heinrich Schütz bent. Work on these two compositions overlapped work on the Symphony No. 2, which, he said, I would find to be between those two poles.

What all three works have in common is a passion for clarity. Some of Harbison's earlier music bothers him now because, he says, it does not have enough precision in harmonic movement and therefore not enough expressive range either, and in recent years he has been eager to escape a style "that reduces your harmonic possibilities." That has meant escaping some of his past, moving away from what his wife, the violinist Rose Mary Harbison, has been open and bloody-minded about calling "Princeton music."

[1]"A Task" copyright © 1975 by Czesław Miłosz. From *Selected Poems* by Czeslaw Miłosz, first published by the Ecco Press, New York, in 1980.

But John Harbison's life began at Princeton, where his father taught history with such brilliance and humanity as to make him a legend in university annals. Like so many composers' biographies, Harbison's begins with piano explorations at an early age, followed soon after by the invention of new pieces. By the time he was twelve he had started his own jazz band.

Beginning in the 1950s, Princeton had a lively music department. The dominant figures on the composition side were Roger Sessions, for whose work and person Harbison's respect and love are virtually limitless; Milton Babbitt, for whose systematic and theoretical approach he has little sympathy; and Earl Kim, for whose patience in working through details with him he remains ever grateful. These are the teachers with whom Harbison did his graduate work, though he had chosen Harvard for his undergraduate studies. The most useful thing he got from Harvard was a traveling fellowship that enabled him to spend a year in Berlin, where he studied composition with Boris Blacher and conducting with Hanns-Martin Schneidt, whose assistant he became at the famed Spandauer Kantorei.

Performance has always been an important part of Harbison's life. At Harvard he conducted the Bach Society Orchestra (his successors in that post include the composer John Adams as well as Hugh Wolff, music director of the Saint Paul Chamber Orchestra). In Cambridge, the Harbisons started a concert series in a basement coffee house where Joan Baez and Tom Rush had given some of their first concerts, and he accomplished memorable things with the Cantata Singers and Collage, a new-music ensemble. He has been on the faculty of MIT for many years, a position from which he has twice taken time off to serve as composer-in-residence to the Pittsburgh Symphony and the Los Angeles Philharmonic. His many awards include a MacArthur Fellowship.

In 1980, Harbison wrote a Violin Concerto for his wife. That was the point at which his musical language reached maximum harmonic clarity; the Concerto was also the work that occasioned the first attacks on him as a turncoat. He wanted to experience at first hand what tonal forces are like. But a composer writes music because he has something to say, and it is in honor of that mission that he struggles with such issues as language, clarity, and style. It was at this point in our conversation that Harbison quoted Miłosz—"pure and generous words were forbidden"—and he spoke with distress of the "screen of style": "For a thing to be acceptable, the veneer has to be hip." (Miłosz explores this subject further in his Harvard Norton lectures, *The Witness of Poetry.*) Harbison has been well aware that "going tonal" is likely to be misunderstood, that one will be abused as an apostate or hailed as born-again, and he is unhappy about people's tendency to hear "pieces under one banner or another without hearing any of the details of the piece. People don't listen well enough or hard enough."

Harbison has written three symphonies (the First was for Seiji Ozawa and the Boston Symphony, the Third for David Zinman and Baltimore), and he has found this a pleasingly American thing to do: "Americans like to assert their independence from dialectical imperatives like 'The Symphony is Dead.' So much of American musical achievement has been stated in this form." High on his list of twentieth-century symphonic heroes are Jean Sibelius ("the Schoenberg of the symphony in the sense of blasting out new ground") and Michael Tippett ("a late emerger . . . whose symphonies take the medium somewhere it hasn't been"). Given his excitement about these two composers, it is not surprising that he describes his own interest as being "in the symphony as a tone poem without a plot." That is a good description of Tippett's Symphony No. 4; the luminous sounds and thaumaturgic gestures of Tippett's Second, especially its Adagio, resonate in Harbison's beautiful symphony.

Harbison initially thought of his Symphony No. 2 as *Four Hymns: Dawn, Daylight, Dusk,* and *Darkness.* "*Four Hymns*" has been dropped, but the four movements retain their individual headings. The first movement, titled *Dawn* and marked luminoso, is in the nature of a prelude whose thematic material is slow to emerge in clearly etched form. It progresses from somewhat fragmentary music to coherent song and then dissolves again; this is also the plan of the entire symphony. The melodic lines are often highly embellished, and the scoring is colorful and active.

The first thing we hear is the bright bell-tone produced by a combination of glockenspiel, vibraphone, crotale, harp, and piano. Next, we become aware of trumpets repeatedly sounding a descending third, and since it is dawn, it is natural to hear this as a cock-crow. The trumpet, in fact, is something like an emblematic signature sound for this symphony. Impassioned string commentary surrounds the almost obsessive trumpet thirds. Woodwinds stir up a busy contrapuntal texture and divergent tempi are in conflict (a quick pulse below, slower violin music on top). All this creates a crescendo of tension, which is suddenly dispelled by the return of the opening music—the sounding bell and the trumpet's cock-crow.

A crash brings us into *Daylight*—"Con brio, non pesante." This movement is built on a scurry of quick sixteenth-notes, presented first in 4/4 time, then in triplets, finally in alternating fours and threes. This triple statement is varied twice, and at its climax the development becomes what Harbison calls "the quarrel of pulses," the music being all but reduced to its rhythms. The other element in this movement, one that comes to demand more and more of our attention, is a simple but arresting gesture of a short crescendo culminating in a bang. *Daylight* has a surprising end, a leisurely coda (grazioso) for the four clarinets. This slows down the pulse, ours as well as that of the music, and so anticipates and prepares the third movement.

"Twilight," says Harbison, "is my favorite time of day and it is the time I do most of my work." *Dusk*—"Poco largo, lambente" (flickering lightly and gently over a surface)—is the slow movement of the symphony and its heart. Violins and violas sing an expansive melody that is several times punctuated but not derailed by flashes of lightning and sudden blazes of sound. As the melody is altered, it takes on a luminous accompaniment of glockenspiel, vibraphone, harp, and celesta, and at moments it opens into chords, like a fan. This is intensely expressive music, poignant in the literal sense of the word. The landing points and punctuations are like suddenly touching a wound.

As in the previous movement, woodwind solos signal that the music is about to arrive at a close. The coda ends with a beautiful passage for soft trumpets and trombones against a sustained and dissolving chord for strings. As the strings disappear, a sextet of reed instruments takes their place, and this closing chord is the bridge into the finale.

Darkness—"Inesorabile"—is a nocturne whose first clearly defined idea is a rhythmically complex one sounded by muted brass. To this, woodwinds add a countermelody of stable, almost marchlike gait. Much later, triplets cut across the 4/4 gait. Although this third element has been slow to arrive, it also proves to have the most staying power. While the other musical ideas tend to dissolve, this one provides most of the material for the coda. There is an immense gathering of strength, every bit of which is needed for the ascent to the climax—a thunderous and terrifying collision, as of meteorites.

Only when the finale was far along did Harbison acknowledge that his original ending was not dark enough to be consonant with the symphony's expressive line up to that point. Long and painful introspection led him toward a newly conceived, quiet close. Thematic fragments appear at ever wider intervals until, finally, we hear another sustained chord for strings, against which woodwinds, impassively marking time, signal The End.

Karl Amadeus Hartmann

Karl Amadeus Hartmann was born in Munich, Germany, on 2 August 1905 and died there on 5 December 1963.

H artmann is one of those composers—Roger Sessions and Luigi Dallapiccola are others who come to mind—with whom the distance between achievement and reputation is absurd. He first worked with Joseph Haas, a student of Max Reger, but he always maintained that his real musical education began when he met Hermann Scherchen in 1927. Scherchen is chiefly remembered as a penetratingly intelligent, individual conductor who made many recordings in the early LP years, but, theorist, writer, editor, passionate advocate of new music, and free spirit generally, he was an amazingly multifaceted musician. He taught analysis and composition as well as conducting, and Bruno Maderna and Luigi Nono were also among his students.

Hartmann treasured Scherchen's teaching because he "was working from practical experience and dealt with the human element first and foremost." Hartmann was equally grateful that Scherchen dragged him into the twentieth century, particularly because he opened the world of Schoenberg and Berg to him. This was always a cause with Scherchen, who had cut his teeth as a professional when, at twenty, he had organized and led the preliminary rehearsals for the first performance of *Pierrot lunaire*.

Not that Hartmann was ever tempted or inclined to become a Schoenbergian. Like Bartók, Shostakovich, and Britten, he was amused on occasion to invent a theme consisting of all twelve notes of the chromatic scale, but as a ruling principle the twelve-note system held no charms for him. What overwhelmed him was the intensity of expression in Schoenberg's and Berg's music and the vocabulary of gestures with which those composers conveyed that intensity. It was like finding the antidote to the New Objectivity (Neue Sachlichkeit) represented by Hindemith, then in the forefront of German musical life.[1] For Hartmann, whose music is, above all, the expression of white-hot emotion, this was like finding a spring in the desert.

Much of the emotion in Hartmann's music arises from his anguish at what he saw happening in Germany. The Nazis, what they stood for and what they did, horrified and nauseated him. At the same time, he could not imagine an existence away from his homeland and language, not even from his native city, and so, after 1933, he entered what came to be called inner emigration. For a time he continued to get performances abroad, but he refused to participate in German musical life in any way, and more and more, what he composed went into a desk drawer.

Once, during the war, he went to Vienna for four lessons with Webern, the third, then totally ignored member of the Viennese trinity. Schoenberg had gone to America, Berg had died, and for Hartmann, working with Webern was a way of getting close to these heroes. In a way, it was comparable to the young Beethoven's having, in Count Waldstein's famous phrase, gone to Haydn to receive the spirit of the recently dead Mozart. Hartmann was happy to find another musician who cared about Mahler and Schoenberg, and analyzing Beethoven and Reger was illuminating, but he had no sense of having made personal contact and felt silenced by Webern's nationalistic and law-and-order-loving tolerance of the Nazis.

At war's end, Hartmann was flung from isolation into the whirlwind of public life. Politically and morally clean, he was in demand. One legacy of the Hitler years was that German musicians found themselves completely unknowing about most of what had happened in their field during the previous twelve years, a period in which Schoenberg, Bartók, Stravinsky, and Webern were among the mature composers doing some of their most significant work and in which a whole new crop of younger talents was beginning to assemble on the stage. With subsidies from the Bavarian government and Bavarian Radio, Hartmann organized and ran for the rest of his life a distinguished and admirably non-ideological series of new-music concerts called MUSICA VIVA, a name he took from a new-music

---

[1] Even though Hartmann rejected Hindemith's "objective" expressive stance and the aesthetics of the Neue Sachlichkeit, he nonetheless found some stimulation in Hindemith's musical vocabulary. This is especially evident in his Concerto funèbre for Violin and String Orchestra (1939, revised 1959).

magazine Scherchen had published in the early 1930s. For a time, he also served as dramaturg to the Bavarian State Opera and as music adviser to Bavarian Radio. The ideal of public service is something Hartmann could well have learned from his first teacher, Haas, who was much inclined that way; among other things, Haas, his own compositional conservatism notwithstanding, was one of the founders of the Donaueschingen new-music festival in 1921.

Most important, Hartmann, who had existed in silence from the age of twenty-eight to forty, years that should be crucially productive ones for an artist, at last began to compose regularly when the war was over—and for human audiences, not for the desk drawer. He destroyed or completely reworked what he had written earlier. This means that while several pieces include material from before the war, his existing oeuvre essentially comes from the brief period 1946 to 1963.

Probably Hartmann's most-played composition is the poignant *Concerto funebre* for Violin and String Orchestra, a work that is an expression both of grief and his desire to set something positive against the seeming "hopelessness of prospects for the spiritual" in 1939 (Hartmann thoroughly revised the concerto in 1959). It does not do, however, to imagine Hartmann as a Cassandra or a mourner in perpetual sackcloth: he was capable of veritable explosions of athleticism and joie de vivre. There are other concertos, chamber music, and an opera, *Simplicius Simplicissimus*. In 1962, he returned to vocal music, planning a major work based on Jean Giraudoux's wartime play *Sodome et Gomorrhe*, with its vision of the end of the world, but was able to complete only one magnificent baritone soliloquy before his death from pancreatic cancer.

His eight symphonies are the center of Hartmann's achievement. Much of No. 1, in which he sets words from Whitman's *When Lilacs Last in the Dooryard Bloom'd* (in German), goes back to 1936, but the work as we have it now dates from 1948, with revisions undertaken in 1950. By 1948 he had already written the work that he called Symphony No. 2— sorting out genesis and chronology is never easy with Hartmann, that constant reviser and recycler—and his first six symphonies were all achieved within an eight-year span.

None of these eight works conforms to a standard symphony pattern. No. 5, the only one whose design is "normal"—three movements, fast, slow, fast—is a *symphonie concertante* for an orchestra with no violins or violas (twice reworked from what was originally, in 1933, a Concerto for Trumpet and Winds); Hartmann's other three-movement symphony, No. 4, for string orchestra, turns that distribution of speeds inside out, a fast movement being enclosed between two impassioned slow ones. A plan Hartmann came to favor was having two large sections, each divided into two or more movements.[2] Fugues abound, and sometimes, perhaps following Beethoven's lead in the Piano Sonata, Opus 110, Hartmann likes to present fugues followed by variations upon them.

A notable feature of Hartmann's orchestral music is his coloristic fantasy and joyous delight in virtuosity. His percussion writing is enterprising, more so than any other of the period except for Bartók's and Varèse's, and he has special feeling for the possibilities of harp and keyboards. Here too he works in contrast, almost in opposition, to the strait-laced Hindemith, but has learned much from his study of Schoenberg's and Berg's imaginative orchestral scores. Hartmann was a composer whose proper instrument was the orchestra, and he had, truly, the lungs of a symphonist.

Adagio (Symphony No. 2)

Hartmann composed his Symphony No. 2 in 1946. Of his first six symphonies, it is the only one in which he uses no material from earlier abandoned or destroyed compositions. The first performance was given at the Donaueschingen Festival on 10 September 1950 by Hans Rosbaud and the Southwest German Radio Orchestra. The dedication is to the Belgian conductor, writer, and champion of new music, Paul Collaer, "great musician and wonderful man."

Three flutes (all doubling piccolo), three oboes (third doubling English horn), three clarinets (third doubling baritone saxophone), three bassoons (third doubling contrabassoon), four horns, three trumpets, three trombones, tuba, timpani, high chimes, vibraphone, cymbals, xylophone, snare drum, bass drum, tam-tam, church bell, harp, celesta, piano, and strings.

The title misleads. The Adagio (Symphony No. 2) is a single movement that takes about fifteen minutes, but it is by no means fifteen minutes of slow music.[3] To be exact, only the first four and nineteen of the last

---

[2] Hartmann could have found a precedent in Nielsen's Symphony No. 5 (1922) or William Schuman's Third (1941), but it is unlikely that he knew either work.

[3] An all-slow symphony is of course quite possible. Henryk Górecki's famous Third Symphony of 1976 is something like fifty-five minutes long, and all of it is lento or largo (when it is not molto lento). In 1986, the American composer Christopher Rouse wrote an impressive Symphony No. 1, which is in effect a single, twenty-five-minute slow movement and intended as a tribute to some of the great adagio composers, among whom Rouse names Hartmann, Allan Pettersson, William Schuman, Shostakovich, and Sibelius.

twenty-five measures are adagio. En route, the music achieves allegro and allegro con fuoco (a fiery allegro), with a metronome mark that indicates a very rapid clip indeed for the allegro. Involved here is what one might call the adagio principle. To offer a generalization that is, like all generalizations, dangerous if swallowed without caution, classical symphonies are essentially allegro experiences with more or less ample slow chapters for emotional and physical contrast; Hartmann's music, especially when he is in his elegiac and what the Germans call *bekenntnishaft* (confessional) mood, is essentially adagio with quick chapters, often quite ample ones, for emotional and physical contrast. "An *adagio*," he once wrote, "is always an introverted process." Inwardness is of the essence for Hartmann; hence the dominance of the adagio principle.

The first music, cellos and basses in bare octaves, is a brooding, Schubert *Unfinished* beginning. It is immediately punctuated by an amazing sound, a ten-note chord that includes the colors of muted trumpets, muted, trilling trombone, and the shimmering, flickering lights of chimes, vibraphone, cymbals (set to vibrating with a knitting needle), harp, celesta, and piano. Virtuoso percussion writing is a Hartmann hallmark. The strings resume their thought, which is again broken by the wild and magic bell-tree. When its ringing ceases, the strings are still there. They describe a rapid descent through more than four octaves and from *fortississimo* to *pianississimo,* and there the introduction ends. The vivid contrast between introversion and exuberance is one we shall constantly meet here, and on a larger scale.

Even before the second starburst, the tempo had begun to speed up. Now, Andante (poco rubato), a solitary baritone saxophone proposes a real theme. It is an extended melody, full of little embellishments, languorous, unpredictable. The meter is 5/4, as in fact it is for the entire symphony. The melody sounds Middle-Eastern, perhaps Jewish: that quality, as well as the choice of the saxophone, suggests to me celebration of the freedom once again to be able to use shapes and colors that had been condemned in the Third Reich as *entartet,* degenerate. This saxophone solo, like the dazzling bell-tree eruptions in the introduction, is defiantly and wonderfully un-German.

Other instruments, beginning with the flute and the first violins, explore the possibilities of the saxophone theme. The accompaniment (string chords with disturbing accents, timpani tattoos, piano trills, harp sweeps, flashes of light from the flute), though almost always in the *pianissimo* range, has a distinctive profile.

A new chapter begins when the tempo moves forward again, con moto e con calore. Not only are the beats themselves faster, they are subdivided into many quick notes. Luxuriant string melodies and rich contrapuntal textures dominate here. The music is caught in the grip of inexorable acceleration—through Andante con moto, poco più mosso, molto più mosso, stringendo (di molto), to Allegro con fuoco. The counterpoint becomes denser, more massy. At the climax, brass and percussion, who are directed to play passionately, let loose a tremendous uproar, and their blustrous fanfare finally clears the way for the next section, the Allegro con fuoco.

Strings and woodwinds have brilliant passages in sixteenth-notes; the piano adds wide-ranging and virtuosic darts of sound; trumpets and trombones, their bells pointed upward, cut through with bright chords. The sound is almost Broadway.[4] The music speeds up still further in a great festivity of sound, but at the climax, *fortississimo* and tempests of notes, Hartmann pulls back to maestoso.

With that begins the voyage home, which is greatly compressed compared to the outbound journey. Violins, *pppp* and molto tranquillo, play a glorious fantasy on the saxophone theme, spread now across a gamut of nearly three octaves. With that, the adagio tempo is reached. Clarinet and violins (now muted) carry the melody. Muted trumpets introduce one last bell-tree sparkler. Then, as at the beginning, the strings descend rapidly into *pianissimo* and to their lowest tones, leaving the symphony to end with the return of its dark opening phrase.

Symphony No. 8

I: *Cantilène*
II: *Dithyrambe:* Scherzo—Fugue

The Symphony No. 8 occupied Hartmann through most of 1960 and 1961, the score being completed at the beginning of 1962. Rafael Kubelik and the West German Radio Symphony Orchestra, Cologne, gave the first performance on 25 January 1963. The dedication is to Karl O. Koch and Dr. Eigel Kruttge, both members of the music staff of West German Radio.

[4] When European critics want to compliment an American orchestra, they write that it doesn't sound American. Hartmann, like many European musicians, seems to have associated "American" with "brilliant," and it is not surprising that his Symphony No. 7, commissioned by the Koussevitzky Music Foundation in the Library of Congress, is the one in which orchestral razzle-dazzle is most prominent.

Three flutes (all doubling piccolo), three oboes, three clarinets (third doubling bass clarinet), three bassoons (third doubling contrabassoon), four
horns, three trumpets, three trombones, tuba, timpani, bass drum, triangle,
tubular bells, two glockenspiels, two marimbas, two snare drums (one with,
one without snares), cymbals, two vibraphones, xylophone, tam-tam, two
harps, piano, celesta, and strings (at least 16-14-12-10-8).

Hartmann's last symphony—and last completed work—is laid out in the
two-movement plan he had come to find more and more stimulating in his
later pieces. The *Cantilène*, the first and slightly the longer of the two
parts, is one great arch; in contrast, the *Dithyrambe* is divided into sharply
profiled sections. There is, however, no break between the *Cantilène* and
the *Dithyrambe*.

The dramatic beginning—lento assai, con passione—jolts us into
wide-eyed alertness. Clarinet and vibraphone together play a jagged line
that traverses a range of nearly three octaves in wide leaps. Not only is
this marked *fff* and *con forza*, the players are explicitly asked to produce a
hard sound. This proclamation is punctuated by a succession of vivid sonorities, a brightly ringing chord for glockenspiel, xylophone, marimba,
celesta, harps, and piano, a flurry of *fortissimo* strings, a flutter-tongued
snarl for muted trumpets and trombones, and the like. Then, after a silence, the first movement proper begins.

The tempo is adagio; the sound is that of solo strings, with marimba,
vibraphone, harps, and piano adding delicate highlights. A fugue begins
to unfold, the second violin leading off. As the title *Cantilène* suggests, the
lines are songful, long, and intensely expressive. As so often in Hartmann,
adagio is but a point of departure: the tempo gets faster and the declamation more impassioned, and as this heightening of expression is in progress,
more and more string players join in to produce a corresponding increase
in the weight of the sound.

The movement consists of three such fugal expositions. The arrival at
the first great crest—fast (estatico)—precipitates a crisis. A huge percussion crescendo brings everything to a halt; then, following some orchestral
aftershocks, a bassoon begins an ornate melody which is passed to the
clarinet and eventually to the oboe. This long line is surrounded by a
constantly varied shimmering and flickering of half-lights. A brilliant passage for violins—Hartmann marks it "sehr virtuos"—initiates another
buildup. A trumpet, two piccolos, and all the violins utter a piercing
scream, which sets the tuned percussion and keyboards to an excited ringing. Now the music unwinds. The close is *pianissimo*, but agitated motion
still enlivens the texture.

Toward the end of the *Cantilène* a four-note figure had become prominent—two pitches in seesaw alternation, three very fast notes leading to a long one. That figure, played by the bassoon and the violas, was the last thing we heard in that movement. Now it continues, persistently and at high speed: the *Dithyrambe* has begun. In a footnote Hartmann explains that this is "a song of jubilation, culminating in wildly rapturous enthusiasm." We immediately sense a new kind of physicality. While in the *Cantilène* the measures are for the most part very large and filled in with patterns that are rhythmically complex, a sense of steady beat is inescapable in the *Dithyrambe*, the entire movement pushing forward in an unbroken 12/16 meter. To put it very simply, the *Dithyrambe*, unlike the *Cantilène*, is an invitation to foot-tapping.

This movement is in two sections, Scherzo and Fugue. The Scherzo itself scuttles by, mostly in *pianissimo*. It is followed by three variations, each at a higher dynamic level. Variation 1, molto leggiero (very light), moves between *piano* and *mezzo-forte*; at least it is supposed to. A *fortissimo* outburst turns the mood nasty, after which the "harmless" element makes a brave attempt at a return. Variation 2, impetuoso—sveglio (impetuous, alert), occupies the ground between *mezzo-forte* and *forte*, and the harmony becomes more dissonant. Variation 3, con fuoco e furioso, raises the dynamic level to *forte-fortissimo*. A finale per tutti, disturbed by constant retards and accelerations and notable for a bravura excursion for the timpani, ends this chapter.

The Fugue follows without break. Its subject contains the four-note figure that began the Scherzo; at the same time, it alludes to the music of the symphony's opening. In the Fugue, Hartmann continues his dramatic play of sudden interruptions and resumptions. With a joyous clatter of pitched percussion and keyboards the Dionysian festivities grow wilder. A jubilant trill for nearly the whole orchestra leads to sudden quiet. The violins sing a slow recitative. Threatening timpani undo the calm in a crescendo that carries them from *ppp* to *fff* in a few seconds; then two tumultuous measures send the symphony crashing to its end.

Joseph Haydn

Franz Joseph Haydn was born in Rohrau-on-the-Leitha, Lower Austria, on 31 March 1732 and died in Vienna on 31 May 1809.

The Early and Middle Years

The little we know about Haydn's early life comes, for the most part, from three biographies that appeared soon after his death: *Biographische Notizen über Joseph Haydn* by Georg August Griesinger, a Saxon diplomat; *Biographische Nachrichten über Joseph Haydn* by Albert Christoph Dies, a landscape painter from Hanover; and *Le Haydine, ovvere Lettere sulla vita e sulle opere del celebre Maestro Giuseppe Haydn* by Giuseppe Antonio Carpani, a Lombard man of letters. Griesinger, Dies, and Carpani all knew Haydn in his last years in Vienna, and in general their books agree. There is reason, however, to question the accuracy of some of the old gentleman's reminiscences, and one cannot be sure that the writers, all dilettantes in music, always understood him correctly. Carpani, moreover, has been suspected of embroidery.

This much seems beyond doubt: Haydn's father was a wagoner who also farmed, and the large family did a lot of singing at home after working hours. (Joseph's younger brother Michael became a very respectable composer.) About the time Haydn was six, he was sent to the house of an uncle and aunt for the furtherance of his musical education. From there he went to Vienna as a cathedral choirboy. By his own account, he listened more than he studied, but acquired a basic education in singing, keyboards, and violin, meanwhile teaching himself out of Johann Joseph Fux's esteemed treatise on composition, *Gradus ad Parnassum*. It is said that Georg Reutter, Haydn's choirmaster at Saint Stephen's, wanted to have the boy castrated when his voice began to change, but that may be one of the dozens of apocryphal stories that have proliferated all over the Haydn biography. At any rate, by about 1749 he was on his own, and for the next few years scraped together a minimal living at musical odd jobs: he told Griesinger that on any one Sunday he might find himself playing violin for the Brothers of Mercy in the suburb of Leopoldstadt at eight in the morning, organ in the private chapel of Count Haugwitz two hours later, and singing at Saint Stephen's for the eleven o'clock Mass. Likely as not, he would have a serenade gig in the evening.

In his early twenties he lived upstairs from the celebrated opera librettist Pietro Metastasio, who shared a large apartment with an old friend, Niccolò Martinez, Master of Ceremonies at the Papal Nunciature.[1] Metastasio got Haydn an appointment as teacher to the nine-year-old Marianne Martinez, a gifted child, and later a favorite duet partner of Mozart's. She was already studying voice with the famous Nicola Porpora, a composer, but best remembered as teacher of some of the most famous castrati of the day, including Farinelli and Caffarelli. For teaching Marianne, Haydn got free meals in the Metastasio-Martinez household; for accompanying her lessons with Porpora (and soon those of his other pupils) and for serving that coarse and irascible eminence as valet, he was remunerated with further training in singing, composition, and Italian.

Not least, through Metastasio, Martinez, and Porpora, Haydn made useful contacts in aristocratic music-loving circles. Thus he came to be music-master in the household of Baron Carl Joseph Fürnberg, for whom he may have written his first string quartets, and it was on Fürnberg's recommendation that at some point between 1757 and 1759 he at last became a capellmeister. His employer was Count Ferdinand Maximilian Morzin, whose castle was at Lukaveč near Pilsen. There Haydn wrote his first symphonies and much music for wind band. Soon, financial difficulties obliged Morzin to dissolve his orchestra. A guest, however, had heard it during Haydn's incumbency. This was Prince Paul Anton Esterházy, whose own capellmeister, Gregor Joseph Werner, was in his sixties and failing. Learn-

---

[1] For a struggling musician to be living in the same house with an eminence like Metastasio is not as unlikely as it sounds, for, as Rosemary Hughes puts it in her beautiful Haydn biography, "the old house, like others of its kind, sheltered a cross-section of Viennese life. Aristocracy lived at street-level, middle-class culture occupied the floors above, and servants, tradespeople, and poor devils such as music teachers lived under the roof." By strange chance, the aristocracy on this particular ground floor in the Michaeler-Haus was the Dowager Princess Eszterházy, whose sons Haydn would be serving for nearly thirty years.

ing that Haydn was free, Paul Anton engaged him as vice-capellmeister, and on 1 May 1761, the two entered into an arrangement that brought security and stimulating working conditions to the twenty-nine-year-old composer and excellent music and eternal luster to the name of Esterházy.

Haydn's three-year contract required him to comport himself as an honorable official in a noble household, to be temperate, mild, lenient, not overbearing in his dealings with his musicians. His work combined the responsibilities of a modern composer-in-residence, music director, principal conductor, general manager, librarian, custodian of instruments, personnel manager (responsible, among other matters, for ensuring that members of the orchestra appeared in clean white stockings and white linen, with a freshly powdered queue or tie-wig), and music teacher. The prince retained performing and publishing rights to Haydn's compositions. Haydn was subordinate to Werner in choral music but otherwise independent, and it was understood that if all went well, he could look forward to becoming Werner's successor as capellmeister.

His Serene Highness was a widely traveled, educated man, an amateur violinist and cellist, and a refined connoisseur. He enjoyed spending money on music and had a splendid library. Two years before Haydn's appointment, he had sent his concertmaster, Luigi Tomasini, himself a composer of repute, on a study trip to Venice. New musicians were engaged along with Haydn, and the orchestra in 1761 consisted of one flutist, pairs of oboists, bassoonists, and hornists, five violinists, two cellists, and a bass player. Many of the players doubled on other instruments, and other players could be borrowed as needed from the parish church or a neighboring town. Haydn led his symphonies from the harpsichord.

In 1766, Haydn became capellmeister upon the death of Werner, more or less retired since Haydn's arrival, but a bitter, difficult emeritus. Haydn's first patron, Prince Paul Anton, had died in 1762, to be succeeded by his younger brother Nikolaus. The new prince was known as "der Prachtliebende" (lover of pomp), and he was indeed a vigorous advocate of conspicuous consumption. Impressed by a visit to Versailles, he undertook to convert a modest hunting lodge south of the Neusiedler Lake near what is now the Austro-Hungarian border into an establishment to rival the famed French palace. The budget for the musical household was ample, and among the Esterházy holdings was a paper factory, one whole division of which was given over to the production of music paper.

Soon after Nikolaus's accession, Haydn's salary was raised by half, but even so, the 1760s were not easy for him. He was overburdened with administrative duties at least as much as with musical (the manuscript of his D-major Horn Concerto of 1762 is marked "written in my sleep"). In 1768, his house burned down: one of the compositions probably lost in the fire was his only Concerto for Double Bass. Nikolaus himself played a difficult instrument called the baryton. It was bowed, but had additional wire strings to be plucked by the left thumb, and over the years Haydn composed a large number of beautiful, now virtually useless trios for this soon-to-be extinct creature.[2]

The entire household was moved for months at a time from Eisenstadt to Eszterháza (whose spelling Haydn usually simplified to "Estoras"): for more on that, see the essay note on the *Farewell* Symphony, No. 45. This Versailles in the marshes of Burgenland—"my desert," Haydn called it— had an opera house and a marionette theater, and much of Haydn's energy went into the composition of operas and incidental music for plays. Many years later, reminiscing with his biographer Georg August Griesinger, Haydn said about that period: "My prince was satisfied with all my works. I was applauded and as leader of an orchestra I could experiment, observe what strengthens an effect and what weakens it, and thus improve, add, eliminate, dare. I was cut off from the world. No one around me could have doubts about me or torment me, and I was forced to become original."

In his isolation, Haydn had little idea how famous he was becoming. Even in the 1760s his reputation had begun to grow beyond the confines of Eisenstadt and Eszterháza. In 1766, a dozen of his symphonies were listed in the catalogue of the Leipzig publisher Breitkopf. A good many of his works were published in Paris, and, a sure tribute, still more that were not by him were issued under his name because that would help sales. His scores were also well represented in the discriminatingly assembled libraries of Bavarian, Austrian, and North Italian monasteries and courts.[3]

But most of this music went out of circulation after Haydn's death. Except for Brahms, the nineteenth century didn't think much of Haydn: Schumann described him as "an old family friend whom one receives gladly and respectfully but who has nothing new to tell us." For more than a hundred years, Haydn's fame rested on just a few of his late string quartets and symphonies, and on *The Creation* and *The Seasons*.

Today you can buy recordings of all the Haydn symphonies and have

---

[2] In the last chapter of his *General History of Music*, Dr. Charles Burney describes hearing Andreas Lidl, a former member of the Esterházy orchestra, play "with exquisite taste and expression upon this ungrateful instrument, with the additional embarrassment of base strings at the back of the neck, with which he accompanied himself, an admirable expedient in a desert, or even in a house, where there is but one musician; but to be at the trouble of accompanying yourself in a great concert, surrounded by idle performers who could take the trouble off your hands, and leave them more at liberty to execute, express, and embellish the principal melody, seemed at best a work of supererogation."

[3] Something to know is that the numbers of the Haydn symphonies are not his own, but were assigned by Eusebius Mandyczewski, the scholar who first tried to bring order into the uncharted territory of the Haydn symphonies at the beginning of the twentieth century. For the most part they give an accurate idea of the chronology, and the consensus has been to keep using them.

a choice of performances for more than half of them. We take this easy access for granted, but I remember well when "Haydn symphonies" meant the great twelve written for London and maybe half a dozen more, such as No. 88, the curious and wonderful No. 86 (Bruno Walter had recorded it), *The Bear* and *The Hen* (Nos. 82 and 83), and of course the *Farewell.* We knew that there must be symphonies to go with all the numbers below 82, but other than the *Farewell* we never heard them. A poorly planned attempt to get a complete Haydn edition under way in 1909, the centenary of Haydn's death, yielded scores of the first forty symphonies (without orchestral parts to go with them), but aside from that, you could hardly even find scores to look at in a library.

All this changed when, in 1949, the twenty-three-year-old H. C. Robbins Landon founded a Haydn Society for the purpose of making another attempt at a complete Haydn edition. This one would be designed for performers as well as scholars, and Landon also intended to get most of Haydn's music recorded. By no means all of this came to fruition. Even now, Haydn alone among composers of his stature is unrepresented by a complete, scholarly edition of his works, though one is at last satisfactorily, if slowly, in progress. Nonetheless, the founding of the Haydn Society was a watershed, and it was also Landon who undertook a massive cleanup job involving hundreds of textual corruptions—changes of harmony, orchestration, dynamics, etc.—that had blurred our perception of Haydn's genius.

Symphony No. 45 in F-sharp minor, *Farewell*

> *Allegro assai*
> *Adagio*
> *Menuet: Allegretto*
> *Finale: Presto—Adagio*

Haydn wrote the *Farewell* Symphony in 1772 and led its first performance at Eszterháza that year.

Two oboes, bassoon, two horns, and strings, plus harpsichord.

The more enchanted Prince Nicholas Esterházy became with the pseudo-Versailles he had built on the Neusiedler Lake near what is now the

Austro-Hungarian border, the longer were the periods of service he demanded there from his musicians. As capellmeister, Haydn enjoyed some perquisites and privileges, but for the rank and file of the orchestra, the long sojourns in the country meant painful separation from their families. (Haydn's own childless marriage was unhappy; he had a long and also unhappy affair with Luigia Polzelli, one of the singers in the Esterházy establishment.)

In 1772 it seemed as though the household would never return to Eisenstadt, and the increasingly depressed musicians appealed to Haydn for help. His response was to write a symphony in which the customary quick finale was broken off in mid-course, the music then continuing as a second slow movement. During the course of this Adagio, one player after another blew out the candle at his desk and departed, leaving just two violinists on stage at the end, concertmaster Luigi Tomasini and Haydn himself. The prince got the point, and the court left for town the next day. This, at least, is the most likely of the various stories tied to this piece.

The *Farewell* Symphony owes a large part of its present fame to that anecdote, but it was one of Haydn's most valued, most circulated, most played symphonies even before the story came to be generally known in the 1780s. Haydn's originality was most strikingly manifested in the extraordinary series of intensely dramatic works in minor keys he wrote around 1770, and the *Farewell* itself is, on any terms and by any standards, one of Haydn's greatest symphonies. Minor-key symphonies are rare and special in this period, but the key of F-sharp minor is rare among the rare. The blacksmith at Eszterháza had to build new crooks, additional lengths of tubing, for the horns in F-sharp needed in the minuet.

Haydn's F-sharp minor Allegro assai, a very quick and forceful allegro, is music of uncommon passion, with its striding arpeggio theme and its tensely syncopated accompaniments. Introducing a completely new theme of enchanting grace in the middle of the development, and not ceasing to elaborate and expand material long after we expect the settling process of recapitulation to have begun, it is as remarkable in form as in feeling.

There follows a limpid and muted Adagio, which, like the Andante in Mozart's E-flat Symphony, seems to promise more innocence than it delivers: the tone of voice stays low, but the modulations are amazing adventures. Then comes a Minuet: robust, but full of surprises at every turn in harmony (the first bass entrance!), rhythm, and scoring. The horn-dominated trio quotes a Gregorian melody from the Holy Week liturgy, one Haydn had used some years earlier in his *Lamentatione* Symphony, No. 26.

The Finale begins at great speed and in a condition of high urgency. Where we expect it to be over—it would be a terse finale, but not implausibly so—Haydn makes a large harmonic loop and comes to rest on the dominant of the home key, as though he were to begin again. A long silence is broken by an adagio in A major, the same key as the "real" slow movement, but quite unprepared and unexpected here. After a colorful little passage for the winds, the first oboe and second horn fall silent. To reassure the puzzled copyist, Haydn writes "nichts mehr" (nothing more) in his autograph.

The music resumes, and one by one, instruments play farewell solos and leave: bassoon, second oboe, first horn, double bass (whose solo, more elaborate than that of the others, moves the music into its final harmonic destination of F-sharp major). The survivors play the gently pathos-filled slow music again. The cello leaves, then all the violins but two, then the viola. The two remaining violins are muted and their music, too, leaving us somewhere between tears and a smile, recedes into silence and darkness.

Symphony No. 64 in A major, *Tempora mutantur*

Allegro con spirito
Largo
Menuetto
Finale: Presto

Haydn wrote this symphony about 1773 and presumably led its first performance at Eszterháza soon after.

Two oboes, two horns, bassoon (to double the bass line), and strings.

The orchestral parts prepared for this symphony at Eszterháza are headed "Tempora mutantur etc." The complete Latin tag runs "Tempora mutantur, nos et mutamur in illis. Quomodo? Fit semper tempore peior homo." In English: "The times change and we change with them. How? As they become worse, so do we." *The Oxford Dictionary of Quotations* attributes this (with slightly different wording) to the *Description of England* by the sixteenth-century historian William Harrison; according to *Bartlett's Familiar Quotations* it also occurs in Raphael Holinshed's *Chronicles of En-*

gland, the book one constantly encounters in footnotes to Shakespeare and which came out in 1578, one year after Harrison's work.

Haydn would have known it from the collection of *Epigrammata* published in 1615 by the Welsh writer John Owen. Jonathan Foster wrote in an article in the *Haydn Yearbook:* "Most Europeans of literary culture in the seventeenth and eighteenth centuries were acquainted with the works of Owen, ten books of epigrams which commanded extraordinary influence, particularly in German literature. The [tempora mutantur] couplet, and especially the first line, became world-famous. To this day the first line can be seen on clocks and sundials." Seeking an explanation for the connection between Haydn's symphony and Owen's epigram, Foster suggests that the first line can be sung to the theme of the Finale, but the jury is still out on that one.

The symphony begins *pianissimo,* which is in itself extraordinary: an opening theme may well be quiet, but the normal thing would be to preface it with a strong chord or even a sequence of them (among many examples in Haydn are the symphonies No. 61 and No. 65). Here Haydn turns the cliché around and gives us two bars of quiet music followed by two that are emphatic (and with thematic material thrust right through the formal dominant and tonic chords). Moreover, the instant replay of these opening measures turns out to be not just a repetition but a subtle variant.

Before he has gone much farther, Haydn demonstrates the polyphonic possibilities of his theme and, in a series of syncopated measures in alternating *piano* and *forte,* makes a strong statement about the range of the harmonic territory he intends to explore. Toward the end of the exposition, in a gently curving melody beautifully scored for violins and violas in octaves, he waxes positively Schubertian in the shadows he casts with his sudden turn to C major.

The second movement is an even more astonishing inspiration. Marked largo and in 3/4 time, it has close cousins in the Adagio of the Symphony No. 75 and the Largo of No. 88, and as in No. 75, the strings are muted. Here, however, the hymn-like tranquillity of the theme is unsettled—quietly, but dramatically and inexorably—by the silences Haydn uses to force its phrases apart, silences that take the place of the phrase-endings and harmonic resolutions we wait for in vain, silences that cancel our expectations of symmetry. Here, too, there are unexpected darkenings of the landscape. Haydn's sense of orchestral resource is wonderful: for a long time we hear only muted strings, but when wind instruments do appear, from the first unassertive addition of oboes to the dramatic (but *pianissimo*) intervention of the two horns in the coda, placement and effect are superb.

Minuet and trio, sharing a predilection for amusing play with wide intervals, provide a moment's respite after the intensity and the surprises of the first two movements. The Finale, with its asymmetries, tensions, and immense forward-moving energy, takes us back to Haydn in a mood where all his craft and discipline are needed to contain the abundance of his wit, invention, and originality.

The Paris Symphonies and Their Aftermath

Even though Haydn himself worked in isolation during his years with the Esterházys, his music had circulated widely, even reaching America. Most particularly there was a Haydn vogue in Paris. Throughout the 1780s Haydn was in correspondence with patrons, publishers, and concert managers there, and in 1784 or 1785 his French admirers commissioned some new music from him.

The initiative came from an educated connoisseur and patron, then in his late twenties, Claude-François-Marie Rigoley, Count d'Ogny, Postmaster-General of France and the owner of one of the largest music libraries of his day. The count was deeply involved in the affairs of a Masonic concert series in Paris, Le Concert de la Loge Olympique, and it was for this organization and its fine and large Paris orchestra (forty violins, ten basses!) and its conductor, the glamorous mulatto composer and violinist from Guadeloupe, Joseph Boulogne, Chevalier de Saint-Georges, that Haydn wrote the symphonies that now bear the numbers 82–87. (Haydn himself became a Freemason in Vienna in 1785, joining the lodge "True Harmony" in February of that year.) D'Ogny offered the impressive sum of 25 louis d'or for each symphony, plus an additional 5 louis for the publication rights. This struck Haydn as "un prix magnifique" and was indeed, and by some margin, the largest fee he had ever received for his music.

The Loge Olympique symphonies, generally referred to now as the Paris symphonies, are Nos. 82–87. We do not know the order of their composition. No. 85 early on had the cachet of being the favorite of Queen Marie Antoinette (it is certainly the one that goes best with her Rococo taste for playing shepherdess) and was thus named La Reine de France or simply La Reine. Especially popular in its own day and all through the nineteenth century, La Reine was one of the first Haydn symphonies to cross the Atlantic, getting performances in Philadelphia and New York in the early 1790s. Nos. 82 and 83, with the zoological nicknames The Bear and The Hen, also became instantly and inextinguishably popular.

No. 86, a marvel of a piece, began to gain some currency in modern times thanks to a delightfully on-its-toes 1938 recording by Bruno Walter and, appropriately enough, the Orchestra of the Paris Conservatory Concerts. At the extreme of obscurity we find the beautiful Symphony in A major, No. 87: it had no publication between the 1780s and 1949, and its performance at a New Friends of Music concert in New York in 1940 was the first in well over a hundred years. The elegant No. 84 is, if anything, even rarer; I have yet to encounter it in concert.

A happy consequence of Haydn's success in Paris was that Count d'Ogny asked for some symphonies for his personal collection, and in 1788–89, Haydn wrote three new ones (90–92) for him and Prince Krafft-Ernst von Oettingen-Wallerstein. They and the two (88 and 89) he wrote in 1787 for Johann Tost, a wealthy Viennese businessman who in his young years had been a violinist in the Esterházy orchestra, were perfect preparation for the achievement of the final great twelve for London.

Symphony No. 86 in D major

> Adagio—Allegro spiritoso
> Capriccio: Largo
> Menuet: Allegretto
> Finale: Allegro con spirito

Haydn composed this symphony in 1786. The first performance was given in Paris the following year in the Concert de la Loge Olympique series under the direction of Joseph Boulogne, Chevalier de Saint-Georges.

Flute, two oboes, two bassoons, two horns, two trumpets, timpani, and strings.

The Adagio introduction begins quietly: Haydn obviously had confidence in the good manners of the Loge Olympique audience. The lyricism of the first sentence soon gives way to the rhetoric of scales, flourishes, and tremolandos. Its close carefully prepares the arrival of the Allegro and with that arrival the resumption of the tonic, D major. The more pleasing our surprise, therefore, when the Allegro begins on a chord situated at a kind of slant to the tonic—the "off-tonic," Robbins Landon calls it. This device is one to which Haydn would return in particularly subtle variants and to equally delightful effect in the *Oxford* Symphony and in the *Surprise*.

This entrance at an angle is more than a momentary pleasure: it invites many a witty touch later on. One of these occurs when Haydn has reached that stage of his exposition where we expect him to establish a new key and perhaps bring in a new theme to go with it. This turns out to be one of those pieces in which he leads us to believe that there will be no new theme, for at the crucial moment it is the old one that reappears, making its slantwise entrance, but now "off-dominant," as it were. Only after that does Haydn close the exposition with a new idea, one as squarely centered harmonically as the other was teasingly tilted. The extensive development, which is actually one measure longer than the exposition, shows us still more about the possibilities of the first theme and its enchanting bias. And, as he is wont to do when the development is extended, Haydn rather compresses the recapitulation.

The second movement is the most remarkable. Haydn calls it a capriccio, and it exhibits a fascinating mixture of whimsy and gravity. The tempo and character mark of "largo," rare in Haydn's slow movements, often implies that something flexible and "speaking" should be brought into the performance. Three notes, quiet and staccato, define a chord of G major. This chord, thus articulated, serves as a springboard both for the theme it introduces and for each important structural event in the movement. (It recurs seven more times in all.)

To begin with, two appearances of this chord initiate an astoundingly varied paragraph that contains pathos, lyricism, gentle humor, and stormy rhetoric. Haydn keeps the staccato articulation under the first lyric/pathetic phrases, thus integrating all the elements he has introduced thus far. The next pair of these chords modulates within itself, the first being in G major as before, but the repeat coming in A minor. The pair after that reverses this procedure, going from E minor home to G major. The final two manifestations are not pairwise; just when and how they occur I shall leave as happy surprises for you. An amazing, amazing movement.

By contrast, the Minuet begins sturdily and plainly. We soon discover, though, that Haydn has something other than simplicity in mind. After the first twelve bars, he develops his theme at length and with a degree of contrapuntal ambition that may well remind us of the corresponding movement in Mozart's still unwritten Symphony No. 40 in G minor. The trio, as irresistible a ländler as Haydn—or anyone—ever wrote, is genuinely and delectably naive.

The Finale is in every way brilliant, and it also feels "big." No doubt the 4/4 meter, with its broader measures, exceedingly rare in a Haydn finale, contributes to this. Here too, one feels Mozart's presence, particularly the *Haffner* Symphony, in a way that is relatively infrequent in Haydn's symphonies. The six Loge Olympique symphonies are not, as a whole, notably Mozartian, but here it is as though Haydn, deeply acquainted with and lovingly in awe of his younger contemporary's work, were mindful of what Mozart had done with his *Paris* Symphony of 1778 to expand Parisian notions of "symphony."

Symphony No. 88 in G major

> *Adagio—Allegro*
> *Largo*
> *Menuetto: Allegretto*
> *Finale: Allegro con spirito*

Haydn wrote this symphony about 1787. Date and circumstances of the first performance are not known, but it is most likely to have occurred in Paris. Some readers may recall seeing this symphony titled "Letter V." The explanation for this oddity is that in the nineteenth century, many Haydn symphonies were identified by their call letters in the catalogue of the Royal Philharmonic Society in London.

Flute, two oboes, two bassoons, two horns, two trumpets, timpani, and strings.

This is one of the last symphonies Haydn wrote before the epiphany of the great dozen for London, and it is already one of those composed, not just *pro domo* at Eszterháza, but for the wider world. The work helped prepare the way for Haydn's conquest of London in the 1790s, being both performed and published there in 1789. Along with No. 89, Haydn sent it to Paris, where Nos. 82–87 had already been enthusiastically received, by way of a certain Johann Tost, one of the Eszterháza violinists, who was to sell the two works at the best possible price. He accomplished this, but at the same time, he foisted off on the publisher Jean-Georges Sieber a symphony by Adalbert Gyrowetz as being yet another work by Haydn. Tost's unscrupulous musical merchandising was not confined to this maneuver, and there was considerable and testy correspondence about it all between Haydn, Sieber, and the Viennese publisher Artaria. (Tost soon switched to being a full-time businessman and part-time violinist and as such, presumably after some sort of reconciliation, became the dedicatee of three sets of Haydn string quartets, opp. 54, 55, and 64.)[4]

No. 88 has long been one of Haydn's most popular symphonies; for years, in fact, it was one of very few outside the London series to get regular performances at all. It is surely one of his most generously inventive. The gestures of the introductory Adagio are grand, but their scoring is contained, trumpets and drums being held in reserve for the time being. The Parisians 200–some years ago must have remarked on the trumpeters and the drummer sitting silent for so long and wondered when they would come into action; today's record and radio listener, not seeing those players, gets a wonderful and very Haydnesque shock when at last they do enter. The Allegro is rustic in manner and big-city intellectual in its working out, a delightful combination.

The Largo begins like a sublime hymn. From the first bars, where the eloquent melody is given to solo cello and solo oboe in octaves, the fascinatingly original scoring has an extraordinary glow. Brahms said, or so the story goes, that he wanted his Ninth to sound like this movement. The theme is richer upon each of its returns. Four times the serenity of the great song is interrupted by powerfully dissonant outbursts, and it is for these dramatic moments, so unexpected in their context, that Haydn has saved his trumpets and timpani.

With the Minuet we return to the country, as it were, and the trio even gives us bagpipe drones. The Finale, among Haydn's most spirited and amusing, is based on one of those themes with a double upbeat that allow for such diverting "when is it going to come back?" games. We can meet several more of such themes, ever more inventively used, in the last movements of the London symphonies.

Symphony No. 92 in G major, *Oxford*

Adagio—Allegro spiritoso
Adagio
Menuet: Allegretto
Presto

Haydn composed this symphony in 1788 or 1789, dedicating it to Claude-François-Marie Rigoley, Count d'Ogny, who had commissioned it. D'Ogny

[4]The title page of the first edition of Mozart's D-major Viola Quintet, K.593, refers to a "Hungarian amateur" as the instigator of that great work. This was probably also Tost.

was backer of a concert series sponsored in Paris by the Loge Olympique for which Haydn had written his symphonies Nos. 82–87 five years earlier; presumably the Symphony No. 92 had its first performance under those auspices. Haydn conducted it at his first London concert on 11 March 1791 and repeated it "by particular Desire" at his concerts on 18 March and 15 April.[5] Most famously, Haydn led a performance of this symphony at the Sheldonian Theatre, Oxford University, on 7 July 1791, when he was awarded an honorary doctorate, hence the symphony's nickname.

Flute, two oboes, two bassoons, two horns, two trumpets, timpani, and strings. The trumpets and drums appear to have been an afterthought.

Haydn's appearance at the Sheldonian is emblematic of his emergence in his late fifties as a celebrity, everything that would be expressed today with getting on the cover of *Time* and being the subject of a segment of *60 Minutes*. It was the historian Charles Burney, having earned his own doctorate in music at University College, Oxford, who proposed that Haydn be given an honorary degree and who made all the arrangements.

Haydn's token degree exercise was the composition of an ingenious three-voice canon on the text "Thy voice, o Harmony, is divine" and the conducting of three concerts. At the presentation of the degree in the Sheldonian Theatre, Haydn responded to the applause by raising the ends of his robe and saying loudly "I thank you," whereupon those present replied by calling up to him, "You speak very good English."

Because Haydn had arrived from London later than expected, he had to conduct a symphony already familiar to the Oxford musicians, there being no time for a rehearsal; however, we do not know which one was chosen. A rehearsal was scheduled for the second morning, and that evening the symphony now called the *Oxford* was played to the same acclaim it had already received at its three performances at Johann Peter Salomon's concerts in London.

It is the last symphony Haydn wrote before the epiphany of the great dozen for London. Rich in invention, melodic charm, orchestral brilliance, humor, and that easy intellectual luxuriance so central to Haydn's musical personality, it was the perfect choice for his introduction to London and for the momentous occasion at Oxford.

Haydn begins with slow music, slow *and* quiet. His slow introductions

[5] The soloist at the April concert was the eleven- or twelve-year-old George Bridgetower, the mulatto violinist for whom Beethoven later wrote his best-known violin sonata, which, however, after an alleged quarrel over a woman he rededicated to Rodolphe Kreutzer.

are predominantly quiet, but most often they start with a forceful call to attention. Not here. For thirteen bars of Adagio he gives us strings alone, and the full complement of woodwinds with the pair of French horns is heard in only two measures of *forte*. The gentle melody is simple, but the flowing second-violin, viola, and cello lines give it astonishing life. Clarity gives way to mystery, and the music disappears into silence in a very strange place indeed.

Stranger still, though, is what happens next. The Allegro begins as if in mid-thought on the dominant-seventh chord of the home key of G major, not in itself a strange chord in the least, but made to sound foreign and surprising by the elaborate non-preparation for it in the last seconds of the introduction. This first theme, boldly answering the quiet question posed in the introduction, dominates the movement from here on. It even reappears where you might well expect a new, second theme, but that is a familiar strategy of Haydn's, wit and husbandry combined. A cute hands-in-pockets whistling theme, charmingly adorned with flute scales, brings the exposition to an end.

Even in this exposition Haydn has shown that he invented the first theme for its contrapuntal potential. Now, in the development, he goes to town in a big way. The polyphony itself is a motor, but the energy of the music is further heightened by all the off-beat accents as the lines intertwine at their densest. Compared with the approach from the introduction, the re-entrance into the first theme is reassuringly normal. What is, however, by no means ordinary is that Haydn has no intention of stopping his development just because he has entered the recapitulation. The exposition is sixty-two measures long, the recapitulation 108, and those numbers tell their own story. The development proper was dazzling, but the recapitulation, with its expansions, reshufflings, its exuberant inability to let anything alone, far outdoes it in adventure. This is as brilliant a sonata movement as any that Haydn ever made up, and that means they don't come more brilliant in anybody's catalogue.

The slow movement is expansively lyrical, with wonderful, delicately dissonant commentary by the solo flute and oboe. For contrast Haydn gives us an energetic tutti in D minor, actually his first forceful trumpet-and-drum music in this symphony. The coda, with the pathos of its broken-off runs for flute and violins, and its cadenza-like woodwind quartet, is amazing.[6]

The Minuet is vigorous and funny. I am not about to explain or other-

---

[6] Haydn's failure as Beethoven's teacher when it came to their formal lessons in Vienna is famous, but these "disintegrating" passages are yet another example of the sort of thing Beethoven learned from his study of Haydn's scores.

wise anticipate Haydn's jokes, but you might just try to keep track of the regular ONE-two-three when the horns with pizzicato strings begin the trio. Beethoven remembered this movement and used it well when he wrote the Minuet in his Eighth Symphony.

The finale begins with one of Haydn's spritziest tunes, parsimoniously unharmonized, with only a single cello rocking back and forth on the keynote G. Haydn shows us not only that this super-simple bass can take on a further dimension of humor when it is assigned to other instruments, but, more subtly, that because the first presentation of the theme is so studiedly neutral there is more room for the inexhaustible scope of his invention. The composer John Harbison once wrote apropos this movement that "some temperaments can remain calm before the onslaught of the Adagio of Mahler's Ninth only to be taken apart by a Haydn Presto." The music moves so surprisingly, so touchingly, so amusingly, above all so swiftly that when it has run its five-minute course it seems as though Haydn had barely started to do all that might be done with his material. If Haydn had actually written this symphony as his degree exercise, his would be the best-earned doctorate in the 800-year history of that university.

The London Symphonies

Seldom have an artist and his audience been so delightedly attuned to each other as Haydn and the enchanted Londoners who crowded his concerts at the Hanover-Square Concert Rooms and the King's Theatre in 1791–92 and again in 1794–95.[7] The English were happy to feel and act possessive toward the most celebrated of living musicians; Haydn, after nearly thirty years of service at an obscure, geographically isolated, but prosperous and artistically enlightened court, rejoiced in this new experience of public success and was far too sane to be crazed by it.

In his music, too, he was a specialist in sanity. Neither a seducer nor a rabble-rouser, he wrote for attentive, quick-witted listeners who knew the language and the conventions, who were alert and responsive enough to be shocked or amused when their expectations were confounded (and who of course wanted an artist to be ahead of them in imagination and

[7]The Hanover-Square hall was a shoebox with seats along the side walls facing inward as well as seats that faced the stage. The capacity was about 800. The King's was a horseshoe-shaped theater with loges. Because seating in the pit was on unnumbered benches, capacity was variable, probably from 750 to 900 plus.

originality rather than resenting that), who noticed when he invented a new harmony and a new scoring for a phrase each time it came around, who were enough of the earth to laugh at the coarser detonations of his humor, who would not assume the lack of a heart because it was not worn on the sleeve. Haydn had felt free and stimulated when writing for the Esterházys; now, in his seventh decade and, as it were, going public, he felt more challenged than ever. He wrote for what Stravinsky, so like him in braininess and wit, called "the Ideal Other," and I have often thought one reason the Londoners loved him so is that he made them feel so intelligent and witty.

Haydn's London symphonies have also been called the Salomon symphonies. Johann Peter Salomon, born in 1745 in Bonn but established in London as a successful violinist and impresario since 1781, happened to be on the Continent when he heard of the death of Haydn's employer, Prince Nicholas Esterházy, and of the disbanding of the family's musical household by his son. He lost no time in setting out for Vienna, where he showed up on Haydn's doorstep, bluntly announced "I am Salomon and I have come from London to fetch you," and made the composer an irresistible offer: £1000 for an opera, six symphonies, and some miscellaneous pieces, plus a £200 guarantee for a benefit concert.

Before leaving, Haydn bade farewell to Mozart, whom he would never see again. Both men shed tears. The journey itself was arduous and the crossing from Calais to Dover rough ("But I fought it all off and came ashore without—excuse me—actually being sick," he wrote to his friend Marianne von Genzinger). Haydn arrived in England on New Year's Day 1791, and the idea was for the first concert to take place on 11 February; however, with delays of various kinds, the series began a month later, on 11 March. Haydn meanwhile had heard his music played at concerts of the Anacreontic Society, the Professional Concerts (Salomon's chief rival), and the New Musical Fund (where one of his symphonies was done by an orchestra of 300!), as well as at a soirée at Carlton House, the residence of the Prince of Wales. He had twice accompanied his cantata *Arianna a Naxos* at the fortepiano and had attended a court ball on the Queen's birthday. At the Handel commemoration at Westminster Abbey, he received the inspiration for the two great works that later crowned his own career, *The Creation* and *The Seasons*. In the summer he would be given an honorary doctorate at Oxford.

In July 1792, Haydn returned to Vienna, where, an ungifted, unrigorous teacher, he briefly gave lessons to the twenty-one-year-old Beethoven, an unhappy encounter for both. Mozart was dead, and so was Frau von Genzinger, almost as young. Haydn's marriage and his now fourteen-year affair with the singer Luigia Polzelli were as wretched and draining as ever.

He was happy to accept Salomon's invitation to return to London, and on 19 January 1794 he left once more for a stay of a year and a half, accompanied this time by his copyist and amanuensis, Joseph Elssler. They arrived on 4 February, a bit later than planned, and actually a day too late for Salomon's first concert. Salomon ceased operations later that year, partly because the war with France made it difficult to engage first-rate singers from the continent, and Haydn transferred his activities to a new series called the Opera Concerts. Salomon had produced three new Haydn symphonies, Nos. 99–101, in 1794; his successor, Giovanni Battista Viotti, violinist, impresario, and considerable composer, had the honor of bringing out Haydn's last three. For other occasions, Haydn wrote piano sonatas, trios, and songs to English texts.

As for the twelve London symphonies, they are bigger, more grandly orchestrated, more brilliantly composed, deeper, and funnier than anything Haydn had done in the genre before. After London, Haydn wrote no more symphonies, and the London twelve were sufficient to keep his Viennese audience entertained for a while. He did go on to write his most miraculous quartets and six great Masses, and then attained the culmination of his achievement in his two oratorios, *The Creation* and *The Seasons*.

Symphony No. 93 in D major

> *Adagio—Allegro assai*
> *Largo cantabile*
> *Menuetto: Allegro*
> *Finale: Presto ma non troppo*

Haydn completed this symphony in 1791 and led its first performance at the Hanover-Square Concert Rooms in London on 17 February 1792.

Two flutes, two oboes, two bassoons, two horns, two trumpets, timpani, and strings.

This is the third of the twelve symphonies that Haydn wrote for London between 1791 and 1795. Like most of Haydn's novelties, it was rapturously received by the English public. It was also lauded in the press for its "very extraordinary merit, . . . [using] all the fire of his bold imagination, . . .

a composition at once grand, scientific, charming and original." *The Oracle* opined that of Haydn's "wonderful powers rapture alone should be permitted to speak"; readers of *The Times* learned that "such a combination of excellence was contained in every movement, as inspired all the performers as well as the audience with enthusiastic ardour." At a repeat performance a week later, Haydn stole his own show with a "madrigal" for soloists, chorus, and orchestra called *The Storm* and set to English words by Peter Pindar.

Haydn begins assertively and simply with a call to attention, *fortissimo tutti.* This prepares the way for two phrases that are all innocence and charm. Having reassured his audience, he now administers the first shock to which his blessedly alert Londoners were so happily responsive. Quietly, he lifts the music and sets it down again in infinitely remote E-flat major, suavely gets back to where he belongs, and is now ready for the main part of the movement.

Here Haydn gauged English taste even better than he knew, for the melody that begins the Allegro made its way into nineteenth-century hymnbooks (at heavy sacrifice of tempo and character). The house must have been full of smiles when the violins first sang out the gracious and spirited second theme. The development is suddenly forceful and full of that "science" eighteenth-century writers refer to. It is also extensive and teasing. The recapitulation is taut, and it adds a witty not-quite imitation by the bassoon to the second subject.

The second movement is in G major, and here Haydn springs another surprise, the sound of a solo string quartet. It is a case of "pay attention now," for he will not repeat the effect. The movement is full of event and adventure, and it is here that Haydn redeems the promise of that first, startling visit to E-flat in the Adagio introduction to the first movement. A slight tendency to grow ruminative becomes, in the recapitulation, almost perilously self-indulgent until Haydn points out rudely—very rudely—that there is such a thing as being too dreamy. The Londoners loved it—I hope they were even uninhibited enough to laugh out aloud at the indiscretion of Haydn's bassoon—and they demanded an encore of the entire movement. (At the second performance, the first movement as well as the second was "encort," as Haydn spells it in his diary.)

The Minuet is vigorous, very physical. Its most remarkable feature is the trio. The basic assumption behind its dialogue between trumpet-and-drum tattoos and sweetly unruffled strings is simple: its details are far beyond our powers to predict.

Then Haydn builds a finale on one of those themes with a double upbeat that allows him to play amusing here-it-comes/no-not-yet games. The ending, well studied by Beethoven when he came to write his own D-major Symphony, No. 2, eleven years later—and Beethoven learned as much from Haydn's scores as he failed to learn in his lessons—must have been the most brilliant and energetic London had ever heard.

Symphony No. 94 in G major, *Surprise*

Adagio—Vivace assai
Andante
Menuet: Allegro molto
Allegro di molto

Haydn wrote this symphony in 1791 and led its first performance at the Hanover-Square Concert Rooms in London on 23 March 1792.

Two flutes, two oboes, two bassoons, two horns, two trumpets, timpani, and strings. This is the only classical symphony to require timpani on three different pitches instead of the usual two on tonic and dominant. In the first movement Haydn's timpanist had to tune his G-drum to A in the development section. Today a timpanist would use three drums.

The *Surprise* Symphony, one of Haydn's first half-dozen for London, became instantly and vastly popular. Credit for the invention of its nickname was claimed by Andrew Ashe, a flutist in Salomon's orchestra, who wrote into his own copy that "my valued friend Haydn thank'd me for giving it such an appropriate name." In its early years much ink was devoted to the issue of the surprise, with biographers and memoirists squabbling irritably about what Haydn had said to whom and what nonsense the other fellow's theory must be. Did he really say, in planting the bang in the second movement, that bang that continues to delight us long after it can surprise, "This will make the ladies jump"? Was he thinking of the elderly gentlemen he had noticed at concerts who unfailingly went to sleep the moment the music began? Sleepers do actually seem to have been a problem, as Londoners staggered from their heavy dinners—plenty of sherry before, hock and Burgundy during, and port afterward—into the cramped Hanover-Square Concert Rooms, and Haydn specified that his new symphonies were always to be placed at the beginning of the second half.[8]

---

[8]No wonder the spell-check on my word processor wants to change the name of the locale of these concerts to "Hangover-Square." It also offers "saloon" as a possible improvement on "Salomon."

The prize for the prettiest exegesis goes to the critic of *The Oracle,* who wrote that "the surprise might be likened to the situation of a beautiful Shepherdess who, lulled to sleep by the murmur of a distant Waterfall, starts alarmed by the unexpected firing of a fowling-piece." Finally, we should note that the surprise was an afterthought: in Haydn's original manuscript page, the repeat of the Andante's first eight bars is literal and indicated by the customary shorthand of colon and double-bar.

Donald Tovey pinpointed "dramatic surprise at the moment" as the essence of Haydn's compositional procedure. This symphony is full of surprises of every kind. The very beginning, a soft cantabile of woodwinds, unprepared by any sort of call to attention, is absolutely original. Strings continue the phrase—another surprise: one doesn't expect a change of color so soon—and when the dialogue offers to repeat itself, the strings let it be known that they have things to say too serious, too dark, too mysterious for flutes and oboes and bassoons.

How the fast part of the movement starts is another surprise: piquantly off-center in its harmony, also a bit ambiguous about which beats are up and which down. Haydn eventually does the expected thing, that is, he goes to the dominant, D major; first, however, he surprises us with an uncommonly adventurous journey there, one that entails dressing the first theme in F major for a moment to see what kind of impression it makes that way. The D-major music, once it arrives, is enchanting: first several measures of accompaniment with funny off-beat accents, then some scales to show off the brilliance of the first violins, finally a comfortably relaxed rustic tune.

The development is chiefly concerned with the first theme, and this gets flung with great enthusiasm through a wide range of harmonies. Haydn has saved his richest invention for the recapitulation, which is in fact a combined recapitulation and coda. Everything returns in due course, just as we hope, but everything is reconsidered, reinvented: the proportions are different, the violins' sixteenth-note scales are laid out in a fresh way so that the players have to find new fingerings, and in the middle of it Haydn even decides that there is room for more development. This is altogether one of Haydn's most liberated symphonic movements, a brilliant play of long-range strategy and colorful detail, ablaze with energy, quickened by humor.

As for the tune of the Andante, we have to make an effort to remember that once upon a time it did not exist. Nine years or so after writing it, Haydn quoted it in *The Seasons,* in the song that describes the farmer whistling as he follows his plow. Haydn's patron and librettist, Baron Gottfried van Swieten, was annoyed. He wanted a quotation from one of the popular operas of the day, and Haydn had to set him straight indignantly: his tune was as popular (in both senses) as anything in any opera. In the symphony, Haydn makes a set of variations on the tune, variations exquisitely tactful in their simplicity, yet breathtaking in their inventiveness. Pathos is rare in Haydn and the more piercing therefore when it does occur. Hardly anything in any classical symphony is more touching than Haydn's half-minute of closing music, the nursery song now heard through a veil of harmonies more mysterious than any we have experienced since the introduction, the lowest notes of horns and a soft drumroll casting their shadows and a single flute contributing its shy flecks of light. (One would like to imagine it was Mr. Ashe, but I fear not, for he more often played second flute.)

What follows is a Minuet in name only: Haydn specifies a very quick tempo, and the first phrase is accompanied by the unmistakable oom-pah-pah of something far more rustic than a Minuet.

The finale is Haydnesque comedy at its richest. It even has a fine *fortissimo* surprise of its own, one obscured for more than a century and a half by corrupt editions that tamed an exuberant explosion into a decorous crescendo.

Symphony No. 95 in C minor

> *Allegro moderato*
> *Andante cantabile*
> *Menuet*
> *Finale: Vivace*

Haydn wrote this symphony in 1791 and led its first performance at the Hanover-Square Concert Rooms in London, possibly on 1 April that year but more probably on 29 April.

Flute, two oboes, two bassoons, two horns, two trumpets, timpani, and strings.

This is the only one of Haydn's twelve London symphonies in a minor key. It is, for that matter, his first symphony in minor since No. 83, the great *La Poule* (The Hen) of 1785. It is also the only one of the London symphonies without an introduction. Haydn had come to think of those slow prefaces as patches of mystery and suspense, of darkness, sometimes hinting at the quick music to come, sometimes unrelated to it, but in either case effectively setting off the major-mode brightness of the Allegro. Preparing a dark Allegro with a still darker introduction is an aesthetic challenge taken up in the generations after Haydn, stuff from the world of Beethoven's *Appassionata* and Opus 111 piano sonatas, Schumann's *Manfred* Overture, and the Brahms First Symphony. (You also find fascinatingly ambiguous cases like Beethoven's *Kreutzer* Sonata or some, like Weber's *Freischütz* Overture, where the "normal" procedure is reversed.)

In the 1770s, Haydn wrote a number of marvelous symphonies in minor, among which No. 45, the *Farewell*, is the most powerful as well as the most famous; all in all, though, the darker mode was never his territory in the sense that it was Mozart's or Beethoven's. Mozart had learned much from Haydn, who was his senior by twenty-four years; later, Haydn was not ashamed to learn from Mozart, whom he loved as a friend and whom he thought greater than himself. It is not surprising that this beautiful and rarely heard C-minor symphony of Haydn's bears Mozartian traces. Mozart made distinctions among minor keys. His G-minor pieces tend to share a family resemblance, as do his D-minor compositions and those in C minor, and these families all differ from one another. What, therefore, this Haydn symphony calls to mind is specifically Mozart in C minor, a Mozart of dramatic gestures, often hard-edged themes, taut chromatic inflections (A-flat and F-sharp hemming in the dominant G are especially characteristic)—the Mozart of the Piano Sonata, K.457, and Fantasia, K.475, the Piano Concerto, K.491, and the Wind Serenade, K.388(384a).

The beginning is arresting: five notes (with the typically Mozartian G/A-flat/F-sharp pattern), *fortissimo*, staccato, unharmonized, and followed by a dramatic silence. If you are experienced in the ways of eighteenth-century music, you will expect two things (and be right both times): that music in soft contrast will follow the silence and that the initial five-note figure will be developed polyphonically. Energetic polyphonic imitations occur almost at once en route to E-flat major and a friendly, beautifully scored new theme. The development is both ample and intense. The recapitulation is filled with lovely orchestral touches. One of these is the quietly penetrating chord for two bassoons with which Haydn settles in C major for the return of the second subject; another, evidently an afterthought from the first rehearsal, was to make the little scale which decorates that theme a solo for Salomon, who was not only the impresario responsible for getting Haydn to London but also the concertmaster.

Adding cantabile to andante in the second movement was also an afterthought. This is almost a theme and variations. Haydn begins with a lyric melody that manages to be simultaneously demure and unpredictable, and he follows this with a variation in which a solo cello emerges from the texture. Next he seems to start a variation in minor; this, however, reveals itself as a transitional passage, full of grand pauses and unexpected harmonic turns, and leading back to an unvaried restatement of the theme. This proves to be another red herring, for after only four measures Haydn launches into a new and full variation with brilliant thirty-second-notes for the violins. He closes the movement with one of those musing chromatic codas he liked to use to surprise the Londoners in his slow movements. "Simultaneously demure and unpredictable" is in fact an apt characterization for the whole movement.

The Minuet is forceful, rich in humor and pathos, and not untouched by a certain Mozartian fever. The trio, in major, belongs to the principal cellist, whose difficult solo is reticently accompanied by plucked strings.

When the Finale begins, Haydn has abandoned C minor and the tragic gesture altogether. He starts with one of his most radiant and inspired melodies and, perhaps with an eye to Mozart's *Jupiter*, builds a movement whose thrust is fueled by concentrated polyphony. Goethe's friend and musical adviser, Carl Friedrich Zelter, wrote appreciatively about this finale in 1798:

> [Haydn] chooses for the last movement a theme that has something light and *galant* about it, but which, for all its simplicity, has much dignity and is especially suitable for the strongest and most varied development. The theme was chosen as being light and gentle, like the theme of a typical rondo: the public was fooled, having expected the usual rondo. But all at once the principal theme's main thought is taken up, played with strength and fullness, and Haydn even works up a fine fugue from it. . . . And quite frankly, you won't learn from this example by Haydn, at least you won't learn how to write fugues. But then, who would want to learn the first rules of poetry from Klopstock's Odes . . . or Greek from Æschylus?[9]

Symphony No. 96 in D major, *The Miracle*

Adagio—Allegro
Andante
Menuetto: Allegretto
Finale: Vivace

Haydn composed this symphony in 1791 and led its first performance at the Hanover-Square Concert Rooms in London that year, possibly on 11 March, the first of his London concerts.

[9] *Der Briefwechsel zwischen Goethe und Zelter*, ed. M. Hecker (Leipzig: Tasel, 1913).

Two flutes, two oboes, two bassoons, two horns, two trumpets, timpani, and strings.

We do not know just which of his symphonies Haydn led at his first London concert on 11 March 1791, the announcement itself being vague ("New Grand Overture—Haydn") and newspaper accounts confined to generalized rhapsody. It may have been No. 92, written in 1789 and known as the *Oxford* because Haydn conducted it at that university in July 1791 when he received an honorary degree; it may have been No. 96, which we know for certain to have been the first of the new symphonies Haydn composed expressly for London. Whichever it was, the slow movement was encored—an unprecedented event in London, Haydn noted in his diary—and there was a strong but unsuccessful attempt to get the Minuet repeated as well. If No. 96 was not the symphony performed on that occasion, it would have had its premiere at one of the Salomon concerts a month later, in April.

What one of Haydn's first biographers, Albert Christoph Dies, called "the flattering name" of *The Miracle*, has become firmly glued to this symphony. It properly belongs, though, to the Symphony No. 102, not this one, and it is in the essay on that work that I let Dies tell the story.

If you saw the first two bars of the Symphony No. 96 in piano score, you might well guess it to be a tutti with trumpets and drums. In fact, Haydn withholds the trumpets and drums for a while, and this first gesture, a unison descent through three notes of a chord of D major, is only *forte*, not *fortissimo*. Altogether, this is a symphony of subtle brilliance compared to the other, more extroverted D-major London symphonies, Nos. 93, 101 (*The Clock*), and 104. The Adagio introduction is also more melodic than declamatory. Haydn sometimes liked in his slow introductions to use the minor mode to set off the major-key Allegro; here, the introduction begins in D major, but more than half of it is in D minor or its near relatives, and it is a lovely and pathos-filled oboe solo that provides the bridge into the Allegro.

This, like the introduction, in 3/4 time, opens with a softly chugging accompaniment across which the first violins partly sing, partly speak a gracefully curved melody. Haydn telescopes its close with the beginning of the next event, throwing us off our rhythmic stride. That next event is the first tutti with trumpets and drums, though Haydn is by no means finished with the first theme, particularly not with its distinctive three-note upbeat. The theme in fact ends with three eighth-notes (on the downbeat) as well as beginning that way, and in the development Haydn invents some delicious play with that ambiguity.

This witty chapter begins with a dramatic call to attention, then goes on to further contemplation of the main theme. Among other things, Haydn isolates the two-note pairs that make up its third measure, gets them started in conversation, but then has them peter out lazily. After an episode whose melodic shape seems to anticipate Mendelssohn's *Hebrides* Overture comes the most dramatic detail in the development, a sudden silence of two and two-thirds measures. This ought to lead to something special, like the recapitulation, and indeed it seems to do just that. If your ear is trained, you will hear immediately that while the tune is right, the key is not; if it is not, in just a few seconds you will discover anyway that Haydn is continuing with his development. The recapitulation—the real thing, not a comic false alarm—is introduced much more demurely. As usual in Haydn, this section is rich in detail, including a dramatic reminder of the D-minor coloration of the introduction.

The Andante is delicately chamber-musical in character, something like an eighteenth-century Concerto for Orchestra. Haydn writes rewarding passages for solo winds, and Salomon, who was concertmaster at these concerts, gets an attractive solo, as he so often does in this first set of London symphonies. So concerto-like is the spirit that the orchestra even draws up on a six-four chord to introduce a cadenza, one that has an unexpected outcome indeed.

The Minuet is vigorous and laid out on a generous scale; the trio is an enchanting oboe solo, and the sound of the high horn accompaniment is delectable. The Finale is a bubbly comedy whose first theme begins with that favorite Haydn device, one of those double upbeats that allow for inventive when-is-it-going-to-begin-again? games.

Symphony No. 97 in C major

Adagio—Vivace
Adagio ma non troppo
Menuetto: Allegretto
Finale: Presto assai

Haydn completed this symphony in 1792 and led its first performance at the Hanover-Square Concert Rooms in London, probably on 3 May 1792.

Two flutes, two oboes, two bassoons, two horns, two trumpets, timpani, and strings.

Haydn kept them waiting for this one. Having arrived in England on New Year's Day 1791, he produced two new symphonies that year, Nos. 96 and 95, and then three more in quick succession at the beginning of the following year, No. 93 in February, and Nos. 98 and 94 in March. Salomon, the impresario who had brought Haydn to London, must have hoped to have the sixth and last symphony of the promised set available to present at one of his April concerts, but he had to content himself and his audiences with repeats of Nos. 98, 94, and 93—always billed of course as "by particular Desire"—plus, by way of a novelty, the first performance in England of No. 91, a work of 1788.

Meanwhile, Haydn was pushing hard to get the new symphony finished, hard enough to worry Mrs. Rebecca Schroeter, a German composer's English widow, with whom he was enjoying a gently amorous friendship:

> M:D:* I was extremely sorry to heare this morning that you was indisposed, I am told you was five hours at your Study's yesterday, indeed my D:L: I am afraid it will hurt you, why should you who have already produced so many WONDERFUL and CHARMING compositions, still fatigue your self with such close application. I almost tremble for your health, let me prevail on you my MUCH-LOVED H: not to keep to your Study's so long at ONE TIME, my D: LOVE if you cou'd know how very precious your welfare is to me. . . . [10]

The concert on 3 May was to be entirely for Haydn's financial benefit, and it was on this occasion that he seems to have presented his new symphony; it was definitely performed at the concerts of 4 May, 11 May, and 6 June. One of the reports mentions that "some of the movements were encored." We do not know which, but in any event Haydn's audience again did not fail him, nor he them.

This is Haydn's twentieth and last symphony in C major. H. C. Robbins Landon has remarked that C major is for Haydn what D major was for Bach, the festive trumpets-and-drums key, and this symphony is very much in that vein. All of Haydn's English symphonies have trumpets and drums, and, even though London could not always provide him with indi-

---

* [Perhaps "my dear."—M.S.]

[10]Quoted in H. C. Robbins Landon, *Haydn, Chronicle and Works* (Bloomington: Indiana University Press, 1976), Vol. 3, p. 157.

vidual virtuosi like those in his Esterházy band, these works are also scored with a wonderful sense for brilliant orchestral effect. At the same time, they differ enormously among themselves, and the first encounter with this joyously outgoing symphony would have given the audience—by now an experienced audience of Haydn connoisseurs—its first recognition of yet another facet of the artistic personality of London's favorite composer.

Haydn begins with a slow introduction, his normal procedure in major-key symphonies from 1786 on. This one is soft except for two *forte* accents and a single beat of *forte/fortissimo* at the outset. Earlier one might have said that a *forte* opening was to get the audience quiet; in fact, though, Haydn had discovered with the *Surprise* Symphony, No. 94, that in London it was safe to begin softly, and four of the six symphonies he wrote for his second London visit do so.[11] So why this *forte* start? I shall suggest an answer in a moment.

After one measure of quiet ticking on the keynote C, the strings enter on a gently dissonant chord. It sounds agreeably colorful to us but, arriving without preparation, it must have come as a poignant shock two centuries ago. The most alert listeners would also have picked up on a subtle joke of Haydn's, namely that this first event of the symphony is a formula for a closing cadence.[12] A wistful melody, with flute joining the violins, continues the thought. This paragraph never lands on a proper final cadence of its own; rather, the arrival on C, *fortissimo* for the whole orchestra, is the first beat of the Vivace. And here we may have an explanation for the symphony's loud—briefly loud—beginning. The *fortissimo* start of the Vivace is a surprise, but it is what you might call a rational surprise in that, by referring back to the symphony's initial C, it ties threads together. The relation of Haydn's Allegros to their slow introductions in his late works is always remarkably ingenious and subtle.

The opening Adagio began with a slightly mysterious harmonic aura. The Vivace begins with something that could not be plainer, nine measures of the chord of C major, the first seven of them not even harmonized but presented as a unison fanfare. In fact, we go twenty measures before something even slightly exotic happens to the harmony. This is music of a kind that Haydn's pupil Beethoven was so good at, music in which deliberately neutral materials yield extraordinary results. What Haydn draws from that C-major chord is indeed remarkable; the effect he makes a little later with fifteen measures of bare octaves, this time on all sorts of strange

[11] There is, however, a question about the loudness of the drumroll that begins the eponymous symphony, No. 103.
[12] A year later Haydn repeated the same joke, this time in amusingly brusque, even crude form, in the C-major String Quartet, Opus 74, no. 1. We shall meet it again in Beethoven's First Symphony.

pitches, is not less so. The new and contrasting theme with its oom-pah-pah accompaniment is of beguiling innocence. It makes a lovely contrast to the high-energy stuff we have just heard; lulling us, it sets up something else unexpected, the reappearance in its original slow tempo of the symphony's opening phrase, now set in a vivace context and serving as the closing cadence of the exposition.

The development begins with one of Haydn's leaps into a strange key, here E-flat major. Turning the vigorous tonic-and-dominant drumming of the exposition's first bars into the pop-pop of a bassoon yields another joke. By now the material is familiar, even super-familiar; what, however, we could not anticipate is its enchantingly irregular and always *pianissimo* surfacing in the strings, while flute and oboes spin out a slightly melancholy three-part invention. Except for one sizable harmonic tremor near the beginning, the recapitulation is nice and regular, and like the exposition, it ends with the tender cadential phrase from the introduction. It is for this moment that Haydn has reserved his biggest surprise, the extension of that cadence into a coda whose length almost equals that of the development and which is of astonishing enterprise and expressive range.

The slow movement, which must not be too slow—it is Adagio *ma non troppo* and in cut time—is, like the corresponding movements in Nos. 94 and 95, a set of variations. Themes intended for variation are usually in two parts, the second a bit longer than the first, each part to be repeated. Here Haydn chooses to play with this convention. In the theme itself he makes the expected repeats, but writes them out in full and makes captivating changes in the orchestration. Moreover, to add yet another layer of subtle play, the theme abounds with internal repetitions of its own.

There are three variations. The first breaks the melody down into triplets. Haydn also continues the repeat game, this time by making no repeats at all! The second variation is in minor, with highly colored harmonies and trumpet-and-drum outbursts. Here the repeats are indicated simply by repeat signs. The third variation is the most astonishing, particularly for its sound: Haydn asks the violinists to play near the bridge, which produces a nasty rasping that must have raised a lot of eyebrows. This effect was suppressed by all publishers of this symphony until H. C. Robbins Landon's edition of 1963, and even now some conductors are timid about it. In this last variation, Haydn again writes out the repeats in full, and in doing so makes delightful use of having first and second violins exchange roles with each other.[13] As he does so often in the slow move-

---

[13] The effect of this is much diminished by the modern seating that puts all the violins on the same side of the stage.

ments of his London symphonies, Haydn appends a generous coda, which, in contrast to the grotesquerie of the last variation, is a page of unbridled pathos. To which the orchestra finally says, "Enough already."

In the Minuet, Haydn continues unconventionally to give us fully written out, fascinatingly varied repeats. No symphony of his contains more lovingly worked detail, and no wonder he worried Mrs. Schroeter with all those hours spent at his "Study's." The trio is a wonderfully flavorful bit of orchestral writing, especially the oboe-violin mixture with the bassoon a tenth below; the high horn accompaniment, elaborated later by the addition of soft trumpets and drums; and finally the concertmaster's moment, marked in Haydn's score as "Salomon Solo ma piano."

The Finale, originally marked "spiritoso," now goes presto assai—very fast. Here is another of those double-upbeat themes that lend themselves to Haydn's "so when *is* it going to come back?" games. Unexpected chromaticisms and endless invention in the field of orchestral textures also play their part in this movement, one of Haydn's most spirited and vivacious comedies.

Symphony No. 98 in B-flat major

> *Adagio—Allegro*
> *Adagio*
> *Menuet: Allegro*
> *Finale: Presto—Più moderato*

Haydn composed this symphony in 1792 and led its first performance at the Hanover-Square Concert Rooms in London on 2 March of that year.

Flute, two oboes, two bassoons, two horns, two trumpets, timpani, a keyboard instrument, and strings.

Haydn is the most economical of composers and in that respect, as in so many, the opposite of the lavish Mozart. He likes, for example, to invent simple, terse, open-ended themes whose harmony and scoring he can easily vary, which he can turn toward new destinations, but which stay remarkably themselves. He begins this great symphony with just such an idea, an ascending common chord of B-flat minor, followed by a descent in quicker notes and in a zigzag that includes a couple of tones outside the common chord:

Ex. 1

After the rhetorical flourish of the chord and the unmeasured silence, Haydn presents the idea twice more:

Ex. 2

and

Ex. 3

    All this is as simple as possible and at the same time extraordinarily subtle. The second statement starts with the same two notes as the first, but with the third note it veers off so as to face the entrance to new harmonic territory, D-flat major. Haydn has also changed the character by switching from *forte* to *piano*, at the same time replacing the sharp accents and staccatos of the opening statement with softening slurs. For the third statement, he reverts to the original forceful character. Again he begins with two of the notes of the first statement, but not the same two. He picks up the harmonic suggestion at the end of the second statement by beginning in D-flat major, but almost immediately—with the fourth note, to be exact—returns to the B-flat minor of the opening. The closing rhetorical flourish is greatly expanded because Haydn is preparing us for an event even more momentous than simply another repetition of this core idea.

That event is the releasing arrival of the major-mode Allegro, the event against which the introduction—so astonishingly dramatic and wide-ranging for its economy and brevity—has been holding us in suspense. Familiar with the conventions, Haydn's audience would have expected a bright, quick movement to emerge from the dark introductory measures, an effect much like that of stepping from a low-ceilinged, shadowy vesti-bule into the nave of a great cathedral. It must have delighted them that the music of this Allegro is both new and not new. What we hear now is another version of the idea Haydn had built the introduction on: the shape of version one, the phrasing of version two, the sound of unison strings, but now in B-flat major and of course at a quick tempo:

Ex. 4

Haydn had worked this trick before in one of the last of his pre-London symphonies, No. 90 in C, and he would do it again in his next one, No. 97, and then still more dramatically and subtly in *The Drumroll*, No. 103. This one theme is almost enough to carry Haydn through an uncommonly rich and complex first movement. To put it another way, he gives us no other formally delineated theme, and when he makes a grand landing in a new key, the place where we would most expect to hear a new, contrasting theme, he makes an outright aggressive point of giving us the old one, punched out with an accent on each of its first three notes. Nonetheless, the movement is full of contrast, and its harmonies, rhythms, and figurations give it a powerfully forward-thrusting character.

The development is both long and intense (though I find it hard to join Robbins Landon in hearing angst in its polyphonic intertwinings). The recapitulation is unostentatiously irregular, reshuffling material in star-tling ways, and it finally allows full play to the theme's potential for ram-bunctiousness. After the premiere, Haydn was able to note in the journal he kept—in part in his newly acquired English—that "in the 3rd concert, the new Symphony in B-flat was given, and the first and last Allegros encort."

Mozart's slow movements are often operatic; Haydn's sometimes sug-gest hymns. Haydn would in fact write music very much like this solemn

Adagio for the prayer *Seid nun gnädig* (Be now merciful) in *The Seasons*. Tovey was the first to point out that both in the oratorio and the symphony Haydn moves into near-quotations from Mozart, the *Quam olim Abrahae* fugue from the Requiem in the former, and here a passage from the Andante of the *Jupiter* Symphony. Mozart had died on 5 December 1791, just a few weeks before Haydn began this symphony. In London it was a day so foggy that he had to light candles at eleven o'clock in the morning. The news from Vienna reached him about two weeks later; he wept.

Haydn had been both model and father to Mozart; at the same time, he recognized in Mozart a gift still richer than his own. After Mozart's death he felt more and more free to incorporate touches of Mozart's more sensuous language into his own work. His immediate response was to make the slow movement of his current work-in-progress into a private Requiem for his friend. Haydn, with his "high spirits . . . occupied with things of the mind," as Tovey puts it, was more inclined to be developmental and concentrated than the lyric Mozart. The placement and effect, therefore, of the "same" idea is strikingly different; nothing here is more touching than Haydn's assertive statement of "This is *not* Mozart" when he plunges from the *Jupiter* music into a grimly powerful development. The movement's opening hymnal phrase is one of those where Haydn reharmonizes and rescores each of its appearances. The last time it comes around, Haydn softens its first chord of F major with a gently alien E-flat in the first violins, who then continue on their Mozartian path by a series of chromatic steps through D and D-flat down to C.[14]

The Minuet is robust in character, energetic in its traversal of the harmonic landscape, and festively scored. The trio is more gently rustic.

The Finale is the biggest and most adventurous in any Haydn symphony. It steps out briskly with one of those double-upbeat themes Haydn teases his listeners with as they wonder which upbeat is actually going to mark the theme's return. But Haydn has richer jokes in mind. A long silence follows the exposition, and what breaks that silence is something utterly unpredictable, in sonority as well as in harmonic placement.[15] Characteristic as well as wonderful is the subsequent discovery that this particular surprise is not a one-time gag, but an idea capable of astonishing and witty expansion.

After all this, Haydn gives us a rich and spacious coda. As he did in the first movement, he alters the character of the theme by changing its

[14] Until H. C. Robbins Landon initiated a massive cleanup in the 1950s, many Haydn symphonies were available only in corrupt editions that perpetuated some appalling nineteenth-century alterations. The Symphony No. 98 was one of the worst treated: trumpet and drum parts were thoroughly and badly rewritten, and someone had thought to remove the violins' magical E-flat.

[15] Hint: Johann Peter Salomon, the impresario who had persuaded Haydn into his London adventure, was also the concertmaster at these concerts.

tempo. We are disconcerted to begin with, first of all by the new and leisurely gait itself, then by the very notion of slowing down, of seeming to reduce physical energy at a point in the piece when, if anything, you expect it to be increased. In a moment, though, Haydn shows us that the new tempo allows for a subdivision of the beat into sixteenth-notes that run faster than anything we have heard in the Finale thus far.

This is the home stretch, but that does not keep Haydn from springing one more surprise, the sudden emergence for eleven measures of a rippling keyboard figuration. By 1792 the retention in orchestral music of a keyboard instrument was a matter of custom, not of musical necessity. The conservative English subscribed to that custom, and the announcements for the concerts that this symphony and its companions were composed for promise that "Dr. Haydn [will] direct the Performance . . . at the Piano Forte." (As late as 1820, the London Philharmonic was startled, even put out, when Louis Spohr first got up to lead them with a little wooden stick in his hand.) Most of the time, Haydn probably played simple chords and often left off doing even that in order to wave his hands. It seems, though, that at a performance of the Symphony No. 98, at an exceptionally sparely scored passage near the end of the Finale, he suddenly let loose a stardust of sixteenth-notes. He wrote down the figuration as an *aide-mémoire* for himself, and Salomon also preserved it in slightly different form in a trio arrangement he made of the piece. The effect is too much fun to miss, though of course it makes sense only if the piano or harpsichord has participated throughout.[16]

Symphony No. 99 in E-flat major

> *Adagio—Vivace assai*
> *Adagio*
> *Menuet: Allegretto*
> *Finale: Vivace*

Haydn composed this symphony in Vienna in 1793 for his return to London and conducted the first performance at the King's Theatre there on 19 February 1794.

---

[16] I have heard this more often on the harpsichord than on the piano. The harpsichord sounds "cuter" and more like "ancient music," but given the date and given that the concert announcements clearly say "Piano Forte," this choice does not make much sense. I would say the same thing about the choice of keyboard instrument for the recitatives in Haydn's oratorios and, for that matter, Mozart's operas.

Two flutes, two oboes, two clarinets, two bassoons, two horns, two trumpets, timpani, and strings.

This magnificent symphony, with its wonderfully rich and warm sonority, is the work Haydn wrote to launch his second visit to London. It is the first time he used clarinets in a symphony, and their sound—one is high, the other very low—makes a telling contribution to the handsome opening chord of E-flat major. Their appearance should probably be counted as another instance of Mozart's posthumous influence on Haydn. Mozart had used clarinets in only three of his symphonies, the *Paris* (1778), No. 39 in E-flat, and the revised version of No. 40 in G minor, but that instrument is prominent in his concertos and operas. With its chocolaty tone, it is an important component of the Mozart sound. Haydn, at least until his last works, tends to go for a leaner texture and cooler sonority.

He begins this lavish symphony with a pair of symmetrical phrases, extending the sentence so as to arrive at the dominant. At least it seems that way. He reaches the dominant, B-flat, on a sonorous *fortissimo* and then goes on to enhance its effect by adding A-flat and turning the chord into a dominant seventh. This, if we can imagine ourselves carrying the work to this point, is where you or I would stop, then presumably returning to the tonic, E-flat, and continuing from there. Not Haydn. As though to give the B-flat extra emphasis, he goes to its upper neighbor, C-flat, then back to B-flat—so far everything is all right—but *then* back to C-flat . . . and there he stays, making a long, unmeasured halt.

The first violins like that note, which Haydn now writes as B-natural. They muse on it. The second oboe takes it seriously, as a B, and using that B as a dominant of E minor, sings a plaintive phrase in that key, willingly supported by the strings. In less than a minute we have strayed incredibly far from home or, to put it another way, phenomenal horizons and possibilities have opened up. But what is going to happen right now? The first oboe gives out a heightened version of the second oboe's phrase, and with the easy shift of just a couple of notes in the accompanying string chords, Haydn moves the music onto G, the dominant of C—C minor in this case, as the emphatic E-flats in the melody make clear. And there, on the doorstep of C minor, he draws up to another grand halt.

But wasn't this supposed to be a symphony in E-flat? the woodwinds and horns inquire softly. They do this by playing a chord of B-flat/D/F/A-flat, that same dominant seventh where a little while back we thought ourselves on such sure ground before those C-flats derailed us. But of course, the violins reply, as, in a new and quick tempo, they initiate a playful melody. The indiscretions of the introduction seem to be forgotten.

But no. As Haydn moves toward his new key area, he reminds us, throwing in an abruptly accented C-flat and bringing back, again with strong accents so that we won't miss anything, the seesawing motion between neighboring notes that had taken us to the big C-flat in the introduction. He also does not fail to throw in a passing but emphatic recall of the C minor the introduction tried to lead us into.

When Haydn reaches the new key, B-flat, he offers a reminder of the first theme before giving us a new one that is, if possible, even more cheerfully jaunty. From there, the way to the end of the exposition is swift. The development begins with a couple of wistful questions about the first theme. Then Haydn begins an energetic voyage across broad areas of harmonic territory, for the most part playing inventively with bits of the second theme. Romantic horns herald the arrival at the recapitulation, which, as almost always in late Haydn, is much more than a simple reprise—with the necessary harmonic adjustments—of the exposition. Everything is reconsidered, redesigned, and tightened, even though Haydn still shows appetite for more developing of the second theme. In two melancholic measures the ghost of Mozart puts in an appearance. The opening of the first theme is summoned to give this excitingly designed movement a firm close, and the surprises continue to the final bars.

In his piano sonatas and chamber music, Haydn enjoys placing the slow movement in a remote key so that its first sounds hit us with a sense of shock. He does it much more rarely in his symphonies, but here is a glorious example. The G-major chord that begins the Adagio is a thunderclap in utterly modest *piano,* and the melody which it initiates—it could almost be a hymn—is one of Haydn's most inspired. Woodwinds echo the end of the first phrase. With the second phrase, the melody expands to travel on paths we could not foresee, and this time the continuation by the woodwinds turns out to be a long fantasy for flute, two oboes, and bassoon, that finally lands in the dominant, D major. There Haydn presents a new and heavenly theme. It is very short and it carries the exposition to its close. These have been thirty-four amazingly packed measures.

With a restrained sort of sadness, the music continues in D minor and, not without drama, makes its way to C major, where Haydn lets us hear the great second theme once more. But the energy for harmonic travel continues unabated, and the voyage takes us to a *fortissimo* climax on reiterated chords of B major. These are followed by an unmeasured pause. This ought to prepare E minor or E major. Instead, Haydn sets us down in G major in the lovely company of the first theme. The recapitulation has begun, and Haydn, with his grand preparation for arriving at a place he did not intend to go to, has contrived to make that G-major chord as fresh, as shocking, as it was at the beginning of the movement.

This recapitulation, too, is wonderfully retouched, with new harmonies for the woodwind echo of the first phrase, with the second phrase omitted altogether, and with the conversation for solo winds given to the strings. The radiant second theme returns twice, separated by one of Haydn's most dramatic pages. The final return of the second theme rises to a resplendent climax in *fortissimo*. The very end, like the end of the exposition, is a surprise better heard than read about. Beethoven was taken with it and used it in his Piano Concerto No. 3, another work where the first chord of the slow movement is a powerful and poetic shock.

The Minuet begins at court but soon finds itself in the country with a hearty oom-pah-pah accompaniment. It is one of Haydn's biggest minuets, full of caprices and surprises, and scored with a marvelously fresh and ample sound. Getting into the trio involves another bold harmonic leap, this one into C major, also no mean distance from E-flat. Oboe and violins, joined briefly by the bassoon an octave lower, do the honors on the gentle melody. Haydn writes a bridge passage, both tender and witty, to get from the trio back into the repeat of the Minuet.

The Finale, which begins with a perky violin tune, is yet one more instance of Haydn's inexhaustible invention in the genre of speedy comedy for wide-awake listeners. The second theme, with its mini-fanfare, unleashes quite a repertory of jokes within itself, and the dialogue moves swiftly from one instrumental group to the next. The conversation gets quite intense in a contrapuntal development. As the movement goes on, the orchestral writing becomes more and more virtuosic and we finally get the gratification of actually hearing a brass instrument, the second horn, play the tumbling little fanfare. To the very end, Haydn does not cease from inventing.

Symphony No. 100 in G major, *Military*

Adagio—Allegro
Allegretto
Menuet: Moderato
Finale: Presto

Haydn composed this symphony early in 1794, probably partly in Vienna and partly in London, and drawing on a 1786 concerto for *lira organizzata* for the second movement. He led the first performance at the Hanover-Square Concert Rooms in London on 31 March 1794, his sixty-second birthday.

Two flutes, two oboes, two clarinets, two bassoons, two horns, two trumpets, timpani, triangle, cymbals, bass drum, and strings.

At the first seven concerts that Johann Peter Salomon arranged for Haydn's second visit to London, two new symphonies, Nos. 99 and 101, were introduced and repeated. The programs also included three of the symphonies Haydn had written for his first stay, the *Sinfonia concertante* (it had been a favorite in 1792), and two string quartets, presumably from opp. 71 and 74, that were new to London, and one of which was repeated. Works by others included a new violin concerto by Viotti and a new piano concerto by Dussek, each presented with its composer as soloist. The Symphony No. 100, billed in the customary fashion as "New Grand Overture," had its turn at the eighth concert. The string quartet played the week before was repeated, and the program included music by Viotti and Pleyel, among others. The soloists were the evidently controversial soprano Gertrude Mara; Mme. Delavalle, a virtuosa on the pedal harp; and the bass Ludwig Fischer, he of the fabulous low D's for whom Mozart had written the role of Osmin in *The Abduction from the Seraglio.*

The New Grand Overture was repeated a week after its premiere, and two days later the *Morning Chronicle* reported:

> Another new Symphony, by Haydn, was performed for the second time; and the middle movement was again received with absolute shouts of applause. Encore! encore! encore! resounded from every seat: the Ladies themselves could not forbear. It is the advancing to battle; and the march of men, the sounding of the charge, the clash of arms, the groans of the wounded, and what may well be called the hellish roar of war increase to a climax of horrid sublimity! which, if others can conceive, he alone can execute; at least, he alone hitherto has effected these wonders.[17]

By the time the benefit concert for Haydn on 2 May was announced, the symphony had acquired its nickname. We read: "By Desire, the Grand Overture . . . with the Militaire Movement, as performed at Mr. Salomon's Concert, Haydn." The frequency of performances that year and the next attest to the immense popularity of the new work, and in the *Morning Chronicle*'s report of the concert on 23 February 1795 we are told that "the Grand Symphony of Haydn, with the Military Movement, which never fails to astonish and enrapture, and which, as usual, was encored, began the second act." On that occasion, however, the performance seems not

---

[17] Quoted in Robbins Landon, *Haydn, Chronicle and Works*, Vol. 3, p. 247.

to have gone well, for the reviewer scolds: "We know not by what accident, but, though the sublimity of the composition overcame every little
defect, we have heard it performed more accurately. Another time, no
doubt, the band will be more determined, and more precise in their time."
For his last London benefit on 4 May 1795 he again chose the *Military* as
a hit certain to draw. Publications, too, followed in short order: full score,
orchestral parts, arrangements for string quartet, for flute and string quartet
with piano ad libitum, for trio with piano and strings, piano solo, piano
duet, and in abridged form as a duet for two flutes.

Like all of Haydn's late symphonies in major keys, this one starts with
a slow introduction. Here, however, the Adagio is less obviously introductory than, say, the mysteries that begin *The Clock* and *The Drumroll*, or
than the sharply defined but highly formalized gestures in No. 104. This
Adagio is lyric, and not until the startling harmonic wrench at the entrance of the flutes, oboes, trumpets, and drums, can we be sure this is not
an independent slow movement rather than a gradual revelation of deeper
perspectives. The Allegro it serves to introduce is itself amazing: the
sweetly shrill sound of a trio for flute and oboes, the swagger of the violin
tune later on, the long silence at the beginning of the development (to
say nothing of how that silence is broken), and the reshuffling of material
for the joyously inventive combined recapitulation and coda.

Then comes the military movement. Here Haydn adds the military
apparatus—or "Turkish music," as it was then called—of triangle, cymbals,
and bass drum to his standard orchestra. He also gives extra richness to the
sound of this second movement by dividing the violas into two sections, a
leaf taken from Mozart's book. The music itself goes back to 1786, when
Haydn wrote a set of little concertos for King Ferdinand IV of Naples. His
Majesty played an odd instrument called the *lira organizzata* (literally
"organ-ized hurdy-gurdy"). The hurdy-gurdy, to quote *The Oxford Companion to Music*, is "a stringed instrument somewhat of the violin type, played
by turning with the right hand a handle which operates a rosined wheel
(in effect a circular bow), and by depressing with the left hand a few
finger-keys like those of a piano. These latter operate an internal mecha-
nism functioning somewhat like the fingers of the left hand of a violinist."
The *lira organizzata* is a hurdy-gurdy that has been "organized" by adding
pipes and a bellows.

The Romance of Haydn's third concerto for this instrument became
the symphony's second movement. In its original form it is entirely demure, and in transcribing it, Haydn gave it extra energy by composing tiny
bridges that propel each episode into the next. For instance, the four notes
on the oboe that lead into the woodwind repetition of the opening strain
are new: in the concerto you simply get three beats of silence at that point.

But of course the most spectacular extension of the earlier version—in length as well as in sonorous and expressive range—is in the military music. The coda, based on a bugle call apparently in use as late as 1938, is new. Musical depictions of war have gone some way in noise and realism in the last 200 years, but the drama of Haydn's gestures and the brilliance of their execution, the drumroll, the great eruption of distant A-flat major, the pathos of the quiet music that follows, the sternly forceful close—these still speak powerfully today.

The Minuet is earthy and Austrian, and it brings an unscheduled small pleasure because Haydn elects to write out and rescore the first eight bars rather than just repeating them literally in the usual way.

The mercurial Finale became so popular that it was sometimes played separately as the closing piece on a concert. Robbins Landon also writes that in the early nineteenth century its main theme began to appear in collections of English country dances as *Lord Cathcart* and thus, in effect, became a folk tune. That the Turkish music comes back must have pleased the London audiences, but the *Morning Chronicle* critic found it excessive. On 5 May 1794 he wrote:

> Was on Friday last in the Hanover-square Rooms. The Company was numerous and splendid. [Haydn's] grand and most admirable military movement produced its full effect, and every auditor seemed delighted to contribute to do honour to this great man. We cannot help remarking, that the cymbals introduced in the military movement, though they there produce a fine effect, are in themselves discordant, grating, and offensive, and ought not to have been introduced, either in the last movement of that Overture, or in the Finale at the close of the Concert. The reason for the great effect they produce in the military movement is that they mark and tell the story; they inform us that the army is marching to battle, and, calling up all the ideas of the terror of such a scene, give it reality. Discordant sounds are then sublime; for what can be more horribly discordant to the heart than thousands of men meeting to murder each other?[18]

But there are more surprises in the wonderfully rowdy finale, one of them being Haydn's best timpani joke. Another is touching and mysterious, when, after a long silence, Haydn begins some music for strings alone, staccato, *pianissimo*, in a remote minor key, with just a suggestion of the texture of fugue. It is a paradox that the most distant and enigmatic moment in this symphony should occur in the midst of the greatest jollity. The place is almost a quotation from *The Magic Flute*. Quickly, in a matter of twelve, thirteen seconds, Haydn moves on. It is as though unexpect-

---

[18] Quoted in Robbins Landon, *Haydn, Chronicle and Works*, Vol. 3, p. 250.

edly, while looking for something else, he had come across Mozart's portrait, but even now the reminder is too painful. When Haydn reveals the depth of his feeling, he does it with a certain diffidence. He speaks, then, to that same ideal and quick listener at whom he directs the best of his unsurpassed humor.

Symphony No. 101 in D major, *The Clock*

Adagio—Presto
Andante
Menuet: Allegretto
Finale: Vivace

Haydn wrote the Minuet of this symphony in Vienna in 1793, completed the score in London in February 1794, and led the first performance at the Hanover-Square Concert Rooms on 3 March that year. Its nickname appeared as early as 1798, when the work was published by Johann Traeg in Vienna.

Two flutes, two oboes, two clarinets, two bassoons, two horns, two trumpets, timpani, and strings.

Three of Haydn's London symphonies in major keys begin with slow introductions in minor: No. 98, this one, and No. 104. In No. 98 the Adagio is dramatic, almost severe; in No. 104, fanfares alternate with wistful and searching music. The introduction of No. 101 is dark and mysterious. It begins *piano*, with a slow rising scale that stops just short of having traversed an octave. The response is a gradual descent—it takes twice as long as the climb—whose destination is F major, the relative major of D minor, where the music began. A still longer sentence goes to a chord of A major, the dominant, where Haydn is poised to begin the main part of the movement. This music, with its edgy harmonies and disturbing accents, is deeply shadowed.

From that closing dominant chord, Haydn executes a graceful leap into D major and a light-footed Presto. Both that tempo mark and the 6/8 meter are unusual for a first movement, being more associated with finales. The new theme moves in five-bar phrases, but the odd fives sound so natural that you could easily not even notice their oddness. This theme, like the introduction, begins with a rising scale: the idea that we first met as a kind of tenebrous specter has been translated into sunlit reality.

Haydn uses the same scale to kick off the transition to the dominant. Presenting a new theme, as he does here, is not at all Haydn's usual custom: more often than not, he prefers to have the first theme do double duty. The new idea, which Tovey aptly characterizes as "full of coaxing and mockery," does, however, share an important feature with the first theme, which is that it too begins with a full measure of unaccompanied eighth-notes for the violin. Haydn likes connections of that sort. From scurrying eighths, he skids downward into long notes, the longest we have heard in this Presto. And there is another connection: those long notes make a rising scale, which, just a few quick measures later, is answered by a powerfully scored and accented—and shadowed—descending scale. The contrast between quick and long notes is effective, and Haydn will use it again.

Of course the exposition is to be repeated, and Haydn finds new and wonderfully witty use for scales in the passage that sends us back to the start of the Presto. The development, which takes notice of both themes, makes an energetic sweep through C major, E minor, B minor (with a most dramatic arrival), G major, and back to the doorstep of D major. The recapitulation is buoyant and, to use a favorite word of praise of eighteenth-century critics, intellectual, with all proportions and sequences of events coming in for reconsideration. All in one, it brilliantly combines the functions of return, of stilling some left-over yen for development, and of completion. The second theme is whirled about some more, but it is the first one that Haydn brings in to round things off jubilantly.

The Andante begins with the tick-tock—bassoons and plucked strings—that gives this symphony its name. This pleasantly monotonous and homely pulsation is of course an accompaniment, and what it accompanies is a sweetly graceful tune which the first violins begin in the second measure. The tune is sly as well as graceful, for its initial four-bar phrase is answered by one of five bars. (No one who knows Haydn's music will be surprised to hear that the second strain of the melody begins with 5 + 4.) As for the ticking, we will notice that while he does not aspire to the technical razzle-dazzle of the Prelude to Ravel's *L'Heure espagnole*, Haydn has a gratifying number of different clocks in his shop, offering "tick-tock" in a happy variety of colors.

As the melody reaches its cadence, it is interrupted by a great *fortissimo* noise in G minor. But if the change of mood is abrupt, continuity is as organic as ever, for this whole episode is simply a matter of taking one measure of the earlier melody and putting it under a powerful magnifying glass. The melody then returns in an orchestration as amazing as it is charming, with ticking flute and bassoon straddling the tune in the violins. After a startling silence, the ticking and the tune resume in a distant key, E-flat. This, however, turns out to be a feint. The tune is broken off after a couple of measures and eventually the music finds its way to the home key, G major, where the full orchestra plays a grand variation with quick sextuplets for the violins. High horns do the clock turn. Haydn leaves that *fortissimo* as abruptly as he entered it, to conclude with seven quiet measures in which horns, cellos, and basses anchor everything in place with their low G's. This movement as well as the opening one were encored at the first performance.

The grandly scored Minuet is the longest in any of Haydn's symphonies. With its contrapuntal imitations when the main theme returns, it is also one of his most elaborate. In the trio, Haydn give us village band music of the kind we will find again in Beethoven's *Pastoral*. Strings quietly churn out an accompaniment that consists of nothing but iambic reiterations of the tonic chord. The flute obligingly adds a tune (beginning with a rising scale), though when its melody moves onto the dominant, the strings refuse to budge off the tonic. Then the whole band wakes up, at least for a moment, and blasts out a four-bar cadence. When this is repeated, at least some of the strings are more alert and accommodate their notes to what the flute tune seems to require, but the cellos and basses remain obdurate about their repeated D's. This produces some strange dissonances. That Haydn meant what he wrote is obvious from the fact that he numbered the measures as a way of reassuring the string players that these wrong harmonies are in fact the right ones. Nonetheless, conductors used routinely to alter these harmonies and make them textbook "correct." As recently as 1981 I witnessed a Viennese conductor attempt to bowdlerize this passage, to be eventually dissuaded by the protests of members of the orchestra.

The Finale begins innocently, but we are in for high adventure. (Here is another theme that starts with a portion of a rising scale.) When Haydn arrives in a new key, the dominant, he gives us two semi-new ideas, both of them fresh in aspect but with clear motivic connections to the first theme. The next return to that theme is diverted into a tempestuous chapter in D minor. This comes to a suspenseful halt on the dominant. What now? The obvious answer is that it is time for the main theme to return. But hasn't the buildup been too dramatic for something so simple? The first violins think that bringing back the main theme is a good idea, but the seconds add a new counterpoint—all this in conspiratorial *pianissimo*— and we are off and running with a double fugue.

This is the moment to note that Haydn had remarkably high expectations of collective string virtuosity from his London players, and presumably with such leaders as Salomon and Viotti they were handsomely met. The violin writing in the first and last movements of this symphony is especially demanding; in fact, it is often daunting to orchestras that dispatch Bartók without a second thought. The fugue, at any rate, runs its course. Beginning with the oboe, several instruments take it upon themselves to play the first three notes of the main theme. Their hint is picked up. The orchestra plays the theme twice more, once *fortissimo* with everybody and then *piano* with strings alone, as we heard it the first time, and at that point the finish line is in sight.

Symphony No. 102 in B-flat major, *The Real Miracle*

Largo—Vivace
Adagio
Menuet: Allegro
Finale: Presto

Haydn composed this symphony in 1794 and led the first performance at the King's Theatre, London, on 2 February 1795.

Two flutes, two oboes, two bassoons, two horns, two trumpets, timpani, and strings.

It is Haydn's Symphony No. 96 in D major that is always called *The Miracle* in honor of the famous incident of the Fallen Chandelier. A chandelier did come down at one of Haydn's London concerts and no one was hurt, but it happened at the King's Theatre in February 1795 at the first performance of this symphony, not, as hoary and stubborn tradition has it, at the Hanover-Square Concert Rooms at the premiere of No. 96. The story, according to the Haydn biography by Albert Christoph Dies, based on twenty-nine conversations with the composer between 1805 and 1809, goes as follows:

> When Haydn appeared in the orchestra and sat down at the pianoforte to conduct a symphony himself, the curious audience in the parterre left their seats and crowded toward the orchestra the better to see the famous

Haydn quite close. The seats in the middle of the floor were thus empty, and hardly were they empty when the great chandelier crashed down and broke into bits, throwing the numerous gathering into great consternation. As soon as the first moment of fright was over and those who had pressed forward could think of the danger they had luckily escaped and find words to express it, several persons uttered the state of their feelings with loud cries of "Miracle! Miracle!" Haydn himself was deeply moved and thanked the merciful Providence that had allowed him in a certain way to be the cause of or the means of saving the lives of at least thirty people. . . .

I have heard this incident related in various ways and almost always with the addition that in London they conferred on the symphony the flattering name, *The Miracle*. It may be that such is the case, but when I made inquiry of Haydn in the matter, he said, "I know nothing about that."[19]

The work itself, a miracle even amid the collective miracle of the twelve London symphonies, begins with a B-flat five octaves deep, unmeasured but long, and with a sound that for all its simplicity has a certain distinctive grit. Violins and violas continue the slow introduction with a phrase of elegiac cast, and as the music continues, the harmonies become richer and darker. In fact, by the time the main, quick portion of the movement is about to start, Haydn has moved the music all the way into B-flat minor. To put an introduction in minor so as to set off the brightness of an Allegro in major is an effective device, and one Haydn uses several times in his late symphonies; here, using major to set off the minor in the first place, he has invented a witty elaboration of that device.

Now the phrase the violins played after that first long B-flat reappears, speeded up, more fully fleshed, with all pathos removed, and in this new guise it propels the Vivace into being. There is irrepressible energy in the forward charge of those sixteenth-notes, and sharp cross-accents in the woodwinds add to the excitement. A *fortissimo* unison, always with a silence on either side, constantly disrupts the flow of the movement. The first time that happens, it is followed by a little phrase whose low register and quiet dynamics set it strikingly apart from all the bustle so far; this, however, is quickly swept out of the path by the insistent reappearance—though standing on its head now—of an ebullient phrase from before.[20]

If that new phrase didn't stand much of a chance in the exposition,

[19] Vernon Gotwals, *Haydn: Two Contemporary Portraits* (Madison: University of Wisconsin Press, 1968).

[20] Actually, which way is up is a matter for debate. We naturally tend to think of the version in which we first hear a phrase as its normal form. Here that is the one that begins with a downward plunge, so the variant, beginning with a leap upward, is the inversion. In this instance, though, I believe that our psychological experience is different: the second version, the one that goes up, is much more powerful, and when we hear *it* our response is, "Aha, so that's how it really goes!"

it plays, from the outset, a considerable role in the development. This section—longer by one-third than the exposition, a unique proportion in Haydn's symphonies—evolves into a contrapuntally intricate, highly competitive conversation among the elements we have met so far: the *fortissimo* unison with its attendant silences, the quiet phrase, and the Vivace's opening melody (both in its original form and reduced to its rhythmic essence as a tattoo of sixteenths). It is the still small voice that does the most to thrust the music from key to key.

Another unmeasured pause allows everyone to draw breath after all this rough-and-tumble, and then, with the flute taking the tune, the recapitulation begins. Or does it? The tune is right but the key is wrong, and after all, the real point of the recapitulation is to re-establish the home key after the journeys begun in the exposition and continued in heightened form in the development. The orchestra interrupts, *fortissimo* and furious, and the development, now almost entirely dominated by the churning sixteenth-notes, rages on for another thirty-five measures. The recapitulation, though full of wonderful detail, is powerfully compressed, as is the turbulent coda.

For the Adagio, Haydn borrows a movement from the Piano Trio in F-sharp minor he had written earlier that year (or possibly the year before). It is music so inspired that it is no wonder he wanted to give it wider circulation. It must also have meant something special to him because, while he normally puts "In Nomine Domini" at the beginning of each symphony and "Laus Deo" at the end, here he inserts an extra blank page with the words "In Nomine Domini" before this movement. It is a solemnly ornate melody presented in a series of free variations. The actual sound of the movement is the most remarkable that Haydn ever imagined. Trumpets and drums are muted, a solo cello injects its gently penetrating timbre into the middle of the texture, and just before the end, the two trumpets in their lowest register contribute a sound so extraordinary (literally) that it still tends to frighten conductors, many of whom remove it.

The Minuet is forceful and, like the first movement, unusually extensive in its development. The trio, by contrast, is gentle. A lovely detail is the quietly affirmative phrase that the flute contributes twelve times.

The Finale is one of Haydn's quickest and also one of his funniest. (An encore was demanded and granted at the first performance.) At the same time, the drama and the harmonic surprises of the first two movements insist on not being forgotten. As one could indeed say of the whole symphony, this last movement is also one of those pieces that remind us how much Beethoven learned from Haydn's scores, no matter how much of a bust the formal lessons were.

Symphony No. 103 in E-flat major, *The Drumroll*

> *Adagio—Allegro con spirito*
> *Andante più tosto Allegretto*
> *Menuet*
> *Finale: Allegro con spirito*

Haydn composed this symphony in London in the winter of 1794–95 and led its first performance at the King's Theatre on 2 March 1795. He made some changes, notably to the end of the Finale, after his return to Vienna that August and reintroduced the work there in its revised form on 21 September.

Two flutes, two oboes, two clarinets, two bassoons, two horns, two trumpets, timpani, and strings.

Here is what the *Morning Chronicle* had to say about the premiere of *The Drumroll:*

> Another new Overture, by the fertile and enchanting HAYDN, was performed; which, as usual, had continual strokes of genius, both in air and harmony. The Introduction excited the deepest attention, the Allegro charmed, the Andante was encored, the Minuets, especially the Trio, were playful and sweet, and the last movement was equal, if not superior to the preceding.[21]

Well might the introduction have "excited the deepest attention." It begins with the long kettledrum roll on E-flat that gives the symphony takes its name. From this there emerges a phrase, quiet, very slow, for low strings and bassoon, with flute and oboes joining in to make a cadence in its fifth and sixth measures.

Right away there is a problem, or at least a question: what to do with the drumroll? Haydn put no dynamic marking on it; neither is there any in the part the London timpanist played from. Salomon made two arrangements of this symphony, one for piano trio and one for piano quintet. Into the former he put a crescendo/decrescendo sign $\mathrel{<\!\!\!-}\ \ {-\!\!\!>}$ (musi-

[21] Robbins Landon, *Haydn, Chronicle and Works*, Vol. 3, p. 295.

cians call this hairpins)—and into the latter a *fortissimo*. The hairpin version with its *pianissimo* start was the one that caught hold in the nineteenth century, making this the first of innumerable pieces from Schubert's *Unfinished* to Bartók's Concerto for Orchestra with mysterious creeping-bass beginnings. On the other hand, the Haydn scholar H. C. Robbins Landon is a *fortissimo* man: at his suggestion, Hermann Scherchen adopted that version to exciting effect in his 1950 recording, undoubtedly startling the hell out of many an unsuspecting record collector, and Robbins Landon also proposes *fortissimo*-decrescendo as the primary reading in his Universal complete edition of Haydn's symphonies. The choice is the conductor's, and the main thing is that this "Intrada," as Haydn labels it, be impressive.

Of what follows the drumroll, Robbins Landon writes: "Without knowing the score and listening to a performance with closed eyes, no one could possibly tell the meter of the opening." He also suggests that the first notes of this theme are an intentional reference, though "oblique," to the *Dies irae* from the Gregorian Mass for the Dead (as quoted so famously by Berlioz and Rachmaninoff).

Ex. 1

Haydn does on occasion quote Gregorian chant in his symphonies, for example in No. 26, *Lamentatione,* and in No. 49, *La Passione.* Even so, I was skeptical about Landon's contention, only to have a friend who was listening to a recording without knowing the score comment both on the mystery of the meter of those slow bass notes and on the fact that the first four notes were those of the *Dies irae.*

With the unfolding of the introduction comes some clarity but also even more mystery as Haydn, with greatest deliberation, prepares an entry into C minor. The moment the Allegro begins, we discover that he meant no such thing. The alternation of G and A-flat that closes the Adagio is picked up and reinterpreted as belonging to E-flat major, which is in fact just what the first twenty-five measures of the introduction—before the C-minor red herring—would have led us to expect. It is an amazingly organic—and subtle—transition from introduction to Allegro: one of the rare precedents is a work Haydn loved well, Mozart's Symphony No. 39, also in E-flat.

But even as Haydn now gets us firmly placed harmonically, he sets us a new metrical puzzle. It takes a full eight measures before we know for certain where "one" is and how to get in step with Haydn's buoyant stride. After so much expansiveness in the Adagio, the exposition goes by at great speed. The contrasting theme is even more of a pop tune than the first one, and just before it—as a present to the sharp-eared and attentive— there is a quick allusion to the matter of the introduction.[22]

The development is long—longer than the exposition by a dozen measures—and adventurous; among its adventures is another appearance, quite ghostly this time, of the music of the introduction. The recapitulation, on the other hand, is startlingly condensed. It also becomes astonishingly serious, assuming a tone and suggesting harmonic shadows we thought we had left behind us with the Adagio. What all this leads to is nothing less than a fourth appearance (assuming the exposition was repeated) of that dark introductory music—drumroll and all—but this time in the original slow tempo![23] A coda, quick and brief, again brings the adagio theme in allegro tempo, which we now hear as a combination that ties everything together. A touch as surprising as any is added by some new high horn calls.

The Andante, which, as we have seen, the London audience liked so much that they demanded an encore, is based on two folk songs from the region around the Esterházy estates, the first in C minor, the second in C major. The movement is a set of variations; however, Haydn obviously chose the two themes for their consanguinity, so that one gets the impression that the second, is itself already a variation of the first. Sharpening the F in the second tune is a clever ruse in the interest of bringing it closer to the first.

Haydn makes two variations on each theme, covering a wide range of musical characters from the martial to the playful. Viotti, his distinguished concertmaster, got a rewarding solo, as had his predecessors Tomasini (at Eszterháza) and Salomon (in London) in earlier symphonies. The coda, with its demonstration on how paradoxically to reaffirm C major by making an excursion to E-flat, is wonderful. Haydn's quickening of andante by adding "più tosto Allegretto" (more like an allegretto) was an afterthought when he had returned to Vienna.

The Minuet is a moment of relaxation; the trio, with its delicately chosen doublings of string lines by woodwinds (or vice versa), is a tour de

[22] In the finale of his Fifth Symphony, Mahler plays engagingly with the idea of taking a theme from a slow movement and translating it into a quick one. He had conducted several performances of *The Drumroll* (one of only two Haydn symphonies in his repertory!) in the years just before writing his own Fifth.

[23] Haydn had learned from Mozart's D-major Viola Quintet, K.593. The young Beethoven, writing his *Pathétique* Sonata, Opus 13, paid close attention to both models.

force of textural subtlety as well as a show of how innocent beginnings can give rise to unlikely complexities.

And now the Finale, perhaps Haydn's greatest. The first movement had suggested two things, one large and one small. First there was the idea that one theme might establish dominance over an entire movement; then, at the end, there was that flourish of horns, so surprising, but so purposefully planted. Haydn now picks up both threads, the second one first. He begins the Finale with a call for two horns alone. This is followed by an unmeasured silence, after which Haydn gives us the horn call again, though now as the accompaniment to a springy violin tune. At this point, ten seconds into the movement, we have met all of its thematic material. Haydn is never lavish with themes; indeed, drawing maximal variety and event from a monothematic design is a singularly characteristic manifestation of his inventive mind. But even by Haydn's standards, this finale is a bravura display of making very little go very far. To the end he keeps us surprised—he wrote only surprise symphonies—both with what he does that is new and with what he reveals about what is familiar.

Back in Vienna, he tightened the last pages. Given his overriding concern with compression, he was undoubtedly right; on the other hand, he heroically sacrificed a joke too good to remain forever unheard. It would be nice if conductors would once in a while give us a chance to hear what Londoners heard in 1795.[24]

Symphony No. 104 in D major

Adagio—Allegro
Andante
Menuet: Allegro
Finale: Spiritoso

Haydn wrote this symphony, his last, in London in 1795 and led its first performance at the King's Theatre on 4 May that year.[25]

---

[24] I have heard it only once, and that was at my instigation—in a performance by Peter Schneider and the San Francisco Symphony in 1984.

[25] This symphony is often called "the *London* Symphony." Given that this could equally well describe eleven other works, it is one of the most pointless of musical nicknames. The Germans, however, outdo us in silliness. They call it "the *Salomon* Symphony," a name that might apply to any one of nine other Haydn symphonies, but not to this one, inasmuch as it was written not for Salomon, but, like Nos. 102 and 103, for Viotti's Opera Concerts.

Two flutes, two oboes, two clarinets, two bassoons, two horns, two trumpets, timpani, and strings.

All the music on the bill when this symphony was introduced was by Haydn; the program included the seventh performance in about as many months of the work that had turned out to be the greatest popular success of his second London visit, the *Military* Symphony, No. 100 in G major. There were also some vocal numbers, and of one of the singers, a certain Madame Banti, Haydn notes in his diary—in English—that "she song very scanty." Of the event as a whole, Haydn remarked (back in German now) that "the whole company was thoroughly pleased and so was I. I made 4000 gulden on this evening: such a thing is possible only in England." The *Morning Chronicle*'s reviewer wrote: "It is with pleasure that we inform the public that genius is not so totally neglected as some are too often apt to confirm," and he also commented on the "fullness, richness, and majesty, in all its parts" of Haydn's new symphony.

Contemporary criticism was apt to stress the complexity, the sense of amplitude and abundance in Haydn's work. But his intoxicating intelligence and invention—and thus also his famous sense of humor—are as much and as inextricably tied to his feeling for economy. It is Haydn's way to work with few, simple, striking, and malleable ideas.

The purely formal fanfare that opens this symphony is an example. We hear it first in its most obvious, "natural" form, but it returns twice in the Adagio introduction, subtly transformed the first time, dramatically the second. And what rich returns Haydn derives from the sighing figure the violins introduce in the first measure after the fanfare!

When, after that, minor gives way to major and Adagio to Allegro, a single theme is almost all it takes to propel this densely and wittily worked movement along. The theme itself is laid out in a neat pair of eight-bar phrases, and it comes across as charming and innocent. Itself quiet, it soon yields to a lively *fortissimo* tutti. In due course the music makes its way to a new key, the dominant, where Haydn, rather than giving us a new melody as we would normally expect even from his thrifty self, serves forth a repetition of the one we already know. We quickly find out that this is not stinginess on his part. Interesting imitations enliven the texture, and at the last minute Haydn produces at least a hint of a new theme.

One of the features of the main theme is the four repeated notes that make up its third measure. Repeated notes are always a potential source of energy, and Haydn now proceeds to make a clever and ebullient demonstration of this. Those four notes and the pair of ever so slightly sighing half-notes that follow them are virtually all the material Haydn needs for

singularly robust, bold, and extensive development. After that, the recapitulation brings its own surprises; nor do we have to wait long for the first
of them, a delicious rescoring and revoicing for flute and oboes of the
second eight measures.

It was melodies like the one that begins the Andante that earned
Haydn his nineteenth-century reputation for innocence. Butter would not
melt in the mouth of the personage who speaks in the first four measures.
But the poignant (and accented) B-flat in the next phrase is fair warning,
and the extraordinary extensions when the opening phrase returns—the
violin sound now edged with a bit of bassoon tone—persuade us that innocence is but a point of departure for adventures both subtle and deep. The
most astonishing of these, the mysterious cessation of motion on remote
and mysterious harmonies and the touching speculation of the flute, is a
late afterthought of Haydn's. This moment is, with *The Representation of
Chaos* in *The Creation*, Haydn's furthest reach into the music of the future.

The strong Minuet is alive with amusing syncopations. The trio,
charmingly scored with its oboe and bassoon doublings of the violin line
and its "naive" pizzicato accompaniment, is gently lyrical. Haydn provides
ten measures of bridge into the reprise of the Minuet, and that is a very
rare feature in his music.

The Finale starts with a Croatian folk song, presented in rustic style
over a bagpipe-like drone. The movement as a whole, though, is full of
big-city wisdom about counterpoint and rapidly swirling dissonance. The
most remarkable thing here is surely the second, contrasting theme, slower
in gait and delicately harmonized, and Haydn uses it to make the most
mysterious and surprising transition into a recapitulation that ever occurred
to him. The final cadence is a powerful epigram.

Paul Hindemith (handwritten signature)

Paul Hindemith

Paul Hindemith was born in Hanau, Hesse-Nassau, on 16 November 1895 and died in Frankfurt on 28 December 1963.[1]

Symphony, *Mathis der Maler (Mathis the Painter)*

Angelic Concert (In quiet motion—Fairly lively half-notes)
Entombment (Very slow)
Temptation of Saint Anthony (Very slow, not in strict time—Very lively—Slow—Lively—Very lively)

Hindemith began preliminary studies for his opera *Mathis der Maler* in 1933, but, in response to a request from Wilhelm Furtwängler for a new piece for the Berlin Philharmonic, wrote the eponymous symphony first. He completed the first movement in November 1933, the second in February 1934, and the third just in time for the premiere on 12 March 1934. It was of course Furtwängler who introduced the *Mathis* symphony with the Berlin Philharmonic. The opera was completed in July 1935. Furtwängler had also hoped to conduct that premiere in Berlin, but this was verboten; the first performance therefore took place in Zürich, Switzerland, and only in May 1938.

[1] Hindemith saved misspellings of his name in letters, telegrams, bills, newspaper articles, concert programs, etc. A few of the many variants are Hindemitch, Hindemouth, Hintelmant, Hindismith, Heldeman, Hinder Mith, Hendrath, Hindemild, Algumuth, Hindemist, Hammermitt, Hairdemith, and Hundemith.

Two flutes (second doubling piccolo), two oboes, two clarinets, two bassoons, four horns, two trumpets, three trombones, tuba, timpani, glockenspiel, snare drum, cymbals, triangle, bass drum, and strings.

Hindemith was about to turn thirty-seven when his publisher, Willy Strecker, or possibly Franz Willms, one of the editors at Schott, drew his attention to Mathis or Matthias Grünewald, his future alter ego. As a musician Hindemith was already middle-aged, having left behind the wildnesses of his young years. I recall a conversation in New York about 1949 in which someone was describing a recording session of Varèse's *Ionisation* he had just attended to a woman who had grown up in Berlin in the 1920s. She listened wide-eyed to the account of this production by thirteen players of thirty-seven percussion instruments (including two fire sirens) and finally said, "My goodness, it must be worse than Hindemith!"

At the time it struck me as strange that she should have picked so mild a composer as Hindemith; only later did I understand that to a German of her age, especially to one not expert in music, Hindemith might well have represented the ne plus ultra of avant-garde craziness. He had even used a fire siren in his *Kammermusik* No. 1 (in 1921, ten years before Varèse), and thousands of Germans of this lady's generation who had never in their lives darkened the doors of an opera house would have recognized Hindemith's name as that of the man in whose opera the soprano sang an aria in the bathtub, nude. The soprano, warbling about nothing more salacious than the delights of an apartment with running hot water, was of course not nude, and her body-stockinged self was concealed in a mass of bubbles. One Berlin opera buff who saw *Neues vom Tage* (News of the Day) at the Kroll Opera in 1929 was the leader of the dissident National Socialist party—a man then taken seriously only by his followers and a few extreme pessimists—and he never forgave Hindemith this immorality.

When the 1930s began, Hindemith had been a public figure for many years. Since the early 1920s—and his own middle twenties—he had enjoyed an international reputation as one of the best and also one of the most "advanced" composers of the day, much admired, much imitated, much decried (the famous bathtub scene being by no means the first Hindemith scandal). He had been active as a performer since childhood and at nineteen was concertmaster of the Frankfurt opera; he was regarded, with Lionel Tertis and William Primrose, as one of the outstanding violists in the 1920s and 1930s; he was enough of a pianist to handle the keyboard parts in his own sonatas; he was an excellent clarinetist and, beyond that, proud of being able to play every part on every instrument in all seven of his *Kammermusiken* (a set of seven 1920s *Brandenburgs*)—some, he admitted, with more effort than others. He was a good conductor, a renowned teacher of composition, a gifted and inventive pedagogue altogether, an important author of books on the theory of music and the craft of musicianship and composition, and not least, an indefatigable organizer of concerts, festivals, and collegia musici.

Hitler became chancellor in January 1933. Hindemith, then working on an opera about the love of a German woman and a French prisoner of war in World War I, at first thought, like many other intelligent Germans, that this was simply the coming to power of the opposition, a nuisance to be ridden out. His wife, though a Catholic convert since her youth, was half-Jewish by birth;[2] even so, Hindemith initially watched the new government's racial and other policies with surprising equanimity, certainly with more irony than fury or fear. As late as 1935 he thought the worst was over, although by then he had seen such Jewish musicians as Schoenberg, Walter, Klemperer, Schnabel, Huberman, and his own string trio partners Emanuel Feuermann and Szymon Goldberg leave the country; he knew that Furtwängler had been forced, at least for a time, out of his positions with the Berlin Philharmonic and the Berlin State Opera, largely because of his support of Hindemith; and he had watched other non-Jewish colleagues, among them Adolf and Fritz Busch and Erich Kleiber, go into exile. His brother-in-law had spent a year in a concentration camp; nonetheless, it was not until September 1938 that the Hindemiths left Germany for a new home in Switzerland, four months after Paul had been prominently featured, along with Schoenberg, Stravinsky, Weill, Irving Berlin, and Louis Armstrong, among others, in a much publicized traveling exhibition of "Entartete Musik"—degenerate music. Still, Hindemith's decision in 1933 to abandon *Étienne und Luise* (to which he never returned) and to direct his attention to *Mathis der Maler*, which became his magnum opus, suggests that he was more troubled by the situation and his position in it than he otherwise let on.

The painter Mathias Grünewald, like El Greco, was a discovery of the 1920s. Born in Würzburg in the third quarter of the fifteenth century, he died in 1528, the same year as Dürer. His real name was Mathis Gothart, to which he added Nithart, his wife's family name, when he married in 1519. His first biographer, the seventeenth-century painter Joachim von Sandrart, called him Grünewald. No one knows why, but that name has stuck. Grünewald's most important work—and one of the most over-

---

[2] Gertrud Hindemith was the daughter of Ludwig Rottenberg, music director at Frankfurt during the composer's concertmastering days. It was apropos of her that Göring made his oft-cited assertion, "*I'll* decide who's Jewish" ("Wer Jude ist, bestimme ich"). Göring had actually taken over this formulation from Karl Lueger, the notoriously anti-Semitic mayor of Vienna at the beginning of the twentieth century.

whelming works in Western art—is his altarpiece for the Antonite monastery at Isenheim in Alsace (now in the Unterlinden Museum at Colmar). The conception and execution of this powerful polyptych play a crucial role in *Mathis der Maler*.

The central themes of the opera, whose libretto Hindemith wrote himself and which he wished to present as an *apologia pro vita sua*, are: What is an artist to do at a time of political crisis, engage in the struggle or attend to his art? Can "non-engaged" art be justified? In a program note for the premiere of the opera, Hindemith wrote:

> If I have attempted to present in a form appropriate to the stage what I read into the few dates in the life of Mathis Gothart Nithart and what they suggest about his works, I have done so because I can think of no more vital, problematic, humanly and artistically moving (therefore in the best sense dramatic) a figure than the creator of the Isenheim Altar . . . a man so obscured by the shadows cast by his own legend that for centuries no one knew his real name, but who speaks to us today through his art with uncanny intensity and warmth.
>
> This man, whose artistic work was blessed with the highest imaginable degree of perfection but who was plagued by all the hellish torments of a doubting, searching spirit, experienced . . . with all the sensibility of such a constitution the coming of a new era with its concomitant over-turning of accepted values. Although he knew well the consequential artistic achievements of the dawning Renaissance, he chose in his own work to develop to their fullest potential the materials of the past, rather like J. S. Bach, who appears as a conservator in the stream of musical progress. Caught in the powerful machinery of church and state, he had the strength to resist these forces, and in his paintings he could report clearly enough how profoundly he was shaken by the wild tumult of his time, with all its suffering, its sicknesses, and its wars.[3]

The historical Mathis seems to have sympathized with the German peasants in the series of bloody and destructive uprisings they began in 1524 and to have lost the patronage of the Cardinal-Archbishop of Mainz because of his stand. Hindemith's Mathis, an anti-hero before that expression was coined, actually joins the peasant army but fails utterly as a man of action. At the end, his great work for Isenheim accomplished, Mathis wishes only to retire from the world, alone.[4]

Hindemith's own agenda is clear: to be an apolitical artist. In what Donald Tovey called "the most emancipating intellectual maxim of mod-

---

[3] Zürich Stadttheater program book, 28 May 1938.
[4] Hindemith alters the chronology for the sake of his drama: the Isenheim altar, commissioned in 1515, was finished several years before the peasant uprisings.

ern times," the authors of 1066 and All That tell us that "history is what we remember." Or, recalling the last line of Edith Sitwell's "Tango"—"For what they hear they repeat"—so aptly set to music by Hindemith's friend William Walton, we might also add that what we hear or read and then repeat becomes history. Something that has become history is the idea that Mathis der Maler was a courageous anti-Nazi manifesto. I certainly don't know that anyone publicly questioned this before 1982, when Fred K. Prieberg published his Musik im NS-Staat (Music in the National Socialist State). Hindemith's publisher, Willy Strecker, described the composer's state of mind in August 1933:

> He is full of enthusiasm for the subject, which suits him extremely well. This can become the German opera. The figure of Grünewald, who went his own way in spite of being misunderstood, and resisted the influence of the Italian Renaissance, is of course a reflection of himself, and that is why it interests him so tremendously. . . . The theme is big and German, yet of international interest.[5]

Rather than being an anti-Nazi manifesto, Mathis seems to have been intended as a salvage operation, as a move on Hindemith's part to establish himself as a good German artist. Surely Strecker's emphasis on the German-ness of the opera was based on conversations between himself and Hindemith, and the "big and German" theme of Mathis is a striking departure from the Francophile "internationalist" one, unwelcome in the Third Reich, of the abandoned Étienne und Luise. And as late as March 1935, Strecker, with Hindemith's approval, penned a defense in which he stressed—and I quote from Geoffrey Skelton's biography—that Hindemith

> had never written "cheap successes" like The Three-Penny Opera or [Krenek's] Jonny spielt auf; he did not owe his success to Jewish cliques and critics—on the contrary, he had often had trouble with Jewish critics; he avoided the use of "fashionable instruments typical of a destructive age" such as vibraphones and wind machines; and his positive, constructive music could not be compared with "the decadent intellectual musical efforts of a Schoenberg," to whose ideas he had always been sharply opposed.[6]

---

[5] Quoted in Geoffrey Skelton, Paul Hindemith: The Man Behind the Music (New York: Taplinger, 1975).

[6] Quoted, ibid. Strecker conveniently forgot the saxophones in Hindemith's operas Cardillac, Hin und zurück, and Neues vom Tage, the banjo in the latter work, and the Kammermusik fire siren. It is interesting to speculate about what Dr. Richard Strauss, President of the Reichsmusikkammer (the arm of the Propaganda Ministry responsible for musical matters), would have said if he had seen Strecker's letter and found the wind machine in his Don Quixote and Alpine Symphony described as a fashionable instrument typical of a destructive age. —M.S.

In the event, the premiere of the *Mathis der Maler* Symphony was a resounding success. Hindemith's continuing turn toward a more conservative style pleased the public and the politicians, and it seemed that the composer's rehabilitation was complete, the dread bathtub forgotten. Hindemith himself conducted the Berlin Philharmonic in a Telefunken recording and received many invitations to lead the work in concert. But German *Kulturpolitik* was anything other than stable, and only a month after Furtwängler's triumph with *Mathis*, Hans Rosbaud was forbidden to conduct the work for Frankfurt Radio.

Both Hindemith and Furtwängler were caught in the political infighting between Dr. Goebbels and Alfred Rosenberg, editor of the official Nazi paper, *Völkischer Beobachter*. Later in 1934, Furtwängler published an essay, "The Hindemith Case," which was featured on the front page of the *Deutsche Allgemeine Zeitung* and made him a hero with the Berlin public (one reads of twenty-minute ovations for him at the Philharmonie and at a *Tristan* performance the day the article appeared). On the other hand, his pertinent question "What is to become of us if political denunciation is to be applied in the fullest measure to matters of art?" got him fired from the Philharmonic, the Opera, and the Reichsmusikkammer that same year. Goebbels himself addressed the Hindemith Case in a major speech, and there could no longer be any question of a performance of *Mathis* at the Berlin Opera.

"There are only two things worth aiming for: good music and a clean conscience," Hindemith wrote to Strecker in his first letter after settling in Switzerland, "and both are being taken care of now. Looked at from this point of view, all our previous efforts were a waste of time. . . . " No question, *Mathis der Maler* is good music, and the *Mathis* Symphony, by virtue of its concentration, is even stronger than the opera.

Each of the three movements is named for one of the panels of the Isenheim Altarpiece. When closed, the center wings of Grünewald's polyptych show the Crucifixion, as horrifying as any ever painted; smaller side panels depict Saint Anthony on the left and Saint Sebastian on the right. Below the Crucifixion and slightly behind it is the Entombment. When the center wings are opened, their reverse sides show a violently excited Annunciation on the left, a radiant Resurrection on the right, and they free the view of the Angelic Concert. The Angelic Concert is also painted on two wings that can be opened, and their reverse sides show the Conversation of Saints Paul and Anthony on the left and the Temptation of Saint Anthony on the right. In the middle are sculpted figures of Saints Augustine, Anthony, and Jerome. The Entombment on the predella can also be opened to reveal a sculpted Last Supper.

Grünewald's Angelic Concert, for which the first movement of Hindemith's symphony is named, depicts a Virgin and Child being serenaded by an angel playing a never-never instrument something like a viola da gamba with a host of seraphic instrumentalists in a pavilion behind. The symphony's opening movement appears twice in the opera—first, unaltered, as the Overture, and then, beautifully developed, in a scene where Mathis has a vision of this picture when he is in flight from his miscarried military career.

The music begins in slow solemnity, three softly luminous G-major string chords punctuating rising woodwind phrases. (Many things in *Mathis* happen by threes.) This introduction done, trombones gently sing an old German song, *Es sungen drei Engel ein' süssen Gesang* (Three Angels Were Singing a Sweet Song). Hindemith himself pointed to folk song, Reformation war songs, and Gregorian chant as the "nourishing soil" in which Mathis grew. "Es sungen drei Engel" is also heard three times, raised at each occurrence by a major third and moving from trombones through horns to the A-major brightness of trumpets with woodwinds and glockenspiel. Then the main part of the movement begins, striding energetically in duple meter. At the height of the elaborately contrapuntal development the three angels return, splendidly illuminated, and after a highly condensed recapitulation the movement ends grandly, in G major.

The second movement, called *Entombment*, opens with touchingly hesitant gestures which introduce an eloquent melody begun by the flute and continued by the oboe. The music moves toward a solemn climax; the coda, one of Hindemith's most beautiful pages, is profoundly peaceful. In the opera, this movement becomes the interlude between the two scenes of the Seventh Tableau, following the death of Regina, daughter of the peasant leader Schwalb; it also underlies the final scene. Hindemith also leaned on it heavily when, in January 1936, he found himself in London with less than twenty-four hours in which to produce a *Trauermusik* (Mourning Music) for the death of King George V.

Originally Hindemith had imagined his *Mathis* Suite (as he then thought of it) as having four movements, with the *Entombment* as finale, as it would be in the opera. When he went to a three-movement design, with *Entombment* in second place, deciding what to do for a finale was what gave him the greatest difficulty in the whole project. He was in fact on the point of leaving it at two movements when he saw how he could use the Temptation of Saint Anthony in the opera, and once that idea was clear he was able to compose the symphony's third movement in four weeks. This movement is the most elaborate of the three, and the relationship between symphony and opera is most complex here.

In a manner that will remind some readers of the way Robertson Davies places and uses Francis Cornish's wedding triptych in *What's Bred in the Bone,* Hindemith has Mathis undergo his spiritual crisis in a scene in which the painter himself becomes Saint Anthony, other characters in the drama assume such roles as Luxuria and a harlot, and the events Grünewald depicted on the panel spring to life on the stage.[7] Hindemith supplies a Latin epigraph for the finale of his Symphony: "Ubi eras bone Jhesu/ubi eras, quare non affuisti/ut sanares vulnera meas?" (Where were you, good Jesus, where were you? Why have you not come to heal my wounds?) This is taken from the altarpiece, and in the opera Mathis/Anthony sings it at the height of his torment. The opening is an orchestral recitative in fiercely twisted lines, an extraordinary passage. The main part of the movement is a thrusting quick music in triple meter. Prepared by a silence, a four-note descending phrase emerges with special emphasis: in the opera it will be sung repeatedly by the chorus to the words "Wir plagen dich" (We torment you). After a brief slow interlude, the finale moves ever more rapidly, first developing the "Wir plagen dich" motif, then superimposing the Gregorian *Lauda Sion Salvatorem* (Zion, Praise the Savior) as a majestic woodwind chant across scurrying strings, finally to reach home in a glorious brass Alleluia.

---

[7]Davies explicitly mentions Grünewald, Hindemith, and *Mathis der Maler* in the scene where Cornish's triptych is unveiled. The literal translation of *Luxuria* is "luxury," but the word carries strong connotations of dissipation and excess.

Arthur Honegger

Arthur Honegger was born in Le Havre, France, on 10 March 1892 and died in Paris on 27 November 1955.

Mention Honegger and, after "hmm," you will probably get "Didn't he write that piece about a locomotive?" or perhaps some head-scratching about Les Six. Yes, he did write that piece about a locomotive. Called *Pacific 231*, it is really an abstract study in the relationship of rhythm and tempo, the colorful title being an afterthought; so at least Honegger maintained years later. As *Mouvement symphonique* No. 1, which is the other, abstract half of its title, this engaging work would not have had one-thousandth the number of performances. (It is a good locomotive piece too.)[1] And yes, Honegger was a member of Les Six—with Auric, Durey, Milhaud, Poulenc, and Tailleferre—but that doesn't mean a thing. Although they were all friends, Les Six were not bound in any aesthetic or musico-political alliance, even though Jean Cocteau, as self-appointed coach, guru, and flak, made a move toward inventing a coherent artistic stance for them. It is ironic that Honegger is remembered for two things so off to one side from his essential artistic personality. Very few orchestral musicians I have asked could remember playing one of Honegger's symphonies recently, if ever.

The New Grove Dictionary of Music and Musicians calls Honegger a Swiss composer, but of course notes that he was born in Le Havre. (In the previous edition he was "a French-born composer of Swiss parentage.") Other reference books list him variously as a "French composer," "com-

---

[1] Ephraim Katz's *Film Encyclopedia* also lists a 1931 film score, *Pacific 231*, but here I must plead ignorance.

poser of Swiss parentage and nationality, but identified with the modern French school," "of Swiss parentage," "a German Swiss Protestant," and a "French-born Swiss composer." David Mason Greene gets more specific in his lively *Biographical Encyclopedia of Composers* and tells us that "despite Honegger's French birth, he was legally Swiss, his parents having come to Le Havre from Switzerland to set up a business in café fixtures."

Honegger himself felt ties both to Zürich, where his parents came from, and to Paris, his elective home, incredibly different though those two worlds are. In the conversations with the critic Bernard Gavoty that make up his book *I Am a Composer*, he said:

> I am what the language of passports calls of "dual nationality," that is to say, a combination of French and Swiss. Born at Le Havre to Swiss parents, I have lived in France most of my life and studied there as though I were French, yet at my core there is a Swiss atavism, that which Milhaud calls my Helvetic sensibility. All the rest—my intellectual blossoming, the sharpening of my moral and spiritual values—I owe to France.
>
> What do I owe to Switzerland? Without doubt, the Protestant tradition, great difficulty in deluding myself about the value of what I do, a naive sense of honesty, a familiarity with the Bible.
>
> What do I owe to Le Havre? My childhood years and the passions of those happy times: the sea . . . [which] had a profound influence and enlarged the horizons of my childhood. . . . And I must not forget my favorite sports—track, swimming, soccer, and rugby. And it was at Le Havre that I began to write music.[2]

There was always music at home: Mrs. Honegger was a fine alto and a good pianist. He learned the Beethoven sonatas from her and, when he had become good enough on the violin, joined her in the violin sonatas and the trios. Beethoven was the object of intense love all Honegger's life, and so was Bach. No wonder he felt out of tune with the anti-German frivolities that Cocteau proclaimed as an artistic program for Les Six. Theater became another passion. Early, he tried his hand at opera and, approaching sixty, he wrote, "It would have been my dream to write only operas."

At seventeen, Honegger went to the Conservatory in Zürich, and it was Friedrich Hegar, the director of that school, who persuaded his parents to allow him to become a musician. For two years he commuted from Le Havre to Paris for instruction from Lucien Capet in violin, Charles-Marie Widor in composition, André Gédalge in counterpoint and fugue, and

---

[2] Arthur Honegger, *I Am a Composer* (New York: St. Martin's Press, 1966). Rugby was the subject of Honegger's *Mouvement symphonique* No. 2, composed 1928, five years after *Pacific 231*. —M.S.

Vincent d'Indy in conducting. In 1913, when the senior Honeggers returned to Switzerland, Arthur settled in Paris for good, beginning an active life as composer and performer, and initiating a rich round of friendships with artists, writers, and other musicians. He lived for a time with the great mezzo-soprano Claire Croiza, admired by three generations of French composers from Saint-Saëns to Poulenc; later he married the pianist Andrée Vaurabourg.

In 1921, because the deadline was too tight for Jean Dupérier, the first composer approached, Honegger was asked to provide music for play about King David to be staged at a festival in the Swiss village of Mézières. Ernest Ansermet had recommended him, and it was as lucky a break for René Morax, the playwright and founder of the Mézières theater who had written the text, as it was for the unknown twenty-nine-year-old composer. Honegger's score for soloists, chorus, and a brilliantly handled ensemble of eighteen instruments was a hit.

He himself saw further possibilities in it. He always had a penchant for the grand utterance. ("I shall never forget L'Impératrice aux rochers at the Paris Opéra," wrote the waspish Virgil Thomson, "which fell as flat as anything could fall in spite of the presence on stage at one and the same time of the Pope, the Emperor, the Virgin Mary, Madame Ida Rubinstein, and twenty live horses.") Honegger rescored King David for large orchestra. That did not fall flat. It had the kind of success all composers dream of and is still a mainstay of the choral repertory. In recent years there has been renewed interest in another extravaganza for Ida Rubinstein, Joan of Arc at the Stake.[3]

After his triumph with King David, Honegger was a major figure. He wrote music across a wide range of genres: operas, oratorios, ballets, incidental music for plays, film scores, music for radio, orchestral works, cham-

---

[3] Rubinstein came from Russia, a tall woman described as of "mysteriously androgynous beauty." She was wealthy, she was demanding (Stravinsky recounts that she commissioned the painter Léon Bakst to arrange the flowers in her Parisian garden in boxes so that the design could be changed every few weeks), she kept a black tiger cub, and it was bruited that she drank champagne out of Madonna lilies. Her real talent was in mime, but she was ambitious to dance, act, and sing. In 1909, Diaghilev introduced her in Fokine's Cléopâtre, and she was sensational in a role perfected suited to her gifts and limitations, as she was the year after in Sheherazade. Later, she was off on enterprises of her own, the d'Annunzio-Debussy Martyre de St. Sébastien being the first of what the dance historian Lynn Garafola calls her "genre-defying spectacles." ("I found the legs of Mme. Rubinstein sublime. . . . For me this was everything", wrote Proust to the composer Reynaldo Hahn after the premiere.) In 1928, she formed her own company. She died in 1960 at, as Nicolas Slonimsky writes, "an uncertain age (but old)." Music lovers are profoundly in her debt: aside from her Debussy and Honegger projects, she got Stravinsky to compose Perséphone and Le Baiser de la fée, and it was for her that Ravel wrote Bolero.

ber music, songs.[4] He himself seemed to be everywhere, conducting, playing, lecturing, teaching, writing criticism, receiving awards. Koussevitzky invited him to teach at Tanglewood in the summer of 1947. On the way there, in New York, Honegger suffered a heart attack. He was never really well again, and the works of the last eight years of his life are few.

Honegger's huge oeuvre is a bewildering mixture of the serious and the frivolous, of severity and hokum, invention and routine, delicacy of utterance and yelling on a soapbox, elegance of texture and racket. Lots of winnowing is in order, but those of his compositions that are the most sincere and focused—the Second, Third, and Fifth symphonies, the opera *Antigone* (his own favorite, and Poulenc's too), *Pacific 231*, the Christmas Cantata, the First and Third string quartets, the *Suite archaïque*, and always the lovable and moving *King David*—are treasures.[5]

Of Honegger's five symphonies, No. 1 (1930), commissioned for the Boston Symphony's fiftieth anniversary, stands apart from the others in chronology and style. The others come from the ten-year span, 1941 to 1950, whose first half is dominated by World War II. Legally and morally, Honegger could have gone to a comfortable existence in Switzerland in 1940; he preferred to stick it out among the people whose life he had been a part of since before World War I. His Symphony No. 2 was commissioned for the Basel Chamber Orchestra's tenth anniversary in 1936. Honegger did not get around to writing it until five years later, and, as a wartime piece, it turned into a powerfully grim composition in which the air brightens only in the last minute, literally, when a trumpet joins the string orchestra in a chorale. The Symphony No. 3, the *Liturgique*, was written in the immediate aftermath of the war; its three movements are titled *Dies irae*, *De profundis clamavi*, and *Dona nobis pacem*, and it explores further the dark temper of the Second. The Symphony No. 4 (1946), another work for the Basel Chamber Orchestra and called *Deliciae Basiliensis* (The Delights of Basel) is a cheerful intermezzo in the series. Honegger's heart attack occurred in 1947; the vivid Fifth concluded the series three years later.

---

[4]The two film scores you might have heard are those for *Crime and Punishment* (1935, directed by Pierre Chanal, with Pierre Blanchard and Harry Baur) and, more likely, the one for *Pygmalion* (1938, directed by Anthony Asquith, with Wendy Hiller and Leslie Howard). Honegger also wrote the original score, since lost, for the Abel Gance *Napoléon* (1927).

[5]It is sad to read in *I Am a Composer* that Honegger grew tired of *King David* in later years. He told Bernard Gavoty that he listened to it "with a certain boredom. . . . I try . . . to pretend that I am a spectator just like the others, and endeavor to sort out the good qualities from the bad."

Symphonie liturgique (No. 3)

Dies irae (Allegro marcato)
De profundis clamavi (Adagio)
Dona nobis pacem (Andante—Adagio)

Honegger composed this symphony in 1945-46. The first performance was given by the Zürich Tonhalle Orchestra under Charles Munch on 17 August 1946. The dedication is to Charles Munch.

Three flutes (one doubling piccolo), two oboes and English horn, two clarinets and bass clarinet, two bassoons and contrabassoon, four horns, three trumpets, three trombones, tuba, piano, suspended cymbal, bass drum, triangle, field drum, tam-tam, and strings.

Honegger described his *Symphonie liturgique* as "a drama in which there are three actors: misery, happiness, and humanity." He gave Latin titles from the Roman Catholic liturgy to each of its three movements: *Dies irae* (Day of Wrath) from the Mass for the Dead; *De profundis clamavi* (Out of the depths have I cried unto thee) from Psalm 129, one of the Penitential Psalms used in the Daily Office of the Roman liturgy; and *Dona nobis pacem* (Give us peace) from the Ordinary of the Mass.[6] As he worked on his *Symphonie liturgique* at the end of the war, Honegger almost certainly did not know that just after the start of that catastrophe the twenty-six-year-old Benjamin Britten had composed a *Sinfonia da Requiem* to whose three movements he gave the titles *Lacrymosa, Dies irae,* and *Requiem aeternam.*

Honegger's *Dies irae* opens with an ominous rumbling in low strings—a sinister variant of the opening of the last movement of Debussy's *La Mer*—and all the strings are quickly drawn into this commotion. More sharply defined material emerges: irritably dissonant, syncopated adumbrations of march music in trumpets and high woodwinds; the beginnings of an angular theme, also marchlike, in the strings; bass instruments stalking threateningly. The march character comes unmistakably to the fore as these elements coalesce. After a time, prompted by cellos with bassoons,

[6]"Out of the depths" is Psalm 129 in the Catholic Bible but 130 in Protestant versions.

then by violas with oboe and English horn, the violins offer a new and ardent melody, but swirling woodwinds and syncopated trumpets cannot leave it undisturbed. This chapter comes to a close with a theme in which strings and woodwinds move in block chords.

This music reaches a crest of intensity; then everything is abruptly choked off. We hear the rumbling opening music again; the field drum adds its own military rhythm and becomes an ever more inescapable presence; the angular phrase introduced by the strings at the beginning is expanded into a powerful melody of great breadth. The return of the theme in block chords leads to the coda. While horns and cymbal create a kind of white-noise background, and with timpani adding punctuation that sets a triple meter against the prevailing march tempo, we hear the last protests of the rumbling *La Mer* gesture. The music is no longer loud, but the rhythmic drive is relentless to the very last note.

De profundis clamavi is a prayer. *I Am a Composer* contains an interesting exchange about this movement. Gavoty says: "You have sought—I have it from your own mouth—a development without recapitulations or joints, a melodic line which, starting from point A, strives to reach its terminus at point B by an unbroken trajectory. It is impossible to imagine a purer or subtler form." Honegger replies:

> You are too kind. True, above all, I have tried for a melodic line which I want to be ample, generous, free-flowing, and not a labored piling up of fragments that do not sit happily next to one another. . . . The large melodic flow in no way excludes punctuation. That is the mark of successful composition, and we find it in all the masters. . . . I think of the highest form of melody as being like rainbows. They rise and come down again, but you cannot at any one moment say, "Here, you see, it has returned to fragment B, there to fragment A". . . . Listeners must be able simply to let themselves be carried along by melodies and rhythms. . . . [7]

The *De profundis* is a handsome realization of Honegger's ideal. The most emotionally penetrating of his inventions as well as the one most persistently present, is a chorale-like melody sung very near the beginning by the cellos, whose line is higher than that of the violins and violas. There is much counterpoint, and the interwoven lines are subtly made, unpredictable in detail. Violas with English horn and second violins with oboe utter agonized cries. At the close, a single flute takes off in flight, a bird soaring over a devastated world, perhaps a symbol of hope that the prayer—"Lord, hear my voice"—may yet be answered.

[7] Honegger, *I am a Composer.*

The *Dona nobis pacem* seems to crush that hope. In Beethoven's *Missa solemnis*, completed eight years after Waterloo but aflame with the composer's memory of twenty-two years of virtually continuous war, the *Dona nobis pacem* is headed "Prayer for inward *and outward* peace." (The italics are mine.) Similarly, *pax*, for Honegger in 1945, means the cessation of war as much as it means peace of spirit. Like Haydn in his *Missa in tempore belli* and, overwhelmingly, Beethoven in the *Missa solemnis*, Honegger must, before praying for peace, evoke the horror of war so as to bring home to us the need for that prayer.

The grim, measured march that dominates this movement was in fact the first music Honegger heard in his mind when he composed the *Symphonie liturgique*. He spoke about this to the composer Marcel Delannoy, who published a book about Honegger in 1953:

> [The theme of the finale] is the theme of human folly, a kind of march that marks time around the same notes, stuttering, constantly repeating the same thing: war, customs regulations, militarism, nationalism, red tape, the gradual transformation of human beings into slaves of a deaf and blind government. A second theme portrays people's defensive response, but human idiocy engulfs everything until a universal cry bursts forth, a kind of "Help! Help!" which, translated into Latin, might come out as "*Dona nobis pacem! Dona nobis pacem!*" And then peace returns. One escapes aloft: an aspiration for purity. A hope of peace . . . serenity. There are even birds left to sing in the trees. It is so clear that with a bit of good will all this could be so easily arranged.[8]

The English critic Felix Aprahamian, whose translation on the sleeve of the Ansermet recording I have adapted, points out that the expression rendered here as "human idiocy" is "bowdlerized even in the original French to 'c . . . e'."

Against a stubbornly dull marking of time by piano and timpani with bass drum punctuations, bass clarinet and double basses in contrary motion begin the dull-witted march of folly. Horns assert themselves with a more aggressive new theme. Low strings rumble thunderously in short phrases like those with which the symphony began. Woodwinds jeeringly plunge through two octaves of chromatic scales. High cellos—again they are set above the other strings—sing out in anguished phrases. Trumpets, using the technique called flutter-tongue, bray their dirty mockery.

All this ascends to a fierce climax. Suddenly everything stops save for a few errant explosions. Now is the time for prayer. In C-sharp major, the first violins and a single cello play a chorale.[9] Flutes and trumpets offer a reminder of the first march theme, heard as though from very far away. Then, as in the last bars of the *De profundis*, and with the solo cello continuing its poignant song, a lark ascends. A single violin speaks the benediction.

Symphony No. 5, *Di tre re*

> *Grave*
> *Allegretto*
> *Allegro marcato*

Honegger wrote his Symphony No. 5 in 1950, completing the composition of the first movement on 5 September and the orchestration on 28 October, finishing the writing of the second movement and its orchestration on 1 October and 23 November respectively, and the two stages of the third on 10 November and 3 December. The title means "Of the three D's." More about that below. The work was commissioned by the Koussevitzky Music Foundation and is dedicated to the memory of Natalie Koussevitzky. The first performances were given by the Boston Symphony on 9 and 10 March 1951 under Koussevitzky's successor, Charles Munch.

Three flutes, two oboes and English horn, two clarinets and bass clarinet, three bassoons, four horns, three trumpets, three trombones, tuba, timpani, and strings.

At my first hearing of this symphony—it was a scorching performance by Charles Munch and the Boston Symphony on tour in Stuttgart—the music brought to mind and heart the racked compositions of Adrian Leverkühn, the tragic central figure of Thomas Mann's *Doctor Faustus*.[10]

[9] This is the first music in clear-cut major, but Honegger notates it in C-sharp minor, indicating each E-sharp by an accidental. Is it too fanciful to read into this the idea that even now there is something tentative and uncertain about the sense of consolation the major mode suggests?

[10] About 1950, the then very young Argentine composer Mauricio Kagel had tried actually to write Leverkühn's pieces on the basis of Mann's descriptions, only to discover the truth of Mann's assertion that it took only one or two good details to produce a convincing description. In other words, there simply was not enough to go on.

Later, as I came to know more music, I learned that Dmitri Shostakovich and his German contemporary Karl Amadeus Hartmann were still more potent post-Mahlerian symphonists of apocalypse. Nonetheless, returning after a long interval to the Honegger Fifth and its predecessors, particularly the wartime Second (1941) and the immediately postwar *Symphonie liturgique* (1946), I found again that Honegger, in a serious mood *and* at his most concentrated, was an authentic and powerfully truthful messenger from the world of the mid-twentieth century.

The Fifth Symphony is compact, its three movements running about twenty-two minutes. Like the Prokofiev Violin Concerto No. 1, it turns the familiar fast-slow-fast design inside out. The opening slow movement's first idea is a series of thickly voiced, fully scored chords in contrary motion, that is, the high voices descend while the low ones climb. The first chord is an unambiguous D minor, and the harmonies that follow, quite dissonant, move around that key. The sense is of an oppressive cloud. After two shorter and quieter echoes of this paragraph, a new kind of music begins, linear, transparent, in quicker notes (though still at the same "Grave" tempo), and dominated by the sound of solo woodwinds. Trumpets, though also quiet, pierce the texture with strange, stuttering fragments of fanfare.

As the counterpoint becomes busier, the music crests to *fortissimo* and recapitulates the massive opening theme. Meanwhile the trumpets, having lost their shyness and hesitation, bridge what would otherwise be a long silence with a harrowing scream. From this there emerges a *pianissimo* transformation of the opening music, now decorated by the winds with fragments of broken chords. For a moment this is reversed, winds playing the theme and strings adding the broken-chord commentary. Then the movement subsides and heads toward its quiet close. Pizzicato strings define the final D-minor cadence, which is given special color by a "foreign" E-flat. The last note is a low D for pizzicato cellos and basses with timpani.

The second movement is an unmerry scherzo that proceeds at a moderate tempo. The clarinet, accompanied by staccato violins, leads off with a chromatic theme. From time to time, string chords slap irritably at the utterances of the woodwinds. The music rises to *fortissimo,* to be immediately interrupted by an Adagio of Tchaikovskian melancholia. This is gorgeously scored, the string parts being arranged so as to put the cellos and sometimes the violas higher than the violins. It is also very short, just nineteen measures; then the Allegretto resumes, newly and inventively scored with lots of chattering sixteenth-notes. Brasses threaten, low strings shudder in tremolando. The Adagio returns, only half as long as before, but more elaborately orchestrated, the strings (now muted) seconded by brass, and with a beautiful overlay of running sixteenths for the woodwinds. The opening music returns once more, its procedures speeded up. The final sound, appearing as though out of nowhere, is the same low D for pizzicato cellos and basses with timpani that ended the first movement.

The finale is obsessive and sinister, a sort of Shostakovich march, but more dissonant. Trumpets establish a firm sense of one-two-three-four, but other instruments do their best to subvert any sense of regularity and safety. Unlike the first two movements, with their flexibilities and changes of pace, this is very much an *in tempo* music. For a moment, a brave tune unfurls itself across the scene like a banner. Then the marchers are transformed into goblins. The rhythm is relentless, but the sounds are *pianissimo* and the texture is in fragments. The bass line makes its way down to the keynote, and without a trace of ritard, the music comes to its exceedingly punctual close. The final, isolated sound is the same low D for pizzicato cellos and basses with timpani that ended the two previous movements.

And thus the three D's, the *tre re*. If Honegger meant anything by the title other than the literal reference to the three closing D's, he never said so.

Chas. E. Ives.

Charles Ives

Charles Edward Ives was born in Danbury, Connecticut, on 20 October 1874 and died in New York on 19 May 1954.

It is, on the face of it, absurd that I, born fifty-four years after Charles Ives, should have been able to attend the premieres of three of his four symphonies—not in utero or as a babe in arms, but as a grown man. The facts are these: Lou Harrison's performance of the Symphony No. 3 with the New York Little Symphony at the Carnegie Chamber Music Hall (now Weill Recital Hall) on 5 April 1946 was the first complete performance of any symphony by Ives; Leonard Bernstein conducted the New York Philharmonic-Symphony in the first performance of the Symphony No. 2 on George Washington's Birthday in 1951; and Leopold Stokowski introduced the Symphony No. 4 in April 1965, nearly eleven years after Ives's death. As for the Symphony No. 1, written in 1897–98, Walter Damrosch rehearsed three movements of it with the New York Symphony in 1910 but pronounced it unsuitable for public performance. It was not heard in concert until November 1965, when the Chicago Symphony played it under Morton Gould.

To Ives, inspired, original, aggressive, untidy, hard-nosed, sentimental, Damrosch represented that genteel tradition of music-making whose very existence enraged him and whose extinction was his lifelong mission. "Nice" was for Ives the ultimate putdown. It was part of his misogyny and, as the Anglo-American musicologist Philip Brett puts it, of being "thoroughly saturated in homosexual panic." With that went an overload of right-wing political fury, a general tendency to be impatient, contemptuous, and to fall into abusive name-calling. Ives had absorbed these attitudes, if not all their specific manifestations, as a child and adolescent, when the great presence in his life was his father, George Edward Ives,

Danbury's bandmaster, a music teacher, leader of theater orchestras, director of music at the Methodist Church, and the only one of four siblings not to follow their father into a respectable life in commerce and industry.

Not only was George Ives a musician, he was an unsettlingly unconventional one, with an unbounded hunger for experimentation inside the home as well as out of it. He accompanied his family in C while they sang *Old Folks at Home* in E-flat, tried to teach them tunes in quarter-tones, played his cornet across the water so as to study the echo, worked with bells and glasses, and rigged up musical machines of his own invention. When his own band and another passed in the park, each playing a different march, he was delighted. Recalling that event more than eighty years later, the ninety-seven-year-old Danbury architect Philip Sunderland confirmed that it had "interested [George Ives] very much," but added that "people in Danbury didn't think it was very interesting to see the two bands blending and playing different tunes. They didn't take George Ives very seriously. He was only the bandleader."

But the handsome and athletic Charlie took his father very seriously indeed, and George, both in his lifetime and afterward, in memory, nurtured his son's fantasy and his courage. It is not only what the Danbury bands played—and Ives's music is always full of reference to hymns, marches, dance music, and other sounds from the vernacular—but their blending and colliding that determined the sound of his compositions. He loved musical collage and gave new meaning to the notion of polyphony: in his scores it is not just the counterpoint of individual musical strands but the coming together of whole different musics. He shocked his listeners by blurring the hallowed line between the cultivated and the popular. He questioned the idea that tempo should be stable and probed the possibility of flexible, evolving speeds. He found his way to polytonality, atonality, polyrhythms, and other devices that, like Leonardo's bicycle and contact lenses and ball bearings, all had to be reinvented by others. He even anticipated ideas dear to some composers in the 1960s: that any sound is potential music, that a stylistically neat and consistent articulation of musical materials is not a necessary part of the musical experience, and that a work need not be "fixed," but might be work-in-progress as long as its creator lived.

What matters more than any of these inventions or discoveries is Ives's personal voice, his transcendent vision, his belief in the power of music to speak to the most central questions of human existence. There are sensitive, intelligent, exploring people whose temperaments will forever make them allergic to Ives's grandly imprecise, al fresco manner. Not every piece by Ives works, but at his best he is one of the most tender and amusing of songwriters, a genre painter of heart-piercing sureness of touch (particularly in the *Holidays* Symphony, the Third Symphony [*The Camp*

Meeting], the Second Orchestral Set, and *Three Places in New England*) and capable of awesome grandeur of utterance. In support of the last claim I would cite especially the Violin Sonata No. 3, both piano sonatas, and the Symphony No. 4.

For a time, after his graduation from Yale in 1898, he worked as an organist, first in Bloomfield, New Jersey, then at Central Presbyterian Church in New York. For a steady job he became a clerk—at five dollars a week—in the actuarial department of the Mutual Life Insurance Company (and star pitcher of Mutual's baseball team). He practiced self-preservation by withdrawal, composing no more music after 1924 or so, passing the last four decades of his life in near-total isolation from that traffic in professional music where careers are made. He stayed with life insurance and, in partnership with Julian Southall Myrick, went on to make a fortune at Mutual Life.

Elliott Carter, Aaron Copland, Henry Cowell, E. Robert Schmitz, and Nicolas Slonimsky in various ways drew attention to his music, to his very existence. In 1939 John Kirkpatrick gave the first performance of the *Concord* Sonata (composed 1910–15), an event that was a landmark in awareness of the composer and of his stature. In 1947 Ives was awarded the Pulitzer Prize for his Symphony No. 3, written forty-three years earlier. Long before that, he had expressed himself on that subject when he remarked that prizes were for little boys. By 1951 he was much too ill to accept an invitation to attend the first performance of his Symphony No. 2—he had not traveled since 1938—but he heard the broadcast on the family cook's portable radio. After his death, John Kirkpatrick and Joseph Braunstein, then at the New York Public Library, independently undertook to sort and catalogue his manuscripts. It was then that his music began to enter the repertory and that serious Ives scholarship began, its most powerful accomplishment being to get works such as the Symphony No. 4 into performable condition.

Symphony No. 4

> *Prelude: Maestoso*
> *Allegretto*
> *Fugue: Andante moderato*
> *Largo maestoso*

Ives worked on the Symphony No. 4 between 1909 and 1916. On 29 January 1927, Eugene Goossens conducted a simplified version of the first

two movements in New York. On 10 May 1933, Bernard Herrmann conducted the third movement in New York in an edition of his own; when
he repeated it with the CBS Symphony in 1946, it was the first time that
any music by Ives was broadcast. This movement, originally part of Ives's
String Quartet No. 1 (1896), was also heard as part of that work, though
not until 1961 or perhaps even later. (The history here is complicated:
Ives took this movement out of the Quartet when he put it into the symphony, with the result that the first performance of the Quartet—in
1957!—lacked that movement. It was restored when the score was published in 1961.) The first complete performance of the Symphony No. 4
was given on 26 April 1965 in Carnegie Hall, New York, by the American
Symphony Orchestra under the direction of Leopold Stokowski. With the
help of the composer Henry Cowell and of two expert editors, Kurt Stone
and Ronald Herder, then curator of the Fleisher Music Collection at the
Free Library of Philadelphia, Theodore Seder prepared the material for that
first performance. Seder was convinced—and convinced Stokowski—that
two assistant conductors would be needed for certain passages in the second
and fourth movements where the music proceeds in several meters simultaneously; accordingly, José Serebrier, then the American Symphony Orchestra's associate conductor, and David Katz were enlisted to take part.
The Schola Cantorum, prepared by Hugh Ross, sang the choral parts.
After Stokowski's performance, the composer and conductor Gunther
Schuller prepared an edition that could be played under a single conductor,
which he introduced with the Berlin Radio Symphony on 28 November 1965. The single-conductor edition has been the standard one ever
since.

Three flutes and two piccolos, two oboes, three clarinets, three bassoons,
tenor saxophone, four horns, two cornets, six trumpets (fifth doubling cornet), four trombones, tuba, two harps, piano four-hands, solo piano, celesta,
organ, "ether organ," timpani, snare drum, military drum, tom-tom, bass
drum, triangle, cymbals, high and low bells, light and heavy gongs, four-part
chorus, and strings. In addition, in the first movement Ives asks for a "distant choir" of four solo violins, solo viola (and/or clarinet ad libitum), and
harp; in the fourth movement he asks for a "distant choir" of five solo violins and two harps as well as a "battery unit" consisting of snare drum, small
timpani or medium drum, cymbals and bass drum, and gong. It is not clear
what Ives meant by "ether organ": "aetherophone" was another name for
the theremin, an electronic instrument developed in the 1920s, and this may
have been what Ives had in mind. A synthesizer makes an acceptable substitute; in any event, the part is optional.

Some years after Ives's death, an inquiry from Germany set into motion a specific search for everything connected with the Symphony No. 4. The projected performance never came about, but the investigations in response to the German inquiry led to the conclusion that, messy though some of the material was, the wherewithal existed for making a usable score of the Fourth Symphony. When Leopold Stokowski expressed interest in conducting the work, it was decided that a workable score and set of orchestral parts should be prepared. When Stokowski led the first complete performance four days after his eighty-third birthday, it was, for him, the culmination of more than half a century's activity on behalf of new music. Later conductors, among them José Serebrier (one of the assistants at the premiere), Gunther Schuller, Seiji Ozawa, and Michael Tilson Thomas, were able to make more of the work, but even so, that night in Carnegie Hall it was amply clear that something overwhelming had taken place.

When Eugene Goossens conducted the first two movements in 1927, the pianist and writer Henry Ballamann, generally recognized as Ives's first real champion, wrote a program note that stems directly from his conversations with Ives. It makes a useful basic road map:

> This symphony . . . consists of four movements,—a prelude, a majestic fugue, a third movement in comedy vein, and a finale of transcendental spiritual content. [In the published score, the "comedy" is the second movement and the fugue the third.] The aesthetic program of the work is . . . the searching questions of What? and Why? which the spirit of man asks of life. This is particularly the sense of the prelude. The three succeeding movements are the diverse answers in which existence replies. . . . The fugue . . . is an expression of the reaction of life into formalism and ritualism. The succeeding movement . . . is not a scherzo. . . . It is a comedy in the sense that Hawthorne's *Celestial Railroad* is comedy. Indeed this work of Hawthorne's may be considered as a sort of incidental program in which an exciting, easy, and worldly progress through life is contrasted with the trials of the Pilgrims in their journey through the swamp. The occasional slow episodes—Pilgrims' hymns—are constantly crowded out and overwhelmed by the former. The dream, or fantasy, ends with an interruption of reality—the Fourth of July in Concord—brass bands, drum corps, etc. . . . [1]

Later, Ives himself wrote down these further thoughts:

> The last movement (which seems to me the best, compared with the other movements, or for that matter with any other thing I've done) . . .

[1] Peter Burkholder, *Charles Ives: The Ideas Behind the Music* (New Haven: Yale University Press, 1985).

covers a good many years. . . . In a way [it] is an apotheosis of the preceding content, in terms that have something to do with the reality of existence
and its religious experience.[2]

The Prelude is brief. Immediately after the powerful opening gesture—
low strings rising and falling, answered by the violins playing a phrase from
the Piano Sonata No. 1—two muted violins (part of the "distant choir"
Ives asks for) play *Nearer, My God, to Thee,* to which a solo cello responds
with *In the Sweet By-and-By.* Then human voices add their sound in another of Lowell Mason's hymns, the sturdy *Watchman, Tell Us of the Night,*
one of Ives's special favorites.

> Watchman, tell us of the night,
> What the signs of promise are:
> Traveller, o'er yon mountain height,
> See that Glory-beaming star!
> Watchman, ought of joy or hope,
> Traveller, yes, it brings the day,
> Promised day of Israel.
> Dost thou see its beauteous ray?

Kirkpatrick lists Arthur Sullivan's *Proprior Deo,* Henry Southwick Per-
kins's *Something for Thee, I Hear Thy Welcome Voice,* and the Westminster
chimes (on the celesta) as further material quoted here.

From the simplicity of the Prelude, Ives knocks us into the wildness of
his Hawthornian "comedy." He in fact uses fragments from the *Hawthorne*
movement of his *Concord* Sonata along with *Tramp, Tramp, Tramp, In the
Sweet By-and-By* (in quarter tones!), *The Red, White, and Blue, Beulah
Land, Yankee Doodle, Marching Through Georgia, Turkey in the Straw, Long,
Long Ago, The Irish Washerwoman,* and the reveille bugle call, often simultaneously and in independent tempi. A quiet interlude for solo viola with
piano is described by Ives as "a take off . . . on polite salon music . . .
pink teas in Vanity Fair social life." The solo piano part in this movement
requires no less virtuosity than one of Ives's sonatas. This Ivesian collage
in excelsis is the symphony's longest movement.

Back to simplicity. Ives often had trouble with the world of "correct"
fugues and the channeling of life into "formalism and ritualism," but here
he treats this world with affection and respect. He even uses the old-
fashioned notation of four half-notes per measure instead of the four quarters we would find in a modern hymnal; perhaps Kirkpatrick is right in

---

[2]Quoted in John Kirkpatrick, *Ives-Memos* (New York: Norton, 1972).

taking this to be parodistic. Ives begins with *From Greenland's Icy Mountains*, to which he later adds *All Hail the Power of Jesus' Name*. At the very end we hear a phrase from *Joy to the World*.

And now, the transcendent finale. Ives's assessment of this as "the best, compared with the other movements, or for that matter with any other thing I've done" is convincing. *Nearer, My God, to Thee* is the principal material, but it is embedded in other hymns, among them *Ye Christian Heralds* and *Jesus, Lover of my Soul*. We also hear the Westminster chimes and, as Kirkpatrick says, "like a gargoyle up in the tower," *As Freshmen First We Came to Yale*. The chorus sings again, but wordlessly. The music builds hugely. Then the waves that have engulfed us recede and the symphony ends in magical quiet.

Finally, a word about some of the hymn-writers whose tunes Ives quotes most prominently in the Fourth Symphony. Ives sang hymns as a boy in Danbury and played them on the organ at church services, also in Danbury (at fourteen he became organist at the First Baptist Church) as well as later at Yale, in Bloomfield, New Jersey, and in New York. He knew the music sung at revival meetings, and because he worked at various times in Baptist, Presbyterian, Congregational, and Episcopalian churches, he came to know a wide repertory of Protestant hymns. A good five dozen of these found their way into his works, along with military marches, college songs, parlor songs, and tunes from the dance hall. Some of these were special favorites of his and occur over and over in his symphonies, sonatas, etcetera.

Joseph Philbrick Webster, composer, singer, impresario, teacher, piano salesman, and abolitionist, was born in Manchester, New Hampshire, on 18 February 1819 and died in Elkhorn, Wisconsin, on 18 January 1875. His teacher was Lowell Mason; he himself was a fertile composer of songs in many genres. He composed *In the Sweet By-and-By* in 1867 on a text by Sanford Fillmore Bennett. Ives quotes this hymn almost as much as *Bethany (Nearer, My God, to Thee)*, and always in especially charged expressive contexts.

John R. Sweney, composer of *Beulah Land*, was born in West Chester, Pennsylvania, on 31 December 1837 and died in Chester, Pennsylvania, on 10 April 1899. For twenty-five years he was a professor of music at the Pennsylvania Military Academy, and for more than ten of those years he directed music at the Bethany Presbyterian Church. He wrote over a thousand gospel hymns and helped compile more than sixty collections.

Charles Heinrich Christoph Zeuner, composer of *Ye Christian Heralds*, was born in Eisleben, Germany, on 20 September 1795 and died in Philadelphia on 7 November 1857. He was a student of Hummel's and became a court musician near Eisleben, then went to Boston in the mid-1820s. Later he became a church organist in Philadelphia. Zeuner compiled collections of church music and composed an oratorio widely performed in its day, *The Feast of Tabernacles.* That was written in 1832, the same year as *Ye Christian Heralds.*

Simeon Butler Marsh (1798–1875), a Presbyterian, was another teacher and prominent nineteenth-century American composer of hymns. The tune he wrote for *Jesus, Lover of My Soul* is known as *Martyn.* The words, nearly a hundred years old when Marsh wrote the tune, are by Charles Wesley, evangelist and founder, with his brother John, of the Methodist church.

Lowell Mason, who composed *Nearer, My God, to Thee* and *From Greenland's Icy Mountains,* was born in Medfield, Massachusetts, on 8 January 1792 and died in Orange, New Jersey, on 11 August 1872. He was immensely active as a composer, church musician, educator, conductor, and editor of hymn books. *Joy to the World,* adapted from Handel, is his most famous song. He composed the tune called *Bethany* for Sarah Flower Adams's *Nearer, My God, to Thee* in 1856. This was the hymn Ives quoted more often than any other. It became part of British and American folklore after the sinking of the *Titanic* on 15 April 1912, when eight of the ship's musicians were drowned playing it. Ives also remembered being at the Café Boulevard in New York when the news came in that President McKinley had been shot and everyone stood up and sang that hymn. Mrs. Adams was an English poet and a prolific writer, mostly of religious and inspirational texts. Mason composed *From Greenland's Icy Mountains* in 1827 as a solo for a meeting of the Missionary Society.

Gustav Mahler

Gustav Mahler was born in Kalischt (Kaliště), Bohemia, on 7 July 1860 and died in Vienna on 18 May 1911.

Mahler once said he was thrice homeless—as a Bohemian among Austrians, as an Austrian among Germans, and as a Jew everywhere in the world. The village where he was born is about sixty miles southeast of Prague, and the trumpet calls he heard from its military garrison ghost through his music. His father, first a carter, then the owner of a small liquor store which he parlayed into a reasonably successful distillery, was an intellectually awake, unhappy, brutal man; his mother, sweet, plain, and with a limp, was forced by her parents to marry Bernhard Mahler whom she did not know and even though she loved someone else. Not surprisingly, she was wretched. Gustav was the second of Bernhard and Marie Mahler's fourteen children; of the fourteen, eight died in infancy or childhood. When Mahler wrote his *Kindertotenlieder*, his two daughters were alive and well, but he was an expert on the deaths of children. In addition, his sister Leopoldine died at twenty-six of a brain tumor or meningitis, and his brother Otto, also a talented musician, committed suicide at twenty-one. His brother Louis, at various times also known as Alois and Hans Christian (!), emigrated to Chicago, where he became a baker and eventually vanished.

A childhood memory, reported by Sigmund Freud, whom Mahler consulted in 1910, not on the famous couch at Berggasse 19, but during a long walk on a beach near Leiden in Holland: once, when Bernhard Mahler was especially abusive to his wife, Gustav, unable to bear the scene any longer, rushed headlong from the house, all but crashing into an organ-grinder who was playing the popular song *Ach, du lieber Augustin*. Startling juxtapositions of the tragic and the frivolous became a hallmark of Mahler's style; indeed, no feature of his music was more disturbing to his listeners.[1] That the name of the Dutch town where they met is the German for "suffering" must have given some grim amusement to doctor and patient.

Mahler was a poor student as a boy; nonetheless, a local businessman got him an audition with the pianist Julius Epstein at the Vienna Conservatory, who was immediately convinced that the fifteen-year-old boy was a remarkable musician. That fall, Mahler began his bumpy career at the Conservatory, where, along with his piano lessons with Epstein, he studied harmony with Robert Fuchs and composition with Robert Krenn, and several times collided with Joseph Hellmesberger, a distinguished quartet-leader and committed anti-Semite. One of Mahler's roommates was Hugo Wolf, one of the greatest of all songwriters; another was the immensely gifted Hans Rott, who died at twenty-four and from whose impressive Symphony in E (1878–80) Mahler learned a lot; a third was the violinist and conductor Rudolf Krzyzanowski. (Wolf, Rott, and Krzyzanowski all died insane.)

At twenty, Mahler took his first job as a conductor, leading the summer operetta season at Bad Hall near Linz. That was starting at the bottom with a vengeance, but over the next few years, Mahler climbed the career ladder, moving to Laibach (Ljubljana), Iglau (Jihlava), Olmütz (Olomouc), Kassel, Prague, Leipzig, Budapest, Hamburg, and eventually—in 1897—Vienna. It was also in 1897 that Mahler was received into the Roman Catholic church. To what extent this was a career move in the face of Viennese anti-Semitism, to what extent a spiritual need or even an aesthetic response, is still debated.

With Arthur Nikisch, five years his senior, and Arturo Toscanini, seven years his junior, he was one of the great conductors in his generation—passionate, personal, electrifying. As in his composition, he never came down on the side of caution. He loved and detested conducting; that is, he loved the opportunity to shape musical objects according to his penetrating vision and hated the constant compromise and the friction with musicians less possessed than himself. Similarly, the sheer rush that came from performance both exhilarated and drained him. Conducting was his source of income from that first summer of 1880 at Bad Hall till the

---

[1]In a haunting coincidence, Arnold Schoenberg, intuitively and profoundly in sympathy with Mahler, had used the same song for just that shocking purpose in his String Quartet No. 2 (1907–08).

end of his life, and of necessity he became a summer composer, finding retreats at Steinbach and later at Lake Wörth in Carinthia and Toblach (Dobbiaco) in the Dolomites. Quiet was a constant quest, and to ensure it was one of the primary assignments of the women in his life: his sister Justine, various friends, and eventually his wife, the gifted, magnetic, and beautiful Alma Schindler, whom he married in 1902. Before Alma, there had been a serious succession of lovers, most of them sopranos at the opera houses where he conducted.

Essentially Mahler was a composer of songs and symphonies, and the two genres crossed interestingly in his lifework. Of Mahler symphonies there are nine or ten or eleven, depending on how you count. The matter of the symphonies numbered 1 through 9 is clear-cut. The difficulty is that, with Beethoven's Ninth and Bruckner's unfinished Ninth in mind, Mahler entertained a deep-rooted superstition about ninth symphonies, thinking of them as a limit beyond which no composer could go. The work that followed the Symphony No. 8 was a song cycle, *Das Lied von der Erde* (The Song of the Earth), but Mahler sought to deceive the counting-gods by calling it a "symphony for alto (or baritone), tenor, and orchestra," though not assigning it a number. Thus *Das Lied* was a secret Ninth Symphony, while the next work, the symphony he called No. 9, was "really" the Tenth. Furthermore, he made sufficient progress on an actual Tenth Symphony for several musicians to have produced "performing versions" that, though controversial, have entered the active repertory.

Mahler's symphonies fall into groups whose members share points of view and even material details, each piece being more richly understood in the context of its group. The first group consists of the first four symphonies. These are to a large extent based on songs by Mahler himself, and three of them actually use voices. In No. 1, the orchestra quotes the *Lieder eines fahrenden Gesellen* (Songs of a Wayfarer) of 1884; the texts of those songs are Mahler's own, but the style of the poetry owes much to *Des Knaben Wunderhorn* (The Boy's Magic Horn), a collection of folk verse assembled and considerably fixed up at the beginning of the nineteenth century by the poets Achim von Arnim and Clemens Brentano. The next three symphonies include vocal settings of *Wunderhorn* texts along with words by other writers, again including Mahler himself.

Then come three purely orchestral and profoundly exploring symphonies; these, too, make references to songs, particularly to the *Kindertotenlieder*, but these references are both rarer and less explicit than those in the first four symphonies. No. 6 is one of the most admired and most passionately loved by those who know their Mahler best (Arnold

Schoenberg, Anton Webern, and Alban Berg at the head of the parade).[2]

The Fifth, Sixth, and Seventh all begin with marches in a minor key, and explicitly funereal ones in Nos. 5 and 7. But No. 6, this central panel of the triptych, stands out in various ways. Nos. 5 and 7 have exuberantly cheerful last movements; No. 6, as already noted, has Mahler's only tragic close. Nos. 5 and 7 are five-movement symphonies. Two linked pairs of movements enclose a central scherzo in No. 5, while two large movements enclose a triple intermezzo (Night Music/Scherzo/Night Music) in No. 7. No. 6 is the only symphony that Mahler planned from the beginning as a four-movement work in the traditional design.[3]

The whirlwind that was the last chapter of Mahler's not very long but tumultuous life began in 1907. Four momentous things happened that year:

On 17 March, Mahler resigned the artistic directorship of the Vienna Court Opera, bringing to a close a ten-year term whose achievement has become legend. Mahler was, however, drained by the struggles and tempests that were the price of that achievement, worn down by anti-Semitic attacks on himself and his young protégé Bruno Walter, and feeling the need to give more time to the composition and performance of his own music. He was not, however, able to resist the lure of the podium nor to do without his income as a conductor, and on 5 June, he signed a contract with the Metropolitan Opera in New York, where he would make his debut conducting *Tristan und Isolde* on New Year's Day 1908.

On 5 July, his daughter Maria, four and a half, died at the end of a two-week battle with scarlet fever and diphtheria, just hours after an emergency tracheotomy had been performed at the Mahlers' summer house at Maiernigg in Carinthia. A few days after the funeral, a physician who had come to examine Mahler's exhausted wife and her seriously ill mother, responding to the composer's half-joking "As long as you're here you might as well have a look at me too," discovered that things were not as they should be with Mahler's heart. Most biographies report a diagnosis of subacute bacterial endocarditis. Recent interpretation of the evidence suggests that what was discovered was a defect in the mitral valve, presumably stemming either from Mahler's family history or rheumatic fever. Subacute bacterial endocarditis would be a result of this defect, but would probably have developed no earlier than the fall of 1910. It is not a condition Mah-

---

[2] Of the Mahler symphonies, the Sixth and Seventh took the longest to enter the repertory.
[3] The Symphony No. 1 is a five-movement work cut down by Mahler to four movements. The other four-movement symphonies, Nos. 4 and 9, are altogether non-traditional in design and in their distribution of weight and proportion.

ler would have been likely to survive for four years. Beginning with Mahler's widow, biographers have tended to dramatize the account of his physical condition after the summer of 1907. In any event, Mahler, that dedicated hiker, cyclist, and swimmer, to say nothing of fiery conductor, was put on a regimen of depressingly restricted activity. Still, what happened from 1907 until 1911 is not the life story of an invalid.

1907: concerts in Saint Petersburg and Helsinki; his meeting with Sibelius; the last opera performance in Vienna (*Fidelio*, played to half a house) and the last concert there (his own Symphony No. 2); departure for New York.

1908: performances at the Metropolitan Opera at the beginning and end of the year; concerts with the New York Symphony; the premiere in Prague of the three-year-old Symphony No. 7; the composition that summer of *Das Lied von der Erde*.

1909: the termination of his association with the Met and the start of a three-year contract with the dilapidated New York Philharmonic; work on the Symphony No. 9.

1910: concerts with the Philharmonic in New York and other American cities; engagements in Paris and Rome; the triumphant premiere in Munich of the Symphony No. 8 (written in the summer of 1906); the completion of the Ninth Symphony, followed immediately by extensive and concentrated work on the Tenth; the meeting at Leiden with Freud.

1911: the last New York Philharmonic concert on 21 February, including the premiere of Busoni's *Berceuse élégiaque—A Man's Cradle Song at His Mother's Coffin*. Then came the onset of a streptococcal blood infection, unsuccessful serum treatment in Paris, and, on 18 May, death in a Vienna sanatorium. "No doubt," Richard Strauss remarked, "he'll now become a great man in Vienna too."

Into this 1907–11 chapter falls the complex and diverse final group of Mahler's works. It begins with two vocal works, the Symphony No. 8 and *Das Lied von der Erde* (The Song of the Earth), continues with the Symphony No. 9, and leads to the unfinished Tenth. No. 9 is in some respects commentary upon and extension of *Das Lied von der Erde*, while the Tenth both quotes that work and further explores certain ideas and features of the Ninth.

Bruno Walter, a friend since he had become a coach and chorus master on Mahler's staff at the Hamburg Opera in 1894, later a devoted advocate during the decades when to regard Mahler as a great composer was to hold an absurd minority opinion, conducted the posthumous premieres of *Das Lied von der Erde* and the Ninth Symphony.

Symphony No. 1 in D major

> Slow. Dragging. Always very easygoing
> With powerful movement, but not too fast
> Solemn and measured, without dragging—Very
>   simple and modest, like a folk song
> With violent movement

Mahler did most of the work on this symphony in February and March 1888, having begun to sketch it in earnest three years earlier and using material going back to the 1870s. He revised the score extensively on several occasions; the second, and last, edition published during Mahler's lifetime is dated 1906. Mahler himself conducted the first performance of the work, then called Symphonic Poem in Two Parts, with the Budapest Philharmonic on 20 November 1889.

Four flutes (three doubling piccolo), four oboes (one doubling English horn), four clarinets (one doubling bass clarinet, two doubling E-flat clarinet), three bassoons (one doubling contrabassoon), seven horns, five trumpets, four trombones, bass tuba, timpani (two players), bass drum, cymbals, triangle, tam-tam, harp, and strings.

Once, contemplating the failures of sympathy and understanding his First Symphony had met with at most of its early performances, Mahler lamented that while Beethoven had been able to start as a sort of modified Haydn and Mozart, and Wagner as Weber and Meyerbeer, he himself had the misfortune to be Gustav Mahler from the outset. He composed this symphony, surely the most original First after the Berlioz Fantastique, in high hopes of being understood, even imagining that it might earn him enough money so that he could abandon his rapidly expanding career as a conductor—a luxury that life would in fact never allow him.

But he enjoyed public success with the work only in Prague in 1898 and in Amsterdam five years later. The Viennese audience, musically reactionary and anti-Semitic to boot, was singularly vile in its behavior, and even Mahler's future wife, Alma Schindler, whose devotion to The Cause would in later years sometimes subordinate a concern for truth, fled that concert in anger and disgust.[4] One critic suggested that the work might have been meant as a parody of a symphony. No wonder that Mahler, completing his Fourth Symphony in 1900, felt driven to mark its finale "Durchaus ohne Parodie!" (With no trace of parody!).

The Symphony No. 1 even puzzled its own composer. No other piece of Mahler's has so complicated a history, and about no other did he change his mind so often and over so long a period. He transformed the total concept by canceling a whole movement, he made striking alterations in compositional and orchestral detail, and for some time he was unsure whether he was offering a symphonic poem, a program symphony, or just a symphony.

At the Budapest premiere, the work appeared as a "symphonic poem" whose two parts consisted of three and two movements respectively. At that stage, the first movement was followed by a piece called *Blumine*— more about that at the end of this essay. What is now the third movement was called *à la pompes funèbres,* but that was the only suggestion of anything programmatic. Nevertheless, the day before the premiere a newspaper article outlined a program whose source can only have been Mahler himself and which identifies the first three movements with spring, happy daydreams, and a wedding procession, the fourth as a funeral march representing the burial of the poet's illusions, and the fifth as a hard-won progress to spiritual victory.

When Mahler revised the score in January 1893, he called it a symphony in five movements and two parts, also giving it the name of *Titan*— not, however, for the terrible and violent figures of Greek mythology, but for the eponymous novel by Jean Paul (Johann Paul Friedrich Richter, 1763–1825), a key figure in German literary Romanticism and one of Mahler's favorite writers. The first part, *From the Days of Youth,* comprised three movements: *Spring Without End, Blumine,* and *Under Full Sail;* the second, *Commedia humana,* consisted of two movements: *Funeral March in the Manner of Callot* and *Dall'inferno al paradiso.*[5]

By the time the next performance came around—that was in Hamburg in October of the same year—Mahler announced the work as *TITAN, a Tone Poem in the Form of a Symphony.* The first part was now called *From the Days of Youth: Flower-, Fruit-, and Thornpieces* (this is part of the full title of *Siebenkäs,* another of Jean Paul's novels), and Mahler added that the introduction represented "Nature's awakening from its long winter

---

[4] The Mahler First is now one of the most super-insured of all pieces for conductors who want to have a clamorous success; as late as the 1940s, though, it was still perceived as a problem piece and began programs more often than it ended them.

[5] Jacques Callot (1592–1635), renowned for his etchings and drawings, was an artist with a special flair for portraying the grotesque.

sleep." For the fourth movement, now titled *Foundered!*, he provided a long note to the effect that his inspiration had been the woodcut after the satirical drawing *The Hunter's Funeral* by Schubert's friend Moritz von Schwind. It depicts a torchlight procession of weeping deer, foxes, rabbits, and other forest animals bearing a hunter to his grave. Mahler says the music is "now ironic and merry, now uncanny and brooding. Upon which—immediately—*Dall'inferno* follows as the sudden despairing cry of a heart wounded to its depths."

Mahler retained most of that through the 1890s. Before the Vienna performance in 1900, he again leaked a program to a friendly critic, and it is a curious one. First comes rejection of *Titan*, as well as "all other titles and inscriptions, which, like all 'programs,' are always misinterpreted. [The composer] dislikes and discards them as 'anti-artistic' and 'anti-musical.' " There follows a scenario that reads much like an elaborated version of the original one for Budapest.[6]

What had happened is that during the nineties, when Richard Strauss's *Till Eulenspiegel, Also sprach Zarathustra, Don Quixote,* and *Ein Heldenleben* had come out, program music had become a hot political issue in the musical world, one to take sides on. Mahler saw himself as living in a very different world from Strauss, and he wished to establish a certain distance between himself and his colleague. At the same time, the extramusical ideas that had originally informed his symphony would not disappear, and, somewhat uncomfortably and unconvincingly, he seemed now to be wanting to have it both ways.[7] He found, moreover, that there was no pleasing the critics on this issue: in Berlin he was faulted for omitting the program and in Frankfurt for keeping it.

"I should like to stress that the symphony goes far beyond the love story on which it is based, or rather, which preceded it in the life of its creator," Mahler wrote. In that spirit, let me move on to the music, stopping just long enough to say that actually two love stories were involved, one in 1884 with the Kassel Opera soprano Johanna Richter, which led to the composition of the *Songs of a Wayfarer* that Mahler quotes and uses in this symphony, and a more dangerous one in 1887 and 1888 with Marion von Weber, wife of the grandson of the composer of *Der Freischütz.* The first time the opening *pianississimo* A, seven octaves deep, was ever heard,

[6]This was one of the occasions when Mahler emphasized the connection between his first two symphonies, saying here that "the real, the climactic dénouement [of the First] comes only in the Second." Elsewhere he stated that the opening movement of the Second was the funeral music for the hero of the First.
[7]Strauss, too, lived uneasily with this question, composing a highly detailed sort of program music, reacting irritably to requests for explications, providing them nonetheless, and always stressing the purely musical integrity of his tone poems.

Mahler sat at the piano and the Webers stood on either side of him to play the notes that were beyond the reach of his hands.

Mahler writes "Wie ein Naturlaut" (like a sound of nature) on that first page, and he instructed the conductor Franz Schalk, "The introduction to the first movement *sounds of nature, not music!*" In the manner discovered by Beethoven for the opening of his Ninth Symphony and imitated in countless ways throughout the nineteenth century, fragments detach themselves from the mist, become graspable, coalesce. Among these fragments are a pair of notes descending by a fourth, distant fanfares, a little cry of oboes, a cuckoo call (by the only cuckoo in the world who toots a fourth rather than a third), a gentle horn melody.

Gradually the tempo quickens to arrive at the melody of the second of Mahler's *Wayfarer* songs. (One of the most characteristic, original, and forward-looking features of this movement is how much time Mahler spends not *in* tempo but en route from one speed to another.) Mahler's wayfarer crosses the fields in the morning, rejoicing in the beauty of the world and hoping that this marks the beauty of his own happy times, only to see that no, spring can never, never bloom for him. But for Mahler the song is useful not only as an evocation but as a musical source, and he draws astounding riches from it by a process, as Erwin Stein put it, of constantly shuffling and reshuffling its figures like a deck of cards. The movement rises to one tremendous climax—to bring that into sharper focus was one of the chief tasks of Mahler's 1893 revision—and the last page is wild. One of its most important constant features, however, is the one to which Mahler drew Schalk's attention in the letter already quoted: "In the first movement the *greatest* delicacy throughout (except in the big climax)."

The scherzo, whose indebtedness to Bruckner was acknowledged by Mahler himself, is the symphony's briefest and simplest movement, and also the only one that the first audiences could be counted on to like. Its opening idea comes from a fragment for piano duet that may go back as far as 1876, and the movement makes several allusions to the song *Hans und Grethe*, whose earliest version was written in 1880. The trio, set in an F major that sounds very mellow in the A-major context of the scherzo itself, fascinatingly contrasts the simplicity of the rustic, super-Austrian material itself with the artfulness of its arrangement.

The funeral music that follows was what most upset the first audiences. The use of vernacular material presented in slightly perverted form (the round we have all sung as *Frère Jacques*, but set by Mahler in a lugubrious minor); the parodic, vulgar music with its lachrymose oboes and trumpets; the boom-chick of bass drum with cymbal attached; the hiccup-

ping violins; the appearance in the middle of all this of part of the last
Wayfarer song, exquisitely scored for muted strings with a harp and a few
soft woodwinds—people simply did not know what to make of this mixture, how to respond, whether to laugh or cry or both. They sensed that
something irreverent was being done, something new and somehow ominous, that these collisions of the spooky, the gross, and the vulnerable
were uncomfortably like life itself, and they were offended. Incidentally,
the most famous detail of orchestration in the symphony, the bass solo
that begins the round, was an afterthought: As late as 1893, the first statement of the *Frère Jacques* tune was more conventionally set for bass and
cello in unison.[8]

Mahler likened the opening of the finale to a bolt of lightning that
rips from a black cloud. The ensuing violence is suspended for some magical minutes as Mahler gives us the gift—in the soft pillows of D-flat major—of one of his most inspired lyric melodies. Using and transforming
material from the first movement, he takes us, in the terms of his various
programs, on the path from annihilation to victory. In musical terms, he
engages us in a struggle to regain D major, the main key of the symphony,
but unheard since the first movement ended. When at last he re-enters
that key, he does so by way of a stunning and violent *coup de théâtre*, only
to withdraw from the sounds of victory and to show us the hollowness of
that triumph. He then goes all the way back to the music that began the
symphony and gathers strength for a second assault. This one does indeed
open the doors to a renewed conquest of D major and a heroic ending.
That achievement is celebrated in a hymn that evokes Handel's *Hallelujah!*
and in which the horns, now on their feet, are instructed to drown out
the rest of the orchestra, "even the trumpets."[9]

A postscript on *Blumine:* the title is yet another tribute to Jean Paul,
who gave the name *Herbst-Blumine* to a collection of magazine articles.
Jean Paul seems to have invented the word *Blumine*. It comes from *Blume*
(flower), and *Herbst-Blumine* might be translated as "autumn flora." Mahler's *Blumine* is an adaptation—or possibly a straight transcription—of part

[8] More often than not, problems get solved over time; here, however, is something that has *become*
a problem. Almost certainly this bass solo just naturally sounded awful a hundred years ago, and
it was meant to as part of the parodic atmosphere. Since then, technical standards of bass playing
have risen sky-high. The bass players of the best orchestras now take pride in playing this solo as
"beautifully" as possible, and in so doing completely undermine Mahler's intent.

[9] Strauss, who conducted preliminary rehearsals for a performance in Weimar in 1894, suggested
to Mahler that he make a cut from the first D-major arrival to the second, which is nearly one-
third of the movement. Mahler of course did no such thing; many conductors, who like Strauss
failed to see the emotional point of the double arrival in D, did make that cut, and as late as the
1950s it was not uncommon to hear the movement mutilated that way.

of the music he wrote early in 1884 for a series of *tableaux vivants* based on Viktor von Scheffel's sentimental poem *Der Trompeter von Säckingen* (in this particular scene, Werner, the trumpeter, plays a serenade to his beloved on the other side of the Rhine).

This music is lost, and so, apparently, is the manuscript of the original 1889 version of the "symphonic poem." The only source for *Blumine* is the manuscript of the January 1893 revision, which was privately owned and inaccessible from the time Mahler gave it to an American former pupil until December 1959, when it was bought at a Sotheby's auction by Mrs. James M. Osborn of New Haven, Connecticut, and deposited in the Osborn Collection of the Yale University Library. The first performance since 1894 of *Blumine* was given by Benjamin Britten and the Philharmonia Orchestra at the Aldeburgh Festival on 18 June 1967. Britten presented *Blumine* by itself; the first modern performance of the whole symphony including *Blumine* was given by Frank Brieff and the New Haven Symphony on 9 April 1968. That performance, like almost all others since, combined the 1884/1893 *Blumine* with the other four movements in a form they achieved much later, thus creating a problematic hybrid, and this will continue to be a problem as long as performance materials for the 1893 version of the symphony are not easily available. The first modern performance to set *Blumine* together with the original Budapest versions of the other four movements was given by Joel Lazar and the Cantabrigia Orchestra at Harvard University on 11 August 1969.

Debate over whether or not to restore *Blumine* to the symphony began immediately after the New Haven performance. The pro-*Blumine* arguments are that the music itself is touchingly delicate and lovely, offering a wonderful opportunity to a sensitive solo trumpeter; that it is interesting to get acquainted with the symphony as Mahler first imagined, composed, and conducted it; that it makes a welcome buffer between the exuberances of the first movement's close and the beginning of the scherzo. The counterarguments are the "hybrid" issue; that *Blumine* is more of an interruption than a buffer; and that Mahler, in word and deed, left no doubt that he thought the inclusion of this movement an error and that he wished to leave the symphony as a four-movement work.[10]

---

[10] Here is a can of worms indeed. As any musician knows who has ever dealt with the different versions of Bach's *Saint John Passion*, Handel's *Messiah*, Mozart's *Don Giovanni*, Schumann's *Kreisleriana*, or Stravinsky's *Petrushka*, questions of the relative validity of composers' first, intermediate, and final thoughts are immensely and vexingly complicated.

Symphony No. 2 in C minor

> Allegro maestoso
> Andante moderato
> In quietly flowing motion
> Urlicht (Primal Light): Very solemn, but simple
> In the tempo of the scherzo—Allegro energico—
> Slow, misterioso

Mahler originally wrote the first movement of the Symphony No. 2 in 1888 as a "symphonic poem," *Todtenfeier* (Funeral Rites). Some sketches for the second movement also date from that year. Mahler long wavered about whether to make *Todtenfeier* the beginning of a symphony, and it was not until the summer of 1893 that he composed the second and third movements. The finale and a revision of the first movement followed in the spring and summer of 1894; later that year, the song *Urlicht* (Primal Light), probably composed in 1892 and orchestrated in 1893, was inserted as the fourth movement. The fair copy of the complete score of the symphony is dated 28 December 1894. Mahler (not Richard Strauss, as was long believed) conducted the premiere of the first three movements with the Berlin Philharmonic on 4 March 1895. He also led the first performance of the entire work on 13 December of the same year; the orchestra was again the Berlin Philharmonic, the soloists were Josephine von Artner and Hedwig Felden, and the choirs were prepared by Friedrich Gernsheim. Mahler revised the scoring again in 1903 and was still tinkering with the score as late as 1909.

Four flutes (all doubling piccolos), two oboes (third and fourth doubling English horns), three clarinets (third doubling bass clarinet) and two E-flat clarinets, four bassoons (third and fourth doubling contrabassoon), ten horns, eight trumpets (four each of the horns and trumpets first play off-stage in the finale, most of these then moving on-stage), four trombones, bass tuba, organ, two harps, two sets of timpani, bass drum, cymbals, high and low tam-tams, triangle (another kettledrum, triangle, bass drum, and pair of cymbals are off-stage), two snare drums, glockenspiel, three deep bells of unspecified pitch, and birch brush (*Rute* in German—the "rod" or schoolmaster's switch, played against the body of the bass drum), and strings, plus soprano and alto soloists, and large mixed chorus.

In August 1886, eight years out of school and with conducting experience at Bad Hall, Laibach (Ljubljana), Iglau (Jihlava), Olmütz (Olomouc), Kassel, and Prague, the twenty-six-year-old Mahler was appointed second conductor at the theater in Leipzig. He soon made the acquaintance of a captain in the Saxon army, Baron Carl von Weber, grandson of the composer of *Der Freischütz*, *Euryanthe*, and *Oberon*, music close to Mahler's heart. The encounter had interesting consequences. First, Captain von Weber invited Mahler to examine his grandfather's sketches for an opera called *Die drei Pintos*, begun and abandoned in 1820 near the end of his work on *Freischütz*. He hoped to interest Mahler in extracting a performing version from those sketches, a project considered but dropped earlier in the century by Giacomo Meyerbeer and Franz Lachner. Next, Mahler and Weber's wife Marion fell in love, and some of their affair is, as it were, composed into the First Symphony, on which Mahler worked with great concentration in February and March 1888.

He did, in the event, take on *Die drei Pintos* and conducted its highly acclaimed premiere on 20 January 1888. Bouquets and wreaths galore were presented to Mahler and the cast. Mahler took home as many of these floral tributes as he could manage, and lying in his room amid their seductive scent, he imagined himself dead on his bier.[11] Marion von Weber pulled him out of this state and removed the flowers, but the experience had been sufficient to sharpen greatly Mahler's vision of a compositional project he had had in mind for some months and which he began a few weeks later. This was a large orchestral piece called *Todtenfeier*. Mahler's biographer Henry-Louis de La Grange points out that *Todtenfeier* was the title of the recently published German translation by Mahler's friend Siegfried Lipiner of *Dziady*, the visionary and epic masterpiece of Poland's greatest poet, Adam Mickiewicz. De La Grange suggests as well that certain aspects of *Dziady* and of Mickiewicz's life were apposite to Mahler's own situation, particularly with respect to Marion von Weber, and that the music might be construed as a requiem for their relationship.

We know, at any rate, that the following things happened: Mahler began the composition of *Todtenfeier* in February 1888, but soon interrupted himself, preferring to work on his First Symphony during the welcome forced holiday brought about by the closing of theaters in mourning for Emperor Wilhelm I. In May, he resigned his Leipzig post, in part because of the increasingly tense situation with the Webers, and became music director of the opera in Budapest. He returned to his *Todtenfeier*

---

[11] Mahler's younger sister Justine, who was his housekeeper before his marriage and later became the wife of Arnold Rosé, the eminent concertmaster of the Vienna Philharmonic, liked as a child to surround her bed with lighted candles and play corpse.

score in the late spring and summer, finishing the composition in August and completing the orchestral score in Prague on 10 September. Five years later—Mahler had meanwhile become principal conductor in Hamburg— he realized that *Todtenfeier* was not an independent piece but rather the first movement of a new symphony. In 1893–94, the rest fell into place as quickly as his conducting obligations permitted.

The Second Symphony is often called the *Resurrection,* but Mahler himself gave it no title. On various occasions, though, and beginning in December 1895, Mahler offered programs to explain the work. As always, he blew hot and cold on this question. Writing to his wife, he referred to the program he had provided at the request of King Albert of Saxony in connection with a performance of the symphony in Dresden in December 1901 as "a crutch for a cripple." He goes on: "It gives only a superficial indication, all that any program can do for a musical work, let alone this one, which is so much all of a piece that it can no more be explained than the world itself. I'm quite sure that if God were asked to draw up a program of the world he created he could never do it. At best it would say as little about the nature of God and life as my analysis says about my C-minor Symphony."

Not only was Mahler skeptical about the programs he could not resist devising—all after the event—but he changed his mind repeatedly as to just what the program was. (La Grange recounts three different versions, one written in January 1896 for Mahler's friend Natalie Bauer-Lechner and the conductor Bruno Walter, another two months later for the critic Max Marschalk, and the Munich-Dresden version of 1900–1901.) Across their differences, the programs share certain features. The first movement cele-brates a dead hero. It retains, in other words, its original *Todtenfeier* aspect, and since the First and Second symphonies were, in a sense, of simultane-ous genesis, it is worth citing Mahler's comments that it is the hero of the First Symphony who is borne to his grave in the funeral music of the Second (to Marschalk, 26 March 1896) and that "the real, the climactic dénouement [of the First] comes only in the Second" (transmitted to Ludwig Karpath, critic of the *Neues Wiener Tagblatt,* by Bauer-Lechner in November 1900). The second and third movements represent retrospect, the second being innocent and nostalgic, the third including a certain element of the grotesque. The fourth and fifth movements are the resolu-tion, and they deal with the Last Judgment, and redemption, and resur-rection.

All this has bearing on Mahler's perception of the structure of his Second Symphony, a matter on which he made various comments that are not so much contradictory as they are complementary. Referring to the frustrating—because partial—premiere in Berlin in March 1895, he said that the first three movements were in effect "only the exposition" of the symphony. He wrote elsewhere that the appearance of the *Urlicht* song sheds light on what comes before. Writing to the critic Arthur Seidl in 1897, he refers to the three middle movements as having the function only of an "interludium."

There is, as well, the question of breaks between movements. The score is quite explicit here, specifying a pause "of at least five minutes" after the first movement and emphatically demanding in German and Italian that the last three movements follow one another without any interruption. Yet in March 1903, Mahler wrote to Julius Buths, who was getting ready to conduct the work in Düsseldorf, a letter worth quoting at some length:

> According [to your suggestion], then, the principal break in the concert would come between the fourth and fifth movements. I marvel at the sensitivity with which you (contrary to my own indications) have recognized the natural caesura in the work. I have long been of this opinion, and furthermore, each performance I have conducted has strengthened this view.
>
> Nonetheless, there ought *also* to be an ample pause for gathering one's thoughts after the first movement because the second movement has the effect after the first, not of contrast, but as a mere irrelevance. This is my fault and not to be blamed on insufficient comprehension on the part of the listeners. Perhaps you have already sensed this in rehearsing the two movements one after the other. The Andante is composed as a kind of intermezzo (like some lingering resonance of *long* past days from the life of him whom we bore to his grave in the first movement—something from the days when the sun still smiled upon him).
>
> While the first, third, fourth, and fifth movements belong together thematically and in mood, the second piece stands by itself, in a certain sense interrupting the grim and severe march of events. Perhaps this is a weakness in planning, the intention behind which is, however, surely clarified for you by the foregoing suggestion.
>
> It is altogether logical to interpret the beginning of the fifth movement as a connecting link to the first, and the big break before the former helps to make this clear to the listener.[12]

This is illuminating and written with great conviction; yet one should probably assume that Mahler's final thoughts on the question are to be found in his 1909 revisions, published 1910, where he sticks with his original directions for a break after the first movement and an attacca between the third and fourth, and the fourth and fifth movements.

[12] Gustav Mahler *Briefe,* edited by Mathias Hansen (Leipzig: Reelam, 1981).

The first and last movements are the symphony's biggest, though the finale is much the longer of the two. In other ways they are as different as possible, partly no doubt because of the six years that separate them, still more crucially because of their different structural and expressive functions. The *Todtenfeier* is firmly anchored to the classical sonata tradition (late Romantic branch). Its character is that of a march, and Mahler's choice of key—C minor—surely alludes to *the* classic exemplar of such a piece, the *marcia funebre* in Beethoven's *Eroica*. The lyric, contrasting theme, beautifully scored for horns, is an homage to Beethoven's Violin Concerto.

Disjunctions of tempo are very much a feature of Mahler's style. At the very beginning, against scrubbing violins and violas, low strings hurl turns, scales, and broken chords. Their instruction is to play not merely *fff* but "ferociously." Here, for example, Mahler prescribes two distinct speeds for the string figures and the rests that separate them, the former "in violent onslaught" at about ♩ = 144, the latter in the movement's main tempo of about ♩ = 84–92. Later, the climax of the development is defined not only by maximal dissonance, but, still more strikingly, by a series of three disruptive caesuras, each followed by an "out of tempo" forward rush.

The thematic material of the second movement, both the gentle dance it begins with and the cello tune that soon joins in, go back to Leipzig and the time of the *Todtenfeier*. Like the minuet from the Third Symphony, this movement was occasionally played by itself, and Mahler used to refer to these bucolic genre pieces as the raisins in his cakes. Three musicians who resisted its charms were Claude Debussy, Paul Dukas, and Gabriel Pierné, who all walked out during its performance in Paris in 1910. Reactionary, they said, and too much like Schubert.

The third movement is a symphonic expansion of a song about Saint Anthony of Padua's Sermon to the Fishes; the text comes from the collection of German folk verse, *Des Knaben Wunderhorn* (The Boy's Magic Horn).[13] Mahler worked on the two pieces simultaneously and finished the scoring of the song one day after he completed the orchestration of the scherzo.

The sardonic *Fischpredigt* scherzo skids into silence, and its final shudder is succeeded by a new sound, the sound of a human voice. In summoning that resource, as he would in his next two symphonies as well, Mahler consciously and explicitly evokes Beethoven's Ninth Symphony.[14]

[13] In his *Sinfonia* of 1968, Luciano Berio created a brilliant trope on this scherzo, superimposing on it a collage of reminiscences from the symphonic literature along with texts by Samuel Beckett and others. It is a profoundly Mahlerian vision.

[14] Mahler's use of the human voice in his Symphony No. 8 and *Das Lied von der Erde* (The Song of the Earth), which he also called a symphony, is different. Had Mahler not called the Eighth a symphony, we would probably call it a cantata, while *Das Lied von der Erde* is really a song cycle.

Urlicht, whose text also comes from *Des Knaben Wunderhorn*, is one of Mahler's loveliest songs and full of Mahlerian paradox, too, in that its hymnlike simplicity and naturalness are achieved by a metrical flexibility so vigilant of prosody and so complex that the opening section of thirty-five bars has twenty-one changes of meter. The chamber-musical scoring is also characteristically detailed and inventive.

Urlicht	Primal Light
O Röschen rot!	O little red rose!
Der Mensch liegt in grösster Noth!	Humankind lies in greatest need!
Der Mensch liegt in grösster Pein!	Humankind lies in greatest pain!
Je lieber möcht' ich im Himmel sein!	Much rather would I be in Heaven!
Da kam ich auf einen breiten Weg,	Then I came onto a broad path,
Da kam ein Engelein und wollt' mich abweisen.	And an angel came and wanted to turn me away.
Ach nein! Ich ließ mich nicht abweisen!	But no, I would not be turned away!
Ich bin von Gott and will wieder zu Gott!	I am from God and would return to God!
Der liebe Gott wird mir ein Lichtchen geben,	Dear God will give me a little light,
Wird leuchten mir bis in das ewig selig Leben!	Will light me to eternal, blissful life.

—from *Des Knaben Wunderhorn*

The peace that the song spreads over the symphony like balm is shattered by an outburst whose ferocity again refers to the corresponding place in Beethoven's Ninth. Like Beethoven, Mahler draws on music from earlier in the symphony; not, however, in order to reject it, but to build upon it. He arrays before us a great and pictorial pageant. Horns sound in the distance (Mahler referred to this as "the crier in the wilderness"). A march with a suggestion of the Gregorian *Dies irae* is heard, and so is other music saturated in angst, more trumpet signals, marches, and a chorale. Then Mahler's *große Appell*, the Great Summons, the Last Trump: horns and trumpets loud but at a great distance, while in the foreground a solitary bird flutters across the scene of destruction. Silence. From that silence there emerges again the sound of human voices in a Hymn of Resurrection. A few instruments enter to support the singers and, magically, at the word *rief* (called), a single soprano begins to float free.

Although thoroughly aware of the perils of inviting comparison with Beethoven, Mahler knew early that he wanted a vocal finale. The problem

of finding the right text baffled him for a long time. Once again the remarkable figure of Hans von Bülow enters the scene—Hans von Bülow,
the pianist who gave the first performance of Tchaikovsky's most famous
piano concerto, who conducted the premieres of Tristan and Meistersinger
(and whose young wife left him for Wagner), and who was one of the most
influential supporters of Brahms. When Mahler went to the Hamburg Opera in 1891, the other important conductor in town was Hans von Bülow,
who was in charge of the symphony concerts. Bülow was not often a generous colleague, but Mahler impressed him, and his support was not diminished by his failure to like or understand the Todtenfeier when Mahler
played it for him on the piano: it made Tristan sound like a Haydn symphony, he said.

As Bülow's health declined, Mahler began to substitute for him, and
he was much affected by Bülow's death early in 1894. At the memorial
service in Hamburg, the choir sang a setting of the Resurrection Hymn by
the eighteenth-century Saxon poet Friedrich Gottlieb Klopstock. "It struck
me like lightning, this thing," Mahler wrote to Arthur Seidl, "and everything was revealed to my soul clear and plain." He took the first two stanzas of Klopstock's hymn and added to them verses of his own that deal still
more explicitly with the issue of redemption and resurrection.

The lines about the vanquishing of pain and death are given to the
two soloists in passionate duet. The verses beginning "Mit Flügeln, die ich
mir errungen" (With wings I won for myself) form the upbeat to the triumphant reappearance of the chorale: "Sterben werd' ich, um zu leben!" (I
shall die so as to live!), and the symphony comes to its close in a din of
fanfares and pealing bells.

Auferstehung	Resurrection
Aufersteh'n, ja aufersteh'n wirst du,	Rise again, yes, you will rise again,
Mein Staub, nach kurzer Ruh!	My dust, after brief rest!
Unsterblich Leben! Unsterblich Leben	Immortal life! Immortal life
Wird der dich rief geben!	Will He who called you grant you!
Wieder aufzublüh'n wirst du gesät!	To bloom again you were sown!
Der Herr der Ernte geht	The Lord of the Harvest goes
Und sammelt Garben	And gathers sheaves,
Uns ein, die Starben!	Us, who died!

　　　　　—Friedrich Gottlieb Klopstock

O glaube, mein Herz, o glaube:	O believe, my heart, but believe:
Es geht dir nichts verloren!	Nothing will be lost to you!
Dein ist, Dein, ja Dein, was du	Yours is what you longed for,
gesehnt!	

Dein, was du geliebt,	Yours what you loved,
Was du gestritten!	What you fought for!
O glaube:	O believe:
Du warst nicht umsonst geboren!	You were not born in vain!
Hast nicht umsonst gelitten!	You have not lived in vain, nor
	suffered!
Was entstanden ist, das muß	All that has come into being must
vergehen!	perish!
Was vergangen, auferstehen!	All that has perished must rise again!
Hör' auf zu beben!	Cease from trembling!
Bereite dich zu leben!	Prepare to live!
O Schmerz! Du Alldurchdringer!	O Pain, piercer of all things,
Dir bin ich entrungen!	From you I have been wrested!
O Tod! Du Allbezwinger!	O Death, conqueror of all things,
Nun bist du bezwungen!	Now you are conquered!
Mit Flügeln, die ich mir errungen,	With wings I won for myself
In heißem Liebesstreben	In love's ardent struggle,
Werd' ich entschweben	I shall fly upwards
Zum Licht, zu dem kein Aug' ge-	To that light which no eye has
drungen!	penetrated!
Sterben werd' ich, um zu leben!	I shall die so as to live.
Aufersteh'n, ja auferstehn wirst du,	Rise again, yes, you will rise again,
Mein Herz, in einem Nu!	My heart, in the twinkling of an eye!
Was du geschlagen,	What you have conquered
Zu Gott wird es dich tragen!	Will bear you to God!

—Gustav Mahler

Symphony No. 3

Part I   *Introduction. Forcefully and decisively.*

Part II   *Tempo di menuetto. Moderately.*
           Comodo. Scherzando. Unhurriedly.
           Very slow. Mysteriously.
           Joyous in tempo and jaunty in expression.
           Slow. Calm. Deeply felt.

Mahler did the main work on his Third Symphony in the summer of 1895,
when he composed the last five of its six movements, and 1896, when he

added the first. Two of his songs, *Ablösung im Sommer* (Relief in Summer) and *Das himmlische Leben* (Life in Heaven), provided source material for some of the symphony, and they go back to about 1890 and February 1892 respectively. Mahler made final revisions in May 1899. The symphony was introduced piecemeal. Arthur Nikisch conducted the second movement, then presented as *Blumenstück* (Flower Piece), with the Berlin Philharmonic on 9 November 1896. Felix Weingartner gave the second, third, and sixth movements with the Royal Orchestra, Berlin, on 9 March 1897. With Luise Geller-Wolter singing the alto solos, Mahler himself conducted the first complete performance at the Festival of the Allgemeiner deutscher Musikverein at Krefeld on 9 June 1902.

Four flutes (two doubling piccolo), four oboes (one doubling English horn), three clarinets (one doubling bass clarinet) and two E-flat clarinets, four bassoons (one doubling contrabassoon), eight horns, four trumpets, posthorn, four trombones, bass and contrabass tuba, timpani, glockenspiel, snare drum, triangle, tambourine, bass drum with cymbal attached, suspended cymbals, tam-tam, birch brush, two harps, and strings, plus solo contralto, women's chorus, and boys' chorus.

"Any ass can hear that," said Brahms when someone pointed out the resemblance of the big tune in the finale of his First Symphony to the one in Beethoven's Ninth. It is not recorded what Mahler said when someone—and someone must have—remarked on his beginning his Third Symphony with the Brahms First. That, too, any ass can hear, and we know what Mahler thought of such asses—cf. his song about the ass, the cuckoo, and the nightingale, *Lob des hohen Verstandes* (Lofty Intellect Condescends to Praise), composed in June 1896, midway through his work on the Third Symphony.[15]

Mahler was neither forgetful nor a plagiarist, and in the 1930s Donald Tovey asserted the view, then considered heterodox, that "we cannot fall back upon the device of classifying Mahler as one of the conductor-

---

[15] Brahms, who looked at the score of Mahler's Second Symphony and found its scherzo to be a piece "bordering on genius," saw none of the Third. Mahler at this time always paid a summer visit to Brahms at Bad Ischl, close enough to his own house at Steinbach for a pleasant bicycle trip. "Von Zeit zu Zeit seh' ich den Alten gern" (From time to time I enjoy seeing the old man), said Mahler, quoting Goethe's Mephistopheles on the subject of his visits to the Lord. "Gloomy and hating life," the old man was nonetheless friendly to Mahler, though impossible to draw out on music or any other subject of intellectual content. That he asked to have one of Mahler's scores sent to him was an amazing departure from his usual reserve.

composers who have drifted into composition through an urge to display their vast memories as experienced conductors." No, just like Brahms's pseudo-quotation of Beethoven, this beginning is allusion and reference, both to a particular monument of the symphonic tradition and to a topos or type of triumphal song. Mahler lived ambivalently in tradition, wanting to be part of it and, in the word of his biographer Henry-Louis de La Grange, to "insult" it. The Third, the biggest of Mahler's symphonies as well as the most out of the ordinary in proportion and design, is the most massive of his insults.

When Mahler, then near to completing his Eighth Symphony, visited Sibelius in 1907, the two composers argued about "the essence of symphony," Mahler rejecting his colleague's creed of severity, style, and logic by countering with "No, a symphony must be like the world. It must embrace everything." Twelve years earlier, while working on his Third, he had remarked that to "call it a symphony is really incorrect since it does not follow the usual form. The term 'symphony'—to me this means creating a world with all the technical means available."

The completion of the Second Symphony in 1894 had given Mahler confidence: he was sure of being in perfect control of his technique. Now, in the summer of 1895, escaped for some months from his duties as principal conductor of the Hamburg Opera, installed in his new one-room cabin at Steinbach on the Attersee some twenty miles east of Salzburg, with his sister Justine and his friend Natalie Bauer-Lechner to look after him (this, along with the usual household chores, most crucially meant silencing crows, water birds, children, and whistling farmhands), Mahler set out to make a world to which he gave the over-all title *The Happy Life—A Midsummer Night's Dream* (adding "not after Shakespeare, critics and Shakespeare mavens please note").

Before he wrote a single measure, he worked out a scenario in five sections titled *What the Forest Tells Me, What the Trees Tell Me, What Twilight Tells Me* ("strings only," he noted), *What the Cuckoo Tells Me* (*scherzo*), and *What the Child Tells Me.* He changed all that five times as the music began to take shape in his mind during the summer. *The Happy Life* disappeared, to be replaced for a while by the Nietzschean *Gay Science* (first *My Gay Science*). The trees, twilight, and cuckoo were all removed, supplanted by flowers, animals, and morning bells. He added *What the Night Tells Me* and saw that he wanted to begin with the triumphal entry of summer, which would include an element of something Dionysian and even frightening. In less than three weeks he composed what are now the second through fifth movements. He went on to the Adagio and, by the time his composing vacation came to an end on 20 August, he had made an outline of the first movement and written two independent songs, *Lied des Verfolgten im Turm* (Song of the Persecuted Man in the Tower) and the magical *Wo die schönen Trompeten blasen* (Where the Lovely Trumpets Sound). It was the richest summer of his life.

In June 1896 he was back at Steinbach. Over the winter he had made some progress scoring the new symphony and had complicated his life by an intense, stormy affair with Anna von Mildenburg, a young, superlatively gifted dramatic soprano newly come to Hamburg. He also discovered when he got to Steinbach that he had forgotten to bring the sketches of the first movement, and it was while he was waiting for them that he wrote his little bouquet for critics, *Lob des hohen Verstandes*. In due course the sketches arrived, and as Mahler worked on them, he came to realize that *The Awakening of Pan* and *The Triumphal March of Summer* wanted to be one movement rather than two.[16]

He also saw, to his alarm, that the first movement was growing hugely, that it would be more than half an hour long, and that it was also getting louder and louder. He deleted his finale, which was the *Life in Heaven* song of 1892 and for which he found the perfect place a few years later as the last movement of his Fourth Symphony. That necessitated rewriting the last pages of the Adagio, which had now become the finale, but to all intents and purposes the work was under control by early August.

Gay Science was still part of the title at the beginning of the summer, coupled with what had become *A Midsummer Noon's Dream*, but in Mahler's eighth and last scenario, dated 6 August 1896, the superscription is simply *A Midsummer Noon's Dream*, with the following titles given to the individual movements:

> First Part: *Pan Awakes. Summer Comes Marching In (Bacchic Procession).*
> Second Part: *What the Flowers in the Meadow Tell Me.*
> *What the Animals in the Forest Tell Me.*
> *What Humanity Tells Me.*
> *What the Angels Tell Me.*
> *What Love Tells Me.*

At the 1902 premiere, the program page showed no titles at all, only tempo and generic indications (*Tempo di Menuetto, Rondo, Alto Solo,* and so on). "Beginning with Beethoven," Mahler wrote to the critic Max Kalbeck that year, "there is no modern music without its underlying program. —But no music is worth anything if first you have to tell the listener

---

[16]Mahler was responsive to omens, and when a letter from Anna von Mildenburg arrived with P A N stamped prominently on the envelope, he was all set to take it as preternatural endorsement of his symphonic plan. His rush dissipated when he looked again and saw that the letters were followed by the number 30, the whole standing for Postamt Nr. 30, Post Office No. 30.

what experience lies behind it and what he is supposed to experience in it. And so yet again, to hell with every program! You just have to bring your ears and a heart along and—not least—willingly surrender to the rhapsodist. Some residue of mystery always remains, even for the creator."

Writing to the conductor Josef Krug-Waldsee around the same time, he elaborated:

> Those titles were an attempt on my part to provide non-musicians with something to hold on to and with signposts for the intellectual, or better, the expressive content of the various movements and for their relationship to each other and to the whole. That it didn't work (as in fact it never could work) and that it led only to misinterpretations of the most horrendous sort became painfully clear all too quickly. It was the same disaster that had overtaken me on previous and similar occasions, and now I have, once and for all, given up commenting, analyzing, and all such expediencies of whatever sort. Those titles . . . will surely say something to you *after* you know the score. You will draw intimations from them about how I imagined the steady intensification of feeling, from the indistinct, unyielding, elemental existences (of the forces of nature) to the tender formation of the human heart, which in turn points toward and reaches a region beyond itself (God).
>
> Please express that in your own words without quoting these extremely inadequate titles. That way you will have acted in my spirit. I am *very* grateful that you asked me [about the titles], for how my work is introduced into public life is by no means inconsequential to me and for its future.[17]

Words a program annotator quotes at his peril. But the climate has changed, and today's audience is very much inclined to come to Mahler with that willingness to surrender he had hoped for. When we look at the titles in the Third Symphony, even though they were finally rejected, we are looking at a series of attempts to put into few words the world of ideas, emotions, and association that lay behind the musical choices Mahler made as he composed. We too can draw intimations from them and then remove them as a scaffolding we no longer need. That said, let us look at the musical object Mahler left us.

The first movement accounts for roughly one-third of the symphony's length. Starting with magnificent gaiety and brio, it falls at once into tragedy: seesawing chords of low horns and bassoons, the drumbeats of a funeral procession, cries and outrage. Mysterious twitterings follow, the suggestion of a distant quick march, and a grandly rhetorical recitative for the trombone. Against all that, Mahler poses a series of quick marches (the

---

[17] Mahler *Briefe.*

realization of the earlier hint of march music) that have tunes you can't believe you haven't known all your life and that used to cause critics to complain of Mahler's "banality." They are elaborated and scored with an astonishing combination of delicacy and exuberance. Their swagger is re-warded by collision with catastrophe, and the whole movement is the con-flict of the dark and the bright elements, culminating in the victory of the bright. For all its outsize dimensions, this is as classical a sonata form as Mahler ever designed.

Two other points should be made. One concerns Mahler's fascination, not ignored later in the century, with things happening "out of time." The piccolo player rushing her imitations of the violins' little fanfares is not berserk: she is merely following Mahler's direction to play "without regard for the beat." That is playful, but the same device is turned to dramatic effect when, at the end of a steadily accelerating development, the snare drums cut across the oom-pah of the cellos and basses with a slower march tempo of their own, thus preparing the way for the eight horns to blast the recapitulation into being. The other thing to point out is that several of the themes heard near the beginning will be transformed into the materials of the last three movements—fascinating especially when you recall that the first movement was written after the others.[18]

In the division of the work Mahler finally adopted, the first movement makes up the entire first section. What follows is, except for the finale, a series of shorter character pieces, beginning with the *Blumenstück*, the first music Mahler composed for this symphony. This is a delicately sentimental minuet, with access, in its contrasting middle section, to slightly sinister sources of energy. It "anticipates" music not to be heard in the symphony at all, specifically the scurrying runs from the *Life in Heaven* song that was dropped from this design and incorporated into the Symphony No. 4. Some time after he finished this movement, Mahler noted with surprise that the basses play pizzicato throughout. In the last measure, Wagner's *Parsifal* flower-maidens make a ghostly appearance in Mahler's Upper Aus-trian pastoral landscape.

In the third movement, Mahler draws on his song *Relief in Summer*, whose text tells of waiting for Lady Nightingale to start singing as soon as the cuckoo is through. The marvel here is the landscape with posthorn, not just the lovely melody itself, but the way it is presented: the magic transformation of the highly present trumpet into distant posthorn, the

---

[18] In the Fourth Symphony, too, Mahler convinces us that the music he composed between 1899 and 1901 leads inevitably to a finale that had existed since 1892. The Verdi Requiem is perhaps the most famous composition in which everything leads with entirely convincing inevitability to a pre-existing finale.

gradual change of the posthorn's melody from fanfare to song, the interlude for flutes, and, as Arnold Schoenberg pointed out, the accompaniment "at first with the divided high violins, then, even more beautiful if possible, with the horns." After the brief return of this idyll and before the snappy coda, Mahler makes spine-chilling reference to the Last Judgment "Great Summons" music in the Second Symphony's finale.

Now low strings rock to and fro, the harps accenting a few of their notes; the seesawing chords from the symphony's first pages return; a human voice intones the Midnight Song from Friedrich Nietzsche's *Also sprach Zarathustra*. Each of its eleven lines is to be imagined as coming between two of the twelve strokes of midnight. *Pianississimo* throughout, Mahler warns. The harmony is almost as static as the dynamics, being frozen in all but a few measures to a pedal D. The beginning and end, which frame D in its own dominant, A, are exceptions, and so is the setting with solo violin of "Lust tiefer noch as Herzeleid" (Joy deeper still than heartbreak).

O Mensch! Gib Acht!	Oh, man, give heed!
Was spricht die tiefe Mitternacht?	What does deep midnight say?
Ich schlief!	I slept!
Aus tiefem Traum bin ich erwacht!	From a deep dream have I waked.
Die Welt ist tief!	The world is deep,
Und tiefer als der Tag gedacht!	And deeper than the day had thought!
Tief ist ihr Weh!	Deep is its pain!
Lust tiefer noch als Herzeleid!	Joy deeper still than heartbreak!
Weh spricht: Vergeh!	Pain speaks: Vanish!
Doch alle Lust will Ewigkeit!	But all joy seeks eternity,
Will tiefe, tiefe Ewigkeit!	Seeks deep, deep eternity.

—Friedrich Nietzsche

From here the music continues without a break and, as abruptly as it changed from the scherzo to Nietzsche's midnight, so does it move now from that darkness into a world of bells and angels. The text of the fifth movement, *Es sungen drei Engel* (Three Angels Were Singing), comes from that famous collection of much-edited folk poetry *Des Knaben Wunderhorn* (The Boy's Magic Horn), though the interjections of "Du sollst ja nicht weinen (But you mustn't weep)" are Mahler's own.[19] A three-part chorus

---

[19] Mahler, who drew on this anthology many times, often approached the poems with the same freedom with which the compilers, Clemens Brentano and Achim von Arnim, treated the original folk verses.

of women's voices carries most of the text, with the solo contralto returning to take the role of the sinner. The boys' chorus, confined at first
to bell noises, joins later in the exhortation "Liebe nur Gott" (Only love
God) and for the final stanza. This movement, too, foreshadows the *Life
in Heaven* that will not in fact occur until the Fourth Symphony: the solemnly archaic chords first heard at "Ich hab übertreten die zehen Gebot"
(I have trespassed against the Ten Commandments) are associated in the
later work with details of the domestic arrangements in that touching depiction of heaven. Mahler loved the sound and atmosphere of these chords
and brought them back years later near the end of the Eighth Symphony.
Violins are silent in this softly sonorous movement.

Es sungen drei Engel einen süßen Gesang,	Three angels were singing a sweet song:
Mit Freuden es selig im Himmel klang;	With joy it resounded blissfully in Heaven.
Sie jauchzten fröhlich auch dabei,	At the same time they happily shouted with joy
Dass Petrus sei von Sünden frei.	That Peter was absolved from sin.
Denn als der Heer Jesus zu Tische saß,	For as Lord Jesus sat at table,
Mit seinen zwölf Jüngern das Abendmal aß,	Eating supper with his twelve apostles,
So sprach der Herr Jesus: "Was stehst du denn hier?	So spoke Lord Jesus: "Why are you standing here?
Wenn ich dich anseh', so weinest du mir."	When I look at you, you weep."
"Und sollt' ich nicht weinen, du gütiger Gott!	"And how should I not weep, you kind God!
Du sollst ja nicht weinen!	*No, you mustn't weep!*
Ich hab' übertreten die zehen Gebot.	"I have trespassed against the Ten Commandments.
Ich gehe und weine ja bitterlich,	I go and weep, and bitterly."
Du sollst ja nicht weinen!	*No, you mustn't weep!*
Ach komm und erbarme dich über mich!'	"Ah, come and have mercy on me!"
"Hast du denn übertreten die zehen Gebot,	"If you have trespassed against the Ten Commandments,
So fall auf die Knie und bete zu Gott.	Then fall on your knees and pray to God.
Liebe nur Gott in alle Zeit!	Only love God forever,
So wirst du erlangen die himmlische Freud'."	And you will attain heavenly joy."

Die himmlische Freud' ist eine selige Stadt,	Heavenly joy is a blessed city,
Die himmlische Freud', die kein Ende mehr hat.	Heavenly joy that has no end.
Die himmlische Freud' war Petro bereit	Heavenly joy was prepared for Peter
Durch Jesum und allen zur Seligkeit.	By Jesus and for the salvation of all.

—from *Des Knaben Wunderhorn*

The delicate tension between the regions of F (the quick marches in the first movement, and the third and fifth movements) and D (the dirges in the first movement, the Nietzsche song, and, by extension, the minuet, which is in A major) is now and finally resolved in favor of D. Mahler realized that in ending his symphony with an Adagio he had made a very special decision. "In Adagio movements," he explained to Natalie Bauer-Lechner, "everything is resolved in quiet. The Ixion wheel of outer appearances is at last brought to a standstill. In fast movements—minuets, allegros, even andantes nowadays—everything is motion, change, flux. Therefore I have ended my Second and Third symphonies contrary to custom . . . with Adagios—the higher form as distinguished from the lower."

A noble thought, but, not for the only time in Mahler, there is some gap between theory and reality. The Adagio makes its way at last to a sure and grand conquest, but during its course—and this is a movement, like the first, on a very large scale—Ixion's flaming wheel can hardly be conceived of as standing still. In his opening melody, Mahler invites association with the slow movement of Beethoven's last quartet, Opus 135. Soon, though, the music is caught in "motion, change, flux," and before the final triumph, it encounters once more the catastrophe that interrupted the first movement. The Adagio's original title, *What Love Tells Me*, refers to Christian love, *agape*, and Mahler's draft carries the superscription "Behold my wounds! Let not one soul be lost!" The performance directions, too, speak to the issue of spirituality, for Mahler commands that the immense final bars with their thundering kettledrums—this is decidedly not a movement in which "everything is resolved in quiet"—be played "not with brute force [but] with rich, noble tone."[20] Likewise, the last measure is "not to be cut off sharply"; rather, there should be some softness to the edge between sound and silence at the end of this most riskily comprehensive of Mahler's worlds.

---

[20] Mahler writes "gesättigt," which carries a range of meanings in the area of "satisfied" and "saturated."

Symphony No. 4

> Deliberately. Do not hurry
> In easy motion. Without haste
> Serene
> Very leisurely

Except for the finale, which was originally composed as a song with piano accompaniment in February 1892, Mahler wrote his Fourth Symphony between June 1899 and April 1901. He continued, however, on the basis of his experience conducting the work, to tinker with the orchestration. He entered his final revisions after the last performances he conducted of this symphony with the New York Philharmonic in January 1911. Mahler led the premiere on 25 November 1901 with the Kaim Orchestra of Munich; the soprano was Margarete Michalek.

Four flutes (third and fourth doubling piccolo), three oboes (third doubling English horn), five clarinets (second doubling E-flat clarinet, third doubling bass clarinet), three bassoons (third doubling contrabassoon), four horns, three trumpets, timpani, bass drum, triangle, sleigh bells, glockenspiel, cymbals, tam-tam, harp, and strings, plus solo soprano.

Having begun by being both wowed and bewildered by Mahler's Second Symphony and just plain bewildered by the First (heard only on a thoroughly inadequate 1930s AM table radio), I finally caught on when the Fourth came my way. That experience of hearing Bruno Walter's New York Philharmonic-Symphony recording in a tiny listening booth in the Baldwin Piano Store in Saint Louis (done in installments because my lunch break at my summer job with an advertising agency was only half an hour) was not acoustically ideal either, but at last I fell in love. Many years later I was delighted to learn that Mahler himself had thought of this sunlit work as one whose transparency, relative brevity, and non-aggressive stance might win him new friends. In fact, it enraged most of its first hearers. Munich hated it, and so did most of the German cities where Felix Weingartner took it on tour with the Kaim Orchestra immediately after the premiere, Stuttgart being, for some reason, the exception.

The very qualities Mahler had banked on were the ones that annoyed. The bells, real and imitated (in flutes), with which the music begins! And that chawbacon tune in the violins! What in heaven's name was the composer of the *Resurrection* Symphony up to with this newfound naïveté? Most of the answers proposed at the time were politicized, anti-Semitic, ugly. Today, we perceive more clearly that what he was up to was writing a Mahler symphony, uncharacteristic only in its virtually exclusive involvement with the sunny end of the expressive range. But naïve? The violin tune, yes, is so popular in tone that we can hardly conceive that once upon a time it didn't exist, but it is also *pianissimo,* which is the first step toward subverting its rustic simplicity. Moreover, Mahler marks accents on it in two places, both unexpected.

The first phrase ends and, while clarinets and bassoons mark the beat, low strings suggest a surprising though charmingly appropriate continuation. A horn interrupts them mid-phrase and itself has the very words taken out of its mouth by the bassoon. At that moment, the cellos and basses assert themselves with a severe "As I was saying" just as the violins chime in with their own upside-down thoughts on the continuation of the opening phrase that the lower strings had suggested four bars earlier. The game of interruptions, resumptions, extensions, reconsiderations, and unexpected combinations continues. When, for example, the violins try their first melody again, the cellos have figured out that it is possible to imitate it, lagging two beats behind (a discovery they proffer with utmost discretion, *pianissimo* and deadpan), until bassoons and low strings call time out, and the cellos sing an ardent something that clearly declares "new key" and "second theme."

"Turning cliché into event" is how Theodor Adorno characterized Mahler's practice. Ideas lead to many different conclusions and can be ordered in so many ways. Mahler's master here is the Haydn of the London symphonies and string quartets of the 1790s. The scoring, too, rests on Mahler's ability to apply an original and altogether personal fantasy to resources not in themselves extraordinary. Trombones and the tuba are absent; only the percussion is lavish. Mahler plays with this orchestra as though with a kaleidoscope. He can write a brilliantly sonorous tutti, but hardly ever does, preferring to have the thread of discourse passed rapidly, wittily from instrument to instrument, section to section. He thinks polyphonically, but enjoys the combining of textures and colors as much as the combining of themes.

Mahler wrote to a friend that he could dream up the most wonderful titles for the movements of this symphony, but would not "betray them to the rabble of critics and listeners" who would then subject them to "their banal misunderstandings." We do, however, have his name for the scherzo:

Freund Hein spielt auf (Death Strikes Up).[21] Alma Mahler explained that here "the composer was under the spell of the self-portrait by Arnold Böcklin, in which Death fiddles into the painter's ear while the latter sits entranced." Death's fiddle is tuned a whole tone high to make it harsher (the player is also instructed to make it sound like a country instrument and to enter "very aggressively"). Twice, Mahler tempers these grotesqueries with a gentle trio: Willem Mengelberg, the Amsterdam conductor, took detailed notes at Mahler's 1904 rehearsals, and at this point he put into his score that "here he leads us into a lovely landscape."[22]

The Adagio, which Mahler thought his finest slow movement, is a set of softly and gradually unfolding variations. It is rich in seductive melody, but the constant feature Mahler always returns to is the tolling of the basses, *piano* under the *pianissimo* of the violas and cellos. The variations, twice interrupted by a leanly scored lament in the minor mode, become shorter, more diverse in character, more given to abrupt changes of outlook. They are also pulled more and more in the direction of E major, a key that asserts itself dramatically at the end of the movement in a blaze of sound. Working miracles in harmony, pacing, and orchestral fabric, Mahler, pronouncing a benediction, brings us back to serene quiet on the very threshold of his original G major, but when the finale emerges almost imperceptibly, it is in E. Our entry into this region has been prepared, but it is well that the music sound new, for Mahler means us to understand that now we are in heaven.

On 6 February 1892, Mahler had finished a song he called *Das himmlische Leben* (Life in Heaven), one of five humoresques on texts from *Des Knaben Wunderhorn* (The Boy's Magic Horn). *Des Knaben Wunderhorn* is a collection of German folk poetry compiled just after 1800 by Clemens Brentano and Achim von Arnim. That, at least, is what it purports to be. In fact, the two poets indulged themselves freely in paraphrases, additions, and deletions, fixing things so as to give them a more antique and authentic ring, even contributing poems all their own. Mahler began to write *Wunderhorn* songs immediately after completing the First Symphony in 1888 (he had already borrowed a *Wunderhorn* poem as the foundation of the first of his *Songs of a Wayfarer* of 1884–85). The *Wunderhorn* then touches the Second, Third, and Fourth symphonies. The scherzo of No. 2 shares material and was composed at the same time as a setting of a poem about Saint Anthony of Padua's Sermon to the Fishes, and the next move-

---

[21] Freund Hein—literally this could be rendered as Friend Hal—is a fairy-tale bogey whose name is often a euphemism for Death.

[22] I am very grateful to the late Erich Leinsdorf for copying out several of Mengelberg's notations for me while on a visit to Amsterdam.

ment in that work is the song *Urlicht* (Primal Light), also on a text from *Des Knaben Wunderhorn*. The Third Symphony's fifth movement is another *Wunderhorn* song, *Es sungen drei Engel* (Three Angels Were Singing), and until about a year before completing it, Mahler meant to end that symphony with *Das himmlische Leben*, the song we now know as the finale of the Fourth. That explains why the Third appears to "quote" the Fourth, twice in the minuet and again in the *Drei Engel* song: those moments prepare for an event that does not, after all, occur (or at least not until five years later and in another piece).

For that matter, Mahler had to plan parts of the Fourth Symphony from the end back, so that the song would appear to be the outcome and conclusion of what was in fact music composed eight years after the song. From a late letter of Mahler's to the Leipzig conductor Georg Göhler, we know how important it was to him that listeners clearly understand how the first three movements all point toward and are resolved in the finale.

The music of the song, though gloriously inventive in detail, is of utmost cleanness and simplicity. The solemn and archaic chords first heard at "Sanct Peter in Himmel sieht zu" (Saint Peter in heaven looks on) have a double meaning for Mahler: here, they are associated with details about the domestic arrangements in this mystical, sweetly scurrile picture of heaven, but in the Third Symphony they belong with the bitter self-castigation at having transgressed the Ten Commandments and with the plea to God for forgiveness. Whether you are listening to the Fourth and remembering the Third, or the other way around, the reference is touching. It reminds us, as well, how much all of Mahler's work is one work. Just as the symphony began with bells, so it ends with them—this time those wonderful, deep single harp-tones of which Mahler was the discoverer.

The poem is a Bavarian folk song called *Der Himmel hängt voll Geigen* (Heaven Is Hung with Violins). About the text: Saint Luke's symbol is a winged ox; Saint Martha, sister of Lazarus, is the patron saint of those engaged in service of the needy. On Saint Ursula and the eleven thousand virgins, I quote Donald Attwater's indispensable *Penguin Dictionary of Saints:*

> Ursula, to avoid an unwanted marriage, departed with her company from the island of Britain, where her father was a king; on their way back from a visit to Rome, they were slaughtered by Huns at Cologne on account of their Christian faith. During the twelfth century this pious romance was preposterously elaborated through the mistakes of imaginative visionaries; a public burial-ground uncovered at Cologne was taken to be the grave of the martyrs, false relics came into circulation and forged epitaphs of non-existent

persons were produced. The earliest reference which gives St. Ursula the first place speaks of her ten companions: how these eleven came to be multiplied by a thousand is a matter of speculation.[23]

Das himmlische Leben	Life in Heaven
Wir genießen die himmlische Freuden,	We enjoy the pleasures of Heaven
D'rum thun wir das Irdische meiden.	And therefore avoid earthly ones.
Kein weltlich' Getümmel	No worldly tumult
Hört man nicht im Himmel!	Is to be heard in Heaven.
Lebt Alles in sanftester Ruh'!	All live in gentlest peace.
Wir führen ein englisches Leben!	We lead angelic lives,
Sind dennoch ganz lustig daneben!	Yet have a merry time of it besides.
Wir tanzen und springen,	We dance and we spring,
Wir hüpfen und singen!	We skip and we sing.
Sanct Peter im Himmel sieht zu!	Saint Peter in Heaven looks on.
Johannes das Lämmlein auslasset,	John lets the little lamb out,
Der Metzger Herodes drauf passet!	And Herod the Butcher lies in wait for it.
Wir führen ein geduldig's,	We lead a patient,
Unschuldig's, geduldig's,	Innocent, patient
Ein liebliches Lämmlein zu Tod!	Dear little lamb to its death.
Sanct Lucas den Ochsen thät schlachten	Saint Luke slaughters the ox
Ohn' einig's Bedenken und Achten.	Without thought or concern.
Der Wein kost kein Heller	Wine doesn't cost a penny
Im himmlischen Keller,	In the heavenly cellars.
Die Englein, die backen das Brot.	The angels bake the bread.
Gut' Kräuter von allerhand Arten,	Good greens of every sort
Die wachsen im himmlischen Garten!	Grow in the heavenly vegetable patch.
Gut' Spargel, Fisolen,	Good asparagus, string beans,
Und was wir nun wollen!	And whatever we want!
Ganze Schüsseln voll sind us bereit!	Whole dishfuls are set out for us.
Gut Äpfel, gut' Birn' und gut' Trauben!	Good apples, good pears, and good grapes,
Die Gärtner, die Alles erlauben!	And gardners who allow everything!
Willst Rehbock, willst Hasen,	If you want venison or hare,
Auf offener Straßen sie laufen herbei.	You'll find them running on the public streets.
Sollt ein Fasttag etwa kommen	Should a fast-day come along,
Alle Fische gleich mit Freuden ange-schwommen!	All the fishes at once come swimming with joy.

[23] Donald Attwater, *The Penguin Dictionary of Saints* (Baltimore: Penguin Books, 1965).

Dort läuft schon Sanct Peter	There goes Saint Peter, running
Mit Netz und mit Köder	With his net and his bait
Zum himmlischen Weiher hinein.	To the heavenly pond.
Sanct Martha die Köchin muß sein.	Saint Martha shall be the cook.
Kein Musik ist ja nicht auf Erden,	There is just no music on earth
Die uns'rer verglichen kann werden.	That can compare to ours.
Elftausend Jungfrauen	Even the eleven thousand virgins
Zu tanzen sich trauen!	Venture to dance,
Sanct Ursula selbst dazu lacht!	And Saint Ursula herself has to laugh.
Cäcilia mit ihren Verwandten	Cecilia and all her relations
Sind treffliche Hofmusikanten!	Make excellent court musicians.
Die englischen Stimmen	The angelic voices
Ermuntern die Sinnen!	Gladden our senses,
Dass Alles für Freuden erwacht.	So that all awake for joy.

—from *Des Knaben Wunderhorn*

Symphony No. 5

Funeral march: With measured step.
    Strict. Like a cortège.
Stormily. With greatest vehemence.

Scherzo: Vigorously, not too fast

Adagietto: Very slow
Rondo-Finale: Allegro giocoso. Lively.

Mahler composed his Symphony No. 5 in 1901–02 and led the first performance with the Gürzenich Orchestra in Cologne on 18 October 1904, having conducted a read-through with the Vienna Philharmonic earlier that year. He continued to revise details of the orchestration until 1907, possibly even 1909.

Four flutes (two doubling piccolo), three oboes and English horn, three clarinets and bass clarinet, three bassoons and contrabassoon, six horns, four trumpets, three trombones, tuba, timpani, cymbals, bass drum, bass drum with cymbals attached, snare drum, triangle, glockenspiel, tam-tam, slapstick, harp, and strings.

In the first movement of Mahler's Fourth Symphony (1899–1901), a sunny exposition leads to a surprisingly shadowed development. Its explosive climax is quickly stifled, and, across the still-unsettled muttering and ticking of a few instruments, a trumpet calls the orchestra to order with a quietly insistent fanfare. It is a variant of that fanfare—at the same pitch even—that opens the Symphony No. 5. There is no obvious explanation for this quotation, this link, but to contend that no explanation is needed will not do. The fanfare, though it comes so close to being a commonplace, is too arresting, and it is too critically placed in both symphonies. Let us speculate. In 1901, at the juncture of completing the Fourth Symphony and beginning the Fifth, Mahler was acutely conscious of taking a new path (as Beethoven had said of himself a hundred years before). Perhaps, as he set out, he wanted to show that the seed for the new was to be found in the old.

In what sense, then, is the Fifth Symphony new? After a run of eccentric symphonies, Mahler comes back to a more "normal" design, one that could in fact be described as concentric as well as symmetrical.[24] In the First Symphony, the orchestra plays long passages from Mahler's own *Songs of a Wayfarer*, and the Second, Third, and Fourth symphonies actually include singing. While the Fifth also alludes to three of Mahler's songs, it is essentially an instrumental conception. This shift toward purely orchestral symphonies is tied to another change in Mahler's work. Except for lines from a hymn by Klopstock in the Second Symphony and a poem by Nietzsche in the Third, for thirteen years Mahler had set only texts from the folk base collection, *Des Knaben Wunderhorn* (The Boy's Magic Horn). But in July 1901, Mahler composed his last *Wunderhorn* song, *Der Tamboursg'sell* (The Drummer Boy), and turned to the writings of Friedrich Rückert, setting six of his poems that month and next.

With that change of literary inspiration, a certain kind of "open" *Wunderhorn* lyricism disappears from Mahler's symphonies. The music becomes leaner and harder. Also around this time, Mahler acquired the complete edition of Bach and, at least partly in consequence of his excited discovery of what was in those volumes, his textures become more polyphonic. (The one time he conducted the Symphony No. 5 in Vienna he preceded it with Bach's motet *Singet dem Herrn ein neues Lied* (Sing unto the Lord a New Song). But this new "intensified polyphony," as Bruno Walter called it, demanded a new orchestral style, and this did not come easily. Mahler was always a pragmatist in orchestration, tending to revise

---

[24] Only in his Sixth Symphony (1903–05) would Mahler return to the familiar nineteenth-century four-movement pattern. The Ninth is also in four movements, but the sequence in that work is not the conventional one.

constantly in response to his experience conducting his own works or hearing them under a trusted colleague like Willem Mengelberg in Amsterdam,
but never did he find he had so thoroughly miscalculated a sound as in the
first version of the Fifth, with its apparently deafening barrage of percussion. He made alterations until at least 1907, which is when he conducted
the Fifth for the last time, and in 1911, looking back at the beginnings of
a work that had proved refractory even with such good conductors as Leo
Blech and Arthur Nikisch, Mahler wrote: "I cannot understand how I
could have written so much like a beginner. . . . Clearly the routine I
had acquired in the first four symphonies had deserted me altogether, as
though a totally new message demanded a new technique."[25]

Mahler's wife, Alma, was ill and could not accompany him to Cologne for the premiere, and to that unhappy circumstance we owe one of
the composer's most remarkable and delightful letters, written 14 October
1904, just after the first rehearsal. Of the symphony he wrote: "Heavens,
what is the public to make of this chaos in which new worlds are for ever
being engendered, only to crumble into ruin the next moment? What are
they to say to this primeval music, this foaming, roaring, raging sea of
sound, to these dancing stars, to these breath-taking, iridescent, and flash-
ing breakers?"

For the composer Ernst Krenek, the Fifth Symphony was the work
with which Mahler enters "upon the territory of the 'new' music of the
twentieth century." And to return for a moment to Mahler's report from
Cologne: "Oh that I might give my symphony its first performance fifty
years after my death! . . . Oh that I were a Cologne town councilor with
a box at the Municipal Theater and at the Gürzenich Hall and could look
down upon all modern music!"

Mahler casts the work in five movements, but some very large Roman
numerals in the score indicate a more basic division into three sections,
consisting respectively of the first two, the third, and the last two movements. Very roughly, the proportions are 3:2:3. At the center stands the
Scherzo, with which Mahler actually began his work on the symphony,
and its place in the design is pleasingly ambiguous in that it is framed
between larger structural units (Sections I and III) but is itself longer than
any other single movement.

Mahler begins the symphony with funeral music. This is a persistent
theme in his work, one that plays a large role in the first three symphonies

---

[25]Our sense of the newness of the Fifth Symphony is somewhat blunted by the fact that almost
all the performances we now hear of the Fourth Symphony are of the final revised version of
1911, a recension whose sound is that of "the new Mahler."

and, later, in the Sixth, the Ninth, and the unfinished Tenth. He starts
here with the summons of the single trumpet. Most of the orchestra is
drawn into this darkly sonorous exordium, whose purpose, we soon discover, is to prepare a lament sung by violins and cellos. At least that is
how it is sung to begin with, but it is characteristic of Mahler's scoring
that colors and textures, weights and balances, degrees of light and shade
shift from moment to moment. In the grave rotation of this kaleidoscope,
clarinets and bassoons and violas emerge momentarily from their place
among the accompanists to add a melodic suggestion of their own (one
that is at once picked up by the violins), the second violins join to reinforce the firsts, and the cellos, piangendo (weeping), make themselves independent as the violins withdraw far into the background. Something else
that changes is the melody itself. Ask six people who know this symphony
to sing this dirge for you and you may well get six different versions, all of
them correct. It is a wonderful play of perpetual variation.

The opening music comes back; indeed, it is almost as though the
cellos' insistent triplets *will* the return of the fanfare. Again this summons
leads to the inspired threnody, unfolded this time at greater breadth than
before and with a more intense grieving. Yet again the trumpet recalls the
symphony's first bars. This time, suddenly, with utmost violence and across
a brutally simple accompaniment, violins fling forth a whipping downward
scale, and the trumpet is pushed to scream its anguish. Mahler marks this
page "impassioned, wild" and adds a footnote for the conductor that the
playing of the violins must be "at all times as vehement as possible!"
Theodor Adorno with grim humor refers to this passage as "pogrom music."

An attempt to introduce a loftier strain is quickly swept aside in the
turmoil. Gradually Mahler returns to the original slow tempo and to the
cortège we have come to associate with it, and it is here that he alludes
for a moment to one of the songs of that rich summer of 1901. This is the
first of the Rückert *Kindertotenlieder,* and the line is the poet's bitter greeting to the first sunrise after the death of his child, "Hail to the world's
joyous light!" When the whipping violin scale returns it is in the context
of the slow tempo. Then the movement disintegrates in ghostly reminders
of the fanfare and a savagely final punctuation mark.

What we have heard so far is a slow movement with a fast interruption. There follows its inversion, a quick movement that returns several
times to the tempo of the funeral march. And more, these two parts of
Section I actually share thematic material. (Adorno's remark that the two
movements stand in the relation of exposition and development simplifies
the situation rather too drastically, but it is an undeniably suggestive way
of pointing to their interdependence.) Still more variants of the great
threnody appear, and the grieving commentary that accompanied the mel-

ody in the first movement pushes its way more insistently into the foreground, to the point even of transforming itself for a moment into a march
of unseemly jauntiness.

Mahler uses yet another transformation of that motif with its upward-
thrusting ninth to say that there will be an end to tears and to lamentation; for now, trumpets and trombones intone a chorale, the symphony's
first extended music in a major key. But it is too soon for victory. The
grand proclamation vanishes as though it had never been, and this movement, too, dematerializes in a passage of the most astounding orchestral
fantasy. We can, however, be sure of two things about the future course
of this symphony: we have not heard the last of the chorale itself nor of
the key, D major, in which it made its dramatic entrance.

Let me, at this point, touch on the question of key. Symphonies from
Haydn to Brahms and Bruckner usually begin and end in the same key,
the harmonic stability thus generated being an essential expressive and
architectonic tool. In his First Symphony, Mahler simultaneously drama-
tizes and questions this plan by delaying extraordinarily the return to his
initial D major. In the Fourth Symphony, about four-fifths of the way
through, he suddenly diverts the harmonic current to remote territory and
simply ends in his newfound land. He has no stable convictions about this
matter: some of his symphonies return to their harmonic starting points,
some do not. The Fifth is one of the latter, and part of the drama is the
emergence of D major as a clearly perceived goal—far from the keening C-
sharp minor of the first movement and the roiling A minor in the second.

Now, as we reach the middle panel of Mahler's symphonic triptych,
four horns in unison legitimize D major by declaring it to be the key of the
Scherzo. The voice of a single horn detaches itself from that call, the
beginning of a challenging obbligato for the principal player. This is country music, by turns ebullient, nostalgic, and a mite parodistic. There is
room even for awe as horns speak and echo across deep mountain gorges.
It is exuberantly inventive too, its energies fed by the bold ingenuity of
Mahler's polyphony (four themes sound at once in the coda), and it is
brilliantly set for the orchestra. It also incorporates a mystery. We know
that it quotes a tune by a certain Thomas Koschat, a slightly older contemporary of Mahler's who specialized in setting Carinthian dialect verse, but
so far no one has identified which theme does the quoting.

The diminutive in the title of the famous Adagietto refers to its brevity and is not meant as a qualification of its adagioness: in the first three
measures alone, Mahler tells the conductor three times and in two languages that he wants it "very slow." This is an issue to which I shall return.
The Adagietto was a celebrated page well before Luchino Visconti raped

and dismembered it for his frivolous film of Thomas Mann's *Death in Venice*. It is one of the movements that used occasionally to be played alone when programming an entire Mahler symphony was too risky, and Mahler's friends Willem Mengelberg and Bruno Walter both recorded it long before Walter was allowed to make the first complete album of the Fifth. Fair enough: if any one movement can convey the essence both of Mahler's heartache and of his melodic style, seemingly so obvious until you get into "deep listening," this Adagietto is it. The orchestra is reduced to strings with harp, and one could go on learning forever from the uncanny sense of detail with which Mahler moves those few strands of sound. If the harp part were lost and one had to reconstruct it, figuring out the right harmonies would be easy, but nobody could ever guess Mahler's hesitating rhythm or his sensitive spacing of those chords.

The Adagietto is cousin to one of Mahler's first Rückert songs, *Ich bin der Welt abhanden gekommen* (I am lost to the world). It is not so much a matter of quotation or even allusion as of drawing twice from the same well. Adagietto and song share characteristic features of contour, harmony, and texture, and our knowledge of the song, which ends with the lines "I live alone in my heaven, in my loving, in my song," confirms our sense of what Mahler wishes to tell us in this page of his symphony.

Recently, however, in the beautiful facsimile edition of both Mahler's and Alma Mahler's manuscripts of the Adagietto, published by the Kaplan Foundation, New York, in 1992, Gilbert E. Kaplan has offered an interesting revisionist interpretation. He proposes that the movement is not a lament, not in any way melancholic, but a love letter to Alma, and he adduces some convincing evidence, both internal and external. This of course affects the tempo. Kaplan's own ardent performance that accompanies his edition comes in at just under eight minutes, which is fast—not for the music, but within the context of a tradition that has this movement taking something like eleven or twelve minutes. (There are even slower versions.) Kaplan's 7:57 is, however, close to Walter's recorded performances (7:58 and 7:37) and to Mengelberg's (7:04). Hermann Scherchen's 1952 recording is still, so far as I know, the slowest, and it verges on the unintelligible, but it is my impression that the current slow-and-slower tradition began to take hold firmly in the aftermath of Leonard Bernstein's performance at Robert Kennedy's funeral service in 1968.[26]

---

[26] This is not an isolated phenomenon: the drift of conductors toward stasis—which they think of as a search for profundity—has affected and continues to affect performance of much repertory from Beethoven forward. Conductors are not alone in this unfortunate trend, but they seem most liable to it.

After the D-major brightness of the Scherzo, Mahler had set the Adagietto in a darker F major. Now, in a most delicately imagined passage, he finds his way back to D. The Adagietto makes its extraordinarily drawn-out cadence on a chord whose top note is A. One horn echoes that note. It is almost as though we had forgotten that there were sounds other than those of strings. The horn is an inspired choice of instrument for this moment: not only does it reintroduce the sound of winds, but it takes us back to the horn-dominated Scherzo, to music before the lost-to-the-world Adagietto brought time to a stop. Softly the violins confirm the horn's recollection. The horn attacks it again, this time with more vigor; then the bassoon treats it quite properly as the dominant of D and as a note against which a cheery song might be introduced. Its melody is close to that of Mahler's bouquet to critics, *Lob des hohen Verstandes* (Lofty Intellect Condescends to Praise).

As abruptly as he had shifted from the tragedy of the first two movements into the joyous vitality of the Scherzo, so Mahler now leaves behind the hesitations and cries of his Adagietto to dive into the radiant, abundant Finale. It is, most of it, superb comedy, so vigorous that it can even include the melody of the Adagietto—in quick tempo—as one of its themes. Adorno points out the likeness of the disruptive blasts of B-flat to the irruptions of C-sharp into the comedy-finale of Beethoven's Eighth Symphony. The brass chorale from the second movement comes back, this time in its full extension, as a gesture of triumph and as a structural bridge across the symphony's great span. When all is done, though, no one is in the mood for an exalted close, and the symphony ends on a shout of laughter.

Symphony No. 6 in A minor

Allegro energico, ma non troppo
Scherzo: Wuchtig
Andante
Finale: Allegro moderato

Mahler composed the Symphony No. 6 during the summers of 1903 and 1904, completing the orchestration on 1 May 1905. He led the Vienna Philharmonic through a reading rehearsal in March 1906 and conducted the first public performance in Essen on 27 May 1906. He later revised the work in various ways (see the note below).

Four flutes and piccolo (third and fourth flutes also doubling piccolo), four oboes (third and fourth doubling English horn), three clarinets with high clarinet (D and E-flat) and bass clarinet, four bassoons and contrabassoon, eight horns, six trumpets, three tenor trombones and bass trombone, bass tuba, timpani, bass drum, snare drum (doubled), cymbals, triangle, rattle, tam-tam, glockenspiel, cowbells, low-pitched bells, birch brush, hammer, xylophone, two harps, celesta (doubled if possible), and strings.

> *"When I describe what the catastrophe of modern man looks like, music comes into my mind—music of Gustav Mahler, the much abused. And not by chance."*
> —Albert Camus

It is not always easy for the outsider to understand that artists do not necessarily produce "happy" works when they themselves are happy, or "sad" ones—whether "tragic" or "*pathétique*"—when their lives are going badly. In the summers of 1903 and 1904, Mahler was as happy as ever in his life—and, though his gift for misery gets more attention, he had a great talent for happiness. In March 1902, only four months after meeting her, he had married the vivacious, gifted, and beautiful Alma Schindler; one daughter, Maria, was born in November of that year, and another, Anna, came along in June 1904. His music was getting more performances and even seemed at times to be meeting with more understanding. His work at the Imperial Court Opera in Vienna, where he had been director since 1897, was going well, and he had just begun a wonderfully harmonious association with that prince of stage designers, Alfred Roller; their productions together of *Tristan, Fidelio, Don Giovanni,* and *Figaro* have become part of operatic legend. During these sunny, energy-filled summers—and as an immensely busy conductor and administrator he had to cram all his composing into the summer months—Mahler wrote the darkest music of his life, the Sixth Symphony (which he himself may or may not have called the *Tragic,* though others certainly have) and the two final songs of the *Kindertotenlieder* (Songs on the Deaths of Children).

Alma Mahler was understandably appalled by the obsession with the deaths of children on the part of a father of two healthy little girls (Friedrich Rückert had written the *Kindertotenlieder* poems in response to the death of his own children), and when the four-year-old Maria died after a combined onslaught of diphtheria and scarlet fever in the summer of 1907, Alma was sure that her husband had tempted providence by composing those songs. Mahler himself saw it differently. He was convinced that an artist has the power to intuit, even to experience, events before they occur, and that he cannot escape the pain of such fore-knowledge.

He imagined the Finale of the Sixth Symphony as a scenario in which "the hero" is assaulted by "three hammer-blows of fate, the last of which fells him as a tree is felled." The summer of 1907 brought him three such blows: Maria's death, the discovery of his own heart disease, and the bitter end of his directorship of the Vienna Opera. Again, as Alma insisted, the Sixth Symphony is Mahler's autobiography, written ahead of time.

Was Mahler writing about himself? Was he predicting the apocalypse of 1914? Auschwitz and Babi Yar? Was he just writing a symphony? We know from Alma—and on matters like this she is dependable—that Mahler was emotionally more engaged, frighteningly so, by this piece than by any other in his life; that after the dress rehearsal for the first performance he walked "up and down in the artists' room, sobbing, wringing his hands, unable to control himself"; that at the concert itself he was so afraid of losing control, so afraid of the demons he himself had unleashed in his music, that he conducted badly. The Sixth Symphony is a work imbued with a tragic vision. Where Mahler's other symphonies end in triumph or exaltation or joyous exuberance, in quiet bliss, or, at their darkest, in resignation and acceptance, and while even the *Kindertotenlieder* draw to their close with a vision of the children at rest "as though in their mother's house, affrighted by no storm, protected by the hand of God," the Sixth is unique in its bleakly hopeless, minor-key conclusion.

Mahler's ambivalence about extra-musical meaning in his symphonies never went away. What is behind the music? How much did he want his listeners to know? He stressed that his First Symphony went "far beyond the love story on which it is based, or rather, which preceded it in the life of its creator," and on another occasion he remarked irritably that his symphonies were not just the memoirs of an opera director. In that spirit, having suggested that the Sixth Symphony carries heavy emotional freight and that it has persistently shown power to provoke intense emotional reactions in its listeners (rejection not excluded), let us now move on to the work itself.

When the first bad (in both senses) reviews of the Sixth Symphony appeared, Mahler remarked: "All of a sudden they like my Fifth. I suppose we'll have to wait till the Seventh for the Sixth to turn out to be any good." And to Richard Specht, his first biographer, he wrote: "My Sixth will propound riddles whose solution can be attempted only by a generation that has absorbed and truly digested my first five symphonies." It was an accurate prediction. The Sixth—"the only Sixth, despite the *Pastoral*," said the twenty-one-year-old Berg in a rush of understandable hyperbole—

was transformed from riddle to communication in letters of fire in he 1960s when Mahler began to be played enough for what Adorno called his "musical physiognomy" to be known. (Nor might Camus now call Mahler the "much abused"—except by certain conductors.)

Mahler's Fourth, Fifth, and Seventh symphonies explore what Schoenberg called "fluctuating tonality" and what the English composer Robert Simpson, writing about Nielsen, identified as "progressive tonality"; that is, they end in keys other than the ones where they began. This is a radical design possibility that interested Mahler as early as 1884 in the third of his *Songs of a Wayfarer*. But the Symphony No. 6, a fascinating mix of the classical and the radical, is anchored firmly to a single key, A minor. This is a special key for Mahler, the one that dominates his early cantata, *Das klagende Lied* (The Song of Lamenting); the key of the Fifth Symphony's ferocious second movement; and later, of that bitterest of toasts to life and death, *The Drinking Song of Earth's Misery*, which opens *Das Lied von der Erde*.

Each of Mahler's three middle symphonies requires a more elaborate orchestra than its predecessor, No. 6 having a large brass section and being especially rich in percussion, and No. 7, along with ample and colorful percussion, calling for such exotica as tenor horn, mandolin, and guitar. Although Mahler always uses his enormous band as a pool from which to draw ever-new chamber combinations, No. 6 is the most "tuttistic" of all his symphonies.

Mahler's instructions to the conductor for the opening march music are bilingual: "Allegro energico, ma non troppo," to which he adds "Heftig, aber markig," which one can translate as "vehement but sturdy." (*Markig*, an adjective Bruckner liked, comes from *Mark*, meaning "marrow.") This march is grim: here is a heightening of that pitiless, terrifying masterpiece of song, *Revelge* (Reveille), that he had written four years earlier. We feel the tramping before we rightly hear the band, but it takes only five measures of fierce crescendo before the music is hugely present. Bruno Walter drew attention to the breadth of Mahler's first themes, and here is a striking example. This powerful paragraph ends in a decrescendo as abrupt as the crescendo that introduced it, one managed, however, by the withdrawal of instruments rather than by a reduction in dynamics.[27] Though brusque, these are formal measures of preparation, and their very

---

[27] Alban Berg read and heard this page with eager excitement. In his opera *Wozzeck*, when Wozzeck has murdered his common-law wife, Marie, the orchestra responds with two terrifying crescendos on B. The second of these is the "normal" kind, that is, a crescendo from *ppp* to *fff* for all instruments, but the first, through most of its duration, is "additive," progressing from the sound of a single horn *pppp* to the full orchestra *fff*.

detachment sets off all the more effectively the cold horror of what they prepare for.

It is a simple gesture. Against a diminishing snare drumroll, two timpanists beat a left/left/left-right-left march cadence. Over that, three trumpeters sound a chord of A major. They too make a diminuendo, and halfway down, the chord changes from major to minor (as the trumpets get softer, three oboes, playing the same notes, make a crescendo). That is all.

Ex. 1

"Fate" or "tragedy" or "Abandon all hope . . ."—no words say it as surely as the music itself.[28] Chillingly, the symphony continues as though this had never happened, with a quiet, chorale-like passage for woodwinds.

Upon those few measures there follows a complete swing-about in mood as violins, seconded in patches by woodwinds, sing a fervent melody which Alma tells us is intended to represent her. ("He came . . . to tell me that he had tried to express me in a theme. 'I don't know whether I've succeeded or not, but you'll have to put up with it.' ") The Italian scholar Quirino Principe made an interesting discovery about this "Alma" theme. In 1883, Mahler was for a brief time the conductor at Olmütz (Olomouc) in Moravia. His predecessor was a certain Emil Kaiser, who, while there, wrote an opera called *Der Trompeter von Säckingen*.[29] Principe found an uncanny similarity between an aria for the hero in Kaiser's *Trompeter* and Mahler's "Alma" theme of 1903:

---

[28] Rapid, nervous alternations of major and minor (Schubert raised to a higher power) are a constant feature of Mahler's style: Adorno calls this the "dialect element" in his language. Here is that trait compressed to the ultimate degree, and for the most drastic purpose. Opera lovers will recall the Prelude to Act 5 of *Don Carlos*, where Verdi, in a context of deep gloom, presents the progression in reverse, minor to major. I have no idea what, if anything, this means. Though he never conducted *Don Carlos*, Mahler certainly knew his Verdi and admired him.

[29] Mahler wrote music for a series of *tableaux vivants* on the poem on which both Kaiser's opera and a once popular one by Viktor Nessler were based, and it was from that score that he drew *Blumine*, the original second movement of his First Symphony.

Ex. 2

Kaiser: *Der Trompeter von Säckingen*

Be-hüt dich Gott, es wär zu schön ge-we - sen, be-hüt' dich Gott, es hat nicht sol-len sein,

Ex. 3

"Alma"

The words of the aria read: "God keep you, it would have been too lovely;/ God keep you, it was not meant to be." Let who will interpret that!

Interrupted briefly by grotesquely staccato march music, "Alma," in tender decrescendo, brings the exposition to a close. This first movement is the only one after the Symphony No. 1 in which Mahler, in another surprisingly "classical" move, asks for a repeat of the exposition. For a long time, the marchers dominate the development, and they are grimmer than ever. One of Mahler's most beautiful songs is on a text by Rückert, in which the poet describes himself as "der Welt abhanden gekommen"— (detached from the world with which I used to waste so much time). Now Mahler puts that world in its place. He withdraws to mountain heights. Celesta and divided violins play mysterious chord sequences, beautifully blurred by the sound of distant cowbells. "The last greeting from earth to penetrate the remote solitude of the mountain peaks," Mahler said.[30]

Some fragments of melody drift aloft, but the major-minor "fate" sequence, though strongly intoned by muted horns and trombones, scarcely penetrates our awareness. The awakening from this vision is sudden and cheerfully unkind—more march music, aggressively jolly and in major. Even the opening theme is recapitulated in major, but not for long: Mahler's major-minor game is played in dead earnest. The recapitulation is

---

[30] In the score itself he writes that the cowbells "must be treated very discreetly—in realistic imitation of the higher and lower bells of a grazing herd, sounding from afar, sometimes combined, sometimes singly. But it must be expressly stated that this technical remark allows no programmatic interpretation."

regular, though powerfully and interestingly compressed; for example, the drummers' left/left/left-right-left that precedes the major-minor "fate" chord, is now telescoped with the formal bars of preparation. "Alma" reappears in due course; in fact the movement ends with "herself" in a gesture of unbridled triumph.

Klaus Pringsheim, Thomas Mann's brother-in-law, who had just been appointed assistant conductor in Vienna, accompanied Mahler to Essen for the first performance of the Sixth Symphony and reported that even during the rehearsals Mahler had difficulty making up his mind about the order of the two middle movements. This was a major issue in the revisions that followed the first performance and the first printing by C. F. Kahnt, Leipzig, that year. The matter is controversial, but Erwin Ratz, editor of the revised score published in 1963 in the Critical Complete Edition, decided in favor of placing the Scherzo second, and most conductors in the last twenty years have followed this order. I shall return to the question in a moment.

Mahler marks the Scherzo "wuchtig," which means "weighty" or "ponderous." It shares motivic material with the first movement: it too begins with stabbing detached low A's, and it is in A minor. But where in the first movement those low A's provided a grimly regular one-two-three-four framework, here rhythmic dissension reigns from the beginning. The basses (and the cellos with them for two measures) scan the repeated A's quite regularly as ONE-two-three, ONE-two-three, but at the same time the timpani insist on THREE-one-two, THREE-one-two: the resulting metrical tension becomes a permanent feature of this Scherzo.

What you notice first is the similarity to the first movement—the A's and the forceful presence of a melodic shape that goes A-C-A.

Ex. 4

first movement

Ex. 5

second movement

This, however, is a grotesque, horrible variant of that earlier music, sardonic commentary filled with mirthless laughter. Mahler may well have been thinking of Liszt's *Faust* Symphony, where the "Mephistopheles" finale is a similar perversion of the "Gretchen" movement, just as Liszt was surely thinking of Beethoven's *Hammerklavier* Sonata, whose nose-tweaking Scherzo is a satirical and miniature variant of that sonata's mighty first movement.

The trio, which comes around twice, first in F major, then in D, is of an extreme metrical irregularity and in that sense one of Mahler's most forward-looking pages; at the same time, because of its deliberate, eerily "cute" gestures, Mahler marks it "altväterisch" (old-fashioned). Alma Mahler heard in it "the arhythmical play of little children." Her reading of the coda, in which this "altväterisch" music is reintroduced with a sinister cock-crow, is that "the childish voices become more and more tragic, finally to die out in a whimper."

After this music of disintegration and suppressed violence, the Andante is balm. The first sonorities—muted *pianissimo* strings in middle and low registers—are like a soothing hand after the insistent woodwinds and high strings of the Scherzo. Even the key itself, E-flat major, is warmly mellow after the sharper harmonic areas explored thus far. Like "Alma" in the first movement, here is a theme that would be dangerous if written by anyone else, "plain," but as composed by Mahler—"cliché turned into event," as Adorno says—this inspired melody, twenty measures long, is a marvel of subtle phrasing. Sometime try listening to it and breathing when it breathes. It is magically scored, with dabs of wind color acutely setting this or that point on the melodic curve into higher relief. When it returns later in the movement, Mahler, as well as adding a softly soaring countermelody for muted violins, has the line trace a path from oboe to bassoon to horn and so on, the changing colors delicately overlapped.

Here is music full of Mahlerian major-minor ambiguities (twenty bars of an E-flat-major melody bring four G-flats, two C-flats, and two F-flats, all notes from the world of E-flat minor and beyond). The movement as a whole is of surprising harmonic sweep, its climax placed in faraway, luminous E major. For that arrival Mahler brings back the mysterious sound of the cowbells. Gentle echoes, drifting as though from great distances, can be heard of a phrase from the first of the *Kindertotenlieder*—"Heil sei dem Freudenlicht der Welt!" (Hail to the World's Joyous Light) and of the "Life in Heaven" finale of the Fourth Symphony. Mahler's final intentions concerning the order of these two middle movements are not entirely clear. The autograph (in the Pierpont Morgan Library in New York) puts the Scherzo before the Andante, as does the first printing, which preceded the first performance. During rehearsals for that event, Mahler changed his mind and placed the Andante ahead of the Scherzo, and he stayed with that ordering on the two subsequent occasions when he conducted the symphony again. The second edition, which he began to proofread almost immediately after the first performance, also puts the Andante second and the Scherzo third. One reads consistently that Mahler eventually wished the original order restored, and Erwin Ratz in his brief editorial report for the Critical Edition simply states this as a fact, but there is no hard and direct evidence for it.

Musically, the case for having the Scherzo precede the Andante is strong and threefold. One: the Scherzo's impact as a kind of parody of the first movement is greater if it follows that movement immediately (cf., as suggested earlier, the *Faust* Symphony and the *Hammerklavier* Sonata). Two: the respite provided by the Andante is more telling when it is offered after the double impact of the first and second movements and just before the emotionally taxing finale. Three: the key relationships, whose effect we all feel even if we cannot put names to them, are more effective for reasons we shall see in a moment.

And with this we come to the Finale. With Beethoven, the center of gravity in symphonies began a decisive shift to the finale, and here we have an extreme case of a "finale symphony." This last movement is not much longer than the first; it is, however, longer than the second and third movements together, and so it feels big—and is meant to. Of course "big" and "long" are not synonymous, and in a good performance the Finale is actually the least likely of the four movements to feel "long." The feeling of "big" that this finale conveys, our sense of the location of the center of gravity, has much more to do with psychological than with clock time, and psychological time here is a matter of weight and density. The Finale of the Sixth Symphony surpasses the earlier movements in richness of musical event and in the oppressiveness that its emotional burden lays upon the listener. This, remember, is the movement in which, to cite Mahler's own mixed metaphor, three hammer-blows of fate fell the hero like a tree.

If, absurdly, I had to pick one passage of Mahler to show him at his uniquely greatest, I would probably go to the first two pages of the Finale of the Sixth Symphony. From the thud of a low C (contrabassoon, eight horns, harps, cellos, and basses, reinforced by a soft blow on the bass drum) there arises an encompassing swirl of strangely luminous dust: harp glissandos, a woodwind chord, chains of trills on muted strings. It is alien and terrifying because, with one exception, everything in the symphony thus far has been lucidly and sharply defined, even in the most delicate *pianissimo*. The exception is the unearthly episode with the cowbells in the first movement. That was a beatific moment; this is its inverse, music of enveloping terror. We have come to an accursed spot.

The first violins, unmuted, detach themselves from this nebula to declaim a wide-ranging phrase of impassioned recitative, which, in its descent, collides with a specter we have not met in a while—the major chord that turns to minor (trumpets and trombones together this time) and the drummers with their fierce marching cadence. And as this recedes, the low strings come slowly to rest on a low A.

If you thought that the blaze of triumph in which the first movement ended promised real victory or that the grotesque apparitions of the Scherzo were Romantic fondness for the bizarre as spice, now is your moment to reconsider. These sixteen measures, not much more than half a minute of music, also define the Finale's harmonic task. The Andante closed in E-flat major. The Finale begins in its nearest related key, that is, the one with which it shares the greatest number of notes, C minor; the arching phrase, however, is slewed about in mid-course to A minor, and that is where it makes its cadence. Here is the Finale in microcosm. The music must now re-establish the primacy of A minor, the symphony's central key.

Mahler's Finale is a design not only of great breadth but of astonishing boldness and originality. Its formal point of reference is the familiar sonata plan of introduction, the presentation of material, its development, its restatement or recapitulation, and coda. This is, however, realized in a totally original way—one hardly more surprising than what we might find in late Haydn, but of course on an enormously larger scale. Thus the introduction, itself a complex sequence of events of which the nebula-plus-"fate"-chord is but the first, reappears, always varied, its components redistributed, at each major juncture of the movement: before the development, before the recapitulation, and to introduce the coda. Part of the exposition is recapitulated before the development, and the main recapitulation itself is, so to speak, out of its proper order.

Let me describe the piece in another way. From the introduction, variegated, but all slow, the music gradually breaks through once again to the world of marches. The hero goes forth to conquer, but in the full flood of confidence and exaltation, a hammer-blow strikes him down. This is literally a hammer-blow, for which Mahler wants the effect of a "short, powerful, heavy-sounding blow of non-metallic quality, like the stroke of an ax," or, as the conductor Frederik Prausnitz has put it, like "a blow to one's own helmeted head."[31] The music gathers energy, the forward march becomes even more determined, even frenzied, in its thrust, only to be halted again by a second hammer-blow.

In Mahler's original conception, a third hammer-blow coincided with

[31] The realization of this effect caused Mahler no end of difficulty and frustration; conductors since his day as well as recording producers have, on the whole, fared little better. The most effective realization I have heard is on Benjamin Zander's recording with the Boston Philharmonic on the Pickwick label. It is accomplished there by bashing a wooden timpani crate with a length of plumber's lead piping.

the A-major "fate" chord after the last appearance of the introductory dust-storm. He eliminated it in his revision. Perhaps he felt that the irrepress-ibility of that monstrous introduction was enough. Perhaps, as Benjamin Zander suggests, he identified so keenly with his hero that, while he him-self was on the podium, he could not face that third, fatal assault. He also lightened the orchestration at that spot by striking out the trombones and tuba, using one timpanist instead of two, and cutting back the dynamics of the horns, trumpets, and percussion. It is possible that around 1910 Mahler considered restoring the third hammer-blow (and presumably the original, heavier orchestration of this passage), but since there was no fur-ther edition of the symphony in his lifetime and no performances after his own in Vienna in 1907, this never came about.

When the duststorm appears for the last time, it begins in A minor, and the "fate" chord is the last music in A major we hear. Over a long drumroll that relentlessly glues the music to A minor, trombones and tuba stammer fragments of funeral music. The symphony comes to a halt, re-cedes into inaudibility. The final, brutal, tragic gesture is a sudden blast of A minor—not even the false hope of an A-major beginning this time—and, behind it, the drummers' last grim tattoo.

Symphony No. 7

> *Slow (Adagio)—Allegro con fuoco*
> *Night Music: Andante molto moderato*
>   *(very measured)*
> *Scherzo: Spectral*
> *Night Music: Andante amoroso*
> *Rondo-Finale: Allegro ordinario*

Mahler composed the Symphony No. 7 during the summers of 1904 and 1905. On 15 August 1905, the day he came to the last page of the draft full score of the first movement, showing off his Latin to his friend Guido Adler, professor of musicology at the University of Vienna, he wrote "Sep-tima mea finita est." "Finita" to him meant *essentially* finished; in other words, at this point, having brought the first movement to its close, he had the whole score under control and in a condition where he could work out the details in whatever moments the coming winter season would allow him. He himself conducted the first performance on 19 September 1908 in Prague. Mahler made a number of revisions both before and after the first performance, and even the best available editions—Erwin Ratz's for the International Gustav Mahler Society (1959) and Hans Ferdinand Redlich's for Eulenburg (1960)—have not yet solved all the problems posed by the tangle of available sources.

Four flutes and two piccolos (doubling second and third flutes), three oboes and English horn, four clarinets with E-flat clarinet and bass clarinet, three bassoons and contrabassoon, tenor horn, four French horns, three trumpets, three trombones, bass tuba, timpani, bass drum, cymbals, tam-tam, triangle, glockenspiel, tambourine, cowbells, low-pitched bells, two harps, mandolin, guitar, and strings.

"Three night pieces; the finale, bright day. As foundation for the whole, the first movement."

—Mahler to the Swiss critic William Ritter

What arresting openings Mahler invented for his symphonies! The First, moving imperceptibly from silence into sound, and that sound not music at all but the sound of nature; the Second, raging strings leaping at you, terrifying, like Magwitch in *Great Expectations* leaping at Pip on the moor; the marches, joyous in the Third, funereal in the Fifth, menacing in the Sixth; the sweetly beguiling song of the Fourth; in the Eighth, the glad shout of *Veni, creator spiritus*; keening violins over a faltering heartbeat in the Ninth; in the unfinished Tenth, the loneliest melody in the world.

And the Seventh? Here is another march, dark and mournful, its harmony oddly oblique. Long chords with heavy brass and bass drum, ponderous even in *pianissimo*, punctuate the shuddering gait of the strings. Across their beat we hear an unaccustomed sound, that of a tenor horn, an oversize cornet whose tone is forceful yet touched by human vulnerability. Its lament, picked up and continued by the woodwinds, is both declamation and song, protest and resignation, graspable and strange. Like the chords that support it, it is aslant—a march, yet something other, something more. Of my own first encounter with this symphony when Dimitri Mitropoulos conducted it with the New York Philharmonic-Symphony in 1948, I most vividly recall my sense of the oddness of this beginning, the sense of the familiar-yet-not.[32]

---

[32] Another distinct memory, not surprisingly, is of amazement at the new and fascinating colors of the *Nachtmusiken* and the Scherzo. Yet another, even more, shocking to my innocent twenty-year-old self, is of the loathing for the music I heard some of the players express as they left Carnegie Hall.

It was not easy for Mahler to find this beginning; he, in fact, began the Seventh Symphony in its middle. The structure is symmetrical: the first and last movements, both on a large scale, flank three character pieces. They, too, are symmetrical in that the first and third are both called *Nachtmusik*.

It was with these two night musics that Mahler began this score in the summer of 1904, a happy summer in a happy year. From his felicity at Maiernigg on the south shore of Lake Wörth, not ten miles from what is now Austria's border with Slovenia, a favorite composing spot for Brahms before him and Alban Berg after, Mahler wrested his most tragic music so far, the shattering close of his Sixth Symphony and the last two *Kindertotenlieder*. Even before the Finale of the Sixth Symphony was complete, Mahler had drawn what he called the architectural sketches for the Seventh. By this he meant the two *Nachtmusiken*, but neither his own nor his wife's account makes it clear whether or not he also made notations for the other movements. It was the first time he had ever worked on two symphonies simultaneously. In an essay written for the San Francisco Symphony's program book in 1985, Anthony Newcomb adduces the parallel instances of Beethoven's Fifth and *Pastoral* symphonies and Wagner's *Tristan* and *Meistersinger*. In each case, a fraught and tension-filled work is followed by one more relaxed; either pair may, consciously or not, have served Mahler as model.

Summer came to an end, and with it the Maiernigg idyll. Mahler plunged into a typically busy year, with new productions in Vienna of *Fidelio, Rheingold,* Pfitzner's *Die Rose vom Liebesgarten,* as well as one-acters by Leo Blech and Eugène d'Albert; the premieres of the Symphony No. 5 in Cologne and of the *Kindertotenlieder* in Vienna; a visit to the Amsterdam Concertgebouw, where the high point was a Sunday concert whose program read MAHLER Symphony No. 4/intermission/MAHLER Symphony No. 4; performances in various cities of the Third and Fifth symphonies; and participation in music festivals at Strasbourg and Graz.

Winter passed, spring was about to turn into summer, and on 15 June Mahler was finally free to get on the train and head back down to Maiernigg. As always, opening the case that held his manuscripts was part joyous anticipation, part nervous apprehension. It was one thing to be at Maiernigg again, another to invent—or discover—the framework to fit his two *Nachtmusiken* into. He could not find the way in. Despairing, plagued by digestive miseries into the bargain, he took off for the Dolomites by himself. In the past, hiking around Lake Misurina had released his creative energies, but this time nothing happened. Profoundly depressed, he returned. He took the express to Klagenfurt, then the local along the north shore of the lake as far as Krumpendorf, where he was to be rowed across the lake. With the first dipping of the oars into the water, he recalled later, "the theme of the introduction (or rather, its rhythm, its atmosphere) came to me."

From that moment forward he worked like a man possessed, as indeed he must have so as to bring this gigantic structure under control by mid-August, even if not to finish it in detail. His Latin message to Guido Adler was jubilant. Englished, it reads: "My Seventh is finished. I believe this work to be auspiciously begun and happily concluded. Many greetings to you and yours, also from my wife. G.M." Thinking about the first performance, Mahler considered the New York Symphony, which he would be conducting in the 1907–08 season, but soon realized that this would be madness in a city and a country that knew so little of his music.[33] A festival in Prague to celebrate the sixtieth year on the throne of the Emperor Francis Joseph provided a more suitable occasion. Prague offered a less-than-first-rate orchestra; on the other hand, Mahler had ample rehearsal time, and the worshipful young conductors—among them Artur Bodanzky, Otto Klemperer, and Bruno Walter—who attended the preparations recounted how he used every night to make revisions on the basis of that day's experience. He was always the most pragmatic of composer-conductors.

The *Nachtmusiken* and the Scherzo made their effect at once, but the first and last movements were harder nuts to crack; that has not changed substantially over time. In the days when conductors sometimes programmed isolated movements of Mahler symphonies as a form of bait, the two *Nachtmusiken*, like the Adagietto from the Fifth Symphony, often served that purpose and served it well. In Prague the reception was respectful rather than spontaneously and uninhibitedly enthusiastic. Mahler himself conducted the Seventh only once more, in Munich, a few weeks after the concert at Prague. It is still the least known of his symphonies: if the Eighth, the so-called *Symphony of a Thousand,* is more seldom performed,

---

[33] New York would have to wait another forty years. Those whose memories do not go back to a time when Mahler was less ubiquitous and certainly less loved than today might be interested to know that it was only at the insistence of the influential Bruno Walter that the Philharmonic-Symphony undertook to perform those Mahler symphonies that were then completely unknown. Walter himself conducted No. 4 in 1944 and No. 5 in 1947, and had sufficient prestige and selling power at Columbia Records to get them recorded, both for the first time. Mitropoulos conducted No. 6 in 1947 (in its American premiere!) and No. 7 in 1948. Leopold Stokowski conducted No. 8 in 1950, but No. 3 did not get its turn until Mitropoulos brought it in 1956. The orchestra gave live Sunday afternoon broadcasts then. These unknown Mahlers were considered too risky for the air, and until the Stokowski broadcast of the Eighth, CBS made the conductors change their programs for Sunday.

it is only because it is the most expensive to put on, but No. 7 has the fewest recordings and is almost always the one conductors learn last.

Mahler's Fifth and Seventh symphonies are both victory symphonies, though they differ sharply from each other: the Fifth wrests triumph from tragedy, while the Seventh, as Mahler's succinct road map for Ritter tells us, depicts the journey from night to day. After the tragic Sixth, the Seventh is Mahler's "return to life," to borrow the phrase Berlioz used for *Lélio*, his sequel to the *Symphonie fantastique*.[34] The focus in the Seventh is on nature, on the world humans inhabit, more than on the humans themselves. One could stretch Newcomb's Beethoven parallel and propose a complex network of connections according to which all three of these middle Mahler symphonies mirror the Beethoven Fifth: No. 5 most directly, with its minor-to-major, darkness-to-light scenario; No. 6 by inversion, in that it is a personal narrative ending in defeat rather than victory; No. 7 in that it replicates or at least revisits (by way of *Die Meistersinger*) Beethoven's optimistic C-major ending. At the same time No. 7 is the counterpart of the *Pastoral* both in its non-narrative, nature-directed attitude and in its five-movement design.

If the parallel with the *Pastoral* suggests Romanticism, then one should add that the "distancing" effect produced by the non-narrative character of Mahler's Seventh can be perceived as classical. For that matter, Mahler's refusal, in contrast to his practice in earlier years, to issue a program for the Seventh beyond the stenographic one he gave Ritter is also part of the work's classical temper. Here I call an expert witness, Arnold Schoenberg, who wrote these lines to Mahler after hearing Ferdinand Löwe conduct the Vienna premiere of the Seventh in November 1909:[35]

> [This time] I had less sense than before of something sensationally intense, something that excites and whips you on, something, in a word, that moves the listener to the point of making him lose his balance without giving him another basis for equilibrium in exchange. On the contrary, this time I felt perfect repose based on artistic harmony—something that got me going without unsettling my center of gravity and leaving me to my own devices, something drawing me calmly and pleasantly into its magnetic field like that force that guides the planets in their courses, letting them go their

[34]Not quite aptly, the Seventh is sometimes called *Song of the Night*.
[35]Löwe was one of the men responsible for the distorted editions of the Bruckner symphonies that were the only ones available until the beginning of the 1930s. Schoenberg writes to Mahler that not having had much time to study the score, he cannot say whether the performance was a good one. Löwe, he says, "was obviously trying very hard to carry out the directions exactly" but adds that "there is after all no reason to expect him to understand this work in particular considering how many years he has been conducting without ever having understood anything else."

own ways, influencing them, to be sure, but in a manner so easy and inevitable that there are never any sudden jolts. This may sound a bit overblown; however, it does seem to me to express clearly something I overwhelmingly felt: I have ranged you with the classical composers.[36]

And now, let us return to the symphony itself. The opening, then, is music in which we may hear the stroke of oars as well as the suggestion of cortège. This is night indeed. The tenor horn roars his song, the verb being Mahler's own: not only does he prescribe "großer Ton!" but he also described this as "nature roaring." Suddenly the tempo changes to something "a little less slow but still very measured," and with that change the character becomes more marcato and severe. The opening music returns, but the tempo soon accelerates into Allegro con fuoco, a fiery allegro. (Mahler seems unworried about shuttling between German and Italian.) With this Allegro we get a third march, this one aggressively impetuous and ablaze with forward-thrusting energy.

What has happened—or one thing that has happened—is that Mahler has carried us from a slow introduction into the main body of a sonata-allegro movement. If we care to seek a model, we can find it in Beethoven's Seventh, the symphony Mahler conducted more often than any other, and perhaps even more precisely in Schubert's *Great* C-major and the Berlioz *Fantastique*. The latter two are works that look toward both the classical and the Romantic manner. Mahler's Seventh, like his Sixth, is similarly Janus-faced. The colors and the expressive vocabulary of this music are so forward-looking, so Romantic, not to say modern, and so suggestive of the idea of symphonic poem that it can be quite a surprise to realize how classical his forms often are. In the first Allegro of the Sixth, for example, Mahler asks for a literal repeat of the exposition, and, while there are a few later examples, 1905 is a very late date indeed for that convention. Hewing to sonata form, as Mahler does here for the last time, to the design that afforded such flexibility and such a range of expressive possibilities to the great symphonists from Haydn to Brahms and Bruckner, is certainly a classical strategy.

As the exposition continues and Mahler settles in a new key—C major after E minor—he brings in a new and gorgeous theme, a highly inflected violin melody full of yearning, but also to be played with great verve ("mit großem Schwung"), even in *pianissimo*. It is also a famous conductor trap. Mahler indicates by three different notational means and in

---

[36] Arnold Schoenberg, *Letters*, selected and edited by Erwin Stein (New York, St. Martin's Press, 1965).

two languages that the tempo must remain the same, but almost without exception conductors slow it down, not just slightly but vastly, sometimes as much as by half, causing immense disorder to the movement as a whole. This melody rises to a tremendous climax and then merges into the marcato music of the second of the three marches.

More such integrating merges lie ahead. At the focal point of the development, there occurs what must be the most enchanted minute in all Mahler. Across a high note in the violins that is *pianissimo* but energized by insistent tremolando, trumpets and high woodwinds, one by one, sound calls and questions. At the same time, low strings with a quartet of bassoons, echoed by soft brass, musingly recall the second march and, in doing so, completely transform its character from sharply focused to veiled. It is the harp that wakens us into an ecstatic vision of the glorious lyric theme, with the march fragments still perceptible in the background. From this heaven, a sudden plunge of violins through two and a half octaves returns us abruptly, shockingly, to the earth of the slow introduction. The recapitulation has begun. It is tautly compressed. The music seems if anything more choleric than before. The coda is fierce and sheer.

Mahler begat extraordinary progeny. Berg in the first generation, Shostakovich (especially "present" in the Seventh with its humor and humors) and Britten in the next, are the most remarkable of his spiritual sons and heirs. Aaron Copland was another, profoundly understanding at a time when Mahler was generally thought of in this country as an eccentric and tiresome preoccupation of Jewish refugees from Germany and Austria. Copland made a revealing observation when he remarked that Mahler's was the first orchestra without pedal. This comes to mind now because the opening of the first of the *Nachtmusiken,* a minute and a quarter of preparation and search, of calling and skirling, plucking and piping, presents a perfect example of orchestra senza pedale.

A tremendous skid downward through five and a half octaves calls the proceedings to order. This artfully stylized version of an orchestra warming up turns into a tidy presentation of a theme that has been adumbrated in the fantastical introduction. The theme itself is part march, part song, given a piquant flavor by that mix of major and minor we find so often in Mahler's music. In later years, the Dutch conductor Willem Mengelberg said that in this movement Mahler had been inspired by Rembrandt's *Night Watch,* but the composer Alphons Diepenbrock, also one of Mahler's Amsterdam friends, both clarified and subtilized the issue:

> It is not true that [Mahler] wanted actually to depict *The Night Watch.* He cited the painting only as a point of comparison. [This movement] is a walk at night, and he said himself that he thought of it as a patrol. Beyond

that he said something different every time. What is certain is that it is a march, full of fantastic chiaroscuro—hence the Rembrandt parallel.[37]

Otto Klemperer catches the atmosphere beautifully when he writes, "The style of the whole is far from reality." The initial march theme is succeeded by an inspired, broadly swinging cello tune. Like many such themes by Mahler—the Fourth Symphony is especially full of them—this one, heard casually, seems utterly naïve; closely attended to, it proves to be full of asymmetries and surprises of every kind. It is a beautiful example of what Theodor Adorno meant when he wrote about Mahler's way of "turning cliché into event." Watch for the return of this tune, even more lusciously scored and with a new countertheme in the woodwind. Distant cowbells become part of the texture, and the wandering woodwinds outline ever more dissonant figurations. Eventually Mahler reveals that he wants some of these skirls played "like bird calls."[38] The cowbells recall the Symphony No. 6, in which they play such a prominent part. Suddenly that great tragedy-in-music, the Sixth, intrudes even more as a *fortissimo* trumpet chord of C major droops into minor: this sound of major falling into minor is *the* expressive and sonorous signature of the Sixth. The music here shrinks away from this horrifying revenant. The string figurations collapse, there is a stroke of cymbals and tam-tam, and then nothing is left but a cello harmonic and a ping on the harp—a high G, oddly indefinite as a close for a piece in C minor.[39]

The direction for the next movement, the Scherzo, is "schattenhaft," literally "like a shadow" but better rendered as "spectral." To this Mahler adds "flowing, *but not fast*," the underlining being his own. Drums and low strings disagree about what the opening note should be. Both, in the event, are right: the timpani A is the logical preparatory dominant for this D-minor movement, while the seemingly contradictory B-flat in the cellos and basses turns out to be the beginning of a climb, step by step, to the keynote D. Notes scurry about, cobwebs brush the face, witches step out in a ghastly parody of a waltz. All three middle movements of the Seventh

---

[37] Quoted in Henry-Louis de La Grange *Gustav Mahler*, Vol. 3 (Paris: Fayard, 1984).

[38] At one of the rehearsals for the first performance, Mahler had asked to have a window closed because he was disturbed by a bird of which he said, "This one's not in my score."

[39] This is the sound Thomas Mann describes as the one that ends *Doktor Fausti Weheklag* (Doctor Faustus's Lamentation), the cantata with which Adrian Leverkühn, the composer-hero of his novel *Doctor Faustus*, closes his tragic career: "One group of instruments after another withdraws, and what remains, that with which the work closes, is the high G of a single cello, the last word, the last vanishing sound, slowly dissolving in a pianissimo fermata. Then there is nothing more— silence and night." Mann heard Mahler conduct the Seventh in Munich. It is also possible that he was reminded of this detail by Adorno, his musical adviser during the writing (or, as Mann would have preferred, the composition) of *Doctor Faustus*.

call to mind images from German Romantic literature, the poetry of Eichendorff and the stories of E.T.A. Hoffmann in particular. Here I am reminded of Eichendorff's haunting *Zwielicht* (Twilight), set with such genius by Schumann in his *Liederkreis:* "Stimmen hin und wieder wandern" (Voices wander here and there). The trio is consoling, or almost. The Scherzo returns, finally to unravel and disintegrate.

The first *Nachtmusik* was a nocturnal patrol; the second is a serenade, which Mahler marks Andante amoroso.[40] Klemperer points out that the opening bars—solo violin leaping an octave "mit Aufschwung" (with enthusiastic impetus)—are like a phrase from Schumann. William Ritter, the Swiss writer and artist for whom Mahler made the summary quoted at the head of this essay, was not only a discerning critic, nearly alone in his time in his understanding of Mahler, but also a colorful writer. His description of the way the second *Nachtmusik* begins is wonderful:

> Heavy with passion, the violin solo falls, like a turtledove aswoon with tenderness, down onto the chords of the harp. For a moment one hears only heartbeats. It is a serenade, voluptuously soft, moist with languor and reverie, pearly with the dew of silvery tears falling drop by drop from guitar and mandolin.[41]

Those exotic instruments, together with the harp, create a magical atmosphere. Once Mahler touches on the Fifth Symphony's Adagietto (which may or may not have been an ecstatically melancholy love letter to Alma, his wife). The movement is full of enchanting detail. When Schoenberg, infuriated by Olin Downes's dismissive *New York Times* review of the Seventh in 1948, wasted an hour of his time on a letter trying to persuade that pompous critic of the worth of this symphony, it was to this so finely imagined, lovingly worked movement that he went for his musical examples.

After these four so differentiated night scenes comes the brightness of day to waken us with a thunderous tattoo of drums. Mahler heads the movement "Rondo-Finale." That sounds like Haydn, and is another classical touch. Horns and bassoon are the first instruments to be roused, and they lead the orchestra in a spirited fanfare whose trills put it on the edge of parody. Cliché turning into event again? Mahler's humor gave trouble to many of his first listeners. Sometimes he maneuvers so near the edge of parody or of irony—like Leverkühn in his Violin Concerto—that unless

---

[40] Here is *Doctor Faustus* once more. Leverkühn's Violin Concerto begins with "an *Andante amoroso* whose tenderness and whose sonority constantly edge up to the very borders of irony." That is a good description of the tone of this second *Nachtmusik*, which in fact begins with a solo violin.
[41] Quoted in De La Grange. *Gustav Mahler*, Vol. 3.

you know his language and his temperament well, it is possible to misunderstand him completely, for example to mistake humor for ineptness. Few listeners here will fail to be reminded of *Die Meistersinger*.

But what is that about? I recall well my own first bewildered encounter with this piece, coming to it with very little experience of Mahler's music at all, and thinking that this Finale sounded like someone's grotesque and futile attempt to remember how the *Meistersinger* Overture goes. I don't know when I finally caught on. The grand-rhetoric *Meistersinger* reference is there on purpose. Again, Ritter understood right away, pointing out that Mahler never quotes Wagner but "re-begins" the Overture in order to take it far beyond. The triumphant C-major Finale is itself a kind of cliché stemming from the Beethoven Fifth and transmitted by way of the Brahms First and, much more significantly for this context, *Die Meistersinger*.[42] Mahler uses *Die Meistersinger* as an easily recognizable symbol for a good-humored victory finale. Other *Meistersinger* references occur: for instance, the chorale tune to which the prize song is baptized, and even the deceptive cadence to which Wagner frequently resorts to keep the music flowing.

This Finale is wild and wonderful. The *Meistersinger* idea turns out to be a whole boxful of ideas that to an adroitly and wittily inventive builder like Mahler suggest endless possibilities for combining and recombining, shuffling and reshuffling. To the city-square music of Mahlerized *Meistersinger* he adds stomping, zesty country music. No part of the harmonic map is untouched, while the rhythms sway in untamed abandon between two-beat and three-beat measures. So high is the humor that even the dread major-into-minor triad from the Sixth Symphony is rendered harmless when it appears. Bells clang, big drum and cymbals cheer the revelers on.

Then we hear music we have not heard or thought about for a long time: the fiery march from the first movement. Or rather, we hear a series of attempts to inject it into the proceedings, though the instruments who propose it—first horns, next violins, later trombones and tuba, then trumpets—cannot seem to get it quite right and settle it squarely on the harmonic floor. Just as we think the attempt has been abandoned, the drums stir everything up again, and finally the theme enters in glory. The circle is complete, and Mahler charges to his thunderous final cadence.

---

[42] Although as a young man Mahler had always enjoyed his summer calls on Brahms, he was surprisingly uninterested in Brahms's music, at least as a conductor. He programmed the First Symphony only three times (and not until 1910), the Second and the Haydn Variations only once each, and the Fourth not at all. The Third came closest to being a favorite, with six performances between 1894 and 1910.

Symphony No. 8

Hymn: Veni, creator spiritus
Final Scene of Faust

Mahler sketched the Symphony No. 8 between 21 June and 18 August 1906, and completed the score the following summer. He conducted the first performance in Munich on 12 September 1910 with a specially assembled orchestra, the Riedelverein of Leipzig, the Vienna Singverein, the Munich Central School Children's Chorus, and soloists Gertrud Förstel, Marta Winternitz-Dorda, Irma Koboth, Ottilie Meyzger, Tilly Koenen, Felix Senius, Nicola Geisse-Winkel, and Richard Mayr.

Five flutes (fifth doubling piccolo), four oboes and English horn, three clarinets with E-flat clarinet and bass clarinet, four bassoons and contrabassoon, eight horns, four trumpets, four trombones, bass tuba, timpani, bass drum, tam-tam, triangle, glockenspiel, tubular bells, celesta, piano, harmonium, organ, two harps, mandolin, and strings. There is, in addition, a group of four trumpets and three trombones, separately stationed. Vocal forces comprise two mixed choruses, boys' chorus, girls' chorus, three sopranos (Magna peccatrix, Una poenitentium, Mater Gloriosa), two altos (Mulier samaritana, Maria aegyptiaca), tenor (Doctor Marianus), baritone (Pater Ecstaticus), and bass Pater Profundus). The dedication is to "meiner lieben Frau, Alma Maria."

Goethe's subject in Act 3 of the Second Part of *Faust* is the union, symbolic and physical, of his tragic hero and Helen of Troy. The association of the two figures is not in itself new. Simon Magus, the first-century sorcerer whose misdeed, as recorded in Chapter 8 of the Acts of the Apostles, gave us the word *simony*, is said to have called himself Faustus—in modern Italian he would be Fortunato and in modern American Lucky—and he traveled and worked with a former prostitute to whom, for a bit of class, he gave the name Helena. His sixteenth-century successor, who had probably read about Simon in a new edition of a book then 1200 years old and titled *Recognitiones*, for professional purposes styled himself Faustus Junior and later simply Doctor Johannes Faust, and he too—"for the sake of order and propriety," as Thomas Mann puts it—acquired a companion called Helena. The conjuring up of the legendary beauty, daughter of Leda and

Zeus, came to be one of the standard entertainments in dramatic representations of the Faust stories. In Christopher Marlowe's *Tragicall History of
D. Faustus* (1604), Helen takes on greater significance, in that it is for her
sake Faust is willing to reject salvation: "Sweet Helen, make me immortal
with a kiss." Nowhere, however, is the bringing together of Faust and
Helen so boldly drawn nor so freighted with meaning and suggestion as in
what Goethe himself called his "Classical-Romantic phantasmagoria," nor
so freighted with meaning and suggestion. In their meeting, Goethe seeks
to portray ideal love, to suggest the fusion of Germanic and Greek civilization, and to resolve "the vehement opposition of Classicists and Romantics." And, as Johann Peter Eckermann, the Boswell of Goethe's later
years, pointed out, "Half the history of the world lies behind it."

We have, in the Anglo-American tradition, no cultural totem quite
like *Faust*, no one work so known, so quoted, so lived with and possessed,
as *Faust* was by cultured Germans during the nineteenth century and at
least the first third of the twentieth. The King James version of the Bible
is the nearest thing. It is significant that on the title page of his symphony
Mahler does not need to say whose *Faust*. But even in that context, Mahler's closeness to *Faust* was remarkable. A Viennese lady whose occasional
houseguest Mahler was reported that he was not really so difficult: she
provided apples at breakfast, lunch, and dinner, and put Bielschowsky's
Goethe biography in her guest room, one volume in her country villa and
one in her city apartment, and "he was in heaven. Goethe and apples are
two things he cannot live without."

Faust is a recklessly inclusive masterwork whose action, to quote
Goethe himself, "covers a good 3000 years from the sack of Troy to the
destruction of Missolonghi" and whose content is expressed in an astounding variety of styles, verse forms, textures, quotations, allusions, parodies,
and in tones sublime and profane. Joining *Faust* to *Veni, creator spiritus*,
linking the complexities of Goethe's humanism to the orthodoxy, the ques-
tionless faith of an eighth-century Christian hymn, Mahler sought to create a similarly encompassing work. Mahler, one imagines, must often have
looked to *Faust* for permission for his own unprecedentedly global symphonies.

In June 1906, when he arrived at Maiernigg on Lake Wörth in southern Austria where he had bought a plot of land in 1899, he had, to begin
with, not a glimmer of an idea for a new composition.[43] According to

---

[43] The Lake Wörth region was the place of which Brahms said that melodies lay so thick on the
ground that one had to be careful not to step on them. He composed his Second Symphony,
Violin Concerto, and G-major Violin Sonata in successive summers at Pörtschach on the north
shore, and fifty-seven years after Brahms, Alban Berg was proud to be writing his own Violin
Concerto just across the water near Velden.

Alma Mahler, he was "haunted by the specter of failing inspiration." He went to his studio, a tiny hut separated from the main house by some hundreds of yards, on the first day "with the firm resolution of idling the holiday away (I needed to so much that year) and recruiting my strength. On the threshold of my old workshop the *Spiritus creator* took hold of me and shook me and drove me on for the next eight weeks until the greatest part of my work was done." He had access only to a corrupt edition of the hymn text and, to his chagrin, also found that he had composed too much music for the words. He wired Vienna, asking to have the hymn sent to Maiernigg by telegram. As Alma Mahler tells it, "The complete text fit the music exactly. Intuitively, he had composed the music for the full strophes." (This is not exactly right inasmuch as Mahler omits the second half of the fifth stanza.)

Mahler was quick to perceive that *Veni, creator spiritus* was but a beginning, to see that he was ready to tackle that Holy of Holies in German literature, the final scene of *Faust*, and that the bridge between the texts was to be found in the third stanza of the hymn:

Accende lumen sensibus,   Illuminate our senses,
Infunde amorem cordibus!   Pour love into our hearts!

He completed the score with astonishing speed.[44] To begin with, he was in no hurry about the first performance, but infected by the excitement of Bruno Walter and Willem Mengelberg when he played parts of the new score to them, Mahler became amenable to having the impresario Emil Gutmann organize the premiere. He asked Walter to choose and coach the soloists, and himself became involved in the planning of countless details, from the placement of the choruses, about which he consulted his Vienna stage designer, Alfred Roller, to the layout of the program book.

That concert was very much an event to have been at, like the premiere of Stravinsky's *Le Sacre du printemps* three years later, and the audience at both has grown tremendously over the years. In his Mahler biography, Egon Gartenberg lists Schoenberg, Klemperer, Stokowski, Clemenceau, Siegfried Wagner, Alfredo Casella, Webern, Stefan Zweig, Thomas Mann, and Max Reinhardt as among those present in Munich, and Berndt Wessling adds Goldmark, Franz Schmidt, d'Albert, Korngold, Elgar, Leo Fall, Vaughan Williams, Rachmaninoff, Weingartner, Muck, Schuch, Leo Blech, Fritz Stiedry, Max von Schillings, the Prince Regent

[44] Theodor Adorno reports that one of Berg's most treasured possessions was Mahler's first jotting down of the symphony's final Chorus mysticus, *Alles Vergängliche ist nur ein Gleichnis*. It is on a piece of toilet paper. Yeats, who noted that "Love has pitched his mansion in/The place of excrement," would have delighted in that.

of Bavaria, King Albert I of the Belgians, and Henry Ford. I have not checked out the entire list, but Schoenberg, Elgar, Vaughan Williams, and Rachmaninoff were definitely going about their business elsewhere. In any case, the concert was a glorious and intensely emotional occasion and Mahler's one experience of being completely accepted as a composer.[45]

Tradition ascribes *Veni, creator spiritus* to Rabanus Maurus, Archishop of Mainz from 847 until his death in 856, but modern scholarship will not have it so. The hymn, which probably dates from just before Maurus's time, is part of the liturgy for Pentecost, the festival that commemorates the descent of the Holy Ghost upon the disciples (Acts 2). It is also sung at grand celebrations such as the elevation of a saint or the coronation of a pope. Mahler's reference to it as "the *Spiritus creator*" is characteristic: he could not leave a text alone, and, aside from the omissions noted, he presents the lines in an incredibly dense growth of repetitions, combinations, inversions, transpositions, and conflations. He manhandles Goethe's text, too, making two substantial cuts, one of thirtysix lines and another of seven, presumably on purpose; other omissions, inversions, and altered word forms (*Liebesband* for *Liebeband*, *ew'ge* for *ewige*, *Frauen* for *Fraun*) should probably be ascribed to his working from memory.[46]

The Faust chapbook of 1587, which is the literary source for the whole legend and which appeared in English in 1592 as *The history of the Damnable Life and Deserved Death of Doctor John Faustus*, is an entertainment and a cautionary tale. For Goethe, the career of the old humbug was not just a tale to tell; it was a story upon which to hang an entire *Weltanschauung*. This became gradually clear to him as he worked on *Faust*, and that was a long time. Goethe harbored plans for a *Faust* as early as the 1760s when he was an undergraduate and he sealed up the manuscript—"ended, but not completed because uncompletable," says Mann—on his eighty-second birthday, 28 August 1831, "lest I be tempted to carry this work further." Being in fact tempted, he opened the packet in January 1832 and tinkered with details until the 24th of that month, eight weeks before his death.

The impresario Gutmann coined the name *Symphony of a Thousand* as part of his marketing pitch, and it was given wide currency by Paul Stefan, author of the first book on Mahler. There was truth in Gutmann's advertising: the performance involved 858 singers and an orchestra of 171, which, if you add Mahler himself, comes to 1030 persons. Stokowski, leading the first American performances in Philadelphia and New York, outdid Gutmann, fielding an army of 1069, counting himself.

For a complete setting of these verses you must go to Schumann's Scenes from Goethe's *Faust*, a inspired, penetrating composition and one of the nineteenth century's underground masterpieces.

Goethe's most radical change in telling the story is that he makes it end not in death and damnation, but in Faust's salvation. The Faustian quest is not arrogance but aspiration.[47] The moment of salvation is the subject of Goethe's final scene and of the mighty close of Mahler's symphony. The story of *Faust I*, of the pact with the Devil and the Gretchen tragedy, does not need to be retold here. *Faust II* seems at first to be less a continuation than a fresh start from another perspective (Goethe himself said as much). Faust has been made oblivious of his past. In a series of steps that Goethe wishes us to perceive as successively higher stages of questing, Faust is in service at the Imperial Court, then in love with Helen of Troy and, in that union, the father of a boy called Euphorion.[48] Finally, after Helen's return to the underworld, Faust challenges nature herself as he takes on a gigantic project of land reclamation.

One hundred years old, Faust receives the visitation of four gray women, Want, Distress, Guilt, and Care. Only Care has the power to enter; as she leaves, she breathes on him and strikes him blind. His pact with Mephistopheles demands that if ever he entreats "the swift moment . . . /Tarry a while! you are so fair!" his life is over and his soul forfeit. Taking, in his blindness, the sound of his own grave being dug to be the sound of his construction plans going forward, enraptured by the vision of the life to arise on land newly claimed from the elements, he cries, "I might entreat the fleeting minute:/O tarry yet, thou art so fair!" He dies, and in a scene of superb comedy—angels pelt the devils with rose petals, which sting and burn them murderously, and Mephistopheles' own attention is fatally distracted by the bare bottoms of the little boy angels— heavenly hosts wrest Faust's entelechy, or immortal essence, from the forces of hell. And with that, Goethe's—and Mahler's—finale can begin.

To say that Goethe composed this finale as though writing a libretto for an opera or oratorio is not simply a matter of justifying Schumann o

---

[47] In this, Goethe was significantly anticipated by the playwright and critic Gotthold Ephraim Lessing, who floated the possibility of a "Faust without evil" in his *Letter on Literature XVII* (1759) taking the idea further in a fragmentary play fifteen years later; Goethe, however, was the first writer actually to carry this plan out.

[48] Euphorion—from the Greek *euphoros*, easy to bear or well-borne—inherits his father's fierce drive toward the absolute and dies attempting to fly. Goethe intends him as an embodiment of the poetic spirit in general and also as a representation of Byron, the one poet among his contemporaries whom, after the death of Schiller in 1805, Goethe totally respected. Byron had died in 1824, having gone to Missolonghi to take part in the Greek war for independence. Goethe mourned Byron deeply, and *Faust II* includes a moving lament for him. When Euphorion launches himself in flight to the chorus's cries of "Icarus! Icarus!/Piteous plight!" the stage direction indicates that the "beautiful youth plunges down at his parents' feet; one seems to recognize in the body a familiar figure, but the corporeal vanishes at once; the aureole rises like a meteor to the sky; robe, cloak, and lyre are left behind." The "familiar figure" is of course Byron. This is one small example of the breadth of reference and the boldness of theatrical vision in *Faust II*.

Mahler. The musical libretto is one among many poetic styles touched in
Faust; besides, we know that Goethe always hoped that at least parts of
the tragedy would be set to music. The ideal composer, he said, would
have been Mozart working "in the manner of *Don Giovanni.*"

The visual inspiration for this scene may include Traini's and Gozzoli's
frescoes in the Camposanto at Pisa and Wilhelm von Humboldt's description of the Benedictine monastery at Montserrat; the scenario evokes the
final cantos of Dante's *Paradiso.* The scene is set in mountain gorges inhab-
ited by hermits who are named, in ascending order of divine knowledge,
Pater Ecstaticus, Pater Profundus, Pater Seraphicus, and Doctor Marianus.
Moving among these anchorites is a group of children who died immediately after birth. Angels come bearing Faust's immortal essence, and we
learn from younger angels that the roses which had played so critical a part
in the capture of that essence were the gifts of penitent women.

Hailed by Doctor Marianus, the Virgin appears in glory.[49] The penitent donors of the roses—the sinner who bathed Christ's feet at the house
of Simon the Pharisee; the Samaritan woman who gave Christ water at
Jacob's well and to whom he first revealed that he was the Messiah; and
Mary of Egypt, who repented a life of sin after an invisible hand had kept
her from entering the temple and who, at her death after forty years in the
desert, wrote a message in the sand asking to be buried there—intercede
with the Virgin on behalf of Gretchen. One more penitent woman (Una
poenitentium, "once called Gretchen") speaks thanks to the Mater Gloriosa for having heeded her prayers on behalf of "my love of old." With
Gretchen's reappearance, the immense circle of the poem is closed. The
Mater Gloriosa grants to Gretchen that she may lead Faust "to higher
spheres." In eight of the most celebrated and the most densely beautiful
lines of Western poetry, a mystic chorus speaks of heaven as the place
where parable becomes reality, where earthly imperfection is made perfect,
where the indescribable is achieved.

Mahler discussed this close in a letter he wrote to his wife in June
1909:

> It is all an allegory to convey something that, no matter what form it
> is given, can never be adequately expressed. Only the transitory can be de-
> scribed; but what we feel and surmise but will never attain (or experience as
> an actual event), in other words, the intransitory that lies behind all experi-
> ence, that is indescribable. That which draws us by its mystic force, that

---

[49] This is the counterpart of Gretchen's scene with the statue of the Mater Dolorosa in *Faust I.*
Much of Goethe's finale is recapitulation and can be understood fully only in the context of the
12,000 or so lines that come before it. In that sense it is similar to the Immolation Scene at the
end of *Götterdämmerung.*

which every created thing, perhaps even the very stones, feels with absolute certainty at the very center of its being, that which Goethe here—again using an image—calls the Eternal Feminine—that is to say, the resting-place, the goal, as opposed to striving and struggling toward the goal (the eternal masculine)—that is the force of love, and you are right to call it by that name. There are countless representations and names for it. . . . Goethe himself reveals it stage by stage, on and on, in image after image, more and more clearly as he draws nearer the end. In Faust's impassioned search for Helen, in the Classical Walpurgis Night, in the still inchoate Homunculus, through the manifold entelechies of lower and higher degree—he presents it with ever greater clarity and certainty right up to the appearance of the Mater Gloriosa, the personification of the Eternal Feminine. And so . . . Goethe himself addresses his listeners: "All that is transitory (everything I have presented to you here on these two evenings) is nothing but images, inadequate, of course, in their earthly manifestations; but there, liberated from earthly inadequacy, they will become reality, and then we shall need no paraphrase, no figures, no images. What we seek to describe here in vain—for it is indescribable—is accomplished there. And what is that? Again, I can only speak in images and say: the Eternal Feminine has drawn us on—we have arrived—we are at rest—we possess what we could only strive and struggle for on earth. Christians call this 'eternal bliss,' and I cannot do better than employ this beautiful and sufficient mythology—the most complete conception which, at this epoch of humanity, it is possible to attain."[50]

In April 1926, Anton Webern conducted what must by all accounts have been two overwhelming performances of the Eighth Symphony. Describing them to Schoenberg, he wrote: "In [the first part] I set a real Allegro impetuoso; in no time the movement was over, like a gigantic prelude to the second." This "impetuous" allegro is precisely what Mahler specifies as he hurls the first words of the *Veni, creator spiritus* at us. Not only is the tempo itself quick, but the musical events themselves—the sequence of ever shorter measures (4/4, 4/4, 3/4, 2/4) and the trombones' compressed variation of the chorus's first phrase—create a sense of utmost urgency. Moreover, as soon as the chorus resumes, the violins, imitated by all the high woodwind, add a new melody of sweeping physical energy.

With "Imple superna gratia," solo voices begin to emerge and the prayer becomes more quiet; the change of key from E-flat to D-flat also has

---

[50]Gustav Mahler *Briefe.* In February 1831 Goethe remarked to his amanuensis Eckermann that it was sometimes necessary "to come to the aid of the spiritual with all manner of arts." Specifically about the final scene of *Faust* he explained that in order to avoid vagueness and gain solidity it was technically useful to turn to something ready-made and to employ these "sharply outlined Christian ecclesiastical figures and ideas." Nietzsche called Eckermann's *Conversations with Goethe* "the greatest book in the German language." Undoubtedly Mahler knew it well.

a softening effect. "Infirma," the plea for strength, is dark, with fantastical commentary from a solo violin; indeed, this symphony is, altogether, a major outing for the concertmaster. After an orchestral interlude in which the metabolic rate is high and Mahler's harmonies are at their most adventurous—Adorno rightly says it looks ahead to the cantatas of Webern— "Infirma" returns with stern power.

Mahler's treatment of what he regarded as "the cardinal point of the text" and the bridge to *Faust*, the "Accende lumen sensibus," tells us something important about his verbal inversions. His first introduction of that line by the soloists is quiet. But the word order is reversed—"Lumen accende sensibus"—and the great outburst with all voices in unison, including those of the children, coincides with the first presentation of the line in its proper order. The change there of texture, tempo, and harmony makes this the most dramatic stroke in the symphony, and the effect is heightened by the breath-stopping comma that breaks the word *accende* in two. Mahler sets "Hostem repellas," the prayer that the foe be scattered, as one of his fiercest marches; the appeal to the leader to go before us, "Ductore sic te praevio," is a dense double fugue. The points of the hymn are vividly differentiated, but all the rich detail is subordinated to the eager thrust of the movement as a whole, calling to mind the shouts of "Credo, credo" with which Beethoven pushes aside doctrinal clauses in the *Missa solemnis*.

Veni, creator spiritus,	Come, Creator-Spirit,
Mentes tuorum visita,	Visit these Thy souls,
Imple superna gratia,	Fill them with heavenly grace
Quae tu creasti pectora.	Whom Thou hast created of Thy spirit.
Qui diceris Paraclitus,	Who art called Comforter,
Altissima donum Dei,	Supreme Gift of God,
Fons vivus, ignus, caritas	Living Fountain, Fire, Love,
Et spiritalis unctio.	And the Anointing of the Soul.
Infirma nostri corporis	Our feeble flesh
Virtute firmans perpeti,	Make ever strong in Virtue,
Accende lumen sensibus,	Kindle our Reason with Light.
Infunde amorem cordibus.	Infuse our hearts with Love.
Hostem repellas longius	Our enemies be driven far from us.
Pacemque dones protinus,	Give us peace continually.
Ductore sic te praevio	Thus shall we, if Thou guide us,
Vitemus omne pessimum.	Avoid all grievous ill.
Tu septiformis munere	Thou of the sevenfold Gifts,
Digitus paternae dexterae	Finger upon the right hand of the Father,

[Tu rite promissum Patris	Thou, True Promise of the Father,
Sermone ditans guttura.]	Giveth the gift of Speech unto our tongues.

Per te sciamus da Patrem,	Grant that we may perceive through Thee, Father,
Noscamus [atque] Filium,	May we know, O son, through Thee;
[Te utriusque] Spiritum	And through Thee, Spirit, in both indwelling,
Credamus omni tempore.	May we ever believe.

Da gaudiorum praemia,	Give us the reward of Joy,
Da gratiarum munera,	Give us the gift of Grace,
Dissolve litis vincula,	Loosen the bonds of Strife,
Adstringe pacis foedera.	Make us to preserve Peace.

Gloria Patri Domino,	Glory be to the Father, our Lord,
Deo sit gloria et Filio	Glory be to God, and to the Son
Natoque, qui a mortuis	Begotten, who was raised
Surrexit, ac Paraclito	From Death, and to Thee, Comforter,
In saeculorum saecula.	From age to age.

[Brackets indicate text omitted by Mahler]

Reflecting the difference between Goethe's discursive and theatrical rhapsodies and the concentrated plainness of the medieval hymn, Part II of Mahler's symphony is as expansive as Part I was ferociously compressed. (*Veni, creator spiritus* is between a quarter and a third of the symphony.) Mahler begins Part II with a miraculous piece of landscape painting, a broadly drawn prelude, hushed and fairly slow, whose elements are recapitulated and expanded in the first utterances of the anchorites and angels. Goethe's spiritual-operatic spectacle elicits lively musical response from Mahler: part of what drew him into the Roman Catholic church in 1897 was his attraction to the aesthetics of ceremony.

In some ways this movement is like a song cycle, as Pater Ecstaticus, Pater Profundus, the angel choirs, Doctor Marianus, and the three penitent women bring us their reflections and prayers, each articulated with marvelous individuality: the urgent pleas of the two *patres* (the one sweetly ardent, the other almost tormented in his passion), the mellifluous song of the Younger Angels, the ecstatic viola and violin rhapsodies that are hung like garlands about the words of the More Perfect Angels, the radiant Doctor Marianus, the all but whispered recollections of the penitent women, the ecstatic vocal line spun by Una poenitentium as she prays to the Virgin for the salvation of the lover who betrayed her. At the same time, and again parallel to this part of Goethe's composition, much of Mahler's music is recapitulation, even hearkening back to parts of the first movement. This symphony, like *Faust* itself, is something to be lived with for a long time so that the richly intricate network of references and allusions might take on clarity.

The final summons of Doctor Marianus to look up to the Virgin's redeeming visage, "Blicket auf!," rises to a rapt climax. This is the beginning of the finale within the finale. Then, after long moments of suspense, the Chorus mysticus intones the poet's reflections on now and later, here and beyond, image and reality. But, as he does in his *Resurrection* Symphony, Mahler gives over the power to music without words. Brass instruments, organ, drums, plucked strings, bells, all invoke the symphony's opening phrase—"Veni, creator spiritus"—but now its dissonances, the tense upward leap of a seventh, stretched now in a still greater leap of a ninth, are dissolved in consonance, in the roar of the final, long chord of E-flat major. We are home. Prayer has become affirmation. "We have arrived—we are at rest—we possess what we could only strive and struggle for on earth."

Final scene from Goethe's *Faust*

Mountain glens, forest, rock, solitude. Holy Anchorites sheltering in the clefts of rocks, scattered at various heights along the cliffs.

Choir and Echo

Waldung, sie schwankt heran,	Upward the forests sway,
Felsen, sie lasten dran,	Great rocks upon them weigh,
Wurzeln, sie klammern an,	Roots here securely cling,
Stamm dicht an Stamm hinan.	Trunks densely pressing in.
Woge nach Woge spritzt,	Wave upon wave breaks to spray,
Höhle, die tiefste, schützt.	Caves, deepest refuge lend.
Löwen, sie schleichen stumm,	Lions, who silent prowl,
Freundlich um uns herum,	Friendly about us come,
Ehren geweihten Ort,	Honor this hallowed place,
Heiligen Liebeshort.	Love's holy hermitage.

Pater Ecstaticus *(floating up and down)*

Ewiger Wonnebrand,	Rapture's eternal fire,
Glühendes Liebesband,	Love's incandescent bonds,
Siedender Schmerz der Brust,	Pain that seethes in my breast
Schäumende Gotteslust.	Gleaming, divine desire,
Pfeile, durchdringet mich,	O Arrows, pierce through me,
Lanzen, bezwinget mich,	Spears, make me to submit,
Keulen, zerschmettert mich,	Cudgels, o shatter me,
Blitze, durchwettert mich!	And, Lightning, storm through me;

Daß ja das Nichtige	That all vain Nothingness
Alles verflüchtige,	Vanish in vaporous haze!
Glänze der Dauerstern,	Gleam of the constant star,
Ewiger Liebe Kern!	Immortal Love's true flower.

Pater Profundus (in the lower region)

Wie Felsenabgrund mir zu Füßen	As rocky chasms at my feet
Auf tiefem Abgrund lasten ruht,	Rest heavy on the deep-cleft gorge,
Wie tausend Bäche strahlend fließen	And as a thousand brooks flow, sparkling,
Zum grausen Sturz des Schaums der Flut,	Toward the foaming torrent's fearsome fall,
Wie strack, mit eig'nem kräft'gen Triebe,	As, straight, the tree of its own powerful bent,
Der Stamm sich in die Lüfte trägt,	Bears itself upward into air,
So ist es die allmächt'ge Liebe,	Even so is almighty Love,
Die alles bildet, alles hegt.	Which fashions all things, and which cares for all.
Ist um mich her ein wildes Brausen,	There is about me here a savage raging,
Als wogte Wald und Felsengrund!	As though the very rocks, the forests heaved!
Und dich stürzt, liebevoll im Sausen,	Yet, the abundant waters, full of love, for all their raging,
Die Wasserfülle sich zum Schlund,	Cast themselves headlong-down, into the gorge,
Berufen gleich das Tal zu wässern;	Summoned forthwith to water all the vale;
Der Blitz, der flammend niederschlug,	The lightning which, bright-flaming, earthward struck,
Die Atmosphäre zu verbessern,	To purify the air,
Die Gift und Dunst im Busen trug:	Which held foul vapors and vile poisons in its breast;
Sind Liebesboten, sie verkünden,	These are Love's heralds, they declare,
Was ewig schaffend uns umwallt,	That which, ever-creating, here holds sway.
Mein Inn'res mög' es auch entzünden,	O that it might suffuse my inmost self with fire,
Wo sich der Geist, verworren, kalt,	Where my perplexed soul, and cold,
Verquält in stumpfer Sinne Schranken,	Vexes itself within the narrow confines of dulled sense,
Scharf angeschloss'nem Kettenschmerz.	Endures the chafe of shackles harshly clasped.
O Gott! beschwichtige die Gedanken,	O God! quiet my thoughts,
Erleuchte mein bedürftig Herz!	Fill my sore-wanting heart with Light!

Choir of Angels (*soaring in the upper atmosphere, bearing Faust's immortal soul*)

Gerettet ist das edle Glied	Delivered is our noble member
Der Geisterwelt vom Bösen	Of the spirits' realm from evil:
Wer immer strebend sich bemüht,	That soul who ever diligently strives
Denn können wir erlösen.	We can redeem,
Und hat an ihm die Liebe gar	And if it be that Love indeed
Von oben teilgenommen,	Lend him of her favor, from on high,
Begegnet ihm die sel'ge Schar	The sainted hosts will greet that soul
Mit herzlichem Willkommen.	With heartfelt welcome.

Choir of Blessed Boys (*circling about the highest peaks*)

Hände verschlinget euch	Hands clasp you
Freudig zum Ringverein,	Joyfully, join in a ring,
Regt euch und singet	With holy fervor now,
Heil'ge Gefühle drein.	Leap you and sing.
Göttlich belehret,	Having been taught of God,
Dürft ihr vertrauen,	You may believe:
Den ihr verehret,	Him whom you have adored,
Werdet ihr schauen.	You shall perceive.

Chorus of Younger Angels

Jene Rosen aus den Händen	'Twas those rose from the hands
Liebend-heil'ger Büßerinnen,	Of pious-loving penitent women,
Halfen uns den Sieg gewinnen	Helped us make the victory ours
Und das hohe Werk vollenden,	And achieve our noble work,
Diesen Seelenschatz erbeuten.	To win this treasured soul as booty.
Böse wichen, als wir streuten,	Evil cowered where we strewed them,
Teufel flohen, als wir trafen.	Devils fled as they were struck.
Statt gewohnter Höllenstrafen,	The specters felt not hell's own torments,
Fühlten Liebesqual die Geister;	But knew Love's agonies instead;
Selbst der alte Satansmeister	Even that ancient prince of devils
War von spitzer Pein durchdrungen.	Himself, was riven with the sharpest pain!
Jauchzet auf! es ist gelungen.	Rejoice! the victory is attained!

More Perfect Angels

Uns bleibt ein Erdenrest	To us remains an earthly relic
Zu tragen peinlich.	We must bear with pain,
Und wär' er von Asbest,	Which, though it were made of asbestos,

Er ist nicht reinlich.
Wenn starke Geisteskraft
Die Elemente
An sich herangerafft,
Kein Engel trennte
Geeinte Zwienatur
Der innigen beiden;
Die ewige Liebe nur
Vermag's zu scheiden.

The Younger Angels

Ich spür' soeben,
Nebelnd um Felsenhöh',

Ein Geisterleben,
Regend sich in der Näh'.
Seliger Knaben
Seh' ich bewegte Schar,
Los von der Erde Druck,
Im Kreis gesellt,
Die sich erlaben
Am neuen Lenz und Schmuck
Der obern Welt.

Doctor Marianus (in the highest, purest
    sphere)

Hier ist die Aussicht frei,
Der Geist erhoben.
Dort ziehen Frauen vorbei,
Schwebend nach oben;
Die Herrliche mittenin,
Im Sternenkranze,
Die Himmelskönigin,
Ich seh's am Glanze!
Höchste Herrscherin der Welt!
Lasse mich im blauen
Ausgespannten Himmelszelt
Dein Geheimnis schauen!
Bill'ge, was des Mannes Brust
Ernst und zart bewegt
Und mit heil'ger Liebeslust
Dir entgegen trägt!
Unbezwinglich unser Mut,
Wenn du hehr gebietest;
Plötzlich mildert sich die Glut,

Is unclean.
When once the strong power of the soul
Hath drawn
The Elements unto itself,
No angel can divide
The conjoint double-nature
Of the ardent pair;
Eternal Love alone
Hath power to part them,

Here now I seem to see,
Drift like a haze among the craggy
    heights,
A spirit life,
Which stirs but closely by.
Of sainted boys
I see a moving host,
Free from the press of earth,
United in a circle.
Who feast their eyes
Upon the new spring and the flowers
Of the celestial world.

Here is the vision clear,
The spirit lifted.
There women's forms pass by,
Drifting into the blue,
The Fairest, in their midst,
Circled about with stars,
The very Queen of Heaven.
I know that radiance,
Supreme Empress of the world!
Grant that, beneath the blue
And far-flung canopy of Heaven,
I may perceive thy mystery!
Receive what moves the heart of man
Tenderly and deeply,
Which, in the sacred joy of Love,
Unto thee he renders.
Nothing can subdue our courage,
If thou, noble one, command us,
But our zeal is swiftly tempered,

Wenn du uns befriedest.

If thou speak to us of peace.

The Younger Angels

Sei er zum Anbeginn,
Steiegnder Vollgewinn,
Diesen gesellt!

As he begins to rise,
To greater, perfect gain,
Let him first find fellowship with these!

Choir of Blessed Boys

Freudig empfangen wir
Diesen im Puppenstand;
Also erlangen wir
Englisches Unterpfand.
Löset die Flocken los,
Die ihn umgeben!
Schon ist er schön und groß
Von heiligem Leben.

With joy we will receive
This youth, as yet unfledged,
For thus may we achieve
Angels' society.
Loosen the silken flakes,
Which yet enshroud him;
Already he grows tall and fair,
Surrounded by this holy life.

Doctor Marianus and a Choir of Men

Jungfrau, rein im schönsten Sinne,
Mutter, Ehren würdig,
Uns erwählte Königin,
Göttern ebenbürtig.

Virgin, pure as pure is lovely,
Worthy to wear Honor's crown,
Our Queen, whom we have chosen,
And the equal of the gods.

Full Choir

Dir, der Unberührbaren,
Ist es nicht benommen,
Daß die leicht Verführbaren
Traulich zu dir kommen.
In die Schwachheit hingerafft,
Sind sie schwer zu retten.
Wer zerreißt aus eig'ner Kraft
Der Gelüste Ketten?
Wie entgleitet schnell der Fuß
Schiefem, glattem Boden.

Hath it not, Untouchable,
Ever been thy way,
That, trusting, such may come to thee
As have been lightly led astray.
Swept away in their own weakness,
They are hard to rescue.
Who in his own strength can break
The shackles of the fleshly lusts?
O how swiftly slips the foot
On ground both treacherous and steep!

Chorus of Penitent Women and
Una Poenitentium

Du schwebst zu Höhen
Der ewigen Reiche,
Vernimm das Flehen,
Du Gnadenreiche,
Du Ohnegleiche!

Thou who dost soar unto the heights
Of the everlasting realms,
Hear our pleading,
Thou, All-Gracious,
O thou Matchless Virgin!

Magna Peccatrix

Bei der Liebe, die den Füßen

By the love, which o'er the feet

Deines gottverklärten Sohnes
Tränen ließ zum Balsam fließen,
Trotz des Pharisäer-Hohnes,
Beim Gefäße, das so reichlich
Tropfte Wohlgeruch hernieder,
Bei den Locken, die so weichlich
Trockneten die heil'gen Glieder . . .

Of thy Son, transfigured of God,
Shed warm tears, for soothing balm,
Faced the Pharisees' derision;
By the vial which so richly
Shed its fragrant odors round,
By the tresses which so softly
Then did dry those sacred limbs . . .

Mulier Samaritana

Bei dem Bronn, zu dem schon weiland
Abram ließ die Herde führen,
Bei dem Eimer, den der Heiland
Kühl die Lippe durft' berühren,
Bei der reinen, reichen Quelle,
Die nun forther sich ergießet,
Überflüssig, ewig helle,
Rings durch alle Welten fließt . . .

By the well, to which aforetime
Abram let his flocks be led,
By the water-jug which, cooling,
Was suffered to touch the Savior's lips,
By the pure, rich-springing fountain
Which pours forth out of that place,
Flooding over, clear forever,
Watering all the Universe . . .

Maria Aegyptiaca

Bei dem hochgeweihten Orte
Wo den Herrn man niederließ,
Bei dem Arm, der von der Pforte
Warnend mich zurücke stieß,
Bei der vierzigjähr'gen Buße,
Der ich treu in Wüsten blieb,
Bei dem sel'gen Scheidegruße,
Den im Sand ich niederschrieb . . .

By that place, above all sacred,
Where they laid the Lord to rest,
By the Arm which from the portal,
With stern warning forced me back,
By my penance, forty years,
Suffered in the wilderness,
By the blessed farewell greeting
Which I traced upon the sand . . .

All Three

Die du großen Sünderinnen
Deine Nähe nicht verweigerst,
Und ein büßendes Gewinnen
In die Ewigkeiten steigerst,
Gönne auch dieser guten Seele,
Die sich einmal nur vergessen,
Die nicht ahnte, daß sie fehle,
Dein Verzeihen angemessen!

Thou, who to grievous-sinning women
Never hast denied Thy presence,
And to penitential merit
Raised them up, eternally,
Grant the same to this good spirit,
Who but once herself forgot,
Who knew not that she should forfeit
Thy just pardon utterly!

Una Poenitentium (once called
    Gretchen, making obeisance to the
    Virgin)

Neige, neige,
Du Ohnegleiche,
Du Strahlenreiche,
Dein Antlitz gnädig meinem Glück.

Incline, incline,
Thou Matchless One,
Thou rich-in-radiance,
Graciously, incline thy face unto my
    joy.

Der früh Geliebte,
Nicht mehr Getrübte,
Er kommt zurück.

My erstwhile love,
No longer sullied,
Now returns to me.

Blessed Boys (*circling ever nearer*)

Er überwächst uns schon
An mächt'gen Gliedern,
Wird treuer Pflege Lohn
Reichlich erwidern.
Wir wurden früh entfernt
Von Lebechören;
Doch dieser hat gelernt,
Er wird uns lehren.

Already he has grown beyond us,
With his powerful limbs.
And the reward of faithful care
Richly he will return in kind.
We were taken early
From the living choirs;
But he has been well-schooled,
And he will teach us.

Gretchen (Una Poenitentium) (*stepping forward*)

Vom edlen Geisterchor umgeben,
Wird sich der Neue kaum gewahr,
Er ahnet kaum das frische Leben,

Surrounded by the noble spirit-chorus,
This newest soul has little sense of self,
'But faintly he perceives the new existence,

so gleicht er schon der heil'gen Schar.

So like is he already to the sacred throng.

Sie, wie er jedem Erdenbande
Der alten Hülle sich entrafft,

See how he strips away each earthly tie,
Each last remaining vestige of his former frame,

Und aus ätherischem Gewande

Till he at last, clothed in celestial vestments,

Hervortritt erste Jugendkraft!

Steps forth in the first glorious strength of youth!

Vergönne mir, ihn zu belehren!

O grant that I may be allowed to teach him;

Noch blendet ihn der neue Tag.

The light of the new day confounds him still.

Mater Gloriosa

Komm! hebe dich zu höhern Sphären!
Wenn er dich ahnet, folgt er nach.

Come! Lift you unto loftier spheres.
If he understands you, he will follow.

Chorus Mysticus

Komm! Komm!

Come! Come!

Doctor Marianus

Blicker auf . . .

Look up . . .

Chorus Mysticus

Komm!   Come

Doctor Marianus

. . . alle reuig Zarten!   . . . all you contrite, tender souls!

Chorus Mysticus

Komm!   Come!

Doctor Marianus

Blicket auf, auf zum Retterblick,   Look up to that redeeming visage,
Alle reuig Zarten,   All you contrite, tender souls,
Euch zu del'gem Glück   Thankfully to be translated
Dankend umzuarten.   Unto blissful happiness.
Werde jeder bess're Sinn   May every nobler instinct be
Dir zum Dienst erbötig;   Set at your disposal;
Jungfrau, Mutter, Königin,   Virgin, Mother, Majesty,
Göttin, bleibe gnädig!   Goddess, be thou ever gracious!

Choir of Boys

Blicket auf!   Look up!

Chorus Mysticus

Blicket auf,   Look up,
Alle reuig Zarten!   All you contrite, tender souls!
Blicket auf! Blicket auf!   Look up! Look up!
Werde jeder bess're Sinn   May ever nobler instincts be
Dir zum Dienst erbötig;   Set at your disposal;
Jungfrau, Mutter, Königin,   Virgin, Mother, Majesty,
Göttin, bleibe gnädig!   Goddess, be thou ever gracious!

Alles Vergängliche   All things which know decay
Ist nur ein Gleichnis;   Are but vain likeness.
Das Unzulängliche,   All we could not attain
Hier wird's Ereignis;   Is here achieved.
Das Unbeschreibliche,   The indescribable,
Hier ist's getan;   Here it is done.
Das Ewig-Weibliche   Eternal-*anima*
Zieht uns hinan!   Compels us on.

        —Johann Wolfgang von Goethe   —transl. Donna Hewitt

This translation, © 1980 Donna Hewitt, was commissioned by the Boston Symphony Orchestra.

Symphony No. 9

> *Andante comodo*
> *In the tempo of a comfortable landler*
> *Rondo Burleske*
> *Adagio*

Mahler began his Ninth Symphony in the late spring of 1909, finished the orchestral draft that fall, and, on 1 April 1910, was able to report to his friend and former assistant Bruno Walter that the score, "a very positive enrichment of my little family," was complete. It was Walter who conducted the first performance with the Vienna Philharmonic on 26 June 1912, thirteen months after Mahler's death.

Four flutes and piccolo, three oboes and English horn, four clarinets (fourth doubling E-flat clarinet) and bass clarinet, four bassoons (third doubling contrabassoon), four horns, three trumpets, three trombones, bass tuba, timpani, cymbals, bass drum, tam-tam, triangle, glockenspiel, low-pitched chimes, two harps, and strings. (Mahler's autograph has only a single harp; the decision to divide the part between two players was Bruno Walter's.)

The Ninth Symphony is the last score Mahler completed. The dark part of him that was superstitious about Ninth symphonies would have wanted it so, but there was also the side to Mahler that caused him, for all his fascination with death, always to choose life. This was the Mahler who was more interested in writing music than in flirting with superstitions or his penchant for morbid fancy; it was also the Mahler who, within days of completing the Ninth Symphony, plunged with tempestuous energy into composing a Tenth, a task on which he had made significant progress when he died of a streptococcal blood infection seven weeks before his fifty-first birthday.

The Ninth was the last of Mahler's completed scores to be presented to the public, something that has surely contributed to the tradition of reading the work as the composer's farewell to life. The gestures of dissolution and parting with which this symphony ends are of an annihilating poignancy, and, as we shall see, the music makes specific reference to the *idea of farewell*; nonetheless, it is important to understand that Mahler did not mean this as *an actual farewell*. To read it thus is to indulge in a sentimentality that weakens the stab of this music.

In this Ninth, Mahler returns to a four-movement design for the first time since the Sixth Symphony of 1903–05. If the four movements of the Sixth still correspond to those of the normal classical and Romantic symphony, Mahler is clearly after another aim altogether in the Ninth. He begins with a very large movement whose basic tempo is semi-slow but which tends to spill over into allegro. Next comes a double intermezzo in the form of a vividly contrasted pair of scherzos, a set of landlers and a "Burleske." The finale is an Adagio whose weight and span approach those of the first movement.

Deryck Cooke proposed that the formal model Mahler had in mind was Tchaikovsky's *Pathétique*, and the correspondences are indeed clear: big first movements between slow and fast, beginning and ending quietly; the landlers and Tchaikovsky's gimpy 5/4 waltz; the "Burleske" and Tchaikovsky's brilliant march; the two Adagio finales. History added another parallel in that each symphony was its composer's inadvertent farewell to work and to life. The *Pathétique* was new music, just sixteen years old, when Mahler began his Ninth Symphony, and Mahler remembered gratefully Tchaikovsky's admiration of his *Eugene Onegin* performances in Hamburg in 1891. In 1901, Mahler had spoken ill of the *Pathétique* to his friend Natalie Bauer-Lechner, especially deploring its lack of counterpoint, but in January and March 1910 he conducted it several times. This of course was after the completion of the full draft of the Ninth Symphony and while the orchestration was in progress.

As for the first movement, it is surely Mahler's greatest achievement in symphonic composition. Shortly before Mahler was born, Wagner wrote to Mathilde Wesendonk: "I should now like to call my deepest and most subtle art the art of transition, for the whole fabric of my art is based upon such transitions." The Ninth's first movement is the high point of Mahler's own practice in the deep and subtle art of transition, of organic expansion, of continuous variation.

In deep quiet, cellos and horn set a rhythmic frame. The notes are oddly, disconcertingly placed in the time flow; Leonard Bernstein suggested that their halting rhythm represents, or perhaps reflects, the irregular pulse of Mahler's own faltering heart. Cellos and horn play the same pitch, A, and it will be more than fifty measures—more than three minutes of playing time—before we meet a bar in which A is not a crucial component, and then it takes a violent deceptive cadence to wrench the music in another direction. The harp begins a kind of tolling about that low A, while a stopped horn projects another thought, also with A as its point of departure and in a variant of the faltering-pulse rhythm.[51] The accompani-

---

[51] The discovery of the harp as an instrument that can do more than accompany or prettily decorate is one of Mahler's important orchestral achievements.

ment becomes denser, though it always remains transparent, with each detail highly individual. All this prepares a melody which the second violins build up step by step, full of literal or subtly varied repetitions.

We soon hear that the melody is in fact a duet, for the horn re-emerges with thoughts of its own on the material. Listening still more closely, we can notice that the accompanying figures in the harp, the clarinet, and the elaborately divided lower strings are using the same vocabulary too—the same intervals and the same rhythmic patterns. Do the accompaniments reflect the melody much as good servants take on something of their masters' style, or is the melody—or better, the melodic complex—an expansion of the elements that make up the ever present, ever changing background? Before the growing of this melody is done, the first violins have replaced the horn as the seconds' duet partner, while the clarinet (anticipated by the English horn) and the cellos cross the border, turning from accompanists into singers.[52] This beginning is a miraculous example of Mahler's inspired art of transition, so painstakingly worked (as we can tell from the orchestral draft, which has been published in facsimile by Universal Edition, Vienna) and so convincing in its appearance of utter spontaneity and natural growth. The transitions, moreover, exist in two dimensions: horizontal, as the melody proceeds through time from one event to the next, and vertical, in the integration of the melodic strands and their accompaniments.

This long opening melody keeps returning, always with new details of shape and texture, and its D-major presence is the soil in which the movement is rooted. Another element of which we become intensely aware is the stepwise descent through a third.

Ex. 1

Mahler marks this "Lebewohl" (Farewell) in his sketches, and he is alluding to Beethoven, whose *Farewell* Sonata, Opus 81a, begins with exactly

[52] The full effect of the first violins' *pianissimo* entrance can be felt only when the orchestra is seated according to the plan Mahler knew and wrote for, that is, with first violins on the conductors left and seconds to his right. Unfortunately, too few conductors care, and too many are pusillanimous about facing down their orchestras' resistance to reseating.

this gesture. Mahler even emulates the way Beethoven makes the phrase overlap with itself to create poignant dissonances.

The most persistent element of contrast comes in the form of an impassioned, thrusting theme in minor, whose stormy character is new, but whose intervals, rhythms, and accompaniments continue the patterns established earlier. In Mahler's harmonic design, the corresponding "opposition" to D major is a pull toward the flat side, sometimes to D minor, more often and more powerfully all the way over to B-flat minor. The "faltering pulse" and the harp tollings persist; dramatic abruptions shatter the long-breathed, seamless continuities; urgent trumpet signals mark towering climaxes. From one of these high points the music plunges into sudden quiet and the slowest tempo so far. The coda is virtually chamber music with simultaneous monologues of all but dissociated instruments: flute, oboe, violin, piccolo, horn, just a few strands of cellos and basses to begin with. The intervals between events become wider—it is as though the music continued, but beyond our hearing—until at last silence wins out over sound. With the completion of this immense and wonderfully poised arch, about one-third of the great symphony is done.[53]

The second movement returns us forcefully to earth. Mahler always had a love for the vernacular, and here is one more of his fantastical explorations of dance music. He shows us three kinds: a landler in C, leisurely, clumsy, heavy-footed, coarse (the adjectives are Mahler's); something much quicker and more waltz-like in slightly soured E major (and taken over almost literally by Shostakovich in the scherzo of his Fifth Symphony); and another landler, this one in F, the slowest of these three musics, gentle, lilting, sentimental. These tunes, tempos, and characters lend themselves to delightful combinations and interchanges.[54] This movement, too, finishes in a disintegrating coda, but the effect here is toward an intriguing mixture of the ghostly and the cute.

Where the second movement was expansive and leisurely, the third is music of violent urgency. Mahler styles it "Burleske" and wants it played "very defiantly." The first four measures, which take about three seconds, hurl three distinct motifs at us. That sort of concentration is fair warning of what is to follow. Mahler inscribed the autograph "to my brothers in Apollo," an invocation of the god who led the Muses in song that refers

[53] This is similar to the haunting close of the second movement of the Seventh Symphony.
[54] There is something specifically "modern" about these transformations and intercuttings, the idea, for example, of bringing back the first landler in the quick tempo of the quasi-waltz. I suspect that the reason so many conductors slow the return of the chorale at the end of Brahms's Symphony No. 1 down to its original tempo is that they cannot come to terms with the "modern" and therefore disturbing idea that it is possible to wed the old theme to a new tempo. See also my essay on the Schubert Great C-major Symphony.

to the virtuosic display of contrapuntal craft unleashed here. A contrasting trio brings a march and even some amiability—also, later, a twisted reminiscence of one of the exuberant march tunes in the Third Symphony's first movement. Most surprising, and deeply touching as well, is the trumpet's shining D-major transformation of one of the Burleske's most jagged themes into a melody of tenderly consoling warmth. It is, however, the fierce music, returning now at still greater speed and in yet more ferocious temper, that brings this movement to its crashing final cadence.

Now Mahler builds an Adagio to balance and, as it were, to complete the first movement. The violins utter a great cry. It is a strange and wonderful phrase, seeming at first to soar into an E-major heaven, but, with a surprising side-slip, moving into distant D-flat major. In the Symphony No. 4, Mahler began to question the assumption that a piece should end in the key where it began. In Nos. 6 and 8 he stays with that convention, but elsewhere he takes the conclusion to another key. In the optimistic Fifth he goes up half a step from C-sharp to D, but for this wrenching close he goes down by the same interval, from D to D-flat.

With D-flat major clearly established as home, all the strings, who are adjured to play with big tone, sound a richly textured hymn. Their song is interrupted for a moment by a quiet, virtually unaccompanied phrase of a single bassoon, but impassioned declamation in the choral style immediately resumes. That other world, however, insists on its rights, and Mahler gives us passages of a ghostly and hollow music, very high and very low. Between the two extremes there is a great chasm. The two musics alternate, the hymnic song being more intense and urgent at each of its returns. We hear echoes of *Das Lied von der Erde* and phrases from the Burleske.

Here, too, disintegration begins. All instruments but the strings fall silent. Cellos sing a phrase which they can scarcely bear to let go. Then, after a great stillness, the music seems to draw breath to begin again, even slower than before: adagissimo, slow, and *ppp* to the end, Mahler warns. As though with infinite regret, with almost every trace of physicality removed, muted strings recall moments of their—and our—journey. The first violins, alone unmuted among their colleagues, remember something from still longer ago, the *Kindertotenlieder*, those laments on the deaths of children that Mahler, to his wife's horror, had written two years before death took their daughter Maria. "Der Tag ist schön auf jenen Höh'n!"—the day is so lovely on those heights.

Ex. 2

[Sonnen] - schein! __ Der Tag ___ ist schön __ auf je ____ nen Höh'n!

Ex. 3

"Might this not," asks Mahler's biographer Michael Kennedy, "be his requiem for his daughter, dead only two years when he began to compose it, and for his long-dead brothers and sisters?" More and more, the music recedes, a kind of polyphony to the last, the cellos and second violins gently firm, the first violins and violas softly afloat. Grief gives way to peace, music and silence become one.

Symphony No. 10

Adagio
Scherzo: Fast quarter-notes
Purgatorio: *Allegretto moderato*
[Scherzo]: With greatest vehemence
Finale: Slow (but not dragging)

Although some of the ideas go back to 1908, Mahler did most of the work on this unfinished symphony in the summer of 1910, completing the work in short score, but leaving a fully orchestrated score only of the first movement and the first twenty-eight measures of the third. Most conductors still prefer to perform the Adagio alone; however, the second performing version of the complete five-movement work by the English writer Deryck Cooke has been often heard and several times recorded. In 1994, a more recent performing version by an American musician, Remo Mazzetti, Jr., thanks to the advocacy of Leonard Slatkin began to achieve some circulation and was recorded. There are also versions by Joe Wheeler, an Englishman, Clinton Carpenter, an American, and Hans Wollschläger, a German.

The first attempt at preparing a practical full score was undertaken by the composer Ernst Krenek in 1924. He presented the first and third movements only, and these sections were performed on 14 October 1924 by Franz Schalk and the Vienna Philharmonic. Alban Berg had gone through Krenek's score and offered criticisms, though these seem not to have been taken into account; yet the first performance did incorporate some re-touchings by Alexander von Zemlinsky and Schalk himself. Deryck Cooke began work on his score in 1959 in connection with the impending Mahler centenary, and on 19 December 1960, Berthold Goldschmidt, who had assisted Cooke, conducted a partial performance with the Philharmonia Orchestra in London. This was a lecture-demonstration for radio, but the objections of Mahler's widow, Alma Mahler Werfel, to any sort of "completion" had to be overcome before there could be a full performance. This, though not easy, was accomplished in 1963, and on 13 August 1964, Goldschmidt and the London Symphony gave the first complete performance of Cooke's score. One who was not satisfied was Cooke himself. With the assistance of two young composers, the brothers Colin and David Matthews, he prepared what he called his "finally revised full-length performing version"—generally known as Cooke II—and this was introduced, also in London, on 15 October 1972 by Wyn Morris and the New Philharmonia.

Having begun to think in 1980 about preparing his own performing version of the Mahler Tenth, Mazzetti began to undertake the task seriously in 1983, completing it two years later. The first three movements were performed by Gaetano Delogu and the Netherlands Radio Philharmonic on 14 November 1986 as part of a symposium on the work at Utrecht. The full premiere was given by the same orchestra and conductor, again in Utrecht, on 3 February 1989. The Mahler-Mazzetti score is dedicated to the late American Mahler scholar and devotee Jack Diether.

To make this essay broadly useful, I have avoided specific references to Cooke's and Mazzetti's orchestrations as much as possible.

Mahler-Cooke II calls for four flutes (fourth doubling piccolo), four oboes (fourth doubling English horn), four clarinets (fourth doubling E-flat clarinet) and bass clarinet, four bassoons (third and fourth doubling contrabassoon), four horns, four trumpets, four trombones, bass tuba, timpani (two players), bass drum, large double-sided military drum with a diameter of at least 80 centimeters ($31\frac{1}{2}$ inches), snare drum, cymbals, triangle, tam-tam, birch brush (*Rute*), xylophone, glockenspiel, harp, and strings. Mahler-Mazzetti is essentially the same, but omits the xylophone and *Rute*, and calls for two harps.

When Bruno Walter conducted the posthumous premieres of Mahler's *Das Lied von der Erde* in Munich in November 1911 and the Symphony No. 9

in Vienna in June 1912, it seemed that all of Mahler's music had been offered to the public. It was assumed that the Tenth Symphony was in too fragmentary a state ever to be performed, and word went about that Mahler had asked his wife to destroy whatever drafts remained. Mahler's biographer Richard Specht wrote about the "gaiety" and "exuberance" of the music, but his wording makes it plain that he had not actually seen the score and did not expect to; his source for this description was Alma.

In 1912, Arnold Schoenberg, that paradoxical confluence of the rational and the mystic, wrote:

> We shall know as little about what [Mahler's] Tenth (for which, as also in the case of Beethoven's, sketches exist) would have said as we know about Beethoven's Tenth or Bruckner's. It seems that the Ninth is a limit. He who wants to go beyond it must die. It seems as if something might be imparted to us in the Tenth which we ought not yet to know, for we are not yet ready. Those who have written a Ninth stood too near the hereafter. Perhaps the riddles of this world would be solved if one of those who knew them were to write a Tenth. And that is probably not going to happen.[55]

Mahler, for that matter, had his own misgivings about going beyond the Ninth. He had called *Das Lied von der Erde* a symphony without numbering it, so that the symphony he called No. 9 was actually his tenth. Thus he had dealt with "the limit" by circumvention, or so he believed. With ten symphonies completed (counting *Das Lied*), he moved virtually without pause, fearlessly and with white-hot energy, from the last pages of the official No. 9 to the first of No. 10. In 1911, the discovery of penicillin was still seventeen years away. Had that antibiotic been available to combat his blood infection, there is little doubt that he would have finished his work-in-progress that summer.

Schoenberg's Mahler/Beethoven parallel was inapt because he had no idea how far Mahler had actually progressed on his Tenth.[56] Only Mahler's widow had any idea until 1924, when she asked the twenty-three-year-old composer Ernst Krenek, then just married to the Mahlers' nineteen-year-old daughter Anna, to "complete" the symphony. Krenek felt this to be an "obviously impossible" assignment, and, as he said later, an "intermediate solution" like Cooke's did not occur to him. The upshot was that Krenek prepared a practical full score of two movements, the Adagio, which was

---

[55] Arnold Schoenberg, "Gustav Mahler," in *Style and Idea*, ed. Leonard Stein (New York: St. Martin's Press, 1975).

[56] A recent attempt to create a Beethoven Tenth from the sketches has proved an unfortunate enterprise, chiefly because Beethoven left nothing like the reasonably complete outline that Mahler had achieved for his Tenth at the time of his death.

complete, and *Purgatorio,* which was nearly complete. At the same time, Alma Mahler Gropius, as she then was, allowed the Viennese publisher Paul Zsolnay (a future husband of Anna Mahler Krenek) to publish a large part of Mahler's manuscript in facsimile.[57]

She had done this on Specht's advice, and it was a surprising decision. In his Mahler biography, passing on what little he knew about the Tenth, Specht had mentioned "mysterious superscriptions [that] hover between the notes." Such superscriptions do indeed exist, but they are not so much "mysterious" as explicit and exceedingly painful. Gustav Mahler, in 1910, was a man in torment, for he believed himself on the point of losing his intensely beloved, very much younger, bright and lively, beguilingly beautiful wife. Alma Maria Schindler, born 31 August 1879, met Mahler in November 1901, became pregnant, and married him four months later. Their marriage was a mixture of passionate mutual devotion and fundamental out-of-tuneness. Eight years into it, Alma, flirtatious by temperament and frustrated by Gustav's sexual withdrawal from her, was restless, and in May 1910, at a spa in Tobelbad just southwest of Graz, she met Walter Gropius, four years her junior and about to embark on one of the most distinguished careers in the history of architecture. Under trying and even bizarre circumstances—Gropius had by accident (!) addressed the letter in which he invited Alma to leave Gustav to "Herr Direktor Mahler"— Alma chose to stay with her husband, who later told her that if she had left him then, "I would simply have gone out, like a torch deprived of air." The verbal exclamations that Mahler scattered through the score of the Tenth Symphony are reflections of this crisis, and it cannot have been easy for Alma to agree to the publication of such painfully intimate material. As we have seen, she still had qualms about it as late as the 1960's.[58]

The so-called Krenek edition of the Adagio and *Purgatorio,* long the only available performing edition of any music from the Tenth Symphony, lacked too much both of science and art to be satisfactory; in any event, with the appearance in 1964 of the Adagio in the critical Mahler edition and that of Cooke II in 1976, it has to all intents and purposes dropped

---

[57] A more complete facsimile, but, disappointingly, much less well printed than Zsolnay's, was published in 1967 by the Munich publisher Walter Ricke. The last remaining pages were published in 1976 in Cooke II.

[58] Alma Mahler was married to Gropius from 1915 to 1919. Their daughter, Alma Manon, died in 1935 of complications from polio, and Alban Berg wrote his Violin Concerto as a memorial to that gifted and beautiful young woman. From 1911 to 1914, Alma Mahler had had an intense relationship with the painter and poet Oskar Kokoschka, who later described this period as "the most unquiet" of his life. In 1929 she married the novelist Franz Werfel (whose sister and Berg were lovers), emigrating with him to France in 1938 and escaping to the United States two years later. She died in New York in 1964, her marriage to Mahler still the dominant fact of her life. All this became the subject of a delicious and irreverent song by Tom Lehrer.

out of circulation.[59] Moreover, the pairing of the intense and expansive Adagio with the epigrammatic *Purgatorio* made a puzzling impression in performance, and without any knowledge of Mahler's intentions as to context it was hard to know what to make of *Purgatorio* at all.

It was again Specht who suggested, after studying the facsimile, that it was a mistake to assume that all that could be done about the Tenth Symphony had been done, and he urged that "some musician of high standing, devoted to Mahler, and intimate with his style" should prepare a performable full score of the entire work. He named Schoenberg as a likely candidate. For a long time nothing happened. In 1942, the Canadian-born Mahler scholar Jack Diether tried in vain to interest Shostakovich in the task. Seven years later, when the fruitless correspondence with Shostakovich had come to an end, Diether also suggested to Alma Mahler Werfel that Schoenberg be approached. "I'll ask him," she said. Diether reported that "she then invited both of us to her next salon, and during the evening she showed the manuscript to Schoenberg, who took it aside for an hour or so in her study, then returned to the parlor to express his regrets." Schoenberg was then seventy-five and had eye problems so severe that even work on his own compositions had become nearly impossible for him. He of course met all of Specht's criteria; however, as we know not only from his recompositions of Monn and Handel but also from his orchestrations of Bach and Brahms, he was temperamentally incapable of dealing with someone else's score in a spirit that was not assertively his own.

We are inconsistent in our feelings about what to do with unfinished compositions. We seem to prefer Bach's *Art of Fugue* to stop where Bach's blindness and last illness halted his hand, but for two centuries we have accepted "completions" in various degrees of competence of Mozart's Requiem. At the premiere of *Turandot*, Toscanini refused to proceed beyond what had been written by Puccini himself, but ever since, the work has flourished with the robustly workman-like conclusion by Franco Alfano. Friedrich Cerha's realization of Act 3 of Berg's *Lulu*—more a secretarial than a creative task—has been accepted, but continuations and "completions" by Peter Gülke and Brian Newbould of some of Schubert's unfinished symphonies (but not including the *Unfinished*) have met with skepticism.

Some considerable voices, including those of Bruno Walter, Leonard Bernstein, Rafael Kubelik, Pierre Boulez, and Erwin Ratz (chief editor for the International Mahler Society), have spoken out against the "complete"

[59] Together with the previously mentioned emendations by Zemlinsky (to whom Alma Schindler had been about to surrender her virginity when she met Mahler) and Schalk, the published score of the Krenek version included changes by Otto Jokl, a Berg pupil working as an editor for Associated Music Publishers, New York, who issued the score in 1951. In sum, "Krenek edition" is a shorthand expression less than fair to Krenek.

Mahler Tenth. In the November 1978 issue of *19th-Century Music*. Richard Swift, writing from a scholarly composer's point of view, cogently states the case against discounting what Mahler might yet have done between "the stage that the work had reached" when he died and his final fair copy.[60] (What adds interest to Swift's article is that, while he has a strong objection in principle, he in fact admires much of Cooke's work.) Yet, if we accept Cooke's score on Cooke's terms—and, mutatis mutandis, Mazzetti's—as a "performing version" of a draft that Mahler would undoubtedly have "elaborated, refined and perfected . . . in a thousand details," in which he would also "no doubt, have expanded, contracted, redisposed, added, or canceled a passage here and there," and where he would "finally, of course, have embodied the result in his own incomparable orchestration," we have before us something of the greatest significance both as a document and as a monument.

Having a Mahler Tenth adds a great human and musical experience to our lives, and that is the first and obvious argument *pro*. The last movement particularly speaks for itself in this respect. Knowing this music also alters our perception of Mahler's life work. To a large extent because of the powerful influence of Alma Mahler, we have been taught to see this as tending toward a conscious, death-possessed farewell in the last song— its very name is *Der Abschied* (The Farewell)—of *Das Lied von der Erde* and the Symphony No. 9. But it is clear that Mahler in no way thought of that last heart-wrenching Adagissimo as the final page of his letter to the world. Ken Russell's film fantasy on Mahler is an assailable interpretation of the composer's life and work, but it contains some ringing truths: one of them—it is factually quite wrong—is the last shot, showing Mahler arriving in Paris from America in March 1911, confidently exclaiming to the waiting reporters, "I'm going to live forever!" The Tenth, on which Mahler excitedly embarked as soon as he could after completing the Ninth, is, for all the tragic elements in the verbal glosses and the music itself, is also informed by the gaiety and exuberance about which Specht had written, as well as by profound serenity at its close.

In the Tenth Symphony, Mahler returned to the symmetrical five-movement design he had used in his Fifth and Seventh and in the original version of the First. This idea was not clear to Mahler to begin with, and the crossing out of numbers and of designations like "Finale" on the folders that contain the material for the several movements indicates that he changed his mind more than once about their order within the whole.

---

[60] For that matter, Mahler would undoubtedly have made changes in *Das Lied von der Erde* and the Ninth Symphony, had he lived to conduct them himself or even to hear them. *Das Lied*, especially, has appalling balance problems in the first and fourth songs.

He wrote "Adagio" on the folder that contains the music for the first movement, but he does not enter that tempo—nor, for that matter, the main key, F-sharp major—until measure 16. He begins, rather, with one of the world's great upbeats: a *pianissimo* Andante for the violas alone, probing, wandering, surprising, shedding a muted light on many harmonic regions, slowing almost to a halt, finally and unexpectedly opening the gates to the Adagio proper. This is a melody of wide range and great *intensity—piano*, but warm, is Mahler's instruction to the violins—enriched by counterpoint from the violas and horn, becoming a duet with the second violins, returning eventually to the world of the opening music.

These two tempi and characters comprise the material for this movement. A dramatic dislocation into B major (Mahler notates it as C-flat, which makes it look more distant), with sustained brass chords and sweeping broken-chord figurations in strings and harp, brings about a crisis, the trumpet screaming a long high A, the orchestra seeking to suffocate it in a terrifying series of massively dense and dissonant chords. Fragments and reminiscences, finally an immensely spacious, gloriously scored cadence, bring the music to a close.

The second movement is a scherzo on a large scale in F-sharp minor: the folder still bears the designation "Scherzo-Finale." It moves in rapid quarter-notes, and its most immediately distinctive feature is the constant change of meter—3/2, 2/2, 5/4, 2/2, 3/4, and so on—that jolts the pulse in nearly every measure. Here is one of Mahler's most astonishing leaps into the future, and even so great a conductor as Mahler himself would have had to acquire some new techniques to manage this exceedingly difficult music in performance. Only the scene of Tristan's delirium would have come even close in his conducting experience. The trio, in a slower ländler tempo, is a variation of the melody of the Adagio. There is a shorter second interlude under chains of trills. At the end, the mordantly sardonic character of the opening is translated into the gaiety and exuberance which Specht cites.

Mahler sometimes divided his symphonies into two main *Abtheilungen* or sections; following that lead, Cooke proposes a major break at the end of the second movement. Another reading of the musical material, however, suggests that the third movement is a miniature pendant to or variation of what immediately precedes it, the relationship being much like that of the first two movements of Beethoven's *Hammerklavier* Sonata. The dominance in both of Mahler's movements of the interval of a third— major in the second movement and minor in the third—is a striking and certainly audible connection. Mahler labeled this movement *Purgatorio oder Inferno*, later striking out *Inferno* with a heavy zigzag line. The ghostly and whirring texture recalls *Das irdische Leben* (Earthly Life) in *Des Knaben Wunderhorn*, a song with which it also shares the key of B-flat minor.

The main tempo is allegretto moderato, and the movement is a tiny da capo form.

Here is where the verbal superscriptions in the manuscript begin. As the middle section becomes more intense, Mahler writes "Tod! Verk!," the latter presumably an abbreviation for "Verklärung" (transfiguration). At the climax he writes "Erbarmen!!" (Mercy!!) at the top of the page and, at the bottom, "O Gott! O Gott! warum hast du mich verlassen?" (O God! O God! Why hast thou forsaken me?). Six measures later, when the same music returns at an even greater level of intensity, he writes "Dein Wille geschehe!" (Thy will be done!).

Up to this point, each movement has been very much shorter than the one before: *Purgatorio* is less than one-quarter the length of the Adagio. The fourth movement is counterpoise to the second, and with it, the dimensions begin to expand again. Everything on the folder is violently crossed out except the Roman numeral IV and these notations:

> Der Teufel tanzt es mit mir
> Wahnsinn, fass mich an, Verfluchten!
> vernichte mich
> das ich vergesse, dass ich bin!
> das ich aufhöre zu sein
> dass ich ver

> The Devil dances it with me
> Madness, seize me, who am accursed!
> destroy me
> that I may forget that I exist!
> that I may cease to be
> that I for

Jack Diether rightly calls this movement "demonic." Mahler quotes the "mercy" motif from *Purgatorio*, alluding as well to *Das Lied von der Erde*—the reference is to the "morschen Tand" ("rotten trumpery") passage in the first song—and the Ninth Symphony. On the last pages the music disintegrates into the mutterings of percussion. A *fortissimo* thud of the muffled military drum is, so to speak, the last word, but Mahler fills the remaining space on the page with sprawling text:

> Du allein weißt was es bedeutet.
> Ach! Ach! Ach!
> Leb' wohl mein Saitenspiel!
> Leb wohl
> Leb wohl
> Leb wohl

with still more and larger exclamations of "Ach" on the left side.

> You alone know what it means.
> Farewell, my lyre!

"Du allein" means Alma. She tells this story in her *Memories and Letters:*

> Marie Uchatius, a young art student, visited me one day in the Hotel Majestic.[61] Hearing a confused noise, we leaned out of the window and saw a long procession in the wide street alongside Central Park. It was the funeral procession of a fireman about whose heroic death we had read in the newspaper. The chief mourners were almost directly below us when the procession halted, and the master of ceremonies stepped forward and spoke briefly. From our eleventh-floor window we could only guess at what he said. There was a brief pause, then a stroke on a muffled drum, then the dead silence. Then the procession moved on and it was all over. The scene brought tears to our eyes, and I looked anxiously at the window of Mahler's room. He too was leaning out, and tears were streaming down his face. That brief drum stroke impressed him so deeply that he used it in his Tenth Symphony.[62]

Michael Kennedy writes in his Mahler biography that "this incident occurred on Sunday afternoon, 16th February 1908. The funeral was of Charles W. Kruger, Deputy Chief of the City of New York Fire Department, commanding the 2nd Division, who died . . . while fighting a fire at 217 Canal Street at 1 a.m. on 14th February. He had been in the fire service for thirty-six years."[63]

The Finale begins without break, with the same sound of the muffled drum, and in the introduction a tentative unfolding of motifs is punctuated by five more repetitions of the drum stroke. The rising scale in the bass and the slower descending one both refer back to *Purgatorio.* Gradually the music gathers speed. At the same time, it begins the long voyage from D minor, where the fourth movement ended, back to F-sharp.[64] A winding flute solo, a variant of the waltzing in the preceding scherzo, leads to a

---

[61] In New York on Central Park West, south of 72nd Street. An apartment building by the same name now occupies that site. —M.S.

[62] Alma Mahler, *Gustav Mahler: Memories and Letters,* ed. Donald Mitchell and Knud Martner (Seattle, University of Washington Press, 1975).

[63] The music at the funeral service at St. Thomas's Church was the hymn *Nearer, My God, to Thee,* Mozart's *Ave verum corpus,* Schumann's *Träumerei,* and Handel's "Largo."

[64] Concluding a symphony in its initial key, while normal classical and Romantic procedure, is by no means to be taken for granted with Mahler. In the Tenth Symphony it was an afterthought, the manuscript showing that Mahler originally intended the Finale to end in B-flat.

newly rapt and still music for strings. The drum of death breaks into this peace to introduce the quick music that forms the central portion of the Finale, again based on themes from *Purgatorio:* what amazing riches this brief, almost incorporeal movement yields! Again, as in the first movement, a breaking point is reached in the trumpet's shrilling high A and the orchestra's brutally dissonant blanketing of that protest. Brass proclaim the opening viola melody, but from there Mahler moves into a music that is ardent, yet singularly at peace—in Michael Kennedy's words, "a great song of life and love—the most fervently intense ending to any Mahler symphony and a triumphant vindication of his spiritual courage."

This love song is to Alma. When the string music fades beyond our hearing, and woodwinds interject their gentle sighs, Mahler writes "Für dich leben! für dich sterben!" (To live for you! To die for you!). At the last, there is one terrible rearing up of violins—they vault through nearly two octaves and in a single beat swell from *pianissimo* to *fortissimo*—and there Mahler has written "Almschi!"[65]

---

[65] In the earlier draft in B-flat, the "Almschi!" is firmly written and twice underlined; in the final version the handwriting is huge, shaky, almost out of control, the exclamation mark nearly illegible, the slant of the word in sharp descent from left to right.

Bohuslav Martinů

Bohuslav Martinů was born on 8 December 1890 in Polička
near the Moravian border of Bohemia, now the Czech
Republic, then part of the Austro-Hungarian Empire. He
died in Liestal, Switzerland, on 28 August 1959.

In the fall of 1948, Martinů, then in his eighth year of uneasy American
exile, began a three-year stint on the faculty at Princeton. I was a
senior and excited at the prospect of meeting a composer whose music
I liked so much and who, moreover, was at the height of his then considerable fame. Tall, thin, gray-haired, blue-eyed, he had a narrow face of distinctly Slavic cast, a face that explored from time to time the risk of a
smile which, when it blossomed, delightfully combined warmth and skepticism. His speech, *pianissimo* and *con sordino*, was strongly accented (I still
sometimes catch myself thinking of "slow," a frequent complaint of his
about performances, as rhyming with "now") and, as we discovered, it was
odd in various ways: fifths and fourths, for example, were "quints" and
"quarts." We knew that he was partially deaf as the result of a bad fall,
since stories about him in newspapers and magazines were plentiful. Listening (with the t pronounced) or speaking, he was infinitely more comfortable in French, but really he was shy in any language.

Another composer had rather suddenly left Princeton for greener (actually crimson) pastures, and the Boston Symphony's Serge Koussevitzky,
long a champion of Martinů (back in 1927), recommended him as a replacement. I don't know whether Koussevitzky had been impressed by Martinů's debut as a teacher of composition at Tanglewood or whether, as
seemed more likely, he was simply eager to help a deserving artist; in the
event, Martinů proved inarticulate and helpless in the classroom. Also, he
really had no one to teach, Princeton just then being poor in student

composers. What students there were soon stopped coming to Martinů's class, and it seemed that the only two people interested in him and his work were a brilliant pianist who was actually a graduate student in Romance languages (Charles Rosen) and a musicology student with no talent for composition (myself).

Martinů dutifully came down from New York to spend Thursday afternoons on campus. Charles and I would meet the two-car shuttle train from Princeton Junction, take him to Lahière's for lunch (at least it had a French name, and one could get a glass of wine there—wine that always caused him to make a face), and then sit in the Pekin Room, a quaint octagonal excrescence to the student center, where we would talk and listen to records. Afterwards we would feed him tea (liberally laced with bourbon) and take him back to the train. It was a strange contrast to one's public views of him receiving and rather shrinkingly acknowledging ovations at concerts and at the American premiere of that future staple of opera workshop productions, *The Comedy on the Bridge.*

I treasured those Thursdays. Martinů didn't much like to talk about music, I think because he was afraid one expected a "pronouncement," which was not at all his style. He enjoyed more talking about what he had been reading (I remember enthusiasms for Spengler, Velikovsky, and Saint-Exupéry) and about pictures he had seen (it didn't surprise me a few years later when he wrote *The Frescoes of Piero della Francesca*). We also talked politics, though it invariably depressed him. He certainly didn't like to talk about his own music, though in response to begging he would occasionally lug cumbersome acetates and heavy glass discs of broadcast transcriptions down with him. He made an exception for his opera *Juliette*, which he wanted us to borrow and read and perhaps even translate. But when I asked him about his *Field Mass*, which I had read about in Miloš Šafránek's biography, he claimed not to remember having written such a piece. I never did figure out whether he had really forgotten or whether the memory of a work so closely associated with the early weeks of the war was simply too painful. (On the other hand, I remember his attempts to recall a string quartet, presumably the powerful No. 5, whose score was lost during the war and which was found only in 1955.)

He enjoyed Princeton's well-stocked library of scores and records, and our Thursdays turned more and more into listening sessions. Sometimes he would make requests; often he asked to be surprised. He revered Bartók and never tired of marveling over the first movement of the Music for Strings, Percussion, and Celesta (one could think of his own Double Concerto for Two String Orchestras, Piano, and Timpani, and of his String Quartet No. 5, as "productive marveling"), and my own love for Bartók dates from those afternoons, but otherwise he was always happy to escape his own century. He shook his head over Stravinsky's newest music, finding the Mass *chiche* (stingy); he had never had much sympathy for the Viennese school, finding its expressive world *exaspéré*, though he insisted that I go to New York to hear Dimitri Mitropoulos conduct the first American performances of *Wozzeck* in twenty years.

Haydn always produced a smile, more even than Mozart. He liked a certain *sec* quality in Haydn (as opposed to Mozart's generous sexiness), and he loved the humor down to its subtlest manifestations. There we were able to repay him in a small way. He mentioned that he had heard Charles Munch conduct a Haydn piece with solo oboe, bassoon, violin, and cello in Paris before the war, and that he had never been able to trace this. We found him a score of Haydn's *Sinfonia concertante* (then not in print) as well as a rare pre-war Munch recording, and eventually an air-check of a Toscanini broadcast. Soon he brought in the score, just finished, of a delightful *sinfonia concertante* of his own for the same combination. Similarly Berlioz, whose *Nuits d'été* had just come out on records for the first time and which delighted him, made him think of writing a *Nouvelle Symphonie fantastique*. How that came out is told in my essay on the *Fantaisies symphoniques* (Symphony No. 6).

Even more, Martinů loved sixteenth-century music, particularly French chansons and Italian madrigals. He himself wrote not only real vocal madrigals but also Madrigals for violin and viola, a Madrigal-Sonata for flute, violin, and piano, and for Princeton's most famous resident, Albert Einstein, Madrigal Stanzas for violin and piano.[1] He liked counterpoint, he liked the airy textures of classical and Renaissance music (maintaining that one could have foretold Brahms's late-in-life liver trouble from his early fondness for thick textures), and he liked the ease and unpretentiousness with which his pre-Beethoven colleagues had gone about their work. Older music was Paradise Lost. It embodied his ideal of *mesure*, or sense of proportion, and it was free of something he abhorred in life and in art, the desire to be greater than one is. But whether it was Lassus or Bartók on the piano rack, Martinů would sometimes point at a chord, at a detail of voicing, at some bit of contrapuntal finesse, and show why it delighted him. That wasn't "pronouncement," it wasn't even teaching in a conventional sense, but being able to watch what touched a real composer certainly was learning.

Martinů's music, long neglected (except in Czechoslovakia), began to come back into favor at the end of the 1980s. It was incredibly popular in

---

[1] Martinů wrote the Madrigal Stanzas in 1943 rather by way of a fan letter to the great physicist. He hardly knew Einstein, and I don't recall there ever being contact while Martinů taught at Princeton. The pianist at the first reading of the Madrigal Stanzas was another celebrated Princeton resident, Robert Casadesus.

the 1940s and '50s; for example, after Erich Leinsdorf conducted the premiere of the Symphony No. 2 with the Cleveland Orchestra in October
1943 to commemorate the twenty-fifth anniversary of the founding of the
Czech republic, the work was picked up that same season by Artur Rodzinski and the New York Philharmonic-Symphony, Fritz Reiner and the Pittsburgh Symphony, and Dimitri Mitropoulos and the Minneapolis Symphony, and in the following year by Vladimir Golschmann in Saint Louis
and by Eugene Ormandy, who took it back to New York as well as playing
it in Philadelphia. Ernest Ansermet, Sir Adrian Boult, Erich Kleiber, Rafael Kubelik, and Manuel Rosenthal were among the conductors who introduced it internationally in 1945-46. Not only is such a triumphal procession nearly unimaginable for any major work today; it was, except for
Shostakovich, virtually unique then. Furthermore, an excellent biography
of Martinů appeared in 1946. His standing was also one of the very few
subjects on which Olin Downes and Virgil Thomson, the warring critics
of *The New York Times* and *The New York Herald-Tribune* could agree.

Of course, to be a Czech exile was a public relations plus. Czechoslovakia was a land whose national aspirations had been repressed under
Austro-Hungarian dominion; that between the wars had impressed the
world as a model democracy; that England and France betrayed to Germany in the Munich pact of 1938; and that, after 1945, had a respite of
less than three years before a Communist coup d'état enslaved it again.
Smetana and Dvořák had sung its beauties and glories as well as its ago-
nies, and Martinů was seen as their heir. His Double Concerto, composed
in 1938, was celebrated as an expression of the angst and anguish of its
time; his *Memorial to Lidice,* an ode for the Czech village whose entire
population was murdered or deported by the Germans in 1942, was recognized as the modern counterpart, dark and tragic, to a patriotic tone poem
like Smetana's *Vltava.*

The political context would have meant nothing had Martinů not
been a very good composer. Though he would never have presumed to
make such a claim, he *is* the heir of Smetana and Dvořák; he himself
would have wanted one to add the Moravian individualist Janáček. (Martinů's native village of Polička is in Bohemia, but he always insisted that
it was really Moravian, ethnically and in spirit.) Martinů's music, especially that of his American years, speaks Czech, though I once heard him
complain, not more than half humorously, that a distinguished compatriot's performance of one of his pieces was "too Czech."

His relationship to his country was complicated. He deplored its pro-
vincialism, but loved it ardently. Nonetheless, he lived outside it more
than half his life, and for fifteen years he did so by choice. He moved to
Paris in 1923, and married Charlotte Quennehen, a seamstress from Pi-
cardy. French became his chief language. In the United States, where he

lived from 1941 to 1953, he was bitterly homesick and pained beyond words by his knowledge of German oppression in Czechoslovakia; still, when the war was over and he was invited to teach at the Prague Conservatory (which had expelled him for "incorrigible negligence" thirty-six years before), he first accepted, then hesitated. After the Communist takeover in 1948, he felt that to return was out of the question.

Martinů's father was Polička's sexton; he himself was born in the tower of Saint James's, where the family had tiny quarters 193 steps up from the street. (It is now a Martinů museum.) He liked to talk about that tower and the beneficent isolation it afforded, just as, later on, Paris delighted him because one could hide there and go unbothered about one's work. He took violin lessons from the village tailor and at ten started to compose, without instruction and without much to go on by way of models beyond his violin études. He moved on to the Prague Conservatory, but, not really interested in his violin and organ studies, he flunked out. Supporting himself by giving music lessons, he continued his precarious progress as a self-taught composer, and, in spite of himself, had become a good enough violinist to join the Czech Philharmonic for five years. Another attempt to study at the Prague Conservatory, this time composition with Josef Suk, also came to grief and led to his being shown the door a second time. Later in life, Martinů would be a remarkably orderly and steady worker, but at this stage, discipline was still alien to him.

Nonetheless, he got a small state grant that allowed him to go to Paris, which he had come to know a little on orchestra tours. His aim, he wrote later, was "to look for the real foundations of Western culture." He was poor, shy, but full of optimism. He took some useful lessons from Albert Roussel, and formed a "groupe des quatre" with three other struggling young composers from abroad, Marcel Mihalovici (Rumania), Tibor Harsányi (Hungary), and Conrad Beck (Switzerland). He composed a lot, and his music was beginning to get around. *Half-Time*, a Stravinskian ode to soccer, made a strong impression when Václav Talich conducted it with the Czech Philharmonic in 1924, and other works were played at major festivals at Baden-Baden and Siena. Koussevitzky, fairly recently arrived from Paris, introduced Martinů's music in America when he led the Boston Symphony in *La Bagarre* (Tumult) in 1927, and a year later, his String Quintet was performed at the Elizabeth Sprague Coolidge Chamber Music Festival. The 1930s saw the composition of some of Martinů's most important music, notably the opera *Juliette* (his favorite among all his works with the possible exception of his 1955 oratorio *Gilgamesh* and the Double Concerto).

On 10 June 1940, four days before the Germans entered Paris, the Martinůs, leaving all their possessions behind, headed south, making their way to Lisbon, not without difficulty and string-pulling in high places. After further delays, they boarded the S.S. *Exeter*, landing in Hoboken,

New Jersey, on 31 March 1941. Friends, acquaintances, and colleagues welcomed Martinů. Koussevitzky, who had conducted several of Martinů's compositions during the 1930s, now programmed his 1937 Concerto Grosso, commissioned an orchestral work, and later engaged him to teach at Tanglewood. Martinů entered upon a period of prolific and first-rate work, in five years composing five symphonies, *Memorial to Lidice*, a violin concerto (for Mischa Elman), a cello concerto, a two-piano concerto, a piano quintet, a string quartet, a violin sonata, études and polkas for piano, three sets of songs on Moravian texts, and more.

But, for all his relief at living in a democracy and his admiration for American ideals, Martinů was not happy. In public, he always spoke warmly of the country that had received him and his work so eagerly; in private, he confided to friends that he detested the oppressive monotony of Manhattan, that life in America seemed to him hectic and dedicated to trivial values, and that he found himself increasingly dismayed by what he saw happening to the political climate. His limited English and his poor hearing aggravated his isolation and unhappiness. At the end of the 1940s he felt he had gone into a slump as a composer, though the last major work he began in America, the *Fantaisies symphoniques*, written for the Boston Symphony's seventy-fifth anniversary, turned out to be the summit of his achievement as a composer of music for orchestra.

In 1953, the Martinůs returned to Europe, settling first in Nice; one further year of teaching in America, this time at the Curtis Institute in Philadelphia, persuaded Martinů that he had been right to leave. The Martinůs lived in Rome for a while, then in Switzerland. Settings of Kazantzakis's *The Greek Passion* and of Prophecies of Isaiah were his last major projects; these final years were also filled with small vocal works crying with love and longing for the country he had not seen since 1938. He died of cancer. Eleven days before, he and Charlotte had supplemented their civil wedding of 1931 with a Catholic ceremony.

Bruckner was forty-two when he completed his Symphony No. 1, Brahms forty-three, and Elgar fifty-one. Martinů was fifty-two. Though he had written for large orchestra in his operas and some of his concertos, he had not composed a major work for large orchestra since *La Rapsodie* of 1928. Instead, his inclinations, in which his unease with grandeur played a large part, had led him instead to fruitful and lively investigations of the concerto grosso style. Tendering his commission, Koussevitzky had not specified a symphony; that was Martinů's choice. Having begun to explore this genre, Martinů delighted in it, writing five symphonies in five years. After the spring of 1946, when he completed his Fifth, the symphony dropped out of Martinů's life, though the *Fantaisies symphoniques* (1953), *The Frescoes of Piero della Francesca* (1955), and the *Parables* (1957) constitute an eloquent triple epilogue to his symphonic endeavors.

Even aside from the stylistic ingredients that make them instantly recognizable as Martinů, the symphonies share certain characteristics: each is
about half an hour, laid out in three or four movements on a familiar
design or a close variant thereof, and scored for more or less the same
ample orchestra, in which the piano (except in No. 6) is a special coloristic component. What Virgil Thomson wrote in 1942 about No. 1 is, with
variations of emphasis, true of them all:

> The Martinů Symphony is a beaut. It is wholly lovely and doesn't
> sound like anything else. . . . The shining sounds of it sing as well as shine;
> the instrumental complication is a part of the musical conception, not an
> icing laid over it. Personal indeed is the delicate but vigorous rhythmic ani-
> mation, the singing (rather than dynamic) syncopation that permeates the
> work. Personal and individual, too, is the whole orchestral sound of it, the
> acoustical superstructure that shimmers constantly.[2]

At the same time, each of the symphonies has a distinctive personality. Martinů's biographer Harry Halbreich has aptly called No. 1 epic and
broad, No. 2 idyllic and intimate (he uses that hard-to-translate German
word *innig,* which carries implications as well of "fervent" and "heartfelt"),
No. 3 weighty and confessional *(bekenntnishaft),* No. 4 radiant, happy, and
sunny, No. 5 complicated and full of contrast. To a considerable extent,
these differences reflect Martinů's mood of the moment. The Largo of No.
1, for example, was his first musical response to Lidice; the dark No. 3,
always the least popular and the one he came to be proudest of, was written at the height of his grieving homesickness; No. 4 was written in that
uniquely emotional spring for Europeans of Martinů's generation when the
war in Europe had finally come to an end.

Fantaisies symphoniques (Symphony No. 6)

Lento—Andante moderato—Allegro—Allegro vivo—Lento Poco allegro
Lento—Poco vivo, adagio—Più mosso—Andante—Allegro—
  Moderato—Allegro—Allegro vivace—Lento

Martinů developed his first ideas for this piece in 1951, in effect finishing
the first movement on 21 April that year. After a considerable interval,

---

[2]*New York Herald Tribune,* 19 November 1942.

he returned to this score, completing it on 23 April 1953. During the next month, he revised the orchestration, drawing the final double bar on 26 May 1953. The score is dedicated to Charles Munch in honor of the Boston Symphony's seventy-fifth anniversary and was first performed by Munch and that orchestra on 7 January 1955. It was awarded the New York Music Critics' Circle Award for that year.

Three flutes and piccolo, three oboes, three clarinets, three bassoons, four horns, three trumpets, three trombones, bass tuba, timpani, triangle, tambourine, snare drum, bass drum, cymbals, tam-tam, and strings.

In my introductory note on Martinů, I mentioned that looking at some Berlioz scores with his students at Princeton in 1950 or 1951 gave him the idea of writing a *Nouvelle Symphonie fantastique.* He actually wrote one movement, then laid it aside in order to work on other projects, mostly chamber music, but also his Rhapsody for Viola and Orchestra. Next, along with Barber, Bernstein, Copland, Hanson, Piston, Petrassi, Poulenc, Schuman, Sessions, and others, Martinů was commissioned to write a work for the Boston Symphony's seventy-fifth anniversary, coming up in 1956. Apart from the obvious pleasure of getting a commission from one of the world's best orchestras, this sat well with Martinů. Back in 1927, the Boston Symphony had given the first performances of any of his music in America, and Serge Koussevitzky, its conductor from 1924 to 1951, had continued to be supportive and helpful. Charles Munch, Koussevitzky's successor in Boston, had been a friend in Paris before the war, and he too had programmed Martinů's music in Boston. Munch had also come to be especially acclaimed for his performances of Berlioz, in particular works such as *Nuits d'été, La Damnation de Faust, Roméo et Juliette,* and the Requiem, all as good as unknown to American audiences in the early 1950s, and so the idea of the *Nouvelle Symphonie fantastique* once again sprang to life in Martinů's mind.

He soon decided that his proposed title was rash and eventually settled on *Fantaisies symphoniques.* When John N. Burk, the Boston Symphony's program annotator, asked Martinů for some information and commentary on his new work, this was the reply:

> There is one reason for this work which is clear and certain for me: I wished to write something for Charles Munch. I am impressed and I like his spontaneous approach to the music where music takes shape in a free way, flowing and freely following its movements. An almost imperceptible slowing

down or rushing up gives the melody a sudden life. So I had the intention to write for him a symphony which I would call "Fantastic," and I started my idea in a big way, putting three pianos in a very big orchestra. This was already fantastic enough, and during work I came down to earth. I saw it was not a symphony but something which I mentioned before, connected with Munch's conception and conducting. I abandoned the title and finally I abandoned also my three pianos, being suddenly frightened by these three big instruments on the stage.

I called the three movements "Fantasies," which they really are. One little fantasy of mine is that I used a few bars quotation from another piece, from my opera *Juliet*, which, to my mind, fitted perfectly well. That is of the nature of fantasy.[3]

When he came to America in 1941, Martinů wrote five symphonies in five years (No. 1 was a Koussevitzky commission for Boston). Eight years elapsed between the Fifth and the completion of the next, and by then Martinů was ready to take a fresh look at the idea of "symphony." As his letter to Burk attests, he was keenly aware that the Sixth differed from its predecessors in important ways—so much so that, after years of back-and-forth, he decided to drop the "Symphony No. 6" part of the title altogether. The published score is simply headed *Fantaisies symphoniques*. I have included it here because, in spite of its strong "fantastic" component, it has the feel and stature of a symphony. If Martinů had continued to call it Symphony No. 6, no one would question the aptness of the title.

By the time Martinů decided to complete what he had begun in the first movement of his *Nouvelle Symphonie fantastique*, he had also made firm plans to return to Europe. He did most of the work on the *Fantaisies symphoniques* in New York, but when he accomplished his final revisions, he was once again living in France. As I have described elsewhere, Martinů was grateful for the shelter the United States had offered him and for its warm welcome to his music, but felt exiled and out of place. Being back in France was a liberation for him.[4] It was in America that he had become a symphonist, and surely it is not just chance that after fulfilling his Boston commission, Martinů did not write another symphony.

[3] Boston Symphony Orchestra program book, 7–8 January 1955. In his book *Martinů: Werkverzeichnis, Dokumentation und Biographie*, Harry Halbreich points out that there never were three pianos in the original version of the first movement, only two. The *Fantaisies symphoniques* turned out to be Martinů's only symphony without a piano in the orchestra. He used to say that the reason he started using the piano in his orchestral scores was that he had not learned to figure out the complicated transpositions that writing for the harp required. —M.S.

[4] When Martinů came back in 1955 to teach at the Curtis Institute in Philadelphia for a year, Munch, with characteristic generosity, repeated the *Fantaisies symphoniques* with the Boston Symphony so that the composer might hear his music played by the musicians for whom he had written it.

If you do no more than look at the tempo indications of the *Fantaisies symphoniques,* you can see that the plan is unusual. Two of Martinů's earlier symphonies, the Third and the Fifth, are three-movement works; both are fast-slow-fast. At first glance it seems that Martinů has turned the design inside out, to slow-fast-slow, but what really happens is that although the first and last movements begin and end with slow music, they work their way into quick tempi in the middle.

Tempi reflect moods and musical character, everything we would sum up under the heading of expressive content. Martinů wrote to his biographer Miloš Šafránek that this side of the work was "completely private in nature. I alone know what it is about—all other speculation on the subject is movie fantasy." The most arresting feature of the *Fantaisies symphoniques* is the complexity of its psychological and dramatic processes. This is striking in itself, but this complexity also defines the essential difference between the *Fantaisies symphoniques* and Martinů's first five symphonies. Those are powerful compositions, gorgeous in sound, and each of distinct and vividly projected personality. It is Martinů's freedom in the matter of form—in other words, everything that made him think of this work as *Fantaisies symphoniques* rather than plain Symphony (or even *Fantastic Symphony*)—that makes possible this visionary score with its mixture, and sometimes collisions, of dreams, reality, nostalgia, harshness, energy, deep sadness, terrors, and peace. We say "as mixed up as a dream," but are dreams stranger than our waking lives?

Something else new here is the sound itself. Martinů always was something of an orchestral magician, but in the *Fantaisies symphoniques* he surpasses himself as he conjures a breathtaking range of coruscations, phosphorescences, and lambent half-lights from the instruments. This, too, was a tribute to Munch, who could make the sounds of Debussy and Ravel dance and shimmer like no one else, and because Munch had inherited a great French orchestra from Koussevitzky, it was indirectly a tribute to Martinů's earlier benefactor as well.

The first sound we hear is a murmur of woodwinds and three muted solo strings, all revolving closely about the keynote, F. This swirl—F/G-flat/E/F—is something like a germinal cell for the entire work.[5] As though from a distance, a muted trumpet adds a vaguely threatening fanfare of stabbing repeated notes. Arcadia is haunted by death. Only when the full strings start to play can we make out the larger rhythmic picture and hear that these scurrying notes are tiny subdivisions of very slow beats (Lento).

The music gains in sonority and arrives at a complete cadence. A solo cello emerges to suggest a melody, which the flutes then carry forward.

[5] The same pattern is also of crucial importance in the Symphony No. 3.

Like the opening music, it is full of chromatic intervals and is confined to a very small compass. Its variants and derivatives will play large roles throughout. The tempo is now half again as fast as at the beginning (Andante moderato), and after some hesitation, the music leaps into an energetic Allegro. Soon, Martinů gives us one of his unmistakably Czech tunes, syncopated, voluptuously harmonized in parallel sixths, and flooded by the pain of homesickness, but the brass are having none of this and blast it out of the way.

The atmosphere darkens. Explosions in the strings cut into a woodwind melody, the harmonies become more chromatic, the rhythms grow more intense: something frightening is in the air. The tempo goes up one more notch to Allegro vivace. A single violin, accompanied by a tattoo of percussion (real percussion at first, then percussive strings), sings out in a transformation of the earlier cello/flute theme. The Czech tune returns and is again cut off, this time by a blurring of the harmony that sends the music to the edge of unintelligibility. Now we find ourselves immersed again in the strange world of the opening music, with its murmuring strings and woodwinds, and the stabbing trumpet—so seductive and so subtly frightening. To this, Martinů adds the briefest of codas. It is the music that had led to the Allegro the first time we heard it, resolved this time in a single, long-held chord of F major.

Overall, the impression is of an "allegro" dream, not all sweet, occurring within the reality of the slow opening and closing music. But paradoxically, it is the opening and closing that sound like dream music and the Allegro that suggests "reality." Martinů loved the story of Lao-tzu, who dreamed that he was a butterfly but wakened to wonder: Am I a man dreaming I am a butterfly or am I a butterfly dreaming I am a man?[6]

The second movement is a scherzo alive with nervous energy. Like the first movement, it begins with muted strings and close chromatic intervals so that it sounds like a variation of that earlier music, only here the meter is a clear and dancelike 6/8. Martinů packs a tremendous amount of event into not many minutes of mercurial music, whose moods range from exuberance and playfulness to deep melancholia.

In the middle section, brass, with firm backing from timpani and snare drum, suddenly cut into the energetically forward-moving music with an assertive proclamation or warning. This nasty disruption is a four-note phrase that Shostakovich often used to spell out his initials, using the German transliteration of his name (Schostakowitsch) and German musical notation (E-flat is called "es", and B-natural is H), so that D/E-flat/C-B spells DSCH. (Martinů's version is transposed and begins on B rather

[6] I think, too, of the German poet Novalis, who wrote, "The more poetic, the more real."

than D, but the shape is the same.) It is possible that Martinů had heard the then very new Shostakovich Tenth, in which the composer "signs" his music in this fashion; however, I don't know whether he actually did and even find it hard to imagine that the prospect would have interested him. If he is indeed quoting DSCH, does he mean Shostakovich to stand for Communist oppression in Czechoslovakia? Or is it all just coincidence?

Like the first movement, the last begins with very slow music. This time, though, the whole orchestra (except percussion) speaks out in searing cries. As the tempo quickens, cellos and violas sing a tristful song related to the cello-flute theme in the first movement. When the clarinet brings it back, Martinů lets it melt into an achingly sad passage in which two clarinets sing in thirds, sixths, and tenths. It is like Dvořák at his most poignantly vulnerable, truly music to break the heart. Yet Martinů moves forward into an agitated Allegro and speeds on. It is here, in a sequence of frightening inner turbulence, a duststorm in *pianissimo,* that he quotes his opera *Juliette.*[7]

Everything points toward a triumphant close when a fiercely dissonant chord, *fortissimo,* throttles this hope. Only the dying vibrations of the tamtam sound in the shocked silence. Then the strings, still remembering the cello-flute theme from the first movement, intone a solemn chorale. Softly, the first violins, alone, show us how that theme sounds unadorned and lonely. Woodwinds take up the chorale, and with three gentle chords, this emotion-laden, visionary set of fantasies arrives at a peaceful close.

---

[7] *Juliette* is a surreal play by Georges Neveux that Martinů may have seen when it was produced in Paris in 1930. It is about a young bookseller obsessed with finding a woman whom he once saw through her window as she sat at the piano, playing and singing. In Martinů's own words, "rejecting sanity and reality, he settles for the half-life of dreams." In a word, the subject of *Juliette* is longing.

Felix Mendelssohn-Bartholdy

Jakob Ludwig Felix Mendelssohn was born in Hamburg, then under French rule, on 3 February 1809 and died in Leipzig, Saxony, on 4 November 1847. Bartholdy was the name of his mother's brother Jakob, who had changed his own name from Salomon, taking Bartholdy from the previous owner of a piece of real estate he had bought in Berlin. It was he who most persistently urged the family's conversion to Lutheranism: the name Bartholdy was added to Mendelssohn—to distinguish the Protestant Mendelssohns from the obstinately Jewish ones—when Felix's father converted in 1822, the children having already been baptized in 1816.

M endelssohn is the most astonishing of all the composing prodigies. Mozart was to go much farther, but as a teenager not even he surpasses or often equals Mendelssohn in assurance and certainly not in individuality. To think of the young Mendelssohn is to think first of all of the Octet for Strings, written 1825, the year he turned sixteen, and of the *Midsummer Night's Dream* Overture, the work of a boy of seventeen. He had found a voice unmistakably his own and he used it with the confidence of a seasoned professional. In a way he was just that. By the time of the Octet, he had seen, heard, read a lot. He had composed a lot, too.

All advantages were his. Moses Mendelssohn, his grandfather, was a philosopher and literary man of stature—a Martin Buber of his time, it has been suggested—who has an enduring monument as the principal character of Lessing's profound and humorous play about religious tolerance, *Nathan the Wise*. It is with Moses that the name Mendelssohn comes into the family: his father's name was Mendel Dessau, and he styled himself Moses Ben Mendel, Moses the son of Mendel. Felix's father was a prosperous banker. His mother played the piano, sang, drew, and read French, Italian, English, and Greek authors in the original.

Felix's sister Fanny, four years older, surprised the family when she was thirteen by giving them a performance, from memory, of the whole of Bach's *Well-Tempered Clavier*. Fanny Mendelssohn-Hensel, the person Felix was closest to all his life (even after his marriage) and whose death hastened his own, is one of the lost women of nineteenth-century history. Her father insisted that music could only be an ornament to her life, never its "fundamental bass." He managed, however, to ignore the letters from Uncle Jakob Bartholdy, with their animadversions against Felix's being allowed to become a professional musician, "which is after all no kind of career, no life, no goal."

With Fanny to one side of him and Rebecka and Paul, two and four years younger, on the other, Felix was Crown Prince. At ten, he gave his first piano recital. He traveled widely with his family, turned into an accomplished linguist, and learned to execute the elegant drawings that adorn his letters and journals. He became the pupil and protégé of Carl Zelter, composer, conductor, Bach-lover, and partner in a prolific correspondence with Goethe. It was through Zelter that Felix met Germany's Great Man himself, improvising for him, upsetting him by thundering through Beethoven's shocking Fifth Symphony for him at the piano, and thoroughly enjoying his rather flirtatious friendship with that seventy-two-year-old Olympian eminence. The deaths of Zelter and Goethe in the spring of 1832 hit Mendelssohn hard; the former brought an additional hurt when the Berlin Singakademie did not appoint Mendelssohn as his successor.

In 1829, Mendelssohn, just turned twenty, had conducted the Singakademie chorus in a performance in Berlin of Bach's *Passion According to Saint Matthew*. Apart from the fact that we would surely find Mendelssohn's reorchestration and huge cuts hard to take, the significance of that performance has been exaggerated over the years, as well as embellished by tales of how the score Mendelssohn conducted from had been rescued in the nick of time from the grocer who had started to use its leaves to wrap cheese in (Eduard Devrient, who sang the part of Jesus in the Berlin performance was responsible for that one).

Still, even if Bach had not been as forgotten as all that, it is probable that nothing even approaching a complete *Saint Matthew Passion* had been heard in two generations. That in itself was sufficient to mark this as an undertaking of considerable moment in the nineteenth-century rediscovery of Bach. The enterprise was impressive and did make its waves.

It was also characteristic of its staggeringly gifted and ruthlessly driven organizer. Mendelssohn, elegant classicist nurturing Romantic fantasies, was amazingly facile and at times no less amazingly self-critical: the twelve-year gestation of the *Scotch* Symphony and his never-resolved doubts about the *Italian* tell their own stories. When he died he was burnt-out by his non-stop composing, traveling, conducting, playing. Being charming all the time must have been draining too. Fanny's death was a blow his fragile ecology could not take. His F-minor String Quartet, a cry of a piercing intensity not heard in his music before, was to be his Requiem for her. Before he could finish it he too had died, annihilated at thirty-eight.[1]

Symphony No. 3 in A minor, Opus 56, *Scotch*

*Andante con moto and Allegro un poco agitato—Vivace non troppo—
Adagio—Allegro vivacissimo and Allegro maestoso assai*

Mendelssohn completed this symphony, which, not counting the string symphonies he wrote as a boy, is actually his fifth and last, on 20 January 1842, though his first idea for it goes back to the summer of 1829. Though Mendelssohn always referred to this in correspondence and conversation as his "Scotch Symphony," he does not use that title anywhere on the score.[2] He conducted the first performance at the Leipzig Gewandhaus on 3 March 1842. He then made a few revisions, and the work was played in its final form for the first time just two weeks later under the direction of Karl Bach, conductor at the Leipzig Opera. The dedication is to "H. M. Queen Victoria of Great Britain and Ireland."

Two flutes, two oboes, two clarinets, two bassoons, four horns, two trumpets, timpani, and strings.

[1] A curious parallel: just a year later, the thirty-year-old Emily Brontë died, devastated by the death of her brother Branwell three months before.
[2] The current rule that *Scotch* is used only for whiskey (or whisky) and that *Scots* and *Scottish* are the correct forms for people, places, customs, and so forth was not yet in force in Mendelssohn's day. This symphony was called the *Scotch* without objection throughout the nineteenth century.

In 1829 Mendelssohn made his first visit to England, the country where he became more appreciated, more adored, than in any other. He conducted his Symphony No. 1 with the London Philharmonic, played Weber's Konzertstück and Beethoven's *Emperor* Concerto with that orchestra (creating a sensation because he did it from memory), gave a piano recital, and capped his stay with a benefit concert for Silesian flood victims, for which he assembled an all-star cast including the sopranos Maria Malibran and Henriette Sontag, the pianist Ignaz Moscheles, and the flutist Louis Drouet. Not to give a false impression of Mendelssohn's London stay, this time he did not just work but had fun as well.

In mid-July he was ready for a vacation, and so, with Karl Klingemann, a friend from Berlin now posted in London as Secretary to the Hanoverian Legation, he set out for Scotland. He was both a diligent and a gifted letterwriter, as was Klingemann, which means we have a remarkably complete picture of their journey to Glasgow, Edinburgh, Perth, Inverness, Loch Lomond, and the Hebrides islands of Iona, Mull, and Staffa. They made a detour to Abbotsford to visit the then worshiped, now unreadable Sir Walter Scott and were disappointed to find him grouchy, distracted, and unwilling to rise beyond small talk. They were good-humored about bad food (sometimes no food), uncomfortable inns, and taciturn Scots ("To all questions you get a dry 'no' "), but Mendelssohn hated, absolutely hated, bagpipes and anything to do with folk music.

On 7 August, after his visit to Staffa and Fingal's Cave, he jotted down the opening of his *Hebrides* Overture. A week before, on 30 July, he had written home:

> In darkening twilight today, we went to the Palace [of Holyrood] where Queen Mary lived and loved. There is a little room to be seen there with a spiral staircase at its door. That is where they went up and found Rizzio in the room, dragged him out, and three chambers away there is a dark corner where they murdered him. The chapel beside it has lost its roof and is overgrown with grass and ivy, and at that broken altar Mary was crowned Queen of Scotland. Everything there is ruined, decayed and open to the clear sky. I believe that I have found there today the beginning of my Scotch Symphony.[3]

And for himself he wrote down sixteen bars of music, the opening, still in preliminary form, of this score.

But it was years before either of his musical mementos from Scotland

---

[3] *Felix Mendelssohn: Letters,* edited by Gisela Selden-Goth (New York: Pantheon, 1945). One reason for Mendelssohn's fascination with Queen Mary and Holyrood was that, like virtually every literate and theater-going German, he loved Schiller's emotional and rousing *Maria Stuart.*

reached final form. The *Hebrides* Overture went through three stages, being first written in 1829 with the name of *Die einsame Insel* ("The Desert Island"), then revised in December 1830 and again in June 1832. Mendelssohn did not even return to his plan for a Scotch Symphony until 1841. He wrote from Rome in March 1831 that he could not "find his way back into the Scottish fog mood," and the matter receded farther and farther from the forefront of his mind. Over the next ten years, he wrote the *Reformation* and *Italian* symphonies, as well as the *Hymn of Praise* (on the invention of printing), two piano concertos, four books of Songs Without Words, the oratorio *Saint Paul*, four string quartets, the Piano Trio No. 1, and much besides.

He had traveled, become music director first at Düsseldorf and then at the Leipzig Gewandhaus, married Cécile Jeanrenaud, had given the first performance of Schubert's Great C-major Symphony, and had just been appointed director of the music division of the Academy of Arts in Berlin. In 1842, on his seventh visit to England, he made two new friends, enthusiastic and competent performers of his songs and chamber music, Queen Victoria and Prince Albert, and Her Majesty graciously consented to accept the dedication of the *Scotch* Symphony. (She herself was later the author of two charming memoirs about Scotland, *Leaves from a Journal of Our Life in the Highlands, 1848–61* and *More Leaves . . . 1862–82.*)

When Breitkopf & Härtel published the score and parts in February 1843, Robert Schumann reviewed the work in the *Neue Zeitschrift für Musik* and, misinformed by someone about the circumstances of its composition, committed one of the most famous gaffes in the annals of criticism:

> We learn from a third party that the beginning of the new symphony was written . . . during Mendelssohn's residence in Rome. . . . This is interesting to know in view of its special character. Just as the sight of a yellowed page, unexpectedly found in a mislaid volume, conjures up a vanished time and shines in such brightness that we forget the present, so must many lovely reminiscences have risen to encircle the imagination of the master when among his papers he rediscovered these old melodies sung in lovely Italy—until, intentionally or unintentionally, this tender tone picture revealed itself; a picture that—like those of Italian travel in Jean Paul's *Titan*—makes us forget for a while our unhappiness at never having seen that blessed land.
>
> And so it has often been said that a special folk tone breathes from this symphony—only a wholly unimaginative person could fail to observe it. . . . We do not find [here] traditional instrumental pathos and massive breadth, no sense of an attempt to outdo Beethoven; rather, it approaches, mainly in character, the Schubert [Great C-major] Symphony—with the distinction that while Schubert's suggests a rather wild, gypsy-like existence, Mendelssohn places us under Italian skies. This is a way of saying that the

latter is of a graciously civilized character, speaking a more familiar language, though we must allow Schubert other superiorities, particularly that of richer powers of invention.[4]

Schumann goes on to remark, "In point of plan, Mendelssohn's symphony is distinguished by its intimate connection of all four movements." Schumann refers to similarities among the movements of melodic shape, character, and so on. But Mendelssohn is also concerned with connection in another sense: the score is prefaced by a note asking that the movements not be separated by the customary pauses, and the composer goes on to suggest that their sequence be indicated in the program as follows:

Introduction and Allegro agitato—Scherzo assai vivace—Adagio cantabile—Allegro guerriero and Finale maestoso.

I have followed this style at the beginning of this essay; however, the markings in Mendelssohn's preface and in the music itself do not exactly correspond. (Max Bruch picked up Mendelssohn's unusual "allegro guerriero" for his own Scottish Fantasia.)

The introduction begins solemnly. Mendelssohn has refined his 1829 sketch, coming up with a more interesting rhythm in the first measure and a less flaccid turn of melody a little later. This hymn-like opening gives way to an impassioned recitation for the violins, and it is from this passage that the rest of the Andante takes its cue. The music subsides into silence, and after a moment the Allegro begins, its "agitato" quality set into higher relief by the *pianissimo* which Mendelssohn maintains through twenty-one measures.[5] The *Scotch* is very much of a *pianissimo* symphony. The scoring tends to be dense and dark in a manner that we, certain of the symphony's title, are much inclined to interpret as Northern and peaty. At the first *fortissimo*, the tempo is pushed up to Assai animato, which is in fact the base speed for the remainder of the movement.

As always, Mendelssohn handles the entrance into the recapitulation captivatingly: as the moment of return approaches, cellos start to sing a new melody in notes much slower than the skipping staccato eighths in the strings and woodwinds, set in delicate *piano* against the surrounding *pianissimo*, and when the first theme returns, it is as a counterpoint against the continuing cello song. Schumann delighted in this sort of thing: "Every page of the score proves how skillfully Mendelssohn retrieves one of his former ideas, how delicately he ornaments a return to the theme, so that

[4]Robert Schumann, *On Music and Musicians,* edited by Konrad Wolff (New York: Pantheon, 1946).
[5]I don't know whether Tchaikovsky had this music in mind when he composed the corresponding pages of his Fifth Symphony, but it certainly sounds that way.

it comes to us as in a new light, how rich and interesting he can render his details without overloading them or making a display of pedantic learning." The coda brings one of those diminished-sevenths tempests that Romantic composers were so fond of, even crypto-classicists like Mendelssohn. Once again the music subsides—very beautifully—and a breath of the introduction brings the first movement to a close.

The Scherzo emerges from this with buzzing sixteenth-notes and distant horn calls (on all sorts of instruments). In spite of Mendelssohn's irritations in the summer of 1829, the flavor of the tunes is distinctly Scots. The Adagio alternates a sentiment-drenched melody with stern episodes of march character. The fiercely energetic fourth movement again seems very Scots indeed, and every bit as macho and athletic as Mendelssohn's "guerriero" promises. He invents yet another of his magical *pianissimos*, this time to emerge into a noble song, scored in surprisingly dark and muted hues for such a peroration: he remarks somewhere that it should suggest a men's chorus. Schumann of course caught the cousinage of this hymn to the one that begins the symphony and remarked: "We consider it most poetic; it is like an evening corresponding to a lovely morning."

Symphony No. 4 in A major, Opus 90, *Italian*

Allegro vivace
Andante con moto
Con moto moderato
Saltarello: Presto

The genesis of the *Italian* Symphony is not entirely clear. It seems that Mendelssohn had some sort of an "Italian" symphony in mind at the end of 1830; however, the concentrated work on the score falls into the period from mid-January to 13 March 1833. He conducted the first performance with the Philharmonic Society, London, on 13 May 1833.

Two flutes, two oboes, two clarinets, two bassoons, two horns, two trumpets, timpani, and strings.

It is hard to imagine that any musician has ever had trouble with the *Italian* Symphony unless it was sheer envy. Berlioz, who found Mendelssohn priggish and unlikable, called it "admirable, magnifique," and thought it deserved a gold medal. The surprising exception is Mendelssohn himself, who revised the work after its first performance in London in 1833 (in the same Hanover-Square Concert Rooms where Haydn had enjoyed his triumphs in the 1790s), introducing changes that distressed both his sister Fanny and his friend the composer, conductor, and pianist Ignaz Moscheles. Furthermore, he remained dissatisfied, never conducted the work again, and refused to publish it. He was still struggling with it in 1835. His last mention of it is in October 1840, and when he died in 1847, he left behind detailed plans for further revisions to the first three movements. These plans have never been incorporated into any published score. We have no clue why this perfectly poised symphony displeased him so.

He began work on it during an extended journey through Italy in 1830–31, referring to it as his "Italian symphony" as well as remarking that it was the most cheerful piece he had yet composed. The impetus to complete the piece came in the form of a resolution passed 5 November 1832 by the general membership of the London Philharmonic Society "that Mr. Mendelssohn-Bartholdy be requested to compose a symphony, an overture and a vocal piece for the Society, for which he be offered the sum of one hundred guineas."[6] The public success of the new symphony was immense. Paganini was in the audience, and he was so taken by Mendelssohn's playing of Mozart's D-minor Piano Concerto that he suggested they ought to play all the Beethoven sonatas together. But because Paganini soon had to submit to surgery on his venereally infected larynx, that extraordinary event never came about.

That the new symphony made such a splash is no wonder. The first movement is music of architectural genius and the highest of high spirits. It presents one captivating invention after another, beginning with that first energizing tattoo of wind chords and the bounding violin melody that begins seconds later. The paragraph given to this idea is both spacious and buoyantly athletic. The second theme is a graceful and leisurely melody of delicious rhythmic subtlety. Next, the clarinet, eager to discover how the first theme sounds stretched and in minor, casts a shadow over the landscape. A new and charming idea—a dialogue for woodwinds, whose implications are musingly explored by the violins—leads us back to the beginning of the movement for a second trip through the exposition. When we come to the end of the exposition the second time, Mendelssohn bypasses this episode, taking a shortcut straight into the development.

[6]One hundred guineas equal £105. From George Eliot's *Middlemarch*, which is set in this period, one can learn that £80 was a reasonable annual salary for a contractor's and surveyor's assistant, that Dorothea Casaubon's annual gift of £200 to Dr. Lydgate's New Hospital was considered exceedingly generous, but that the doctor, at the time of his recent marriage, had spent £600 on silver plate and jewelery.

Here, too, we get a surprise in that Mendelssohn begins by expanding in fugue upon a brand-new theme. This episode rises to a point of vigorous swagger, though Mendelssohn keeps finding occasion to remind us that he really has not forgotten the movement's first theme. The moment of recapitulation is wonderfully managed: it is out of phase, which is something of a Mendelssohnian house specialty, the melody reappearing while the bass is still finding its way back to the tonic. In this adventure, the oboe is the sweetest and most seductive of tour guides. A place is found for the fugue subject from the beginning of the development, and the elusive theme Mendelssohn had used to steer us into the repeat of the exposition gets its due in the coda.[7]

The Andante is a chaste processional, perhaps a souvenir of one of the religious ceremonies that captured Mendelssohn's imagination on his Italian journey. He invents utterly simple, utterly fresh sounds for his gently melancholic hymn, first oboe, bassoons, and violas in octaves, then violins in octaves with the two flutes adding a decorative counterpoint. Did Verdi, who devised something similar in the Agnus Dei of his Requiem, have Mendelssohn's Italian postcard in mind? For contrast, the clarinets offer an easygoing tune in major. Fragments of the chant-like introductory measures and of the hymn reach us as though carried by a capricious wind, and so—most beautifully—the procession moves beyond our hearing.

Next, Mendelssohn gives us a minuet, at least a Romantic translation of minuet, delicate and surely quite un-Italian. Distant horns and bassoons color the gentle trio. The minuet returns and drifts to an enchanting, lightly sentimental close.

Last comes a rarity, a minor-key finale to a symphony in major. This movement is brilliant in every way, perfectly gauged for exhilaration to the end. A saltarello is literally a leaping dance, but the continuously running music that begins a minute or so into the movement is that of a tarantella, so named because it was believed that the only cure for the bite of a tarantula was to keep the victim in perpetual motion. The tarantula, it seems, has been maligned: its bite, though painful, is harmless. At harvest-time, though, fiddlers would walk through the fields of Italy, hoping for therapeutic engagements, and who after all would wish to knock anything that provides musicians with gainful and reasonably honest employment?

---

[7]Since Mendelssohn builds the coda on a theme that has occurred only once before in the movement, in the lead-in to the repeat of the exposition, it is obvious that to include this one previous occurrence is essential; in other words, because that one occurrence is the lead-back to the repeat of the exposition, it is necessary—not optional—to observe this repeat. But never underestimate the potential for insensitivity among conductors: a few of the most celebrated have charged through this movement without the repeat, creating the irrational and exceedingly un-Mendelssohnian effect of introducing a brand-new theme seconds before the end.

Wolfgang Amadè Mozart

Joannes Chrisostomus Wolfgang Gottlieb Mozart, who began to call himself Wolfgango Amadeo about 1770 and Wolfgang Amadè in 1777, but who never used Amadeus except in jest (signing the occasional letter Wolfgangus Amadeus Mozartus), was born in Salzburg, Austria, on 27 January 1756 and died in Vienna on 5 December 1791.

Symphony No. 35 in D major, K.385, *Haffner*

Allegro con spirito
[Andante]
Menuetto
Presto

Mozart wrote the *Haffner* Symphony between 20 July and 7 August 1782, but in a form rather different from the present one. It was played in Salzburg soon after. He revised it early the next year and led the first performance of the new and final version at the Vienna Burgtheater on 23 March 1783.

Two flutes, two oboes, two clarinets, two bassoons, two horns, two trumpets, timpani, and strings.

Although Mozart wrote the *Haffner* Symphony in Vienna, it is tied to his earlier life in Salzburg. Sigmund Haffner would not think it inappropriate that the town he served as mayor and where he made his fortune as a wholesale merchant name a street for him, but the visitor to Salzburg who smiles upon seeing the enameled sign that says Sigmund-Haffner-Gasse does so because the name conjures up music, Mozart's music.

Haffner, who had come from Imbach in the Tyrol, had been a useful friend to the young Mozart and particularly to his father, Leopold, sometimes providing introductions and letters of credit as the two traveled about Europe. Haffner died in 1772. Four years later, his daughter Marie Elisabeth—Liserl—married Franz Xaver Späth, a shipping agent; the bride's brother, another Sigmund Haffner, commissioned a festive music for a garden party on the wedding day, 29 July 1776. That is the *Haffner* Serenade, K.250.

In 1782 the Haffners had new cause to celebrate: the young Sigmund—he was exactly Mozart's age—was ennobled and took the name von Imbachhausen. Once again, he wanted music by Mozart. Leopold forwarded the request to Vienna. The timing, for Mozart, could hardly have been worse. As he wrote to his father on 20 July, he was up to his eyeballs in work. He had students. Complications threatened his imminent marriage to Constanze Weber on 4 August. *The Abduction from the Seraglio* had just had a hugely successful premiere at the Burgtheater, and by the 28th he had to arrange the score for wind instruments,

> . . . otherwise somebody else will beat me to it and get the profits. And now I'm supposed to produce a new symphony! How on earth can I manage? You have no idea how hard it is to arrange something like that for winds so that it really suits them and yet loses none of its effect. Oh well, I must just spend the night over it, otherwise it can't be done—and for you, dearest father, I'll make the sacrifice. You'll definitely get something from me in every mail—I'll work as fast as possible—and so far as haste permits, I'll write well.[1]

What he sent to Salzburg between 27 July and 7 August was not, however, the *Haffner* Symphony we now know, but another serenade with introductory march and two minuets. We encounter the piece again in a letter of Mozart's dated 21 December: he has decided to play it at his Lenten concert in Vienna and asks his father to send the score along from Salzburg, a request he has to repeat a couple of times. By 15 February, though, it has arrived, because he writes: "The new *Haffner* Symphony has

[1] W. A. Mozart, *Briefe und Aufzeichnungen*, edited by O. E. Deutsch and J. H. Eibl (Kassel: Bärenreiter, 1962–75).

positively amazed me, for I had forgotten every single note of it. It must surely produce a good effect."

It did. Mozart had converted the *Haffner* from party music to symphony by dropping the introductory (and closing) march and one minuet. He also enriched the sound by adding two flutes and two clarinets to his original wind group with its pairs of oboes, bassoons, horns, trumpets, and kettledrums; plus strings. The new winds have, however, nothing independent to do: they only double what is there already, but the doublings, particularly those an octave above or below, are cannily done and sound splendid. Mozart uses these additional winds only in the first and last movements. That they are omitted from the generally quiet Andante is not surprising, but their absence from the minuet, which is scored in a grand tutti style, is.

Mozart's most provocative alteration, though, is in crossing out the double bar with repeat signs at the end of the first movement's exposition. This he does with heavy red crayon. He also puts no repeat signs in the newly added flute and clarinet parts, which go into the empty staves at the top and bottom of his original pages. As a general rule, certainly, Mozart asks that the exposition of his symphonic first movements (and those in sonatas, quartets, quintets, etc.) be repeated. There are, however, three important exceptions, and they occur in the three big symphonies immediately preceding the *Haffner*—the *Paris* and No. 33, both of 1779, and No. 34, of 1780.

The *Haffner*'s first movement is unusual and striking. Mozart had been studying Haydn's newest quartets, the Opus 33 of 1781 (published 1782). His carefully worked and magnificent response to this collection was a set of six quartets of his own, written between December 1782 and January 1785, and dedicated to Haydn in generous and loving words. One of the ways Mozart, by temperament, most remarkably differs from Haydn is in being as lavish with material as the man he called father, guide, and dearest friend is economical. In this sense, the *Haffner* Allegro is also a response to Haydn, and specifically to his tight-knit monothematicism.

We have seen that this Allegro "amazed" him when he got it back from Salzburg after not having thought about it for six months. Some of his shock—and delight—would have come from seeing a score in which he had done something unprecedented for him, namely to build an entire movement where the first idea is virtually never absent and where no other theme of comparable weight or profile is introduced. Part of the reason for the convention of the repeat is to consolidate the listener's acquaintance with the material to be developed and then interestingly recapitulated. With the one theme already so dominant, that necessity disappears, and convention can go with it. Furthermore, the impulse to move powerfully ahead without a formal and literal repetition of ninety-four measures grows naturally from that so striking tautness. Hence the great crayon slash down the eleventh page of the manuscript.

The opening of the symphony is magnificent, the sources of its energy twofold. One is the very nature of the musical gesture: the commanding unisons, the tremendous leaps, the violins' crackling grace notes, the whirring trill, the dynamic silences. The other is the rhythm, the bold asymmetry of the five-measure phrase, three answered by two. Mozart compresses incredibly: the two C-sharps in the third measure happen too quickly—for our most banally "normal" expectations, that is—and the silence following them is too short. And to answer an already compressed phrase with one that does not rhythmically "rhyme" but is in fact still shorter compounds the effect. The sweet phrases for strings and bassoons that come right after give us properly well-mannered symmetry, and later we shall re-encounter the first idea when it feels like being more expansive, even to the point of stretching beyond four-plus-four normality.

After adventure, the Andante and Minuet come as stuff for relaxation. These movements are courtly, enchanting Salzburg party music in excelsis, and the Danish scholar Jens Peter Larsen perfectly characterized the trio in the Minuet as "a little marvel of unproblematical music-making."

The finale's main theme is a variant of a hit from the *The Abduction from the Seraglio,* which he had been so busy arranging for wind ensemble— the harem-keeper Osmin's *Ha, wie will ich triumphieren.* This movement, about which Mozart said that it should "go as fast as possible," is naughty, conspiratorial, like the *Figaro* Overture. It is full of surprising extensions and diversions, and as effervescent as the Haffners' champagne.

Symphony No. 36 in C major, K.425, *Linz*

Adagio—Allegro spiritoso
Andante
Menuetto
Presto

Mozart composed the *Linz* Symphony in about four days, beginning sometime after his arrival at Linz at 9 a.m. on 30 October 1783 and having it ready for performance by Count Thun's orchestra on 4 November.

Two oboes, two bassoons, two horns, two trumpets, timpani, and strings.

Linz is Austria's third-largest city, an industrial center with busy steel mills and, in spite of some fine buildings, not especially attractive. Hitler grew up in Linz, and Johannes Kepler, the great novelist and storyteller Adalbert Stifter, and Anton Bruckner spent important parts of their working lives there. But the city is most happily renowned for a heady torte of raspberry jam, almond, clove, and cinnamon, and for this symphony of Mozart's.

Wolfgang and Constanze Mozart visited Linz for three weeks in the fall of 1783 as guests of Count Johann Thun-Hohenstein, an old friend of the Mozart family. The young couple had gone from Vienna to Salzburg to present Constanze to Leopold Mozart in the hopes of reconciling that most difficult and possessive fussbudget of a father to what he was convinced was a precipitate and unwise marriage. Leopold, however, was resistant, the visit was awkward, and the couple, unhappy about the storm clouds *chez* Papa, were relieved to get away.[2]

When the Mozarts arrived at Linz on their way home after stops in Vöcklaburg, Lambach (where Mozart was just in time to accompany the *Agnus Dei* at Mass), and Ebelsberg, they were met at the city gates by a servant of the Thun household to make sure they would not stop at an inn but go instead to the family *palais* in Minorite Square. It was 30 October, and the next day, Mozart wrote to his father about learning that Count Thun had already scheduled a concert for the following Tuesday, 4 November, and that he was evidently expected to perform a symphony that evening. He had no symphony with him, and so he would have to "work on one at head-over-heels speed." By the way, Franz Xaver Niemetschek, Mozart's biographer and tutor of his son Carl, tells us that the count's orchestra was "first-rate."

It is a grandly inventive work that Mozart made in such a hurry: one gets the sense of an enormous advance in ambition and skill since the *Haffner* Symphony of the previous year. For the first time, Mozart begins a symphony with a slow introduction, declamatory at the outset, then yielding and full of pathos. Cannily it creates suspense, which is dissolved with the entry into the energetic and festive Allegro spiritoso. How delightful the first theme is, with those slow notes that so carefully fail to prepare us for the sudden rush of the third and fourth bars. That first phrase, four

[2] Only when Wolfgang and Constanze got home did they learn that their infant son Raimund Leopold, whom they had left in Vienna in the charge of a wet-nurse, had died about three weeks after their departure after bouts of severe intestinal cramps.

bars long, is answered by one of six bars; this in turn is followed by a variant of the opening phrase, *forte,* with trumpets and drums, and extended to seven measures.

Nothing is ordinary here, and even the seeming formalities that drive the music into the next key, G major, are full of subversive detail. A particularly beautiful one is a brief passage, beginning with violins alone, where Mozart again plays with our sense of time by slowing the music down to half-notes. He continues in this spirit. No sooner, for example, has he landed in G than he leaves it in favor of a stern outburst in E minor. Here, in fact, the music is in such a hurry that the E-minor eruption doesn't even wait for the beginning of a new bar, instead, exploding right into the middle of the one where the G-major landing was accomplished. The strings make a gentle attempt to correct this indiscretion, but it is a few more measures before G major "takes" for sure. A few E-flats momentarily darken the exuberant progress to the end of the exposition.

A nicely arched phrase for violins leads back to the beginning of the Allegro and, the second time we come to it, directly into A minor and the start of the development. It is the violins' bridge phrase, itself derived from an earlier passage in the course of the transition to G major, that first occupies Mozart. Shadows fall in a wonderful page of chromatic woodwind harmony with sighs for the violins. Then, almost before we know it, Mozart has brought us back to C major and into the recapitulation. Only in its regularity, and that of the finale's recapitulation, are we reminded of the daunting deadline Mozart faced. Afterwards, he gives us the surprise of a fairly extended coda that corresponds to the first phase of the development.

Some editions give a marking of Poco adagio for the second movement. That is incorrect, though not altogether wrong in spirit. This Andante, touched by the 6/8 lilt of a siciliano, is in F major, but yearns always for minor-mode harmonies. Unusual is the presence of trumpets and drums, most often silent in the not necessarily so slow "slow movements" of classical symphonies. It seems likely that it was from this Andante that Beethoven got the idea for using trumpets and drums so effectively in the second movement of his Symphony No. 1, and the Mozart scholar Neal Zaslaw suggests that here could be the inspiration for the dramatic trumpet-and-drum interventions in the great Largo of Haydn's Symphony No. 88 (probably 1787).

The development, like the whole movement, begins with strings alone, and in C major, where the exposition ended. Quickly, though, it turns to C minor and from there to even darker F minor. At the same time, the texture becomes startlingly severe. Mozart softens the music by going into A-flat major for a moment, then makes his way back to F major.

It is interesting that here, just as he had done in the first movement, he uses a fragment of chromatic scale to carry him into the recapitulation, and he will do so again in the finale. In the recapitulation itself, he embellishes the melody almost as though he were the soloist in a concerto or the singer of an aria. There is no coda: the music comes to a punctual close with the last measures of the recapitulation.

The Minuet is courtly; the trio, which is *piano* all the way through, demurely rustic. The scoring in the trio, for oboe an octave above the violins and bassoon an octave below (sometimes in canon, sometimes a sixth below), is delicious.

The finale brings back the first movement's exuberance, but in heightened form: the first page alone contains three distinct ideas. Similarly, there is not one "closing theme" but a whole bubbling and irresistible series of them. Nor is there any stinginess with themes en route, and there is even room for one of the most beautiful of his darkening clouds. This is Mozart at his most dazzlingly prodigal. The development begins with an ordinary G-major chord, made not at all ordinary by being laid out as a descending zigzag—like lightning in slow motion. This zigzag proves to be a powerful motor indeed as first violins, cellos, bassoon, oboe, and violas (in a most striking touch of color) explore it by turns. The recapitulation proceeds as expected, which is to say, delightfully. There is no coda.

Symphony No. 38 in D major, K.504, *Prague*

Adagio—Allegro
Andante
Finale: Presto

Mozart entered this symphony into his catalogue on 6 December 1786 and first conducted it in Prague on 19 January 1787.

Two flutes, two oboes, two bassoons, two horns, two trumpets, timpani, and strings.

As Vienna began to lose interest in Mozart in the middle 1780s, Prague adopted him. *Le nozze di Figaro* was staged there on 10 December 1786, seven months after its premiere in Vienna, and so great was its triumph that the Prague musical community invited Mozart to attend and conduct some of the performances as well as to give some concerts. He arrived on 11 January 1787 in the company of his wife and sister-in-law, amazed and touched by the universal *Figaro* mania: everyone, he reported, was "writing about it, talking about it, humming it, whistling it, and dancing it." For Prague, Mozart played his newest piano concerto, the magnificent C major, K.503, and at a Grand Musical Academy on 19 January, he offered them his newest symphony. On the basis of paper studies, the English musicologist Alan Tyson has presented the idea, admittedly speculative, that Mozart had originally intended to perform his *Paris* Symphony, then decided to write a new finale for it, and finally added new first and second movements to that finale. As an encore, he improvised at the piano one dozen variations on *Non più andrai* from *Figaro*—this after half an hour's free extemporization at the keyboard! When he returned to Vienna in February, it was with a commission for a new opera: that contract was met with *Don Giovanni*, first staged in Prague that October.

"My orchestra is in Prague," Mozart wrote to the musicians who had invited him, "and my Prague people understand me." When the news of his death reached them, in five days they prepared a chorus of 120 voices to sing a Requiem, all the bells in the city were set to ringing, and people stood by the hundreds in the bitter December cold because the cathedral could not hold them all. Reporting on an all-Mozart concert three years later, a Prague journalist wrote that it was

> easy to imagine how full the hall was if one knows Prague's artistic sense and its love for Mozart. . . . This evening was fittingly and admirably devoted to an act of homage to merit and genius. It was a rewarding feast for sensitive hearts and a small tribute to the inexpressible delight that Mozart's divine tones often drew from us. . . . It is as though Mozart had composed especially for Bohemia. Nowhere was his music better understood and executed than in Prague, and even out in the country it is universally popular.[3]

The *Prague* is one of three Mozart symphonies to begin with a slow introduction, the others being the *Linz* Symphony of 1783 and No. 39 of 1788.[4] Mozart begins with gestures of utmost formality, but it becomes evident at once that these are points of reference against which to project an astonishing series of diversions and extensions. The music moves con-

---

[3] O. E. Deutsch, *Mozart: A Documentary Biography* (Stanford: Standford University Press, 1965).
[4] The work that is confusingly listed as Mozart's Symphony No. 37, K.444, is actually a symphony by Michael Haydn with a slow introduction by Mozart. Before the author of everything after the introduction was identified, this symphony was much admired. It is still an attractive piece.

tinually forward, eschewing repose, and when we think that a firm cadence is inevitable—and we are now about to enter the sixteenth measure of a very slow tempo—Mozart stops our breath with a dramatic turn into minor. This D minor, with drums and pungently flavorful low trumpets, points back to the piano concerto in that key, K.466, and ahead to *Don Giovanni.* Beethoven studied all this carefully when he came to write his Symphony No. 2.

Having reached that D-minor harmony with all its sense of foreboding, Mozart gives us first a powerful rising sequence, then music of gradual, tensely anticipatory subsidence. Our attention thus captured, the Allegro can begin quietly, subtly off-center in its harmony, and against an accompaniment of taut syncopations. It is a beginning that strikingly sets off the festive trumpet-and-drum music to come. When a new theme arrives, it is one of ideal freshness and charm. Yet neither the drama of the Adagio nor the urgent elegance of the Allegro prepares us for the coming together of learning and fire that produces the densely polyphonic, irresistibly energetic development. This, by the way, is one of the few passages for which Mozart left elaborate sketches. The extraordinary spirit of these pages also informs the recapitulation and the blazing coda.

If we pay but casual attention to how the Andante begins, we could take it to be simply another instance of exquisite Mozartian grace. Listen, however, to the specific coloration with which Mozart has here invested the familiar gestures—listen, that is, to the effect produced by the gently unyielding bass and to the poignant chromatic embellishment when the first phrase is repeated—and you quickly get the idea that nothing is going to be ordinary. Strange shadows on the harmonies, the quiet force behind the contrapuntal imitations, the sighs in the closing melody—all these contribute to what caused Mozart's biographer Alfred Einstein to exclaim, "What a deepening of the concept of Andante is here!"[5]

Here is another symphony without minuet; rather, Mozart forges straight ahead into one of his most miraculous finales, a movement that has strength without heaviness, crackling energy of rhythm, a challenge to the most virtuosic of orchestras, and, as always, grace. We think of Mozart's last three symphonies as a special group. If, however, we think not about chronology, but about quality, we shall hear that the attainment of miracle in the genre is reached first, and no less, in the *Prague.*

---

[5] Alan Tyson, the English expert on Mozart manuscripts, suggests that the ten-bar G-major fragment, K.504a, was Mozart's first stab at a middle movement for this symphony.

The Last Three Symphonies

The very perfection of Mozart's last three symphonies, No. 39 in E-flat, the great G-minor, and the *Jupiter*, is miraculous, and the more so given how quickly they were composed. No less impressive is their diversity, and the clarity with which, in three quite different directions, they define the possibilities of Mozart's art. Eric Blom puts it thus: "It is as though the same man had written Shakespeare's *Twelfth Night*, Racine's *Phèdre*, and Goethe's *Iphigenie* within whatever period may be equivalent for the rapid execution of three plays as compared to three symphonies."

In view of how much Mozart's compositions are as a rule bound to particular occasions, commissions, or concerts, another wonder is that these symphonies exist at all. They were completed respectively on 26 June, 25 July, and 10 August 1788. By then Mozart's public career had begun to go badly. There had been a time when he could report, as he did in a letter to his father on 3 March 1784, that he had had twenty-two concerts in thirty-eight days: "I don't think that in this way I can possibly get out of practice." A few weeks later he wrote that for his own series of concerts he had a bigger subscription list than two other performers put together.

Not many years later all this had changed. *Figaro*, new in 1786, was popular in Vienna, but not more so than other operas by lesser composers, and certainly not sufficiently to buoy up Mozart's fortunes for long. *Don Giovanni*, first given in Vienna on 7 May 1788, failed to repeat the enormous success it had enjoyed in Prague, and the performance on 15 December of that year was the last one in the capital in the composer's lifetime. By then, Mozart was in catastrophic financial straits. In June 1788, he wrote the first of the agonizing letters in which he entreated his brother Mason, Michael Puchberg, for help. He mentions a series of concerts about to begin at the Casino "next week" and encloses a pair of tickets. There is no evidence in newspapers or anywhere else that these concerts ever took place: this time, perhaps, the subscribers were too few. Nor did Mozart give other concerts of his own in Vienna after that.

It seems reasonable to connect Mozart's last three symphonies with the projected Casino concerts. Little is known about their early history. Orchestra parts for them were printed by Johann André in Offenbach, Hesse, two years after Mozart's death, but various libraries have also yielded manuscript copies, some of which certainly date to the composer's lifetime. The G-minor Symphony was played in its revised version with added clarinets in April 1791, but whether Mozart ever heard the *Jupiter* or the E-flat we do not know.

Symphony No. 39 in E-flat major, K.543

Adagio—Allegro
Andante con moto
Menuetto: Allegretto
Finale: Allegro

The Symphony No. 39 is dated 26 June 1788. Nothing is known about its early performance history.

Flute, two clarinets, two bassoons, two horns, two trumpets, timpani, and strings.

Mozart begins the Symphony in E-flat with an imposing slow introduction. This in itself is worthy of comment, for slow introductions are rare in his work: the only other instances are the *Linz* Symphony of 1783 and the *Prague* Symphony of 1786 (and the introduction he contributed to a symphony by Michael Haydn). The *Linz* introduction is superb, declamatory at first, then yielding and full of pathos, and it cannily creates suspense before the arrival of the Allegro. With the *Prague* Symphony, Mozart rises to another level of ambition and accomplishment. In that Adagio, the details are more fanciful, and more richly and subtly suggestive of the music to come; above all, Mozart commands now a new and vast sense of scale. This is the music of a man ready to write the great exordium to *Don Giovanni.*

The introduction to the E-flat Symphony again draws on that fund of drama, suggestion, and a feeling for splendor. It is also the most sumptuous-sounding chapter to be found in any of his symphonies. The musical gestures themselves are monuments of formality and regularity, but at the same time, the harmonies grow darker, syncopations trouble the rhythmic picture, the scale passages begin to take odd turns, the dotted rhythms become obsessive and mount to dissonance as biting as any Mozart ever conceived. The last very slow notes for flute, violins, and bassoons (with cellos and basses beginning to imitate at the distance of one bar) propose mysteries unimaginably far from the grandly untroubled opening measures.

In the Allegro, whose softly forward-moving start does not lead us to expect the outbursts of fierce energy soon to come, Mozart realizes much of what he has suggested in the Adagio, while the prevalence of brilliant violin scales provides an explicit link between the two sections of the movement.

One of my recollections from my days of conservatory teaching is that most of my students seemed at an early age to have been inoculated with the idea that Haydn and Mozart invariably composed in nicely even four- and eight-measure phrases, while only the Romantics, encouraged by Bee- thoven, indulged in such licentious pleasures as five-bar units. (Had they all slept with copies of Robert Haven Schauffler's *Beethoven: The Man Who Freed Music* under their pillows?)

I used to try to disabuse them of this notion by having them listen and breathe to the Andante of Mozart's C-major Piano Concerto, K.467, then not yet known as the *Elvira Madigan,* and to the second theme of the first movement of this E-flat major symphony. The concerto theme, though its unfolding is wondrously natural, also has something a bit subversive about it, perhaps because of its length, but the example from this sym- phony was always particularly interesting because it seems so "normal," so perfect an example of classical equipoise, that one would really like to use it to demonstrate what an ideally balanced Mozartian phrase sounds like. But five bars it is. And ideally balanced it is as well—who says you can't achieve perfect balance by putting two measures in one pan of the scales and three in the other?

The second movement, too, begins in deceptive charm and inno- cence. That is to say, the charm and the innocence are real, but they are by no means all that Mozart gives us here. The final cadence of the long opening melody is strangely shadowed, and almost immediately an outburst in the minor mode suggests the presence of dark places to be explored. Here, too, dotted rhythms are insistently present, and the tension they build is heightened by the firm processions of slow and steady notes in the wind instruments and by the distance of Mozart's harmonic voyages.

The magnificently sturdy Minuet and its lyric trio are an oasis. Here, too, the sound of wind instruments is prominent, both in the band-style accompaniments in the minuet itself and in the trio's melting clarinet solo.

The Finale, on the other hand, with its syncopations, its probing of distant harmonies, its rowdy basses, its silences, is—from that first extrava- gantly long upbeat to the epigrammatic ending—Mozart at his most wildly and wittily inventive.

Symphony No. 40 in G minor, K.550

> *Molto allegro*
> *Andante*
> *Menuetto: Allegretto*
> *Allegro assai*

Mozart entered this symphony into his own catalogue on 25 July 1788. This date refers to Mozart's original version; the one most often heard, which adds a pair of clarinets, was probably made for concerts in Vienna on 16 and 17 April 1791. The conductor on that occasion was the composer Antonio Salieri, who, ironically, is most apt to be remembered today in connection with the libel that he poisoned Mozart.

Flute, two oboes, two clarinets, two bassoons, two horns, and strings. As noted above, the original version has no clarinets.

Which version? Almost always nowadays the answer is "with clarinets." Lazily, I had assumed that this had been true ever since 1791—that the clarinet version had in effect immediately supplanted the earlier one—until, leafing through some old Boston Symphony program books, I found this in William F. Apthorp's notes for the concerts of 16-17 March 1894:

> Johannes Brahms has in his possession a score of this symphony, in the composer's autograph, with added parts for two clarinets; but he has steadily refused to let this score go out of his hands. And, such is the completeness and perfection of the original score, in its now universally known shape, that no one can well imagine what Mozart could have found for a pair of clarinets to say in the work that had not already been said by the other instruments.[6]

Apthorp's information was not quite up-to-date. He was right about Brahms's ownership of the autograph—now in the collection of the Society of Friends of Music in Vienna, to whom he bequeathed it—but the clarinet version had in fact been published in 1882, though with considerable inaccuracies, as part of Breitkopf & Härtel's collected Mozart edition. As for

[6] Boston Symphony Orchestra program book, 16–17 March 1894.

the answer to Apthorp's implied question, Mozart redistributed rather than added material, and accommodating the clarinets involved extensive re-casting of the oboe parts. He did not write out a whole new score, but only a nine-page supplement with the new oboe and clarinet lines. It caused editors a lot of trouble, and it was only in 1930, with the appearance of the Eulenburg miniature score edited by Theodor Kroyer, that all the details were straightened out.

The first version has more bite and it is a pity for it to be neglected as much as it now is.[7] The revised version, on the other hand, has a special appeal in that the clarinet is so much the Mozartian instrument par excellence: think of the Concerto, the Quintet, the Trio with viola and piano, all written for Mozart's friend Anton Stadler; of the wind serenades, of the basset horns in the Requiem, of Donna Anna's *Non mi dir*, the farewell trio in *Così fan tutte*, the stirrings of Tamino's heart in *The Magic Flute*'s portrait aria, not to forget the extraordinary solos (also for Stadler) in *La clemenza di Tito*. And it is the clarinet version that comes closer to the condition described by Charles Rosen in *The Classical Style*:

> In all of Mozart's supreme expressions of suffering and terror—the G-minor Symphony, *Don Giovanni*, the G-minor Quintet, Pamina's aria in *Die Zauberflöte*—there is something shockingly voluptuous. Nor does this detract from its power or effectiveness: the grief and the sensuality strengthen each other, and end by becoming indivisible, indistinguishable one from the other. . . . In his corruption of sentimental values, Mozart is a subversive artist. It is with some surprise that one remembers how rarely the clarinet appears in the symphonies: clarinets are part of the original design only in the *Paris* and in No. 39 in E-flat, while they were afterthoughts in the *Haffner* as well as in the G minor.[8]

The great Stadler was almost certainly the inspiration for the revision of the G-minor Symphony, for we know that he and his younger brother Johann took part in Salieri's concerts at the Burgtheater in April 1791: in any event, from what we know of Mozart's work habits, we can be sure that he would not have put himself to the trouble of the revision except with a specific performance in view. (This was a pair of benefit concerts for widows and orphans; besides the Mozart symphony that opened the program, the music consisted of excerpts from Giovanni Paisiello's opera

---

[7] Wilhelm Furtwängler championed it, and his extraordinary recording with the Vienna Philharmonic is very much worth knowing, not just for its sonority but also for its "authentic" tempi—surprising, perhaps, from a "Romantic" conductor who died in 1954 and hadn't the slightest interest in questions of historical performing practice.

[8] Charles Rosen, *The Classic Style* (New York: Viking, 1971).

Fedra.) If Mozart was present at one of those concerts, it would have been his last opportunity to hear one of his symphonies. That he had heard the G-minor Symphony before (or, for that matter, that he had heard either of its companion pieces, the E-flat and the *Jupiter*) is doubtful.

Robert Schumann surprises us by speaking of the G-minor Symphony's "weightless, Hellenic grace." At the other extreme, some conductors surprise us—to be polite about it—by converting the first movement into a pathetic Andante. But what the score suggests above all is urgency, something that at once distinguishes the symphony from the other members of Mozart's G-minor family: the Viola Quintet, K.516; Pamina's aria in *The Magic Flute*; and even the precocious and impressive Symphony No. 25 of 1773.[9]

The violas' breathless accompaniment that, for a second or two, precedes the melody—and how astonished the first audience must have been by such a beginning, an accompaniment only, and *piano*—immediately establishes a sense of tremendous urgency. This is reinforced by the melody itself, upbeat leading to upbeat leading to upbeat. We know, too, that Mozart altered the tempo marking from "Allegro assai" to "Molto allegro," which in eighteenth-century usage is a change toward the faster.

The subtle voicing for instruments is a wonder in itself: the transparency Mozart achieves by never duplicating notes in the melody with notes in the accompaniment; the new atmosphere that is generated when the cellos and basses first play sustained rather than detached notes; the stretching of horizons when he first brings in the woodwinds; the discreet supporting chords of oboes and bassoons that make the repetition of the first melody not just a repetition but a continuation and a development. And all this is just the first half-minute. The harmony in these opening pages is simple, the more effectively to prepare the violent dislocations to come.

A contrasting theme in B-flat major is, by comparison, all pathos. It, too, is beautifully scored in subtle dialogue between strings and woodwinds. It is momentarily disturbed by fever, then the exposition charges energetically to its conclusion. A single brusque chord—the dominant of G minor, but in its most unusual distribution—sends the music back to the beginning. When, after a second trip through the exposition, we arrive at the same place again, two more short chords follow this unsettling dominant. The first of these chords is actually the most logical one possible, namely the tonic, a good, firm chord of G minor. But before we have a chance to feel grounded, Mozart throws a second chord at us. This one is more

[9]Pamina's aria is traditionally taken at a tempo absurdly slow for its figurations, musical character, and for Mozart's direction of "andante."

disconcerting in harmonic color, and the effect is enhanced—or exacerbated—by the fact that it comes half a bar sooner than we expect. It is as
though Mozart had suddenly doubled the speed.

Flute, oboe, and bassoon pick up on one of that ambiguous chord's
possible meanings and spin us into a very remote place indeed, F-sharp
minor. There the movement seems to start over, as though from the beginning, though just seconds later it is clear that urgent intensifications are
on the agenda. Mozart whirls the opening theme across great harmonic
spaces, focusing more and more closely on its first three notes. The harmony becomes more chromatic and more anguished until a long descent—
flute in dialogue with clarinets (oboes in the original)—sends us into the
recapitulation. This time the second theme is in dark G minor, and the
coda rises to still hotter temperatures and deeper pathos.

The Andante is both somber and sensual, another, if milder, instance
of that combination of suffering with voluptuousness of which Rosen
speaks. The opening music is rich and strange. Violas begin with an idea
in repeated notes, but, as second violins and then first violins join them
in imitation at successively higher pitches, what we hear is not so much a
theme as a texture. Just as we accept this unexpected idea, the response to
these opening measures turns out to be sweet and graceful melody. When,
after the completion of the first eight-measure phrase, the repeated-note
idea begins again, this time in cellos and basses, the first violins add a
soaring countermelody whose course is completely unpredictable. It is clear
that, for all the drastic change of character wrought by the difference in
tempo, Mozart continues—more quietly—to explore the first movement's
world of aching chromatic harmony. For the little descending two-note
figures that are such prominent features here, the eighteenth century had
a technical term, *Seufzer*, or sighs.

Polyphony, powerfully used in the first movement, comes to the fore
again in the ruggedly stern Minuet, in which Mozart comes close to the
corresponding movement in Haydn's Symphony No. 39, also in G minor.
Mozart's sense of harmonic strategy also creates the pathos of the Minuet's
pastoral trio, where, for the only time in this symphony, the composer
settles in G major (the trio being, as well, the only part of the symphony
that he did not rescore).

The finale brings the most explosive music Mozart ever wrote: those
eight measures of rude octaves and frozen silences that launch the development.[10] The context for this disruption, though, is music more consistently

---

[10] The British critic Hans Keller showed how Mozart, to counter the centrifugal tendency of these
wild measures, has entirely saturated the passage with the presentation in straightforward form, in
retrograde, in inversion, and in retrograde inversion, of a single three-note figure.

regular in rhythm than any we have heard in the first two movements and in the main part of the Minuet. It is the normality of most of the finale and the sense of direct momentum it generates that most markedly establish the difference between this movement and the first Allegro. The first movement raises questions, posits instabilities, opens abysses. But for all the anguish Mozart still feels and expresses, and even though it is in this movement that he brings his language closest to the breaking point, the finale must at the last be a force that stabilizes, sets solid ground under our feet, seeks to close wounds, and brings the voyager safely—if bruised— into port.

Symphony No. 41 in C major, K.551, *Jupiter*

> *Allegro vivace*
> *Andante cantabile*
> *Menuetto: Allegro*
> *Molto allegro*

Mozart completed the *Jupiter* Symphony, about whose early performance history nothing certain is known, on 10 August 1788.

Flute, two oboes, two bassoons, two horns, two trumpets, timpani, and strings.

A word, first, about the symphony's name. It is not Mozart's, but it is old and perhaps the brainchild of Johann Peter Salomon, the German-born violinist and impresario most famous for having twice enticed Haydn to London. At any rate, in 1829, thirty-eight years after Mozart's death and fourteen after Salomon's, the English composer, organist, and publisher Vincent Novello and his wife Mary visited the Continent and spent a few summer days in Salzburg with Mozart's widow and son. The Novellos kept separate journals, and in Vincent's, on 7 August 1829, we may read the following: "Mozart's son said he considered the Finale to his father's Sinfonia in C—which Salomon christened the *Jupiter*—to be the highest triumph of Instrumental Composition, and I agree with him."

In terms of Eric Blom's literary comparison, the *Jupiter* is *Iphigenie:* noble, at once subtle and grand, "classical." The fences so recklessly torn down in the G-minor *Phèdre* are restored. The opening gestures, with their orderly contrasts and symmetries, are more formal, indeed more formulaic, than anything else in the last three symphonies. But whatever Mozart touches becomes personal utterance. After an impressive drawing up to a halt (that "rattling of dishes at a feast" of which Wagner was wont to complain in eighteenth-century pieces), the opening music reappears; but what was assertive before is now quiet and enriched by softly radiant commentary from the flute and the oboe.

Another cadence of extreme formality, and a new theme appears. This, too, being full of gentle, unobtrusive complexities such as the imitation in the bass of the violin melody or the deft addition to the texture of bassoon and flute, is not so innocent as at first it seems. One tune in this movement is catchier than the rest, more singable, and for good reason: Mozart is quoting one of his own arias, *Un bacio di mano* (A Hand-kiss), K.541, written a couple of months earlier for Francesco Albertarelli, his first Viennese Don Giovanni, to insert in Anfossi's opera *Le gelosie fortunate*.

When he comes to his Andante—the strings are muted now—Mozart becomes more overtly personal, writing music saturated in pathos and offering one rhythmic surprise after another. The destiny of the thirty-second-note serpents that the violins append to the first theme when the basses initially take it over is especially wondrous. The coda, which adds miracles at a point when we can hardly believe more miracles are possible, was an afterthought appended by Mozart on an extra leaf. Haydn, wishing to set an unobtrusive memorial for his beloved friend, alluded to this deeply touching movement in the Adagio of his own Symphony No. 98 in B-flat.

The Minuet, aside from having the proper meter and speed, is not particularly minuet-like. It is fascinating what a wide-ranging category "minuet" is for Mozart. In these last three symphonies alone we have the bandstand high spirits of the one in No. 39, the fiercely serious sense of purpose and drive in the G-minor, and here the perfect embodiment of elegance. The *Jupiter* Minuet is wonderful in a quiet way: here is music that constantly blossoms into *richesses* Mozart carefully leads us not to expect. The trio is, for the most part, an enchanting dialogue of ever so slightly coquettish strings and winds so soberly reticent that they seem able to do no more than make little cadences. There is one *forte* outburst lasting just a few seconds: here the orchestra sounds a new and brief phrase of striking profile. It demands attention, and, although just then it seems to pass without consequence, we shall soon discover why.

That happens the moment the finale begins. Here Mozart picks up the four-note idea that had made such a startlingly forceful appearance in the trio. When first we heard it, it was on an odd harmonic slant; now it is set firmly in C major. This idea is in fact part of the common stock of the eighteenth-century vocabulary; Mozart himself had used it before on several occasions—in Masses, in the Symphony No. 33 in B-flat, in the great E-flat Sonata for Piano and Violin, K.481—and as he is quick to remind us, it lends itself to contrapuntal elaboration.

The music moves at a tempo swifter than any we have yet heard in this symphony. All the themes in this finale are short: they are material to work with more than objects presented for the sake of their intrinsic charm, and Mozart whirls them by us with a fierce energy that is rooted in his dazzling polyphony. Especially when the development gets going, the expressive intensity generated by that energy is exhilarating, shocking, uplifting all at once.

Six years earlier, Mozart had come to know the music of J. S. Bach. Having begun by transcribing and imitating, Mozart has now achieved a complete and easy integration of Baroque polyphony with the galant language that was his most direct inheritance, which he had learned at the knee of Sebastian Bach's youngest son, Johann Christian. In his exuberantly energetic coda, Mozart unfurls a dazzling glory of polyphony to cap, in one of music's truly sublime pages, a movement that is one of the most splendid manifestations of that rich gathering-in we call the classical style.

Carl Nielsen (signature)

Carl Nielsen

Carl August Nielsen was born at Sortelung near Nørre
Lyndelse on Funen, Denmark, on 9 June 1865 and died in
Copenhagen on 3 October 1931. The FS numbers refer to
the chronological catalogue of Nielsen's works by Dan Fog
and Torben Schousboe.

When twenty-second-century musicologists write the history of
the symphony, they may well see the twentieth century as even
more of a glory period for that genre than the nineteenth. This
is to take nothing away from Beethoven and Schubert, Bruckner and
Brahms, Tchaikovsky and Dvořák, but the century that saw the creation of
the symphonies of Elgar, Mahler, Sibelius, Nielsen, Stravinsky, Martinů,
Sessions, Shostakovich—and this is to make only a beginning—offers
something extraordinary in scope, richness, originality, and urgency of expression. The six symphonies of Carl Nielsen make up one of the most
remarkable and, to a constantly growing number of listeners, indispensable
treasures in that great flowering.

Nielsen began his life as a musical explorer when he was three and
found out that logs in the woodpile when struck yielded different pitches
according to their thickness and length. But home provided real instruments as well. His father, a house painter, played the fiddle and cornet to
earn the odd extra penny; his mother sang, and so did most of his eleven
brothers and sisters. Carl was six and making progress on his father's three-
quarter-size violin when he encountered a piano for the first time at an
aunt's house. The great engine enchanted him. On the violin you had to
look for the notes; the piano laid them "in long shining rows before my
very eyes; I could not only hear but see them, and I made one big discovery after another."

At fourteen, after a boyhood spent herding geese, he became a bandsman in the 16th Battalion of the Royal Danish Army, acquiring new instrumental skills. A kindly older musician showed him the central classics of European music: Mozart, Beethoven, and eventually Bach. With these models before him, he began to compose, and in 1884, after examination by Niels W. Gade, the elder statesman of Danish music, he was admitted to the Copenhagen Conservatory as a scholarship student in violin and piano. After two years there, he continued theory studies privately, also getting a general education: in a biographical essay appended to Robert Simpson's *Carl Nielsen: Symphonist,* Torben Meyer lists Nordic and Greek mythology, Plato, Shakespeare, Goethe, and Ludvig Holberg as Nielsen's favorite reading. Meanwhile, he supported himself by playing violin in the orchestra at the Tivoli Gardens, joining the Royal Orchestra in 1889, and for many years yet, Nielsen would depend financially on his playing and conducting, in Copenhagen at the Royal Theater and with the Music Society Orchestra, and later in Gothenburg, Sweden, with that city's Music Society Orchestra (now the Gothenburg Symphony).

The catalogue of his compositions grew: Symphony No. 1 (1892); Symphony No. 2 (*The Four Temperaments*) and the opera *Saul and David* (1901); the comic opera *Maskerade* (1906); Symphony No. 3 (*Espansiva*) and the Violin Concerto (1911); Symphony No. 4 (*The Inextinguishable*) and two major works for piano, the Chaconne and the Theme and Variations (1916); the Suite for Piano (1919); Symphony No. 5 and the Wind Quintet (1922), all interspersed with other chamber and piano music, choral works, and strikingly beautiful songs.

The year 1922 marks the beginning of the breakdown of Nielsen's health. Angina pectoris was diagnosed, and with it came loss of energy, and for a time depression. His great Symphony No. 4 had been a celebration of "the Inextinguishable . . . the elemental Will of Life," those forces of regeneration that would prevail even after "the devastation of the world through fire, flood, volcanoes, etc." Nielsen's last ten years showed that he could live that principle as well as write a great symphony about it.

He returned to life, frail though he now was and wracked by repeated heart attacks, but the music of his later years—Prelude and Theme with Variations for Solo Violin (1923); Symphony No. 6 (1925); the Flute Concerto (1926); Preludio e Presto for Solo Violin, the Clarinet Concerto, and Three Pieces for Piano (all 1928); and *Commotio* for Organ (1931)—proceeds from a mind bolder and more inquisitive than ever. And good musical citizen that he was, he wrote, as needed, cantatas for the centenary of the Copenhagen Polytechnic High School, for the fiftieth anniversaries of the Young Merchants' Education Association and the Danish Cremation Union, and for the opening of the Copenhagen Municipal

Swimming Pool. In the aftermath of the sinking of the *Titanic,* he promptly prepared a wind band paraphrase on *Nearer, My God, to Thee.* He also gave time to educational projects like Piano Music for Young and Old and to patriotic ones like the songbook *Danmark.*

But Nielsen was no Boy Scout of music. His works from the 1920s can be full of rage (the gun battle of the timpani in *The Inextinguishable* is an anticipation of this), and their intent is often to be profoundly disturbing: try, for example, his last large-scale composition, the visionary and altogether astounding *Commotio.* As Robert Simpson put it, "Nielsen is one of those rare individuals who know the shortest route to the truth." His prose writings, too, fascinatingly inject an alarming measure of resentment and anger into the folksy friendliness. He really ought to have written at least a *Sinfonia irritabile;* the *Choleric* movement in his *Four Temperaments* hardly does justice to his potential in this direction.

In 1931 Nielsen took on the extra burden of the directorship of the Copenhagen Conservatory. That fall a new production of *Maskerade* was mounted at the Royal Theater. At a rehearsal, impatient with a stagehand's slowness, Nielsen climbed a rope into the flies to set right some matter or other. Walking home with the conductor Egisto Tango, he nearly collapsed in exhaustion. He managed to get to the performance, but felt so ill that he had to leave during Act 2. A week later he died, an honored figure at home—his funeral was a great public event, like Verdi's—but still only a name to most musicians abroad.

Nielsen's reputation outside Denmark dates from the 1950s, a result of the first international tours of the Danish State Radio Symphony and of Danish conductors, notably Erik Tuxen. The publication in 1952 of Robert Simpson's *Carl Nielsen: Symphonist* was of immense importance, and I am deeply indebted to it. Not least, Nielsen's belated conquest was a product of the long-playing record.

Finally, a word on keys, a subject that comes up a lot in my essays on Nielsen's symphonies. Contrary to classic procedure from Haydn to Shostakovich, Nielsen often ends a symphony in a key different from the one where it began. (His contemporary Gustav Mahler often does that, too, but to different purpose and with different effect.) For Nielsen, the acquisition or conquest of the final key is the crux of the symphonic drama. Simpson points to this as an essential feature of Nielsen's style and gives it the name "progressive tonality." Nielsen knew perfectly well that most listeners could not "follow" a harmonic structure in the sense of being able to say, "Ah, this is E major" or "What a neat modulation to the flat submediant"—in other words, to put names to their experience. On the other hand, he also knew that listeners can and do respond to the events themselves, to unexpected juxtapositions, to departures and homecomings. That faculty, that unconscious but acute memory, is what Nielsen addresses in his symphonic dramas—which of course, in the broadest sense, makes him no different from the other masters in the tonal tradition.

The Inextinguishable (Symphony No. 4), Opus 29, FS76

> *Allegro*
> *Poco allegretto*
> *Poco adagio quasi andante*
> *Allegro*

Nielsen began to sketch his Symphony No. 4 in 1914 and completed the score on 14 January 1916. He conducted the first performance with the orchestra of the Copenhagen Music Society in Odd Fellows Hall, Copenhagen, on 1 February 1916.

Three flutes (one doubling piccolo), three oboes, three clarinets, three bassoons, four horns, three trumpets, three trombones, tuba, timpani (two sets and two players stationed opposite each other), and strings.

Inextinguishable is not—like *Military, Unfinished, Scotch, Pathétique,* or *Gothic*—an adjective qualifying Symphony. Rather, *Det uudslukkelige,* as the neuter definite article makes clear, is an abstract noun. A prefatory note in the score is an attempt at an explanation:

> Under this title the composer has endeavored to indicate in one word what music alone is capable of expressing to the full: *The Elemental Will of Life.* Music *is* Life and, like it, is inextinguishable. The title given by the composer to this musical work might therefore seem superfluous; the composer, however, has employed the word in order to underline the strictly musical character of his task. It is not a program, only a suggestion as to the way into this, music's own territory.[1]

Nielsen was more lucid in a letter written four years after he had completed the score:

---

[1] Carl Nielsen, *The Inextinguishable* (Symphony No. 4) (Copenhagen: Hansen, no date).

The title *The Inextinguishable* is not a program but a pointer to the proper domain of music. It is meant to express the appearance of the most elementary forces among human beings, animals, and even plants. We can say: in case all the world were to be devastated by fire, flood, volcanoes, etc., and all things were destroyed and dead, then nature would still begin to breed new life again, begin to push forward again with all the fine and strong forces inherent in matter. Soon the plants would begin to multiply, the breeding and screaming of birds would be seen and heard, the aspiration and yearning of human beings would be felt. These forces, which are "inextinguishable," are what I have tried to present.[2]

These words—and the music they offer to elucidate—reflect ideas that Nielsen carried with him and that nourished him all his life, ideas that must have begun to form when, as a little boy on the island of Fyn, he watched with astonishing powers of observation the life of the fields and woods and ponds, ideas reinforced by his constant reading in Greek and Norse mythology when he was a student in Copenhagen.

In the summer of 1914, right before Europe did its best to destroy itself and put Nielsen's idea of regeneration to the test, the composer, having just freed himself from conducting at the Royal Theater, tackled the problem of translating his vision of "The Inextinguishable" into music. One of the first things he seems to have known about his new composition is that it would proceed without a break. He was excited by Liszt's Piano Sonata in B minor, whose single movement encompasses the contrasts and the rhetorical-expressive progress of a multi-movement work, and like Liszt, he was deeply interested in questioning traditional formal procedures.[3] Nielsen came to know that most remarkable carrying forward of Liszt's plan, Arnold Schoenberg's Chamber Symphony of 1906, only late in life. He disliked Schoenberg's style, but he found such music as he knew of the Second Viennese School challenging and provocative.

On 24 July 1914, Nielsen wrote to a friend that he was "well under way with a new large-scale orchestral work, a sort of symphony in one movement, which is meant to represent all that we feel and think about life in the most fundamental sense of the word, that is, all that has the will to live and to move." What Nielsen finally produced was a work that sounds perhaps more like a four-movement symphony with no breaks. There are four distinct tempo areas that are even quite traditionally ordered as an allegro, an intermezzo in medium tempo, a slow movement, and an allegro finale. One of the first movement's themes, however, has a

[2] Quoted in Robert Simpson, *Carl Nielsen, Symphonist* (New York: Taplinger, 1979).
[3] Liszt had stimulating models in Schubert, notably the *Wanderer* Fantasy, and the late Beethoven quartets and sonatas.

significant role to play later in the work; more crucially, from the point of view of harmonic architecture, the symphonic argument is one continuous whole from beginning to end.

The symphony begins with woodwinds and strings (plus an initial blast of brass to reinforce the explosive opening). The two lines, the winds and the strings, sound independent, though they are in fact different views of the same matter. Part of the difference is in harmonic bias, the winds leaning toward D minor (acknowledged by the key signature as the official key at this point), the strings tending more toward C. Syncopation, the unexpected distribution of long notes and short, and sheer speed all convey a sense of wild energy, and the way the timpani gleefully join in whenever the winds play the unstable interval of E-flat/A contributes to the feeling that this is music reluctant to settle. It does, however, calm down to the point where clarinets in thirds, like ladies in Romantic opera, sing a long, serene, smoothly molded melody. It is a spacious paragraph, whose gentle dying away is interrupted by a cross comment from the violas. The unruffled clarinets offer to recommence their song, but almost the whole orchestra breaks in with a rambunctious variant. This makes a dramatic introduction of a new key, E major, and it is in fact the place of this key that will become the most passionately argued issue in the symphony.

A long development and an extraordinarily compressed recapitulation (ending in E) subside into music rather in the manner of those intermezzi, neither fast nor slow, that Brahms often put in place of a scherzo. Nielsen's Poco allegretto, charmingly antiquated in manner, dominated by woodwinds and opening up yet another harmonic area (G major), provides stillness after the aggressively eventful first movement.

This intermezzo is, however, soon over, and all the violins—which Nielsen of course imagined spread all across the front of the stage rather than with the seconds bunched behind the firsts on the left—sparely accompanied by pizzicato strings and drums, begin the slow movement with a melody of great breadth and intensity. Violas and cellos, entering to tremendous effect at a pitch higher than that of the violins, continue the thought until a single violin, delicately supported by just a few strings and woodwinds, suggests a new idea, one of loveliest serenity (and in E). The woodwinds, however, clamor for more action, and the ensuing fugued discussion leads to the most sonorous climax so far. Fragments of both themes move through the orchestra, some stated with urgency, some reticently. Violins disport themselves in grand preparatory gestures, and after a suspenseful pause the new Allegro begins.

The theme that opens this new section is the sort that wants to run freely, but everywhere it meets with interference. There are rhythmic disruptions, tense dissonances, and suddenly a ferocious onslaught from both timpanists. As the first timpanist did at the beginning of the symphony, both drummers now play tritones (F/B and D-flat/G), those unstable, unstabilizing intervals once thought of by theorists as *diabolus in musica*. You deal with the devil by showing him a cross, and you exorcise his interval with perfect fourths and fifths. Nielsen marks his victory "glorioso"; however, the victory is only provisional, because we are still in A major. There is a long diminuendo, a device Nielsen often uses to effect transitions, and the music in fact shoots right past its E-major goal to B major. That sets off a renewed attack on the part of the drums, who now mark the chord of D minor, the key of the symphony's tumultuous opening. The piccolo, the clarinets, and all the strings scream in protest. What they scream is B, over and over. This is not only the tonic of the key the drums have tried to force them to abandon; it is also the dominant of E, and therefore the most powerful springboard from which to reach that key. The high strings and woodwinds gain support from the brass, who not only cast a vote on the issue of key but also intone the beginning of a familiar melody. It is the clarinets-in-thirds theme from the first movement. The rest of the orchestra quickly catches on, and the music drives home to its destination, with E major firmly achieved and with the drums joining in the celebration of The Inextinguishable.

Symphony No. 5, Opus 50, FS97

> *Tempo giusto—Adagio non troppo*
> *Allegro—Presto—Andante un poco tranquillo—Allegro*

Nielsen began work on the Fifth Symphony in February 1921, completed the score on 15 January 1922, and conducted the first performance in Copenhagen just a few days later on 24 January. The dedication is to the composer's friends Vera and Carl Johan Michaelsen.

Two flutes and piccolo, two oboes, two clarinets, two bassoons, four horns, three trumpets, three trombones, bass tuba, timpani, cymbals, triangle, snare drum, tambourine, celesta, and strings.

Nielsen's Second, Third, and Fourth symphonies have titles; Nielsen also thought of one for the Sixth, but decided against using it. That the Fifth does not is surprising, given the drama that takes place in it. There are two movements, each divided into distinct, sharply characterized sections. The first begins in tempo giusto, a direction hardly seen since Handel's day (except, surprisingly, in a couple of Chopin's waltzes and later, perhaps less surprisingly, in Stravinsky's *Dumbarton Oaks* Concerto). "The right tempo" is as good a translation as any, meaning "Look at the score and if you're any kind of musician you'll see what the tempo is."[4] Here Nielsen makes it easy by adding a metronome mark, 100 to the quarter-note.

Violas are stuck on C and A. A certain obsessive quality, a sense of being, stuck to certain ideas is characteristic of this symphony. Winds wander about in pairs, strings introduce a more sinuously winding theme, and in the middle of all that, a snare drum insists, though in *pianissimo* at first, on a simple but distinctive rhythmic figure. ("Insists" seems about right to describe its fifty-seven-fold statement of that figure.) Meanwhile, the lower strings and the timpani are equally committed to a manic repetition of two notes, F and D. The celesta becomes involved with its own preoccupation with the note D and soon infects others.

It is a threatening and uneasy sort of music, and almost nothing about it is scarier than the fact that it just goes away, its place taken by a lusciously scored, expressive Adagio. A sudden timpani roll is a warning signal. The obsessed snare drummer returns, charged now by Nielsen with improvising in a manner as though determined at all costs to break up the performance. It takes the full, ferocious force of the orchestra to silence him, but even in the epilogue to this movement, with the still small voice of the clarinet heard across a motionless G-major chord in horns and strings, the remembrance of the threat stays with us. What Nielsen has imagined and portrayed here is a profoundly frightening vision of madness and of the invasion of order by disorder.

Nielsen's music, beginning with the Fourth Symphony, is full of conversations, if that is the word, or confrontations, of the kind initiated here by the snare drum. These can be comic, like the irascible dialogue of clarinet and bassoon in one of the variations in the Wind Quintet or the trombone's repeated offers to turn the Flute Concerto into a double concerto; menacing, like the drumming here and the timpani onslaughts in the Fourth Symphony; or ambiguous, often disturbingly so, like the insistent snare drum in the Clarinet Concerto or the interventions of the clownish and by no means harmless trombone in the Symphony No. 6.

B major is the key into which Nielsen leaps to open his second move-

---

[4] In her diaries, Cosima Wagner records a visit from an almost pathologically timid, indecisive composer. After his departure, Wagner remarked that if this man ever wrote a symphony, surely the tempo mark would be "tempo giusto, ma non troppo."

ment, and a long and bold leap it is after the F-to-G voyage of the first. Now we enter the world of the really energetic Allegro. It too is a world of obsessions: the B from all the strings and the timpani, and the return of that ticking D from the first movement (to which the violins keep offering A-flat as an alternative). Then there are two fugued sections, one very rapid and on a subject that can't seem to get past its initial upbeat, the other on a carefully stepping, exploring theme, Andante un poco tranquillo. Finally, Nielsen makes a return to something like the opening music. There is one last mania: its subject is B-flat, which provides the entry to the drama's resolution on a grandly triumphal, affirmative E-flat major.

Symphony No. 6, FS116

Tempo giusto
Humoreske: Allegretto
Proposta seria: Adagio
Theme and Variations: Allegro

Nielsen began his Symphony No. 6 in August 1924, reached the end of the first movement on 20 November, and completed the score a little over a year later, on 5 December 1925. That was one day before the first rehearsal for the premiere, which Nielsen himself conducted with the Royal Orchestra in Copenhagen, to which the work is dedicated. The concert, part of an extended celebration of the composer's sixtieth birthday, was on 11 December. Nielsen originally called the work *Sinfonia semplice* (Simple Symphony), but withdrew this title before publication. The most commonly available edition incorporates slight revisions by Nielsen's son-in-law, the Hungarian violinist Emil Telmányi.

Two flutes, two oboes, two clarinets, two bassoons, four horns, two trumpets, three trombones, tuba, timpani, glockenspiel, triangle, cymbals, and strings.

Thirty-three years separate the quizzical Sixth, Nielsen's last symphony, from his First. The strangest and most private of the series, the funniest, in some ways the grimmest and in many the most touching, the Sixth is a fascinating and brave voyage of musical and personal discovery. Mahler

once wrote: "I should like to stress that [my First] Symphony goes far beyond the love story on which it is based, or rather, which preceded it in
the life of its creator." Symphonies are not autobiographies, not even the
Fantastique, but sometimes the life clarifies the work. That is true of the
Nielsen Sixth Symphony. I, at least, am persuaded by Robert Simpson's
biographical and profoundly musical interpretation of the work in the 1979
edition of his book *Carl Nielsen: Symphonist.* What follows here is, like
much of my love and understanding of Nielsen, greatly indebted to
Simpson.[5]

When he began work on his Sixth Symphony, Nielsen told his daughter Anne Marie that it would be "completely idyllic" in character. He
planned to call it *Sinfonia semplice.* When he was done, he wrote that there
were "serious and problematic things in the first and third movements" but
that "as a whole I have tried to make the symphony as lively and gay as
possible." Still, something in the sixteen months he had worked on the
piece had kept him from writing a "completely idyllic" and "simple" symphony. "Something" was his life, his struggle to come to terms with his
failing heart. The aged Thomas Mann, marveling at the unexpected turns
the decades had brought, liked to address his own life by quoting Hamlet's
"Thou com'st in such a questionable shape." Nielsen, too, looked and
wondered. He could be gloomy, but he was not, in Keats's wonderful adjective, gloom-pleased. He was not Mahler or Tchaikovsky, and so the
Sixth did not turn out tragic, nor even *pathétique,* not at all. But it surely
is emotionally ambiguous and complex: this is what makes it difficult and
at least part of what makes it endlessly fascinating.

We come once again to the subject of "progressive tonality." Usually
the final key is a goal to be ardently sought; here Simpson proposes that it
is an end the protagonist—Carl Nielsen living in and speaking through his
symphony—seeks to evade, as a sick and aging man seeks to evade knowledge of mortality. The goal is reached not because it is sought but because
it is inevitable. The Sixth Symphony is a story not of "because," but of
"despite." It is a drama not of quest and conquest, but of acceptance.

What happens? The glockenspiel, an important instrument throughout, sounds four soft D's, and the violins begin a serene melody in G
major. It *is* idyllic and simple. A clarinet, joined by a bassoon, hangs garlands on the violins' top D. But a shadow falls across Arcady. In those
garlands are B-flats, even E-flat, D-flat, A-flat, all fleeting, but each a re-

[5]I specify the 1979 edition because in the original version of 1952 Simpson had, in his own later
words, "seriously misjudged" the Sixth Symphony. In his 1979 Preface, Simpson recounts his slow
journey toward comprehension. That so acute a critic, himself a fine composer and deeply committed to Nielsen, found himself thus blocked should give pause to all of us with our rush-to-
judgment propensities.

minder that there is such a thing as G minor in the world, that even in Arcady there is death.[6] We know such shadows in Mozart. The music tumbles in dejection, but just for a moment. Then the violins, back in G major, begin a little dance. This is a scene we shall encounter often in this symphony: the voice of innocence, determined not to notice shadows but confronted by them just the same, and by realities that cannot go unnoticed. Half a minute has passed, and we have heard almost the last of the idyllic and the *semplice*.

The music is extremely varied. Themes occur in many different lengths and shapes, and they suggest many moods. This first movement is full of physical vigor but also has passages that are, in Brian Duke's words, "as lifeless as an Easter Island statue, gazing sightlessly out to sea." Textures are polyphonic more often than not, and the effect can be either athletic or severe, even stark. The scoring emphasizes clarity and definition. "Each instrument," Nielsen said, "is like a sleeper whom I have to wake into life."

A crucial focal point, and a moment of unforgettable beauty, is the first return of the violins' opening melody, now embedded in a rich polyphonic tissue of glorious euphony—"tranquil and intense as a blue sky," as Simpson says. But the key is F-sharp major, not G—"so near and yet so far," Simpson remarks—and this is less return or grounding than further voyaging into new worlds.

Catastrophe occurs without warning. It comes in the form of a sudden jolt forward in speed, of thundering drums, shrilling triangle and woodwinds, a terse fanfare, a wild rush of strings. The key is B-flat, hinted at so early and so often. B-flat was the symphony's first alien note, back in the fifth measure, in the clarinet and bassoon garland; now it asserts itself brutally. The fanfare sounds twice more, culminating in a dissonant shriek through which the glockenspiel rings its alarm and the violas and cellos sing a piercing, keening lament. The aftermath is drear and strange, and the interweaving string lines suggest Shostakovich at his most disconsolate.[7] After a renewed outburst of energy, the music takes a turn into a new landscape. In A-flat major, the same distance from G as F-sharp but

---

[6] See, by all means, Erwin Panofsky's classic essay, "Et in Arcadia ego: Poussin and the Elegiac Tradition," in *Meaning in the Visual Arts* (New York: Doubleday Anchor paperback, 1957).

[7] Both in his sense of humor and his melancholia, Nielsen often reminds me of Shostakovich. I don't know whether there is a good historical explanation for this—how well, for example, Nielsen knew Mahler, who is principal godfather to Shostakovich, or whether Shostakovich knew Nielsen at all. I have never seen Nielsen mentioned in any writings about Shostakovich, though it may be that the missing link is Jascha Horenstein, a great conductor of both composers, active in the Soviet Union between the wars, and through his Mahler performances an important force in the life of the young Shostakovich.

in the opposite direction—another instance of "so near and yet so far"—
the violins, now muted, again begin the symphony's opening melody. This
time they continue it, oddly and touchingly. Two bassoons decorate the
long closing note, and the last sound is that of the glockenspiel. A peaceful cadence, it is a sad variant of the idyllic beginning.

"I have in my symphony," Nielsen said at the time of the premiere,
"a piece for small percussion instruments—triangle, glockenspiel, and snare
drum—that quarrel, each sticking to its own tastes and delights. Times
change. Where is music going? What is permanent? We do not know!
This idea is found in my little Humoreske, which is the second
movement."

Triangle and piccolo start off, a bassoon drops a B-flat that is at the
same time sotto voce and rude. Piccolo, clarinets, bassoon, percussion—
each has something to say, none cares to listen. The clarinet begins an
uncouth, disturbing theme, spawning a raucous polyphony. After the percussion try to bring a bit of military discipline into the proceedings, the
clarinet and the two bassoons respond with an almost orderly little tune.
It could be a footling caricature of the symphony's opening phrase, but
whatever it is, the trombone greets it with a derisive yawn. Harpo Marx
in *A Night at the Opera* is not more disruptive. The contemptuous trombone succeeds in distracting everybody, and the music gradually collapses,
not quite in disarray, but to escape into a nap. (Simpson writes that "it is
perhaps not inapt to regard each movement . . . except the last as eventually going to sleep.")

The strings were silent in the Humoreske, silent and appalled. Next
comes a Proposta seria, a Serious Proposal (or Proposition), and here they
are in their element. Cellos begin this poignant music, violins follow
them, entering below the cellos, and then come the violas, very high. The
downward pull on the melodic lines is powerful, and so is the threat of
B-flat. The movement comes close to settling in B-flat minor, but at the
last moment the strings pull gently away, violins tolling A-flat, violas and
cellos leaning on D-flat. The harmonies merge in a soft blur. As at the
beautiful A-flat close of the first movement, the direction is "molto tranquillo."

The second and third movements are short: together they are not
three-quarters as long as the first movement, and having nothing of the
highly developed nature of that movement they seem even shorter. The
finale, though also shorter than the first movement, is nevertheless bigger
than the two middle movements together; being a set of variations, and
one that is deliberately episodic and discontinuous, it introduces yet another sense of how time passes.

Nielsen moves without a break out of the calm close of the Proposta seria to begin a cascade that Simpson provocatively links to the corresponding gesture in Beethoven's *Eroica*. The Sixth Symphony, he suggests is Nielsen's *Eroica*, not in the sense of that symphony in which Beethoven "is contemplating heroism," but in the spirit of the rondo finale of the Quartet, Opus 130, "the last thing [Beethoven] completed, [where] he was being heroic, achieving a gaiety beyond all reason, expressed with perfect organization."

Nielsen's cascade dissolves in a very long, low, and soft note for flute and clarinet. When that has disappeared, a single bassoon, unaccompanied, gives us a theme to be varied, a neat sixteen measures long, but not as symmetrical nor as innocent harmonically as is suggested by its butter-won't-melt-in-my-mouth beginning. The theme is firmly in B-flat major, and here is the first spot in this symphony where Nielsen uses a key signature. Officially there are nine variations, which bring many surprising departures. There is no need to describe them in detail—not the earlier ones, at any rate.

Variation 6 is a shocker, a waltz whose naïveté is immediately compromised by the fact that the accompaniment, though not dissonant, is out of phase with the tune. (It is a bit like the village band in Beethoven's *Pastoral*.) Whatever poise is left goes by the boards when, in the next variation, trombones, tuba, and bass drum interrupt with a two-beat version of the tune—in B-flat. Strings and woodwinds desperately continue their waltzing—in B-natural—and go down to a paradoxical defeat: The brass and drums join them in their triple meter, but somehow nothing is left of the waltz. Once more I must quote Simpson: "I used to represent this as the vandalistic brass smashing up the exquisite waltz. But it is the waltz, exquisite though it be, that is refusing to face the facts with which the brass is sternly (and brutally) confronting it."

The conflict, the non-quest, the attempted escape, are nearly over. Variation 8 is a grave and expressive lament, in B-flat minor, and extremely slow. It gives way to Variation 9, a passage that Thorvald Nielsen (no kin) said the composer described as "Death knocking at the gate." A brief and sinister page for percussion with tuba and bassoons, it is like a glimpse into some evil toy shop.[8] (In an interview, Nielsen called this finale "all jolly!") A fanfare intervenes, opening the way for the coda, which in fact begins as a tenth variation—rushing strings egged on by one of Nielsen's disturbing snare drums. B-flat major is here now, and beyond dispute: foreign chords are there for color, not as threats or as moves to escape the inevitable. Suddenly, and for the first time, B-flat major be-

---

[8]Once again Shostakovich comes to mind, this time the Symphony No. 15, with its evocations of toy instruments.

comes luminous. Strings cheerfully lead the way to the final cadence, which is itself both a firm acceptance and a good joke.

If we come back to my fancy that Carl Nielsen, like Thomas Mann, looked at his life and thought, "Thou com'st in such a questionable shape," we may perhaps go the next step and imagine him voicing Hamlet's thought entire:

> Be thy intents wicked or charitable,
> Thou com'st in such a questionable shape
> That I will speak to thee.

His last symphony was that speech.

Walter Piston (signature)

Walter Piston

Walter Hamor Piston, Jr. was born in Rockland, Maine, on 20 January 1894 and died in Belmont, Massachusetts, on 12 November 1976.

Belmont is a pretty town northwest of Boston, and Walter Piston lived in his hilltop house there from the day he came to teach at Harvard in 1926 until he died. He was a remarkable teacher, not only of those who sat in his classroom in Paine Hall—among them Elliott Carter, Arthur Berger, Irving Fine, Leonard Bernstein, Daniel Pinkham, and Yehudi Wyner—but also of three generations of students who learned harmony, counterpoint, and orchestration from his still current textbooks. He was proud that he himself had drawn the illustrations for his orchestration book—all but the violin, which was by his wife, Kathryn Nason, an excellent painter—and he wrote a musical manuscript so fine that his scores could be printed without being engraved, and with no hardship on players.

"You write, I will play," said Serge Koussevitzky, appointed conductor of the Boston Symphony in 1924, when Piston, with a letter of introduction from his teacher, Nadia Boulanger, presented himself. Five of Piston's eight symphonies were among the works to be given their first performances by the Boston Symphony under Koussevitzky and his successors Charles Munch and Erich Leinsdorf. It was a happy symbiosis. Piston's compositions were part of what kept the Boston Symphony's repertory lively, and the encouragement especially of Koussevitzky and Munch was very much part of what turned Piston into a composer primarily of orchestral music.

Piston's grandfather Antonio Pistone sailed his schooner from Genoa to Maine, where he married a woman from Vinalhaven called Experience Hamor. One's first impression of Piston was of a stereotypical laconic New Englander; however, the sculpting of his face and the flash of his eyes told another story, and if one watched him closely and listened attentively, one might for a moment catch something of the Mediterranean creature inside that buttoned-down exterior. Piston's music is rather like that too. The heart is there, but it is not worn on the sleeve.

Walter Piston went from Mechanics Arts High School in Boston, where he learned blacksmithing, to a job as draftsman for the Boston Elevated Railroad, to Massachusetts Normal Art School, to the United States Navy (his rank was Musician, Second Class), and eventually to Harvard, where he was by some nine years the oldest graduate in the class of 1924. After that, for two critical years, he studied with Nadia Boulanger and Paul Dukas in Paris. There he also took violin lessons with Georges Enescu and played viola in the orchestra of the École Normale. With all this variety of life experience, Piston became a richly educated man who read French, German, and Italian as easily as English, and who was blessed with endless curiosity. And of course there was Piston humor, alert, tight-lipped, *pianissimo*, ironic, and a source of joy to his friends and to all who heard him speak.

For Piston, clarity was the sine qua non of respectable art (or utterance of any kind): his New England sense of economy and his French training saw to that. Stravinsky delighted him, as did Roussel, the later Fauré, and Ravel in his more linear manifestations. Piston was a conservative—in his life as much as in his art—who found that there was much to be said for holding to certain traditional ways of doing things.

Audiences never ceased to take pleasure in his music, but he himself came to feel isolated near the end of his life when so much musical activity, particularly in American universities and in professional journals, was focused on the so-called avant-garde. He once said he had come to be taken for granted like the old sycamores that line Memorial Drive as it snakes its way along the Charles River in Cambridge. He could be wryly funny about that too. When Harvard put on a concert of his chamber music in honor of his seventieth birthday, Piston, after he was called to the stage, thanked the players "for taking so much trouble over all that mid-Victorian music." I should add that he stayed thoroughly informed about what his more "advanced" colleagues were up to, skeptical though he was about a lot of their doings. When I was asked to speak at the presentation (in absentia) of the MacDowell Medal to Piston in 1976, what came to my mind to serve as text for my sermon, so to speak, was a line of Emily Dickinson's "Pardon my sanity in a world insane."

I have chosen to write about Piston's Second and Sixth symphonies.

The latter is a wonderful example of his ebullient "Boston Symhony" manner; the former gives the most touching glimpses of the deeply sentient Italian inside the shell of the Harvard professor.

Symphony No. 2

Moderato
Adagio
Allegro

Piston composed his Symphony No. 2 in 1943. Commissioned by the Alice M. Ditson Fund of Columbia University, it was first performed on 5 March 1944 in Washington, D. C., by the National Symphony Orchestra, Hans Kindler conducting.

Two flutes and piccolo, two oboes and English horn, two clarinets and bass clarinet, two bassoons and contrabassoon, four horns, three trumpets, three trombones, tuba, timpani, tambourine, triangle, snare drum, cymbals, bass drum, and strings.

The date is 1943, the year the war began to turn around, the year of Guadalcanal and the recapture of the Aleutians, the German surrender at Stalingrad and long retreats by Rommel in North Africa, the American invasion of Italy. It was, Aaron Copland declared, "a time for mass singing, not poignant Lieder." Copland himself contributed the hardiest of all the topical rah-rah music to the sound of that half-decade, the inescapable *Fanfare for the Common Man*. Piston wrote a *Fanfare for the Fighting French* for the same project, a series of commissions by Eugene Goossens, then conductor of the Cincinnati Symphony. It is neatly done, quoting the *Marseillaise*, but not stirring; later, in his Symphony No. 3, he twitted Copland with a lightning-quick allusion to the *Common Man*. But Piston was hardly one for "mass singing," and his Second is not one of the noisy wartime symphonies—physically or spiritually noisy—like those being written by Harris and Schuman in America, Prokofiev and Shostakovich in the Soviet Union.

Not that Piston was untouched by the war. His grandfather's homeland was the Fascist enemy (at least until October 1943, when the Italians switched sides and declared war on Germany) and the swastika flew in his beloved Paris. He told the composer Arthur Berger, who had taken his class at Harvard, that he had suffered a slump at the beginning of the war, "feeling that music was about the most futile occupation." What got him out of it was letters from former students, now in military service, "who said they hoped I was keeping on composing because that was one of the things they were out there for. I have now completely recovered my sense that it is important and that I am meant to do that job (along with other things like teaching and civilian defense). I am now on my second symphony. . . ."

The Symphony No. 2 was taken up by the Boston Symphony, the New York Philharmonic-Symphony, and the Cleveland Orchestra, won the New York Music Critics' Circle Award (which carried some prestige), and was generally liked, but it did not make the impact of the famous American Thirds—Harris's, Schuman's, and Copland's—nor that of Piston's own Third, a Pulitzer Prize winner in 1948. When Michael Tilson Thomas revived and recorded the Second in Boston in 1970, it was a rediscovery of a work virtually unknown; even so, it was not until the 1990s that this beautiful symphony really came into its own.

I am baffled by Howard Pollack's contention in his useful book on Piston that the Second "beautifully expresses the heroic struggle of American involvement in the Second World War." It is, as is most of Piston's music, a celebration of civility, reason, and, in its most memorable moments, emotional generosity, none of them attitudes held in much esteem in time of war. For a clenched-fist response by Piston to the war, one expressive not of ferocity but of pain, go to his concentrated and powerful Passacaglia for Piano (1944).

This work in which Piston rediscovered his sense of vocation comes closer than most of his to being unembarrassed about warmth, even about a certain *italianità*. Its first movement is a beautifully laid-out sonata-allegro. Piston begins by spreading a deliciously unpredictable, rhythmically flexible melody for violas and cellos across the spacious 6/4 measures. It is easy enough to write the word *espressivo* into a score, but Piston's broad-spanned theme really invites that kind of playing. A forceful transition in deliberately dry octaves leads to a new idea, a dance tune, seasoned with bright percussion, and with a more prominent "Made in America" label than we usually find in Piston, and in well-lit C major after the more shadowed A minor of the beginning. To conclude the exposition, Piston gives us four measures of quiet but energetic fugue, something he doesn't ever seem to like to do without.

The development begins with a lower and darker revisiting of the opening melody, then grows into a large and vigorous series of paragraphs for the full orchestra. Expressive attributes are heightened in the recapitulation: what was dark seems even darker, while the dance episode takes on a stagedoor-canteen jauntiness. The coda returns to the opening melody one more time, *pianissimo*, first on cellos and basses, then in the woodwinds, softly, hauntingly accompanied by off-the-beat wind chords and quiet, dark thuds on the kettledrum. It is one of the most touching pages in any twentieth-century symphony.

A bassoon and muted strings suggest the possibility of a theme for the Adagio. The clarinet—*dolce, espressivo*—listens and responds, and a beautiful, long-breathed melody begins to grow, one that we gradually recognize as being cousin to the first movement's opening theme. Other woodwind solos and eventually the strings spin out what seems a spontaneous and wondrous improvisation, though Pollack points out that "the sketches reveal that Piston worked long and hard on this theme" and, presumably, its inspired continuation. At the close, which is singularly lovely, the clarinet has been given bass hormones and the strings are muted. Here is music where the conductor must forget Harvard and think Genoa. When Piston died, this Adagio is the music Leonard Bernstein played for his memorial tribute at the New York Philharmonic. He could not have chosen more aptly.

The finale, with three themes of highly profiled and varied character, is brisk and full of energy. For Pollack it is "a call to arms," and the movement does indeed begin with a theme whose first gestures are those of fanfares—back in the A-minor tonality of the first movement. The first contrasting theme is dance-like, the second an expansive and expressive melody introduced by the English horn and the clarinet together. Toward the end, the brass issue some commanding proclamations. Trumpets sound a chord that becomes the occasion for a forceful gathering-in—it always reminds me of the return of the Sorcerer in the little masterpiece by Piston's teacher Dukas—and then the finale charges to its assertive conclusion.

Symphony No. 6

Fluendo espressivo
Leggerissimo vivace
Adagio sereno
Allegro energico

Commissioned to celebrate the 75th season of the Boston Symphony Orchestra, Piston's Symphony No. 6 was composed in 1955 and first performed by Charles Munch and the Boston Symphony on 25 November of that year. The dedication is "to the Memory of Serge and Natalie Koussevitzky."

Two flutes and piccolo, two oboes and English horn, two clarinets and bass clarinet, two bassoons and contrabassoon, four horns, three trumpets, three trombones, tuba, timpani, bass drum, triangle, snare drum, military drum, tambourine, cymbals, tam-tam, two harps, and strings.

> *"This symphony was composed with no intent other than to make music to be played and listened to."*
>
> —Walter Piston

Many composers enjoy writing for particular performers. Handel and Mozart, relishing the challenge of tailoring their arias to the gifts (and limitations) of their singers, are famous examples; so, in later times, are the partnerships, as it were, of Schubert and Michael Vogl, Robert and Clara Schumann, Brahms and Joseph Joachim, and on to Bartók and Zoltán Székely, Prokofiev and Richter, Poulenc with Pierre Bernac and Denise Duval, Shostakovich with Oistrakh and Rostropovich, Britten with Peter Pears, Kathleen Ferrier, and Fischer-Dieskau. Some composers have experiences in listening that establish a certain ideal of sound in their memories; thus, for example, Roger Sessions used to say that whenever he wrote for orchestra it was with the imprint of the Boston Symphony under Karl Muck and the London Symphony under Arthur Nikisch in his mind, and that when he wrote for contralto in his cantata *When Lilacs Last in the Dooryard Bloom'd*, he imagined the voices of Ernestine Schumann-Heink and Marian Anderson.

The Boston Symphony provided Walter Piston with an ideal model of what orchestral execution might be. From 1926, when he settled for life in the Boston area, until a few months before his death fifty years later, he could be found in his balcony seat at Symphony Hall virtually every Friday afternoon the orchestra performed, and between 1928, when Koussevitzky introduced his Symphonic Piece, until 1972, when Doriot Anthony Dwyer and Michael Tilson Thomas gave the first performance of his Flute Concerto, the BSO played twenty-two of his works. Several were written expressly for that orchestra, and in the matter of the four symphonies on that list, he prided himself in having captured not just something about the orchestra itself but also certain qualities of its conductors, Koussevitzky for the First and Third, Munch for the Sixth, and Leinsdorf for the Eighth.

Working on his Symphony No. 6 he was intensely aware of writing
for the orchestra:

> I had grown up with and . . . knew intimately. Each note set down sounded
> in my mind with extraordinary clarity, as though played immediately by
> those who were to perform the work. On several occasions it seemed as
> though the melodies were being written by the instruments themselves as I
> followed along. I refrained from playing even a single note of this symphony
> on the piano.[1]

Hearing the recording made by Munch and the Boston Symphony
remains an extraordinary experience. Mozart wrote of wanting an aria to
fit a singer like a perfectly made suit: in that spirit, the solos in this symphony for flute, English horn, cello, among others, the star-bursts of harp
tone, belong forever to Doriot Dwyer, Louis Speyer, Samuel Mayes, and
Bernard Zighera, the musicians whose special eloquence and tone Piston
had held in his mind's ear while inventing them. In the same way, no
conductor I have heard since Munch has come close to capturing the spontaneity, fluidity, charm, and fizz that Piston saw as the essence of that
mercurial conductor and that he injected into this symphony.

Piston begins with a long melody, *fluendo espressivo*, for strings and a
few winds; the accompaniment is lean. *Fluendo* is not a marking I recall
seeing elsewhere, but it perfectly characterizes this suavely flowing, sweetly
temperamental first theme. It spins itself out into a spacious, elegantly
proportioned paragraph; then a bridge passage—crisp, quicker figurations
and descending harp scales borrowed from that Munch favorite, the *Symphonie fantastique*—introduces a new idea. This is another long melody,
more poignant than the first; whereas the earlier theme remained consistent in color, this one is kaleidoscopic, being passed from one solo wind
instrument to the next. The development focuses on the first theme,
which, since it gets so much attention at this stage, is not recapitulated
until almost the end of the movement. This subsides into deep quiet. Cellos and basses continue to reflect on the first theme, to which wind instruments in pairs add subtle punctuation.

The scherzo is emblematic of the brilliance and finesse of the Boston
Symphony in the Koussevitzky and early Munch years. The percussion department sets it into motion; violins, playing scales and arpeggios, muted
and *pianissimo*, add airy melody to the whirring and ticking. A bit later,
woodwinds contribute a more sustained theme. For a long time the music
continues as an etude in lighter-than-air *pianissimo*, but after a time it rises

---

[1] Boston Symphony Orchestra program book, 25-26 November 1955.

to *forte,* at least briefly. At the end, all the little clocks and machines run down. In a puff of smoke the music is gone.

The slow movement is Piston's most special achievement in the Sixth Symphony. Here is his vulnerable self. Against a backdrop of low strings, one cello alone—sostenuto e tranquillo—begins a beautiful melody, which is continued first by the oboe, then in the first violins. There are varied episodes, the first of them a quietly elegiac conversation among solo wind instruments (Doriot Dwyer's flute begins this), but Piston always returns to the cello theme. The first time it comes back it is rapturously embellished by all the violins—dolce e liberamente; later it returns in a sonorous scoring for the full orchestra. Near the end, the cello, playing alone, invokes the name of BACH, a composer especially revered by Munch.[2]

Piston began in A minor; now, having gone through a D-major scherzo and an F-sharp-minor Adagio, he returns to A, though now it is A *major.* By the way, he uses no key signatures, indicating all sharps and flats by accidentals—a surprising choice for a composer and theorist of such conservative cast of mind. Piston favors what I think of as Haydn finales, movements that are witty and orchestrally brilliant rather than weighty and "significant." Here is one of the best of them, full of delightfully varied themes and sonorities. He was also a composer who could write irresistible bring-down-the-house closes, not by any means a common skill, and the Sixth Symphony ends jubilantly in just that way.

---

[2] B, A, C, H are the German names for B-flat, A, C, B-natural. Munch, *né* Münch, was a Protestant from Alsace who grew up with the Bach cantatas and Passions. Albert Schweitzer was often the organist at the performances conducted in Strasbourg by Munch's father.

Serge Prokofieff

Sergei Prokofiev

Sergei Sergeievich Prokofiev was born in Sontsovka (now Krasnoye), Government of Ekaterinoslav (Dniepropetrovsk), Ukraine. The date, according to his birth certificate, was 27 April 1891, although he himself always gave out 23 April. He died in Nikolina Gora near Moscow on 5 March 1953, not quite an hour before Stalin.

Prokofiev, a much-cosseted only child (two sisters had died before he was born), began composing at five, and before he was out of his teens he had written four operas, two symphonies, and a stack of piano music. His mother, a cultivated player, was his first piano teacher, and in 1902 the composer Reinhold Glière was brought into the household as musical tutor to the eleven-year-old Sergei Sergeievich.

At thirteen, Prokofiev was admitted to the Saint Petersburg Conservatory. He gave Rimsky-Korsakov and Liadov a hard time in their classes and did poorly in them. Happily, he found friends who kept his musical spirits alive, most significantly two fellow-students, the composer Nikolai Miaskovsky and the critic and musicologist Boris Asafiev, and two teachers, the pianist Anna Esipova, who, after a bloody battle of wills instilled discipline into the boy and turned him into a remarkable pianist, and the composer and conductor Nikolai Tcherepnin, who of all the faculty at the Conservatory was most informed about and in sympathy with the newest musical developments.

Prokofiev's exit from the Conservatory in 1914 was grand: he won the Rubinstein Prize, the highest honor available to a pianist, for the performance of his own Piano Concerto No. 1, completed and already performed in Moscow two years earlier. By this time he had already composed and played the first version of his Piano Concerto No. 2, an imposing advance over No. 1. In the next few years he wrote a touching setting of Hans Christian Andersen's *The Ugly Duckling,* two ballet scores, *Chout* (The Buffoon) and *Ala and Lolli* (drawing the *Scythian* Suite from the latter), and the opera *The Gambler.*

The critic Vyacheslav Karatygin wrote that the premiere of the Piano Concerto No. 2 "left listeners frozen with fright, hair standing on end." Prokofiev was called "the piano cubist and futurist" and reviewers talked of "a Babel of sounds heaped upon one another without rhyme or reason"; one thought that the cadenza might have been "created by capriciously emptying an inkwell on the page." But Karatygin was right when he predicted that ten years hence the same audience would be "unanimously applauding a new composer with a European reputation."

Almost right, anyway. In 1923 Prokofiev had a European and even the beginnings of an American reputation, but his own country had been changed beyond recognition by the October Revolution of 1917. Who knows what had become of the listeners who had hissed his Second Concerto at the Imperial Park at Pavlovsk in 1913. As for Prokofiev himself, he persuaded Serge Koussevitzky, his publisher as well as his chief champion among conductors, to give him a substantial advance, raised some money through concerts (conducting the premiere of the *Classical* Symphony at one of these), talked an official into issuing a passport with no expiration date, and on 7 May 1918 boarded the Trans-Siberian Express for Vladivostok to begin the life of an émigré.

From Vladivostok Prokofiev went by ship to Tokyo, where he gave some concerts, then crossed the Pacific. The immigration authorities suspected him of being a Bolshevik spy and detained him for three days on Angel Island in San Francisco Bay. He recalled this interrogation: "Have you ever been in prison?" "Yes, I have." "That's bad. Where?" "Here, on your island." "So you like to make jokes, do you?"

With few dollars but a hefty package of scores, he got on a train to New York as soon as he could. There he gave a piano recital that gave him a reputation as a sort of musical *fauve,* a wild man, and he recorded a few piano rolls. At a concert in Petrograd, Prokofiev had once met Cyrus McCormick, president of the International Harvester Company (his father had invented the first mechanical reaper). Prokofiev liked machines, and McCormick, who liked modern music, had given the young composer his card, urging with expansive American bonhomie, "Look me up if you're ever in Chicago." On that basis, Prokofiev took off for the Midwest, where things began to improve: Frederick Stock programmed the *Scythian* Suite with the Chicago Symphony, and the Chicago Opera undertook to produce *The Love for Three Oranges,* whose march would years later become the theme music for *The FBI in Peace and War.*

In America, Prokofiev continued to compose, conduct, and play the piano, the latter two pursuits enjoying mixed success with critic and public. He fell in love with, lived with, and eventually married Lina Llubera, a soprano with a Spanish father and an Alsatian-Polish mother. He crossed the Atlantic several times, tried living in Bavaria, and eventually, toward the end of 1923, settled in Paris.

Parisian audiences, particularly those for the Concerts Koussevitzky, which had a bit of a snob *cachet,* liked their modern music to carry a certain shock value. They welcomed the spiky *Buffoon* and the savage *Scythian* Suite, the latter, let's face it, a successful go at capitalizing on the sensation Stravinsky's *Le Sacre du printemps* had made just before the war. Prokofiev's Violin Concerto No. 1, on the other hand, was thought simply too Romantic. The composer Georges Auric brought out the most wounding adjective in his vocabulary: Mendelssohnian. When Prokofiev returned to Russia for the first time in 1927, he had the opposite experience: they loved the Violin Concerto, but *The Buffoon* and the *Scythian* Suite did not please. The gradual process of homecoming continued in 1933, when he gave concerts in Russia and was asked to score the film *Lieutenant Kijé.* His visits became more and more frequent, and in 1936, he, his wife, and their two children took an apartment in Moscow. One of his first projects was a modest work for a children's theater there: he called it *Peter and the Wolf.*

The issues surrounding Prokofiev's stay in the West and his return to Russia have skewed responses to his music by politicizing them. Soviet critics, notably Israel Nestyev, still his most important biographer, could find no value in what Prokofiev had written in Chicago or Paris, and insisted that only the return to native soil freed his voice and led him from corruption to redemption. Conversely, Western writers tended to deplore his decision to go home, many implying that the change in his musical language in his later years was a concession to official hostility to "Western formalism" and that he was defeated artistically by the demands of Socialist Realist aesthetics. It is a bitterly amusing irony that when the Nazis condemned what was essentially the same phenomenon, namely the modernism represented by such composers as Schoenberg, Bartók, Stravinsky, Webern, Berg, and Hindemith, they called it "cultural Bolshevism."

As for Prokofiev's music, no question, it did change. In his earlier years he often wrote a sharp-edged and fairly dissonant sort of music, which he himself, like many of his critics, might, with Stravinskian self-irony, have called brittle and "heartless." In his later years in the Soviet Union, he turned to a more mellifluous style, painted with a broader brush, and was less inclined to humor. He can even seem downright self-conscious in his concern not to rub the wrong way. It is an issue of hard versus soft, and as such it is also a matter of taste. Listeners who find their ideal Prokofiev in *Romeo and Juliet* may well be uncomfortable with *The Fiery Angel*. One can also understand that those whose favorite Prokofiev is the Symphony No. 2 might find the famous Fifth disappointing.

It is a complicated question. Other "Western formalists" or "cultural Bolsheviks," including Bartók, Hindemith, and Schoenberg, came to move away from the "modernism" of their early or middle years without the kind of direct political pressure to which, for example, Prokofiev and Shostakovich were subjected.[1] Nor did this phenomenon cease with the generation of modernism's founding fathers: think of George Rochberg or Henryk Górecki. It is hard to know just what roles were played in these choices by aesthetic conviction, nostalgia (no small consideration for Schoenberg), or the desire to reach a larger audience.

In Prokofiev we cannot really find a clear-cut division between early and late, Western and Soviet. True, there is little like the lushness of *Romeo and Juliet* and *War and Peace* in his early music, and not much like the sharpness of *Chout*, *Visions fugitives*, or *Suggestion diabolique* in his work after 1936. Nonetheless, the beautiful melody that opens the Violin Concerto No. 1 came to Prokofiev in 1915 and was not rejected by him in Paris; the Sixth Symphony is not exactly soft. He himself recognized four "basic lines" in his lifework, which he called classical, modern, motoric, and lyrical. These do not, however, correspond to particular periods in his life; though the balance among the components varies from work to work, all are present all the time.

Classical Symphony in D major (No. 1), Opus 25

> *Allegro*
> *Larghetto*
> *Gavotte: Non troppo allegro*
> *Finale: Molto vivace*

Prokofiev began his *Classical* Symphony in 1916, but did most of the work during the summer of 1917, completing it on 10 September of that year. He conducted the first performance in Petrograd on 21 April 1918. The

---

[1] Had Stravinsky died at seventy, shortly after completing *The Rake's Progress*, he too would belong on this list. As it is, he swung back and in the last years of his long life composed some of his most exploring and radically "modern" music.

score is dedicated to Prokofiev's former classmate the critic and musicologist Boris Asafiev.

Two flutes, two oboes, two clarinets, two bassoons, two horns, two trumpets, timpani, and strings.

For a Russian composer, 1917 cannot have been an easy year to concentrate on his work. A series of strikes, anti-war marches, and the refusal of soldiers to fire on the demonstrators led, step by step, to the overthrow and abdication of the Tsar; the Black Sea fleet mutinied; there were terrible food shortages in the big cities; the Kerensky government was turned out in the October Revolution (which actually took place on 7 November according to the Western European calendar); after ten years of exile, Lenin arrived at Petrograd's Finland Station and became Chairman of the Council of People's Commissars; and an armistice with Germany was signed at Brest-Litovsk. Nonetheless, 1917 was the most richly productive year of Prokofiev's life, the one in which he composed the Violin Concerto No. 1, the *Classical* Symphony, the Third and Fourth piano sonatas, the *Visions fugitives* for piano, and began both the Piano Concerto No. 3 and the ambitious and remarkable cantata on Chaldean texts, *Seven, They Are Seven.*

Here is Prokofiev's own account in his memoir, *Prokofiev by Prokofiev:*

> I spent the summer of 1917 in the country near Petrograd all alone, reading Kant and working a great deal. I deliberately did not take my piano with me, for I wished to try composing without it. Until then I had always composed at the piano, but I noticed that thematic material composed away from the piano was often better. . . . I had been playing with the idea of writing a whole symphony without the piano, thinking that such a piece would have more natural and transparent colors.
>
> So that is how the project for a symphony in the style of Haydn came about. I had come to understand a great deal about Haydn's technique from [Nikolai] Tcherepnin [at the Saint Petersburg Conservatory], and thought it would be less scary to embark on this difficult pianoless journey if I were on familiar stylistic ground.
>
> It seemed to me that if Haydn had lived to our day, he would have retained his own style while absorbing something new at the same time. This was the kind of symphony I wanted to write: a symphony in the classical style. And when I saw that my idea was beginning to pan out I called it the *Classical* Symphony. I called it that in the first place because it was simpler,

and secondly for fun, to "tease the geese," and in the secret hope that . . . it would really turn out to be a classic.[2]

Through Tcherepnin, Prokofiev had developed not only knowledge of Haydn and Mozart but a real liking for their music, "a taste for the bassoon playing staccato and the flute playing two octaves higher than the bassoon etc." His first musical experiences had been centered on Beethoven, Chopin, Grieg, and Tchaikovsky; a little later, Debussy, Reger, Strauss, and Scriabin came to be favorites as well. When he was eleven, Prokofiev had been taken to meet the composer Sergei Taneyev, who taught at the Moscow Conservatory. He recalled later that Taneyev had given him some excellent chocolate and told him that his harmonic vocabulary was too simple. He liked the chocolate, but the criticism horrified the young composer of the opera *Desert Islands,* and the pepper mill was immediately put to work. Fourteen years later it must have been quite a wrench for Prokofiev, by then a notorious "modernist," to cut dissonance back to something like eighteenth-century levels.

If the radio announcer told you he was going to play something by Haydn and then started a recording of the *Classical* Symphony, it would take you only a few seconds to figure out that you were being put on. But then Prokofiev was not trying to produce a forgery that would conceivably pass as a newly discovered Haydn symphony.[3] Nor did he intend a parody. As the American musicologist Laurel Fay has written, this is "a high-spirited and sparkling salute."

Prokofiev thoroughly enjoyed doing what he set out to do, which was to write a symphony for classical orchestra, transparent in texture, harmonically "cool," on a modest scale, with clearly articulated periods and cadences, buoyant, comedic in spirit, and without weltschmerz and angst. All this was especially challenging to accomplish and striking in effect in the aftermath of the symphonies of Mahler, Strauss's *Elektra,* and Schoenberg's *Gurrelieder.* Prokofiev not only had a good time doing it, he achieved his goals, including that of composing a classic.

The symphony begins with a 1917 translation of what 140 years or so earlier was called a Mannheim skyrocket, a tonic chord rising rapidly into the air, a specialty of the composers who worked in the capital of the

[2] Sergei Prokofiev, *Prokofiev by Prokofiev* (New York: Doubleday, 1979).
[3] I wonder whether anyone could in fact manage such a deception without proceeding so cautiously that the result would be unbearably dull and therefore unconvincing for that reason. Good forgers inject too much of themselves and their own time. This is why their work might convince at the moment but seem totally implausible only a generation later. We look at the famous Van Meegeren "Vermeers" of the 1930s and can only wonder. Similarly, actors in Hollywood costume dramas have cut reasonable figures when the films were new, but a generation later they look like their 1950s selves and absurd.

Bavarian Palatinate and were associated with the superb orchestra there. Among other things, this effervescent opening immediately gives notice that Prokofiev means to write rewarding virtuoso music for a modern orchestra. Prokofiev's friend, publisher, and advocate on the podium, Serge Koussevitzky, came to make a specialty of the *Classical* Symphony, and his 1929 recording with the Boston Symphony is still unsurpassed for sheer scintillating brilliance; it is interesting, therefore, to read in *The Orchestra Speaks*, the fascinating memoir by Bernard Shore, who was principal viola in the BBC Symphony in the 1930s, that Prokofiev as conductor took a much more relaxed view of this music.

The D-major skyrocket sets in motion a continuous purling of rapid eighth-notes. The main theme itself descends, nicely balancing the upward thrust of the rocket. Not even Haydn with all his harmonic daring would have repeated the theme in distant C major within ten seconds; in fact, one of the charms of the *Classical* Symphony lies in Prokofiev's skill at conveying something of the essence of Haydn while not writing a single measure that could possibly occur in a Haydn symphony. Prokofiev immediately returns to D from his C-major escape, and with utmost nonchalance, after which the woodwinds offer a little pendant to the opening theme. With textbook orthodoxy, Prokofiev moves to the dominant, A major. The running eighths stop, and we hear a new theme in which violins play pert grace notes and negotiate precipitate leaps *pianissimo* and *con eleganza*. In its combination of ease with just a touch of danger, it is the essence of rococo charm.[4]

Unlike Shostakovich in his somewhat related Ninth Symphony a generation later, Prokofiev does not do the "classical" thing and ask for the exposition to be repeated. He leaps into the development with a great bound, gives some time to each of his themes, and decks the music with thoroughly twentieth-century syncopations. The recapitulation arrives joyously, but in C major, not the home key of D: this is reaping what was sown in that tiny excursion to C in the first few seconds of the piece. We can also think of it as one of Prokofiev's typical harmonic sideslips writ large. Everything else happens as scheduled, and one last skyrocket brings the movement to a close.

Writing in a somewhat aggrieved tone about his Violin Concerto No. 1, Prokofiev remarked that his "lyric line was not noticed until late. For a long time I was given no credit for any lyric gift whatever, and for want of

---

[4] A conductor I knew had what for him was a rare opportunity to lead one of the world's most celebrated orchestras in a set of concerts. His first thought, when the invitation came, was to put the *Classical* Symphony on the program because he wanted to hear a really great violin section negotiate this treacherous passage as though it were child's play.

encouragement it developed slowly. But as time went on I gave more and more attention to this aspect of my work." He cites the wonderful opening melody of the concerto as an example of his unappreciated lyric bent, but could as well have called attention to the beautiful, high-flying second movement of the *Classical* Symphony from the same year. Except in sweetness and restraint, the music here makes no pretense at being "classical." Harmony and scoring are exquisite in every single measure.

Classical symphonies have minuets; the *Classical* Symphony has a gavotte, a somewhat weightier dance with four beats to the bar, and always beginning on 3. The harmony is full of Prokofievian skids and quick recoveries. The trio is a musette over a bagpipe drone; its delicacy leaves its mark on the return of the Gavotte itself, which is markedly less robust the second time around. Prokofiev liked this movement well enough to revive it back twenty years later in a considerably expanded version in Act 1 of his ballet *Romeo and Juliet.*

The Finale brings us back to the mood of the first movement (this time with the classical repeat of the exposition), only now there is no stopping to smell the roses. This is sheer uninhibited delight in energy and forward movement.

Symphony No. 5 in B-flat major, Opus 100

> *Andante*
> *Allegro moderato*
> *Adagio*
> *Allegro giocoso*

Using some material dating back to the late 1930s, Prokofiev composed his Symphony No. 5 during the summer of 1944 and on 13 January 1945 led the Moscow State Philharmonic Orchestra in the premiere.

Two flutes and piccolo, two oboes and English horn, two B-flat clarinets plus E-flat and bass clarinets, two bassoons and contrabassoon, four horns, three trumpets, three trombones, bass tuba, piano, harp, timpani, triangle, cymbals, tambourine, snare drum, wood block, bass drum, tam-tam, and strings.

Although he never returned to his native country after the Revolution and became an ardent American patriot, Serge Koussevitzky, the Boston

Symphony's conductor from 1924 to 1949, maintained a profound inner identity as a Russian. As such, he sympathized passionately with the Soviet Union's war effort against the Germans, and his performances of Prokofiev and Shostakovich, many of them American premieres, were acts of commitment that went beyond ordinary considerations of professional responsibility, ambition, and rivalry with colleagues. Aware of the material difficulties in wartime Russia, Koussevitzky arranged for regular shipments of music paper to the Soviet Composers' Union. When he began to study the Prokofiev Fifth before introducing it in America, it gave him special pleasure to see that the score was written on paper that had made the long round-trip from a music store on Boylston Street, just a few blocks from Boston's Symphony Hall.[5]

I have sometimes wondered what went through Prokofiev's mind when he saw the E. C. Schirmer imprint on his manuscript paper. Was he touched by Koussevitzky's caring gesture? What memories did it bring back of Koussevitzky in Moscow, Paris, and Boston, and of his concerts with the Boston Symphony as conductor and pianist? Unlike Koussevitzky, who seemed never to be more than a degree or two below the emotional boiling point, Prokofiev was a chilly character, certainly not much given to sentimentalities. Still, he and Koussevitzky had been in each other's lives a long time. They had known about each other at least since 1908, when the thirty-four-year-old Koussevitzky, then the world's leading double bass virtuoso and beginning two other careers as conductor and head of Editions Russes de Musique, began repeatedly to reject the scores submitted to his publishing house by the teenage composer. Eventually, though, Prokofiev succeeded in softening Koussevitzky up, and in 1914 he was invited to play his Piano Concerto No. 1 with him in Moscow. This marked the beginning of more than thirty years' devoted sponsorship on Koussevitzky's part. Between 1916 and 1937, he published many of Prokofiev's works, including the *Visions fugitives,* the Third and Fourth piano sonatas, the *Scythian* Suite, the Dostoyevsky opera *The Gambler,* the ballet *Chout,* the *Lieutenant Kijé* Suite, and several books of songs. In addition, he invited Prokofiev to appear with the Boston Symphony in five different seasons as pianist or conductor. And appropriately enough, it was Koussevitzky who gave the first American performances of Prokofiev's Fifth Symphony in November 1945.

Prokofiev composed his Fifth Symphony at Ivanovo, some 150 miles northeast of Moscow, where the Composers' Union had set up a House of Creative Work to give members a setting more peaceful than the hubbub

---

[5] Prokofiev's autograph manuscript of the Fifth is now at the Boston Public Library, so it too has come home.

of wartime Moscow or Leningrad. The population of the House in 1944 was a Who's Who of Soviet music: among those whom Prokofiev joined there or who arrived later were Glière (his first composition teacher), Shostakovich, Khachaturian, and Kabalevsky. A mood of optimism was in the air. A few days before Prokofiev's arrival at Ivanovo, the Allies had invaded Normandy, and only a couple of weeks later, the Soviet armies launched massive and successful offensives in Byelorussia and Poland. Seven months later, when he stood on the podium of the Great Hall of the Moscow Conservatory to lead the first performance of the Fifth Symphony, the Soviet armies had just begun—literally, the day before—what would prove to be their final push to victory. As Prokofiev raised his baton in the silent hall, the audience could hear the gunfire celebrating the news, arrived only hours before, that the army had crossed the Vistula.

The new symphony was a triumph and that evening was the high point of Prokofiev's career. A few days later, apparently as a result of previously undetected high blood pressure, he blacked out, fell, and suffered a concussion. (The accounts of exactly when and where he fell are slightly conflicting.) He was never in full good health again. In 1946 he won a Stalin Prize, First Class, for the Fifth Symphony (and another at the same time for the Piano Sonata No. 8), but no new work of his was ever again acclaimed with the same enthusiasm. In 1948, along with Shostakovich, Khachaturian, and others, he was subjected to brutal bullying by Andrei Zhdanov's government committee. He continued to compose, but when he died—not quite an hour before Stalin—he was a defeated man. In his *Music and Musical Life in Soviet Russia,* Boris Schwarz reports that "*Sovietskaya Muzyka,* the official music journal, carried the obituary of Stalin on page 1, the one of Prokofiev on page 117 of the April 1953 issue."

In America, too, the Fifth Symphony was a tremendous success when Koussevitzky introduced it in Boston, New York, and Washington. The week after, Prokofiev's picture was on the cover of *Time.* Within the year, Victor and Columbia, then our only two important classical labels, both came out with first-rate recordings. When Artur Rodzinski, Eugene Ormandy, and George Szell played it with their orchestras in New York, Philadelphia, and Cleveland, their success equaled Koussevitzky's. No question, the Fifth was a repertory piece from Day One. Five years later, the political climate in America had changed to the point that when the Utah Symphony announced the Salt Lake City premiere, the conductor, Maurice Abravanel, received an anonymous death threat over the telephone.

At the time Prokofiev began work on his new score, he had not written a symphony since 1930, when he had completed his Fourth, a Koussevitzky commission to celebrate the Boston orchestra's fiftieth anniversary.

This was also the first time he set out to write a symphony from scratch since No. 2 in 1924–25. The Third and Fourth had both been byproducts of his work for the theater, the Third using material from the opera *The Fiery Angel*, the Fourth from the ballet *The Prodigal Son*. The Fifth had no program, but Prokofiev announced that it was music "glorifying the human spirit . . . praising the free and happy man—his strength, his generosity, and the purity of his soul." Soviet composers at this time often sent their new works into the world freighted by rhetoric of this sort; some of their American colleagues, notably Roy Harris, leaned that way as well.

More interesting and consequential was Prokofiev's statement that he thought of his new Fifth Symphony as "[crowning] a great period of my work." All rhetorical and political considerations aside, these words can be taken to refer to purely musical issues. The Prokofiev of the Fifth Symphony is a composer in command. Many composers in the nineteenth and twentieth centuries, even very good ones, were baffled by the problem of how to confront the sonata style defined by Haydn, Mozart, and Beethoven, how to get at its substance and not just its shell. Here, in his Symphony No. 5, the fifty-three-year-old Prokofiev takes on the challenge with the confidence, the skill, and the fresh approach of a master.

The work is in four movements, but they are not quite the conventional four of the classical and Romantic symphony; rather, what Prokofiev gives us here is a slow/fast/slow/fast sequence familiar from Baroque music. (I doubt that Prokofiev deliberately modeled his Fifth on Bach sonatas or anything of that sort.) At any rate, he begins with an Andante in handsomely made sonata form. As most nineteenth-century composers did, Prokofiev thinks of "andante" as "slow" (literally it means "moving"); indeed, his metronome mark of $\quarternote = 48$ indicates a tempo slower than any I have ever heard in performance.

The opening melody itelf soars, but Prokofiev's presentation of it is austere, in woodwind octaves and almost unharmonized. He continues the theme with one of his characteristic harmonic sideslips, sending it from B-flat major to A. The harmonies move rapidly, and before he arrives at his real destination, the dominant, F major, Prokofiev has also made landings in D-flat major and B major. Once arrived in F, he gives us a new theme, more lyric than the first, and in a more flowing tempo. But for all his fondness for quick key changes, Prokofiev means us to take the big motion from B-flat to F very seriously, and to make sure of that, he anchors the music to a pedal F for eighteen measures in the original slow tempo. Over that pedal he offers one more new idea, a theme characterized by a nervous flurry of sixteenth-notes. And with that, we arrive at the end of the exposition.

Prokofiev now picks up from Beethoven (the first movements of the String Quartet in F major, Opus 59, no. 1 and the Ninth Symphony) and Brahms (Symphony No. 4, first movement) the device of seeming to embark on a formal repeat of the exposition, only to have a dramatic turn of harmony reveal that the development has in fact begun. (In the Beethoven and Brahms, one could literally be deceived; Prokofiev, while keeping the musical substance, changes the scoring of the opening theme from woodwinds to low strings.) The actual moment of throwing the switch, a soft rain of pizzicato and tremolando violins and violas, is lovely indeed. The development ruminates on all the material, cresting in two impassioned statements of the lyric second theme.

The recapitulation begins when B-flat major is regained and the first theme strides onto the scene *fortissimo*, scored band-style for brass. As though to make up for the near-absence of harmony at its first appearance, it is now supported by strikingly dissonant chords. The sequence of events for the recapitulation is normal, but their unfolding is compressed. The coda, which twice attains a towering *fortissimo*, reflects at length on the first theme. The scoring for the percussion, including piano, is especially arresting.

The second movement is a scherzo. With violins marking the time, the clarinet proposes an impertinent little tune, to which the oboe and the violas make equally impertinent response. Here is a touch of the old Prokofiev, the wry humorist from whom Shostakovich learned so much. This is material initially sketched for his *Romeo and Juliet* ballet of 1935–36. A slightly slower passage leads into the trio, which itself is actually a little faster than the main section of the movement. Clarinet and violas lead off with a sinuous and high-spirited tune that has something of the atmosphere and charm of Khachaturian's *Masquerade*. The same bridge that brought us into the trio takes us out again. The repeat of the scherzo is twisted, even sinister, and it ends with a good smack.

Then comes a weighty slow movement, and here Prokofiev gives what turns out to be a surprisingly fast metronome mark of $\quarternote = 60$ faster in fact than most conductors find comfortable. The music is both somber and lyric. An accompaniment figure, which moves in triplet broken chords in the manner of the first movement of the *Moonlight* Sonata, sets the pulse. The dynamic level is *mezzo-piano*, but the sound is weighty and dense. It supports an expansive and richly eloquent melody, begun in F major but soon, by one of those Prokofiev dodges, shifted into E. Prokofiev's biographer Harlow Robinson points out that this theme goes back to 1936, when Prokofiev wrote it for a never completed film of Pushkin's *Queen of Spades*. The middle section of the movement is darker in character, suggesting a cortège, even though it is still in triple meter. After an intensely emotional climax, the first theme returns, *pianissimo*, but in a newly elaborate scoring. The coda is ingeniously and touchingly built on the *Moonlight* accompaniment, and a slow clarinet arpeggio ushers the music into silence.

The finale brings us back to B-flat major, the symphony's home key. It begins in a reflective mood, with woodwinds and strings engaged in quiet dialogue. This is followed by something surprising and extraordinarily beautiful, the return of the first movement's opening theme, scored now for the cellos divided four ways. Abruptly, these moods are swept away. Violas start an energetic vamp-till-ready, the horns and the other strings join in, and the clarinet supplies a delightfully exuberant tune. Except for a single brief solemn interlude, the mood is joyous, the motion athletic. Throughout, Prokofiev keeps finding new ways of heightening the voltage until, after a dizzying swirl of music in an original and tasty combination for solo strings, piano, harp, and percussion, he brings his symphony to an end on a rush to a final B-flat bang.

Symphony No. 6 in E-flat minor, Opus 111

> *Allegro moderato*
> *Largo*
> *Vivace*

Using sketches that go back to 1944 and therefore antedate the completion of the Fifth Symphony, Prokofiev worked on his Sixth from 1945 until 18 February 1947. Yevgeny Mravinsky and the Leningrad Philharmonic gave the first performance on 11 October 1947.

Two flutes and piccolo, two oboes and English horn, two clarinets with bass clarinet and E-flat clarinet, two bassoons and contrabassoon, four horns, three trumpets, three trombones, tuba, timpani, triangle, cymbals, tambourine, snare drum, wood block, bass drum, tam-tam, piano, harp, celesta, and strings.

For anyone trying to understand Prokofiev's trajectory, both musical and personal, it would be absurd to discount the cultural and political climate in the USSR, but equally misleading to ignore the fact that many of the best twentieth-century composers, working in quite different sorts of political and social situations, found themselves drawn toward an "easier" manner as they grew older. In Prokofiev's Sixth Symphony, we sense a wrench of nostalgia for a language he had spoken earlier in his life—less the humorous, tart, slightly sardonic, crackling idiom commanded so brilliantly in, say, the Piano Concerto No. 3 (1921), than the more problematic, quasi-expressionist tone of his opera *The Fiery Angel* (1919) or the Symphony No. 2 (1924).[6]

Prokofiev himself, never a wordy man, had only this to say about the Sixth Symphony: "The first movement is agitated, at times lyrical, at times austere; the second movement, Largo, is brighter and more tuneful; the finale, rapid and in a major key, is close in character to my Fifth Symphony, save for reminiscences of the austere passages in the first movement." Not much, and in one important aspect misleading, namely that the second movement, though indeed much of the time "brighter and more tuneful," begins and ends with music whose harmony and texture are dense and exceedingly difficult to penetrate. Leopold Stokowski, who conducted the American premiere in 1949, remarked then of these pages that it would surely take years to understand them.

The Fifth Symphony, to which Prokofiev alludes in his laconic note, is the most equilibrated work of his later years. It is unambiguous in expression and, at least when a good conductor is on the box, acoustically lucid. Its popularity is completely understandable. The premiere under Prokofiev's own direction in January 1945 was an occasion of triumph. That of the Sixth in October 1947 was one of respectable success. Three months later, the harassment of Soviet composers by the Central Committee of the Communist Party and Andrei Zhdanov (whose name, by the way, does not appear in Nestyev's biography of Prokofiev) was at its height, and the Sixth Symphony was singled out for attack as too obscure for the ordinary Soviet citizen to understand.

That observation was, of course, correct: the Sixth was not the uncomplicated victory symphony for which many listeners had hoped, even two and a half years after the end of the war, and in no sense is it "easy listening." Prokofiev had told Nestyev that to some extent the work had been inspired by the feeling of the last months of the war in 1944 and 1945, but he added these words: "Now [in October 1947] we are rejoicing in our great victory, but each of us has wounds that cannot be healed.

---

[6] As I was writing this, I thought to look again at what Nestyev has to say about the Sixth Symphony. Here he is: "It seems as though the two Prokofievs, the old and the new, were engaged in a struggle, revealing in the course of this struggle both powerful, genuine lyricism and sudden outbursts of unrestrained expressionism utterly incomprehensible to the listener."

One has lost those dear to him, another has lost his health. This must not be forgotten."

The Sixth Symphony, then, is a work of conflicting and unresolved emotions. Who can say what produced the difference between it and its predecessor? The need to respond to the hideous war years must have played its part; so, I imagine, did the internal pressure of Prokofiev's irrepressible creative spirit. The composer Nicolas Nabokov, who left Russia permanently in 1920 and continued to be close to Prokofiev through his Parisian years, wrote in his book of essays *Old Friends and New Music* that Prokofiev's "remaining artistic integrity quite naturally revolted against the very idea of conformity for conformity's sake, a conformity which was not based on his own beliefs and ran counter to his artistic freedom."

For whatever combination of reasons, the Sixth Symphony is a work in which Prokofiev took risks, human and artistic. To compose such a work in such a place and at such a time took courage. Perhaps, paradoxically, Prokofiev found that courage in part in his own declining health. Since the first frightening symptoms of severe hypertension had appeared early in 1945, he was a dying man—a very slowly dying man, to be sure—and he knew it. He also knew that ultimately he was beyond the strictures and ukases of the Zhdanovs of this world. Dutifully he attended the hearings to which he had been summoned, and there he sat, his arms folded, his back to the commissar.

In the first movement of the Sixth Symphony, we pass through a landscape of melancholy pastoral music, funeral cortèges, and warring furies. Prokofiev begins with the sharp barking of muted trumpets and trombone. They start a descending scale which is continued by the other two trombones, the tuba, and plucked cellos and basses. The distribution of half and whole steps in this scale is unusual, and the harmonic drift uncertain. The beginning of the lyric 6/8 melody played by muted violins and violas is similarly ambiguous. The paragraph is long and its unpredictable unfolding is disturbed by distant snare-drum rolls. A second theme for oboes in octaves—"dolce e sognando" (sweet and dreaming)—brings both contrast and sameness: the tempo is slower and the key, B minor, is distant from where we have been, but this melody too flows with the freedom of chant and the orchestral sound continues austere. A great cadential broadening marks the end of the first chapter.

At this point we might expect a development. In fact, Prokofiev delivers a double surprise: he returns to his home key of E-flat minor, and, at a slower tempo, he gives us something new.[7] It is a grim march that to

---

[7] Prokofiev's marking is Andante molto; clearly he is using "andante" in its traditional nineteenth-century sense of "slow."

begin with consists only of two levels of accompaniment, dry chords for bassoons with piano, and barely articulate fragments proposed by low brass with plucked strings and supported by the bass drum. Then he adds a melody. The sound is that of English horn with violas, the irresistible combination Tchaikovsky discovered for *the* tune in *Romeo and Juliet*. We have entered a new world both of sound and expression. For a moment this music rises to *fortissimo*. Then the first theme returns, played by the strings in octaves. This is expanded and leads to an aggressive, tormented climax full of percussion crescendos and sharp accents. This subsides, and when the broadening cadential passage reappears, the horns make it sinister with their approaching and receding waves of sound. The oboe theme is transformed into a horn solo. The funeral music also returns, and the movement comes to a close with restless mutterings in bass instruments and a drumroll to cast a deep shadow. It is *pianissimo* but it is certainly not quiet.

The second movement, *pace* Prokofiev's description, is intensely conflicted, and its lyrical cantilena is always liable to disruption by harshly scored sounds of rage. It opens with a cry. Basses, contrabassoon, tuba, and timpani firmly lay down a tonic pedal, A-flat, but against this, horns and woodwinds begin a chromatic ascent in grinding parallel seconds, while on top of that, more woodwinds, high up, sing a keening lament. Prokofiev had not written such lacerating music in more than twenty years. As though this were not allowed, as in a sense it really was not, Prokofiev dismisses this extreme and uninhibited expression of anguish after just five measures. Like Beethoven in the Ninth Symphony commanding "nicht diese Töne," he summons more agreeable sounds.

More agreeable perhaps, but surely no less intense. In a mood of inspired lyricism, Prokofiev spins out a melody that brings to mind the most impassioned pages of *Romeo and Juliet* and *War and Peace*, after which the cellos offer another broad-spanned melody in a more tranquil vein. Then comes a tempestuous episode, remarkable not least for its extraordinary, sharply defined color. The percussion, both real (timpani tattoos and alternating accents for tambourine and wood block) and surrogate (piano, muted trumpets, and pizzicato strings), plays an especially effective role here. As a not quite twenty-one-year-old student, the soprano Galina Vishnevskaya heard the first performance of the Sixth Symphony, and all her life she remembered the sound of this work, "sharp and ringing, like the dripping of snow in spring." The horn quartet provides contrast with a passage of musing that another of Prokofiev's biographers, David Gutman, calls "tenderly nostalgic." The two lyric themes are recapitulated, in reverse order. Then, lest we forget, Prokofiev brings back the tortured opening music. This time it is even briefer than before, but we shall not forget. For a moment it seems as though the oboe, dolcissimo, wants to start something new in faraway D major, but the basses have already begun their final confirmation of this movement's home key of A-flat major, and there this eloquent movement finds its close. To the last, flute, celesta, and second violins keep slipping from the keynote to its neighbor, G. This is not perfect peace.

The third movement takes a drastic leap into optimism. The clarinet brings the finale of Prokofiev's Fifth Symphony to mind, but this is a sinister cousin, darker in coloration and temperament. The sound is sometimes "classical," sometimes balletic. Long, dissonant brass notes mock, like scoffers sticking out their tongues, and strings add their sardonic commentary in down-skidding glissandos. Eventually the momentum evaporates, the texture thins out, and bassoon and bass clarinet bring the music to a suspenseful halt. It resumes with the oboe theme from the first movement; we are back in the world of those austere, sparsely punctuated octaves. Over a string tremolando, played near the bridge so as to produce a fleshless buzzing, oboes and English horn add a new and reticent lament. Then reticence is no more. The orchestra screams its protest, molto espressivo, *fortissimo*. But this stuff is too dangerous, and Prokofiev hastily sweeps it aside.

Sergei Rachmaninoff

Sergei Vasilievich Rachmaninoff was born at Semyonovo, district of Starorusky, Russia, on 1 April 1873 and died in Beverly Hills, California, on 28 March 1943.

Rachmaninoff is one of those composers whose popularity rests upon an excessively small and unrepresentative group of works. (Handel and Dvořák are two others who come immediately to mind.) We know the symphonist and even the writer of solo piano music and songs too little, the composer of church music and opera almost not at all.

His fifty-year career can be reckoned as having started in 1890, when the seventeen-year-old Moscow Conservatory student began working on his Piano Concerto No. 1, a work we always hear in its 1917 revision; it closed in 1940 with the Symphonic Dances, composed, like the Third Symphony, for the Philadelphia Orchestra. Both beginning and end of the career were unhappy. Rachmaninoff's first important teacher, Nikolai Sergeievich Zverev, who ran a sort of pianists' hothouse in his apartment, permitted this most gifted pupil of his to stretch his horizons by taking some lessons with Alexander Siloti, Rachmaninoff's cousin and a Zverev alumnus, but bitterly resented his growing interest in writing music and his enrollment in the composition classes of Sergei Taneyev and Anton Arensky. A break with Zverev was both necessary and painful. It left Rachmaninoff free to be a composer, but the brutal reception accorded his First Symphony in 1897, horrendously conducted by Alexander Glazunov, threatened to silence him for good. Rachmaninoff's miseries in the last fifteen years or so of his life had to do chiefly with his sense of being out of touch with his public, or rather, that the public was out of touch with his aspirations. That is a story I tell in my essay on the Symphony No. 3.

Having really become a composer with the completion of the Piano
Concerto No. 1 and the tone poem *Prince Rostislav* (1891), Rachmaninoff
wrote prolifically during the next few years: the two *Trios élégiaques*, the
opera *Aleko*, the tone poem *The Rock*, the Suite No. 1 for Two Pianos,
several sets of songs, that C-sharp-minor Prelude whose outlandish popularity was to be a source of gloom and frustration to him all his life, and
the Symphony No. 1. It took three years of psychotherapy and hypnosis
before Rachmaninoff could again face writing a large-scale composition
after the catastrophic premiere of that last work. He withheld it from publication and further performance, but after his death there came to light
first a two-piano transcription, then a set of orchestral parts, and so the
symphony had a second premiere in Moscow in 1945. It is a strong and
interesting work.

Treatment with Dr. Nikolai Dahl, who had trained with Charcot in
Paris, enabled Rachmaninoff to compose his much-loved Piano Concerto
No. 2 in 1900–1901, and it was the success of that work in turn that freed
him. Even so, it was a long time before the notion of "symphony" ceased
to make him shudder. The Second came along ten years after the First,
and after finishing it, Rachmaninoff swore he would never write another
symphony. It was twenty-eight years before he changed his mind and began
work on his third and last essay in the form.

Symphony No. 2 in E minor, Opus 27

> *Largo—Allegro moderato*
> *Allegro molto*
> *Adagio*
> *Allegro vivace*

Rachmaninoff composed the Symphony No. 2 between October 1906 and
April 1907 and conducted the first performance in Saint Petersburg on 26
January 1908. The dedication is to Rachmaninoff's teacher, the composer
Sergei Taneyev.

**Three flutes and piccolo, three oboes, two clarinets and bass clarinet, two
bassoons, four horns, three trumpets, three trombones, bass tuba, timpani,
glockenspiel, bass drum, cymbals, and strings.**

When Rachmaninoff was working on this symphony, he was living in Dresden, where he had gone to escape the constant clamor for his services as a conductor. There he also composed his Piano Sonata No. 1, the tone poem *The Isle of the Dead* after the Böcklin painting he had seen in Dresden's Semper Gallery, and, for his first American tour in 1909, the Piano Concerto No. 3. Thirty-three years old, he was in his fifth year of contented marriage, a father (his second daughter, Tatiana, was born about the time the symphony was completed), an experienced composer in many genres, an unsurpassed and scarcely equaled pianist, and a highly esteemed conductor. As a composer he was original as well as experienced, with a tone of voice and melodic style all his own and, as many attempts, particularly in film studios, have proved, inimitable. In his Preludes and *Études-Tableaux* for piano he developed an impressive skill at composing a highly economical sort of music, but in his symphonies and concertos he preferred, at least at this point in his development, a more expansive manner.

Expansive enough in this instance to have disturbed conductors into making many cuts. Some of the standard deletions consist of petty impatiences like reducing the four measures of accompaniment at the start of the first Allegro to two, but they have also entailed such brutal surgery as the removal of the entire principal theme from the recapitulation of the Adagio. Cuts do not solve formal problems: they merely shorten the time you have to spend dealing with them. Paradoxically, a work may feel longer when it is cut because the proportions are off and the distribution of light and shade is all wrong.

Rachmaninoff himself was strangely passive about this. In 1940, Leslie J. Rogers, the Boston Symphony's librarian in the early part of this century, sent Pierre Monteux the twenty-nine cuts "supposedly given to [Josef Stransky, conductor of the New York Philharmonic] by the composer" as well as the list of different excisions made by Serge Koussevitzky, conductor of the Boston Symphony. In his cover letter Rogers writes: "I asked [Rachmaninoff] about the Stransky cuts. He told me that Stransky made them and he 'approved' them. I asked him if he wanted cuts made and he said that if he conducted it himself there would be no cuts but had no objections to others cutting if they thought it should be cut." In a note for his wonderful 1973 London Symphony recording, André Previn writes that, having begun by making the standard cuts, he had decided, "on re-examining the score . . . to re-instate every note. . . . It makes the symphony undeniably long, but I feel that its honesty, its power, its heart-felt lyricism can stand it."[1]

[1] Until the appearance in 1994 of new recordings by Valery Gergiev and Yuri Temirkanov, Edo de Waart is the only conductor in my experience to have taken the repeat of the first movement's

Rachmaninoff begins in mystery, with *pianissimo* low strings.[2]

Ex. 1

What the cellos and basses play here is a motto that turns out to have a large role in the symphony, sometimes on the surface, sometimes beneath it. Immediately, sonorous wind chords vary its first three notes, and the violins make lachrymose response. The texture becomes more tightly woven, with imitative entrances following fast upon one another; at the same time, the melodic flow is gorgeous. The penetrating high writing for violas, who enter on the same high C as the violins, is especially effective. Rachmaninoff slowly works this up to an intense climax from which he then descends rapidly. Harmonically, this whole introduction describes one great half-cadence from tonic to dominant.

Alone, the English horn muses on these events for a moment. Strings, in softly shuddering tremolando, play a fragment of a rising scale, and the main part of the first movement has begun. The first theme, which the violins introduce, is yet another variant of the introduction's motto, now urgent and forward-thrusting. It is presented in a broad paragraph, and Rachmaninoff's command of such spans is very impressive indeed. Accelerating, the music moves toward a new key, the relative major, G. The theme is new, yet both the design—wind chords leading to a melancholy violin response—and the actual shapes of the phrases are familiar from the introduction. Violins and cellos carry the music forward and, though the key is now officially G major, the yearning for the darker E minor is strong. One of Rachmaninoff's beautiful ever-descending melodies brings the exposition to its quiet close.

A violin solo reminds us of the introduction. After the brief moment

---

exposition, and very effective it was, too. The numbers are interesting. The early and uncut Boston Symphony performances under Max Fiedler and Karl Muck took sixty-five minutes. André Previn's uncut performances average fifty-nine minutes and change. Monteux, making the twenty-nine "Stransky" cuts, came in at fifty-two, but Koussevitzky, making fewer cuts than Monteux, gave consistently quicker performances (forty-one to forty-six minutes). So far as I know, the speed record is held by Izler Solomon, who brought the Boston Symphony to the last double bar in thirty-eight minutes!

[2]This type of opening, so popular in works from Schubert's *Unfinished* Symphony to Bartók's Concerto for Orchestra, was invented by Haydn in his Symphony No. 103, the *Drumroll.*

of quiet, the music pushes forward. Slowly the bass descends from A to G to F-sharp. The cellos recall the motto, the violas interject violent tremors. The bass skips over E—Rachmaninoff is not yet ready to re-establish the tonic and begin the recapitulation—but sits for a long time on E-flat. Then, as the bass starts to rise again, a great crescendo begins. We hear some triumphant fanfares, but this is just a way station. The agitated journey resumes: Rachmaninoff has learned well from Tchaikovsky how to build suspense. Through the storm, we can make out fragments of the opening theme. At last the long dominant pedal on B is resolved to E, the keynote. We are home; the recapitulation has begun.

The fragments we heard in the tempest are as much of a return of the opening theme as we are going to get. When at last we land back in E, we are given the second theme, the one with the wind-string dialogue. And once home, Rachmaninoff moves swiftly into a powerful coda. The final E-minor chord is followed by a thump on low E for cellos and basses alone.

The second movement, the scherzo, is wildly energetic; it is in fact rare for Rachmaninoff to write a movement so consistently athletic. It is particularly brilliant as orchestral writings. The key is A minor, and the reason the beginning rings as it does is that the violins playing their rapid anapests get to use their open A and E strings so much. A little later the glockenspiel adds a nice edge. Midway, Rachmaninoff also gives us one of his broadly Romantic tunes. That provides its own pleasure, but even greater is the delight of the quietly stalking retransition to the driving main theme. The close is humorous disintegration.

Then the trio: as Haydn is supposed to have said of the big bang in his *Surprise* Symphony, "This will make the ladies jump." The second violins start a brilliant fugue, and probably every one of the violinists you hear play this passage today had to present this excerpt at his or her audition. A swift transition leads us into the return of the scherzo, in whose coda Rachmaninoff, as he was so fond of doing, cites the *Dies irae* (Day of Wrath) from the Gregorian Mass for the Dead. This phrase is suggested by the horns at the opening of the movement; toward the end it becomes explicit.

In the beautiful Adagio we find Rachmaninoff's melodic genius working at full power. He begins as though in mid-phrase, with violas winding long garlands of triplets, over which the violins play a phrase that begins with an unforgettable upward thrust. That one is the phrase people usually come out singing after this symphony. But all this is just introduction. The main matter is a lovely clarinet solo, a wonderful instance of Rachmaninoff's way of expanding an idea on and on. The melody takes twenty-three measures to have its say, never repeating itself literally, though circling, as many Russian melodies are apt to do, around a few notes within a limited compass. It is, among other things, a reminder that Rachmaninoff was also a marvelous songwriter. But even when the clarinet stops, the melody is not over, and the violins carry it still further.

When this long and arresting paragraph ends, which it does with the great yearning phrase that began the movement, the violins bring back their lamenting phrase from the symphony's introduction, though it is now more than twice as fast. In fact, the introduction now yields material for the violins, for English horn and oboe, and eventually for the full orchestra to explore. Again Rachmaninoff brings in one of his gradually descending bass lines. This leads to a grand arrival in C major. There is a swift drop to *pianissimo*, a long silence, and then a lovely passage, full of mystery, in which solo instruments, one after one and beginning with the horn, briefly caress the yearning phrase. When the flute takes its turn, the violins softly interject their phrase from the introduction.

This touchingly intimate passage proves to be the transition to the return of the great melody the clarinet played at the beginning of the movement, but which is now given to the violins. (This is one of the passages that used to be cut.) Woodwinds now decorate the melody with the yearning phrase. From here, the movement sinks to a spacious and quiet close.

The finale, back in E, but now E major, begins headlong. The first contrasting theme is a hushed conspiratorial march; the transition to this, with timpani, plucked low strings, and muted horns, is particularly fine. The march is just an interlude. The forceful and speedy opening music returns, to lead to one of Rachmaninoff's "big tunes." If we know the Second and Third piano concertos, we can safely guess that this, grandly presented, will be the material for the final cresting.

But there is much adventure before we get to that point. First comes the surprise of a return for just six measures to the tempo of the slow movement and to its beautiful introductory phrase. Then the high-speed tempo resumes, and in this development section Rachmaninoff gives us one of his most amazing passages, a network of descending scales, slow and fast, high and low, syncopated and straight, that generate such a swirl of sound, that all the bells in Russia seem to be ringing. It is rather like Arvo Pärt eighty years ahead of time.[3] From here on, matters develop much as we would expect, with a recapitulation in whose first pages the carillon scales are not altogether forgotten, with a grand peroration based on the big lyric tune, and a blood-stirring rush to the close, which is sealed with

---

[3] Most of the earlier conductors did not find these scales as magical as I do. At any rate, this was a passage subjected to brutal cutting; I am sure I never heard it until Previn's uncut performance in the early 1970s.

Rachmaninoff's familiar "signature" cadence—YUM-pa-ta-TUM (this time slightly zipped up to YUM-pa-ta-ta-TUM).

Symphony No. 3 in A minor, Opus 44

Lento—Allegro moderato
Adagio ma non troppo—Allegro vivace—Tempo come prima
Allegro—Allegro vivace—Allegro

Rachmaninoff composed the first movement of his Symphony No. 3 between 18 June and 22 August 1935, the second between 26 August and 18 September of the same year, and the third between 6 and 30 June 1936. The first performance was given on 6 November 1936 by what he called his "very favorite orchestra," the Philadelphia; Leopold Stokowski conducted. Rachmaninoff subsequently made some revisions, which were completed by July 1938, and the work was reintroduced in its definite form that fall, again by the Philadelphia Orchestra, this time with Eugene Ormandy conducting.

Two flutes and piccolo, two oboes and English horn, two clarinets and bass clarinet, two bassoons and contrabassoon, four horns, three trumpets (preferably with an alto trumpet in F for the third trumpet), three trombones, tuba, timpani, xylophone, triangle, snare drum, bass drum, cymbals, tambourine, celesta, harp (preferably doubled), and strings.

On 23 December 1917 Rachmaninoff left Russia, never to return. He gave concerts in various Scandinavian cities, lived in Copenhagen for almost a year, then sailed for America. The uproar that kept the Rachmaninoffs awake on their first night in New York was not, as they feared, the sound of Revolution but celebration of the Armistice. Their first American home was a rented house in Menlo Park, California, but they eventually found it more convenient to settle in New York and Locust Point, New Jersey. In 1929, the family returned to Europe, building a villa near Lucerne which they called Senar for SErgei and NAtalia Rachmaninoff; in 1939 they came back to America, first to a house at Orchard Point, Long Island, then to Beverly Hills, where they first rented, then bought a house in 1942.

Rachmaninoff left Russia a famous composer, a highly esteemed conductor, and a most distinguished (part-time) pianist. He was also a man troubled by the problem of keeping those three lives in satisfactory balance. He arrived in America well remembered from his 1909–10 tour (for which he had written his Piano Concerto No. 3), with his Piano Concerto No. 2 well established in the repertory, and with the C-sharp minor Prelude as inescapable as it was in Europe. When word got out that Rachmaninoff had left Russia, he was offered the music directorships of the Boston and Cincinnati orchestras, but decided not to take on the burden of a permanent position; in fact, he hardly ever conducted again, one fortunate exception being a magnificent recording with the Philadelphia Orchestra of the Symphony No. 3. With a family to support, he resigned himself to the life of a traveling piano virtuoso, full-time. As for Rachmaninoff the composer, so fertile between 1900 and 1917, he did not write a single major work between March 1917, when he completed the *Études-Tableaux*, Opus 39, and January 1926, when he began the Piano Concerto No. 4.

His sense of exile, which he felt keenly in spite of his popularity in America and the presence of such friends and colleagues as Josef Hofmann (his favorite pianist and the dedicatee of the Concerto No. 3), Fritz Kreisler (an occasional sonata partner with whom he made some memorable recordings in 1928), Efrem Zimbalist, Mischa Elman, and Eugène Ysaÿe (who took the Cincinnati job)—must have had something to do with the lack of new works, as did his characteristically concentrated commitment to his new bread-winning career as a pianist. But there was another reason: Rachmaninoff, forty-five when he arrived in America, was changing as a composer.

Reviewing Verdi's achievement a few weeks after his death in 1901, Bernard Shaw tried to lay to rest the current saw about the Wagnerization of his later music; rather, he suggested,

> The real secret of the change from the roughness of *Il trovatore* to the elaboration of the last three operas is the inevitable natural drying up of Verdi's spontaneity and fertility. So long as an opera composer can pour forth melodies like *La donna è mobile* and *Il balen*, he does not stop to excogitate harmonic elegancies and orchestral sonorities which are neither helpful to him dramatically nor demanded by the taste of his audience. But when in process of time the well begins to dry up, when instead of getting splashed with the bubbling over of *Ah, si, ben mio*, he had to let down a bucket to drag up *Celeste Aida*, then it is time to be clever, to be nice, to be distinguished, to be impressive, to study instrumental confectionery, to bring thought and knowledge and seriousness to the rescue of failing vitality.[4]

[4] *Shaw's Music*, Vol. 3, edited by Dan H. Laurence (London, The Bodley Head, 1981).

Not, perhaps, an account of *Aida, Otello,* and *Falstaff* that one would want to accept entirely without question, but it does have truth and bring understanding. For Rachmaninoff, too, the well that had yielded the expansive melodies of the Second Symphony, the first three concertos, and many of the Preludes and songs, seemed to have gone dry, though in the late years it produced, suddenly and fantastically, the wonderful 18th Variation in the Paganini Rhapsody. ("That one is for my manager," he said.)

Rachmaninoff needed to make the change that Shaw describes, which meant making the most of that talent for economy, concentration, and precision which had been consistently in evidence in his shorter piano pieces ever since the Preludes, Opus 23, of 1901–03. The essence of late Rachmaninoff, music whose discourse is based on the play of figuration and texture as well as on the energy generated by the thrust of strong and sometimes arrestingly bold harmony, is thoroughly established in the *Études-Tableaux,* surely the summit of what he wrote for his own instrument.

Stravinsky recalled an unannounced visit late one night in July 1942 from Rachmaninoff, who was bearing a pail of raw honey and an invitation to dinner. What they talked about at dinner is not recorded, but if they discussed music and the music world at all, one subject that may well have come up—and that perhaps they are even now discussing with Beethoven, Schumann, Wagner, Debussy, and Schoenberg, among others—is the problem of a public, lay and professional, that wants an artist to repeat his early successes over and over.[5]

Stravinsky's answer to someone who had asked plaintively why he had stopped writing beautiful music like *The Firebird* was, "Why did *you* stop?" Rachmaninoff's public looked yearningly for the grandiloquence and the honey-flow of the Second Piano Concerto. To some extent the market was accommodated when this side of Rachmaninoff was picked up in debased form by the composers of the *Warsaw* Concerto and the *Cornish* Rhapsody. And, ironically, that part of the public that might have responded to Rachmaninoff being nice, clever, distinguished, and so forth, considered him beneath its notice and was probably off listening to Stravinsky.

[5] That Stravinsky was not much in tune with Rachmaninoff's music is not surprising; however, the final paragraph of his account in Robert Craft's *Conversations with Igor Stravinsky* (1959) of this Hollywood meeting with his older compatriot (whom he had never met, neither in Russia nor when they were both living in Switzerland) is worth quoting: "I remember Rachmaninoff's earliest compositions. They were 'watercolors,' songs and piano pieces freshly influenced by Tchaikovsky. Then at twenty-five he turned to 'oils' and became a very old composer indeed. Do not expect me to spit on him for that, however. He was . . . an awesome man, and besides, there are too many others to be spat on before him. As I think about him, his silence looms as a noble contrast to the self-approbation which are the only conversations of all performing and most other musicians. And he was the only pianist I have ever seen who did not grimace. That is a great deal."

That said, let us not do Rachmaninoff the disservice of overstating his case. He was not a giant like Verdi or Stravinsky, and it is silly to suggest that his Third Symphony is to his Second what *Falstaff* is to *Trovatore* or *Rake's Progress* and *Threni* are to *Petrushka* and *Sacre*. At the same time, I would insist that the "unpopular" late works of Rachmaninoff—the Corelli Variations, the Symphony No. 3, and the Piano Concerto No. 4 (in its 1941 revised version)—represent their composer at his most formidably intelligent and imaginative, that they have strength, integrity, vision, and atmosphere.[6]

Rachmaninoff found few friends for these pieces when they were new. In July 1938, for example, we find him writing to his former secretary, Yevgeni Ivanovich Somov, that counting people who loved the Third Symphony, he so far had had to use only three fingers, one for the conductor Sir Henry Wood, one for the violinist Adolf Busch, and a third for himself. "When I run out of fingers on both hands I'll stop counting. Only when will this be?" Earlier he had written to his friend Vladimir Robertovich Wilshaw that at the first performances, which had been played "wonderfully" by the Philadelphians under Stokowski, "both audience and critics responded sourly. Personally I'm convinced that this is a good work. But—sometimes the author is wrong, too! However, I maintain my opinion."

Picking up a Tchaikovskian idea, Rachmaninoff had begun his Second Symphony with a musical motto whose subsequent appearances were intended to have both unifying and dramatic effect. He does the same thing in his Third, beginning in mystery, with a melody of a certain ecclesiastical cast, restricted to just three notes, and played *pianissimo* by clarinet, two stopped horns, and a single muted cello. This disappears into silence. Then the tempo changes abruptly for a "get ready now" outburst by the full orchestra with those satisfying bass drum and cymbal smacks so typical of Rachmaninoff's earlier orchestral style. And now, after this taut double introduction, the first movement proper begins with a melody of extraordinary rhythmic subtlety, flexibility, and span. Rachmaninoff's own sharply inflected reading of this in his 1939 recording shows the importance he attached to the special properties of this melody, with its irregular breathing and its unexpected extensions. Besides clarifying so beautifully what is happening, the performance communicates a touching pride on the part of the composer-conductor in his own invention.

Pattering triplets scatter the atmosphere. They lead to a new idea that

---

[6] At one time I would have added the Symphonic Dances to this list, but in the 1980s they began more and more to find persuasive interpreters and persuaded audiences.

strikes us at first as being in the composer's old manner but whose phrasing and range are the work of a mind more complex than that of the ante bellum Rachmaninoff. A leap forward in tempo, then a subsidence, and the exposition comes to an end. Rachmaninoff directs that the exposition be repeated but unfortunately does not follow his own instructions, maybe in response to pressure from the record company, perhaps because reviews had tended to harp on the length of his recent pieces.

Everything thus far has been tightly packed, but now, as the development begins, Rachmaninoff allows himself more space. The two bassoons in thirds that start this section off against triplets rising through the strings sound positively Wagnerian. We do not readily associate Rachmaninoff with Wagner, but he had in fact heard a lot of Wagner's music when he lived in Dresden at the beginning of the century, been profoundly stirred by his visit to Bayreuth in 1902 (it was part of his and Natalia's honeymoon), and was for years inseparable from his pocket score of *Meistersinger;* once, when Arthur Nikisch, nervous about a cholera epidemic in Moscow, canceled a tour, Rachmaninoff even conducted an all-Wagner program. In any event, the Wagnerian presence flits across the scene more than once in this symphony.

The triplets are the single most pervasive element. The motto intrudes sternly upon the climax, but it is interrupted by a little passage, at once sinister and grotesque, for piccolo, bassoon, and xylophone against a chord of muted horns and violas, the latter played with the stick rather than the hair of the bow. The Debussyan harmony is equally alien. The recapitulation, beautifully introduced by a rising passage for violins (a touch of *Siegfried* here), is full of surprises in its proportions, scoring, and harmony. One last muttering reference to the motto closes the movement.

The second movement begins with a variant of the same chant, now a horn solo heard against a splendidly spreading bouquet of harp chords. Rachmaninoff moves rapidly from idea to idea. The sequence of events has an upbeating, expectant quality, so that it all feels more like an introduction than a fully settled slow movement. Suddenly the music takes a leap forward, a new quick tempo is set, and a scherzo has begun. Like so much of this symphony, it is full of triplets. Though it is of considerable dimensions, it is only an episode within the Adagio. The return to the earlier music is imaginatively made through a passage of sliding chords for woodwinds with buzzing strings, leading to a chain of ominous violin trills. The reprise itself is so compact as to seem hardly more than a fleeting, dreamy recollection of what was. Again Rachmaninoff ends with a dark reminiscence of the motto. Throughout, the scoring is marvelously rich in fantasy, including such pleasures as a flute solo with harp-and-celesta ripples and a soft curtain of chords on four solo violas, flutter-tongue trumpets mocking the military snare drum, or the single drop of celesta sound in the midst of a sequence of Stravinskian chords for trumpets and horns.

The finale is vigorous and in a bright A major. There is an uneasy moment when Rachmaninoff seems to promise one of his big tunes and then fails to deliver, but that disturbance aside, this is an eventful, confident, handsomely shaped, brilliantly scored movement. Much as he had inserted a scherzo into the middle of his Adagio, Rachmaninoff here offers a faster middle section in the form of a virtuosic fugue. This leads to a brief episode of a rather sour funeral music, which in turn introduces an old obsession of Rachmaninoff's, the Gregorian *Dies irae* from the Mass for the Dead. (He had quoted it for the first of many times in the Symphony No. 1.) With unflagging invention, Rachmaninoff drives the symphony to a roaring (and slightly capricious) conclusion.

Franz Schmidt

Franz Schmidt was born in Pozsony, Hungary (now Bratislava, Slovakia) on 22 December 1874 and died in Perchtholdsdorf, a suburb of Vienna, on 11 February 1939.

Fourth Symphony

Allegro molto moderato
Adagio
Molto vivace
Tempo I°, un poco sostenuto
(played without pause)

Schmidt composed his Fourth Symphony in 1932–33. Oswald Kabasta and the Vienna Symphony gave the first performance on 10 January 1934. The score is dedicated to Oswald Kabasta.

Two flutes (second doubling piccolo), two oboes and English horn, two clarinets and E-flat clarinet, two bassoons and contrabassoon, four horns, three trumpets, three trombones, contrabass tuba, timpani, cymbals, bass drum, snare drum, tam-tam, two harps, and strings (as many as possible).

Franz Schmidt is the composer of four symphonies, three of them among the strongest this symphony-rich twentieth century has produced. It is not music for everybody, but if Bruckner speaks to you and if in general you are susceptible to expansive utterance, it may well be music for you. The Fourth Symphony especially is an eloquent and arresting document.

Bratislava was in the Hungarian part of the Austro-Hungarian "dual monarchy" when Schmidt was born there.[1] Hungarians know it as Pozsony and Germans as Preßburg. Located at what is now the juncture of Austria, Hungary, and the Slovak Republic, it is one of those border towns whose ethnic makeup has changed several times over the centuries. Today it is Slovak, in the nineteenth century it was Hungarian, before that it was German. Schmidt's first language was Hungarian, and as a boy he planned, with his parents' blessing, eventually to take his Hungarian mother's family name of Ravasz. (Schmidt's father was German on his father's side and Hungarian on his mother's.)

Franz Schmidt Sr. dabbled with a number of wind instruments; Maria Schmidt was an excellent pianist who had studied with Liszt. She was Franz Junior's first teacher and, he thought, his best. He passed through the studios of some pretty indifferent instructors in Pozsony, but managed to become a proficient pianist and organist anyway. At fourteen, he was sent to Vienna to study with Theodor Leschetizky, a great eminence in the world of piano pedagogy whose remarkable roster of students over the years included Esipova, Paderewski, Schnabel, Gabrilowitsch, Vengerova, Friedman, and Moiseiwitsch. Schmidt took a few lessons, but Leschetizky, who thought his playing "correct, technically excellent, but wanting in *charme,*" seems not to have been very attentive to him.

Matters came to a head at one of Leschetizky's Wednesday teas, when the boy played Liszt's Hungarian Rhapsody No. 12 and Balakirev's razzle-dazzle *Islamey.* The guests and Anna Esipova, then married to Leschetizky, responded warmly, but the great man himself was dismissive: "There's potential, even quite a lot . . . [but] someone with a name like Schmidt shouldn't become an artist." That was the moment at which young Franz decided to stick with his paternal name. He took no more piano lessons.

He was supposed to join Bruckner's counterpoint class, but Bruckner was on what turned out to be a permanent leave of absence, so nothing happened there. Schmidt got a little instruction and a lot of moral support from a Franciscan monk, Felician Josef Moczik, took a few composition lessons with Robert Fuchs, and studied cello with Ferdinand Hellmesberger of the famed Hellmesberger Quartet. At twenty-one, Schmidt was taken into the Vienna Court Opera Orchestra and the Philharmonic, and for some years, playing the cello was his main source of income.

He did not fare well in that intrigue-ridden world. Whenever Mahler conducted and the repertory included an important cello solo, he insisted

[1] Johann Nepomuk Hummel was born there in 1778 and Ernö (or Ernst von) Dohnányi in 1877.

on having Schmidt play it. This naturally aroused the ire of Friedrich Bux-baum, the official principal cellist, and Arnold Rosé, the concertmaster, tended to side with Buxbaum, who was also the cellist in his quartet, rather than with his brother-in-law, Mahler. On some occasions when the atmosphere was calmer, Schmidt played second cello with the Rosé Quartet, for instance in the first performance of Schoenberg's *Verklärte Nacht* (Transfigured Night) in 1902, and he once joined the Rosés in a Schubert program, playing piano in the *Trout* Quintet and the dramatic second cello part in the C-major String Quintet. On a less happy occasion, when Rosé appeared minutes before the curtain was to rise on a performance of *Lohengrin* to order him out of the principal cello chair, Schmidt spat on his concertmaster's shoes and went home. (Schmidt recounts all this in numbing "he said, then I said" detail in the *Autobiographical Sketch* he wrote circa 1914.)

In 1911, he liberated himself from orchestral life. Thereafter he taught piano, counterpoint, and composition, also serving for some years as director of Vienna's two most important music schools, the Staatsakademie and the Musikhochschule. He was a musician with exceptional gifts of ear, memory, and technical facility. (He was known to practice very little.) His knowledge of the standard repertory from Bach to his own day was both extensive and profound; it astounded everyone, as did his ease at transferring what was stored in his memory through his fingers onto the keyboard. Although in the context of the first thirty years of the twentieth century he must be counted as conservative, his range of musical interests was large. For example, he admired what he called Schoenberg's "wide ear" and, like another great conservative, Puccini, he was fascinated by *Pierrot lunaire*—fascinated, in Schmidt's case, to the point of preparing an impeccable performance with students at the Staatsakademie.

Unlike Webern, he had no Nazi sympathies whatever. He was, however, a political naïf, capable on the one hand of recommending Variations on a Hebrew Theme by his student Israel Brandmann to a musical group associated with the proto-Nazi German National Party, on the other of expressing amazement that his Jewish friend, physician, and sonata partner, Oskar Adler, was anxious to leave Austria after the *Anschluß*.[2] The Nazis did Schmidt a bad turn after his death. In 1938, Schmidt was pressured into accepting a commission to write a cantata (*Deutsche Auferstehung* (German Resurrection), to celebrate the *Anschluß*. His heart was not in it and, already very ill, he achieved only a few sketches and fragments; after his death, one of his former students concocted the cantata, which was then performed in Vienna as a genuine work by Schmidt!

---

[2] For more on Adler, see my essay on Schoenberg's Chamber Symphony No. 1.

Playing at the Court Opera had given Schmidt a yen to write for the theater, and he did venture into that bear-pit twice. *Notre Dame*, after Victor Hugo's *The Hunchback of Notre Dame*, is an opera in a robust ve-rismo style that had some success when it was produced in Vienna in 1914; its vibrant Intermezzo, which sounds like a slightly modernized version of the slow part of one of Liszt's Hungarian Rhapsodies, still delights audi-ences when they get a chance to hear it. A later work, *Fredigundis*, disap-peared from view almost immediately, but Peter Pachl in *The New Grove Dictionary of Opera* praises it and its distinctive contrapuntal style.

Schmidt wrote handsome organ music that attests to the impression the work of Reger made on him. He composed extensively for piano, works with orchestra as well as chamber music; almost all of it is for piano left-hand, written for the Austrian pianist Paul Wittgenstein, who lost his right arm in World War I.[3] Schmidt's masterpiece and last completed work is his powerful oratorio on the Apocalypse, *The Book with Seven Seals*.

His one major orchestral work other than his four symphonies is an engaging set of Variations on a Hussar Song (1931). The symphonies themselves span nearly four decades of Schmidt's life. He started the First, in E major, in 1896, the year he joined the Vienna Opera Orchestra and began what he called his galley years (Verdi used the same phrase to de-scribe the period from 1842 to 1853, when he wrote sixteen operas at the rate of about one every nine months); he completed it in 1899. It is curi-ous that he does not mention it in his *Autobiographical Sketch* at all; it was his first major work and was awarded a prize by the Vienna Society of Friends of Music after its first performance in 1902. The work is a bold declaration by the young composer of his intention to be a major sympho-nist. The English writer Harold Truscott remarks that something, possibly the music of Reger, perhaps that of the East Prussian composer Adolf Jen-sen, "blew a gust of the Baroque in [Schmidt's] direction in time for it to affect the E-major Symphony." In this sense, the Symphony No. 1 stands a bit apart from the other three, though this polyphonic vein is one that Schmidt would tap later in *Fredigundis* and *The Book with Seven Seals*.

The Symphony No. 2 followed in 1911, breaking the twelve-year si-lence of Schmidt's "galley years." Here we get a more three-dimensional picture of Schmidt's lyric, expansive, and exuberant style. His harmonic

---

[3] Wittgenstein was wounded on the Russian front a few weeks after the outbreak of war and only a year after his debut as a pianist. Between 1923 and 1940, he commissioned works by Hindemith, Strauss, Korngold, Schmidt, Prokofiev, Ravel, and Britten, among others. He played all except Prokofiev's Piano Concerto No. 4, but seems really to have liked only the five pieces Schmidt wrote for him: a piano concerto, a set of charming variations with orchestra on the scherzo of Beethoven's *Spring* Sonata, a beautiful quintet for piano and strings, and two quintets for piano, clarinet, and strings.

language is chromatic, often to the point of restlessness, and he likes a sumptuous orchestral sound. He shares Schubert's and Brahms's fondness for the Gypsy idiom: I have mentioned the *Notre Dame* Intermezzo; a splendid—and subtler—example can be found in the "Hallelujah!" chorus near the end of *The Book with Seven Seals*. Bruckner is often a presence in Schmidt's music; we feel it in many melodic and harmonic turns as well as in Schmidt's penchant for close connections between first and last movements, especially in the Second and Fourth symphonies. The first movement of Schmidt's Symphony No. 2 ends with a real Bruckner coda (as learned from the Beethoven Ninth), progressing from dark mutterings to a blaze of sound, and it is magnificently done.

The Symphony No. 3 dates from 1928, when it won a prize given by the Columbia Graphophone Company in honor of the centenary of Schubert's death. For Truscott it is the greatest of the four; by any standards it is an advance over No. 2. In particular the slow movement, dissonant and ecstatic, is a most marvelous achievement. Overall, the orchestration is more transparent, though nothing has been sacrificed in richness. It is the most Viennese of the four symphonies and the most Romantic in atmosphere: it suggests visiting an encrusted shipwreck or a ruined castle, Romantic concepts both. The expressive span is wide: this symphony smiles more often than the others, but, as Peter Franklin remarks in his notes to Neeme Järvi's recording, it is also a work touched by "darker knowledge."

Dark is a word that the Fourth Symphony calls to mind as well; we will not find unbuttoned high spirits here, nor the delights of local color, whether Viennese or Gypsy. In 1932, Schmidt's daughter Emma died in childbirth at the age of thirty. He had always felt especially close to her, and he conceived of the symphony that he began soon after this blow as a Requiem for her. It is not a tragic or pessimistic work, though it is full of pain; I hear it as elegiac and contemplative, music of love, and the close is strangely peaceful.

The Fourth Symphony is the largest of Schmidt's symphonies, even if it is not quite as large as the excessively slow tempi of some conductors make it appear. (Two current recordings take forty-nine minutes each; Schmidt's own performance with the Vienna Philharmonic in 1935 took thirty-nine minutes.) Schmidt's music needs space and ample breathing room, but the fast passages really have to move; the most crucial component of a good performance is the conductor's feeling for that ingredient, both mysterious and instantly recognizable, fine Viennese rubato. I stress "fine" because I do not mean the taffy-pull style so often heard in performances of Strauss waltzes; rather, I am thinking of something as natural—and as unmetronomic—as breathing. Flexibility, flexibility all the time, is the watchword.

There is no break between any of the four movements, but the unfolding of the work—what the conductor Andrew Massey calls the plot—is easily apprehended. In brief, the symphony begins with a movement in medium tempo, continues with a slow movement (a great one), then a kind of scherzo, and concludes with a finale that is both recapitulation and transformation of the first movement.

The Fourth happened to be the first music by Schmidt that I ever heard (in a wonderful recording by Rudolf Moralt), and I can recall only a few other occasions when I was so gripped at first encounter by the opening of a work. A trumpet plays alone.

Ex. 1

It is a haunting thing, this melody, and it is also an amazing architectural design in miniature. One of its musical functions is to establish C major as the symphony's principal key, and Schmidt accomplishes this firmly and subtly. The melody gives the impression of something free and harmonically wide-ranging, and for good reason: two notes outside the C-major scale, A-flat and D-flat, are prominent. Yet three of the six phrases end on C, and two others on the dominant, G; furthermore, the first two phrases end respectively on G and C, thus spelling a dominant-to-tonic cadence. The two prominent foreigners, A-flat and D-flat, also turn out to be members of the C-major family. They are respectively a semitone higher than the dominant and the tonic, and these so-called Neapolitan relationships, savory harmonic devices that Beethoven and Schubert used especially effectively, are of great importance harmonically.[4]

----

[4]For no truly convincing reason, the chord based on the note one half-step up from the tonic, for example, D-flat in the key of C, is called Neapolitan. A normal G-C final cadence in the key of C is most often approached by way of a chord based on D; to approach it instead from a chord of D-flat makes for a colorful variation. By extension, we can also think of the note one half-step up from the dominant, for example, A-flat in the key of C, as a kind of secondary Neapolitan.

Not least, the melody is beautifully shaped. It starts in mid-range, rises gradually to the high G (the suspense-building dominant), and comes to rest on the long, low C (enhanced by its Neapolitan neighbor, D-flat). The way the melody moves through time—five-measure phrases at the beginning and end, shorter phrases of various lengths in the more urgent middle part—corresponds to the way it is shaped in melodic space.

I have written at such length about this not-quite one minute of music both because what happens in it is so characteristic of Schmidt's musical thought and because the entire symphony is pervaded by this melody, or elements of it. When the trumpet reaches its final low C, it is joined by the first violins and, a moment later, the violas. Immediately, all the strings move up to D-flat, which is held in the bass for a very long time, while the violins reflect on the trumpet melody. The paragraph builds grandly and culminates in a strong resolution in C major. As the bass slowly rises from C through a whole octave to C-sharp, woodwinds play fragments of arpeggios and hesitant scales; meanwhile, the violins still cannot quite let go of the trumpet theme. This is a moment of expectation and suspense.

Release comes in the form of an arresting new melody in distant F-sharp major: the first violins play it, and Schmidt marks it passionato. It crests and recedes again, after which the trumpet melody returns, played this time by the English horn. Once again tension accumulates powerfully, but the orchestra's striving is abruptly cut off. Fragments of the *passionato* melody endeavor to set things in motion again. The music reaches one more gloriously scored *fortissimo* peak before it subsides with a single cello playing one last recollection of the *passionato* melody's first phrase.

That sound creates the link between the first movement and the second. The principal theme of the Adagio is an eloquent song begun and completed by the solo cello; violins, with support from flute and English horn, take it over in the middle. Then the atmosphere changes abruptly. Against a drumming whose relentless beat begins in the timpani but bit by bit affects the whole orchestra, the cellos begin a mournful threnody. Mahler might have marked it, "Wie ein Kondukt" (Like a cortège). Here is music of searing grief and shattering power, a funeral march that can stand beside the greatest of these by Beethoven, Berlioz, Wagner, Mahler, Elgar, and Shostakovich. Its mountainous climax, marked by a mighty stroke on the tam-tam, is the focal point of the entire symphony. The solo cello prepares the way for the return of the opening music, but the melody itself is now delicately scored for woodwinds, echoed by pizzicato violins, and hung with garlands of gently flowing sixteenth-notes. When it has run its course, the solo cello is heard in a moment of fantastical free flight, there is a last recall of the fearful drumming, and then the scherzo begins.

This third movement starts by pretending to be a fugue on a tarantella-like theme, but it is soon obvious that Schmidt has no intention of being serious about the fugal component for long. The first movement's trumpet theme was absent from the Adagio, but there are reminders of it here, along with recollections of the *passionato* theme and the Adagio's cello melody. There is a trio, or a least a passage that brings thematic contrast, though, departing from his usual practice, Schmidt does not switch to a slower tempo. The trio comes round twice, and the scherzo is attractively reorchestrated on each of its new appearances.

What starts out to be a normal and energetic coda is suddenly interrupted by a wild *fortissimo* outburst, this, too, marked by a great crash of the tam-tam. I assume that this catastrophe is a reliving for Schmidt of Emma's death, though one must not be too literal-minded about this sort of thing. At any rate, it leads to a complete collapse into all but silence— only a *pianissimo* timpani roll still sounds.

As this distant rumble continues, a French horn plays the opening trumpet melody. The symphony's finale has begun. The other horns join in for a polyphonic elaboration of the haunting melody, quickly carrying it to a firm resolution that corresponds to the one in the first movement. Exhaustion from the catastrophe and the collapse dominates the atmosphere, and so there are differences: here the music is in F major rather than C, the whole process has taken only thirty-seven measures compared with eighty the first time, and the dynamic level has not risen above *piano*. The transition with the arpeggios and scales follows and leads to the return of the *passionato* theme.

The trumpet theme returns, again played by the English horn. Its notes are stretched, as though it lacked the energy to produce the fine rhythmic differentiation it had in its original form. It attempts to rise to a climax comparable with the one in the first movement, and thus perhaps to crown the symphony with a great Brucknerian apotheosis, but it is not to be done. The best thing is to bring that inspired melody back in its original simplicity, on the lambent trumpet, and at home—in C major. *Pianissimo* strings furnish it with an escort part of the way, but section by section they drop out. Playing the two final notes—D-flat and C—the trumpet is alone, as it was in the beginning. Schmidt thought of this melody as "a last music to take along into the next world." One could choose worse.

Arnold Schoenberg

Arnold Franz Walter Schönberg (who spelled his name Schoenberg after settling in the United States in 1934) was born in Vienna, on 13 September 1874 and died in Brentwood, California, on 13 July 1951.

Chamber Symphony No. 1, Opus 9

Slow—very fast—much slower—flowing—very fast
Very fast
Much slower, but flowing
Very slow
With élan—much calmer—very fast
(played without pause)

Schoenberg began the Chamber Symphony No. 1 in April 1906 and completed it on 15 July that year. The first performance was given in Vienna on 8 February 1907 by the Rosé Quartet and members of the Vienna Philharmonic. By 1912, Schoenberg had the idea of multiplying the strings and, where necessary, doubling the winds for performances in large halls, and in 1914 his publisher announced the availability of an orchestral version upon request. Nothing is now known of that version; however, in 1935 Schoenberg made a completely new edition for full orchestra, which was published as Opus 9b. (There is no Opus 9a.) The first performance of Opus 9b was given under the composer's direction in Los Angeles in December 1935.

Flute, oboe, English horn, clarinet, D clarinet, bass clarinet, bassoon, contrabassoon, two horns, two violins, viola, cello, and bass. The version for full
orchestra calls for two flutes and piccolo, two oboes and English horn, clarinet, E-flat clarinet, bass clarinet, two bassoons and contrabassoon, three
horns, two trumpets, three trombones, and strings. (In conformity with the
practice he adopted in America, Schoenberg changed the tempo and character directions from German to Italian.)

The Chamber Symphony No. 1 is the work of a man just about to turn
thirty-two. Schoenberg had been composing since he was eight, beginning
with blatant imitations of the duets by Viotti and others that he had played
at his violin lessons, as well as of the opera medleys and marches he had
heard bands play in the park of a Sunday. He even tried his hand at a
Räuber-Phantasie after Schiller's blood-and-thunder protest drama. Home
was not especially prosperous, Samuel Schönberg being the owner of a
small shoe store, and neither parent was musical—at least, their son liked
to say, not more than any other Viennese who was not explicitly a music-
hater. More remotely, though, there was music in his mother's family, and
his cousin Hans Nachod was the Kiel Opera's heldentenor and later the
first Waldemar in Schoenberg's great cantata *Gurrelieder*. With money he
earned giving German lessons to a Greek, Schoenberg bought some sec-
ondhand Beethoven scores, which left him burning to write string quartets.
    At this point a new friend, Oskar Adler, came into Schoenberg's life
and taught him some elementary harmony. He also found him a large viola
strung with zither strings, which Schoenberg, with viola fingerings and
other desperate improvisations, used as a cello. Playing chamber music became an essential part of Schoenberg's existence and, as he told the story
many years later, "I started writing string quartets. In the meantime, *Mey-
ers Konversations-Lexikon* (an encyclopedia, which we bought on installments) had reach the long-hoped-for letter S, enabling me to learn under
'Sonate' how a first movement of a string quartet should be constructed.
At that time I was about eighteen years old, but had not obtained any
other instruction than that which Oskar Adler had given me."[1]
    Schoenberg took a job in a bank, which he hated, and the day the
bank went broke was one of the most joyous of his life. His decision to
seek no further employment along those lines—a change from "solid citizen
to bohemian," as he says his parents saw it—caused a family crisis. From

---

[1] Adler was a physician and astrologer as well as a violinist. His major work was a book published
in 1950, *Das Testament der Astrologie*. He also left a large unpublished manuscript, *The Critique of
Pure Music*. He and Schoenberg were in affectionate correspondence as late as April 1951, three
months before Schoenberg's death. Adler died in London in 1955. —M.S.

then on, he made his living as a musician, to begin with by conducting amateur choruses such as the one of the Metal Workers' Union in the factory town of Stockerau, and by orchestrating other people's operettas. He joined Polyhymnia, an ensemble that rather exaggerated in calling itself an orchestra. It was led by the twenty-three-year-old Alexander von Zemlinsky, a composer whose first efforts had been encouraged by Brahms; he was also a future conductor of distinction. Zemlinsky quickly made friends with the young man whose "fiery mishandling" of the cello he found so engaging. Schoenberg, for his part, acknowledged Zemlinsky in later years as the man from whom he had acquired most of what he knew "of compositional techniques and problems"—in effect, as his only teacher. From this teacher and friend, Schoenberg, the confirmed Brahmsian, learned to value and love Wagner, and in 1901 the personal side of the relationship was consolidated when he married Zemlinsky's sister Mathilde.[2]

In 1897, Schoenberg completed his delightfully Dvorákian String Quartet in D major (unnumbered) and saw it taken into the repertory of the esteemed Fitzner Quartet. But a year later there was a disturbance after the performance of some of his songs, "and since then," Schoenberg told his pupil and biographer, Egon Wellesz, "the scandal has never stopped." On 1 December 1899, he completed his first masterpiece, *Verklärte Nacht* (Transfigured Night), but even that gorgeous and powerfully composed wonder proved controversial, though more to theorists than to audiences. In 1901, he completed the composition of his cantata, *Gurrelieder*, though he only got to the orchestration ten years later. Two other hyper-Romantic masterpieces on the way to the Chamber Symphony were the tone poem *Pelleas und Melisande* and the String Quartet No. 1. For a change of pace, Schoenberg wrote songs for a literary cabaret in Berlin; he also painted, expressively and disturbingly, later exhibiting with Kandinsky's Blue Rider group.

When Schoenberg completed the Chamber Symphony No. 1 in 1906, he told his friends: "Now I have established my style. Now I know how I have to compose." He quickly realized this was not true: as he put it, he was "not destined" to continue in this post-Romantic manner. Looking back, he saw that the Chamber Symphony was only a way station—but an important one—on the road toward his goal, which was to master what he

---

[2] The marriage was not unclouded. In 1908, Mathilde eloped with her husband's painting teacher, the twenty-four-year-old Richard Gerstl, one of the most interesting of the early Expressionists. Schoenberg's student Anton von Webern persuaded her to return to her husband, after which Gerstl committed suicide. The Schoenbergs were reasonably at peace when Mathilde died in 1923. In 1924, Schoenberg entered a happy marriage with Gertrud Kolisch, the sister of another close musical associate, the violinist and quartet leader Rudolf Kolisch.

described as "a style of concision and brevity in which every technical or structural necessity was carried out without unnecessary extension, in which every single unit is supposed to be functional."[3] Within a few years, Schoenberg was composing an astoundingly dense, non-repetitive, richly detailed, unpredictable new music: the Stefan George song cycle *Das Buch der hängenden Gärten* (The Book of the Hanging Gardens); Three Pieces for Piano, Opus 11; Five Pieces for Orchestra, Opus 16; and the one-character opera *Erwartung* (Expectation), all completed in 1909 and all masterpieces of astounding fantasy and concentration, had gone far away from the luxuriant Romanticism and the expansive gestures of *Verklärte Nacht* and *Gurrelieder*.

Something that did not change was Schoenberg's artistic personality and his temperament. From *Verklärte Nacht* to the last scores, passion is a constant, and the most immediate and ultimately overwhelming impression the Chamber Symphony No. 1 makes is that of urgent, ardent, even wild utterance. As he wrote to Mahler in 1904, "I have no middle-ground feelings" (Mittlere Empfindungen gibt es bei mir nicht).

Forty years after composing it, Schoenberg gave a lecture at the University of Chicago on "Heart and Brain in Music." He began by quoting Balzac's description of a character in his novel *Seraphita*, whose "chest and shoulders were broad and [whose] neck was short, like that of all men whose heart must be within the domain of the head." For Schoenberg, heart and brain—the two sources, the two motors—work marvelously and fruitfully together. He was one of the brainiest of artists *and* he believed in inspiration—*Einfall* (literally something that falls in)—and when *der Einfall* hit, he wrote at white heat. He kept that ability into old age: at seventy-two, almost blind and in the aftermath of a near-fatal illness, he wrote his blazingly inspired, richly complex String Trio in thirty-five days. In the Chamber Symphony, we are swept along as though on a cataract of Ein-fälle: vibrant melodies, thrusting rhythms, swirling harmonies, all richly connected.

The Chamber Symphony is in one movement. It is also in five movements. Schoenberg uses a formal device that had served him well in *Pelleas*

---

[3] Schoenberg began two chamber symphonies in 1906. No. 1 in E major was finished quickly. No. 2, in E-flat minor, resisted him, probably because the First, as it developed, pointed so compellingly to such an interesting and promising future that it became impossible for Schoenberg to continue to work in the old vein. Sketches for No. 2 continued to appear until 1910, to be abandoned, then picked up again much later, leading at last to the completion of the work (Opus 38) in America on 21 October 1939. Nine years later, Schoenberg wrote an essay for *The New York Times* titled *On revient toujours* in which he confesses his musical nostalgia and describes his pleasure at sometimes returning to writing tonal music such as the Chamber Symphony No. 2.

und Melisande and the String Quartet No. 1: he combines the traditional four-movement plan—sonata allegro, scherzo, slow movement, finale—with that of a single sonata movement. You can map it out like this:

I. Exposition (sonata allegro)
II. Scherzo—trio—scherzo
III. Elaboration (Schoenberg's preferred term—the more usual word is *development*)
IV. Slow movement
V. Finale, which recapitulates the material of I, but in a different order.

Sections I, III, and V are characterized sharply enough to encourage you to hear five distinct movements; at the same time, their mutual connectedness is so clear that the symphony's master plan as a single sonata movement with extended interludes on either side of the development is also readily audible.

Schoenberg plays resourcefully and imaginatively upon the ambiguities of his design. Here is a case in point. Section I, the exposition, ends with the return of its first theme. You might suppose for a moment that, like a classical composer, he is going to repeat the exposition. Or you might remember what, for example, Brahms does in the first movement of his Symphony No. 4, where what appears to be an old-fashioned repeat of the exposition suddenly veers off course and reveals itself as the start of the development. Schoenberg shares Brahms's relish for mystery and surprise. His doubling back is neither a repeated exposition nor a revisiting of Brahms's feint, but a transition into the next movement, the scherzo.

Schoenberg also has another reason for his maneuver. The reappearance of a theme from the beginning acts as closure and helps to establish Section I as a movement in its own right instead of merely an unfulfilled exposition. This is an instance of Schoenberg's beautifully imagined extension of formal ideas found in Liszt, notably the Piano Sonata and the Piano Concerto No. 2. In the draft of a 1949 program note on the Chamber Symphony, Schoenberg specifically refers to Liszt's symphonic poems, suggesting further that Liszt, in his exploration of encapsulated forms, was following the model of Beethoven's C-sharp minor String Quartet, Opus 131.[4]

The Chamber Symphony opens with a great pile-up of notes that coalesce into a luscious five-note chord, which resolves ever so suavely into a chord of F major: it sounds like a wonderfully round-the-bend version of

[4] More immediately, Liszt was following the model of Schubert's *Wanderer* Fantasy, of which he made an arrangement for piano and orchestra.

a barbershop quartet's opening swipe. (The author and conductor Erwin Stein recalled that in student days, when he and his friends met, they would greet each other by singing the Chamber Symphony's first cadence.) Fourths are prominent in these opening harmonies; both in his theoretical work and his compositions, Schoenberg was much taken at this time with the idea of fourths as raw material to supplant the thirds whose use he was beginning to think of as a harmonic dead end. Neither for Schoenberg nor for his Russian contemporary Alexander Scriabin did fourths prove to be any kind of harmonic panacea; nonetheless, Schoenberg's use of them in the Chamber Symphony is amazing, especially for the intensity with which they come to saturate the entire work.

From the outset, Schoenberg uses his fourths vertically and horizontally, that is, in chords and in melodies. As soon as the very fast main tempo begins, which is immediately after the F-major cadence, Schoenberg has the horn rush impetuously up the steep slope of fourths from D below middle C to the F at the top of the treble staff. Then, as Schoenberg describes it, chords of fourths spread "through the whole architecture of the work, putting their stamp on everything that happens." Inventing a unit to be treated harmonically and melodically at the same time, Schoenberg has anticipated an essential aspect of the serial technique he was to develop much later.

In Schoenberg's earliest sketches, the opening harmonic pile-up heads directly toward the principal key, E major. Only as he worked did Schoenberg discover how much more dramatic an effect he could achieve by approaching his principal key obliquely. The four-measure slow introduction, in itself a beautiful example of "concision and brevity," therefore leads—mysteriously and wonderfully—to F major, and the first clear E-major harmony occurs only in the seventh bar of the Allegro.

Concerning the relationship of musical ideas, Schoenberg tells an instructive story about the inspiration/brain connection. After the horn call, the cello plays an energetic, upward-rushing theme easily recognized by its persistent triplets as well as by its Debussyan whole-tone steps. This moves forward to an intense climax, which is followed by a new melody for violin and horn in a broad, singing style. This second theme had come to Schoenberg quickly and spontaneously, but it bothered him because he could not intellectually and analytically discern any connection between it and the beginning of the movement. "Directed only by my sense of form and the stream of ideas, I had not asked such questions while composing," Schoenberg recalled, "but as usual with me, doubts arose as soon as I had finished. They went so far that I had already raised the sword for the kill, taken the red pencil of the censor to cross out the [second] theme. Fortunately I stood by my inspiration and ignored these mental tortures."

Twenty years later, he suddenly saw that in its intervallic structure the second theme is an inversion of the first. "[The relationship] is of such a complicated nature that I doubt whether any composer would have cared deliberately to construct a theme in this way, but our subconscious does it involuntarily."

The first movement presents a series of fervent, spirited, and variegated themes in rapid succession. The return of the energetic cello theme is, to use Schoenberg's word, "converted" into a transition to the scherzo. The scherzo itself is even faster than the first movement; the horn fourths, this time going down, make a forceful appearance. The ghostly trio takes about twenty seconds; it is followed by an almost equally brief development and the reprise of the scherzo. Another transition leads to the symphony's main development section, in which the themes of the first movement are reconsidered, recombined, and recostumed with captivating energy.

Rising fourths introduce the slow movement, but now they take the form of incorporeal double-bass harmonics, delicate six-note woodwind chords, clarinet arpeggios rising weightless like dandelion seeds, a dreamy melody for the violin, all in *pianissimo*. The music that ensues, richly melancholic, is a feast of lyric inspiration. The textures become more involved as Schoenberg prepares for the finale. This recapitulates and sometimes further transforms earlier themes with great freedom in their order of appearance. The rising fourths and the excited theme from the beginning of the first movement return in the coda. The close, with exultant horns and emphatic assertions of E major against the chromatic current, is joyously exuberant.

A postscript about Schoenberg's full-orchestra version of the Chamber Symphony No. 1: It eliminates any problems of balance in the original. Because the strings are not anxious about being audible and therefore not tempted to force, the transcription does away with what Stravinsky, not altogether unjustly, called the neurasthenic sound in the chamber version. The big-band scoring also shows how Janus-faced a work Opus 9 is. To a large degree because of its novel—and still novel—scoring, the chamber ensemble draws the listener's attention to everything that is forward-looking and "modern" in the music; the magnificent and easy sound of Opus 9b gets us to listen in the opposite direction, and perhaps we then hear for the first time how much the opening comes from the same family as Strauss's *Don Juan* or how much Mahler there is in the slow movement. Opus 9b is a handsome piece of (barely) post-Romantic orchestral music, and it is both surprising and a pity that so few conductors play it.

Franz Schubert

Franz Peter Schubert was born in Liechtenthal, a suburb of Vienna, on 31 January 1797 and died in Vienna on 19 November 1828.

Cautiously, one can hope that the commemorative concerts, publications, and scholarly conferences called into being in 1978 by the 150th anniversary of Schubert's death began an overdue reevaluation of his work and stature as an artist. But we still read sometimes that he was something of an amateur as a composer, albeit an inspired one, and there are still writers who portray him as the most seductive of charmers but deny him greatness.

How much of Schubert's music is in the active repertory? An eighth? Less? Two or three of the symphonies, the *Trout* Quintet, the Cello Quintet, the Impromptus and *Moments musicaux,* a few songs such as *Gretchen am Spinnrade* and *Der Erlkönig,* the *Ave Maria* and *Die Forelle, An die Musik* and the most famous of the Serenades, are insistently with us. Some of the other orchestral and chamber music has a growing audience, as do the great song cycles, while more and more pianists find the courage to play the sonatas. (At the end of the 1920s, Rachmaninoff admitted he had not known that Schubert had written any piano sonatas.) But how vague we are likely to be about all but two or three of those sonatas and the masterpieces for piano duet (unless we play them ourselves), and how many hundreds—literally—of songs we have probably never heard. And what, even on the most trivial level, do most of us know about Schubert's "social" choral works, his sacred music, his operas?

Of Schubert himself most of us have some sort of image: short (five feet exactly) and a bit on the pudgy side, potato nose, curly brown hair, gold-rimmed spectacles; consuming whatever wine and coffee and cigars he could afford or charge; the center of a circle of adoring friends who looked after him, found him places to live, joined him on hiking tours (how much "walking" we find in his music), and with whom he played cards and charades; an unassuming little man whose Viennese accent was as dense as the Knödel in his soup and who somehow, blithely, without laborious sketching or erasing, jotted masterpieces onto tablecloths and the backs of menus.

Much of that is true. He could compose at incredible speed—we know quite a lot about that because his teacher, Antonio Salieri, got him in the habit of dating his manuscripts—and at least one song, his setting of "Hark, hark the lark" from "Schakespear's" *Cymbeline*, actually was written in a sudden seizure of inspiration, among friends, at a café table, on the back of a menu.

But those witnesses to his life whose rich and moving testimony is collected in *Schubert: Memoirs by His Friends*, edited by Otto Erich Deutsch, also noticed that when he sat at the piano to accompany the great Michael Vogl or when he himself sang his songs in his own composer's falsetto, something transformed him beyond their recognition. He could compose music that frightened and dismayed them, the death-possessed songs of *Winterreise* (Winter Journey), for example, which they rejected even though he insisted it was the best thing he had done. "My productions came about through my understanding of music and through my pain," he wrote in his diary, "and those that are produced by pain alone seem to please the world least." He had warned his friends that these songs would make them shudder, and the friends' rejection was, paradoxically, a form of understanding and of love, because in rejecting the songs they were rejecting his knowledge of death, his own death, then just a year away. John Harbison's assertion that Schubert "got closer to full metaphysical revelation than any other composer" is a challenge we do well to take seriously.

"At last I can pour out my whole heart to someone again," the twenty-seven-year-old composer wrote to his friend the painter Leopold Kupelwieser:

> You are so good and faithful, you are sure to forgive me things that others would only take very much amiss. To be brief, I feel myself to be the most unhappy, the most wretched man in the world. Picture to yourself a man whose health will never be sound again and who, out of sheer despair over that, does everything to make matters constantly worse instead of better. Picture to yourself, I say, a man whose brightest hopes have come to nothing, to whom love and friendship at best offer only pain, someone whose response (creative response at least) to all that is beautiful threatens

to vanish. . . . "My peace is gone, my heart is heavy; never, but never again, shall I find peace."[1] That could be my daily song now, for each night when I go to sleep I hope never to wake again, and each morning brings back to me yesterday's grief.[2]

At the same time, Schubert's self-awareness comprised a keen sense of his own worth, of his artistic goals and possibilities. He grew up in the shadow of Beethoven, who himself had had to mature in the shadow of Haydn and Mozart, but bit by bit, Schubert came to understand that he was qualified to step forward as the heir of Beethoven. (I tell some of that story in the essays on the *Unfinished* and the *Great* C-major symphonies.) His last musical wish, fulfilled five days before his death, was to hear Beethoven's Quartet in C-sharp minor, Opus 131. ("The King of Harmony had sent the King of Song a friendly bidding to the crossing," said Karl Holz, one of the violinists at that gathering.)

We also know now that the imposing series of works in which Schubert declared himself—from the Octet, the A-minor and *Death and the Maiden* quartets, and the Grand Duo for piano, all of 1824, to the Cello Quintet and the three piano sonatas of the last year, 1828—was not written without sketches and erasures, without intense concentration and *Sitzfleisch*.

We have, furthermore, the wrong idea if we imagine his work going unnoticed and Schubert himself hopelessly neglected except within the circle of his friends. True, his fame was local, and the E-flat Piano Trio was his only work published abroad in his lifetime, but Vienna was an important musical center, and it meant something to be known there. True also that Schubert never attained the success in the theater that he longed for so ardently, nor did he ever hear a professional performance of one of his symphonies, but for the rest, his music was sung and played, admired, and talked about. On 7 March 1821, Michael Vogl, a star of the Court Opera, sang *Der Erlkönig* at an important charity concert, and that put an end to Schubert's obscurity in the capital. Something like an eighth of his music was in print when he died, not bad for a prolific musician with no connections, without a significant career as a performer, and lacking all talent for self-promotion.

Finally, a word about the numbering of Schubert's symphonies. There is no entirely satisfactory or universally accepted system. Up to the *Little*— or at least littler—C-major Symphony, D.589, there is no problem. (The

---

[1] Schubert is quoting *Gretchen am Spinnrade*, the poem from Goethe's *Faust* that he had set at seventeen with a knowledge of the human heart no boy of that age ought to have. —M.S.

[2] *Franz Schubert's Letters and Other Writings*, edited by O. E. Deutsch (London: Faber & Gwyer, 1928).

D numbers are those assigned by Deutsch in his thematic catalogue of Schubert's works; they are useful in that for the most part they indicate the chronology accurately, but they have not become "naturalized" and familiar.) We have, up to that point, six complete Schubert symphonies, rationally numbered in order of their composition from No. 1 in D major, D.82 (October 1813), to the *Little* C-major, Number 6, D.589 (February 1818). These six works are preceded by a fragment of another symphony in D major, a slow introduction plus nineteen bars of allegro, which Deutsch places as "probably written about 1812." Number 6 is followed by sketches and fragments of two more symphonies, one in D major, D.615 (May 1818), and one in E minor/major, D.729 (August 1821).[3]

From here on, we have confusion. Next come the two fully orchestrated movements in B minor and E major (plus part of a scherzo) which we know as the *Unfinished* Symphony, D.759, the beginning of whose full score is dated October 1822 and which was lost—or rather, hidden—until 1865. Then comes the *Great* C major, which was completed early in 1826, though the manuscript bears the date of March 1828, a confusing discrepancy that has never been cleared up. Finally, in the last weeks of his life Schubert made considerable progress on what would have been yet another symphony in D major, D.966a, parts of which have been realized in "performing versions" by the German musicologist and conductor Peter Gülke and by Brian Newbould. The Italian composer Luciano Berio has used the sketches of the D-major Symphony to compose a work titled *Rendering*. This posthumous collaboration is not, however, a scholarly "performing version" but something Berio himself has described, perhaps with more candor than the musicologists, as a work of "dual authorship."

The *Great* C-major, as the English musical lexicographer Sir George Grove was the first to call it, has been listed as No. 9 and sometimes— rather less often in recent years—as No. 7.[4] Calling it No. 7 made sense while the *Unfinished* was still buried in the attic of Schubert's friend An-

---

[3] Deutsch notes that "Mendelssohn, [Arthur] Sullivan, and Brahms are said to have contemplated finishing the sketch" of the E minor/major Symphony. John Francis Barnett, an English composer, actually did so about 1863, as did Felix Weingartner, the Austrian composer and conductor, in 1934. A stylistically more accurate edition was made in 1977 by the English musicologist Brian Newbould.

[4] *Great* is a problem adjective. *Groß* in German means great in the sense of big as well as of magnificent, whereas the English "great" has all but lost its non-valuative meaning (as one used to find it in, for example, "great toe"). When Schubert voiced his plan to write a "große Sinfonie," he meant one on a large scale, though he undoubtedly hoped it would also turn out to be "great." (There used to be a gag to the effect that Schubert wrote two symphonies, one unfinished and the other endless.) It would be good to find something equivalent to *groß*, but to call this work Schubert's *Large* C-major Symphony or *Big* C-major Symphony sounds weird. And most of us would, after all, agree that D.944 is indeed great.

selm Hüttenbrenner and the *Great* C-major was the next-known symphony after No. 6. But the editors of the complete Schubert edition that came out in Germany between 1883 and 1897 chose to disregard chronology and put the *Unfinished* Symphony after the seven complete ones. This is how that work came by its familiar number, 8. The next step—of designating the *Great* C-major Symphony as number 9—was sensible insofar as it got the chronology of this work and the *Unfinished* straight, but a nuisance in that it left the number 7 unaccounted for.

There is some rational justification for calling the *Unfinished* No. 7 and the C-major No. 8, as the 1979 revised edition of the Deutsch catalogue does; on the other hand, there is a real psychological obstacle to accepting this reshuffling of familiar titles and familiar numbers to make new and unfamiliar combinations. (To confuse things further, the Leipzig Gewandhaus Orchestra, which feels proprietary because it gave the first public performance of the work, calls the *Great* C-major No. 10 in its programs!) Hoping to make things both comfortable and sensible, some program editors simply call the one work *Unfinished* Symphony in B minor, D.759, and the other *Great* C-major Symphony, D.944, getting rid of the No. 7/8/9/10 business altogether.

Then there is a ghost to be exorcised, the so-called *Gastein* Symphony, named for a village with mineral springs, some fifty miles south of Salzburg, where Schubert spent a brief period in the summer of 1825. There, and a little earlier in the year at Gmunden, where he had stayed rather longer, Schubert worked on a symphony. Several of his friends attest to this, and it is mentioned in the obituary notice by his friend Eduard von Bauernfeld. We know now that this was the *Great* C-major, but when it had not yet been shown that this work was written in 1825–26 and was still believed to date from 1828, there remained the question, what became of the *Gastein* or *Gmunden-Gastein* Symphony? Many assumed that this mystery piece would someday turn up, much as the B-minor *Unfinished* had come out of hiding thirty-seven years after Schubert's death. That was part of the attraction of calling the *Great* C-major No. 9: we saved the number 7 for the *Gastein*, much as one sets a place at a Seder for the Prophet Elijah. Deutsch even assigned the *Gastein* a number, 849, in his catalogue. But it is now as good as certain that the allegedly missing *Gastein* is not going to appear; or rather, that it has already done so in the form of the *Great* C-major.[5]

---

[5] It has also been proposed that the C-major Grand Duo for Piano Duet, D.812, is the *Gastein* Symphony, but which Schubert never got around to orchestrating. This has no foundation in reality at all; there are, however, orchestrations of the Grand Duo by, among others, Joseph Joachim and Raymond Leppard.

Unfinished Symphony in B minor, D.759

> *Allegro moderato*
> *Andante con moto*

The score of the two completed movements of this symphony is dated 30 October 1822. A scherzo exists in a fairly complete piano sketch, and the first nine measures of that movement, fully scored, are on the reverse of the last page of the second movement. The first performance of the *Unfinished* was given under the direction of Johann von Herbeck in Vienna on 17 December 1865, the last movement of Schubert's Symphony No. 3 in D major, D.200, being appended as an incongruous finale. August Ludwig (1865–1949), a German composer and critic, was the first to be seized by and to execute the unhappy idea of finishing the *Unfinished:* he added a "Philosopher's Scherzo" and a "March of Destiny."

Two flutes, two oboes, two clarinets, two bassoons, two horns, two trumpets, three trombones, timpani, and strings.

The most obvious question about this symphony we cannot answer. In the 1940s, there was a Victor record album of the work played by the Boston Symphony under Koussevitzky. The picture on the cover showed part of a desk with a page of musical manuscript, purportedly of the *Unfinished.* I remember an inkwell and a quill. The pen lay on the page and had left a few artfully placed inkblots when it dropped from the writer's hand. I think there was a glass with a rose, some of whose petals had also fallen onto the page—at least there ought to have been. But that was not it. Schubert did not leave the score unfinished because Death forbade. He lived a full six years after he abandoned it, six years during which, so far as we know, he did not give it another thought.

The title page is signed and dated—Vienna, 30 October 1822—but beyond that there is no reference to the work in Schubert's lifetime. Johann von Herbeck, who conducted the first performance in 1865, had retrieved the manuscript from Anselm Hüttenbrenner in Ober-Andritz near Graz earlier that year. By then the existence of the work was a matter of public knowledge since it was mentioned in Hüttenbrenner's entry on himself in the *Biographisches Lexikon des Kaisertums Oesterreich* (1836) as well as in the big Schubert biography by Heinrich Kreissle von Hellborn (1864). Anselm Hüttenbrenner had received the manuscript from his younger brother, Josef, who seems to have had it directly from Schubert; however, the details of its journey from Schubert to Josef to Anselm are obscure.

First of all, who were the Hüttenbrenners? Anselm, born 1794 in Graz, a university city some ninety miles southwest of Vienna, was a composer and critic who met Schubert in 1815 as a fellow-student in Antonio Salieri's composition class. Anselm returned to Graz in 1821, but remained on terms of warm friendship with Schubert. He wrote a popular set of *Erlkönig* waltzes based on Schubert's famous song and performed his friend's music. It was Anselm's Requiem that was sung at the memorial service for Schubert in January 1829. He led a long, active, and varied life in the service of music, but in his last years—he died in 1868—he stopped composing, became pious and withdrawn, and occupied himself mainly with questions about theology and magnetism.

Josef Hüttenbrenner, born in 1796, was introduced to Schubert by Anselm in 1817. He became a civil servant, but was passionately devoted to music, at least to Schubert's and Anselm's, with perhaps not much sense that there was a difference. Nowadays we might call him a groupie: he hung around and made himself useful, he was aggressive, his friendship often turned out to be self-serving, and he sometimes irritated Schubert with his uncritical adulation ("Why, that man likes every single thing I do").

In April 1823, half a year after the date on the manuscript of the *Unfinished,* Schubert was awarded the Diploma of Honor of the Styrian Musical Society in Graz. Anselm was a member of the Society and later its president, and the diploma was transmitted to Schubert via himself and Josef. In 1860 Josef first mentioned the symphony to Johann von Herbeck, explaining that "Schubert gave it to me for Anselm as thanks for having sent him the diploma through me." In a letter to an unnamed recipient, and dated 1868, Josef tells it a little differently: "Schubert gave it to me out of gratitude for the Diploma of Honor from the Graz Music Society and dedicated it to the Society and Anselm. I had brought the diploma to Schubert."

In the same letter, Josef states that he and Anselm had been unable to "find an orchestra anywhere that would accept [the symphony]." We don't know when the Hüttenbrenners had stopped trying to get someone to perform the *Unfinished,* but Josef's failure is quite believable for the first decade after Schubert's death; in 1838, Schubert's brother Ferdinand lamented to Robert Schumann that he had been unable to get performances for the symphonies in his possession. It is strange, though, that even after Schubert's *Great* C-major Symphony, with Schumann's help, began to gain recognition as a masterwork, albeit a possibly problematic one, the Hüttenbrenners seem to have made no new efforts to get the *Unfinished* out into the open.

Schubert's letter of thanks to the Graz Society is dated 20 September 1823. This is not a reflection on his manners: though the diploma is dated 6 April, Schubert did not receive it until September. The letter says: "In order also to give musical expression to my sincere gratitude, I shall take the liberty before long of presenting your honorable Society with one of my symphonies in full score." Presumably the two movements of the B-minor Symphony came into Anselm's possession because Schubert intended them for the Society. I would guess that he sent only two movements because he foresaw difficulties with completing the piece, but also wanted to send something substantial fairly quickly. What we don't know at all is when he gave the manuscript to Josef Hüttenbrenner, nor why it remained in Anselm Hüttenbrenner's chest of drawers rather than going to the library of the Styrian Musical Society.

When Josef Hüttenbrenner first told Johann von Herbeck about the *Unfinished* in March 1860, these were his words: "[Anselm] possesses a treasure . . . in Schubert's Symphony in B minor, which we *place on a level* with the great Symphony in C major . . . *and with any of Beethoven's.* Only it is not finished." Josef's point was to use the *Unfinished* as a bribe to get the influential Herbeck to perform some of Anselm's songs, quartets, choruses, operas, overtures, symphonies, Masses, and Requiems. For some reason Herbeck delayed five years, but on 1 May 1865, after Kreissle von Hellborn had publicly urged Anselm to release the manuscript of Schubert's symphony, the conductor finally made the trip to Ober-Andritz. The account that follows is from an article, "The Riddle of Schubert's Unfinished Symphony" by the great Schubert scholar Otto Erich Deutsch (*Music Review* 1940):

> Herbeck arrived in the village and, finding that the inn where he had gone by chance was the one which [Hüttenbrenner] daily frequented, awaited him there. "I have come," he said when Hüttenbrenner arrived, "to ask you to allow one of your compositions to be performed in Vienna." Anselm thereupon escorted Herbeck to his home . . . and into his study that looked like a lumber-room. Furniture, including a close-stool, had to be pushed out of the way before all the manuscripts could be reached and spread out—first, of course, those of Anselm himself. Herbeck while still in Vienna had chosen for the performance Anselm's Overture in C minor . . . and had obtained the manuscript from Josef, but now he also took from Anselm two overtures to play. This being settled, Herbeck said, "I intend to bring the three contemporaries, Schubert, Hüttenbrenner, and Lachner before the

Vienna public in a single concert.[6] Naturally I would like very much to have Schubert represented by a new work." Anselm replied, "Well, I still have a lot of things by Schubert." Then from a drawer crammed with papers in an old-fashioned chest, he pulled out the symphony. Herbeck maintained his outward calm while he held the desired manuscript in his hand. "That would be quite suitable," he said, then with consummate diplomacy, "Will you allow me to have the manuscript transcribed immediately at my expense?" But Anselm, who had been completely won over, replied, "There is no need to hurry, you are welcome to take it with you". . . . So these manuscripts, the decoy and the game, arrived on that very day in Vienna where the Schubert manuscript, after its long exile, was thenceforth to remain.

Between the fall of 1813 and the winter of 1817–18, Schubert, without inhibition, almost casually, had written six symphonies. Then, as he enlarged his idea of symphony, a process that culminated in his admission in 1824 that he was making his way *"zur großen Sinfonie"* and his composition of the *Great* C-major in 1825–26, work became more complicated. In May 1818, he wrote and abandoned twenty-five pages of closely written piano sketches for a symphony in D major. In August 1821, he made more progress with but also abandoned a symphony in E minor/major, whose Adagio introduction is impressive and new in manner. In the fall of 1822 we have the great work in B minor that is the subject of this essay, and which, by the way, was not commonly called the *Unfinished* until the 1890s. This period, 1818–22, is altogether one in which Schubert left many fragments.

The B-minor Symphony he was able to carry a lot farther than the fragments of 1818 and 1821. We know of no external circumstances or pressures that would have kept him from finishing it. That he intended to leave it as a work in two movements in not very closely related keys is a notion totally out of tune with everything else we know about Schubert's thought and practice. Probably most of us today share something of the Romantic fascination with ruins and fragments, with blurred beginnings and endings, but that was not part of Schubert's aesthetic.

The most convincing explanation is that he was at a loss how to go on. The year 1822 was a good one, begun with the completion of his wonderfully imaginative opera *Alfonso und Estrella,* and closing with the stunning and original *Wanderer* Fantasy for piano, composed at about the

---

[6] Franz Paul Lachner (1803–90) was a Bavarian composer and conductor, active chiefly in Vienna and Munich. Wagner likened his conducting of the Andante of Mozart's G-minor Symphony to the swinging of a bronze pigtail. The recitatives in the familiar performing edition of Cherubini's *Médée* are Lachner's. In the event, nothing by Lachner was played at the Vienna concert. After the Hüttenbrenner and Schubert works, the program was completed by some *a cappella* choruses of von Herbeck's own and Mendelssohn's *Italian* Symphony. —M.S.

same time as the two-and-a-fraction movements of the *Unfinished* Symphony. Those movements were altogether new in melodic style, the bold mixture of breadth and concision in their structure, and the warm glow of their orchestral sound. It was music like no other ever heard before, music fit to claim a place in the tradition of the *große Sinfonie*. Schubert's standards were now immensely high.

But the delightful Scherzo is not on the level of the first two movements. Above all, Beethoven had turned the planning and composing of finales into a problem ever since he had begun to write symphonies whose center of gravity was at the end rather than the beginning, works in which the finale was not merely whatever came last but was the movement toward which the entire work tended and in which all its tensions were resolved. This problem unsettled composers as far into the nineteenth century and beyond as Franck, Bruckner, Dvořák, Mahler, and Shostakovich. Even in later years and in works otherwise as miraculous as the G-major String Quartet, D.887, and the C-minor Piano Sonata, D.958, Schubert could not always match earlier movements with finales of comparable concentration and intensity.

Michael Griffel, an American Schubert scholar, had the interesting idea that Schubert, with the Beethoven Fifth in mind, imagined his B-minor Symphony as culminating in a heroic finale in major, but was baffled as to how to accomplish this. Griffel also proposed—and this, too, is a fascinating and provocative thought—that when Schubert wanted to take lessons from the great pedagogue Simon Sechter, an arrangement barely begun at the time of Schubert's last illness and death, it was not in order to study counterpoint and fugue just generally, but to get tips on how to end a minor-key symphony by means of contrapuntal techniques. However much we may mourn the complete B-minor Symphony we don't have—and had Schubert been able to continue on the level of the first two movements, he would have achieved a symphony even greater, certainly more personal, than the *Great* C-major—for Schubert himself in 1822, looking at those two movements, it was just easier to shelve the problem, get the manuscript out of the house, and go on to something else.[7]

I said earlier that the *Unfinished* is music like no other ever heard before. This mysterious opening—yes, we might remember Haydn's *Drum-roll* or the Beethoven Fourth, but in both those pieces, before the stealthy strings begin (the adjective is John Harbison's) there is some sort of formal

---

[7] To mention one other speculation about the *Unfinished*: the English musicologist Gerald Abraham, seconded later by a younger colleague, Brian Newbould, believed that Schubert had in fact written a finale but because of the pressure of another deadline diverted it to the incidental music for Helmina von Chézy's play *Rosamunde*. The movement in question, the Entr'acte No. 1 in B minor, is a fine piece, but the notion of its being a symphonic finale seems preposterous.

announcement, the drumroll in the one, the five-story B-flat in the other. Schubert's *pianissimo* cellos and basses begin their creeping progress without warning. There is another, more important, difference. Beginnings of this kind—at least before Schubert—belong to the world of slow introductions. The Haydn and Beethoven examples are typical. In the *Unfinished* we can't tell right away what the tempo is—is the first note a single beat in a very slow tempo, or what?—any more than we can tell whether the long note on which the first phrase ends is something in tempo or an unmeasured fermata.

After that long note we get some clarity. An accompaniment begins, *pianissimo*, with nervous, rustling violins, pizzicato below. We can now make out what the tempo is—a moderate allegro in 3/4 time—and in retrospect we can understand that the mysterious opening measures were in that tempo too. In other words, in a daring game of ambiguity, those measures implied "introduction" by their gestures but were in fact the real beginning. After a few measures, oboe and clarinet add the melody to the string accompaniment. The sounds stay low, but the heart is disturbed: the melody is quick to stray from its B-minor moorings, and sharply accented chords interrupt its progress. The interruptions are like the pruning of a plant: their result is that the melody stretches, extends itself, until it arrives at a powerful cadence, still in B minor.

Nothing about that cadence is ordinary. The crescendo leading to it is brief and thus very forceful, *fortissimo* arrives unexpectedly, on a weak beat, and the last two measures are tense with cross-rhythms. It was not usually Schubert's way to modulate over a period of time into the new key where he would introduce a new theme; rather, he preferred a sudden and dramatic stepping into new harmonic territory. So it is here. Horns and bassoons, with emphatic accent, pick one note out of the closing B-minor chord, hold it for a long time (but in tempo), then make the gentlest of landings in G major.

And there, to a syncopated accompaniment, Schubert gives us one of the most famous tunes in the world. That both tune and accompaniment are *pianissimo* is of the essence, though this is not always remembered by conductors: the temptation to lean into the cellos is strong. Nonetheless, this restraint—repression is not too strong a word—is everything. This is the only moment of sweet lyricism in a movement otherwise dark, troubled, fierce. No less remarkable than the tune itself is that it, too, is unfinished—broken off in extraordinary gestures of pathos and drama. In a passage that sounds and feels like development rather than exposition— remember the "developmental" tendency of the first theme to stretch and extend—fragments of the melody are tossed violently about. When, however, the tune tries to resume in its original sweetness and innocence, we are made to understand that the *fortissimo* outbursts after it had faded away the first time have made its survival impossible.

These outbursts also introduce a problem that is a plague to interpreters of Schubert's music. The printed score has these disruptive chords marked with *ffz* (meaning *fortissimo* with an accent) and the standard diminuendo sign a wedge pointing to the right. Some diminuendos in Schubert have troubled scholars and musicians (more of the former than the latter) because they make no musical sense: the last notes of the *Great* C-major Symphony and the C-major String Quintet are notorious instances. The difficulty is that the symbol for an accent is also an arrowhead pointing to the right, only shorter. Many of us believe that most of these musically nonsensical diminuendos are accents drawn by Schubert with excessive exuberance. These violently disruptive chords in the first movement of the *Unfinished* are prime examples.

I remember being taught as a college freshman that Schubert, though talented, couldn't compose very well. Specifically, his trouble was that he didn't understand that in sonata form he was not supposed to start developing themes until he was through with the exposition (no dilly-dallying), safely crossed the double bar, and arrived in the proper development section. He is still faulted sometimes for his audacity in writing sonata movements that are not like Haydn's, Mozart's, and Beethoven's—not that those are always like each other's or even, so to speak, like themselves— and not like ex post facto descriptions of sonata form. Here, in the exposition of the first movement of the *Unfinished*, we have twice experienced Schubert's going with his drive to start development, and in just those places we have, twice, experienced some of his most gripping utterances.

Now he is in the development proper, and the music is incredibly focused and concentrated. His subject, all but exclusively throughout this entire section, is the eight-measure cello-and-bass phrase at the very beginning. We hear it first shrouded in even deeper mystery and in a state of tense repression; then it takes over in assertive *fortissimo*. Three times the ghost of the famous G-major melody appears, but the melody itself dare not raise its head: only the syncopated accompaniment, forlorn and without function, is heard. The harmonies change slowly. That is the characteristic of exposition; the harmony in a development typically moves quickly. Schubert, having put something of development into his exposition, now redresses the balance by putting something typical of exposition into his development. Now if that is not a musician who understood composition, balance, sonata form. . . .

The recapitulation begins with the nervous *pianissimo* accompaniment and the oboe-clarinet melody: the eight bars for cellos and basses need no further attention for the moment.[8] The coda is like a compressed re-living of the development. These few bars are an anguished farewell both to and from the movement's dark opening measures. The final cadence is taut, and its strength should *not* be dissipated by the traditional misreading of accent as diminuendo.

The tempo of the second movement is Andante con moto, the time signature 3/8. In spite of the differences between Allegro moderato in 3/4 (as in the first movement) and Andante con moto in 3/8, the two movements go very comfortably at about the same speed, and without any sense of monotony. Something the two movements have in common is that in each, the real rhythmic unit is not the individual beat, whether quarters in the first movement or eighths in the second, but the whole measure. It is an interesting demonstration that tempo is a complex category, involving much besides the speed of beats per minute—such things as weight, how the measures and the individual beats are filled in, and most crucially, the rate of harmonic change.

The second movement, in E major, is calmer in spirit than the first, but here, too, Schubert constantly disturbs the flow and our expectations. The first melody, *pianissimo* again, is wondrously peaceful, but it has barely arrived at the close of its second phrase when the harmony is pierced by dissonance. What appears to be recovery in fact leads to an unawaited, startling excursion to G major—startling especially for occurring less than half a minute into the movement.[9]

The Andante's most memorable feature is the still, almost incorporeal passage for violins alone that introduces the second theme. The theme itself, a melody begun by the clarinet and continued on the oboe, is gentle in demeanor, but deeply disturbing in its unpredictable, strangely shadowed progress over a syncopated accompaniment. Except for two brief swells to *forte,* this is all in *pianissimo/pianississimo.* It is as though Schubert had taken two elements from his first movement—the oboe-clarinet color (separated now instead of blended) and an accompaniment of agitated syncopations—and, through alchemy, had made them yield this new and wondrous music. (In the recapitulation, the oboe begins and the clarinet continues.)

---

[8] Tchaikovsky had learned this lesson well when he composed the first movement of his *Pathétique.*
[9] Speculation beginning in the late 1980s that Schubert was gay has inevitably led to the question of how, if at all, this affects the way we hear his music. One answer that was proposed in what turned into quite an acrimonious debate is that Schubert's inclination to develop or go on excursions at stages in a composition when his classical models did not do so can now be accounted for by the preponderance of the feminine element in his psychological makeup. That is, women stop to smell the roses, while men charge straight to the goal, knocking stuff over as they go.

Reviewing the first performance of the *Unfinished,* Eduard Hanslick had just one reservation: "As if he could not bear to part from his own sweet song, the composer postpones the conclusion of the [Andante], yes, postpones it all too long." Hanslick is dead wrong, but no question, he noticed a most inspired moment—and one very dangerous in performance. (Perhaps his complaint tells us that the conductor lingered too long.)

Schubert begins his coda with music like that which began the movement, but goes at once to the still and mysterious passage for violins alone that had previously introduced the second theme. Only this time it is skewed in its harmonies so as to lead to a harmonically very far away place (G-sharp major, which Schubert for humanitarian reasons notates as A-flat major). There, clarinets and bassoon sing the opening strain once more, as quietly as possible. The violin passage, with another twist of its intervals, brings us safely back to E major and to the last, soft cadences.

We hear it as beautiful, unresolved mystery (that is, if we don't, like Hanslick, hear it as unsatisfactory disturbance). I am sure, though, that Schubert had intended to resolve that mystery in the finale, to explain it, to "compose out" the possibility he hints at in that wonderful last minute. And perhaps there, for just a moment, you might hear the symphony as incomplete as well as unfinished. But then, it might have gone worse: in 1848, Josef Hüttenbrenner's maid used as kindling the manuscript (and only extant copy) of Acts 2 and 3 of Schubert's opera *Claudine von Villa Bella.*

Symphony in C major, D.944 (Old No. 9 or No. 7), *The Great*

> *Andante—Allegro ma non troppo—Più moto*
> *Andante con moto*
> *Scherzo: Allegro vivace*
> *Allegro vivace*

The *Great* C-major, the seventh and last symphony Schubert completed, was long believed to have been composed in 1828, the year of Schubert's death, and the first page of the autograph manuscript is dated "März 1828." However, through examination of the manuscript paper itself, the American scholar Robert Winter has established that the symphony was begun in the summer of 1825, composed primarily during the second half of that year, and completed in the first months of 1826. The discrepancy has not been cleared up. Among the ideas that have been advanced to explain it are that Schubert made some revisions in March 1828 or, aware that the most recent possible date would be most attractive to a buyer, he entered "März 1828" when he was hoping to sell the symphony to a publisher. Otto Erich Deutsch, the Viennese scholar whose thematic catalogue of Schubert's works is the source of the identifying D numbers, believed the *Great* C-major to have been composed in 1828, and his belief is reflected in the high number he assigned to it. Something in the 880s, however, would give a more accurate picture of the symphony's place in the Schubert chronology. (For more on the vexed question of chronology and the numbering of Schubert's symphonies, see page 472.)

Sometime between the summer of 1827 and Schubert's death in November 1828, the work received at least a reading at a rehearsal of the orchestra of the Vienna Society of Friends of Music. Otto Biba, the current archivist of the Society, writes that "paper and scribal evidence make it clear that sometime in the early 1830s, and for an undetermined occasion, several duplicate orchestral parts were prepared. Moreover, the finale of the symphony was performed at a public concert in Vienna in 1836." The first fully authenticated performance of all four movements, though heavily cut, took place on 21 March 1839, Felix Mendelssohn-Bartholdy conducting the orchestra of the Leipzig Gewandhaus.

Two flutes, two oboes, two clarinets, two bassoons, two horns, two trumpets, three trombones, timpani, and strings.

Schubert was twenty-eight in the summer of 1825. Though personally shy and awkward, he was an ambitious and confident young musician. The year before, he had written to his friend Leopold Kupelwieser that, having just finished two string quartets and preparing to begin another, he was ready "to pave the road toward a big symphony." He meant a symphony in the manner and on the scale of one of Beethoven's and mentions the impending premiere of the Beethoven Ninth in the next paragraph. In his teens, Schubert had subscribed to the conventional view that Beethoven was responsible for the current taste for eccentric music, but he had meanwhile come to think of Beethoven, his senior by twenty-six years, as the very ideal of all that a composer might be. The *Great* C-major is Schubert's Beethoven symphony, and its composition and completion were important steps in Schubert's process of putting forward his claim eventually to assume the mantle of Beethoven. Bearing in mind that in 1822 he had abandoned a symphony with an equally magnificent beginning—the famous B-minor *Unfinished*—that he felt able to carry this project to its conclusion is especially significant.

It would, in the event, be a while before the *Great* C-major Symphony became a fixed feature on the musical landscape. The Viennese performance of the finale in 1836 led nowhere. In 1838 Robert Schumann visited Vienna and, having first gone to see Schubert's grave at the Währing cemetery, he called on Schubert's older brother, Ferdinand. Schumann knew that Ferdinand Schubert possessed a number of Franz's manuscripts in which he had been unable to interest publishers or performers; nonetheless, Schumann was stunned by what Ferdinand showed him. Among these treasures, Schumann reported, were several symphonies, unperformed and rejected because "too difficult and bombastic" ("schwierig und schwülstig"). He immediately arranged for the *Great* C-major to be sent to the Leipzig Gewandhaus, where Mendelssohn was the conductor, and that is how that 1839 performance came about.[10]

But the players in Paris and London would not allow François-Antoine Habeneck and Mendelssohn to finish rehearsing the symphony, the London violinists collapsing with laughter when they came to the eighty-eight consecutive bars of triplet eighth-notes accompanying the finale's second theme. Paris finally heard the work in 1851, and the devoted August Manns, who had given the first public performances of Schubert's first three symphonies, got his Crystal Palace Orchestra through it five years later. (Interestingly, New York heard it before Paris or London, and even Boston preceded London.) By the 1850s it was established in the repertory, and in 1868 Schubert's friend Josef Hüttenbrenner was able to refer to it as "now taking first place" in Germany after Beethoven.

Even before the music begins, there is a puzzle. Each measure has four quarter-notes, but the time signature in the manuscript is $\mathdutchcal{C}$ or *alla breve*, to indicate that the motion is to be felt as two beats in each measure, not four. Yet all the printed material, going back to the first publication of orchestral parts in 1840, gives a time signature of C, indicating four beats in each measure. This, combined with a tempo mark of Andante (moving, flowing), means that while this introduction is slower than the Allegro it leads to, it is not *slow*. This not only affects the pace, and thus the character, of the introduction itself, but makes a huge difference to what happens later on.

---

[10]Later, when Schumann wrote about his visit to Ferdinand Schubert, he tells how on Beethoven's grave he found a steel pen nib, which he picked up. He goes on: "But only on festive, solemn occasions such as this one do I put it to use."

In his excited review after Mendelssohn's performance, Schumann particularly praised the originality of Schubert's orchestral concept. We get a sense of that with the first enchanting sounds as two horns, in unison, softly play this melody:

Ex. 1

The entire introduction, with its combination of delicacy and vigorous, inventive life, is an amazing achievement of orchestral fantasy. But the horn theme itself is even more wonderful than its evocative, sylvan sound. It is one of those that feel completely natural, yet are craftily made. Like thousands of themes in the central tradition of Western concert music, it is eight measures long, but unlike nearly all of those thousands, it is not designed according to the easy formula of 4 + 4 = 8. Rather, the first two-measure unit is followed by a kind of inverted echo of the second measure, so that the first unit consists of an odd three measures, 2 + 1. The next three measures echo the first three in rhythm, and the tune is in effect complete at the end of measure 6. Then Schubert does the utterly unforeseeable and adds an echo of measure 6, but at half tempo! This is magic.

On this melody, Schubert builds something like a series of variations. Variation 1, with the tune given to woodwinds, leads to a continuing sentence, sumptuously scored for strings with divided violas and cellos. Mozart would have been proud of the sound of these twelve measures. Variation 2 brings the horn theme in grand *fortissimo* with trombones, the echo measures coming in the woodwinds. This time the extension is twice as long as the one after Variation 1, and Schubert continues the contrast between declamatory *fortissimo* and ruminative *piano*. Variation 3 returns the theme to the woodwinds, *piano*, and the string accompaniment is dominated by *pianissimo* staccato triplets for the violins. This time the continuation, with the violin triplets becoming ever more prominent, is a volcanic crescendo that leads quickly to the main tempo of the movement.

It would not be outlandish to trace some indebtedness here to the Poco sostenuto with which Beethoven's Seventh Symphony begins; however, the overwhelming impression is that here are three minutes of music that, in the freshness of design, in the way Schubert creates the effect of growing momentum while not increasing the tempo at all, in the tone, with its haunting mixture of confidence and vulnerability, are unlike any previous "slow introduction." Altogether, the compositional and rhetorical plan of this symphony as a whole is no less striking than its radiant sound, and this, too, Schumann understood better than virtually all critics until Tovey in the 1920s. (Certainly better than Mendelssohn with his pruning shears.)

The arrival at the Allegro is a moment of splendid triumph, of breaking into the bright, unshadowed light of day. Schubert's original tempo marking was "Allegro vivace"; he changed it to "Allegro ma non troppo." Whatever the adjective, finding the right tempo is a cinch—or should be. Between the significant thematic measures of Schubert's theme come bars of joyously chugging triplets for woodwinds and horns.

Ex. 2

Those triplets go at exactly the same speed as the eighth-note triplets that accompanied the third variation of the theme of the introduction. It is the neatest imaginable fit: each measure of the Allegro equals a half-measure of the Andante. Schubert intended these two parts of the movement, so disparate in many ways, to be joined by a common pulse. Why then the change from "vivace" to "ma non troppo"? I can't say. I can imagine, though, that Schubert, mindful of writing a difficult movement that goes at a fair clip, figured that the sight of "ma non troppo"—not too much—would be conducive to a sense of rhythmic stability and damp any tendency to rushing and gabbling. Schubert made a more important alteration than that. As he originally wrote the movement, the first measures—and all the parallel ones—went

Ex. 3

He changed them to this.

Ex. 4

It was a happy afterthought, turning a friendly banality, a timpani accompaniment, into a theme with a real profile.

Schubert proceeds cheerfully with this theme and its continuation, a scale that strides vigorously down, then up. Briskly, with nearly no transition, he goes to a second theme in an unexpected and pleasingly piquant key, E minor. The flavor is from somewhere a bit east of Vienna. After a while—a joyous while—this tune finds its way to G major, the dominant, and the most likely location for the second group of themes in an exposition. Here the exposition could come to its end, but again Schubert does the unexpected and magical. Having found the dominant, he turns his back on it. The energetic rhythm machine keeps bubbling along—plucked basses, staccato wind chords, swirling strings—but *pianissimo*, in the background. Into the foreground step the three trombones with a series of solemn animadversions in distant A-flat minor, also *pianissimo*. What they speak here is a transformation of measure 2 of the introduction. The music finds its way back to G major, where it boils up to a great climax, *fortississimo*, and then the exposition does indeed come to its beautifully delayed close.

The development begins with the east-of-Vienna theme, now moved into A-flat major. It is wonderfully fresh; at the same time, it makes, through the choice of key, this remarkable connection with the most mysterious and "special" part of the exposition. The triplets return, ominous and loud in horns and trumpets, and now combined with the scalar continuation of the first theme. The great warning utterances of the trombones also reappear *fortissimo*. Most marvelous is the transition to the recapitulation, still preoccupied with the stepwise rising third of the "warning" theme, but utterly mysterious in atmosphere. The closer we get to home, the more hushed the music becomes, and, as though to compensate for having made soft things loud in the development, Schubert now brings back the first theme in *piano*, but as on-its-toes as can be.

Schubert speeds up a bit for the coda, a chapter of tremendous harmonic and rhythmic energy. It culminates in the triumphal return—*fortissimo* and *ben marcato*—of the horn melody that began the movement, now metamorphosed into a rush of fierce and headlong energy. Here is a place that has become, quite unnecessarily, a notorious performance problem. The passage can go wrong in two ways.

Schubert means the theme to reappear in the tempo of the coda, that is, faster (he does not say how much faster) than the basic Allegro ma non troppo: the score is unambiguously clear on this point. If the tempo relationship between the introduction and the Allegro is right, that is, with the triplets in each understood as common ground, the horn theme will reappear at a tempo slightly faster than its original one. If, on the other hand, the introduction was too slow because it was taken in four rather than in two and because Andante is misunderstood as a species of slow tempo, then the horn theme will reappear at a tempo very much faster than the original one. This has generally made conductors nervous, and that, combined with sensing quite correctly that this moment is intended as an apotheosis, leads them, suddenly and irrationally, to pull back the tempo terrifically. That negates all the energy Schubert has built up in the course of his brilliantly planned coda. Besides, the closing measures are not designed to bear the weight of a *slow* apotheosis, and so the end of the movement is ineffectual.

But even if the introduction has been too slow, it is still possible to get the end of the movement right. This involves conceding the possibility that a theme first heard in one tempo can recur at a crucial juncture in a different one; in other words, that the transformation of musical character from lyrically musing to triumphant could entail a change of tempo as well as a change of orchestration and dynamics. Most conductors in the past have choked on this radical idea, just as they choke on the parallel place in the Brahms First when the chorale returns in glory at the end of the finale; there, too, they frantically apply the brakes. There have also always been a few who chose to believe that Schubert meant what he wrote, that he knew how to write *molto rit.* had he wanted that, and who brought the horn tune back in all the jubilance of the coda's allegro. Toscanini, Szell, Levine are names I recall gratefully in this connection; in the 1990s it is less rare to find conductors who go with the music rather than with their habits and the dead weight of "tradition."

You need to take a big breath before going from the blazing close of the first movement to what Tovey so aptly called the wintry introduction to the second. The tempo is Andante con moto, the precautionary "con moto" being an afterthought. The upper strings mark the meter, cellos and basses outline the beginnings of a march. Enter the oboe to move the march from adumbration to reality. Tovey calls this A-minor tune a "heart-breaking show of spirit in adversity," but I also recall being touched and totally persuaded by a performance conducted by Kurt Sanderling, who got the oboist beautifully to suggest the subtly seductive dance of a young Romany woman. This is an ethnic flavoring Schubert loved, and we have of course already encountered it in the first movement's second theme. Schubert continues his melody in major and with *pianissimo* drumming by the cellos and basses. The change from minor to major intensifies whichever quality you hear in the oboe solo, the heartbreaking or the sexy. Indeed, why not both? A third element is an emphatically *fortissimo* continuation of the march.

More lyric music comes with a wonderful violin theme. Schubert gives the beginning to the second violins, after which the firsts take it over in rhapsodic (but still *pianissimo*) flight. The effect is of course lost in the modern seating that places the seconds behind the firsts rather than opposite them. The scoring, with a bassoon a tenth below the violins and the basses an octave below that, is a quiet miracle, as indeed the whole movement is, characterized by a singular sonorous charm.

The passage that prepares the return of the oboe solo is one Schumann described in a famous poetic image: "where a horn calls as though from afar—this seems to me to have come down from another sphere. Here everyone is hushed and listening, as though some heavenly visitant were quietly stealing through the orchestra."

When the oboe theme returns, a distant trumpet and horn add little fanfares that seem to come right out of Mahler. This time, the *fortissimo* continuation of the march culminates in a crisis so shocking that its only possible consequence is dead silence. Then the cellos pick up the musical thread with a song of deep pathos.[11] The lyric theme returns, now given to the flute and clarinet with a beautifully detailed accompaniment for the strings. When Schumann's "heavenly visitant" returns, it is in the guise of a clarinet, magically surrounded by pizzicato violins and *pianissimo* trombones. The possibility of storms stays alive until the last measures, and the sky is dark.

The Scherzo is boisterous and sweet. It is also on a scale commensurate with the expansive first and second movements. One of the things Schubert learned when he went to hear the first performance of the Beethoven Ninth in 1824 was that an effective way to design a big scherzo was to make it a fully developed sonata form, and that is what he does here. He is also lavish in pouring out theme after new theme, and his rhythmic invention is unendingly fresh and buoyant. The Scherzo includes an important episode in A-flat major, a key that played a big role in the first movement. For the trio, Schubert veers off in the opposite direction,

---

[11] Another instance of Tchaikovsky learning from Schubert: compare the crisis/silence climax in the slow movement of Tchaikovsky's Symphony No. 5.

to A major, thus re-entering the world of the second movement. The music, a sublime version of country dance, is gloriously rich in sound, and its melody is one of those that must have been there since the beginning of the world. Some conductors like to double the winds in this symphony: here is one of the passages where this pays off most wonderfully, not because the melody is louder but because it can be played with such effortless richness of tone.

The intoxicating finale begins with a rhythmic summons to attention that Schubert recycled from his own earlier C-major symphony, the *Little* No. 6. He spins this out so that it becomes a whirlwind of wild energy. This reaches the dominant, where this chapter is concluded with a bang and a silence. Four notes played by two horns in unison start the motor up again. Schubert first thought that this was the perfect place for a little fugue; fortunately he thought again, crossed out the few measures he had begun, and, using the horns' four repeated notes as point of departure, wrote a new, simple, inspired, quiet, and irresistibly propulsive theme. The swirling accompaniment is the one that disabled the London violinists and violists. It is those fast triplets that one notices, but the pizzicato bass line in hugely swinging arpeggios contributes no less to the momentum.

Two more features must be mentioned. When the development begins, two clarinets take one phrase out of the second theme, the one with the wild accompaniment, and extend it to create an unmistakable allusion to the Beethoven Ninth, the work that had become *the* symbol for the "große Sinfonie" which Schubert had aspired to and was now in the process of achieving.

Ex. 5

The other point concerns the four horn notes that both introduced and became part of the second theme. Like the second movement, this one shows astounding capacity for drastic, shattering climaxes. Those four notes, so harmless and friendly when we first hear them, assume titanic power. In the coda, it takes all the exuberant and positive energy that has been built up in the course of the symphony to keep that four-note summons, huge and terrible, from blowing the work apart.

In my essay on the *Unfinished* Symphony I discuss the problem of accent marks written so large in Schubert's manuscripts that they have been mistaken for and printed as diminuendo signs. The final long unison C has one of those. Diminuendo makes no more sense here than it would on the last long note of the Beethoven Fifth, and I am glad to see that Roger Fiske, editor of the 1984 Eulenburg miniature score, boldly went where no editor had gone before and printed it as the accent it is obviously meant to be.[12]

---

[12] But you never know. Some years ago I heard one of the best conductors of our time rehearse this symphony, and when he got to the final note he sank into a deep knee-bend to produce the diminuendo in his score. Afterwards I suggested that this ought really to be an accent, and he said, "Oh no, that is Schubert's gesture of humility before Beethoven."

William Schuman

William Howard Schuman was born on 4 August 1910 in New York and died there on 15 February 1992.

Virgil Thomson's book *American Music Since 1910* contains a photo taken about 1950 by John Stewart of five composers in Thomson's living-room. The host, seated, is commanding, self-pleased, wearing just a touch of smile, and managing to not quite look at any of his guests. Behind him stands Barber, eyes cast down. He appears distressed. Copland, leaning on the piano, observes him coolly. Menotti, seated to Thomson's left but facing the opposite way, his handsome face open and alert, looks up at Barber, his longtime lover and friend. And off to one side—he might be in a different picture, even in a different room—sits William Schuman. His gaze is straight ahead and his face is tight. Like that character in Molière, does he wonder about himself, "Que diable allait-il faire dans cette galère?"

Unlike Barber, but very much like Thomson, Copland, and Menotti, Schuman was endlessly and usefully busy attending to matters other than composition: he was at various times professor at Sarah Lawrence College, director of publications for G. Schirmer Inc., president of the Juilliard School, president of Lincoln Center, besides holding board appointments and the like with the Koussevitzky Music Foundation, the MacDowell Colony, the United States Information Agency, the Hall of Fame for Great Americans, and many more. Probably no other musician's name has appeared on the letterheads of so many academies, foundations, and festivals. He held so many honorary doctorates that he was able to have the hoods made into a full-size quilt, allowing him, as he liked to say, to take his naps by degrees.

Had you found yourself sitting beside him on an airplane, you would at once have pegged him as a prosperous businessman, of course in a business with no taint of racketeering or gangsterismo. His knowledgeable conversation about baseball and politics would not have disabused you.[1] But he was also the first composer to win the Pulitzer Prize (for *A Free Song*), the first to win the New York Critics' Circle Award (for the Symphony No. 3), and the first to get a commission from the United States government (*Credendum*).

Like most composers, but in fact unlike his colleagues in the photo, Schuman went into college teaching because he had to make a living. Inventive and vigorous at Sarah Lawrence, he was appointed president of Juilliard. Quietly urbane revolution was his aim. He changed the teaching of theory in ways that made waves all over the country. He went after that ever-elusive goal of lightening the trade-school atmosphere and turning conservatory students into Compleat Musicians. He decided the school needed a resident string quartet to represent professionalism to the students and Juilliard to the world, and, not so incidentally, to bring twentieth-century music, particularly twentieth-century American music, to the head table. He thought that a conservatory should include dance and theater divisions (the latter came into being only after his time).

Through his competence, energy, and an uncommon gift for politics, helped of course by geography, Schuman turned the Juilliard presidency into a major power base. He saw the possibility, for the good of the arts and for the good of those who would get a cut of the pie, of binding Juilliard, the New York Philharmonic, the Metropolitan Opera, the New York City Ballet, the New York City Opera, and other organizations into an alliance which, one hoped, would not be too uneasy. He was a man with a sense of possibilities *and* a sense of realities. Inevitably, he became the first ruler of the new empire, of the Lincoln Center for the Performing Arts. To slightly change a phrase of the philosopher Ernst Bloch, he loved power and the tools of power. He understood the tools too. His musico-political power was different from the power of Thomson (local and laser-sharp), Bernstein (engulfing eros), and Copland (all in the magic of his music), but it was real power and, for many years, immense.

Political though he was, Schuman was a courteous and generous musical citizen, always scrupulous about congratulating colleagues on their new works, pleasing them because his comments were so attentive and specific. (No other composer wrote letters on such creamy paper.) And, a quality not to be taken for granted in his world, Bill Schuman could laugh about

---

[1] To his passion for baseball, Schuman paid affectionate and delightful tribute in 1953 when he made an opera of what he called Ernest L. Thayer's American tragedy, *Casey at the Bat*.

himself. He loved the story of the woman in Macon, Georgia, who told him how much she had enjoyed his Violin Concerto "even though it was atonal." With exquisite graciousness he pointed out that none of his music was atonal, that it was always centered on a key. His new admirer set him straight. "Mr. Schuman," she said, "in Macon your music is atonal." The last time I saw him was at Carnegie Hall. His Symphony for Strings was to be played, and so, among other works, was Beethoven's Second Piano Concerto. He looked over the program, nodded, turned to me, and said: "I think I'll take a bow after the Beethoven. I'll get a bigger hand."

He was nearly twenty when he encountered classical music. That happened when he was reluctantly dragged to one of Toscanini's New York Philharmonic concerts, and the Symphony No. 3 by the other Schuman(n), the Funeral Music from *Götterdämmerung* (played in memoriam Cosima Wagner), and Kodály's *Summer Evening* were on the program. Among the things that impressed him were that the strings bowed in unison and that the drums didn't play all the way through the way they did in Billy Schuman and his Alamo Society Orchestra, the dance band he had organized at George Washington High School in New York City. He had gotten his start in popular music and, by the time he quit the field, he had written some 200 songs, one of them, "In Love with a Memory of You," with his friend Frank Loesser, who later found fame and fortune as lyricist and composer of *Guys and Dolls* and other Broadway hits.

When his near-namesake, Wagner, Toscanini et al. turned his life around, Schuman was a student at the New York University School of Commerce and, with all his practical experience, still a musical illiterate. He stopped in at the Malkin School of Music and said, "I want to be a composer. What do I have to do?" He was told he would have to study harmony, which would be $1 per class or $3 for a private lesson. Next thing, he was a pupil of Max Persin, who had studied with Arensky at the Moscow Conservatory and whom Schuman described as "something of a visionary . . . a wonderful influence and a marvelous teacher."

Another pivotal experience lay ahead. He heard the *Symphony 1933* by Roy Harris and thought it "the most exciting piece of new music" he had ever encountered. Harris, furthermore, was teaching at the Juilliard School, then just around the corner from Teachers College at Columbia University, where Schuman was now enrolled, and he lost no time going to look up his senior colleague. Harris's declamatory, tough, broad-spanned, extroverted style affected Schuman powerfully. His own leaning was in just those directions, and he came away from his lessons with a vocabulary, the beginnings of a technique, and a validation of his own expressive stance. He was to become a far more accomplished craftsman than his teacher, and it was evident before long that he had a remarkable feeling for orchestral sound.

When Schuman's Symphony No. 2 was broadcast in 1939, a listener wrote to him saying that the work "had made me lose faith in the power of aspirin." But when Aaron Copland had heard the same piece the year before, his response had been to write in the influential magazine *Modern Music* that "Schuman is, so far as I am concerned, the musical find of the year." (Schuman himself was more inclined to agree with the aspirin man and withdrew both his First and Second symphonies.) More important was that Copland called Serge Koussevitzky's attention to the young composer, and from that moment on, Schuman had an enthusiastic and powerful champion in the Boston Symphony's conductor. With the introduction in Boston of Schuman's *American Festival* Overture in 1939, recognition was his. His success was affirmed two years later when Koussevitzky introduced the Symphony No. 3. It is still the most played of Schuman's symphonies and together with the equally grandiloquent Thirds of Harris and Copland it has achieved what virtually amounts to canonization as Official American Symphony.

Schuman composed some of our best music, music of hard-edged, deeply felt Romanticism. He wrote in many forms and genres, and with notable success for dance and chorus; it is, however, the series of symphonies that has particularly ensured his place as the sonorous rhetorician, the great Public Orator among America's composers. His music can be muscle-bound and loud-mouthed, but the best of it is tender, rich, fiercely athletic, funny, imposingly, forthright. Barber told him how much he envied his ability to write that gigantic crescendo in the Third Symphony. Schuman's stuff could be wildly optimistic, and he enjoyed that mood, but he had the emotional range that encompassed the marvelous Symphony No. 6, which is, with the Sessions Seventh, the darkest American one we have.

Symphony No. 3

Part I: Passacaglia and Fugue
Part II: Chorale and Toccata

Schuman completed his Third Symphony on 11 January 1941, and it was first performed by Serge Koussevitzky and the Boston Symphony Orchestra on 17 October that year. The dedication reads "for Serge Koussevitzky."

Piccolo (doubling flute) and two flutes, two oboes and English horn, two clarinets with E-flat clarinet and bass clarinet, two bassoons, four horns, four trumpets, four trombones, tuba, timpani, snare drum, xylophone, bass drum, cymbals, and strings. To this basic complement, Schuman adds as "optional, but very desirable," one more flute (doubling second piccolo), oboe, clarinet, and bassoon, plus contrabassoon, another four horns, and piano.

This, characteristically, is a symphony for large orchestra, used without inhibition. The design is unusual, each of the symphony's two parts being in two movements, Passacaglia and Fugue, Chorale and Toccata.[2] Schuman stressed that his four movements have no standard models. The whole edifice is also grandly effective.

The normal definition of passacaglia is a set of variations over a reiterated bass. Many variants exist of this basic scheme, the most common being that the bass line eventually moves into the upper reaches of the texture. Schuman's is also a passacaglia with a difference. It begins normally—and very beautifully—with violas quite gently playing a seven-measure bass. Seven is an odd number, but Brahms, with his passacaglia on a five-measure bass in the Variations on a Theme by Haydn, would not have found it strange. The bass begins on E and more or less ends there. The tone is grave, the line itself is jagged, containing many intervals of the fourth.

With the arrival of the first variation, we encounter something unusual: the new iteration of the passacaglia bass in the second violins starts not on E, but half a tone higher, on F. In the second variation, the cellos play the bass line and take it up yet another half-tone, to F-sharp. Having the bass travel not only from one register to another but actually to different pitches is something we can find in Bach, for example in the Adagio of the D-minor Harpsichord Concerto; what is special here is that it begins immediately and that it is so systematic. In the second variation we also hear that Schuman has a whole other plan going: each variation adds one voice or line to the texture, and each new voice proceeds in exact imitation of the previous one. In other words, this movement is at the same time a passacaglia and a canon. In successive variations, the entrances by the first violins (G), low woodwinds (A-flat), horns (A-natural), and high woodwinds (B-flat) continue the process of making the texture more elaborate and heightening the tension by raising the pitch.

After six variations, Schuman breaks this pattern. Against an agitated

[2] Independently, Schuman's German contemporary Karl Amadeus Hartmann evolved similar ground-plans for his symphonies.

triplet accompaniment in the strings, horns and trumpets proclaim a new and expanded version of the bass. Then, after a series of assertive rhetorical flourishes, a new chapter begins. Cellos sotto voce play rapid scales while the violins sing a slow, serious melody. That melody becomes the subject of new variations, each more compressed than the one before, until the trombones—*fff, molto sonore*—return with a larger-than-life-size version of the original bass. And with that, the passacaglia spills into the fugue. For the progression from passacaglia to fugue, Schuman did have a great model in Bach's Organ Passacaglia in C minor.

The fugue subject is short, spiky, and eruptive; plucked violas and cellos, along with all four horns, present it. The marking is "vigoroso," very much a Schuman word. Aside from general temper, one other feature is carried over from the Passacaglia, which is that the first entrances of the four voices once again occur by rising semitones: B-flat, B-natural, C, D-flat. The movement becomes in effect a fugue with variations. This makes a neat pairing with the first movement: a set of variations in imitative texture (the Passacaglia) followed by a piece whose essence is imitation (the Fugue) but with variations. Among the events that follow are a set of Baroque trumpet flourishes in which the voices enter in very tight succession (the technical name is *stretto*, which means "tight"), a tranquillo episode for solo woodwinds, and a dolce melody in slow notes for muted strings.

A violent outburst from the timpani initiates a new chapter. The strings, now rid of their mutes, whip up excitement with their sharply dotted rhythms; horns snarl (Schuman directs that the playing be "brassy"); and before long it is evident that while the texture is still contrapuntal, any idea of formal fugue has been abandoned. One weighty final proclamation for the full orchestra brings Part I of the symphony to an emphatic close.

The Chorale is the movement that Schuman said "really represents the spirit of the composition." It is calm and for the most part quiet; the tempo is andantino. Schuman starts with softly sonorous polyphony for low strings; the viola and cello sections are divided into two parts each, and their sound is darkly beautiful. Countless Baroque chorale-preludes begin with this kind of polyphony; you might also be reminded of the Hymn of Thanksgiving in Beethoven's A-minor Quartet, Opus 132.

After twenty-one such measures of introduction, a solo trumpet plays a beautifully vocal melody, which is continued by the flute and concluded by the violins. The style is more lyric-rhapsodic than hymnic. The fourths and the bold zigzags so typical of the language of this work are prominent. A hushed passage of swifter, more decorated polyphony for the strings (minus basses) leads to a hugely resonant, full-orchestra statement of the trumpet melody. Then, by way of a striking page for muted horn quartet, which is followed by a duet for muted trumpets, the Chorale moves to a quiet close. This kind of "organistic" scoring, emphasizing one choir at a time rather than inventing colorful mixtures is characteristic of Schuman.

As the bassoon and contrabassoon hold their last low B-flat, a snare drum introduces a catchy rhythm. The concluding Toccata, athletic and virtuosic, has begun. Once again, as oboe and English horn respond to the jaunty tune of the bass clarinet, Schuman alludes to the fugal textures of which he has already made so much in this symphony. Woodwinds add a broader melody. Then comes one of Schuman's most arresting inventions, a recitative, first for a single cello and then for the entire cello section. This leads to an impassioned declaration for all the strings, a sound Schuman would explore further in his Symphony for Strings (1943).[3] The music returns to the swift Toccata tempo, and after more—and ever more assertive—rhetorical flourishes, the work reaches its stunning conclusion.

Symphony No. 6

Largo—Moderato con moto—Leggeramente—Adagio—Allegro risoluto
—Larghissimo

Schuman composed his Symphony No. 6 in 1948-49 in fulfillment of a commission from the Dallas Symphony League. The first performance was given on 27 February 1949 by the Dallas Symphony Orchestra under Antal Dorati.

Three flutes, two oboes and English horn, two clarinets and bass clarinet, two bassoons and contrabassoon, four horns, three trumpets, three trombones, tuba, timpani, cymbals, snare drum, bass drum, bells, and strings.

Schuman's most famous symphony, the Third, ends in an explosion of athletic energy; No. 6 is one in a group of symphonies whose emotional coloration is darker. Its companions in spirit are No. 7, written in 1960 for the seventy-fifth anniversary of the Boston Symphony, and No. 9, *Le*

---

[3] This powerful and concise work was commissioned by Koussevitzky and the Boston Symphony in response to the overwhelming success of the Third Symphony.

Fosse Ardeatine, composed in 1968 after Schuman's visit to the Ardeatine Caves, where in 1944 the Germans murdered 335 Italian civilians in reprisal for the killing of 32 soldiers by the Roman underground.

Of the ten Schuman symphonies, No. 6 has pretty consistently been the one most admired by musicians. Schuman acknowledged it as his own favorite too. I share that view and would add that it occupies a very high place indeed in a time, the middle of the twentieth century, singularly rich in strong symphonies. For audiences it is an accessible but challenging piece. Schuman's musical language is lucid, his expressive gestures are vivid, and you sense readily that his invention is driven by an emotional current that is strong and clear. At the same time, Schuman challenges—and, we might say, compliments—us by assuming both the willingness and ability to pay attention, to sustain concentration. For what he has done here is to cast his twenty-eight-minute symphony as a single movement. It changes character and speed quite as much as any "normal" three- or four-movement symphony. We can even say that, much as in such one-movement masterpieces as Liszt's Piano Sonata or Schoenberg's Chamber Symphony No. 1, the familiar four movements are in fact embraced by the single movement. The transitions, however, ask our attention quite as much as the matter they lead from and lead to. In other words, Schuman needs us to stay with him without letup for every moment of the ride.

To repeat, you can hear a four-movement symphony within the single continuous movement of the Symphony No. 6. Its sections are marked Moderato con moto, Leggeramente, Adagio, and Allegro risoluto. Before we get to any of that, however, Schuman gives us three or four minutes of extremely slow music (Largo) and he will conclude his symphony with three minutes of epilogue in even slower tempo (Larghissimo). Antal Dorati, writing about the Symphony No. 6 at the time of its first performance, pointed out that these parts of the music "provide a frame for the work; or rather, to use an architectural analogy, have a function similar to [that of] the two piers of a bridge—to hold and support the span of the whole structure."

Schuman draws us in with the beginnings of a soft chorale for trumpets and trombones, each of whose phrases is followed by a comment for woodwinds. Two features here play a large role in this symphony, as indeed they do in most of Schuman's music. One is this kind of almost Brucknerian separation of orchestral choirs. The other, manifest in the very first chord, is the collision—or simultaneity, if you prefer—of major and minor (the trumpets play two-thirds of an A-major chord, the trombones two-thirds of one in A minor). Quickly we discover that this wind music is but the introductory part of the introduction, as it were. Muted violins connect with the second of the woodwind comments and begin the spinning out of a long, supple, expressive melody, behind which we always hear some form of the chorale. As the violin melody rises, finally to vanish on a high C, there enters a new voice, that of a piccolo in a staccato figuration that is also completely different from anything we have heard thus far. The flute takes over from its small relative and adds a dancing counterpoint to the melodies we already know, the cellos continuing the chorale and woodwinds extending and developing the violin line.

A short group of chords and a compact (three-note!) fanfare propel us into a new tempo, Moderato con moto. The music is still polyphonic in texture, but the gestures are now emphatic, and the accompaniment of barking low brass and basses playing with the wood side of their bows verges on the savage. (The actual material of this accompaniment is derived from the earlier violin melody which, in expression, is its diametric opposite.) The material is richly varied and includes passages for wind instruments in a state of high rhythmic excitement as well as a new and expressive string melody.

This leads to a huge climax, which clears the air for a passage for timpani alone, one whose pitch content is restricted to just E-flat and C, with the variety provided by the rhythm. That sets the stage for the quasi-scherzo (Leggeramente, which means "lightly"), in which *pianissimo* dancing strings alternate with rhythmically more eccentric excursions for winds. The chorale from the beginning is not forgotten either. After a while, this all settles into an agreeable 6/8 lope.

Without warning, the tempo slows to one-fourth of its leggeramente self, and after some measures of quiet but highly expressive music for strings, Schuman admits that he is now in his Adagio. These pages, handsomely scored and with the melodic lines imbued with magnificent tensile strength, are the symphony's central pillar, a structural and expressive counterpart to those largo/larghissimo piers that support it at its outer limits.

This time it is a gradual series of accelerations that makes the transition into the exciting finale of the inner four-part symphony. The main tempo and character mark is Allegro risoluto, but to this Schuman adds the exhortation "wild." Again, his orchestral antiphonies are ever present. The tempo changes to Presto, and with that speeding up comes a tremendous intensification on every other front: more counterpoint, more cross-rhythm, a richer harmonic stew, more happening altogether. There is a powerful sense of climax and arrival.

Again it is the timpani that define end, transition, and new beginning. All the busyness is suddenly halted and, as though after an opening of great portals, the epilogue begins: huge sweeping melody in strings and woodwinds, nervously insistent punctuation in the brass. The music grows quiet and pensive and, over a swaying of mixed major/minor chords, it begins to dissolve. All this is recapitulation of material we already know. The G-sharp in the mixed E chord drops away. The last sounds, deep in violas, cellos, and basses, and sinking to the threshold of audibility, are of E minor only. Thus it ends in darkness, this great American symphony.

Robert Schumann

Robert Schumann was born in Zwickau, Saxony, on 8 June 1810 and died, insane, possibly of the consequences of syphilis, perhaps a suicide by self-starvation, at Endenich, near Bonn, on 29 July 1856.

In 1839, Clara Wieck, soon to become Clara Schumann, noted in her diary that "it would be best if [Robert] composed for orchestra; his imagination cannot find sufficient scope on the piano. . . . His compositions are all orchestral in feeling." Clara, already a celebrated pianist for more than half her twenty years, was in love with success and with the tools of success (to borrow a phrase from the philosopher Ernst Bloch) and aware that her glittery recital pieces by Herz and Hünten, Kalkbrenner and Moscheles, produced more applause than her moody and poetic fiancé's *Carnaval*. In other words, her remark, which seems at first blush an odd one about the composer of the *Davidsbündler, Carnaval, Phantasiestücke*, Symphonic Etudes, *Scenes from Childhood, Kreisleriana*, the C-major Fantasy, and the *Humoresque*, may mean little more than that she was not yet convinced by, converted to, Robert's piano style. It makes, in any event, ironic reading in view of the hard-dying notion that Schumann did not understand the orchestra and that his symphonies are "inflated piano music" (as the late Gerald Abraham wrote not only in the fifth edition of *Grove's Dictionary of Music and Musicians* [1954] but again in *The New Grove* of 1980).

The story of Schumann's relations with the world of orchestras and orchestral music starts in 1832–33, when he began and then abandoned, at a fairly advanced stage, a symphony in G minor, having witnessed the failure of its first movement at a concert in Leipzig. Otherwise, from 1830, the year of his official Opus 1, the *Abegg* Variations, until 1839, he composed only piano music. In 1840, the year his long and troubled courtship of Clara was resolved in marriage, he concentrated on songs—121 of them, including *Dichterliebe, Frauenliebe und -leben,* the Heine and Eichendorff *Liederkreise, Myrthen,* and cycles on poems by Justinus Kerner and Friedrich Rückert.

Presumably, Clara had voiced her aspirations to her fiancé as well as to her diary. In 1841, Schumann concentrated on orchestral music, writing the *Spring* Symphony; the Overture, Scherzo, and Finale, which he sometimes referred to as his "symphonette"; the beginnings of a symphony in C minor, whose scherzo survived as one of the *Bunte Blätter* for piano, Opus 99; and the D-minor Symphony, now known almost exclusively in its revised form of 1851 and assigned the number 4 to reflect the date of that later version. In the same year, he also wrote a Fantasy for Piano and Orchestra that, four years later, revised, and with an intermezzo and finale attached, became the famous and loved Piano Concerto. As the decade went along, Schumann added, in the realm of music for or with orchestra, the secular oratorio *Das Paradies und die Peri,* the Symphony No. 2, the *Requiem für Mignon* after Goethe's *Wilhelm Meister* as well as some of the Scenes from Goethe's *Faust,* the Concertstück for Four Horns, the Introduction and Allegro appassionato for Piano, the incidental music for Byron's *Manfred,* and the opera *Genoveva.*

When the *Spring* Symphony burst forth in a torrent of confidence and inspiration—it was sketched in four days and completed in not quite four weeks in February and March 1841—Schumann was not only a newcomer to orchestral music; he had written little music of any kind in the sonata style, with its grand strategies based on thematic development and far-ranging harmonic design. Some of what he had done along those lines was magnificent, particularly the Sonata in F minor, Opus 14, which he also called Concerto Without Orchestra, but such works were just occasional departures from that special world of character pieces and lyric songs he had so much made his own. He had entered his thirties; he had established himself as a family man; thanks to an honorary degree from the University of Jena he was now Herr Doktor Schumann; and, no doubt with plenty of urging from Clara, he was eager to prove himself in the more ambitious calling of the larger forms of the symphony, the string quartet, and the oratorio.

Here we encounter Beethoven, as we will almost anywhere in a study of nineteenth-century instrumental music.[1] While Schumann was still a schoolboy, a probable future poet, and a rather promising pianist in the mining and manufacturing town of Zwickau, Franz Schubert wrote to a friend about his own ambition to pave his way "toward the big symphony," by which he meant a symphony in the manner and on the scale of one by Beethoven. Long after Schumann's tragic death in an asylum outside

---

[1] And of course in Wagner.

Bonn, Johannes Brahms was lamenting the impossibility of writing a symphony while one still heard "the footsteps of the giant" (that is, of Beethoven) just behind. For Schumann, Schubert was in many ways master and model; indeed, hearing his "große Sinfonie," the *Great* C-major, for the first time in 1839 was a real spur to Schumann's ambition.

In crucial ways, Brahms was Schumann's pupil in spirit as well as his protégé. Schumann's symphonies are not, however, always the link between those of Schubert and Brahms. Schubert's and Brahms's Beethoven was the Beethoven of the quartets and even more of the symphonies; Schumann, on the other hand, was especially drawn to the later piano sonatas, which, in the words of the composer John Harbison, "suggested a new kind of narrative style, free of the necessity to define in sonata-allegro terms each movement in the form." Even as Schumann prepared to make his own way to "the big symphony," the impulses *away* from the sonata style, impulses of temperament and habit, nourished by his reading of older music, were as powerfully insistent as those that pulled him toward it. The result is five symphonies (if we count the "symphonette") that are problematic, risky, utterly personal, stunningly original, inspired, ever fresh and awaiting our delighted rediscovery.

Symphony No. 1 in B-flat major, Opus 38, *Spring*

> *Andante un poco maestoso—Allegro molto vivace*
> *Larghetto*
> *Scherzo: Molto vivace—Molto più vivace—Tempo I*
> *Allegro animato e grazioso*

Schumann sketched the *Spring* Symphony in just four days, 23 to 26 January 1841, and completed the score less than a month later, on 20 February. Felix Mendelssohn-Bartholdy conducted the first performance at a pension fund concert of the Leipzig Gewandhaus Orchestra on 31 March that year. The dedication is to Friedrich August, King of Saxony, who sent Schumann a golden snuffbox in thanks.

Two flutes, two oboes, two clarinets, two bassoons, four horns, two trumpets, three trombones, timpani, triangle, and strings.

In his great Symphony No. 2, Schumann chose to confront Beethoven the symphonist head-on. In the Symphony No. 1, the debt to Beethoven is less direct, but more than once we shall hear echoes of Beethoven's Fourth, beginning with the fact that the works are in the same key.

Schumann himself thought of this symphony as the *Spring*, though the word does not appear on the title page; originally, he also planned to give each movement a title. He told the composer Louis Spohr he had written the music "with a vernal passion . . . that always sways men even into old age and surprises them anew each year. Description and painting were not part of my intention, but I do believe that the season in which this symphony was born influenced its structure and helped make it what it is." Remember that the symphony was "born" in January and February. The determining mood, therefore, is not spring itself, but the longing for spring in a cold and gray Leipzig winter.

This becomes clear when Schumann writes to Wilhelm Taubert, court conductor in Berlin, who was about to introduce the work there:

> Could you breathe a little of the longing for spring [Frühlingssehnsucht] into your orchestra as they play. That was what was most in my mind when I wrote [the symphony] in January 1841. I should like the very first trumpet entrance to sound as if it came from on high, like a summons to awakening. Further on in the introduction, I should like the music to suggest the world's turning green, perhaps with a butterfly hovering in the air, and then, in the Allegro, to show how everything to do with spring is coming to life. These, however, are ideas that came into my mind only *after* I had completed the piece.[2]

Something else that made this time special for Schumann and nurtured his exuberance was the knowledge that by summer's end he would be a father (Marie Schumann was born on 1 September).

The symphony also had a literary inspiration, one of the *Spring Ballads* by Adolf Böttger, two lines of which are secretly set in the opening phrases:

> O wende, wende deinen Lauf—
> Im Thale blüht der Frühling auf!
> [Oh turn, oh turn and change your course—
> Now in the valley blooms the spring!][3]

---

[2] Quoted in *Hans Gál, Schumann Orchestral Music* (Seattle: University of Washington Press, 1979).
[3] Böttger (1815–70), to be found today only in the most detailed reference works, was quite a popular poet in his day. In 1842, Schumann sent him a sheet with the opening bars of the *Spring* Symphony with a brief message acknowledging his poem as a source of inspiration. That same year Böttger helped Schumann with drawing the libretto for *Das Paradies und die Peri* from Thomas Moore's *Lalla Rookh*.

The metrical correspondence is not to be missed. To quote Harbison once more: "This opening makes explicit a secret condition of most of Schumann's instrumental music—hidden words behind the notes."

This reveille of brass instruments gave Schumann a rude shock when Mendelssohn began the first rehearsal. The opening phrase originally began not on D as in the published score (and in Ex. 1), but on B-flat, which also corresponds to the start of the Allegro. The Schumann scholar Jon Finson writes that both versions had been in the composer's mind early on, but he settled on the one beginning with B-flat.

Ex. 1

Ex. 2

Schumann, however, had forgotten that on the Gewandhaus Orchestra's valveless horns the G and the A could only be produced by hand-stopping and that they would sound, as he later described it, "as though they had caught a violent head cold." Moreover, the valveless trumpets could not play those notes at all. Moving the call up a third was quick thinking on Mendelssohn's part, though it has always seemed surprising that he had not anticipated the problem. No question, Mendelssohn's alert makeshift is weaker than Schumann's original: you lose the buildup from B-flat ("O wende") to D ("Im Thale"), and the change vitiates the tremendous D-minor outburst in the fifth measure. Only a few years later, valve horns and valve trumpets had become standard in the most important orchestras including the Gewandhaus, and the problem disappeared. So why did Schumann not go back to what he had written? Either he got used to the emendation or even came to like it, or, as the English writer Brian Schlotel suggests, "he did not want to bother Breitkopf and Härtel . . . to whom he was constantly, and most deferentially, offering new works." Beginning with Mahler, many conductors have restored Schumann's B-flat opening.[4]

Schumann originally planned to give each movement a title. The first was to be called *Beginning of Spring*, and we have seen how Schumann's letter to Taubert expands on this idea. After the double summons associated with Böttger's spring poem, the music takes a dramatic plunge in the direction of D minor. With the fierce tremolando in the violas and the sharp, interestingly varied punctuations in the rest of the orchestra, there is something almost sinister in this introduction. Are these the sounds of winter's death struggle?[5]

The world turns green by degrees; in other words, Schumann makes his way into the Allegro, which is molto vivace, by way of a gradual acceleration. The rhythm of the symphony's first notes provides a splendid, driving motor for this fervent movement. A new theme for woodwinds is gentler in temper, but the pace does not let up. The exposition, which Schumann wants repeated, passes quickly. The development, three-quarters again as long as the exposition, begins with further exploration of the initial motif, but almost immediately Schumann offers the surprise of a poignant new melody for the oboe.

The moment of recapitulation is managed with a powerful sense of drama. The swift measures of the Allegro continue, but the return of the double fanfare is spread over so many of these that it actually appears at its original andante tempo.[6] It happens in a terrific blaze of sound, *ff* and *fff*. This time the music moves very rapidly to the second theme, after which Schumann gives us a wonderful double coda. The first phase brings the speeding up that we might most naturally expect at this juncture. Though the last measures are triumphant and let us hear the jubilant fan-

---

[4] It used to be assumed that the scoring of Schumann's orchestral music needed considerable help, that is, alteration; current opinion among conductors tends to hold that with some care and a few minor adjustments of dynamics the original orchestration works quite well. Mahler lavishly reorchestrated all four symphonies. The results are fascinating, not as a necessary clarification of Schumann, but for what they tell us about Mahler. Mozart's revisions of Handel, including *Messiah*, are a parallel case.

[5] Remembering the power of the slow introductions in three of Schumann's four symphonies, it is interesting to find him writing in 1835 in a review of a symphony by Christian Gottlob Müller: "What a pleasure when Mozart (in the G-minor Symphony) and Beethoven (in most of his later symphonies) plunge us immediately into rich and exuberant life. Yes, for me, even in some of Haydn's symphonies, that sudden plunge from the Adagio into the Allegro is a grave aesthetic offense."

[6] To always astonishing effect, no matter how often you have heard it, Mozart does the same thing at the recapitulation of the first movement of his *Posthorn* Serenade. I have no idea whether Schumann knew this work.

fare once more, the second phase astonishes and moves us with a tender, hymn-like song, miraculously afloat and free in rhythm. As we soon discover, it looks ahead to the next movement, and its presence is one of those beautiful nonclassical touches Schumann's symphonies abound in.

As for that next movement, originally titled *Evening*, it is a lovely song, a new variant of the "summons to awakening," and given delicate, nervous life by the syncopated accompaniment in the second violins and violas. This Larghetto is rich in orchestral felicities—the soft just-after-the-beat woodwind punctuations when the cellos take the tune, to cite just one—that are as typical of Schumann's orchestral fantasy as his naïveté about the rheumy stopped-horn notes in the introduction. The stirrings of staccato thirty-second-notes most especially recall the Adagio of Beethoven's Fourth Symphony. At the end, the trombones, which have been silent since the end of the first movement, enter—*pianissimo*—for another of those mysterious, anticipatory codas that are a hallmark of the *Spring* Symphony. The music ends very softly and poised on the dominant of G.

What the trombones played in the coda of the second movement is now translated into an energetic, quick, strongly accented Scherzo. Its title was to have been *Merry Playmates*. What comes to mind here is the stormily cross-rhythmed Minuet of Mozart's G-minor Symphony, a work Schumann knew by heart. Even the key is right. Or so it seems—and given that G minor is the relative minor of B-flat major it would be a plausible choice—but we quickly hear that this is a subtle deception: the real key is D minor, but Schumann has chosen to make this curiously slantwise entry into it. Also the atmosphere changes quickly, for after the initial sixteen-measure paragraph, which is repeated, everything becomes quite blithe.

Two trios, as much in contrast with each other as with their surroundings, loosen this vigorous movement. The first, in D major, plays charmingly with antiphonal effects and eventually turns into a country dance. The other, in B-flat major, is on the wild side. The last appearance of the scherzo is drastically abbreviated, moving into another and still more wondrous coda. The speed changes capriciously several times. The last word, back in D major, is a remembrance, scarcely audible, of the first trio. The Swiss composer and scholar Hans Gál writes beautifully about this strange harmonic mosaic of pseudo-G minor, D minor, D major, and B-flat major: "The tonic [D minor] has asserted itself not as an ever-present fact but as the center of events in a complicated system of gravitation, with the effect of a rich, colorful spectrum of harmony. In details of this kind Schumann reveals himself as a close contemporary of Wagner and a forerunner of Brahms, both most ingenious explorers of sophisticated tonal relationships."

Schumann's name for the finale was *Spring at Its Height*, though he later told Taubert that it was "a farewell to spring, therefore not to be taken too frivolously." It begins with a call to attention for the full orchestra. The bubbling first theme always reminds me of Sullivan in his "Never mind the why and wherefore" vein; Sullivan did, after all, study in Leipzig for three years and knew his Schumann very well indeed. A second theme in minor alludes both to the last movement of Schumann's own *Kreisleriana* and to Mendelssohn's E-flat-major String Quartet, Opus 12. The development begins by darkening the scene, but this is, at most, play-spook. Schumann enters the recapitulation with a touch of sheer magic: a melancholy song from the oboe, horn calls from elfland, and a sweetly ornithic cadenza for the flute. From there on, it is all jubilance to the end.

Symphony No. 2 in C major, Opus 61

> *Sostenuto assai—Allegro ma non troppo*
> *Scherzo: Allegro vivace*
> *Adagio espressivo*
> *Allegro molto vivace*

Schumann began work on the Symphony No. 2 in the latter part of 1845 and completed it the following year. Felix Mendelssohn conducted the first performance at the Gewandhaus in Leipzig on 5 November 1846. It was not a happy event. The first half of the concert consisted of excerpts from Weber's *Euryanthe* (Overture, Recitative and aria *Wo berg' ich mich?*, and the Act II finale) and Rossini's *William Tell* (Overture, a recitative and aria, and the Act II finale), and Schumann's symphony was performed by a tired orchestra and conductor to an audience too tired to absorb this difficult new work. Moreover, the *William Tell* Overture had been encored, and Schumann's rancorous supporters accused those who had demanded the encore—and even Mendelssohn—of sabotaging his symphony. The dedication is to King Oscar I of Sweden and Norway, the one who is on the sardine and anchovy tins.

Two flutes, two oboes, two clarinets, two bassoons, two horns, two trumpets, three trombones, timpani, and strings.

Here is another work in which Schumann chose to confront Beethoven the symphonist. Like Beethoven's Fifth, Schumann's Second traces a

course *per ardua ad astra,* most listeners in Schumann's own day had no
difficulty in recognizing. Schumann's boldness was rewarded: this became
the greatest of his symphonies, a judgment about which most mid-
nineteenth-century listeners, professional and lay, found themselves in
ready agreement.[7]

Like its two predecessors, the *Spring* Symphony and the first version
of what we now know as No. 4 in D minor, the Second Symphony No. 2
starts with a slow introduction—not one that exudes assurance, as in the
Spring Symphony, but one that is troubled, as in the Symphony in D minor. Brass instruments sound a summons (as they did in the *Spring*), but
the music of the wandering strings casts strange shadows across it. The
summons itself, the keynote and the fifth note of the scale, is so simple as
to be virtually a cliché. We know something like it, for example, from the
opening of Haydn's last symphony; indeed, it is probable that the resemblance is deliberate and that Schumann's near-quotation is a gesture he
uses to claim a place in the great symphonic tradition. What a world of
difference there is, though, between Haydn's firm and simple statement
and Schumann's unpredictable and "soft" rhythmic placing of the notes:

Ex. 1.

Ex. 2.

There is of course also the difference between Haydn's *fortissimo* and Schumann's *pianissimo,* as well as that between the textural clarity of the Haydn
and the blurring effect of Schumann's strings, which also have their own
rhythmic oddities.

[7]In the 3 April 1984 issue of *19th-Century Music,* Anthony Newcomb published an insightful
article, one to which I am deeply in debt, titled "Once More Between Absolute and Program
Music: Schumann's Second Symphony." He has, among other matters, interesting things to say
about the difference between the high regard the Second Symphony enjoyed in the nineteenth
century and the relatively low esteem accorded it by most twentieth-century critics. In December
1994, the autograph manuscript of this work fetched $2,567,185 at a Sotheby auction, a record
to date for a manuscript of a single musical work.

The Allegro, which this dark exordium struggles to find, is a jagged thing, pierced even on its last pages by the summons of the first measures. And no wonder, for this symphony, sketched quickly in December 1845 and worked out at leisure during the following year, is music written in convalescence. Schumann had suffered his first bout of what "alienists" then called melancholia in 1828, and more such sieges, many of them accompanied by frighteningly concrete suicide fantasies, followed in 1830, 1831, 1833, 1837, 1838, 1839, and 1842. His breakdown in August 1844, with trembling, tinnitus, and phobias (especially with regard to heights and sharp metallic objects), was the worst of any. Several years after this misery, he wrote to D. G. Otten, a conductor in Hamburg, that he feared the "semi-invalid state [could] be divined from the music [of the Second Symphony]. I began to feel more myself when I wrote the last movement and was certainly much better when I finished the whole work. All the same, it reminds me of dark days."

The Allegro is long in coming; that is, the introduction is unusually extended. The music in these preludial pages takes on an eventful life of its own, but, at the same time, never ceases to convey the message that it is preparatory. Its initial meditative gait gives way to a slightly faster pace, as does the steady flow of quarter-notes to more sharply profiled rhythmic figures. When suspense has reached its highest point, the music at last flows into the Allegro.

This is an interestingly eccentric movement. The first theme is sharply rhythmic, with biting accents on the second of the three beats in each measure. The harmonies veer far to the flat side before settling in the dominant, G major, with a new theme, smooth in outline, urgent in expression. The exposition is very short, and the development, mostly concerned with material from the later part of the exposition, is about two and a half times as long. Schumann, I suspect, had been studying Beethoven's *Eroica*. Similarly, the coda is extraordinarily and powerfully expansive.

To offset the intensity of the first Allegro, Schumann brings not the slow movement we expect, but a Scherzo. Like the one in the *Spring* Symphony, it has two trios. The first one here is rustic, while the other offers a touching blend of the dreamy and the learned. The second trio also presents, first shyly, then with growing confidence, the name BACH (B-flat/A/C/B-natural if you use the German names of the notes): Schumann had spent the recuperative months of 1845 in an intensive study of Bach, which he felt had greatly contributed to his recovery, and his two sets of fugues, Opus 72 and Opus 60 (the latter also on the name BACH), date from that time. On the Scherzo's last page, the fanfare rings out in triumph. The Scherzo itself is the only out-and-out virtuoso piece in the four (or five) symphonies: in all probability, every violinist in every major orchestra today has had to play its opening page at his or her audition.

All four movements of this symphony are anchored to the same tonic, C; the Adagio, however, is in C minor. Here Schumann invokes Bach again: the resemblance of contour between the melody of Schumann's Adagio and the opening of the Trio Sonata in Bach's *Musical Offering* is no coincidence:

Ex. 3

Ex. 4

Neither of the two Schumann symphonies that preceded this one, the D-minor and the "symphonette," has a true slow movement; here Schumann gives us one of heart-stopping beauty. The accompaniment throbs poignantly beneath the broad-spanned melody. Halfway through, Schumann begins a fugue. For all his devotion to Bach, he does not take fugue seriously as a compositional device within a larger context; though, to be sure, what happens as the counterpoint loses impetus and recedes, becoming simply another form of restless background to the melody, is wonderful in its own quintessentially Romantic way.

The finale is an original and in every way extraordinary conception in expression and structure, and, I would say, a sign of marvelous mental health. It begins with a fierce rush of energy—to be specific, a scale followed by four chords—which clears the path for an athletic, jolly, and perhaps surprisingly neutral first theme. Next, the melody of the Adagio is revisited at high speed in a manner Mahler would remember well when he came to write his Fifth Symphony.[8] The first theme returns briefly, after which the initial scale, followed now by *six* chords, provides fuel for a

---

[8] According to the biography by Henri-Louis de La Grange, Mahler conducted Schumann's Symphony No. 2 only once, at a pair of New York Philharmonic concerts in 1910. Nonetheless, he is one of the sons of Schumann and had long known his music. See also note 4.

vigorous development, in which remembrances from the first and third movements also have a part to play.

This driving music sinks to a quiet and spacious close in C minor. What follows is one of the most tenderly poetic moments in the whole symphonic literature. It turns out that the oboe had listened carefully, as we perhaps did not, to the way the four chords of the opening gesture turned into six. At any rate, it now transforms those macho chords into a lyric melody of the most poignant sweetness, the sense of distance and mystery being enhanced by the strangeness in this context of the key, E-flat major.[9]

Ex. 5

With this, Schumann plays a game similar to the one where you take a word and, changing one of its letters, produce a new word, continuing that way until none of the original letters is left. For Schumann this is a deeply serious game, and through the rest of the development, he spins out variants of Ex. 5. Again, he speaks by allusion. After a tremendous buildup over rolling drums and rushing scales, the melody appears in the strings as an all but literal quotation from Beethoven's song cycle *An die ferne Geliebte* (To the Distant Beloved). The words of the song are "Nimm sie hin denn, diese Lieder" (Take them, then, these songs).

Ex. 6

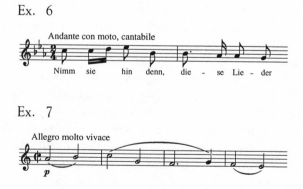

Ex. 7

[9] In the article to which I referred in footnote 7, Newcomb remarks that he has "heard no performance that finds for this moment the proper mood of hesitant, gentle wonder." More than ten years and I don't know how many performances and new recordings later, I haven't either.

Schumann had cited the same phrase in the glorious Piano Fantasy of 1836. That had been a year of enforced physical separation from Clara. Now they were together as husband and wife, as parents of four children, but in some painful way there was still a void between Lover and Beloved.[10] Nevertheless, the tender melancholy of this allusion is swept aside by the gestures of triumph, by the sound of the C-major summons with which this beautiful and enigmatic symphony began. Moreover, it might be some time before you realize that, while the opening four-measure flourish assumed greater and greater significance throughout the finale, the "official" first and second themes had vanished from circulation altogether.

Symphony No. 3 in E-flat major, Opus 97, *Rhenish*

Lively
Scherzo: Very moderate
Not fast
Solemn
Lively

Schumann composed this symphony between 2 November and 9 December 1850, and conducted its premiere at Düsseldorf on 6 February 1851.

Two flutes, two oboes, two clarinets, two bassoons, four horns, two trumpets, three trombones (in the fourth and fifth movements only), timpani, and strings.

More than just a another river, the Rhine has been a political object and the cradle of legend and poetry. Moreover, although it rises in Switzerland and the complicated delta through which it drains into the North Sea is in the Netherlands, the Germans have always thought of it as very much their own.

Schumann and the Rhineland were new to each other in 1850. Except for a period of study at Heidelberg, a winter in Vienna, and occasional travels with his wife, Clara, he had lived in his native Saxony all his life,

---

[10] Aside from its poignant significance in his personal life, *An die ferne Geliebte* had been a crucially important model for Schumann in the composition of his own song cycles—far more so than the Schubert cycles were.

and in Dresden, the capital, since 1844. Dresden was a lively musical center, not least because of Wagner's presence there until 1849, but the Schumanns found it personally and artistically stultifying. Robert had a good friend in the conductor and composer Ferdinand Hiller, and when Hiller left Dresden for Düsseldorf in 1847, he recommended that Schumann succeed him as conductor of the Dresden Liedertafel. Three years later, when Hiller was ready to move again, this time just a few miles upriver to Cologne, he once again proposed Schumann as his successor. On 31 March 1850, Schumann formally accepted his appointment as Düsseldorf's municipal music director.

When Schumann arrived in Düsseldorf on 2 September 1850, he had much to look forward to. The Düsseldorfers, for their part, did everything they could to make their new music director feel welcome, unleashing an exhausting round of speeches, serenades, celebratory concerts, banquets, and balls. The Schumanns' first apartment was horribly noisy in a way that told badly on the nerves of both Robert and Clara; nonetheless, Robert's creative energies were not to be suppressed, and in just fifteen October days he composed his Cello Concerto. The day he finished it he conducted the first of his ten subscription concerts; Clara was his soloist in Mendelssohn's G-minor Concerto and, except that Robert was miffed because she got more attention than he did, it went well.

The venture in their new home quickly turned into disaster. Clearly unequal to the requirements of his position, Schumann was asked to resign in October 1852. The matter was smoothed over, but a year later he had conducted his last concert in Düsseldorf. Always subject to depressions and the survivor of more than one suicide attempt, Schumann threw himself into the Rhine on 27 February 1854. He was rescued and committed into Dr. Richarz's hospital at Endenich, where he died two and a half years later. But all that is part of another story. The *Rhenish* Symphony reflects Schumann's optimism in the face of new challenges and a fresh start among a people more outgoing than any he had known and whose ebullience—not yet perceived as aggressiveness—delighted him.

Schumann begins the *Rhenish* Symphony with one of his most glorious themes, a puissantly forward-thrusting idea, part of whose energy is in its artful cross-rhythm. If you have never seen the score and are not watching the conductor, you probably hear a melody with three rather broad beats to the bar, something like this:

Ex. 1

In fact, though, the measures are half as long, the beats twice as fast, and the melody is syncopated across the written pattern:

Ex. 2

The real 3/4 reveals itself only in the seventh measure, at the point marked with a bracket; indeed, while the ♩ ♩ 3/4 continues in the melody, the bass almost at once reverts to the broader half-tempo triple-meter ³₄. ♩ ♩♩♩ ♩.♪ The tension generated by this difference pervades the entire movement, and the opening theme itself is never absent for long. There is much Beethoven to be heard along the way, especially the *Eroica* and Eighth symphonies, but the spirit of the movement, characterized by minimal contrast and relaxation, is all Schumann's own, as is the highly individual touch of introducing new material when the piece is almost over.

Now Schumann moves away from classical models, except insofar as Beethoven's *Pastoral* Symphony provided a precedent for a five-movement symphony. Schumann's Scherzo is an agreeably galumphing country dance, country cousin perhaps to the minuet in the Beethoven Eighth, with a secondary, decorative idea shared by the main part of the movement and its rather brooding trio. *Morning on the Rhine* was Schumann's original title for the Scherzo. The pace relaxes even further for the next piece. It is not really a slow movement, but something more by way of a middle-tempo intermezzo, an original genre with Schumann.

Then comes the symphony's first truly slow music. On 30 September 1850, four weeks after their arrival in Düsseldorf, the Schumanns made the thirty-mile trip on the new railway line to Cologne to witness the installation of Cardinal/Archbishop von Geissel in the cathedral. Schumann was stunned by this, the largest Gothic building in northern Europe, and, as a newcomer to a Catholic land, he was excited by the splendor of the ceremony.

Here, in the fourth movement of the *Rhenish* Symphony, is his musical monument to a building that was almost as much of a national totem as the river next to which it stands. It is a movement of remarkable rhythmic subtlety and one in which Schumann skillfully uses the evocative properties of antique polyphonic style. He reserves the sound of trombones, still in 1850 associated more with church and theater than with the concert hall, for this tone picture and (with effective restraint) for the finale. This fifth movement begins by being uncomplicatedly cheery; only gradually does it reveal itself as a kind of extension or completion of the cathedral section. As it moves to its brilliant close, it makes allusion as well to the symphony's opening.

Symphony No. 4 in D minor, Opus 120

> *Fairly slow—Lively*
> *Romance: Fairly slow*
> *Scherzo: Lively*
> *Slow—Lively—Faster*

Schumann composed this symphony in what he called a "brainstorm" between 29 May and 9 September 1841. It was premiered as his Symphony No. 2 by the Leipzig Gewandhaus Orchestra on 6 December that year, Ferdinand David conducting. Having withheld it from publication and further performance meanwhile, Schumann gave it a thorough going over between 3 and 19 December 1851 and reintroduced it with the Düsseldorf Municipal Orchestra on 3 March 1853. Its familiar title of Symphony No. 4, Opus 120, therefore refers to the revised edition of 1851, since what we now know as the Second and Third symphonies had been completed in 1846 and 1850 respectively.

Two flutes, two oboes, two clarinets, two bassoons, four horns, two trumpets, three trombones, timpani, and strings.

As I noted in the introduction to these Schumann essays, 1841 was a year rich in orchestral music for him, ending with the Overture, Scherzo, and Finale, Opus 52, which Schumann sometimes called his "symphonette," and ended with this Symphony in D minor. Opus 52 and the D-minor failed to please as much as the *Spring* had seven months earlier. Perhaps, the composer suggested, there had been too many Schumann premieres, and Mendelssohn's good offices on the podium had definitely been missed. (Ferdinand David, who led the first performances of both new works at the same concert, was the Gewandhaus Orchestra's concertmaster and a distinguished musician, but he was not a first-rate or greatly experienced conductor.) Schumann, confident that the new symphony was in no way inferior to the *Spring* and that its quality would eventually be recognized, was relatively unconcerned by this momentary failure. He did, however, put the score away until the successful premiere of his *Rhenish* Symphony in February 1851 encouraged him to look at it again and revise it for a second premiere.

Like all of Schumann's revisions of his own works, which occurred most often in his piano music, this one is problematic. Compositionally, it is an improvement: in particular, the transitions into the first and last movements out of their slow introductions are better paced and thus more tellingly realized—and these are some of the most poetic and original passages in the symphony. The orchestration, on the other hand, is worse, the thick impasto of doublings reflecting Schumann's growing angst on the podium. The year 1851 had been one of some especially unhappy experiences with the Düsseldorf orchestra, whose conductor he had become the year before. It was at Brahms's urging that the 1841 score was published in 1891: Clara Schumann, the force behind many of Robert's not always fortunate revisions, was furious.[11]

Schumann's First Symphony, the *Spring*, begins with what he called a "summons to awakening," continues with a depiction of the gradual greening of the earth, and arrives in a world where "spring is coming to life." The D-minor Symphony, started just four months later, also begins with a drama of emergence, but here it is not spring struggling free of winter: this is a darkly mysterious work, troubled and troubling.

The music begins with an A, five octaves deep, *forte* with an immediate diminuendo. A listener looking neither at a score nor at the conductor takes this to be a downbeat. It is not: the A comes on the last beat of a 3/4 measure and is held over through the next three measures. Why bring this up? What difference does it make? This: beginning on "3" with the note tied over the barline is not a "natural" musical gesture like beginning on "1," and so there is more tension in the attack. This delicate psychological refinement, by the way, is also one of Schumann's later thoughts: the 1841 version begins on the downbeat.[12] Schumann also made the intro-

---

[11] An obvious move is to take the 1851 composition but restore the 1841 orchestration, and Tovey writes that this was done in Germany in the first half of this century. I have never encountered such a performance; nor, for that matter, have I ever heard the 1841 version, though it has been recorded.

[12] In his great overture for Byron's *Manfred*, Schumann goes even further in creating expressive tension by making things difficult for conductor and orchestra. The three powerful chords at the beginning are preceded and followed by unmeasured silences so that there is no audible sense of rhythmic context, but they are placed in the measure and notated so as to create maximal anxiety for the performers.

duction slower in 1851—from Andante con moto (moving along) to Ziem-
lich langsam (fairly slow)—and to the extent that it is slower it is also
darker. Perhaps even the dynamic marking of *forte* contributes to the tension: *fortissimo* or even *pianissimo* would be clear-cut, but *forte* hovers.

As the A continues, now *pianissimo,* string and bassoons play a brooding music under it, all moving in small steps. The flute and the first violins
seek to dispel the ominous atmosphere with a sweetly consoling cadence.
The orchestra will have none of this, and just before its resolution the
cadence is cut off by another A, sharply accented, on "2" (more rhythmic
tension), and fully harmonized. The brooding stepwise music invades more
and more of the orchestra, and the harmonic range widens. While the
basses become fixated on just two of the notes of the brooding theme—A
and G-sharp—the violins explore a variant of it in double tempo. The
ostinato bass and the ever-more-active violins —an opposition that produces still more tension—function as a double motor that pushes the music
forward until it bursts forth in a new, quick tempo and in 2/4 time.

The theme is that of the introduction but speeded up, metamorphosed
into something fiercely energetic by an almost unbroken tattoo of
sixteenth-notes. The key is still D *minor,* and so the energy is not joyous.
Patches of syncopation add to our sense of being in the presence of an
almost frighteningly excitable temperament. Schumann barely takes time
for some passionately yearning sighs before bringing the exposition to a
febrile finish.

Silence. Then catastrophe. Trombones and strings sound an immense
E-flat, a note that comes harmonically out of nowhere. The strings seek to
resume their churning sixteenths, but another blast of E-flat cuts them off.
Once again they try. This time they are allowed to proceed, but the trombones stay on as a menacing presence: now, however, they speak their
monitions quietly, to even more chilling effect. Schumann had come to
know Schubert's *Great* C-major Symphony two years before: these quiet
trombone warnings as well as the way he managed the transition from the
introduction to the quick tempo are emulation and homage to that masterpiece.

The development evolves into a forceful march. After a sudden halt,
Schumann offers us a lyric melody, tender and rapturous. It is not uncon-
nected to the main theme, but the overwhelming effect is that of something unexpected and new. In the 1841 score, the main theme is played
along with it. In a way it is a pity to lose this counterpoint; over all,
though, the contrast, the simple, songful freshness of the melody, is more
vivid when it is very simply accompanied, and it does seem to me that
contrast and freshness are of the essence here.

Once, as I listened to a particularly inspired and revelatory performance of this symphony, one in which the catastrophe, the trombones' disruptive E-flats, was terrifying as never before, and this melody, in contrast, ineffably ecstatic—yes, there can be such a thing as a fiery *piano*—a line of poetry came into my head: "Hier ist die Aussicht frei" (Here the prospect is clear). Placing it took me a moment in the midst of the emotional turmoil Schumann was creating, but then I found it in the final scene of Goethe's *Faust.* Schumann set it gloriously; so did Mahler sixty years later. What was the connection?

Everything to this point, beginning with the word *symphony,* has thrown cues that what we have here is a movement in sonata form. We have heard an introduction, an exposition, a development. We expect a recapitulation. There is none, there will be none. First of all, and with just that sense of drama that often marks the entry into the recapitulation, Schumann gives us a radiantly beautiful new melody that I have characterized as tender and rapturous. Then, instead of returning to the first theme in the home key, he keeps moving, to find fresh angles from which to shed light on his material, to show it in new glory. Above all, it is the tender melody that, late as it was in coming, now turns out to be the goal, the point of the movement. Schumann spins exuberantly through the harmonic universe until he is drawn into the magnetic field of D—now D *major*—and there he brings the first movement to a forceful stop.

In sum, it is as though with the arrival of the new, tenderly ecstatic melody, Schumann had suddenly seen the way ahead, the prospect. With miraculous clarity, he had perceived that the goal is not a return to D minor and a formal recapitulation, at least not now. That melody is an epiphany, a liberation, permission to invent a new and delightfully unorthodox formal design, a moment of understanding that his task is the enjoyment, in the fullest sense of the word, of the world of feelings the melody evokes. As he remarks somewhere in his critical writings: "Those of the first rank are granted the right to enlarge" the traditional classical forms. Indeed, "Here the prospect is clear."

We need respite after these extremes, after this whirlwind of passions, and, with a break of only one beat, stretched slightly by a fermata, Schumann begins his slow movement. He calls it Romance. Remembering the second movement of Beethoven's Seventh Symphony, he sets the scene with a wind chord, without, however, replicating Beethoven's daring in placing this chord in its most unstable position. Oboe and a solo cello sing a melancholy song. The scoring—the two singers in octaves with the lightest possible accompaniment—is exquisite (unchanged from the 1841 original), and the sound, deliciously antiqued, suggests a little Renaissance band, imagined of course through Romantic ears.[13]

Shadows fall as the brooding music of the introduction returns, but oboe and cello reappear briefly to put a cadence to their song. The middle section is another transformation of the introduction, now in D major, with a solo violin adding delicate arabesques to the texture. The two measures for *pianissimo* trombones between stanzas of the violin solo are a marvelous orchestral touch. (The music itself just there is a sudden and surprising visit from Mendelssohn.) The Romance itself returns, and this time it is allowed to complete itself undisturbed.

One of Schumann's 1851 alterations was to ask for the four movements to be played without break. He also thought of titling the work Symphonic Fantasy rather than Symphony No. 4, but pulled back from that at the last moment. He had admired the effect of going from movement to movement without break in Mendelssohn's *Lobgesang* (Song of Praise) Symphony, but more important, he had understood its applicability for his own work, so involved in returns, cross-references, metamorphoses.

The theme of the thunderously energetic Scherzo is yet another transformation of the introduction. Here Schumann dropped some joyous horn calls from his original score, and it is a pity. The trio is a variant of the middle section of the Romance, this time with all the first violins playing the arabesques. This recollection is Romantically (and romantically) blurred by artful rhythmic confusion: the music moves in 3/4 time, but the running eighth-notes of the arabesques float freely against that meter or actually contradict it by dividing the measures into two beats rather than three.[14]

The Scherzo returns, after which Schumann brings back the trio once more. This time, however, it begins to hesitate, to disintegrate. Writing longer and longer notes, Schumann composes a retard. With the miraculously soft and distant voices of clarinets and bassoons, divided violas and cellos, the music all but comes to a halt. We are in near darkness when we hear, as though from a great distance, the rising theme of the first movement. Trombones and horns sound solemn warnings. Day breaks, the music draws nearer, and we are in a lively D-major movement. The theme

---

[13] Max Alberti writes in the introduction to the Eulenburg miniature score that Schumann included a guitar in the original version of this movement, but the Breitkopf & Härtel edition of the 1841 score does not show this.

[14] It is of course possible to straitjacket the violins and make them shape their eighth-notes into rigid 3/4 bars, but the most illuminating performances I have heard (Furtwängler, Skrowaczewski) make the most of this polyphony of rhythms. Skrowaczewski was the conductor of the performance I referred to earlier.

of the first movement is a powerful presence in the lower strings to enrich the finale's own sturdy theme. It is as though this were at last the recapitulation Schumann had bypassed in the first movement.

The finale is vibrant, exultant music. Still, when the exposition has come to an end (and presumably been repeated), Schumann again evokes the specter of catastrophe with great trombone unisons. The movement grows ever more jubilant and Schumann twice increases the speed for his whirlwind coda. But before the final presto, the orchestra sounds a dramatic cry, a great *fortissimo* chord whose harmony and orchestration evoke the moment when the Commendatore appears in response to Don Giovanni's frivolous invitation to dine. Schumann's volatile, explosive symphony ends in virtuosic brilliance, but to the end, harbors the threat of insurrection, violence, terror, and madness.

Roger Sessions (signature)

Roger Sessions

Roger Huntington Sessions was born in Brooklyn, New York, on 28 December 1896 and died in Princeton, New Jersey, on 16 March 1985.

"Program notes . . . . I think they're for the birds"
—Sessions to his biographer, Andrea Olmstead

essions is a figure of gigantic stature on the landscape of American music. He was one of the most effective and influential teachers of his time (of Milton Babbitt, David Del Tredici, John Harbison, Leon Kirchner, Fred Lerdahl, Peter Maxwell Davies, Conlon Nancarrow, Hugo Weisgall, Ellen Taaffe Zwilich, among others—a list that attests to how non-doctrinaire he was) and his essays and lectures constitute a significant and increasingly appreciated body of writings about music. Most important, he was a great composer.

A slow writer in his youth, who later chose to preserve virtually nothing he composed before he was thirty, an ever more fluent one as he grew older, Sessions produced a catalogue of works that, while not extremely large, is one of remarkable weight and value: nine symphonies and other compositions for orchestra, three concertos, two operas, choral works, chamber music, and solo pieces. He began as something of a Stravinskian but moved steadily into a more chromatic style, all the while evolving a highly inflected musical language characterized by long melodic lines of great tensile strength and by a luxuriant polyphonic texture. It is active music, maximalist to the max. Sessions has never received the critical attention given to such innovators as Babbitt, Elliott Carter, and John Cage.

His work stands firmly in the mainstream. As Arthur Mendel once wrote about Bach, nothing is new except the notes.

As an undergraduate at Princeton in the second half of the 1940s, I came to know Roger Sessions by awesome reputation several years before the first of many, never enough, and always cherished personal encounters. In absentia but incessantly invoked and quoted, he was a more vivid presence than most of the flesh-and-blood professors actually on the scene and certainly more so than the two composers who succeeded him in the department. Even the characteristically compact signature that I constantly ran across on library cards conveyed an astonishing sense of personal force. He had recently left for what would be a nine-year stay at the University of California at Berkeley, and it was also the time he had begun to work on his Second Symphony.

In retrospect it seems amazing that such a reputation was founded on what, for a composer entering his fifties, was a rather small group of pieces: incidental music for Andreyev's *The Black Maskers*, a symphony, a piano sonata, a string quartet, a violin concerto, a set of piano pieces called *Pages from a Diary* (to his distress renamed *From My Diary* by the publisher), a short duo for violin and piano. Few, I daresay, would have guessed that ahead lay, among other matters (these include several books), another eight symphonies, three concertos, two operas, three large-scale vocal works (*The Idyll of Theocritus*, choruses on biblical texts, and the great Whitman cantata *When Lilacs Last in the Door yard Bloom'd*), two more piano sonatas, another string quartet, a viola quintet, a sonata for unaccompanied violin. Most of this imposing body of work, every note of it on the highest level, would be achieved by a man in his sixties and seventies.

Sessions had a formidable intellect: that he entered Harvard at fourteen is concrete, if trivial, evidence of his braininess. I remember him as a man in many ways wondrously uncomplicated, a loving husband devastated by his wife's death three years before his own, a devoted and sometimes bewildered father, an impassioned and demanding teacher, on occasion a more than slightly absent-minded professor, a political idealist who was profoundly depressed by evil and by the sheer folly of the world, a man who loved music and words with heart and mind and who was grandly opinionated about both. He had a rich sense of humor and, for all his settled awareness of his own worth, he was altogether down to earth. He could speak with an apocalyptic rumble that gave new meaning to the phrase "rolling periods," and he could be drastically terse and four-lettered. His last words were, "What a goddam nuisance."

He loved polyphonic authors like Thomas Mann and Hermann Broch, and his own music revels in intricacy of texture and reference. Its riches are sometimes piled recklessly high—the first movement of his beautiful Violin Concerto, for instance, can sound like two Bach cantatas played simultaneously—but he always gives you the possibility of hearing more and more in each piece the longer you know it.

To me, his music is inexhaustible. I love his complex, unpredictable melodies (he always said he never wrote a phrase he couldn't sing), I love his sense of color, I love his intensity of feeling, I love a quality that I relate to a kind of New England toughness I remember in him, I love the conviction his work conveys that music is important and can speak to us of important things, even last things. In all these ways, ruggedness and awkwardnesses not excluded, he has always seemed to me to come the nearest of any musician in our time to being the heir of Beethoven. I was thrilled to find Dimitri Mitropoulos describing Sessions in a letter to his lifelong friend Katy Katsoyanis as "the only one who could compete with the rest of the great."

The composer Alfredo Casella told Sessions that his music was "nato difficile"—"born difficult." Dense, full of event, free of redundancy or routine filler, it allows no time to coast. It challenges the listener, who for him was someone alertly intelligent, though not necessarily learned, someone with hair-trigger emotional responses, and rejoicing in his or her God-granted gifts of attention and memory. Sessions's music is also unforgiving. Difficult music by some composers sounds more or less OK in an approximation (as distinct from a real performance); his sounds like hell unless everything—spiritual, technical, and acoustic—is in place. He heard many awful misrepresentations of his music and was aware that people blamed the horrible sounds they heard on him, not on the performers.

He sometimes quoted what Luigi Dallapiccola, his closest friend among composers, wrote to him: "Si sa chè il nostro mestiere è la scuola della pazienza"—(We all know that our profession is the school of patience). He was thankful to the roots of his being to those musicians who had the integrity, imagination, and skill to bring his difficult compositions to life in performance, Mitropoulos and Jean Martinon being two names he spoke with special gratitude, and he was correspondingly, though never publicly, scornful of the hackers and slammers in the profession. He himself remained imperturbably confident and patient. It was part of his toughness that he never felt sorry for himself.

Even as a boy in Hadley, Massachusetts, a town he always referred to as "my ancestral hangout," Sessions was sure he had to be a composer. His head was always full of music, and as he biked home from school one afternoon he was suddenly aware that the music he heard was new and his own. He was twelve and he had been taking piano lessons since he was four. A year later he wrote an opera, *Lancelot and Elaine*, based on Tennyson, and he was ready to admit his vocation to his parents.

At Harvard he studied with Archibald Davison and Edward Burlingame Hill, and then, because the outbreak of war interfered with a plan to go to Ravel in Paris, he worked with Horatio Parker at Yale. As a young instructor at Smith, sure that he knew too little, he continued his education through treatises of Cherubini and d'Indy, and after that, in a crucial decision, by going to Ernest Bloch. He became Bloch's assistant at the Cleveland Institute of Music and left in protest when the board decided they needed a better fund-raiser and more willing socializer than Bloch.

Bloch sharpened Sessions's musical faculties and confirmed his sense of a place in the central tradition of European music. For all his cosmopolitanism—he was, for example, a superb linguist—Sessions was American through and through in speech and attitude, particularly in his idealism; at the same time, he believed that America's cultural heritage was essentially European. Bloch began his first lessons by analyzing the opening bars of Beethoven's Piano Sonata, Opus 2, no. 1, "and I must say," Sessions recalled, "that these ten or twenty minutes . . . were about the most important thing in my whole musical education."

Cleveland was "bad enough with Bloch; without Bloch it would be impossible." A series of fellowships and grants enabled Sessions to escape to Europe, and there his distinctive style began to take shape. Stravinsky, the most exciting and "public" personality in the music world of the 1920s, is very much a presence in *The Black Maskers* score of 1923 and the Symphony No. 1 (1926–27), with its steady rat-tat of eighth-notes. But from the beginning, Sessions was Sessions, writing music stockier than Stravinsky's and, as John Harbison has pointed out, with a "total lack of Stravinskian irony and distance."

The Stravinskian surface eventually disappeared, but even while it was still prominent, as it is in the Violin Concerto (1930–35), elements from another, more German tradition—long-breathed melody, broad gestures, polyphony—were becoming more pronounced. Stravinskian athleticism has been crossed with the Romantic, always noble diction of Brahms and with Sebastian Bach's sinuously winding melos, Sessions all the while coming more and more to assume Bach's love for entwining these lines in elegantly elaborate contrapuntal tracery. As time passed, Sessions's melodic and harmonic vocabulary became increasingly chromatic, and by the end of the 1950s, he had adopted—by slipping into it almost unconsciously, as he liked to tell the story—Arnold Schoenberg's twelve-note mode of composition. But more than ever he sounded like himself.

As man and artist, Sessions was infinitely and quickly responsive to the world around him. A humanist and idealist, he composed powerful threnodies for Franklin D. Roosevelt (Symphony No. 2), John F. Kennedy (Piano Sonata No. 3), and Martin Luther King and Robert F. Kennedy (his greatest work, the setting of Walt Whitman's lament for Abraham Lincoln, *When Lilacs Last in the Dooryard Bloom'd*). His operas *The Trial of*

Lucullus and *Montezuma* were responses to the large political events of the day, as was what he thought of as his Vietnam trilogy of the Sixth, Seventh, and Eighth symphonies). And there were more private acts of reflection, celebration, and mourning, such as the *Pages from a Diary*, the Symphony No. 4 with its elegy for his brother, the Five Pieces for Piano with their *tombeau* for Dallapiccola, and the Symphony No. 9, inspired in part by Blake's *The Tyger*. But if there is much in Sessions's music of what Harbison has called "melancholy without self-indulgence, loneliness without isolation," his vocabulary also encompassed the exuberance of the Symphony No. 3 and the Double Concerto, and the abundant sensuality and *joie de vivre* of *The Idyll of Theocritus*.

From *The Black Maskers* to the Concerto for Orchestra he completed for the Boston Symphony in 1981, whatever he composed is possessed of electrifying energy, physical and intellectual. This energy produces a densely active music in which hardly anything is neutral, in which even accompaniments become so specific as to take on an assertive life of their own. The music throws events at you at a tremendous rate and, to quote Harbison once more, it is all "abundance and sublime willfulness." It is also profoundly traditional in the tensions and releases of its arching melodies, in its commitment to "the long line," in its expressive and ethical intent, its address to what Sessions called the "energies which animate our psychic life." Music, Sessions knew and insisted,

> reproduces for us the most intimate essence, the tempo and the energy, of our spiritual being; our tranquillity and our restlessness, our animation and our discouragement, our vitality and our weakness—all, in fact, of the fine shades of dynamic variation of our inner life.[1]

Symphony No. 2

Molto agitato—Tranquillo e misterioso—Tempo I—Tranquillo e misterioso—Tempo I
Allegretto capriccioso
Adagio, tranquillo ed espressivo
Allegramente

Sessions began work on the Symphony No. 2 in Princeton in 1944, though some of the ideas go back to 1934, and he completed it in Berkeley in

[1] Roger Sessions, *The Musical Experience of Composer, Performer, Listener* (Princeton, Princeton University Press, 1950).

March 1946 (the score is dated "Princeton-Gambier-Berkeley, 1944–46"; Gambier, Ohio, is the seat of Kenyon College, where Sessions taught in the summer of 1945). The work was commissioned by the Ditson Fund of Columbia University, which granted the first performance rights to the San Francisco Symphony. Pierre Monteux led that orchestra in the first performances on 9 and 11 January 1947. The dedication is "To the Memory of Franklin Delano Roosevelt," who died while Sessions was working on the Adagio movement.

Two flutes and piccolo, two oboes and English horn, two clarinets and bass clarinet, two bassoons, four horns, three trumpets, three trombones, bass tuba, timpani, xylophone, snare drum, gong, tambourine, cymbals, bass drum, tenor drum, triangle, piano, and strings.

The moods of the Symphony No. 2 cover the range from a muscular and spirited optimism that is compellingly evocative of its time—victory at the end of World War II—to a brooding lyricism that is altogether Sessions's own and timeless. A rough road map of the first movement shows us this design: fast/slow/fast/slow/fast. But Sessions contrasts temper as well as speed, and it is useful to know that the fast and slow sections are marked "molto agitato" and "tranquillo e misterioso."

In a program note whose musical detail must have been bewildering even to the experienced and educated audiences of half a century ago, Sessions allowed that the symphony

> with reasonable accuracy . . . may be considered as in the key of D minor—the movements being in D minor, F minor, B-flat minor, and D major respectively. The subject of tonality is complex and even problematical nowadays, and if I use terms which I myself find inadequate to the facts of contemporary music, it is because they express certain essentials more satisfactorily than any others I know.[2]

In other words, this movement's D minor is not quite like the D minor of Mozart's great piano concerto in that key, nor like that of César Franck's Symphony. (Nor of course are those D minors like each other.) At the same time—and Sessions even uses the D-minor key signature of one flat in his score—D is the anchor, the point of departure, and, very clearly, the point of final cadence.

[2] San Francisco Symphony program book, 9-11 January 1947.

The first sound we hear is this chord:

Ex. 1

The notes that belong to the chord of D minor are white, the others are black. This is, in other words, a D-minor chord that even in this, its first presentation, comes with considerable dissonant interference. Some of the instruments let it go immediately, others sustain it quietly, and with the chord still sounding, the strings take off on a brilliant flurry of sixteenth-notes. The horns come in with a steady march of eighth-notes, the trumpet climbs a staircase of march-like melody to which the violins respond with a broad swing down and up, after which the all the trumpets continue their vigorous march forward.

Now all this happens in not quite the first half-minute; among other things, then, it is a good example of what I mean when I say that Sessions's music is dense. But that last is an aside. When we are actually listening to the music, the point is that these tightly packed events with which Sessions pelts us provide the material that will be discussed in this Agitato section. It is more likely to be varied than restated literally, and it tends to become more sharply profiled as the music unfolds.

As for that mordant chord: it is the first sound we hear, and that alone, even if it were less full of character and flavor, makes it something we are likely to remember. Sessions therefore uses it as a marker that sets off the major sections of the movement. Each recurrence is a signal that a significant juncture in the progress of the music has been reached. Nor is this chord itself an unvaried, static entity: Sessions always maintains enough of its characteristic tang to keep it recognizable, but at the same time he can ring many variations on its color and voicing. Andrew Imbrie put it beautifully in a program note he wrote for the San Francisco Symphony in 1985:

> The use of this chord neatly demonstrates a fact that is crucial to the understanding of Sessions's music, namely that function does not follow formula. The identity of the chord is not literal but approximate. The deviations from literal identity are small enough to permit the listener confidently to form the necessary association. Yet these same deviations are large enough

to give variation of light and shade, allowing the chord to take on a coloration appropriate to its immediate context.[3]

The "tranquillo e misterioso" music is a lyric violin solo (Sessions loved the high register of that instrument) played against a background of soft sustained chords with gently swirling figures in the solo cello to enliven the texture. The swirls become more prominent; in fact, they turn into a bridge to the string flurry at the beginning of the agitato when that section returns. Both the second agitato and the second tranquillo e misterioso are more developmental in character, more richly figured and orchestrated than before. The third and last agitato brings new material, both at its beginning and its end. At the close, as the music calms down we hear a wide-ranging melody passed from one solo woodwind to another, while under that, a single viola, muted, murmurs a commentary of running sixteenth-notes, a final and surprising transformation of the dazzling sixteenth-note flurry, high, unmuted, and *fortissimo*, with which the movement began. Bass clarinet, cellos, basses, and timpani make a firm cadence onto D, and that note, repeated by all the strings pizzicato, closes the movement.

Now Sessions does something quite unexpected. Capriccioso in the tempo direction for the second movement (Allegretto capriccioso) refers not only to the spirit in which the music is to be played but also to the composer's mood in placing just this movement just here. After the densely packed, intensely serious first movement, Sessions gives us the shortest and lightest movement he ever put into a major work. One of the things "lightest" means is that, so unlike Sessions's usual way, the first tune is unvaried upon its returns, though the continuations are full of delectable surprise. It is an ambling, wryly good-humored scherzo, whose slightly off-center chords remind me a bit of the delightfully tilted harmonies in Nielsen and Prokofiev. It takes less than two minutes and disappears in a puff of air.

The scherzo is just the breather we need before we enter the awesome and dark world of the next movement, Adagio, tranquillo ed espressivo. Here is the heart, the tragic center of the symphony. Muted violas sing the first melody, which leads to a most beautiful extension for the oboe. A change of key (from B-flat minor to C-sharp minor), of tempo (poco più mosso), and color (clarinet with piano accompaniment) introduces a contrasting middle section. Soaring violins pick up the eloquent melody and lead it to a climax. The darker opening music returns. Weighty chords for brass and clarinets seem to signal catastrophe. I never asked Sessions whether this was perhaps the place in the movement he had reached on

[3] San Francisco Symphony program book, 2-5 October 1985.

12 April 1945, the day the country was shocked to its roots by the news of the President's sudden death.[4] Perhaps it is as well. He did not like to talk about such things, and in his program note for the premiere he wrote that

> as composer of the work I do not wish to go beyond this [the indication of a few general expressive points such as the prevailing darkness and somberness of the Adagio]; to do so would imply a kind of commitment and could be taken to indicate conscious intentions which did not exist. The music took the shape which it had to take—I strove, as always, to be simply the obedient and willing servant of my musical ideas. But it must be remembered that for a composer musical ideas have infinitely more substance, more reality, more specific meaning, and a more vital connection with experience than any words that could be found to describe them.[5]

The movement closes quietly, with a wondrously beautiful passage for strings alone: second violins and violas suggest a "walking" melody, which is picked up and carried to its touching conclusion by the first violins.

Once again, Sessions proceeds by extreme contrast. The finale is, for the most part, music of assertive brilliance, beginning with a series of trumpet chords (with cellos and piano) descending in parallel. It is a rondo of generously varied substance and, except for one dramatic interruption, in high spirits. At the end, Sessions leaves no doubt about the "D-ness" of this symphony. Bass instruments sit down firmly on a double pedal of D and A (the crucial two-thirds of a D chord). Suddenly everything wheels into focus, as when the optometrist has found the perfect lens at last, and, beginning with flute and piccolo on a high A, the wind instruments rapidly descend the D-major staircase to land us on the solid floor of a final low D, *fortissimo,* of low brass, basses, and kettledrum.

---

[4] An irreverent memory intrudes, of the autograph manuscript of *La Bohème*, in which Puccini marked the brass chord indicating the death of Mimì with a neatly drawn skull and crossbones. And, unlikely though it seems, there is a Sessions-Puccini connection in that in 1910, Sessions's father consulted several important composers, Engelbert Humperdinck being one and Puccini another, about the thirteen-year-old Roger's future. Puccini, Sessions later learned, paced the floor for a long time but finally felt unable to take the responsibility for giving advice on so important a matter.

[5] San Francisco Symphony program book, 9-11 January 1947.

Dmitri Shostakovich

Dmitri Dmitrievich Shostakovich was born in Saint Petersburg on 25 September 1906 and died in Moscow on 9 August 1975.

When a good life-and-works of Shostakovich at last appears— one, that is, based on thorough study of sources, free of political *parti pris,* and written by someone of musical and human sensibility—we shall have one of the most gripping of all artistic biographies. The subject is a critic's and historian's dream: a composer who added essential works to the repertory, a man who could not commit himself to heroism or to moral and intellectual slavery, one whose actions and statements cover the gamut from the noble to the base, whose music exhibits staggering divergence between public and private works, whose achievement is so uneven, not just between compositions but within them, who functioned in a society tyrannically demanding of its artists, and whose every anguished photograph screams for an answer to the question "Who is this man?" The scores exist and are open to our scrutiny. It is hard, though, to think of another composer whose work is so intensely, so immediately, so drastically affected by life—his own, but also that of the world in which and for which he wrote.

Shostakovich grew up amid music. His mother was a good pianist, his father sang, he and his older sister were given piano lessons. An engineer in the next apartment had chamber music evenings, and young Mitya used to sit in the hallway listening to Haydn, Mozart, Beethoven, Tchaikovsky, and Borodin. An aunt remembered him as "a very serious and sensitive child, often very meditative . . . rather shy," fond of fairy tales, forever composing or improvising at the piano, reading Gogol, practicing Liszt, but loving Mussorgsky and Rimsky-Korsakov best of all. It was clear early on that music was to be central in his life and that in spite of financial hardships—and these were considerable in the Shostakovich family—his gift had to be nurtured. At thirteen, well prepared, first at home, then at Glyaser's Music School, he was admitted to the Conservatory in Petrograd.[1]

He was unsure whether to concentrate on composition or the piano. "If the truth be told, I should have done both," he said years after he had chosen composition. He was in fact an excellent pianist whose graduation recital included Beethoven's *Hammerklavier* Sonata. His piano playing was also useful in that it enabled him to contribute to the household income by accompanying silent movies, but gradually it receded from the center of his musical life. He gave his last solo recital in 1930, but continued for some years to participate in performances of his chamber music, and as late as 1958 and 1959 he made sparkling recordings of his two piano concertos.

He was nineteen when his professional life got off to a brilliant start with an amazing First Symphony, his graduation exercise for Maximilian Steinberg's composition class at the Conservatory. (Steinberg, an excellent teacher, had studied with Rimsky-Korsakov, Glazunov, and Liadov.) Thanks to Bruno Walter, who heard the Symphony No. 1 in Leningrad and himself introduced it in Berlin soon after, this was the work that first spread the young composer's name abroad. Two more symphonies followed in quick succession, both with chorus, both explicitly political, one called *To October,* commemorating the 1917 revolution, the other *The First of May,* honoring International Workers' Day.

The first performance in 1930 of his Gogol opera *The Nose* was delightful confirmation of his gift for satire; four years later, *Lady Macbeth of Mtsensk,* that seamy and brilliant masterpiece of raw verismo, achieved 180 performances in Leningrad and Moscow in its first year and a half. His Cello Sonata and his String Quartet No. 1 were admired, as were his film scores. He began his Symphony No. 4 in a state of high confidence and energy. The leap into it was immense: we are looking at something like the difference between Beethoven's First Symphony and the *Eroica.*

Then, the bombshell. In January 1936, Shostakovich was on a concert tour with the cellist Victor Kubatsky. At Archangel on the 28th he went to the railroad station to buy that morning's *Pravda.* In it he found an unsigned article titled "Chaos Instead of Music." Together with Molotov and other Party funcionaries, Stalin had been to see the much talked about *Lady Macbeth* on the 26th. Shostakovich, passing through Moscow, had been present at that performance too, and had already been a bit worried because Stalin and his group had left after the third of the opera's

---

[1] Saint Petersburg became Petrograd in 1914 and Leningrad in 1924. In 1991 it became Saint Petersburg once again.

four acts and because he himself had not been summoned to his box for congratulations and "criticism." (Just a few days earlier, the composer Ivan Dzerzhinsky had been thus blessed after a performance of his opera, *The Quiet Don*.) Stalin had been scandalized by *Lady Macbeth*, and *Pravda* now attacked the opera for its "formalism," lack of melody, a generally fidgety and neurasthenic style, immorality in the choice of story and the manner of telling it, and all round for exemplifying " 'Leftist' muddle instead of natural human music."

"I'll never forget that day," Shostakovich said later, the one on which began "the bitterness that has colored my life grey." The next week, another article in *Pravda* assailed Shostakovich's score for the ballet *Bright Stream*, which Stalin had gone to see at the Bolshoi. "Two editorial attacks in *Pravda* in ten days—that was too much for one man. Now everyone knew for sure that I would be destroyed. And the anticipation of that noteworthy event—at least for me—has never left me. From that moment on I was stuck with the label 'enemy of the people' and I don't need to explain what the label meant in those days."

That several of his fellow-composers opportunistically joined the campaign against him was a bitter blow. He completed his exploratory and adventurous Symphony No. 4, which he had begun four months earlier, but withdrew it from performance at the last minute. It was 1961 before he dared take it from the drawer and allow it to be played. At that, Shostakovich was lucky to be a composer and not a writer. Composers were thought ultimately harmless and, though harassed, bullied, terrorized in various degrees, they lived. Writers were treated as true enemies of the people and they were silenced like Anna Akhmatova, killed like Isaac Babel, Maxim Gorky, and Osip Mandelstam, or like Marina Tsvetaeva, driven to suicide.[2]

The immense success of the Fifth Symphony in November 1937 rehabilitated Shostakovich somewhat, and a reviewer's phrase that characterized the new work as "a Soviet artist's creative answer to just criticism" came in handy. (The words have been widely but wrongly attributed to Shostakovich himself.)[3] Nonetheless, his position was never wholly secure

---

[2] Another of Stalin's murder victims was the great theater director Vsevolod Meyerhold. The 1936 *Pravda* article on *Lady Macbeth* said that the opera manifested "the most negative features of 'Meyerholdism' infinitely multiplied."

[3] The Kalmus score of Shostakovich's Violin Concerto No. 1, a reprint of a Soviet edition of 1955, has a preface by a certain B. Yagolim, a critic or musicologist who stuck close to the party line and wrote: "Shostakovich's creative work in music, complex and often contradictory in its nature, was not free from modernistic influences and mistakes. His [Second and Third] symphonies, opera *The Nose* . . . , ballets *The Golden Age*, *Bolt*, and some other compositions bear the imprint of formalism and false experimentation. Overcoming his mistakes and misconceptions the composer has created many outstanding works pithy and rich in emotions. The first of them to appear was the Fifth Symphony."

again. Soviet arts policy was committed to the idea that to be worth anything, a work had to make a political or ideological statement—of course
a correct one. The *Leningrad* Symphony filled the bill and won Shostakovich a position of favor for a time, although he said much later that the
piece did not really mean and say what it purported to mean and say back
in 1942 when it was new. On the other hand, the beautiful but non-
ideological Sixth (1939) had fallen by the wayside precisely because it gave
critics no extramusical handle; the powerful Eighth (1943), arguably the
greatest European symphony since the Sibelius Seventh, infuriated many
with its darkness, aka "defeatism"; while No. 9 (1945), expected to be
a great Victory Symphony and of course to live up to the challenge of
being a "Ninth Symphony," disappointed—in some cases more than disappointed, infuriated—by turning out to be a wry comedy on a modest
scale.

In 1948, Shostakovich was again subjected to brutal bullying at an
extended musical court-martial run by Andrei Zhdanov, Stalin's henchman
in ideological and cultural matters and one of his entourage at the *Lady
Macbeth* performance.[4] This time he found himself in the company of Prokofiev, Khachaturian, and others. The Central Committee even found a
way of using the *Leningrad* Symphony against him. In partial atonement,
Shostakovich was obliged to become a spokesman for anti-Western propaganda. His first visit to the United States, where his music was so much
played, admired, and enjoyed, was for a Cultural and Scientific Conference
for World Peace, which took place in New York in 1949. He muttered his
way through a speech in which, along with criticizing American foreign
policy and again recanting his own past sins as a musical "formalist," he
attacked Prokofiev and Stravinsky in terms ironically close to those in
which Commissar Zhdanov and his committee had reviled him and others—including Prokofiev—the year before.

Shostakovich had already expressed "gratitude for all the criticism
contained in the Resolution of the Central Committee." The composer
Ernst Hermann Meyer told the German musicologist Detlef Gojowy that
on visits to the former German Democratic Republic, "Shostakovich had
comported himself as a 'Russian patriot' and in discussions with [German]
colleagues had even defended Zhdanov's cultural politics." In partial rec-
ompense for his cooperation, he was awarded the Stalin Prize for his *Song
of the Forests*. As Arnold Schoenberg noted: "There are heroes and there
are composers. Heroes can be composers and vice versa, but you cannot
require it."

Zhdanov died in 1948, not long after the inquisition of the compos-

---

[4]Shostakovich believed Zhdanov to have been the author of the two *Pravda* attacks in 1936.

ers, but the climate did not change. Shostakovich found it prudent to add four of his most beautiful compositions to the desk drawer that held the score of the Fourth Symphony: the Violin Concerto No. 1 and the song cycle *From Jewish Folk Poetry* (both completed in 1948), the String Quartet No. 4 (1949), and the String Quartet No. 5 (1952). His decision to suppress the song cycle was undoubtedly tied to the fact that anti-Semitism became more rampant and more openly part of public policy in 1948.

Between 1948 and 1953, Shostakovich composed several film scores and a couple of politically orthodox choral works. Beyond that he concentrated on the "private" genres of piano music (the Twenty-four Preludes and Fugues, inspired by serving on the jury of a Bach competition in Leipzig in 1950), song cycles on texts by Lermontov, Pushkin, and Dolmatovsky, and chamber music (the two string quartets already mentioned), avoiding the public forum of the symphony. The eight-year interval between the Ninth and the Tenth is the longest between any two of his symphonies. After being officially rehabilitated for a second time in 1958, Shostakovich lived his remaining years a chain-smoking nervous wreck, but in some semblance of peace. He wrote as he pleased, and his music was performed, published, and acclaimed at home.

For about thirty years after the war, Shostakovich at orchestral concerts in America meant chiefly the Fifth Symphony. The First was brought out from time to time, while the Ninth and Tenth were a third echelon. The other symphonies were rarely played—nos. 2 and 3 almost never to this day—and few soloists took on the violin and cello concertos. Aside from what had virtually become knee-jerk responses to certain of these works ("precocious" for No. 1, "magnificent, stirring" for No. 5, "sparkling, charming" for No. 9), Shostakovich's critical standing was not high, and he was paid little attention in teaching, analysis, and scholarship.

Around the time of his death in 1975, things began to change. The later symphonies began to show up on programs, as well as the neglected Fourth, Sixth, and Eighth. The Symphony No. 11, *The Year 1905*, came to be recognized as a powerful tragic statement, and conductors also discovered that it was a super-insured source of success. The Symphony No. 14, really a song cycle along the lines of Mahler's *Das Lied von der Erde*, made a powerful impression whenever it was adequately sung and played, and No. 15, though perhaps too subtle for most audiences, was much admired. A few opera companies produced *Lady Macbeth* and *The Nose*. One began to hear complete cycles of the fifteen string quartets, the Piano Trio No. 2 became a repertory piece, and violists gratefully played their Sonata from the last year of the composer's life wherever and whenever they could.

Major critical reassessment began as well. By the end of the 1970s,

Shostakovich was no longer the composer of one hugely popular symphony in grandly rhetorical public-meeting style and of a handful of other fringe pieces; neither, historically, was he just remembered as someone whose music we had listened to as part of the war effort, and who had later shamed himself and us at that conference at the Waldorf-Astoria. We had come to agree with Schoenberg: Shostakovich had the breath of a symphonist. We had come to accept him simply as a composer. Schoenberg also says somewhere that what the Chinese philosopher says matters more to him than that he speaks Chinese. In that spirit, Shostakovich emerged as an artist who became an essential reporter on the human condition in the middle of the twentieth century.

Our hearing of Shostakovich's music is very different now from what it was in the first heyday of his American popularity. We are free to hear it all more "musically" now; specifically, we are much more aware of Mahler's place in Shostakovich's heart and in what the Germans would call his *Klangvorstellung* (conception of sound—"speak in German when you can't think of the English for a thing," almost said the Red Queen to Alice). Mahler is in our ears now as he was not in the 1940s, and he is the source for such features as diverse as Shostakovich's fondness for an often desolate two-part counterpoint, his sometimes startling colloquialisms, the tension in his long-range harmonic strategies, to say nothing of a myriad of deliberate and specific allusions to the symphonies of his hero. But for all the love of Mahler and the conscious assumption of his heritage, Shostakovich's voice is very much his own. For all the receptivity of his musical temperament and through all the badgering of the commissars, he never forgot the last part of the Red Queen's advice: "Remember who you are!"

Finally, there is the problem of *Testimony, the Memoirs of Dmitri Shostakovich* "as related to and edited by [the Russian émigré musicologist] Solomon Volkov," which came out in 1979. Experts on Soviet music and musicians who knew and worked with Shostakovich are divided about its genuineness and reliability. The scholarly apparatus that would be so reassuring is not there, and some details are called into question by the material in Elizabeth Wilson's disorderly and fascinating compilation, *Shostakovich: A Life Remembered* (Princeton). For all that, much of *Testimony* has the ring of truth. It is a book that is hard to ignore, in spite of the awkward questions about authenticity that it raises and leaves unanswered. We cannot escape the consonance between what we read in the book and what so much of Shostakovich's music says with such searing urgency. I quote it several times in the notes that follow.

Symphony No. 1 in F major, Opus 10

Allegretto
Allegro
Lento
Allegro molto

Shostakovich completed his Symphony No. 1 in December 1925 as his graduation exercise for Maximilian Steinberg's composition course at the Leningrad Conservatory, though some of the material must go back to an earlier date. When Nadezhda Galli-Shohat, the composer's aunt, first heard this work at its American premiere by Leopold Stokowski and the Philadelphia Orchestra in 1928, she recognized in it many fragments she had heard young Mitya play on the piano as a boy, some of them associated with, among other matters, La Fontaine's fable of the grasshopper and the ant, and with Hans Christian Andersen's tale *The Little Mermaid*.[5] Nikolai Malko and the Leningrad Philharmonic gave the first performance on 12 May 1926.

Three flutes (two doubling piccolo), two oboes, two clarinets, two bassoons, four horns, two trumpets, tromba contralta (defined in Sibyl Marcuse's *Musical Instruments* as a "valved trombone in trumpet form . . . devised and first introduced by Rimsky-Korsakov"), three trombones, bass tuba, timpani, triangle, snare drum, cymbals, bass drum, tam-tam, bells, piano, and strings.

In Maximilian Steinberg, Shostakovich found a good teacher. Even though Steinberg's musical inclinations were academic-conservative, he was able to help his staggeringly gifted pupil become articulate in a language many of whose features can hardly have been to his taste. Moreover, when the plan for a Leningrad Philharmonic performance of this First Symphony seemed about to be derailed because the nineteen-year-old composer had no money to pay for the copying of orchestral parts, the Conservatory

---

[5] *The Little Mermaid* was to have a remarkable and sinister musical future in Thomas Mann's *Doctor Faustus*.

undertook to foot the bill, something that would not have happened without Steinberg's support.

The opus number is always a bit startling. Shostakovich eventually selected only one of his pre-First Symphony works as worth publishing, the Three Fantastic Dances for Piano, Opus 5, but he faced the challenge of writing his ambitious graduation symphony as a surprisingly experienced composer, including even orchestral works (two Scherzos, Opp. 1 and 7, a set of variations, Opus 3, and a group of fables for mezzo-soprano, Opus 4).

In the First Symphony itself, the assurance with which Shostakovich both imagines and realizes a large-scale structure is as impressive as his vigor and freshness of gesture. Of course one can hear what music he has been listening to and what has delighted him. He owes some of the details of his nose-thumbing, wrong-note humor to Prokofiev, he is fascinated by Mahler and his way of twisting the tails of commonplaces, and more than once we see Petrushka raging in his cell or fixing us with his stare from the top of his master's booth. The basic design is that of the conventional four movements, with the scherzo second and the slow movement third (in itself a very conventional unconventionality). Throughout, though, Shostakovich finds ways of playing interestingly within that convention, producing events in unexpected order, interrupting, linking, reverting.

When the first movement has made its transition from a provocatively discontinuous introduction into the "real discourse," the clarinet plays a cheeky phrase which always suggests the amusing possibility that the instrument all on its own is remembering Strauss's *Till Eulenspiegel*. In one way or another, that phrase turns out to be common ground for much of the material of the entire symphony; indeed, it has already been adumbrated in the introduction itself. We should probably have been much less surprised than most of us were by Shostakovich's late-in-life fascination with serial composition (most strikingly in the String Quartet No. 12).

Shostakovich's orchestral ingenuity is already highly developed, such points as the passages for divided solo strings in the first and last movements, the piano writing in the scherzo, and the famous timpani solo in the finale being merely the most immediately noticeable instances. The slow movement in particular is evidence that at eighteen and nineteen Shostakovich had much to say, and much of astonishing depth. Every phrase is a heartening signal of the arrival on the scene of a new, eloquent, and personal voice.

Symphony No. 4 in C minor, Opus 43

Allegretto poco moderato
Moderato con moto
Largo—Allegro

Shostakovich began his Fourth Symphony on 13 September 1935 and com‑
pleted it on 20 May 1936. Fritz Stiedry and the Leningrad Philharmonic
were to have given the first performance in December of that year, but
Shostakovich withdrew the work while it was in rehearsal. By his own
account, he "came back to it several times [and] revised it over a number
of years." He permitted publication of a two‑piano reduction in 1946, but
the symphony was not performed until 30 December 1961, with Kiril Kon‑
drashin conducting the Moscow Philharmonic.

**Four flutes and two piccolos, four oboes (one doubling English horn), four
clarinets plus E‑flat clarinet and bass clarinet, three bassoons and contrabas‑
soon, eight horns, four trumpets, three trombones, two bass tubas, timpani
(two players), triangle, castanets, wood block, snare drum, cymbals, bass
drum, tam‑tam, xylophone, glockenspiel, celesta, two harps, and strings (16–
20 first violins, 14–18 second violins, 12–16 violas, 12–16 cellos, and 10–
14 basses are requested).**

Shostakovich was about to turn twenty‑nine when he began work on his
Fourth Symphony. He was about halfway through when *Pravda*, under di‑
rect orders from Stalin, mounted a ferocious attack on him, his opera *Lady
Macbeth of Mtsensk*, his ballet *Bright Stream*, and "modernism" in general.
Even so, Shostakovich finished the symphony not quite four months later,
and seven months after that, the work was duly put into rehearsal by the
Leningrad Philharmonic. The conductor was Fritz Stiedry, a Viennese mu‑
sician who had been active in the Soviet Union since 1933. Stiedry, who
later went to the Metropolitan Opera in New York, had a reputation as an
able musician, but in *Testimony*, Shostakovich attacks him savagely as lazy,
unscrupulous, unprepared, and cowardly.

In any event, Shostakovich withdrew his score. (That he withdrew it
after the *tenth* rehearsal is enough to make any composer in America today
berserk with envy.) What made him decide to do so, and what made him

decide to do it *then?* There is no one clear answer. Obviously the *Pravda* articles were a major factor. In its wake, *Lady Macbeth of Mtsensk* had been stricken from the calendar of every opera house in the Soviet Union, and it only returned to the repertory in 1962 (somewhat revised, and renamed *Katerina Ismailova*).

Although Shostakovich himself had gone unmolested in other respects, reprisals after a second offense could have been terrible, and the symphony was dangerously close to the opera in style. You have to remember the political context: 1936 was the year of the Moscow show trials, the climax of the first phase of the Stalinist purge. Knowledge of how the government dealt with its enemies could no longer be evaded. It was not just politicians who were targets either. The campaign against writers had begun, Maxim Gorky was liquidated while under medical treatment in June 1936, and there was no reason to assume composers were safe.

Another and quite different explanation for Shostakovich's decision to withdraw the Fourth Symphony is that he was not satisfied with it. Years later, he did in fact call it "a very imperfect, long-winded work that suffers, I'd say, from 'grandiosomania.' " (It is a strange self-castigation from the composer of the *Leningrad: The Year 1905,* and *The Year 1917* symphonies.)[6] As late as a year and a half before his death, he said in a BBC Television film that, in spite of repeated attempts at revision, he did not think he had ever succeeded in getting the Fourth Symphony quite right.

What do we make of that? I find it believable that even in 1974, Shostakovich thought it best not to bring up the 1936 *Pravda* article, believing it safer, certainly wiser, to stick with the explanation that he had not considered the work good enough. Not that I would totally discount the sincerity of this explanation, but over the years Shostakovich said too many expedient things for us always to be able to take his self-criticism at musical face-value. I am sure that both self-preservation and musical judgment played a role in Shostakovich's decision to sequester the Fourth Symphony in his desk drawer; what we cannot determine is the exact weight of each of those two issues.

Trying to sort this out, we bump into both political and artistic questions. The success of his Fifth Symphony when it was introduced in November 1937 prompted Shostakovich to make his first, guarded public response to the events of 1936. In an article, "My Creative Answer," he mentioned that one review of the Fifth had given him special pleasure "where it said that [the work] is a Soviet artist's creative answer to just criticism." We read those words with acute discomfort, even while under-

[6]The Symphony No. 4 *is* the first of Shostakovich's really long pieces.

standing the self-protective instincts that caused Shostakovich to quote them. The story of an artist pushed into withdrawing an extraordinary if problematic work and recanting with a very strong but less shocking one fits only too well with what we know about life in Stalin's Soviet Union. It is also difficult for us comfortably to accept the idea that "just criticism" in the pages of *Pravda* may actually have set Shostakovich on a productive path and that the road not taken—the road, that is, of *Lady Macbeth* and the Fourth Symphony—was one well abandoned.

What was that road? The striking features of this music are dissonance, dissociation, and an exuberant orchestral style. Some of the chamber music of Shostakovich's last decade is based on more radical compositional means, but the controversial opera (in its original version) and the Fourth Symphony are two of the works that come across as his most "modern." (The first few minutes of the so-called Symphony No. 2—its actual title is *To October, a Symphonic Dedication*—are his boldest venture into the world of "modern" and "radical.") The high dissonance factor is crucial. Also, carrying certain of Mahler's methods several steps further, Shostakovich juxtaposes the most disparate musical elements and moves by startling abruptions. Finally, while he later developed an impressively economical technique of making his orchestra sound bigger than it is, a skill he shared with Tchaikovsky and Rimsky-Korsakov, Shostakovich scored his Fourth brilliantly but without stint. This is in fact the biggest orchestra he ever used in one of his symphonies.

We find Shostakovich here, on the verge of thirty, exploring, expanding, conquering for himself some of the territories of recent European music, and not minding being at times reckless in procedures and consequences. Perhaps, without *Pravda*'s "just criticism," he might have traveled farther along that road: we cannot know. As it was, he chose another way, and his voice became one of the most eloquent in our time on the side of musical conservatism. We cannot write Stalin and *Pravda* out of this story, but we must acknowledge that Shostakovich might have chosen to change even without external pressure, as, for example, Hindemith had a little earlier, as Bartók soon would, and as George Rochberg and Henryk Górecki would a whole generation later.[7]

"Conservative" is in any event not the same as "conventional," and in a provocative article in the Autumn 1966 issue of the English magazine *Tempo*, the composer Tim Souster pointed out that Shostakovich's Fifth Symphony is by no means as unadventurous as received opinion would have it. An analogy with Beethoven's Second and Third *Leonore* overtures

---

[7] When I wrote "external pressure" I was thinking of political pressure; on the other hand, the longing for larger audiences and the desire for larger royalty checks are external pressures too.

comes to mind. No. 2 is the more daring, the more original; No. 3 is the more controlled, the more classical, and the more dramatic and exciting for it. We may return more often to No. 3, but we also need the stubborn and maverick individuality of the other. Without it we cannot know Beethoven, and without the experience of working his way through the problems of the Second *Leonore* Overture he could not have achieved the Third.

A triple spasm begins the Fourth Symphony with a gesture of characteristic violence, and at once the first theme with its chugging bass is thrown at us. Its energy is abruptly choked off, and we now hear an expressive violin melody, as quiet as the first idea is rowdy, as irregular in gait as the other is relentless. Shostakovich immediately begins to develop these themes and creates a profusion of collisions and parodies as he does so. Considerably later, he introduces a new theme, a melancholy melody for bassoon with minimal accompaniment on low strings and, with just a few very effective notes, the two harps.

Hugh Ottaway put it aptly in his monograph on the Shostakovich symphonies when he described what happens in this movement as "a hide-and-seek relationship with sonata form." We hear contrasting themes as in a "normal" sonata-form movement, we hear them developed and recapitulated, and one key, C minor, anchors the structure. At the same time, the proportions are unusual. In this twenty-five-minute movement, only about three or four minutes are exposition, and the recapitulation is shorter than that. The bulk is development. Older English books on music used to refer to the development in a sonata movement as the "free fantasia"; I don't think I have ever encountered a (more or less) sonata-form movement where that designation was more apt. It is only in this development that the despondent bassoon theme turns up, and the changes Shostakovich rings on his material include some really wild and violent slewings away from the main stream of discourse. The most dramatic of these is a crazed, high-speed fugue for the strings.

Ferocious brass-and-percussion dissonances pile up at the end of this long fantasia, culminating in a chord—*ffff* crescendo to *fffff*—made up of all twelve notes of the chromatic scale. (Tim Souster points out correspondences between this movement and the first of Beethoven's *Eroica*: the appearance of a significant new theme some way into the development is one, this sort of climax built on savage dissonance is another.) This immense and digressive development is resolved in a drastically compressed recapitulation, one in which Shostakovich, with superb assurance, banks on the stunning effect of the contrast itself as well as on the strength and density of his allusions. One more great swelling of dissonance, and this movement, after all its prodigality and brio, collapses in a bleak shadow play.

There follows a movement about a third as long as the one just finished. It is a kind of intermezzo in which two contrasting themes appear in alternation, both being fascinatingly transformed and recombined upon their various returns. A variant of the second of them, a lyric violin melody, makes an appearance a year later as the principal theme of the Fifth Symphony's first movement. This is the most obvious instance of recycled material from this work, and I imagine that Shostakovich assumed at the time that the Fourth Symphony had gone into the desk drawer for good. This movement ends in the playful tinkle of castanets, wood block, and snare drum.

The finale begins with the most explicitly Mahlerian music in all of Shostakovich, a C-minor cortège that owes much to the first two movements of Mahler's Fifth Symphony and to the orchestral interlude in the last song of *Das Lied von der Erde*. This is the most stable chapter in this symphony, the only one in which we are not buffeted by constant and sudden changes of temper.

This poignant march spills at last into an Allegro in triple meter. It is generously inventive music and a real feast of humor, but its laughter, now high-spirited, now sardonic, is wiped from its face by ghosts from the first two movements. The music subsides into mutterings of cellos and basses. At this point the timpani decide to anchor the symphony to its initial keynote, C, and everything suggests that we are to get ready for a Big Finish. Suddenly, blazing C major is darkened into C minor. The building crumbles. This intense and impassioned symphony has unfolded on the broadest scale, and now, very slowly, it subsides over a C-major chord held for many minutes, with the sounds of trumpet and celesta providing the last flickers of independent light. It is deeply affecting, this mixture of stability and question mark.[8]

Not everyone has been convinced by this finale, particularly by the sequence of funeral music, unbuttoned fun, and the double swerve of seeming to rise from comedy to triumphant climax, only to deny that resolution. Hugh Ottaway, who did some of the best writing in English about Shostakovich, thought the close "a magnificent *non sequitur*." Perhaps I was fortunate that I heard the Fourth Symphony on Kiril Kondrashin's recording and in concerts by Ormandy and Rozhdestvensky before Ottaway's excellent monograph came out. Yes, the unfolding of the finale was frighteningly unsettling and the progress from event to event, from mood to mood, was neither what I could have predicted nor what would have seemed most desirable and satisfying. But it was—and still seems to me to be—just like life.

---

[8] The ending of the Symphony No. 8 is similarly protracted and also set upon a long-sustained C, but the mood is very different.

Symphony No. 5 in D minor, Opus 47

Moderato
Allegretto
Largo
Allegro non troppo

Shostakovich began work on his Symphony No. 5 on 18 April 1937 and completed it three months later, on 20 July. Yevgeny Mravinsky and the Leningrad Philharmonic gave the first performance on 21 November that year.

Two flutes and piccolo, two oboes, two clarinets and E-flat clarinet, two bassoons and contrabassoon, four horns, three trumpets, three trombones, bass tuba, timpani, snare drum, triangle, cymbals, bass drum, tam-tam, bells, xylophone, two harps, piano, celesta, and strings.

In the introduction to Shostakovich's symphonies and the essay on No. 4 in particular, I tell the story of the unhappy early history of that work. Four months after Shostakovich decided to withhold the Fourth Symphony from performance, he began his Fifth. Its completion and the jubilant embracing of it by the public constituted the most significant turning point in the composer's artistic life. His political rehabilitation was the least of it: in 1948, at the hands of Andrei Zhdanov and the Central Committee of the Communist Party, Shostakovich was subjected to attacks far more vicious and brutish than those of 1936. (A second rehabilitation followed in 1958.) But in 1937 Shostakovich found a language in which, over the next three decades, he could write music whose strongest pages—in, for example, the *Leningrad,* Eighth, Tenth, Fourteenth, and Fifteenth symphonies; the Third, Seventh, Eighth, Twelfth, Thirteenth, and Fourteenth string quartets; the Violin Sonata; and the Michelangelo Songs—reveal his voice as one of the most eloquent in our time.

He begins his Fifth Symphony with a gesture both forceful and questioning, one whose sharply dotted rhythm stays on to accompany the broadly lyric melody the first violins introduce almost immediately. (The melody itself is a variant of one in the second movement of the Symphony No. 4.) Still later, spun across a pulsation as static as Shostakovich can make it, the violins play a spacious, serene melody, comfortingly symmetrical (at least when it begins). With that, we have all the material of the first movement. Yet it is an enormously varied movement, and across its great span there take place transformations that totally detach these thematic shapes from their original sonorities, speeds, and worlds of expression. The climax is harsh; the close, with the gentle friction of minor (the strings) and major (the scales in the celesta), is wistfully inconclusive.

So convincing is the design that one can hear the movement many times without stopping to think how original it is, a quality it shares with the first movement of Tchaikovsky's *Pathétique*. Shostakovich is his own best witness in confirming the assessment of Arnold Schoenberg, not much given to praising his contemporaries and not fond of Shostakovich's music either, but who had no doubt that his young colleague had "the breath of a symphonist."

The scherzo is brief and functions as an oasis between the intensely serious first and third movements. Its vein of grotesque humor owes something to Prokofiev and a lot more to Mahler, whose music was much played and studied in Russia in the 1920s and whose work early on defined symphonic ambition for Shostakovich. One thing that both linked and separated Schoenberg and Shostakovich is that each thought of himself—legitimately—as Mahler's son.

After the assertive trumpets of the first movement and the raucous horns of the second, the Largo uses no brass at all. The string scoring is unusual in that Shostakovich calls for three sections of violins rather than the usual two and two each of violas and cellos. (Throughout this book, I have repeatedly pointed out instances of string scoring that is completely effective only when the second violins are seated opposite the firsts; here you have scoring in which all the violins *must* sit together on one side so that the three-part division can be arranged.) String sound dominates in this movement of beautiful, long melodies, and Shostakovich inserts intermezzi for solo woodwinds with exquisite sense of timing and form. Harp and celesta also play prominent roles here. For a moment, the music rises to a crest of hot emotional intensity, a passage of powerful declamation for high and low strings. This anguished dialogue is the most Tchaikovskian page in all of Shostakovich. After a final appearance of celesta and harps, the movement ends with the serene sound of just two sumptuous major chords for the eight-part string orchestra.

Brass, silent for the last twelve minutes, is the pre-eminent color of the finale. This movement picks up the march music—the manner, not the specific material—that formed the climax of the first movement, but the purpose now seems to be to express not threat and tension, but triumph. "The theme of my symphony," Shostakovich declared at the time of the premiere, "is the making of a man. I saw man with all his experiences as the center of the composition. . . . In the finale, the tragically tense impulses of the earlier movements are resolved in optimism and the joy of living."

Just before the coda there is a moment of lyric repose, and Shostakovich's biographer David Rabinovich notes that the accompaniment, first in the violins, then in the harp, for the cello-and-bass recollection of the first movement is a quotation from a song the composer had written in 1936. It is a setting of Pushkin's *Rebirth,* and the crucial lines read:

> And the waverings pass away
> From my tormented soul
> As a new and brighter day
> Brings visions of pure gold.

From that moment of reflection the music rises to its assertive final (and Mahlerian) climax.

Shostakovich carefully organized his finale by means of the relationships of the tempi of its various sections. He begins with ♩ = 88, then stepping the up tempo through ♩ 104, 108, 120, 126, 132, 144, to 184. From there, he goes back to slower tempi, 160, 100–108, 116, to 92. Thus, at the end, the pulse is just a hair faster than at the opening; however, the march with which the movement began is now written in notes twice as long as at the beginning, so that it and its accompanying drumbeats proceed at half its original tempo. It is—or should be—obvious that this relationship between the opening and closing tempi matters is a purely musical and structural issue. The tempo that Shostakovich asks for in the coda is extremely slow, and very few conductors dare it. Yevgeny Mravinsky gets it right, but he does not relate it to the opening of the movement, where he bolts away at something like one-and-a-half times the speed indicated in the score. Kiril Kondrashin and the composer's son, Maxim Shostakovich, come close, but only Kondrashin catches the proper relationship between the opening and closing tempi. Most of the big-name conductors seem to proceed entirely at random.[9]

But tempo also has a bearing on the expressive content of these closing pages. In an early version of this essay, written before the publication of *Testimony* in 1979, I had added this sentence: "[The close] works just as it was intended to work, though many a listener may find that the impact

---

[9] Shostakovich's indication of his metronome mark for the last pages of the Fifth Symphony is idiosyncratic; that is, instead of writing ♩ 92, which would be the usual procedure where the meter is 4/4, he writes ♪ 184. Some conductors have explained their fast tempo for the coda by saying that this must be a misprint for ♩ 184. There would seem to be no justification for this assumption.

and the memory of the questions behind this music are stronger than those of the answer." Clearly I did not believe in the answer, in the claptrap about "optimism and the joy of living," though I was doing my best to live by Tovey's rule that the program annotator is always the counsel for the defense. It was a strange and moving confirmation to find this passage in *Testimony:*

> Awaiting execution is a theme that has tormented me all my life. Many pages of my music are devoted to it. Sometimes I wanted to explain that fact to the performers, I thought they would have a greater understanding of the work's meaning. But then I thought better of it. You can't explain any-thing to a bad performer, and a talented person should sense it himself. . . .
>
> I discovered to my astonishment that the man who considers himself its greatest interpreter does not understand my music.[10] He says I wanted to write exultant finales for my Fifth and Seventh symphonies but I couldn't manage it. It never occurred to this man that I never thought about exultant finales, for what exultation could there be? I think it is clear to everyone what happens in the Fifth. The rejoicing is forced, created under threat, as in [Musorgsky's] *Boris Godunov.* It's as if someone were beating you with a stick and saying, "Your business is rejoicing, your business is rejoicing," and you rise, shaky, and go marching off, muttering, "our business is rejoicing, our business is rejoicing."
>
> What kind of apotheosis is that? You have to be a complete oaf not to hear that. . . .[11]

Well, there were a lot of us oafs around between 1937 and 1979. We may not, all of us, have been convinced by the ending of the Shostakovich Fifth, but I never knew anyone to doubt that this was a genuine attempt to write an "exultant finale." Leaving aside the issue of structure and tempo, I am convinced that the tradition of taking the coda quite fast—sometimes with a grand rhetorical retard, is rooted in the attempt to make the ending jubilant, to *perform* the apotheosis that Shostakovich did not in fact com-pose. Taken at the tempo in the score, and of course without a further grandstanding retard, the close is profoundly in tune with the grim "our

---

[10] Shostakovich is referring to Yevgeny Mravinsky, conductor of the Leningrad Philharmonic from 1938 until his death in 1988. He led the first performances of five of Shostakovich's symphonies (the Eighth is dedicated to him), but the friendship went sour toward the end. On the evidence of his recordings and the one concert I heard him conduct with his orchestra, and in spite of the reservation I expressed earlier about his 1978 recorded performance of the Shostakovich Fifth, I would say that he was one of this century's great conductors. —M.S.

[11] *Testimony: The Memoirs of Dmitri Shostakovich* as related to and edited by Solomon Volkov (New York: Harper & Row, 1979).

business is rejoicing" image drawn by the man who also said, "The majority of my symphonies are tombstones."

Symphony No. 7 in C major, Opus 60, *Leningrad*

Allegretto
Moderato (poco allegretto)
Adagio
Allegro non troppo

Shostakovich began work on the Symphony No. 7 in Leningrad on 15 July 1941 and completed the score on 27 December in Kuibyshev, where he and his family had been evacuated. The first performance was given on 1 March 1942 in Kuibyshev by Samuil Abramovitch Samosud and the Bolshoi Theater Orchestra, also evacuated there. Shostakovich dedicated the work to the city of Leningrad; he did not, however, actually name it the *Leningrad* Symphony as, for example, he named the Symphony No. 11 *The Year 1905*.

Three flutes (second doubling alto flute, third doubling piccolo), two oboes and English horn, three clarinets (third doubling E-flat clarinet) and bass clarinet, two bassoons and contrabassoon, eight horns, six trumpets, six trombones, tuba, timpani, triangle, tambourine, snare drum (the composer recommends the use of two or even three for the big crescendo in the first movement), cymbals, bass drum, tam-tam, xylophone, two harps, piano, and strings.

Perhaps in one of those seductively musty stores where they sell old magazines you can still find a copy of the 20 July 1942 issue of *Time*, whose cover shows Dmitri Shostakovich in a fire helmet, gazing into the distance with determined eyes and fiercely set mouth. Behind him, gutted buildings burn and anti-aircraft shells burst in air.[12] It had been thirteen months

---

[12] It is fascinating to compare this "artist's rendering" with the photograph that is its source. There, too, we see Shostakovich, helmeted and elaborately belted, as he stands on the roof of the Leningrad Conservatory taking his turn at fire warden duty; but it is daylight, the sky is clear, no fires are to be seen, and the composer, though serious, seems a little abstracted, as though he had

since Hitler invaded the Soviet Union, and less than two years since he and Stalin had signed a non-aggression pact.

We, in America, were still trying to get used to the idea of the USSR as our gallant ally after a quarter-century of suspicion and, for many, out-and-out hostility. The movie industry, mobilized to make the new alliance convincing to us, responded with heavy-handed propaganda like *North Star* (which came with an ersatz-Shostakovich score by Aaron Copland). Music was also enlisted in the cause, and Shostakovich's symphonies were conspicuously made to serve this new political purpose. The Fifth even remained very popular after the end of the war and the disintegration of the wartime alliance, but it would take decades for Shostakovich's American reputation to fully recover from the image of him as a political artist, a process not helped by his abject performance as a propaganda mouthpiece for the Soviet Union during the early stages of the ugly Cold War. In 1942, however, Shostakovich was a hero, in the Soviet Union and in the United States.

In the grim winter of 1941–42, Leningrad was in the first year of its 900-day siege by the German army, and the only supply line was across the ice of Lake Ladoga to the east of the city. Stories from that time remind one of accounts of Napoleon's siege and bombardment of Vienna in 1809, when Beethoven, working on the *Farewell* Sonata and the *Emperor* Concerto, covered his head in pillows to protect the remaining shreds of his hearing against the onslaught of the French artillery. In all, about a million people, amounting to one-third of Leningrad's inhabitants, perished in bombings and shellings, in fires, and of cold, starvation, and disease. Those were the conditions under which the *Leningrad* Symphony was conceived and begun.

The precise genesis of the work is still controversial. In Solomon Volkov's *Testimony*, Shostakovich is quoted as saying that it was planned before the war and therefore "simply cannot be seen as a reaction to Hitler's attack. I was thinking of other enemies of humanity. . . . I feel eternal pain for those who were killed by Hitler, but I feel no less pain for those killed on Stalin's orders. . . . I have nothing against calling the Seventh the *Leningrad* Symphony, but it's not about Leningrad under siege; it's about the Leningrad that Stalin destroyed and that Hitler merely finished off." (Almost obsessively, *Testimony* makes the point that Shostakovich's music consists of one secret anti-Stalin protest after another.) Disputing that account, Maxim Shostakovich, the composer's son, declared in 1981, two years after the appearance of Volkov's book, that "the *Leningrad* Sym-

---

fallen to pondering a tricky problem of invertible counterpoint at the twelfth. The photo looks extremely posed.

phony was written under the impact of events; it was not preconceived. On this point *Testimony* is wrong: every movement is dated."[13] Other sources, for example, the monograph by the German writer Detlef Gojowy, tell us that the original plan was for the Seventh to be a *Lenin* Symphony with a choral finale on texts by the founder of the Third International and by the composer himself.

It does appear, though, that it was in July 1941, with the German army about to arrive in the outskirts of Leningrad and the Finns advancing rapidly from the north, that Shostakovich began to write down the Seventh Symphony as it exists in its final form. By autumn, the Germans had also penetrated to within 150 miles of Moscow, and in the south they had reached the Black Sea. The Soviet government organized the evacuation of its cultural elite, including whole schools, theater and dance companies, and orchestras. Shostakovich wanted to stay in Leningrad, but on orders from Moscow, he, his wife, Nina, and their two children, five-year-old Galina and three-year-old Maxim, flew to Moscow on 1 October. Two weeks later they traveled another 600 miles to Kuibyshev, a large manufacturing city some 175 miles northeast of what was then Stalingrad (now Volgograd) and about 300 miles due north of Astrakhan and the Caspian Sea. The day they arrived, Kuibyshev was declared the temporary capital of the Soviet Union because of the German advance. Among those who had also been on the train from Moscow were the composers Vissarion Shebalin and Dmitri Kabalevsky, the violinist David Oistrakh, the pianist Emil Gilels, the filmmaker Sergei Eisenstein, the playwright Valentin Katajev, and the novelist and journalist Ilya Ehrenburg.

In Kuibyshev, Shostakovich resumed work on the Seventh Symphony and completed its final "victory" movement on 27 December; the first performance was given there two months later. Leningrad and its musical institutions got their due in August 1942: the Leningrad Radio Orchestra, brought back to the city for the occasion, introduced the symphony at home, after which the Leningrad Conservatory Orchestra and the Leningrad Philharmonic, evacuated to Tashkent and Novosibirsk respectively, played the work.

Meanwhile the clamor from abroad had begun. Sir Henry J. Wood secured the first performance outside the USSR for his Promenade Concerts in London; the emotional impact of that concert was heightened by the fact that Queen's Hall, London's finest large concert room and the home of the Proms since Wood had founded them in 1895, had been

[13] Maxim Shostakovich was presumably referring to the dates when the movements were completed, but it still possibly, as is asserted in *Testimony*, that at least some of the plan for the symphony goes back to before the war. We need a scholarly biography to clear such points up.

destroyed in a German air raid the previous year. One who was not se-
duced or about to be co-opted for any patriotic/political cause was the great
Wagner biographer and veteran critic Ernest Newman. "To find its place
on the musical map," he wrote in *The Sunday Times*, "one should look
along the seventieth degree of longitude and the last degree of platitude."

Competition for the United States premiere was madly keen. Naturally, the two conductors who had championed Shostakovich's music for
years, Leopold Stokowski, about to begin a term as co-conductor of the
NBC Symphony with Toscanini, and Artur Rodzinski, then in Cleveland,
were particularly eager, but so were several new passengers on the Soviet
bandwagon, among them Toscanini himself, Koussevitzky in Boston, Monteux in San Francisco, Mitropoulos in Minneapolis, and Ormandy in Philadelphia. Stokowski, who had given the American premieres of Shostakovich's First and Sixth symphonies, was especially excited at the prospect of
the Seventh, and before it was even finished, he persuaded NBC to move
quickly to buy the first American performance rights. Given Stokowski's
previous association with Shostakovich and the huge audience for the
weekly NBC Symphony broadcasts, this offer was welcome in the Soviet
Union. It was also remembered that the NBC Symphony, on that occasion
under Rodzinski, had introduced the Fifth Symphony in America.

The score began its journey from Kuibyshev to Radio City. It was
transferred to microfilm, sent by air from Kuibyshev to Tehran, by automobile across western Iran, Iraq, Jordan, and Palestine (Israel) to Cairo, by
air again to Recife in Brazil, where it was put on board a U.S. naval
aircraft that took it to New York. Representatives of the Am-Russ Music
Corporation then delivered it to NBC, where it came into the hands not
of Stokowski, but of Toscanini, who decided that he wanted to conduct
it himself.

Stokowski reminded Toscanini that not only had he been the one to
urge NBC to obtain the rights but that they had made an agreement
whereby he would stay away from Toscanini's repertory and concentrate
on modern music. "Now that you know these facts," he continued, "I feel
confident that you will wish me to broadcast this symphony, and that it
will be with your approval and in harmony with [our] agreement. . . ."
What he got from Toscanini was a smiling reply: "Don't you think, my
dear Stokowski, it would be very interesting for everybody, and yourself,
too, to hear the old Italian conductor (one of the first artists who strenu-
ously fought against fascism) play this work of a young Russian anti-Nazi
composer?"

Toscanini would not budge, and NBC, to whom he was a much more
valuable asset than Stokowski, supported him. That is how the American
premiere of the *Leningrad* came about in July 1942, and it was that week-

end that *Time* put Shostakovich on its cover.[14] In *Testimony*, Volkov cites Shostakovich in a screaming two-page diatribe that begins, "I hate Toscanini." Toscanini's recording of the Seventh, Shostakovich is quoted as saying, "made me very angry. Everything is wrong. The spirit and the character and the tempos. It's a lousy, sloppy, hack job." Did Toscanini's ruthless treatment of Stokowski affect Shostakovich's hearing of this performance? But the Toscanini performance is indeed a mixed bag, high on fervor, but cavalier about tempo relationships. There are small flaws of ensemble of the kind that do occur at public concerts, especially at first performances. Sometimes Toscanini is simply unidiomatic; for example, the violin sighs that accompany the first movement's second theme sound too much like the sighs in the *Traviata* Prelude. A 1944 broadcast of the Symphony No. 1 shows Toscanini to have had no ear for Shostakovich's humor.

Toscanini's was the first of sixty-two performances the *Leningrad* Symphony received in the United States between the summers of 1942 and 1943. Yet even while the war continued and American emotional sympathies were still engaged with Russia, the *Leningrad* Symphony disappeared from the repertory. To the extent that we wanted a modern Russian victory symphony, we preferred Shostakovich No. 5. This is of course ironic in view of Shostakovich's statement in *Testimony* that the grand D-major conclusion of that work portrays not genuine triumph, but forced cheering.

The *Leningrad* Symphony was slow to emerge from the obscurity that engulfed it after the first storm of excitement, and even now opportunities to hear it are rare. When it was new, the specificity of imagery and ideological slant worked for it just as the generality—or universality—of statement in the Eighth Symphony worked against it. Now those values are reversed. It is long, which makes it difficult to program, and it is a hard piece for a conductor to organize. It would be dishonest to pretend that it is an unflawed work, but it is one that bears witness eloquently, one that merits a high place in our musical and human experience.

The first movement is marked "allegretto," an example of Shostakovich's eccentric use of that term. The word refers to a speed between andante and allegro, but it has also taken on an affective connotation of something "perhaps a little more light-hearted than allegro" (*Grove's Dictionary*). Shostakovich's often far from light-hearted allegrettos can be out-and-out grim; perhaps he even intended the dissonance between our associations with the word and its use in his scores to startle and awaken performers. Certainly the mood here is intensely and unremittingly serious.

Shostakovich had planned to give each movement a descriptive title.

---

[14]Stokowski conducted the NBC Symphony in another performance of the *Leningrad* that November. He continued to champion Shostakovich and later introduced the Eleventh and Twelfth symphonies in America.

Like Mahler, his great model as symphonist, and like Strauss, he blew hot and cold on the issue of extramusical meaning and information. He finally withdrew his titles; nonetheless, it is not bad to be aware that his original title for the first movement was *War*. He begins, as he so often does, with a starkly unharmonized theme, though this one is punctuated by basses with trumpets and drums. It is march-like, firmly articulated, and covers a wide range. Shostakovich expounds on it at some length, then gives us a contrasting, more softly lyrical violin melody in the dominant, G major.

So far this is virtually a textbook sonata-form exposition. Slowly the music dissolves into what we expect to be a development section; Shostakovich, however, has something quite different in mind. Here, in fact, comes the episode that has aroused the most discussion. A piccolo reflects on the lyric music we have just heard and a violin continues the piccolo's musing. Cutting across the violin's last note, a snare drum begins to play a march rhythm, quietly, as though from a distance. In E-flat, a key that is both new and not new—it was lightly suggested in the unfolding of the first theme but there has been no settling in it—violins (tapping their strings with the wood side of the bow) and violas (pizzicato) quietly sound a march to go with the drum's obsessive march rhythm. In another context this tune could be as jaunty as *Colonel Bogey*; in this setting and this orchestration it is menacing.

Next, the flute plays it, still *pianissimo*; then piccolo and flute together; then oboe, with the bassoon repeating each phrase so that this becomes a double statement; then trumpet; clarinet and E-flat clarinet with echoes by oboe and English horn, though here the echoing phrases overlap rather than follow the original statements; violins (by now the music has reached *forte*); oboe, clarinet, violins, and cellos together; bass clarinet, bassoon and contrabassoon, horns, violas, cellos, basses; trumpets and trombones; all the high woodwinds with violins and violas; trumpets, trombones, and tuba. By now everyone is at *fortissimo* or *fortississimo*. Nine minutes of music, obsessively concentrated in tremendous crescendo on a single idea. What comes to mind is *Boléro*, and Shostakovich did not disavow that model. Not as famous but actually more similar in procedure and context, and certainly well known to Shostakovich, are the stunningly effective repetitions in the finale of the Sibelius Second Symphony—first threefold, then eightfold.

What was Shostakovich trying to do here? In a 1951 article "On True and So-called Program Music" he refers to these pages as "The Invasion." Earlier he had told the critic David Rabinovich that this passage represented the sudden irruption of war "into our peaceful lives." In another commentary, Shostakovich writes that "the theme of war governs the middle passages." From there, drawing ever nearer, seeming to push all the air out of the room, it is just one step to equating this music, not merely with the image of war breaking "into our peaceful lives" but specifically with the invaders—as though this were actually the march of the German armies in the same sense that the sinister *Peregrinus expectavi* chorus in Prokofiev's *Alexander Nevsky* actually is the song of the invading German crusaders. This misunderstanding—if it is a misunderstanding—was to cost Shostakovich dear. Clearly this is the most memorable and most immediately impressive episode in the work, and when the Bolshevik Central Committee went on the warpath in 1948, one of the charges against Shostakovich was that he had done so much better at portraying the enemy than at conveying the heroism of the Russian people! Once again the critics— this time the politicians-as-critics—were unable to deal with anything in Shostakovich's music except at the most crassly "realistic" level.

Before we leave it, the tune itself is worth a look:

Ex. 1

The section marked A may sound familiar. First of all, it is very close to Danilo's *Da geh' ich zu Maxim* in *The Merry Widow*. (Volkov suggests that this near-quotation may have been some sort of family joke involving baby Maxim Shostakovich.) Another reason it possibly sounds familiar is not that it quotes, but that it is quoted. This is the tune that appears in the marching-band episode in the "Interrupted Intermezzo" of Bartók's Concerto for Orchestra, written in 1943, one year after the great *Leningrad* furor. Exiled, impoverished, ill, and neglected in New York, infuriated by what to him was the banality of Shostakovich's music and its popularity, Bartók inserted into his Concerto a brutal and funny parody of what was both the most notorious and most spectacular part of the famous new symphony.[15]

---

[15] Detlef Gojowy implausibly suggests in his Shostakovich biography that Bartók quoted the *Leningrad* in admiration. In his memoirs, the conductor Antal Dorati recounts that Bartók, his former teacher, asked him whether he knew what the "interruption" in the Concerto for Orchestra was: " 'Of course I do, Professor.' 'Well?' 'It is a quote from *The Merry Widow*.' 'And who is that?' "

The phrase marked "B" also sounds like a quotation to me, of the second movement—another obsessive piece in its own way—of Sibelius's Symphony No. 5. I don't recall ever seeing any comment on this, but I wonder whether this too might not have topical and political significance. In 1939, a few weeks after the beginning of the war, the Soviets wanted to establish military garrisons in Lithuania, Latvia, Estonia, and Finland. The three Baltic states consented, but the Finns refused, and on 30 November, Russia responded by invading Finland. By early March 1940, Finnish resistance was over, but at the start of this lopsided conflict, the Finns, to the astonishment of the entire world and the delight of much of it, inflicted some extraordinary and humiliating setbacks on their invaders, and Field Marshal Mannerheim was briefly an international hero. The next year, three days after the German invasion of Russia, Finland also declared war on Russia, and Mannerheim's troops joined the march on Leningrad. In sum, Sibelius was The Enemy.

After the twelvefold onslaught of the tune, Shostakovich extends and varies it, building this passage into a crushing climax. He then recapitulates the opening music, *fortissimo*, while echoes of the "invasion" theme continue to sound. The lyric music returns, transformed into a threnody for the solo bassoon accompanied by piano and low strings. In a spacious coda the first theme returns once more, *piano* and espressivo, but the sounds that dominate the closing moments are the *pianissimo* yet still relentless snare drum and fragments of the "invasion" march.

This huge movement accounts for more than a third of the symphony. Shostakovich had at first planned the Seventh as a one-movement work, but as he progressed, he saw that he needed to resolve the conflicts posed by the opening movement. The second movement, originally titled *Memories*, is the symphony's shortest. It has no heading other than its tempo direction of Moderato (poco allegretto), but Shostakovich referred to it both as a scherzo and as a lyric intermezzo. It begins in the latter vein, wistfully and gently, with a dancing tune for the second violins. This leads to an expansive lyric episode begun by the oboe, continued by the English horn, and concluded by the cellos. Only after that does the music speed up into a rapid 3/8. The shrill, sardonic voice of the E-flat clarinet is heard, while the other clarinets and the bassoon offer the first approach to cheerful music in this work. No matter what the situation, said Shostakovich, he could not do without humor. The opening music returns, the oboe melody now played by the bass clarinet, and the movement ends quietly with just a few dancing shadows of the initial theme.

The original title for the Adagio was *Our Country's Wide Spaces*. Elsewhere, Shostakovich stated that he hoped to portray his beloved Leningrad by twilight, its streets and the Neva embankments suspended in stillness. He begins with big chords whose voicing for woodwinds, horns, and harps gives them an arrestingly gritty sound. In contrast, all the violins, with almost no accompaniment, state an impressive declamatory theme in a luminous D major. We hear each of these elements once more, after which the music moves on to a haunting flute solo. Shostakovich introduces a faster and fiercer episode, upon which he then superimposes the opening chords in one of those climaxes that Berlioz liked to label "réunion des deux thèmes." After a wonderfully poetic passage for the violas and reminders of the two opening ideas, this evocative movement arrives at a quiet close.

Without break, Shostakovich moves into his *Victory* finale. To begin with, though, all is dark as the violins suspend a long arch of melody over a *pianissimo* drumroll. With great richness and variety of thematic material, the momentum builds to a confident climax. At this point Shostakovich pulls back to reflect on those who have lost their lives. Now he is free to move toward his peroration. Trained as we are by the Beethoven Fifth and the Brahms First, we expect the darkness of C minor to give way to the brightness of C major, but the E-flats, A-flats, and B-flats of C minor abound right up to the last affirmative C-major chord. It is victory, unmistakably, but it is not an easy victory.

How one does wish that Dmitri Dmitrievich Shostakovich could have lived to enjoy an eighty-fifth-birthday present of watching the statues of Lenin toppled, seeing *Pravda* stop publication, even for a single day as it did in the summer of 1991, and knowing the city where he was born and to which he set such a monument was Saint Petersburg again!

Symphony No. 8 in C minor, Opus 65

Adagio
Allegretto
Allegro non troppo
Largo
Allegretto

Radio Moscow announced the completion of Shostakovich's Eighth Symphony on 20 September 1943, and soon after, the composer gave a piano reading of it in Moscow for an invited audience of composers and conductors. The first orchestral performance was given at the Moscow Conservatory for another invited audience of musicians, artists, critics, and journalists on 3 November 1943; the first public performance took place the following evening. Yevgeny Mravinsky, to whom the score is dedicated, conducted the State Symphony Orchestra. Both evenings were part of a Festival of Soviet Music to celebrate the twenty-fifth anniversary of the Soviet Union.

Two flutes and two piccolos, two oboes and English horn, two clarinets with E-flat clarinet and bass clarinet, two bassoons and contrabassoon, three trumpets, four horns, three trombones, tuba, timpani, xylophone, snare drum, cymbals, bass drum, tam-tam, and strings.

After the gigantic effort and at least momentary triumph of the *Leningrad* Symphony, Shostakovich, newly awarded the title of Honored Art Worker and granted a professorship at the Moscow Conservatory in addition to the one he already held in Leningrad, composed a number of songs on texts from Pushkin to *Comin' thro' the Rye,* a piano sonata, and what turned out to be an unfinished opera on Gogol's *The Gamblers.* Then, in the summer of 1943, he settled at the House of Creative Work that the Union of Soviet Composers maintained near Ivanovo, about 150 miles northeast of Moscow, and began composing his Eighth Symphony. It was performed immediately, by the conductor of Shostakovich's choice, and upon an important occasion. Within a year it was heard in the United States and England. It was not badly received—the chronicler of the People's heroism at the siege of Leningrad had too much credit just then—but commentary was respectful, reserved, puzzled, and the work was fairly quickly lost from view.

The composer suggested that it was the second part of a symphonic war trilogy, but instead of going ahead with a heroic Ninth Symphony victory celebration, he produced a scherzando "little symphony" instead. When the Eighth was remembered again, it was in an unhappy context: in January 1948, when Andrei Zhdanov of the Central Committee of the Communist Party was promulgating resolutions on the proper conduct of music and musicians, this work was singled out for special attack.

Zhdanov was a master at playing on mutual antagonisms and jealousies among artists, and the nastiest assault on the Eighth Symphony was delivered by another composer, Vladimir Zakharov, a writer of light music who was soon to become a Secretary in the "new order" presidium of the Composers' Union. Zakharov began by declaring that "our symphonists have put up an iron curtain [!] . . . between the People and themselves. . . . These composers are alien and completely incomprehensible to our

Soviet People. . . . There are still discussions around the question whether the Eighth is good or bad. Such a discussion is nonsense. From the point of view of the People, the Eighth is not a musical work at all; it is a 'composition' which has nothing whatever to do with art."

Critics such as Shostakovich's biographer Ivan Martynov who had praised the Eighth were called to account for their opinions and to revise them. (Those who had written approvingly of the Ninth were in trouble too.) In 1956, however, when there was something of a thaw, Shostakovich actually dared to voice a public lament "that the Eighth Symphony has remained unperformed for many years. In this work there was an attempt to express the emotional experiences of the People, to reflect the terrible tragedy of war. Composed in the summer of 1943, the Eighth Symphony is an echo of that difficult time, and in my opinion quite in the order of things." On 28 May 1958, the Central Committee adopted a resolution "On Rectifying the Errors in the Operas *Great Friendship, Bogdan Khmelnitzky,* and *From All One's Heart,*" in which, astonishingly, Vano Muradeli, Konstantin Dankevich, and Herman Zhukovsky, all brutally drubbed a decade earlier, were "rehabilitated," and in which it was also noted that "comrades Shostakovich, Prokofiev, Khachaturian, Shebalin, Popov, Miaskovsky, and others, whose works at times revealed the wrong tendencies, [had been] indiscriminately denounced as the representatives of a formalist anti-People trend." With that, the Eighth Symphony returned to the repertoire.

Perhaps if Shostakovich had given the Eighth the sort of slam-bang ending he had found for six of his first seven symphonies—the great and long-suppressed No. 4 is the exception—most of this discussion, questioning, and acrimony would never have come up. But then nothing in this symphony is conventional, except perhaps the opening, where Shostakovich returns to the striking formula of the Fifth Symphony of 1937: declamatory, quasi-canonic dialogue of low and high strings in sharply dotted rhythms, subsiding into a lyric melody for violins. How unexpected, though, is the shape of the work as a whole. The first Adagio (which, however, traverses a range of tempi up to an extremely energetic allegro) is itself nearly half the symphony. Next what the critic Daniel Zhitomirsky called a sequence of three marches: a heroic march, a scherzo-march, and a funeral march. Then the finale, reserved and brief. Shostakovich articulates all this in a special way by making his last break after the "heroic march," the last three movements then being played without pause.

A plan like this puzzles us less than it did audiences in the 1940s. That is because we know our Mahler better now. Shostakovich knew him all along: Oskar Fried and Fritz Stiedry held permanent conducting posts in the Soviet Union; Bruno Walter, Otto Klemperer, Hermann Scherchen, Jascha Horenstein, and William Steinberg visited there, and they were, all of them, Mahlerians long before it was trendy. Mahler's symphonies are one adventure after another in rethinking symphonic design, with only the First (in its revised version) and the Sixth built according to familiar four-movement schemes. Such Mahlerian ideas as a first movement hugely larger than any other (Symphony No. 3), linked pairs or groups of movements (No. 5), a series of character pieces in the middle of a symphony (Nos. 2 and 7), a finale surprisingly gentle and modest after what has gone before (No. 4)—all these have left their mark on the Shostakovich Eighth.

Something that is all Shostakovich's own is the sound, and the beginnings of that personal palette are already present in the Symphony No. 1, which he wrote at nineteen. Here in No. 8, he uses a normal large orchestra and, like Tchaikovsky and Rimsky-Korsakov, writes for it with the knack of making it seem much larger than it is. He divides his orchestra into clearly defined blocks, and any one sonority is likely to dominate for a substantial amount of time, whether it is a tutti of a particular coloration, an accompanied solo, or one of his eccentric combinations (there is much play with these in the second movement, with its shrilling piccolos and E-flat clarinet). It is a sound that is hard-edged and lean rather than lush, tending more toward high treble and low bass than into the middle. Much of this, too, Shostakovich learned from Mahler, but the result is quite individual.

For Serge Koussevitzky, the opening Adagio was a movement "which, by the power of its human emotion, surpasses everything else created in our time." It is a masterfully controlled flow of sound, and rich in event: the beautiful, stretched, *pianissimo* melody with which the first violins enter (and how skillfully Shostakovich uses flute and trumpets briefly to support the melody and its accompaniment at the climax); the second, even more expansive violin melody, now espressivo, and in an enigmatic 5/4 meter over quietly pulsing chords; the first intervention of military music; after the first climax, over bounding strings, the scream of oboes and clarinets; the wonderful English-horn recitative, turning gradually into arioso (the greatest opportunity since the *New World* Symphony for a real artist on that hauntingly plangent instrument); and in the coda, the subtly new combinations of ideas from earlier until the last four quiet notes on the trumpet set the music with gentle firmness into its C-major haven.

One could argue with Zhitomirsky about his characterization of the next two movements. The first of these seems grotesque, a parody, and not possibly something genuinely heroic. Nor am I convinced by the third movement as scherzo: I hear a savage, relentless machine. Only Shostakovich could persist so long, longer than anyone else would dare, with such a brutal ostinato. Its most insistent feature, other than the pounding quarter-notes, is again a scream. I think every time of the cellars of the Gestapo and the GPU.

Two great cries pierce the nightmare and open the way to the next slow movement. This is a solemn march indeed, written as a passacaglia, variations over a repeated bass. Shostakovich used this form with great power in a number of other situations, including the Trio No. 2, the Second, Third, Sixth, and Tenth string quartets, the Violin Concerto No. 1, and the Symphony No. 15. Here, the ten-measure bass, which begins with energy and concludes with a broadly composed-in retard, is first played by itself in a marvelously scored decrescendo, and then repeated eleven times. What Shostakovich achieves in the seventh and last variations with his combination of flutter-tongued flutes and muted, plucked strings is one of the eeriest moments in all orchestral music.

Then, quietly, as though it were no feat at all, the clarinets lift the music from G-sharp minor into C major. The finale has begun. Shostakovich had made his public and militant victory statement in the *Leningrad* Symphony. To know only the Shostakovich of the most famous symphonies and concertos is to know him very incompletely: the private Shostakovich of the chamber music, particularly the fifteen string quartets, travels in worlds of which the big orchestral works scarcely dream.[16] This finale gives some hint of what that world is like. The war music, the scream, intervene once more. But before and after, this is music of timidly awakening life. Shostakovich offered to put it into words: "Life is beautiful. All that is dark and ignominious will disappear. All that is beautiful will triumph."

An expectation to be at best timorously entertained, as he knew better than most. He was charged with having written a gloomy symphony. But in those last pages, so spacious in the way they draw breath, so lovely in sound, with the memory of tragedy still present in the hushed dissonances, there is firmness, acceptance, serenity. Perhaps even something of hope.

---

[16]*Mutatis mutandis*, this is no less true of Mozart, Beethoven, Schubert, and Brahms, among others. For Bach, substitute "cantatas" for "chamber music"; for Schumann, the way to the interior goes through the piano music.

Symphony No. 10 in E minor, Opus 93

> *Moderato*
> *Allegro*
> *Allegretto*
> *Andante—Allegro*

Shostakovich composed the Symphony No. 10 in the summer and fall of 1953, and it was introduced on 17 December that year by Yevgeny Mravinsky and the Leningrad Philharmonic.

Two flutes and piccolo (second flute doubling piccolo), two oboes and English horn (English horn doubling third oboe), two clarinets and E-flat clarinet (E-flat clarinet doubling third clarinet), two bassoons and contrabassoon (contrabassoon doubling third bassoon), four horns, three trumpets, three trombones, tuba, timpani, triangle, tambourine, snare drum, cymbals, bass drum, tam-tam, xylophone, and strings.

Joseph Stalin died on 5 March 1953, less than twenty-four hours after word went out that he had suffered a stroke a couple of days earlier. He had become Secretary General of the Communist Party's Central Committee in 1922, and there were millions in the Soviet Union who could not remember a time when he had not been dictator. "We had long lost sight of the fact that [he] was mortal," wrote the novelist and journalist Ilya Ehrenburg.

Shostakovich began work on the Symphony No. 10 a few weeks after Stalin's death, and it was ready in plenty of time for performance at the end of the year. Shostakovich always worked quickly: "That, perhaps, is not a virtue," he remarked wryly in connection with this very score. The Tenth was received enthusiastically in Leningrad and Moscow, as well as in New York the following season.

It also became the subject of a three-day discussion at the Composers' Union in March and April 1954. Shostakovich himself expressed some reservations: in the first movement he had still not succeeded in writing the "real symphonic allegro" he had long dreamed of; the second movement was perhaps too short, especially in relation to the other, rather long movements; the third movement, though "more or less successful," was too long in some places and too short in others. He did not, however, attempt to mend these defects, real or imagined. In the same talk to the Composers' Union he said: "As soon as a work is written, the creative spark dies. When you see its defects, sometimes large and substantial, you begin to think that it wouldn't be a bad thing to avoid them in your next work, but as for the one just written, well, that's done with, thank goodness."[17] Shostakovich's Western critics have, on the whole, been more lenient than he himself was, and the Tenth has often been proclaimed as his finest symphony.

As for the tone of the debate, Boris Schwarz tells us in *The New Grove Dictionary of Music and Musicians* that "the hard-line opposition maintained that the work was 'non-realistic' and deeply pessimistic in approach, but in the end the liberal faction won with the slogan that the new symphony was 'an optimistic tragedy.' "

Shostakovich was of course asked whether the new symphony had a program. "No," he replied, "let them listen and guess for themselves." To this he added only that he had "wanted to portray human emotions and passions." On the other hand, Solomon Volkov states flatly in *Testimony* that "Shostakovich summed up Stalin's era in the Tenth Symphony. The second movement is inexorable, merciless, like an evil whirlwind—a 'musical portrait' of Stalin." He also attributes the following to Shostakovich himself:

> I did depict Stalin in my [Tenth Symphony]. I wrote it right after Stalin's death, and no one has yet guessed what the symphony is about. It's about Stalin and the Stalin years. The second part, the scherzo, is a musical portrait of Stalin, roughly speaking. Of course there are many other things in it, but that's the basis. . . . [It is hard] to draw the image of leaders and teachers with music. But I did give Stalin his due, the shoe fits, as they say. I can't be reproached for avoiding that ugly phenomenon of our reality.

Testimony, I should add, almost obsessively makes the point that Shostakovich's music consists of one secret anti-Stalin protest after another.[18]

What happens in the music itself? Here is another of Shostakovich's darkly brooding first movements. It is also long, longer than the third and fourth movements together. "There are," he himself said, "more slow tempi and lyric moments than dramatic, heroic, and tragic." He begins with low strings, quiet and unharmonized at first.

---

[17]He was speaking for himself. Some composers, Shostakovich's great model, Gustav Mahler, prominent among them, are inveterate, even neurotic, revisers.

[18]*Testimony: The Memoirs of Dmitri Shostakovich.*

Ex. 1

After only two measures, this dissolves into silence. That silence is characteristic of this troubled, wandering music, which stops more than once, as
though uncertain of its direction. So far as I know, Haydn invented this
manner of beginning with low unison strings in his *Drumroll* Symphony;
Schubert's *Unfinished* is a still more familiar example. Hugh Ottaway wrote
in his BBC Music Guide on the Shostakovich symphonies that "Soviet
admirers were quick to remark on the resemblance between Shostakovich's
opening and that of Liszt's *Faust* Symphony: according to Rabinovich [au-
thor of several studies of Shostakovich], an intended and meaningful association of ideas." Liszt's beginning also features silences and a sense of
harmonic ambiguity, and Ottaway adds that "the opening of the Fifth, too,
had been considered Faust-like."

This opening grows into a long passage for strings alone, which con-
tinues until, after several starts and an increase of the tempo, a clarinet
melody brings matters more into focus. So far as I know, Klaus George
Roy, then the Cleveland Orchestra's program annotator, was the first to
point out that what the clarinet plays is a quotation, a poignantly apt one.
The source is the song *Urlicht* (Primal Light), the fourth movement of
Mahler's Symphony No. 2. (Shostakovich was always the son of Mahler.)
In translation, the words the contralto sings are: "Man lies in direst need!
Man lies in greatest pain!"

Ex. 2.

Ex. 3

Shostakovich even takes over Mahler's direction to the performer, just translating "einfach" to "semplice."

The first minutes of the symphony are music of wandering, drifting. By contrast, this clarinet theme is anchored to a long-held low E, the keynote. The violins continue and extend this melody, the full orchestra carries it forward to a crest in *fortissimo,* and then the quiet clarinet completes this chapter. Over rhythmically irregular plucked strings and at a still quicker tempo, a solo flute introduces a new theme, narrow in range, nervous in temperament. As they did with the Mahler theme, the strings pick it up and greatly extend it.

When the texture has thinned down to nearly nothing, bassoons and contrabassoon, accompanied by a series of soft timpani rolls, begin the development by exploring the Mahler theme further. Shostakovich stirs it up to a brutal triple *forte,* at which point the nervous flute theme is brought back, quite transformed in character with snarling trumpets and horns. This high level of tension is sustained for a long time, fierce interventions from timpani and snare drums fanning the flames still further. Moving rapidly from key to key, the music at last quiets down for a recapitulation. The opening music and the Mahler theme, having had so much attention in this grim development, are quickly dispatched; the flute theme, on the other hand, is enhanced by being played by two clarinets in operatic thirds.

The coda revisits the introduction. With characteristic fantasy, Shostakovich assigns the burden of the discourse, a farewell imbued with reluctance and regret, to the duetting of two piccolos. At the close, the wandering chromatics are banished. What is left is a single piccolo, firm in the conviction that the music is in E minor, and unambiguously supported in that by the timpani and the strings.

Listening to this movement, I find myself wondering about the composer's lament that he had still not succeeded in writing a "real symphonic allegro." Tchaikovsky uttered similar complaints about himself, often with more cause, though he was capable of a design so magnificent—and magnificently original—as that of the first movement of the *Pathétique.* It seems to me that Shostakovich's lament is about not producing a textbook sonata-allegro that he should not have written anyway.[19] Here, as in many of his other symphonic first movements—I think particularly of nos. 4 through 8—he has planned and built something unorthodox, but totally in harmony with his material and his expressive intentions. Such movements also show yet again his remarkable command of broad paragraphs

---

[19] He had demonstrated in the first movement of the Symphony No. 9 that he could do this as deftly as anyone.

and chapters. It is worth remembering that Arnold Schoenberg of all people pointed to him as one of the few among his contemporaries with "the breath of [a symphonist]."

The next movement, the supposed Stalin portrait, is less than one-fifth the length of the preceding one, and by far the shortest in the symphony. It crashes across the land at relentless speed, and the dynamic level is at an almost unbroken *forte/fortissimo*. The final explosion is prepared by a brief passage in *piano/pianissimo*: this, with its suggestion of barely suppressed fury, is, if anything, still more sinister.

Shostakovich's misgivings about the brevity of this bitter scherzo were unnecessary. For something so intense, this movement is as long as is manageable or even tolerable without introducing a major contrasting section, and such a contrast would only weaken the effect of this terrifying outburst. As for the idea of following a weighty first movement with a startlingly brief second movement, Shostakovich might well have found his models in late Beethoven, specifically the *Hammerklavier* Sonata (which was in his repertory in his young piano-playing days), and the B-flat-major String Quartet, Opus 130.

This consummate savagery is succeeded in the third movement by another quasi-scherzo of a very different kind. After these terrors, something human stirs in a scene part pathetic, part comic. Someone peeks cautiously around the corner. Is the room clear of threats? Only the head shows, and it is quickly pulled back. Another look—perhaps it is safe to enter. The music itself is a rhythmically ambiguous, ticking theme for the violins, a new version of a shape previously explored in the Violin Concerto No. 1 (not yet heard at the time of the Tenth Symphony) and the String Quartet No. 5 (introduced only five weeks before the symphony).

Before long, the violins introduce an idea that is strikingly different in character, espressivo instead of dryly detached.

Ex. 4

This modulates until it reaches C minor, the home key of this movement. Here it takes on new significance in that Shostakovich now spells out his own initials in musical notation, using the German transliteration of his name (Schostakowitsch) and German notation, where E-flat is called "es"

and B-natural is called H. In other words, the sequence D/E-flat/C-B spells DSCH.[20]

Ex. 5

The Stalin juggernaut is gone; it is the nervous Shostakovich himself who has made his apprehensive entrance.

This imprinting of his own presence is a device Shostakovich used several times in his later works, the most prominent occurrences being in this symphony, the Violin Concerto No. 1, the String Quartet No. 8, and the last symphony, No. 15. Example 4 is the first *explicit* appearance of DSCH in the Tenth Symphony; by this point, however, Shostakovich has several times edged close to his motto by presenting themes that use its component intervals of semitone and minor third in other permutations. If, for example, you transpose the opening of the symphony (Ex. 1) from E minor to C minor, the first four notes spell CDSH, and at the end of the first movement's exposition, the violins, virtually unaccompanied, slowly spell out DCHS. The third movement's opening theme, the one derived from the Violin Concerto No. 1 and the Fifth Quartet, also begins by spelling CDSH.

ex. 6

This means that when DSCH first appears, it sounds like one more absolutely organic variant of a musical idea we have become thoroughly

[20]This kind of encoding of significant names is an old story. The best-known example is the use of a BACH (B-flat/A/C/B-natural) motif by at least a hundred composers, including J. S. Bach himself.

familiar with by now. (Even the "Stalin Portrait" begins with a transposition of CDS.) When, a little later, Shostakovich wants us to hear DSCH as an especially significant version of these notes, he has no trouble finding ways of making it stand out by means of repetitions, scoring, or framing.

A pensive horn call changes the atmosphere. This mysterious summons, which will occur eleven more times before the movement is done, always elicits an intensely serious response in the orchestra. At its first appearance it introduces a recollection of the symphony's opening measures—specifically, of those opening measures as they are evoked in the first movement's coda. This in turn leads to one of the few passages of slow music in the symphony. A single violin, muted, timid, reminds us of the way the movement began. The last of the horn calls introduces a wispy, hesitant version of DSCH, played by flute and piccolo. On this ghostly note the movement ends.

The finale begins with slow music. Two elements make up this Andante, a meditative theme for low strings and a series of intensely expressive, faintly Eastern-sounding woodwind solos. Just as the music seems about to lose itself in melancholy, the violins begin a cheerful romp in E major. Although Shostakovich wrote some great serious symphonic finales, and I think particularly of the Fourth, Eighth, and Fifteenth symphonies, I have sometimes imagined that he would have been happy had circumstances allowed him to be a latter-day Haydn, unburdened by any obligation to devise weighty, "significant" endings. Here, at any rate, is one the most brilliantly vivacious of his Haydn finales, though it finds room for fleeting and always touching moments of a darker, sadder music. In the closing minutes, DSCH, with horns and then timpani to speak his name, steps forward to take a bow—and not a bit shyly.

Symphony No. 15, Opus 141

Allegretto
Adagio
Allegretto
Adagio—Allegretto

Shostakovich completed his Symphony No. 15 in 1971, and his son, Maxim, conducted the first performance with the USSR Radio Symphony in the concert hall of the Moscow Conservatory on 8 January 1972.

Two flutes and piccolo, two oboes, two clarinets, two bassoons, four horns, two trumpets, three trombones, tuba, timpani, triangle, castanets, soprano tom-tom, snare drum, wood block, slapstick, cymbals, bass drum, tam-tam, xylophone, glockenspiel, vibraphone, celesta, and strings. (The composer asks for sixteen first and fourteen second violins, twelve each of violas and cellos, and ten basses, adding that while these numbers are "not mandatory . . . [they] would give the best results.")

In his later years, Shostakovich felt at least a little safer than before about bringing some of his discontent and dismay with life into the open, setting provocative texts by the controversial Yevgeny Yevtushenko in his Thirteenth (1962) and making his annihilating Fourteenth (1969) a cycle of songs about death, something far removed from the official optimism of public Soviet art. Even so, his government found it more useful or politic to exploit than to harass him, and he was loaded with honors at home (Deputy of the Supreme Soviet, USSR State Prize, Hero of Socialist Labor, Order of the October Revolution) even as he was abroad (Honorary Member of the International Music Council of UNESCO, Gold Medal of the Royal Philharmonic Society, Honorary Member of the French Academy, and similar tokens from the German Federal Republic, Austria, Yugoslavia, Italy, and Finland; the Danish Sonning Prize; and honorary doctorates from Trinity College, Dublin, and Northwestern University). In those last years, he devoted most of his energy to the composition of songs and chamber music. This, then, is the context for the enigmatic Fifteenth and last of his symphonies.

It starts brightly. Over an ever so slightly capricious accompaniment of glockenspiel with plucked strings, a flute bounces through a jaunty tune. It is long, and also a little skewed in its harmony: the first phrase, for example, goes up a chord of A-flat major but comes down a scale in A minor. Shostakovich symphonies often begin with stretched and meandering melodies, usually solemn ones, and the critic Andrew Porter has convincingly suggested that the flute here "seems to be making a merry, mocking allusion to those long, low, slowly wandering themes." The rhythm is that of a quickstep and sends the music right into the most famous tune in Rossini's *William Tell* Overture, played on a trumpet and with one of the chords wrong.

What is going on here? Shostakovich often quoted himself, particularly in the last fifteen years of his life, but making so explicit a reference to such a familiar tune by someone else is new. *William Tell*, moreover, will pop up four more times during this movement. The program note at the first performance explained that this music depicts a toy shop at night, the toys all springing to life in their keeper's absence. That seems too innocent. About this "call to arms [sounding] as if from a toy trumpet," Porter asks: "Would it be too fanciful to suggest that, whereas William Tell was an active fighter for freedom, a musician—Shostakovich now feels—has the power to make only small, ineffectual gestures?" Later events in the symphony make it impossible to believe that any quotation, and particularly one so aggressively identifiable, could have been placed in the interests of nothing more than a cute bit of genre painting. It cannot be as trivial as the composer so carefully makes it seem.

In the rambling conversations that make up *Testimony*, Shostakovich says the music of his Fifteenth Symphony is tied to his plans for an opera, never finished (or perhaps never started), based on Anton Chekhov's study of megalomania, *The Black Monk*. He more than once refers to *The Black Monk* as a work he is "determined to write"; he also makes it plain that, along with Mussorgsky, Chekhov, wry, unembarrassed, incorruptibly clear-sighted, full of knowledge of the gray in life, was the Russian artist who meant the most to him and whose work, whose very style of existence, most surely sustained and nourished him.[21]

In the Adagio, Shostakovich alludes to an earlier work of his own, the first movement, also an Adagio, of his Symphony No. 11. Writing to commemorate the fortieth anniversary of the October Revolution of 1917, Shostakovich had taken the year 1905 as his subject, the year of Russia's humiliating defeat in her foolish war against Japan, a year also of strikes, uprisings, and some significant left-wing victories in the Duma. Shostakovich chose, however, to concentrate on "Bloody Sunday," 9 January, when thousands of workers and intellectuals with their families gathered in peaceful petition before the Winter Palace in Saint Petersburg. The tsar's police and armed Cossacks fired into the densely packed crowd. At least a thousand unarmed civilians were killed and many more wounded. Shostakovich was writing ostensibly about Nicholas II, but he was not forgetting the tyrants who had replaced the tsar. To quote *Testimony* again: "[The Eleventh Symphony] deals with contemporary themes even though it's called *1905*. It's about people, who have stopped believing because the cup of evil has run over. . . . Our family discussed the Revolution of 1905 constantly."

The *Palace Square* movement from the Eleventh Symphony is the source for the solemn brass chorale that begins the Adagio of the Fifteenth and comes back as a refrain. Its soft contour is contrasted against the

---

[21] Another urgent project was the completion of the opera *Rothschild's Violin* begun by his student Veniamin Fleishman, killed while serving in the People's Volunteer Guard in the war. Shostakovich had suggested to Fleishman that he set this Chekhov story.

twelve-note melodies sung, unaccompanied, by the solo cello and solo violin.[22] Later, when the orchestra plays a funeral march, the imagery becomes still more explicit. For what happens next, I again quote Porter: "The earlier lyricism turns to ice when the celesta, in a quiet solo that steals into a hushed hall, spells out the cello's theme in inversion: sad, soft-falling transformation of what had been ardent and aspirant."

Without break, the Adagio dissolves into a scherzo in the sardonic tone Shostakovich often used in such movements. So at least it begins (with another twelve-note theme). Trumpet fanfares try for something nobler, but, against sneering trombones, their gestures are as impotent as the Lilliputian calls to arms of the first movement. As the trombones mock, the horns pronounce the composer's own name, that is, the DSCH motto that occurs so often in Shostakovich's later music. The scherzo ends with the chatter of tambourine, castanets, wood block, and xylophone.

To begin his finale, Shostakovich again reaches into a world of music long and profoundly familiar and full of associations. We hear the solemn sequence of brass chords from the Annunciation of Death scene in Act 2 of Wagner's *Die Walküre*. Brünnhilde, beautiful and stern, appears before Siegmund to tell him that he will die in his battle with Hunding. The key words are:

> Only those destined for death
> Can see me;
> Whose gaze finds me
> Must part from the light of life.
> On the field of battle
> I appear to noble heroes;
> Those who become aware of me,
> I choose, and they must follow me.

Wagner brings that music back in the final act of *Götterdämmerung* when Hagen, punishing perjury, has plunged his spear into Siegfried's back. Here, too, as he had in the first movement, Shostakovich slightly alters what he quotes, changing the pitch of the drumbeats and setting their rhythm somewhere between the simple pattern in *Die Walküre* and the more complex one in *Götterdämmerung*. But the more significant change comes in what follows the brass and the pulsing drums. In *Walküre*, it is the nobly impassioned dialogue of Siegmund and Brünnhilde; in *Göt-*

---

[22] Beginning in 1968 with the String Quartet No. 12, Shostakovich repeatedly explored the expressive possibilities of twelve-note melodies, always in contexts of deaths and despair. In the liner notes to Bernard Haitink's recording of the Symphony No. 15, Clive Bennett points out that the melody immediately preceding the *William Tell* quotation is one that uses all twelve pitches.

terdämmerung, the radiant transformation of Brünnhilde's greeting to the sun, to light, to day, to life. Here we get one of those long and meandering Shostakovich melodies. Wanly disconsolate, it begins with another Wagner reference, the grieving, yearning A-F-E with which *Tristan und Isolde* opens.

The climax of the movement is a citation, dark and twisted, from the heroic *Leningrad* Symphony, a work which, according to *Testimony*, is "not about Leningrad under siege, it's about the Leningrad that Stalin destroyed and that Hitler merely finished off." Like the Fourth Symphony and the tragic Eighth, the Fifteenth ends with strings softly holding a single chord for many pages. Here the chord is incomplete: there are just two notes, A and E. Across it, timpani recall the passacaglia from the *Leningrad* Symphony, while snare drum, castanets, wood block, xylophone, glockenspiel, celesta, and tom-tom clack and ping and patter away. The chattering xylophone turns the strings' hollow chord to clear A major, and with a bell-tone, quiet and bright, like the one with which the story began, the symphony vanishes.

Jean Sibelius

Jean (Johan Julius Christian) Sibelius was born at
Tavestehus (Hämeenlinna), Finland, on 8 December 1865
and died at Järvenpää on 20 September 1957.

Symphony No. 1 in E minor, Opus 39

Andante, ma non troppo—Allegro energico
Andante (ma non troppo lento)
Scherzo: Allegro—Lento (ma non troppo)—Tempo I
Finale (Quasi una Fantasia): Andante—Allegro molto

Sibelius began his Symphony No. 1 in the last week of April 1898
and completed it early the following year. On 26 April 1899, Sibelius himself conducted the Helsinki Philharmonic in the first performance. In March 1900, he revised the orchestration somewhat, and this
new and final version was first played on 4 July 1900 in Stockholm at the
start of a Helsinki Philharmonic tour. This time Robert Kajanus conducted.

**Two flutes, two oboes, two clarinets, two bassoons, four horns, three trum-
pets, three trombones, tuba, timpani, bass drum, cymbals, triangle, harp,
and strings.**

At thirty-two, when Sibelius began this symphony, he was a national hero
in the making. *Kullervo*, a seventy-minute symphony with two vocal move-

ments (or a cantata with three instrumental movements) based on the Finnish national epic *Kalevala,* had marked the first step in that direction when he introduced it in 1892. Just back from two years of study in Berlin and Vienna, Sibelius found his homeland in political ferment. Since 1809, Finland had been an autonomous grand duchy of the Russian Empire, though strong cultural traces remained of its previous status as part of Sweden, which had conquered the territory in the twelfth century. In the 1890s, however, the Russians began to reconsider Finland's autonomy, introducing tough censorship and other repressive measures. *Kullervo* not only celebrated a distinctively Finnish treasure but also signified Sibelius's commitment to the new Finnish-language movement, even though his own first tongue was Swedish, as was his name.

Resistance movements develop their own forms of ingenuity, and the Finns were clever at finding unobjectionable pretexts for mounting patriotic pageants—raising funds for politically innocent charities, for example. Music was an essential component of these events, and Sibelius wrote both his *Karelia* Suite and *Finlandia* for such occasions. When the repressed cannot openly cheer their political heroes, they can make their artists into heroes and cheer them. What a wonderful bit of serendipity it had been for champions of the Risorgimento that the name of the great composer *and* great patriot Verdi was an acronym for *Vittorio Emanuele, re d'Italia.* Who could object to cries and graffiti of *Viva Verdi!?*

Well, Italians are Italians and Finns are Finns, but in their own septentrional way the Finns did make Sibelius into a hero, an image he came to cherish and, in his later years, to cultivate assiduously. Now, at the end of both the decade and the century, the official First Symphony by the composer of *Kullervo* and *Karelia* was keenly awaited. It brought him great success and even some international attention when the Helsinki Philharmonic took it on tour to Stockholm, Göteborg, Malmö, Kristiania (Oslo), Copenhagen, Lübeck, Hamburg, Berlin, Amsterdam, and Paris. A few months after the symphony's premiere came *Finlandia,* "a relatively insignificant piece" as far as Sibelius himself was concerned, but the one that would carry his name to more people and places than any other.

As a child, Sibelius took violin lessons and played trios with his older sister and younger brother. In his teens he began more serious studies, which included slogging on his own through a treatise on composition by the early nineteenth-century theorist, A. B. Marx. He was briefly distracted by a notion of pursuing a respectable profession, specifically law, but soon went back to music. His principal teacher was Martin Wegelius, the first head of the Music Institute in Helsinki and the founding father of music education in Finland, but Sibelius was deeply impressed as well by a brilliant musician, actually a few months younger than himself, whom

Wegelius had added to his faculty, the Italian-German pianist and composer Ferruccio Busoni. Done with the Institute, Sibelius went to Berlin on a government grant, got engaged to his best friend's sister, then moved on to Vienna.

For all his interest in composition, he still thought of himself as a violinist. His most painful task in Vienna was to come to terms with the reality that, handicapped by a late start, the provincial level of even the best teaching that had been available to him at home, and his lack of both the physical coordination and the temperament for such a career, he was not going to make it. While studying composition with Robert Fuchs and managing to get an occasional lesson from Karl Goldmark, he played in the Conservatory orchestra (its intonation gave him headaches), and on 9 January 1891 he auditioned for the Philharmonic. "When he got back to his room," we read in Erik Tawaststjerna's biography, "Sibelius broke down and wept. Afterwards he sat at the piano and began to practice scales." That day Sibelius the imagined violin virtuoso vanished, and perhaps it was also that day that Sibelius the great composer was born.

Busoni had given him a letter of introduction to Brahms, but Brahms was not interested.[1] The other great figure among Viennese composers was Bruckner. He had virtually withdrawn from public life, and Sibelius did not meet him either, but Bruckner's Third Symphony, which Sibelius heard Hans Richter conduct at a Philharmonic concert, made a stunning impact. (Not the least of what impressed Sibelius was that the audience booed Bruckner, but his admirers carried him to his coach "amid much cheering and general commotion.") Though their artistic temperaments were vastly different, Bruckner's voice would never be altogether absent from Sibelius's music. For now, it was one more vital infusion to add to the heady experience—heady especially for one whose upbringing had been centered on Haydn and Beethoven—of learning something about Wagner and the young Richard Strauss, the latter only a year and a half older than Sibelius but already the composer of two orchestral knockouts, *Don Juan* and *Death and Transfiguration*.

Sibelius even began a Wagnerian *Kalevala* opera as a kind of sequel to his *Kullervo* symphony, but a good soaking in Wagner at the 1894 Bayreuth Festival brought him to his senses. Realizing he was not an opera composer, he abandoned his new *Kalevala* project, but rescued some of the material for his Four Legends (*The Swan of Tuonela* is the best known of them). Over the years, his continuing fascination with the theater found

[1] Years later, Sibelius told his biographer Johan Ekman a story about having met Brahms in a café. He did not mention this in any letter at the time, and since Sibelius was something of an expert both at covering his tracks and inventing new ones, there is reason to be suspicious.

a happy outlet in the writing of incidental music for plays by Shakespeare, Strindberg, Maeterlinck, and others. Sibelius's extreme turning away from the grand rhetorical stance of Wagnerian theater came in 1907 with the composition of the Symphony No. 3, a marvel of neoclassicism, though it has never been burdened with that label. Later, at his most characteristic and most eloquent, Sibelius invented symphonies that are an entirely individual and wonderful synthesis of classical economy and Romantic, passionate gestures.

The Symphony No. 1 is nourished by Sibelius's love of such gestures; we can hear as well that Tchaikovsky, whose recent *Symphonie pathétique* had been given in Helsinki in 1894 and 1897, and won a place in Sibelius's heart, though this was not a love destined to last.[2] More important, it is music in which we encounter, again and again, personality traits and techniques we recognize as Sibelian. True, the former are just beginning to assume sharp profile and the fairly young and relatively slow-blooming composer has yet to discover the full possibilities of the latter. Nonetheless, the essential message is unmistakable: Jean Sibelius is here.

The beginning is magical. Across a soft drumroll, a clarinet sings a long melody, dark in mood, and in slow descent. Shimmering violins catch it at its cadence. We have now arrived in the main tempo, Allegro energico, as against the Andante, ma non troppo of the melancholic clarinet meditation. Sibelius, by the way, uses "andante" the way most nineteenth-century composers did, with Brahms as the notable exception; that is to say, meaning "slow," so that when he writes "meno andante" he means "faster."

With the new tempo comes a new theme; more precisely, it is a shape already suggested in the clarinet melody, but so transformed in character as to produce the effect of a new theme. It is a strong declamatory phrase pronounced by the first violins and imitated in simpler form by the violas and cellos. This, to begin with, is delivered *poco forte,* so that the dynamics are interestingly at odds with the force of the gesture. For a moment, too, the harmony is ambiguous: the theme sounds like G major, which the accompaniment does not contradict, and it takes a while for the balance to tip clearly toward E minor. This is a touch that would have got Brahms's pleased attention (compare, for example, the opening of his Clarinet Quintet, whose D-major/B-minor ambiguity is itself borrowed from Haydn's B-minor Quartet, Opus 64, no. 2).

Sibelius extends this idea into a broad paragraph, finally arriving at a

[2] Tchaikovsky had died in 1893, the year of *The Swan of Tuonela;* Bruckner died in 1896. In other words, these were figures as immediate as Messiaen or Cage might be to a young composer working today.

full-voiced *fortissimo.* A new, chattering theme for woodwinds appears, but this soon withdraws into the background to become the accompaniment of an eloquent melody, also in woodwinds and yet another offspring of the clarinet introduction. Meanwhile the strings anchor everything to a single, rapidly reiterated chord. There is a powerful counterpoint of different speeds going on here: the new melody is broad, the chattering theme feels quick, the buzzing in the strings conveys restlessness but no specific sense of tempo. On all this, Sibelius imposes a general speeding up of the pulse, reinforcing the effect by placing a series of sharp accents at ever closer intervals. All his life he will play with speeds in this way.

This exciting buildup is abruptly cut off and we are left with three bleak measures of plucked strings and timpani in gray *mezzo-forte.* The strings cry out in protest, and a turbulent development begins. Much of it is concerned with what was once the chattering woodwind theme, but which has radically changed character to become something quite troubled and generally more grown-up. Strings intervene with a passionate new idea—again and characteristically it is *mezzo-forte*—and we are quickly swept into the recapitulation. This time, when the music arrives at the top of the exciting crescendo and accelerando, instead of the gray *mezzo-forte* plunks we hear forceful chords for trombones and timpani. These initiate the terse and intensely dramatic coda. The final bars also show how impressed Sibelius was—as well he might have been—by the end of Act 2 of *Parsifal* when he saw it at Bayreuth.

Now he takes us into a different world. The soft sonorities are new, and the first chord of E-flat major comes as a real shock after the first movement's E minor. This Andante—Sibelius warns us in words, with his alla breve time signature, and with his metronome mark, that it must not be *very* slow—is warm-hearted Romanticism, or at least as close to that as Sibelius can bring himself to come. Muted violins and cellos sing a quiet melody to which woodwinds assent from time to time with a kind of "yes, Lord, amen." In the first movement, Sibelius had shifted fluently and subtly from tempo to tempo, even superimposing different tempi. Here, too, he plays with the contrast of speeds as he inserts sharply differentiated episodes.

A bassoon, whose instrumental color Sibelius thought of as peculiarly Finnish in character, begins the first of these as a kind of fugato, and this leads, by way of some reminiscences of the main theme, to a passage (molto tranquillo) where horns sound sweetly against a forest-murmurs accompaniment. What the horns play is a variant of the first movement's second theme: the idea of symphonic unity is constantly on Sibelius's mind. The music is violently interrupted by the sudden appearance of the first two bars of the main theme. This ought to pull things together; instead, the effect is jarring more than anything, in part because of the abrupt change of tone color (just horns, low woodwinds, and timpani emerging from a rich tutti), and in part because this phrase arrives in a totally unrelated, much slower tempo.[3] With equal suddenness, Sibelius resumes the main Andante tempo, and with it the principal theme, now hung about with spooky scales and trills. The music accelerates again until it has arrived at double its original pace: at this point the first theme sings out across the tumult, but at its own slower tempo. Then the movement can come to a quiet close.

The Scherzo is a vigorous foot-stomping affair, full of sharp cross-accents. But if this is a tipping of the hat to Bruckner, the trio is the music of a new composer. It is all Sibelius's own. The tempo is much slower (Lento, after Allegro), the harmonies are enigmatic, the forward motion is all spasms and disruptions, and the atmosphere is uncanny and altogether unsettling.[4] Full of drastic and immediate contrasts, this is music for conductors who take the trouble to differentiate between *mezzo-forte, forte,* and *fortissimo,* and between *piano* and *pianissimo.* Here is the most remarkable page in the First Symphony and certainly the one most predictive of the Sibelius of the Fourth and Seventh symphonies and *Tapiola.*

The Finale, which Sibelius marks Quasi una fantasia, begins with music we know. This is the clarinet melody with which the symphony began, but what was melancholic and hesitant before is now boldly impassioned, though no less dark. All the violins, violas, and cellos play it in a sonorous *forte.* But we hear no more than half of it before it is interrupted, tentatively resumed by woodwinds, then pushed aside by an anguished and fierce quick movement (not without its Tchaikovskian gestures). In due course this in turn gives way to a grandly lush theme to be played on the violins' G-string. Like the return of the clarinet theme at the beginning of the movement, here is another place where one yearns for the orchestral seating in use in Sibelius's time, one that spreads the violins clear across the entire stage instead of crowding them to the left. The English composer and critic Bayan Northcott points out a subtle connection here, namely that the harmonies of this theme are virtually identical to those of the second movement's principal theme.

This magnificent melody, too, is interrupted by the agitated Allegro

---

[3] As he leads up to this moment, Sibelius uses a tempo and character direction I do not recall seeing in any other score: "sollecitato," which means "speeded up" but which is derived from the primary meaning of *sollecitare*—to urge, plead, or entreat.

[4] Sibelius is erratic in the matter of metronome marks. In the first movement, for example, he gives a mark for the Allegro but none for the preceding Andante; here he gives one for the Scherzo itself but none for the trio. He is therefore no help when it comes to determining the relations of neighboring speeds to one another.

molto. The agitation subsides and again the grand tune returns, now intoned softly by a clarinet. This crossing of one theme with a color so
specifically associated with another is one more fine symphonic subtlety.
Striding across the harmonic landscape, the melody crests to a great climax
with a romantic harp accompaniment of a kind we will not hear from
Sibelius again. Then—and this is another glimpse of the Sibelius of the
years to come (and also of Beethoven nearly a hundred years before)—the
music seems to break apart. It stays *forte* and *fortissimo*, but the sequence
of gestures is strangely disjunct. We reach the tonic chord of E minor.
Swirling strings surround it. More E-minor chords follow, well separated,
but with a *fortissimo* timpani roll underneath. Then, as in the first movement, the drums back off; as they do so, we hear two more chords of E
minor, in gray pizzicato, *mezzo-forte* and *piano*. It is a strange and
haunting close.

Symphony No. 2 in D major, Opus 43

> *Allegretto*
> *Tempo Andante, ma rubato*
> *Vivacissimo—Lento e suave—Tempo primo—Lento e suave*
> *Finale: Allegro moderato*

Sibelius began his Symphony No. 2 in 1901, completing it early in 1902,
and conducting the Helsinki Philharmonic in the first performance on 8
March that year.

**Two flutes, two oboes, two clarinets, two bassoons, four horns, three trum-
pets, three trombones, tuba, timpani, and strings. The work is dedicated to
Baron Axel Carpelan.**

And who was Axel Carpelan? Erik Tawaststjerna tells us in his masterly
Sibelius biography:

> As far as most people were concerned, he was a hypochondriac who
> had done little with his life, had precious little money, and eked out a lonely
> bachelor existence in lodgings in Tampere. After taking his *studenten*, the
> school-leaving certificate that qualified one for university entrance, he

wanted to devote himself to the violin but met with strong parental opposition. His response to their ban was to smash his violin in a fit of rage and frustration and throw the bits and pieces into the stream at Turku. The whole affair seems to have had a traumatic effect on him. He sank into apathy, refusing pleas from his parents to go to the university, and retired into a private world of his own, taking refuge in books and music. He began a correspondence with his idol, the Swedish poet Viktor Rydberg, and another with his country man, Axel Tamm, a wealthy lover of the arts who for many years had made Carpelan an allowance. For all this he lived in something approaching penury and it was only by exercising the utmost frugality and economy that he was able to afford the luxury of spending some weeks in the country during the summer. For a time he paid court to an aristocratic and highly intellectual lady with a fiery, enigmatic temperament, waiting devotedly outside her house for a glimpse of her. She sent him packing in no uncertain terms, brutally telling him to get out of her sight and preferably out of town; this, it seems, he actually did.

As he could not become a musician, Carpelan did the next best thing. He did all in his power to bolster his illusion of being in the midst of musical activity. He had never been outside Scandinavia but was nonetheless extremely well informed about musical life on the continent; composers, conductors, orchestras, musical periodicals and so on. He was in short an amateur in the truest and best sense of the word, but had little real stamina: he never brought himself as far as doing sustained criticism, let alone playing or composing.

. . . In his dealings with Sibelius he showed real flair (the idea of a piece called *Finlandia* was his) and at his best, was a source of inspiration. . . . The Violin Concerto, [the Second] Symphony, a few years later the quartet *Voces intimae*, all of these were spurred into being by Carpelan.[5]

Carpelan had entered Sibelius's life anonymously shortly before the composer was to accompany the Helsinki Philharmonic on a journey to the 1900 World's Fair in Paris. It was then that he suggested a "really devilish" overture that "surely must be called *Finlandia.*" He appeared, still anonymously, at dockside when the orchestra set out by ship for Stockholm, the first stop on the tour, and, a somewhat absurd figure with his foppish gestures, he presented a bouquet to each player.

He first introduced himself to Sibelius that October at the premiere of the composer's choral work *Snöfrid.* Carpelan's letters, full of advice, suggestions, interference, trivia, insight, gossip, hypochondriac laments, and unsolicited opinions, began to arrive more frequently. Even before their meeting, Carpelan had commanded Sibelius to go to Italy—"You

[5] Erik Tawaststjerna, *Sibelius,* Vol. 1. translated by Robert Layton (Berkeley: University of California Press, 1977).

have sat at home long enough, Herr Sibelius"—and, having no money of his own, badgered a Swedish and a Finnish patron into contributing 5000 Finnish marks. "You can spend the late autumn and winter in Italy," he told Sibelius. "Everything there is lovely—even the ugly.[6] You remember the important role that Italy played in Tchaikovsky's development and Strauss's." The importance for Tchaikovsky and Strauss of their Italian journeys is at the very least debatable—it is not as though we were talking about Dürer or Schütz or Goethe—but characteristically, Carpelan's intuition about Sibelius was absolutely on target. Sibelius did not get there in late autumn, but in February 1901 he arrived in Rapallo, just below Genoa.

Still depressed by the death from typhus of his youngest daughter Kirsti the year before, worried about the tough line recently taken toward Finland by Russia, inclined as always to drink and smoke too much, his marriage uneasy, the thirty-five-year-old composer was in poor shape. But, although Sibelius still frightened friends and family with moments of crazy behavior, the tonic effect of Italy was extraordinary. By May, he and his family were home again, and he had accomplished much, particularly by way of sketching what he thought of as a four-movement orchestral fantasy: "I've now fallen fatally in love with [it]. I can't tear myself away from it." What is now the bassoon theme at the beginning of the symphony's second movement first occurred to him in slightly different form as part of a *Don Juan* project. The very quiet theme for strings alone after the first big climax in that movement appears in sketches labeled "Christus." But during the course of the year it became clear to Sibelius that he was writing neither a set of four tone poems nor an orchestral fantasy, but a real symphony.

There were interruptions. Sibelius's reputation in Germany was growing, and he had been invited to take part in a festival of contemporary music organized at Heidelberg by Richard Strauss. *The Swan of Tuonela* and *Lemminkäinen's Journey Home* had great success there, and Strauss, just eighteen months older than Sibelius but already an international eminence on the grandest scale, was complimentary.[7] Nevertheless, on 9 November Sibelius was able to report to Carpelan that the new symphony was "near

---

[6] Carpelan had never been there. —M.S.

[7] Strauss noted in his diary that "Sibelius is the only Scandinavian composer who had real depth. Though he lacks a total mastery of instrumentation, his music has a freshness that presupposes a virtually inexhaustible fund of melodic invention." The comment about instrumentation can be translated to mean that Sibelius wrote for orchestra in a manner that was not in the brilliant post-Wagnerian fashion of the day, the manner that Strauss himself commanded with such stunning mastery. It should also be noted that Carl Nielsen, the other Scandinavian composer with "real depth," had not yet emerged in 1901.

completion." Final polishing took longer than anticipated, and the original date for the premiere could not be met; when, however, the first performances did take place—there was a run of four on 8, 10, 14, and 16 March 1902—the triumph for Sibelius was complete and worth the wait.

Almost at once there appeared an article by Sibelius's friend the conductor Robert Kajanus, who offered a political interpretation of the work:

> The Andante strikes one as the most broken-hearted protest against all the injustice that threatens at the present time to deprive the sun of its light and our flowers of their scent. . . . The scherzo gives a picture of frenetic preparations. Everyone piles his straw on the haystack, all fibers are strained and every second seems to last an hour. One senses in the contrasting trio section with its oboe motif in G-flat what is at stake. The finale develops toward a triumphant conclusion intended to rouse in the listener a picture of lighter and confident prospects for the future.[8]

The Kajanus-Sibelius friendship was never free from friction, and this was one of the occasions when Sibelius was distinctly annoyed. Nonetheless, such readings would surface again. Philip Hale's Boston Symphony program note from 1924, for example, is full of terms like "oppression," "patriotic feeling," "brutal rule," "the awakening of national feeling," and "the desire to organize in defense of their rights." This sort of thing had a comic pendant sixteen years later when Virgil Thomson, who thought the Second Symphony "vulgar, self-indulgent, and provincial beyond all description," wrote in *The New York Herald-Tribune* that the only reason American orchestras played so much Sibelius was that Finland alone had paid her war debts. Thomson enjoyed swimming against the current; in 1940 Sibeliomania was at its zenith in America, sustained by such conductors as Serge Koussevitzky, Eugene Ormandy, Artur Rodzinski, and Leopold Stokowski, as well as by Olin Downes, the chief music critic of the powerful *New York Times,* and soon to be intensified even more by Finland's heroic resistance to invasion by the Soviet Union. By the time of his death in 1957, Sibelius had, most astonishingly, sunk into oblivion, to become the object of excited rediscovery toward the end of the 1970s.

The Sibelius Second is a very familiar piece. That makes it easy to forget how strange some of it, but particularly its first movement, must have sounded to the audiences that heard its early performances. The overall four-movement design is not strange, and the symphony brings no "forbidden" chords, but contemporary listeners had never experienced music that begins and builds like this.

[8] Tawaststjerna, *Sibelius.*

At an easygoing pace, strings fairly quietly play a series of chords, eleven of them, that might be the beginning of a theme or perhaps just a form of "vamp till ready" or an accompaniment in search of a theme. The eleven chords are repeated, then just the first five, twice. Now, in darker colors—the violins have dropped out—the process begins again. Only this time, when the eleven chords are repeated, woodwinds and clarinets add a prettily chirping melody. (A striking difference: the strings always start just *after* the beat, whereas the wind tune sits squarely *on* the beat. Those silent downbeats are an important expressive feature of this movement.) So the chords *were* just an accompaniment waiting for something to accompany. Or were they? Before the oboes and clarinets have gotten very far with their tune, the horns tell them they have the character all wrong, it should be soulful and slower. The woodwinds resume their version. The strings, having first experimented to see what the woodwind tune sounds like when you play it pizzicato, upside down, and very slowly, return to a basic-Finnish version of their chords; that is, only the gesture remains, the tune is gone. The horns carry on with their ruminations. And they all seem pretty much to ignore one another.

It turns out, though, that the clarinets were listening after all, because they now play a bit of the soulful horn phrase as a tag to their own cheerful song. Flutes timidly suggest a new tack. The bassoons pick it up, swirling it upward into a more extended phrase. The violins latch on to the bassoons' last note and, all by themselves, introduce a new, tensely impassioned melody. This describes about a minute and a quarter of music. And so it goes, with more such events to follow—fragment after fragment, some connected to their context and others not, some more assertive than others, and offering a wide range of musical characters.

Gradually we come to feel the coherence of this music. What Sibelius wants us to perceive as most important, he positions accordingly, playing it more often or more emphatically. It is as though he had set himself the task of discovering the coherence and hierarchical placement of all these fragments. He himself put it more picturesquely when he once wrote, "It is as though the Almighty had thrown the pieces of a mosaic down from the floor of heaven and told me to put them together." So, stones into mosaic, that is the scenario of this movement.

Sibelius has in fact ordered his materials in the familiar design of sonata form: the presentation of ideas, their so-called development by means of reassembly and other kinds of alteration, and their restatement. One thing different here is that whereas in most classical and Romantic examples of sonata form the development takes coherent material and fragments it, here, since he is working with fragments in the first place, Sibelius uses the development section as part of the process of binding them together, of assembling the mosaic. That also has the effect of giving the development a different function within the movement. In a "normal" sonata movement, the development is an island, distinctly different from the stable exposition and recapitulation on either side. Here it is an integral part of the overarching process that leads from fragments to mosaic. At the end, something like disintegration supervenes again. It is not so much that the mosaic breaks apart; rather, it is as though the lights have dimmed more and more so that it becomes less and less possible to distinguish anything. Finally, only the string chords are left. They recede into the distance, but because the downbeats are sounding rather than silent, they are also more stabilized than before.

A timpani roll sets the scene for the second movement. Basses alternating with cellos, both pizzicato, spell out a long line. They move in short measures of 3/8. It sounds like the beginning of a movement in a medium tempo, a kind of intermezzo perhaps, and it is only when the bassoons enter with a melody marked "lugubre" that we hear that each group of three bass notes is actually a single beat, in triplets, of a quite slow measure of 4/4.[9] It is a characteristic Sibelius touch that each phrase of the bassoon melody is underlined by a timpani roll. Thus we hear in retrospect that the first timpani roll was not just atmosphere and scene-setting but an organic part of the vocabulary of this movement.

Horns add punctuation to the bassoon melody, and quickly the heat is turned up, everything becoming louder, faster, and more agitated. Antiphonal cries flung back and forth between winds and strings push the music to an almost strident climax; from there, it falls back in exhaustion from *fff* to *ppp*. When the music resumes after a long silence, it is as though the world had changed. A figure that had been the prime motor of agitation before is now totally at peace, and with this gentle entrance into F-sharp major an entirely new harmonic horizon is exposed. (There is a touch of Wagner to these measures.)

Peace, however, is short-lived. A fierce and disturbed development intervenes. The music is full of rushing scales, and we hear much of a device that is a real Sibelius thumbprint, strings buzzing in a kind of impotent fury, circling over and over around a few notes. Familiar materials are variously transformed and the Wagnerian climax returns, leading this time to a more melancholy resolution. Here the process of the first movement is reversed. Fragmentation overpowers coherence, and the music ends with a troubling abruptness.

Another version of Sibelius's buzzing-string music sets the very quick

---

[9] For a more detailed discussion of this kind of play with tempo in Sibelius's music, see the essay on his Symphony No. 7.

scherzo in motion. Woodwinds attempt to start a more sustained melody, but the rushing eighth-notes carry all before them. A long silence, broken only by five drumbeats that descend from *p* to *pppp*, clears the air for the trio, an oboe melody, distinctly *triste*, that begins with nine repetitions of its initial note. (Sibelius likes melodies with repeated notes, but this is extreme even for him.) The measures are broad and slow, but even so, this trio is startlingly short. The scherzo begins again, but this time with a *fortissimo* snarl in the brass. Altogether, on this go-around, the atmosphere is more tense than before. The trio returns. It seems this time to want to be more expansive, but before long we hear that it is moving away from itself, that it is on the way to something else. A new idea—three ascending notes—insists on making itself heard, and this soon bursts forth as the principal theme of the finale.[10]

This theme, simple as it is, generates powerfully thrusting forward motion. The most fascinating feature of this Finale, however, is a wistful melody played obsessively over running eighth-notes in the lower strings. This passage, Tawaststjerna learned from the composer's widow, was written in memory of her sister-in-law, Elli Järnefelt, who had recently taken her own life. The issue of this obsession when it seizes the music for the second time is the renewed blaze of D major in which the symphony so triumphantly ends.

Symphony No. 3 in C major, Opus 52

Allegro moderato
Andantino con moto, quasi allegretto
Moderato—Allegro (ma non tanto)

A letter from Sibelius, dated 21 September 1904, closes with the remark, "Have begun my Third Symphony." He promised the premiere to the Royal Philharmonic Society, London, for 17 March 1907, but the score was not ready. He finished it that summer and conducted the Helsinki Philharmonic in the first performance on 26 September. *Pohjola's Daughter* and the incidental music for Hjalmar Procopé's play *Belshazzar's Feast* were

---

[10] The three ascending notes—D/E/F-sharp—are the exact inversion of the F-sharp/E/D with which the perky woodwind tune at the beginning of the first movement. Indeed, we already had something like a preview of their ascending version when the strings tried the experiment of playing part of the perky tune pizzicato, upside down, and very slowly. Again, something that simply seemed to be an eccentric detail explains itself.

on the same program; with the incidental music for Maeterlinck's *Pelléas et Mélisande*, the revised version of the Violin Concerto, and several songs, these were the chief projects that had occupied Sibelius during the three-year period in which he worked on the Symphony No. 3. The work is dedicated to the composer and conductor, Granville Bantock, one of Sibelius's first and most effective champions in England.

Two flutes, two oboes, two clarinets, two bassoons, four horns, two trumpets, three trombones, timpani, and strings.

> *"Don't eat so much!"*
> —An *apparition to Emanuel Swedenborg, London, 1745*

Salome and the *Symphonia domestica* of Richard Strauss, Ravel's *Alborada del gracioso* and his Introduction and Allegro, Schoenberg's *Pelleas und Melisande*, the Scriabin *Divine Poem*, Debussy's *La Mer* and his first book of *Images* for piano, Mahler's Sixth Symphony and *Kindertotenlieder*, the first books of *Iberia* by Albéniz, Rimsky-Korsakov's *The Invisible City of Kitezh*, the Opus 23 Preludes by Rachmaninoff, Elgar's Introduction and Allegro for Strings, *The Kingdom*, and the fourth of his *Pomp and Circumstance* marches, Puccini's *Madama Butterfly*—that was new and recent music in 1907. How unexpected the stubborn anti-Romanticism of the new Sibelius symphony must have been to the audiences that first heard it in Helsinki, Saint Petersburg, Birmingham, and London. To many it must have been puzzling and annoying. After all, even Sibelius's recent music—the Symphony No. 2, first heard in 1902 and now beginning to make a reputation for its composer throughout Europe; the Violin Concerto, launched in its final form in Berlin, 1905, with Carl Halir as soloist and Richard Strauss conducting; *Pohjola's Daughter*, first played in Saint Petersburg in 1906—had been lush in sound and grand in rhetoric.

During the next decade many composers would hear a voice summoning them to a leaner life. Sibelius heard it sooner. Twenty years later he would heed the voice that told him to spend what turned out to be the last third of his life not composing at all. In any event, in 1904 at the age of thirty-eight, he began work on a classical symphony. He wrote:

> Since Beethoven's time all so-called symphonies, with the exception of those by Brahms, have been symphonic poems. In some cases the composers have given us a program or have at least suggested what they had in mind;

in other cases it is evident that they were concerned with describing or illustrating something, be it a landscape or a series of pictures. That does not correspond to my symphonic ideal. My symphonies are music—conceived and worked out as musical expression, without any literary basis. I am not a literary musician: for me, music begins where words leave off. A symphony should be music first and last. . . . I am particularly pleased to see it explicitly stressed that my [symphonies] are founded on classical symphonic form, and also that wholly misleading speculations about descriptions of nature and about folklore are being gotten rid of.[11]

Sibelius's principal target was his slightly senior contemporary Gustav Mahler. The two composers spent some time together in Helsinki in 1907, and it was in response to Sibelius's saying that what he valued in "the essence of symphony [was] severity of style and the profound logic that created an inner connection among all the motifs" that Mahler pronounced his oft-quoted creed, "No, a symphony must be like the world. It must embrace everything."

Sibelius once wrote: "Homer and Horace had a significance in my development that I cannot value highly enough." He may have meant the two names to stand together for what he got out of his Greek and Latin studies at the University of Helsinki, but actually his music is often interestingly nourished by the tension between the Homeric and the Horatian, the epic and the classical sides of his temperament. Nor are those tensions always resolved. His symphonic poems, he maintained, were quite different from his symphonies; yet, at its Stockholm premiere in 1924, his Seventh Symphony was billed as *Fantasia sinfonica,* and it took Sibelius another year to make up his mind to acknowledge that work as a real symphony.

Horace said of himself that it was his special delight "to enclose words in feet." In that spirit, the Third Symphony is the work in which we meet Sibelius at his most Horatian. It is about the pleasure of making music. Certain pieces by Beethoven are tours de force in composing interestingly, even dramatically, with the most neutral materials imaginable: the Triple Concerto and the *Consecration of the House* Overture are two unpopular examples and the *Emperor* Concerto is a popular one. The Sibelius Third is part of this tradition. Its chief traits are modesty and energy. The orchestration, for 1907, is unassuming. The basic, very "classical" sonority is that of strings and woodwinds, and one seems to hear more of the soft-edged flutes and clarinets than of the sharper double-reeds. The horns and drums are busy, but the trumpets and trombones intervene rarely and economically. The first movement has not a half-dozen measures of *fortissimo,* the

[11] Quoted in Tawaststjerna, *Sibelius,* Vol. 2.

second none at all, and the third only two measures before the last minute of peroration.

The first movement throws three ideas at you in quick succession: the subterranean march of cellos and basses, the swingingly syncopated contribution of the violins, and the jaunty woodwind tune whose sixteenth-notes will dominate the movement more than any other single element. Donald Tovey writes that "a very typical feature of Sibelius is the emergence of a long-drawn melody from a sustained note that began no one can say exactly when." Such a melody soon provides contrast after the propulsive vigor of the first half-dozen pages; it also sets up fascinating tension between its expansiveness (it unfolds for fifteen measures before dissolving into scurrying sixteenths) and the rigorous economy that keeps it circulating around just four notes through most of its length. The coda is a surprise, and I shall not describe it except to comment that the final "amen" cadence—plain *forte*, not emphatic enough for *fortissimo*, nor ready for the pathos of *piano*—is especially characteristic of this symphony.

There is no real slow movement, though the second movement—Andantino con moto, quasi allegretto—brings contrast and repose. Its key, G-sharp minor, is fresh, and remote from any of the places the first movement has visited. In character, the music suggests one of those wistful Schumann or Brahms intermezzi that are neither slow nor quick. Sibelius plays enchantingly with the metrical ambiguity of the melody. After the two-note upbeat, are the next three notes –'–, or are they –''? In other words, are the six beats in each measure to be heard as three times two (ONE two THREE four FIVE six) or as two times three (ONE two three FOUR five six)? As so often with what seem to be either/or questions, the answer is both. Not only can you yourself reverse your hearing of the melody much as you can make the tick-tock of a clock change step, but Sibelius also calls in the basses ever so softly to contradict the flutes and clarinets or the violins in their rhythmic reading. And those basses, though they hardly rise above *mezzo-forte*, want very much to be heard.

Which brings me to another aspect of Sibelius's classical symphonic style. There is no imagery and no drama for you to lose yourself in except that of the musical events themselves. This is like Haydn: you can't do anything with it except listen to it, and it is meant for people who really listen. Just before the end of this second movement, and just for a moment, the conflict of two-against-three becomes troubling rather than charming, and this ambiguous, discreetly mysterious movement ends on a curiously inconclusive note.

The finale is restless. The tempo changes all the time, sometimes abruptly, sometimes gradually. At certain moments, Sibelius can hardly crowd as many notes as he would like to into each measure; at others, he will take time to stand still on a single note, or a pair, or a trill, or an intricately figured chord. Fragments whisk by, some so fast we can hardly apprehend them. Bits of the first two movements whir across the landscape. Shadow becomes substance. Again I quote Tovey: "Then comes the one and all-sufficing climax. All threads are gathered up in one tune that pounds its way to the end with the strokes of Thor's hammer."

Symphony No. 4 in A minor, Opus 63

> *Tempo molto moderato, quasi adagio*
> *Allegro molto vivace*
> *Il tempo largo*
> *Allegro*

Sibelius began work on his Symphony No. 4 in the spring of 1910 and completed the score early in 1911. He conducted the premiere at Helsinki on 3 April 1911 along with *The Dryad*, the Canzonetta for String Orchestra, *In Memoriam*, and *Night Ride and Sunrise*, all composed after 1907. Sibelius dedicated the Symphony No. 4 to his wife's brother, the painter Eero Järnefelt.

Two flutes, two oboes, two clarinets, two bassoons, four horns, two trumpets, three trombones, timpani, "Glocken." (see below), and strings.

The Fourth Symphony, completed not quite four years after the Third, is the extreme point Sibelius reaches as a composer of problematic "modern" music (as Messrs. Damrosch, Muck, and Rogers bear witness below). The most important of his later compositions—the three remaining symphonies and the symphonic poems *Luonnotar*, *The Bard*, *The Oceanides*, and *Tapiola*—affirm the conquests made in the Third and Fourth symphonies.

When Sibelius began work on his new symphony in the quiet of Ainola, the log house he had built at Järvenpää and named for his wife, he had a rich fund of human and musical experience to draw on. He had traveled, most recently to the Koli district in Karelia, where the impact of the rugged hills, unsurveyable expanses of forest, and lead-gray and silver lakes in the crazily changeable, sometimes violent weather was tremendous. New people had come into his life, among them Mahler, Debussy, Arnold Bax, Eugene Goossens, Vincent d'Indy, and Ruskin's and Grieg's friend Mary Wakefield. He had heard new music, including Debussy's *Nocturnes* and *Trois Chansons de Charles d'Orléans*, Elgar's Symphony No. 1, and the cantata *Omar Khayyám* by his friend Granville Bantock, and at Busoni's urging he had bought Schoenberg's Three Piano Pieces, Opus 11. Then, too, there were his own recent compositional explorations: music for Strindberg's *Swanwhite*, the string quartet he called *Voces intimae*, the tone poems *Night Ride and Sunrise* and *In Memoriam*, a good many songs, and the final and remarkable version for strings and percussion of the suite *Rakastava*.

As the Russians began to respond to nationalist stirrings in Finland with new repressive measures, Sibelius had to confront the question of what an artist must or indeed, can do in the face of political crisis and public savagery.[12] He wrote: "I have always hated all empty talk on political questions, all amateurish politicizing. I have tried to make my contribution another way." Now he chose to concentrate on his new symphony, which, he was able to report in December 1910, was "breaking forth in sunshine and strength."

Most crucially, he faced death. The persistent pain in his throat turned out to be caused by a malignant tumor. Surgery in Helsinki was unsuccessful, and Sibelius submitted to a second operation in Berlin. It was a grim experience, physically and emotionally, and even after the removal of the growth the doctors' prognosis was gloomy. But they were wrong. Sibelius survived his tumor by forty-nine years and, after a short period of grumpily endured abstinence, even returned to his black cigars.

How much of all this directly fed the work-in-progress it is impossible to say. The Fourth Symphony is not a tone poem about Karelia, the Russian police, or cancer surgery.[13] Sibelius rejected indignantly one critic's attempt to link the Fourth Symphony to the Koli landscape, detail by

---

[12] In 1809, to punish the Swedes for their refusal to join the blockade of England, Napoleon took Finland away from Sweden, which had conquered it in the twelfth century, and gave the territory to Russia. Under Russia, Finland was an autonomous Grand Duchy, whose Grand Duke, however, happened to be the Tsar of all the Russias. Under Tsars Alexander I and Alexander II, the arrangement worked out not too badly for the Finns. The most brutal of the bad phases began in 1908, the fifteenth year of the reign of Nicholas II, and conditions steadily worsened until his abdication in 1917. Finland proclaimed independence that year.

[13] Composers have on occasion translated their medical experiences into music. Most notably, about 1720, the French composer and bass viol virtuoso Marin Marais wrote a sonata particularizing the operation he had recently undergone for the removal of stones in his bladder, and in Arnold Schoenberg's String Trio of 1946 there are episodes depicting the near-fatal heart attack the composer had suffered that summer. Leonard Bernstein believed that the strange rhythms in the opening moments of Mahler's Ninth Symphony reflected the rhythms of Mahler's own faltering heart.

detail. We should also recall what he wrote in 1931 to Walter Legge, then of the London *Daily Telegraph,* about the difference between his symphonic poems and his symphonies, the latter being "music conceived and worked out in terms of music and with no literary basis. . . . Of course it has happened that, quite unbidden, some mental image has established itself in my mind in connection with a movement I have been writing, but germ and fertilization of my symphonies have been solely musical."

We know, too, how unhappy, really desperate, Sibelius was about the path he thought new music was taking—"All I heard," he wrote to his biographer Karl Ekman, "confirmed my idea of the road I had traveled and had to travel"—and the Fourth Symphony has also been read as a musical protest piece. That Schoenberg's early works for piano did not win his sympathy is hardly surprising. (Sibelius could not have known *Erwartung* and the Five Pieces for Orchestra, both of which would have alarmed him very much more, nor would he have seen or heard anything by Webern or Berg.) More puzzling is what would have disturbed him so deeply about *The Firebird,* Bartók's String Quartet No. 1, and the scores completed in the previous couple of years by Debussy, Ravel, Strauss, Reger, Nielsen, Rachmaninoff, Elgar, Vaughan Williams, or Mahler—to the extent that he even had a chance to get to know them. Perhaps we can find a clue to his alarm in his oft-quoted outburst of scornful irritation: while other composers served gaudy cocktails, he said, he offered the world cold, clear water. It is the rare Sibelius composition whose alcohol and sugar content are zero, though the Symphony No. 4 comes as close as any. And if Sibelius heard and dreaded the "modernism" of Schoenberg's Opus 11 as prophetic, he was amazingly clairvoyant, by gift or by fluke, because to virtually everyone else those pieces would have seemed to exist in terrible, if not mad, isolation—*Zukunftsmusik* with no *Zukunft.* To us, looking at 1911 from the secure distance of more than three-quarters of a century, it is Sibelius's Symphony No. 4 that stands as one of the few visionary and fearless "modern"—permanently "modern" and "difficult"—masterpieces of that time.

Apropos the modernity of the Fourth Symphony: when Walter Damrosch gave the first American performance with the New York Symphony on 2 March 1913, H. E. Krehbiel wrote in the next morning's *Tribune* that the conductor had prefaced the work "with some remarks setting forth the fact that it was music of an anomalous character and protesting that the fact of its performance must not be accepted as an expression of opinion on his part concerning the merit of the composition in whole or in part. He had placed it on the programme only because he considered it a duty toward a distinguished musician whose other beautiful and important works had won admiration." After Karl Muck had led performances in

Boston in 1913 and 1917, Leslie J. Rogers, the Boston Symphony's librarian, wrote into the score what Dr. Muck had said to him after the last of those concerts: "I have rehearsed this symphony nine times and given eight performances and I haven't the faintest idea what the composer means." Mr. Rogers added his own comment: "Futuristic awful!!!"

The hills and winds and waters of Karelia are often described as a landscape to make one feel small. Political powerlessness has the same effect, and the prospect of death—the ultimate powerlessness—does so infinitely more. So should the Fourth Symphony. Aloneness, a sense of the contrast between human and superhuman scale, the impact of enormously concentrated experience—these are perhaps the images that, unbidden, lodged in Sibelius's mind as he conceived and began to fix the musical gestures of his unsettling masterwork.

Sibelius begins with a question. Basses and cellos, *fortissimo* but muted, and also bassoons sound a huge C, from which two other notes, D and F-sharp, detach themselves. The F-sharp falls back to E, and for a long time we hear only a timeless rocking, back and forth, between those two pitches. It is the kraken's roar. I have called it a question. These four notes—C/D/E/F-sharp—are part of a whole-tone scale, an elusive, ambiguous creature all of whose intervals are alike, which therefore presents no articulation and seems to have neither beginning nor end. (It is a famous Debussy trademark, and it is not surprising that, among the new pieces Sibelius had recently heard, he found his French contemporary's *Nocturnes* especially stimulating.)

Then from C to F-sharp is exactly half an octave, that is, halfway from C to the next C. That half-octave interval—it is usually called a tritone (three whole steps)—has, since the Middle Ages, occupied a special place in harmonic reckoning. The keys based on tones a tritone apart are as remote from each other as two keys can be, meaning they have the smallest number of notes in common. The interval itself has a peculiarly pungent sound, and to medieval theorists it was "diabolus in musica." It is a dissonance that demands resolution. The most natural resolution is outward, to a perfect fifth, and that is indeed eventually accomplished in this symphony—in the finale. The possibility of such a resolution is, however, adumbrated as early as the short, sharply rhythmic recitative of trumpets and trombones that interrupts the string tremolandos and tranquil horn calls of this first movement. Moreover, the music heard in the first minutes, including the melody for solo cello and the sevenths it outlines, provides the stuff from which all the rest of the symphony will be drawn. Throughout, as Lionel Pike observes in his remarkable study *Beethoven, Sibelius, and "the Profound Logic,"* harmony and rhythm work hand in hand, always being either restless and off balance together or centered together.

When this questioning, almost slow movement finds its end—curiously, troublingly, inconclusively afloat—the scherzo emerges from it at once: the violins' last A is the cue for the oboe's melody. The tritone disturbs the calm, the dactyls in duple meter disturb the lilt of the opening tune, and the elaborately developed and somber second half of the movement—at half tempo!—disturbs the architectural and expressive set of the whole piece. Such unconventional partitionings are a Sibelius specialty; in the finale of the Third Symphony, for example, he had done the same thing, though with opposite emotional coloration.

The third movement—and this is truly slow music, unlike the first movement, which is *molto moderato and* **quasi** *adagio* (emphasis added)—is the symphony's center, and here—tentatively at first, then more openly—Sibelius sings. He allows himself one lacerating, laconic climax. This music can remind us that when Sibelius heard Bruckner's Fifth Symphony in Berlin it moved him to tears. The Largo ends, as does the first movement, in repetitions and a question mark.

The finale emerges immediately, as the scherzo did from the first movement, its first note being the C-sharp sustained quietly in horns and strings through the Largo's last fifteen measures. The melody itself expands upon an idea proposed softly by clarinets and bassoons when that calm C-sharp in the Largo begins. The allegro quality of the music—in its literal sense of "cheerful" as well as in its musical use to denote a quick tempo—is instantly and seriously compromised by the grinding dissonance that occurs as the second violins join the firsts.

The issue of the tritone is very much alive, and the attempt of the strings to settle on E-flat major (a tritone away from the keynote, A) leads to quite a spat within the orchestra, half amusing, half grim. Now—and the effect is especially striking after the almost ostentatious economy of the first three movements—Sibelius overwhelms us with ideas. The richness of his presentation sets off the coda in which all this music is brought down to the irreducible.

The conductor Herbert Blomstedt has aptly characterized this finale as "an essay in trying to be happy which fails—on purpose." Sibelius's key scheme is interesting in light of this idea. He has gone from the A minor of the first movement to the A major of the finale. This would seem to be the classic symphonic journey *per ardua ad astra*. His route has taken him—and us—through the F major of the second movement and the C-sharp minor of the third, to the finale's A major. Here I suspect a specific—and ironic—reference to the Brahms First. The keys in that work, a true "victory" symphony modeled on the Beethoven Fifth, progress by rising major thirds—C minor to E major to A-flat major to C minor/major. Sibelius, in this Fourth Symphony, also progresses by major thirds, but *his* descend. He has inverted and thus subverted the victory scenario.

Everything is at least reasonably bright until the descending chromatic figure first played by the violins as a strange pendant to the Brucknerian horn chorale demands another way. The music falls back into the minor mode and disintegrates into scarcely audible tremolandi. A single flute voices an appeal, to which the oboe makes crowing and heartless response. The end, *mezzo-forte,* neither affirmative nor pathetic, is shattering in its matter-of-factness.[14]

Finally, a word on bells. In the finale of the Fourth Symphony, Sibelius introduces a sound not used in the first three movements, that of bells. But what kind of bells? The score, first published in 1912 by Breitkopf & Härtel, says "Glocken."—and that is all. "Glocken" means "bells," and it suggests tubular bells. Many conductors have, however, taken this indication to be an abbreviation of "Glockenspiel." To this there are two objections. First, "Glocken." is not a standard abbreviation for Glockenspiel; I have never seen it so used. Second, to cite the period after "Glocken" as evidence that this is an abbreviation won't wash because the printers have put a period after the name of every instrument on the first page of each movement, from "2 Flauti." down to "Contrabasso." To be sure, it is odd that "Glocken." is the only German word amid an otherwise entirely Italian nomenclature, and in at least one case where Sibelius clearly wanted a glockenspiel, in *Lemminkäinen's Journey Home,* he used the Italian word "campanelli."

There would be no problem if the preference for the glockenspiel were not so prevalent among Finnish conductors who worked within ready range of the composer's criticism, if one did not find the glockenspiel on Sir Thomas Beecham's composer-authorized recording for HMV's Sibelius Society, or if in 1935 Sibelius had not written a letter to another English conductor, Leslie Heward, saying "I would suggest to you the using of the Glockenspiel in the Fourth Symphony and of Stahlstäbe for *The Oceanides.*" It would seem that the letter to Heward settles the question; Robert Layton, author of a good book on Sibelius, makes exactly that

---

[14] The score indicates no modification of tempo for this coda, and there are two sharply divergent performance traditions. A few conductors stay rigorously in tempo to the end. (One is Sir Colin Davis, whose haunting image for the last measures is that "a brusque hand smooths the earth over the grave.") Their feeling is that "in tempo" is, like *mezzo-forte,* the stern denial of pathos, and their authority is the score itself. Most conductors soften the tempo to one degree or other so that the decrease in motion matches the decrease in musical action. Their authority is a letter permitting the slackening, from Sibelius to Serge Koussevitzky, whose temperament would not have allowed him to conduct these measures in tempo even with a gun held to his head.

claim. But "Stahlstäbe" (literally steel bars) is another word for the high, bright glockenspiel, and Sibelius clearly intends a distinction between the sounds he wants in the Fourth Symphony and in *The Oceanides*.

Could it be that Sibelius, tangled in two languages, neither one his own, writing "Glockenspiel," was thinking of "Röhrenglockenspiel," a German term sometimes used for a set of tubular bells? Erik Tawaststjerna, the leading Sibelius scholar and biographer in the postwar years, cites another letter in which Sibelius objects to very deep bells—those used, for example, in *Parsifal*, with their gorgeous muddle of overtones—as being "too Oriental," but that is not an objection to standard tubular bells notated, like Sibelius's "Glocken.," in treble clef. Sibelius revised a number of details as the score went through various printings, but he never changed "Glocken.," apparently feeling untroubled by the consequences of any possible unclarity or ambiguity.

In any event, for conductors, variously choosing glockenspiel (these seem the majority at the moment), tubular bells, or even both together, this is an occasion when they must, as interpreters, make a decision. The expressive effect of the icily frivolous glockenspiel is very different from that of the solemn tubular bells, solemn by association as well as by sound.

Sibelius: The Final Three

Plans for Sibelius's last three symphonies grew simultaneously. Here is the composer on 20 May 1918 in a letter to an unknown recipient:

> My new works, partly sketched and planned. The Fifth Symphony in a new form—practically composed anew—I work at daily. . . . The whole— if I may say so—a spirited intensification to the end (climax). Triumphal.
>
> The Sixth Symphony is wild and impassioned in character. Somber, with pastoral contrasts. Probably in four movements, with the end rising to a somber roaring of the orchestra, in which the main theme is drowned.
>
> The Seventh Symphony. Joy of life and *vitalité* with *appassionata* passages. In three movements—the last a "Hellenic Rondo."
>
> All this with due reservations. . . . It looks as though I shall come out with all three of these symphonies at the same time. . . . As usual, the sculptural is more prominent in my music. Hence this hammering on the ethical line that takes hold of me entirely and on which I must concentrate and hold out. . . .
>
> With regard to symphonies VI and VII, the plans may possibly be altered, depending on the way my musical ideas develop. As usual I am a slave

to my themes and submit to their demands. From all this I see how my innermost self has changed since the days of the Fourth Symphony. And these new symphonies of mine are more in the nature of professions of faith than my other works.[15]

The version of the Symphony No. 5 with which Sibelius was then occupied was already the third, and it would be completed and performed in the fall of 1919. The Sixth and Seventh symphonies were finished in 1923 and 1924 after an interval, one of many in Sibelius's life, filled with works of relatively little substance.

Sibelius's ideas did indeed develop differently and the plans were altered accordingly. The Sixth, an oddly shy and veiled work, deliciously ambiguous, defies characterization in just two adjectives, but "wild and impassioned" is nowhere near right. "Somber, with pastoral contrasts" is possible, and it does have four movements. And very little of what Sibelius imagined about the Seventh Symphony in 1918 was realized in the score he completed six years later.

Speaking later to his biographer Karl Ekman, Sibelius acknowledged:

My due reservation about the two new symphonies was fully justified. The Fifth . . . was not completed in its final form until the fall of 1919, and a long time was to elapse before its successors appeared [in February 1923 and March 1924], and then not in the form I had originally intended. The final form of one's work is indeed dependent on powers that are stronger than oneself. Later on one can substantiate this or that, but on the whole one is merely a tool. This wonderful logic—let us call it God—that governs a work is the forcing power.[16]

In an article on "Some Aspects of Form in the Symphonies of Sibelius" (*Music Review*, May 1949), W. G. Hill pointed out a number of thematic correspondences among the later symphonies. It is as though, while Sibelius worked, the contents of the two imaginary drawers labeled VI and VII got themselves mixed up, eventually to be sorted out in quite different ways. The Seventh Symphony is intense, frighteningly appassionato (if not "wild"). In its amazing close—a musical gesture that should leave a witness bereft of speech and to which one responds with concert-hall applause only in order not to explode—we can recognize the "somber roaring" Sibelius had imagined as the ending of the Sixth.

[15] Karl Ekman, *Jean Sibelius* (London: Alan Wilmer, 1936).
[16] Ibid.

Symphony No. 5 in E-flat major, Opus 82

Tempo molto moderato—Allegro moderato—Presto
Andante mosso, quasi allegretto
Allegro molto—Misterioso—Un pochettino largamente

Sibelius completed his Symphony No. 5 in time for his fiftieth-birthday celebrations in 1915 and conducted the Helsinki Municipal Orchestra in the first performance on the day itself. With the same orchestra, he introduced a radically revised version on 14 December 1916. The edition always used today is the result of still further revisions, completed in the fall of 1919; this too was first played in Helsinki under the composer's direction, on 21 October 1921.

Two flutes, two oboes, two clarinets, two bassoons, four horns, three trumpets, three trombones, timpani, and strings.

On the evening of his fiftieth birthday, an event celebrated in Finland as a national holiday, Jean Sibelius led the Helsinki Municipal Orchestra in a program of his own music: the two Serenades for violin, a symphonic poem called *The Oceanides* that he had written for his first visit to America the year before, and the new and eagerly anticipated Fifth Symphony. His status as a cultural hero at home had been established almost twenty-four years earlier with the premiere of *Kullervo*, a massive work for voices and orchestra based on the *Kalevala*, the Finnish national epic. The success of his Second Symphony of 1902 had made him a name abroad. Audiences in Latin countries tended—and still tend—to resist Sibelius, but he was taken very seriously in Germany and received in England and the United States with a welcome that bordered on idolatry. He had been granted a government pension designed to keep him in Finland, and that allowed him to concentrate wholly on composition. Until 1920, when the long-distance runner Paavo Nurmi won two gold medals at the Antwerp Olympic Games, Sibelius was the only Finn whose name was known throughout the world, and his compatriots were fiercely proud of him.

Sibelius's visit to America, where the festivities included the conferral of an honorary doctorate at Yale, was, for him, the zenith of international recognition. Coming home, he heard in mid-Atlantic the news of the assassination at Sarajevo of the heir to the Austrian throne. He had scarcely settled into his life again when, to his disbelief and horror, virtually all Europe was at war. Feeling sure that his best contribution to the world was through music, he concentrated on the composition of the new symphony he had promised to deliver in time for his birthday celebration.

Most of Sibelius's compositions were with a German publisher, which meant he was cut off from his royalties for the duration of the war. Trying to deal with the resulting financial hardship, he produced some potboilers for the Danish house of Hansen. Professional and public distractions made it hard to work, but the Fifth Symphony was completed on time.

Sibelius revised it twice before he was satisfied, pulling the original four movements together into three, striving ever for concentration. A letter written in May 1918 describes hopes and progress of the third version: "The Fifth Symphony in a new form—practically composed anew—I work at daily. Movement I entirely new, movement II reminiscent of the old, movement III reminiscent of the end of movement I of the old. Movement IV the old motifs, but stronger in revision. The whole, if I may say so, a vital climax to the end. Triumphal." Not until the spring of 1919 did political stability return to Finland, and it was only in the fall of that year that the Fifth Symphony attained its final form.

At the end of September 1914 Sibelius had jotted these words into his notebook: "In a deep valley again. But I already begin to see dimly the mountain that I shall certainly ascend. . . . God opens His door for a moment and His orchestra plays the Fifth Symphony." God's orchestra begins with an utterly distinctive sound, a chord of E-flat major so idiosyncratically voiced and scored that it says "Sibelius Five" as unmistakably as certain other E-flat chords say *Emperor* or *Eroica*. The chord presents itself in its least stable position, with B-flat in the bass. The B-flat is a soft timpani roll, the G and E-flat are played by French horns. Two more horns add their voices, and one of them detaches itself to play a softly musing call. This in turn elicits a three-note echo in flutes and oboes.

These are characteristically Sibelian materials: brief, and emerging a bit mysteriously from the orchestral texture. Sibelius offers a few more ideas: a slowly whirling figure in thirds, played by various woodwind couples and leading directly into a conjunct, slower phrase for flute and clarinet; an exclamation, also with woodwinds, and beginning with a Scotch snap, that is, a short and accented note followed by a long and unaccented one; a sequence of chords in crescendo, cutting through the prevailing 12/8 meter in tense cross-rhythms; and yet another Scotch snap idea.

This gives Sibelius plenty from which to generate a movement whose originality is as remarkable as its clarity. First he lets us hear all this music again, but with the harmonic perspective interestingly realigned. That is to say, the first "exposition," like its counterpart in every classical symphony, modulates to a new key; the repeat, however, stays in the original key. Now that he is sure we know the material, Sibelius transforms it with captivating diversity. To describe the first phase, I cannot find better words than Donald Tovey's: the conjunct flute and clarinet phrase "is worked up into a wonderful mysterious kind of fugue which quickens (by 'diminution') into a cloudy chromatic trembling, through which its original figure moans in the clarinet and bassoon."[17] (Sibelius actually marks these moans "lugubre" and "patetico.")

In the second phase, the exclamation with the Scotch snap makes its presence known again, but at a broader tempo than before and with new passion. Suddenly the tempo quickens, and the very first theme becomes part of a dance tune. This is in effect the symphony's scherzo, made of already known materials. As this scherzo unfolds, Sibelius gradually accelerates from allegro moderato via vivace molto to presto and più presto. Forgetting that it started out as part of the first movement's development, the scherzo behaves as though it were an independent entity entitled to a trio, and the trumpet does in fact begin a trio. The scherzo's recapitulation then pulls the whole structure together dramatically, reaffirming the original key and serving as recapitulation for the entire movement. The last, obsessively repeated chord that spins the whole orchestra into dizziness consists of the four notes of the horn call that was the symphony's very first thematic idea.

The second movement is best described as variations on a rhythm. This thematic rhythm is simple: two groups each of five quarter-notes and separated by a quarter rest. Six different tunes occur in this movement, and they are all variants of this twice-five-note pattern. But before the five-note figures begin, we hear some sustained introductory woodwind chords. They do more, however, than prepare the five-note theme. They are a constant presence in this movement, throughout whose course we feel the contrast between the leisure of those chords and the gentle but persistent energy of the five-note rhythm. Contrast becomes tension. This movement can be played for charm, but it is deeply resistant to treatment that so constricts its expressive range. Those long notes in the woodwinds generate dissonance, and there is an element of unease in this music that the touchingly sweet final cadence fails to dispel. One detail should be mentioned. Twice the variations are supported by a bass in broadly swinging half-notes:

---

[17]Diminution means the appearance of a theme in smaller note values, therefore at a quicker tempo. —M.S.

Ex. 1

Of this we shall hear more.

The second movement was in G major, the first movement's secondary key. Now Sibelius restores the symphony's long-range harmonic balance by beginning the finale in a tremendous whirring and buzzing in the original key of E-flat. When the agitation subsides, the two pairs of French horns set up a kind of antiphonal tolling that is in fact the broadly swinging bass from the second movement. Much-divided strings accompany this by playing the same music subtly out of phase. Woodwinds and cellos turn the horn theme itself into an accompaniment by superimposing a new melody of their own, one that begins in characteristically Sibelian fashion on a long note emerging from a weak beat. Sibelius traverses all this territory once more, with new harmonic perspectives revealed the second time around. And that, in a sense, is all.

It is not, of course, all. This finale is an extraordinary object, entangled almost to the end in musical complexity. Strings sing impassioned melodies in *forte* and *fortissimo,* but with their mutes on! The thicket of dissonance becomes so tangled that the great tolling cuts through only with effort, even when the trumpets take it up. We know from the Second Symphony that Sibelius can write a victorious ending with the best of them, but that is not what he gives us here. He resolves the ferocious harmonic and textural dissonance by drastic means. There is an imperious command for silence. Then, four chords and two unisons enforce order, six sharp reports that, as the English writer Harold Truscott puts it, "carry without effort the weight of the whole work." And no matter how often we hear the Fifth Symphony, their sound and their timing can never cease to stun.

Symphony No. 6, Opus 104

> *Allegro molto moderato*
> *Allegretto moderato*
> *Poco vivace*
> *Allegro molto*

Sibelius made his first plans for his Symphony No. 6 in 1918, but completed the score only in February 1923, himself conducting the first performance in Helsinki on the 19th of that month.

Two flutes, two oboes, two clarinets and bass clarinet, two bassoons, four horns, three trumpets, three trombones, timpani, harp, and strings.

This is as strange a symphony as I know, and there are few after Schubert I love so much. The second half of that sentence is autobiography and not important; let me, however, try to explain the first. In the Sibelius Sixth, breezy Beethoven Eighth physical energy keeps house with music that is mysteriously discarnate. There is no slow movement; indeed, there is virtually no slow music. The beautiful and distinctive orchestral sound is black and white, though without ever inviting such a word as "austere." It is also singularly weightless, the bass instruments underemployed, as though gravity tended up toward the treble. (For another contradiction, the bass clarinet, which Sibelius used in no other symphony, most particularly contributes to defining the special sound of the Sixth.)

More than anything, it is the harmony. It is not dissonant like the music Sibelius's younger contemporaries Schoenberg and Bartók were writing at the same time, not even as dissonant as some of Ravel's music of the early 1920s. It is not as ambiguous, as allusive-elusive, as what Debussy had written in the previous decade or as the mysteries Sibelius found in the work of his friend Busoni. It is not as impacted and dense, therefore not as "difficult" as some of what Beethoven had written a hundred years before. Sibelius does, however, defy custom and expectation by his embrace of modal rather than tonal harmony. This choice also removes many familiar rhetorical devices from his thesaurus.

The dominance of major and minor keys in Western music is a relatively recent phenomenon, one that began in the seventeenth century. (It has been seriously questioned through much of the twentieth century.) Earlier, melodies and harmonies were derived from patterns other than the particular distributions that form our familiar major and minor scales. These other modes, which still bear the Greek names arbitrarily assigned to them by medieval theorists, have never quite gone away. They survived in folk music and by that avenue made their way into some concert music that is nourished by folk idioms: Mussorgsky's *Boris Godunov*, for example, before its gentrification by Rimsky-Korsakov, or some of Vaughan Williams. Composers have also found the modes useful for the evocation of a certain religious atmosphere: Beethoven provides notable examples in the *Hammerklavier* Sonata, the *Missa solemnis*, and the Song of Thanksgiving in his String Quartet, Opus 132.

Every recording I have seen of the Sibelius Sixth, and most concert programs as well, get the tag "D minor" into the title. But Sibelius's autograph says nothing about D minor; neither does the first edition of the printed score by Hirsch (Stockholm) or the currently available one by Hansen (Copenhagen). Sibelius and his publishers are of course right. D is the all-important central note of the Sixth Symphony, the note that exerts the magnetic pull of a keynote, but what Sibelius builds upon that note is not D minor but D Dorian. Play all the white notes from D to D on the piano, and you have entered the Dorian mode. A D-minor scale has a spicier distribution of whole- and half-steps at the upper end, and those raised and lowered notes, make all the difference. It is the C-sharp in the D-minor scale, or its counterpart in other scales, that makes possible the physicality, the definiteness, of the most familiar cadence in Western music, that big dominant-to-tonic landing. Here Sibelius tends to avoid the C-sharp and everything it implies, and from that avoidance—or from his choice of the other way—comes that atmosphere of mystery and incorporeality that is so characteristic of the Sixth Symphony.

It begins with two soprano voices: the second violins divided into two sections. It is as though we had suddenly tuned in to them in mid-phrase; indeed, to begin in medias res is a favorite Sibelian strategy, one we find in all his symphonies from No. 4 on. These sopranos descend, but slightly out of phase, so as to create expressively dissonant suspensions, and they are soon joined by violas (to make a bass) and by another pair of sopranos (first violins, also divided into two sections).[18] As critics have pointed out since Cecil Gray's *Sibelius* (1931), this is Sibelius's productive channeling of his love for Palestrina and other Renaissance masters. Especially characteristic is the dynamic marking, neither an assertive *forte* nor a "sensitive" *piano* but a neutral *mezzo-forte*.

This vocal music continues for some time until a new color and a new dimension are added: the first sound of wind instruments (two oboes, one holding a D, the other climbing a scale from D to A) and the first real bass line (cellos, descending stepwise from F through E to D). Sibelius makes it characteristically anti-emphatic by introducing both oboes and cellos in mid-measure (though not together) and by placing each of the bass notes to one side of the downbeat rather than squarely on it.

Now that he has acknowledged he is writing an orchestral piece, Sibelius allows himself first one of his special thumb-prints, the Noah's-Ark pairing of woodwind couples in undulating phrases, then another, one of those mysteriously receding and swelling chords for brass and drums. Some-

---

[18] Here is another depressing instance of bartering away a beautiful musical effect for the sake of the alleged convenience of seating the second violins on the left, screened by the firsts, instead of on the conductor's right, where the composers who wrote our central orchestral repertory thought they belonged and assumed them to be sitting.

thing else needs to be said about the drums (aside from quoting Sibelius's cross comment that most people seem not to realize that percussion players should be musical too), which is that the timpani are tuned to A, C, and F in the first movement, with nothing for the central D. Similarly, the second movement has no drum tuned to G, the note on which that part is centered, and the first time we hear a drum play the keynote is in the last four measures of the third movement. Here is another means of producing the Sixth Symphony's anti-emphasis and anti-gravity.

Earlier I made much of the absence of C-sharp from Sibelius's harmonic cosmos in this work, that C-sharp whose presence would define D minor. There is in fact a C-sharp in the opening music, just one, played by the lowest of the four sections of violins and held for two beats. To be sure, it appears on a weak beat, but the striking and expressive chord whose bass it is also gets the only accent mark in the first forty-eight measures. The chord is a discreet but distinct invitation to alertness, and sure enough, after the woodwinds have begun their pairwise wanderings, the same chord reappears, more fully scored this time for all the strings plus oboes, clarinets, and bassoons. Not only does it appear, it appears quite insistently. It is immediately contradicted by a chord gradually built up by brass and drums (trombones, then trumpets making their first appearance here) and—by now one can say "of course"—all on weak beats and offbeats. This interfering chord is a chord of C major, the firmest possible message of "No, not C-sharp, C-natural!" In the context of the Renaissance polyphony of the strings and the mellifluous thirds of the Noah's-Ark winds, this dissonance stands in bold relief. And with that, Sibelius has established one of the basic assumptions for the dialectic of his Sixth Symphony, the clash of tonal and modal elements, and, beyond that, the tension between adjacent semitones (for example, C-sharp and C-natural).

I have given all this space to just two minutes of music because attention to what Sibelius posits here is a way into the symphony as a whole. The first movement has, at the moment of this C-major interruption, found its real sense of pace, an Allegro—molto moderato—swinging along in ample steps. Sibelius gives us music greatly varied in density and of many characters: winding melodies in thirds, phrases of broad string tunes, restless kaleidoscopic series of canons for plucked strings. Sometimes exuberant, more often reticent and oblique, it all moves toward a coda full of mysterious buzzings and silences. This coda brings the first *fortissimo,* and this occurs abruptly on a chord of E-flat major, one dangerous semitone away from the central D. There is a great buildup to C major—brass and drums and another *fortissimo*—and in four laconic measures, weightless, unsentimental, in tempo, and back on D Dorian, Sibelius brushes the whole thing away.

The second movement starts with a soft triple rap on a drum, the same gesture he would use to begin his Seventh Symphony. The response to this quiet call for attention is a series of soft chords for flutes and bassoons. These chords are strangely and beguilingly afloat, and for a while you have no idea what the tempo, the meter, or the harmonic center will turn out to be. At first the chords are all placed delicately between the beats of the emerging 3/4. In the most leisurely way, the harmony moves toward the Dorian, though transposed so that the magnet note is G. (Those first drum notes were on F-natural, the very note that defines G Dorian as distinct from G minor, which would have F-sharp.) The harp, which Sibelius uses in no other symphony, makes a significant contribution here. The opening music is the nearest Sibelius comes to a slow movement, and it is not very near. This is fascinating music, asymmetrical, continuously evolving, each new element bringing quicker subdivisions of the beat, until once again, in a phrase that is curt but not brusque, Sibelius says "Thank you, that will be enough."

The third movement, the scherzo, is as close as Sibelius comes here to "normal" music, but you should take nothing for granted. We are back in D Dorian, but the chord behind the engagingly hopping violin melody is queerly distributed, with just one horn playing D against a rich supply of A's and F's. The drum does not admit to having a D until the very last bars, so here it adds to the F's. Sibelius draws a delightful diversity of rhythmic patterns from his steady 6/8 meter. The hopping tune in fact sounds like a dotted 2/4 whose dottedness is a bit exaggerated in performance, but we also hear flowing eighth-notes, great swirls of sixteenths, and a wide-eyed stalking canon for woodwinds and harp in slow notes. Twice the heavy brass, abetted by harp and drums, divert the harmonic flow with a peremptory bark, and after the second of these, the movement flees toward its emphatic close.

The finale begins with music that sounds like the Tchaikovsky Serenade arranged for antiphonal Renaissance choirs, basses answering trebles. This kind of grandeur does not return, but Sibelius has saved his most impassioned and dramatic outbursts for this movement. It is also here that, for the only time other than the end of the scherzo, he permits himself the non-oblique gesture of a *fortissimo* on D, thus actually lining up harmonic, rhythmic, and dynamic stresses. The music gains constantly in intensity and speed, suddenly to broaden out into a coda in whose brief duration Sibelius extracts a moment of passion unlike any other in the work. This he does with amazing economy—through the force of his harmony and through the rhythmic distension he creates with just two fermatas. From there he moves into one of his chillingly detached endings. Violins alone hold a D, disappearing into the silence from which, a short half-hour earlier, Sibelius had conjured those soprano singers. The final fermata is not over the D but over the silence that follows it.

Sibelius must have the last word. Of his Sixth Symphony he once said: "You may analyze it and explain it theoretically. You may find that there are several interesting things going on. But most people forget that it is, after all, a poem."[19]

Symphony No. 7, Opus 105

Adagio—Vivacissimo—Adagio—Allegro moderato—Adagio

Sibelius completed his Symphony No. 7, as he noted in his diary, "on the second day of March 1924, at night" and conducted the first performance in Stockholm three weeks later, on 24 March.

Two flutes, two oboes, two clarinets, two bassoons, four horns, three trumpets, three trombones, timpani, and strings.

The Seventh Symphony begins with a soft triple rap on a drum. It is a call to attention, a summons, to which the strings respond with a scale that rises mysteriously from the depths of the orchestra, the basses slightly out of phase in the Brahmsian manner. The music lands on a chord as strange in sonority as it is in harmonic implication. The quiet matter-of-factness of the triple drumbeat, the nature of the response, its quickness, the range of conversational possibilities suggested by the disparity between the C-major scale and the A-flat-minor chord (itself poised uneasily on an E-flat timpani roll)—all these things make it seem not like the beginning of a discourse but like the resumption of one long in progress and but briefly interrupted.

So in a sense it is. Sibelius is one of those artists—Mahler and Thomas Mann, Stravinsky and Picasso, Balanchine and Gide are others—whose lifework is of a piece, whose major statements are in conversation

---

[19]Yes, elsewhere Sibelius does maintain that his symphonies are symphonies, not symphonic poems, but artists do contradict themselves and we have to let them.

with one another, extending, confirming, arguing, contradicting, but always continuing. The seven symphonies of Sibelius with their grand precursor *Kullervo* reward study as a group.

The Seventh Symphony did not, as Sibelius had projected in 1918, turn out to be in three movements; rather, it is a single movement, some twenty-one or twenty-two minutes long. Almost up to the day of the first performance, Sibelius called it *Fantasia sinfonica.*[20] Within that span, tempo and character change often. The sequence reads this way (the stresses are mine):

Adagio—Vivacissimo—Adagio—Allegro molto moderato—*Allegro moderato*—Vivace—Presto—Adagio—Largamente molto—Affettuoso—Tempo I.

These changes are not of equal weight, and we do not hear them all as structural or expressive markers. The *Allegro moderato*, for example, is a real tempo and a real movement, but the preceding Allegro molto moderato is only a brief transitional upbeat to it.[21] Similarly, Vivace and Presto are only successive intensifications of that *Allegro moderato*. Largamente molto and Affettuoso are intensifications of the *Adagio*, and the final Tempo I is only four measures long. The purpose of my italics, therefore, is to indicate the "real" movements. The twice-recurring Adagio is the same music. This now suggests that something does after all remain of Sibelius's original three-movement plan: Adagio, Vivacissimo, and Allegro moderato. Or, elaborating a bit, we can say Sibelius gives us an Adagio, which is the symphony's single biggest section; a scherzo-like Vivacissimo; a sonata-like Allegro moderato, reached by way of a brief reappearance of the Adagio; and a spacious and weighty coda, which actually begins with a brief (and immediately decelerating) Presto, but most of which consists of a final return to the Adagio.

What makes this interesting, what makes it arresting and powerful, is that Sibelius has made these three movements plus coda into a single piece—and *how* he has done it. Robert Layton has written: "The Seventh consummates the nineteenth-century search for symphonic unity." That search for a formal principle which enables a composer to write one movement that is at the same time several movements—or, if you prefer, several movements that function as the parts of a single movement—is usually reckoned to have begun with Schubert's *Wanderer* Fantasy. Liszt was one of the bold explorers, and his Piano Sonata is his magisterial achievement in this realm. The symphonic poems of Strauss are in this tradition, and

---

[20] Schumann went through the same thing with the revised version of his Symphony No. 4, planning to title it *Symphonische Phantasie*, but withdrawing from that idea at the last moment.
[21] The Italian for "movement" is "tempo."

before Sibelius, the great twentieth-century examples were given to us by
Arnold Schoenberg in his String Quartet No. 1 and Chamber Symphony
No. 1.

The changing tempi in the Seventh Symphony are not merely a condition of Sibelius's task; his control of speed is the very key to his awesome
mastery of transition both on the grandest as well as on the minutest scale.
Gratefully, I quote a fancifully evocative paragraph by Donald Tovey, who
particularly emphasizes this aspect of the Seventh Symphony:

> If [the listener] cannot tell when or where the tempo changes, that is
> because Sibelius has achieved the power of moving like aircraft, with the
> wind or against it. An aeronaut carried with the wind has no sense of move-
> ment at all; but Sibelius's airships are roomy enough for the passengers to
> dance if they like: and the landscape, to say nothing of the sky-scape, is not
> always too remote for them to judge of the movement of the ship by external
> evidence. Sibelius has not only mastered but has made a system of that kind
> of movement which Wagner established for music-drama. . . . He moves
> in the air and can change his pace without breaking his movement. The
> tempi in his Seventh Symphony range from a genuine adagio to a genuine
> prestissimo. Time really moves slowly in the adagio, and the prestissimo
> arouses the listener's feeling of muscular movement instead of remaining a
> slow affair written in the notation of a quick one. But nobody can tell how
> or when the pace, whether muscular or vehicular, has changed. [22]

I have described the way the work begins—the soft rap for attention
on the drum, the measured ascent of the strings, the strange minor chord
that so quietly yet so firmly disrupts this process. We hear a quick phrase
for flutes and bassoons, as Marc Mandel has written in a Boston Symphony
program note, "fluttering like birds against an ocean backdrop," and a compressed echo of it on clarinets. We hear fragments of scales, in contrary
motion, at different speeds, in various rhythmic articulations.

Then, and more powerful for being set in this context of epigrams
and interruptions, Sibelius lays down an extraordinary sustained passage, a
rich polyphony for all the strings, which he has divided into nine sections.
In this passage there is more than a touch of Palestrina, whose music had
first engaged his imagination in Italy in 1901 and which assumed increasing
importance to him over the years. The crescendo in this paragraph is a
journey into daylight and also a journey toward C major. It is characteristic
of Sibelius that important entities in his music do not always announce
themselves as important; thus it is that a phrase played quite unassumingly

[22] D. F. Tovey: *Essays in Musical Analysis*, Vol. 6 (Oxford: Oxford University Press, 1939).

by the violins immediately after the ocean-bird woodwinds now turns out to be of considerable significance and is sung forthrightly by flutes, oboes, and horns. But even this turns out to be preparatory for the most critical event so far, a solemn proclamation of a single trombone asserting itself with effortless splendor through the polyphonic thicket.

This statement by the trombone is the culmination of a process of concentration, of gathering in. Now the music begins again to diffuse, to move by fragments, by suggestion, also to escape from the magnetic field of C major. The pace quickens until we find ourselves in the midst of a wild dance with rapidly alternating tattoos of woodwinds and strings. After a while we realize that the exceedingly fast notes have been subordinated to an enormously broader tempo. As Tovey, staying with his flight image, has it: ". . . this muscular energy becomes absorbed quite imperceptibly into the vast cloud-laden air currents through and over which [the trombone theme] returns in solemn adagio with C-minor harmony." In other words, the fast notes are still there, but they are now the swirling accompaniment to the immensely slow beats of the adagio measures. This second appearance of the trombone's command, more insistent than before and embedded in the sounds of heavy brass, marks one of the major articulation points in the Seventh Symphony.

Again the pace quickens, this time to arrive at the energetic, forward-thrusting "third movement," the Allegro moderato. The music gets faster, but it is a typically Sibelian paradox that the attainment of highest speed, the presto, marks the beginning of yet another great slowing. The pounding quarter-notes themselves are held back and, as in the earlier transition from scherzo to Adagio, the quick notes change their meaning and become the accompaniment to an immensely slow music. This music is the third great *tuba mirum* summons of the trombone. This time it leads to a climax more wrenching, more anguished than any we have yet experienced in this symphony. Woodwinds and brass abandon the strings, leaving them to their outcry. Then comes collapse, a scattering of echoes of the ocean-bird phrases, harmonies that descend and descend, a fierce gripping of C major, a sudden and violently dissonant crescendo that is cut off with terrifying finality. As Sir Colin Davis, one of the great Sibelius conductors, has said, it is the closing of the coffin lid.

No non-work in the history of music has been so much written and talked about as the Eighth Symphony of Jean Sibelius. Several conductors claimed to have had it promised to them. Many musicians, scholars, and other visitors to Ainola, the composer's country villa, reported that Sibelius had hinted at or even confirmed its existence. There is no Eighth Symphony. There may have been, at least there may have been some sketches, but there is not now. After 1926, Sibelius wrote no major composition in the remaining thirty-one years of his life. Perhaps whatever he got down of the Eighth, assuming there was something, did not meet his standards, which were, for his symphonies, of the utmost severity. Perhaps he felt—it is arrogant to say "realized," though it is the word I want—that, while he had left room for that darkly elusive postscript, the great tone poem *Tapiola,* he could not add another symphony. He was, almost incomparably, a master of final cadences, the handsomely satisfying kind and the deeply disturbing. In that crunch of instruments converging on a chord of C major in his Seventh Symphony he had said, and has said beyond recall, The End.

Igor Stravinsky

Igor Fedorovich Stravinsky was born at Oranienbaum, Russia (now Lomonosov in the Northwest Petersburg Region of Russia) on 18 June 1882 and died in New York City on 6 April 1971.

Stung by the Dadaists' dislike of his most recent novel, *Les Caves du Vatican*, André Gide wrote in his journal for 24 June 1924: "Each of my books turns against those who were enthusiastic for the preceding one. That will teach them to applaud me only for the right reasons and to take each of my books simply for what it is: a work of art."

Mutatis mutandis, this is something Stravinsky might have said. An admirer of Stravinsky's early ballet scores asked the composer why, since he used to write such beautiful music, had he stopped. Came the reply, "Why did *you* stop?" For the last fifty-some years of his life, Stravinsky infuriated his admirers by refusing to develop predictably, by constantly turning to new borrowed conventions with which to extend and modify his personal style, by writing works that seemed to turn "against those who were enthusiastic for the preceding one."

In his seventies, when the music world had come to assume that a Stravinsky-Schoenberg dichotomy was as God-given as sunrise in the East, Stravinsky shocked everyone by writing serial music (which naturally sounded unmistakably—and wonderfully—like Stravinsky). Of course, he was then a revered figure, indulged even in that unpopular departure. As a younger man, not at all revered, he had enraged the musical world far more in his so-called neoclassical period, which extends from 1920, the year of *Pulcinella*, to 1951, when he finished *The Rake's Progress*. He was rebuked for turning his back on his Russian heritage (a crucial point particularly, but by no means exclusively, in Soviet commentary) and even more for indulging, as his critics saw it, in a series of stylistic masquerades, something that demonstrated to them his lack of a true artistic and moral core. When I wrote the first version of this essay around 1970, I remarked that except in the Soviet Union and perhaps *The New York Times,* one was no longer likely to encounter such criticism, and even 1963 was a surprisingly late date at which to find so pungently representative an example of the genre as Paul Henry Lang's poison-pen introduction to the collection of essays he edited under the title *Stravinsky, a New Appraisal of His Work.* In the 1990s, the Russians seem to have calmed down on the subject of Stravinsky, and the *Times* is busy bashing other composers of "advanced" tendencies.

In 1907, when he was still studying with Rimsky-Korsakov, Stravinsky wrote a symphony—in part, I suppose, to be respectable, in part as an exercise of craft. It is rather like some of the Glazunov symphonies, Stravinsky then much admiring this semi-senior of his: in hindsight (about fifty-two years' worth), Stravinsky remarked that the only bad omen at the first performance was that Glazunov came to him afterward saying, "very nice, very nice." That early Symphony in E-flat is an attractive piece and not bad at all; it's just that from the composer of *The Firebird* and the *Requiem Canticles* and two or three dozen masterpieces in between, one expects so much more.

In any event, it was years before Stravinsky wrote another symphony. *Symphonies of Wind Instruments* (1920) suggests "symphony," but Stravinsky really meant "symphonies" literally as "sounding together," and this great tombeau for Debussy, once thought so forbiddingly austere, now so enjoyable with its spiky rhythms and piercing colors, in no way occupies symphonic space. The *Symphony of Psalms* (1930), which would be my candidate if I could save just one twentieth-century score from a new Flood, is obviously a special case, too. So the two real Stravinsky symphonies are the Symphony in C, begun in 1938 in his second country, France, and finished in 1940 in his third, the United States, and the "all-American" Symphony in Three Movements.

They make a wonderful pair, these two 1940s siblings. First you notice the differences: the Symphony in C, Apollonian, rooted in Haydn, so generously melodic, a work of polished surfaces and sharply defined corners; the Symphony in Three Movements totally a child of the twentieth century, making unimaginable capital of studiedly neutral material (like Beethoven), Dionysian, fierce, and sometimes even unmannerly in its energy. Then, as you listen harder and get to know them better, you hear how, while the distinctness of character never blurs, both works, like all of Stravinsky's best, are Apollonian and Dionysian together, and how both are so personal and unmistakably Stravinskian.

Symphony in C

Moderato alla breve
Larghetto concertato
Allegretto
Largo—Tempo giusto, alla breve

Stravinsky began the first movement of the Symphony in C in Paris in the fall of 1938, completing it at Sancellemoz, Switzerland, on 17 April 1939, and composed the second movement at Sancellemoz between 27 April and 19 July. (Work on both movements was interrupted for concerts in Italy, Stravinsky then being to a dismaying degree an admirer of the Fascist enterprise.) He wrote the Allegretto in Cambridge, Massachusetts, during the winter of 1939–40, completing it on 28 April (he dated it in the manuscript according to the Russian calendar, "Easter, April 15. Boston"), and finished the finale in Beverly Hills, California, on 17 August 1940. The work was commissioned by Mrs. Robert Woods Bliss for a fee of $1500; with the blessing of Mrs. Bliss, the work was offered as a gift to the Chicago Symphony Orchestra in celebration of its fiftieth anniversary. Stravinsky earned an additional $1000 from the sale of the manuscript to the Library of Congress, to which, new to this country, he referred to as "the National Library of the White House." Stravinsky conducted the Chicago Symphony in the premiere on 7 November 1940.[1] The manuscript bears the dedication "À la gloire de Dieu," but this is omitted from the printed score.

[1] Mildred Bliss, described by Sir Kenneth Clark as "the Queen of Georgetown," was a discerning and generous patron of music and the visual arts, as was her husband, Robert Woods Bliss, former ambassador to Argentina. Their Washington mansion, Dumbarton Oaks, which houses the Blisses' formidable collection of Byzantine, Early Christian, and Coptic art as well as an important library, was the site of a conference in 1944 at which representatives of China, Great Britain, the Soviet Union, and the United States met to make the first plans for what would become the United Nations. In 1937, Mr. and Mrs. Bliss commissioned Stravinsky's *Dumbarton Oaks* Concerto, which had its first performance in their home on their thirtieth wedding anniversary. The Bliss money came from the manufacture of Castoria, an evil-tasting dark brown patent medicine concocted from castor oil and cough repressants with which millions of American children were threatened, dosed, and perhaps cured in the first half of the twentieth century.

Three flutes (third doubling piccolo), two oboes, two clarinets, two bassoons, four horns, two trumpets, three trombones, bass tuba, timpani, and strings.

The Symphony in C, with its defiantly anti-modernist, almost insolent title, was regarded with deep suspicion when it was new. Conductors would not touch it, and for some years it was played only where Stravinsky himself had an opportunity to program it, a broadcast by Leopold Stokowski and the NBC Symphony in 1943 being the single exception in America.[2] Robert Craft gave New York its first concert performance of the work in April 1948, an event of singular and unforeseen significance in that the correspondence preparatory to it—the score was still unpublished!—was the beginning of the important Stravinsky-Craft friendship. Virgil Thomson suggested in his review of Craft's concert that

> the attractiveness of Stravinsky's whole neo-Classic production lies . . . less in the expressive power of any given work than in the musical language in which they are all written.
>
> This is a compound of grace and of brusqueness thoroughly Russian in its charm and its rudeness and so utterly sophisticated intellectually that few musicians of intellectual bent can resist it. The general public has never cared much about modern neo-Classicism, but does listen to it more easily than it used to. I don't think musical ticket buyers are overfond of indirectness, and certainly most of anybody's neo-Classic works are indirect. Every now and then, however, one of them forgets its game of reminding you about the history of music and starts saying things of its own. To me the Symphony in C does just that.[3]

This shrewd and perceptive commentary is characteristic of Thomson at his best. In a stimulating essay on "The Uses of Convention: Stravinsky and His Models" Edward T. Cone looks at the question in more depth, centering his discussion on the parallel relationships between the Symphony in C and Haydn's String Quartet, Opus 54, no. 2, and between Stravinsky's 1959 Movements for Piano and Orchestra and Schoenberg's

---

[2] Virgil Thomson remarked in his *Herald Tribune* review of Stokowski's broadcast that any new work by Rachmaninoff, Shostakovich, or Prokofiev would have been played everywhere immediately after its first performance. It seems, though, that the Stokowski performance was bad. "I only ask what anyone could understand in this performance," Stravinsky wrote to the violinist Samuel Dushkin. The second movement, according to the composer, was "pitilessly [dragged . . . and] deformed," while the third "was simply beyond [Stokowski's] technique. . . . He plunged the music into a chaos of disordered sounds." Craft, after hearing an air-check of the performance, pointed out that "the bassoon solos were impeccably played but in the wrong clef, and the third movement was unrecognizable."

[3] *New York Herald Tribune*, 12 April 1948.

Phantasy for Violin and Piano, Opus 47. Cone makes the point that Haydn, through his witty play with his listeners' expectations (specifically in the finale of this quartet),

> was attacking certain conventional presuppositions of the Classical style from the inside, since he had grown up within it—or rather, it had grown around him. Almost every moment in his quartet movement represents a questioning, a reexamination of these standards, and in every case the solution avoids the obvious on one side and the arbitrary on the other. It is a narrow path, but one that Haydn maintains successfully to his goal: a broader redefinition of his own style.
>
> Stravinsky, approaching the Classical from outside, as a historically defined manner, superficially follows its conventions more closely than Haydn. The influence of his personal idiom, however, is so strong that the resulting reinterpretation goes far beyond that of the earlier composer. The result is not an extension but a transformation of his model. . . .
>
> With Stravinsky, as with Haydn and Schoenberg, the contrast between the expectations aroused by the accepted conventions and the actual use to which they are put produces tensions—but with Stravinsky, the resultant pull is in a different direction. In listening to the Haydn and Schoenberg examples we are engrossed by the way in which the personal style is constantly reshaping the general convention. We should hear Stravinsky in just the opposite sense: what is of prime importance is how the borrowed convention extends and modifies the personal style.
>
> We have already come to hear the neo-Classical works in this way, and that is why the Symphony in C and other compositions of its period are now, after years of attack as parodistic pastiches, being recognized as masterpieces.[4]

Having composed a charming—and unassailably Russian—symphony in 1905–07, Stravinsky had planned to write another in the winter of 1925–26, but his energies were diverted into the massive task of *Oedipus Rex*. He began working on the Symphony in C without a commission, an unusual action for him at that point in his career, but it was not long before Mrs. Bliss, still happy about the *Dumbarton Oaks* Concerto that Stravinsky had written for her in 1937–38, offered to pay for it. (Since *Apollo*, written in 1927–28 for the Elizabeth Sprague Coolidge Foundation, and the *Symphony of Psalms*, composed in 1930 for the fiftieth anniversary of the Boston Symphony, American commissions were coming Stravinsky's way in increasing number, including *Jeu de cartes* for Lincoln Kirstein's and George Balanchine's American Ballet in 1937.

---

[4] *Stravinsky, A New Appraisal of His Work*, edited by Paul Henry Long (New York: Norton, 1963).

Stravinsky composed the Symphony in C during the unhappiest period of his life. He was ill—"a New York doctor discovered a lesion in my left lung and clusters of staphylococci in my sputum"—and was ordered to Sancellemoz, the Swiss sanatorium where his wife, Catherine, and two daughters, Liudmilla (called Mika), thirty, and Milena, twenty-four, were gravely ill. Mika died on 30 November 1938, Catherine Stravinsky followed her on 2 March 1939, and the composer's mother three months after that, on 7 June. Looking back in 1963, Stravinsky wrote: "It is no exaggeration to say that in the following weeks [after Mika's death] I was able to continue my own life only by my work on the Symphony in C. But I did not seek to overcome my grief by portraying or giving expression to it in music, and you will listen in vain, I think, for traces of this sort of personal emotion."

A revised and subtly different version of Stravinsky's account reads: "I think it is no exaggeration to say that in the following weeks I myself survived only through my work on the Symphony in C—though, I hasten to add that I did not seek to overcome my personal grief by 'expressing' or 'portraying' it in music, and the listener in search of that kind of exploitation will search in vain, not only here but everywhere in my art."[5]

Stravinsky distinguished between the European and the American movements of the Symphony in C, pointing particularly to differences in rhythmic character. In the liner note he wrote for his 1962 recording with the CBC. Symphony, he even goes so far as to say, "I fear the Symphony is divided down the middle." Elsewhere, he cites several details as things that "would not have come to my ears in Europe" or that "would not have occurred to me before I had known the neon glitter of the California boulevards from a speeding automobile."

I quote again from this note:

> But what can one say about a score that is so unmysterious and so easy to hear on every level and in all its relationships? And the stylistic features, are they not equally obvious, the severely restricted diatonicism (it is probably my most extreme score in this respect); the more concentrated development of the motive in the first movement (compared to other scores); the use of Italianate song-and-accompaniment in the second movement, and of

---

[5] Igor Stravinsky and Robert Craft, *Themes and Episodes* (New York: Knopf, 1966). Stravinsky and Vera Sudeikina, whom he married in Bedford, Massachusetts, on 9 March 1940, had been lovers since 1922; however, he remained uneasily attached to Catherine, his wife since 1906. Stravinsky's relationship with his first wife is discussed by Robert Craft with exemplary fairness in the section "Igor, Catherine, and God" in *Stravinsky: Selected Correspondence*, Vol. 1 (New York: Knopf, 1982).

a suite-of-dances in the third movement (though the symphony flirts with ballet in other movements as well); and of fugato in the two ultimate movements? To answer a common question, the fugato in the fourth movement, abandoned there like a very hot potato, may or may not have been in my mind when I began the Symphony in Three Movements; I do not know.

And how do I regard the Symphony now after twenty-five years? It is so far removed from my present work [Stravinsky was then working on the *Variations (Aldous Huxley in Memoriam)*] that in fact I am unable to judge it at all. Nor will I, from my present position, rehearse what are weaknesses only according to another point of view: the succession of *ostinati*, above all. . . .[6]

Again, the version in *Themes and Episodes* is fascinatingly different:

. . . what can one say about a score that is so unmysterious and so easy to follow at all levels and in all its relationships? The answer is that critics (who must also earn their livelihood) will find a great deal of nothing to say, finding factitious comparisons with other music, then drawing attention to the severity of the diatonicism while tracing the development of the motive in the first movement and accusing me, in it, of consistency (which I dislike because only mediocre composers are consistent, as only good ones are capable of being very bad). They will also uncover my supposed use of Italianate song-and-accompaniment in the second movement, and of fugato in the last two movements *, and discover the existence of a suite-of-dances in the third movement and of flirtations with ballet in other movements, but anyone who had failed to notice this much would require a different sort of commentary in any case.

"How would I evaluate the Symphony today? I cannot answer, for it is so far from my present work that I am unable to judge it at all, and I will not apply the obvious criticisms from my present position, namely, the episodic effect of the many *ostinati*, the heavy emphasizing of key centers; this, as I say, is my point of view today, not that of the Symphony. . . .[7]

* To answer one of their comparison questions in advance, the fugato in the finale, abandoned there like a very hot *pomme de terre*, may well have been in my mind when I began the Symphony in Three Movements, but I do not remember.

Another facet of this "unmysterious" symphony that merits mention is the Haydnesque economy—a better word than the "consistency" that offended Stravinsky—with which the material is treated, especially *the* motif:

[6] Liner note to Columbia recording MS6548 (1963).
[7] Stravinsky and Craft: *Themes and Episodes.*

Ex. 1

which is immediately varied as

Ex. 2

and then very soon spun out into this wonderful and unpredictable melody, the "real" first theme:

Ex. 3

Stravinsky recalled that scores of Haydn and Beethoven were constantly on his piano and his desk during the early stages of his work on the Symphony in C, and he refers to "those celestial powers [standing] behind at least my first and second movements." And further apropos Haydn: Cone shows in his essay how Stravinsky's first movement is based on a balance "not of exposition against recapitulation, but rather of the exposi-

tion on the one side against the recapitulation plus coda on the other,"
but he does not point out that this conflation of recapitulation and coda is
typical of first movements in late Haydn, the *Surprise* Symphony being a
spectacular example. Stravinsky's first movement, by the way, is virtually
unique in his music in proceeding through its entire length without a
change of meter, except insofar as he distinguishes between those measures
where he wants his four quarters beat in two, as at the beginning, or in
four. He makes up for this metrical chastity when he gets to the third
movement!

Other extraordinary features of the Symphony in C are its lucid, incredibly varied scoring (occurring in one of Stravinsky's very few pieces for
more or less "normal" classical orchestra); the "double melody"—more than
a counterpoint of two melodies—of oboe and violins at the beginning of
the second movement (with other pairings later),

Ex. 4

which Stravinsky always took rather faster than his own metronome mark,
about 63 for the eighth-note rather than 50; the enchanting variety
throughout of those Italianate song accompaniments; also in that Larghetto, the transcendent single measure for divided violas, and its counterpart, later, for divided cellos; the Tchaikovskian bassoon duet that introduces the finale (Stravinsky also had Tchaikovsky's Symphony No. 1,
Winter Daydreams, on his desk); the beautifully resolved, coming-full-circle
ending, reminiscent in that quality and in its transition to a slower tempo
of the Brahms Third, a work Stravinsky did not care for at all; the rapt
chorale transformation of the motif, and the loveliness—as well as the
surprise—of the very last orchestral gesture.

Symphony in Three Movements

> [quarter] 160 ([half] 80)
> Andante ([eighth] 76)
> Interlude: L'istesso tempo—Con moto ([quarter] 108)

The first sketches of the Symphony in Three Movements are dated 4 and 9 April 1942, and the first movement was finished on 15 June and ready in full score on 15 October. Stravinsky made the first notations for the second movement on 15 February 1943 and finished that section of the work on 17 March. The third movement was completed on 7 August 1945. Stravinsky conducted the first performance with the New York Philharmonic-Symphony on 24 January 1946, and the work is dedicated to that orchestra.

Two flutes and piccolo, two oboes, three clarinets (third doubling bass clarinet), two bassoons and contrabassoon, four horns, three trumpets, three trombones, bass tuba, timpani, bass drum, piano, harp, and strings.

The Symphony in Three Movements, which Stravinsky occasionally regretted not having called Three Symphonic Movements, was the composer's most interrupted piece. For a long time, the first movement stood by itself. Soon after its completion, Stravinsky wrote the Four Norwegian Moods. Next, he worked on the music that is now the symphony's Andante, but, as we shall see, with quite another purpose in view. And before he pulled all the threads together and invented a finale, he had written the Ode (a memorial for Natalie Koussevitzky, but begun as a score for the Orson Welles film Jane Eyre); the cantata Babel; the Scherzo à la Russe in both its forms, for Paul Whiteman's band and for symphony orchestra; Scènes de ballet for the Billy Rose revue The Seven Lively Arts; the Sonata for Two Pianos; and the Elegy for unaccompanied viola in memory of Alphonse Onnou, leader of the Pro Arte Quartet. Except for the not-quite-one-minute Greeting Prelude for Pierre Monteux's eightieth birthday, the Symphony in Three Movements was also Stravinsky's last work for big orchestra and in the big-orchestra style.

That was also a style in which Stravinsky had not worked for years, not really since Le Baiser de la fée of 1928. He had used large, or fairly large, orchestras in the years between, but either in a subordinate function (*Perséphone*), or to produce what is essentially an aerated chamber-orchestra sound with an eighteenth-century flavor (*Jeu de cartes*, Symphony in C), or both (Violin Concerto). At the premiere of the Symphony in Three Movements, the densely packed orchestral sonority came in for a good deal of comment, as did the unbridled physical energy of the first and third movements. In the 1930s and 1940s, it was widely assumed that Stravinsky was, in effect, dead, and the rugged sounds and exciting syncopations of the new symphony raised hopes that the effete Parisian neoclassicist had, thank heaven, reverted to his *sacrale* Russian roots. (Of course the brash final chord was also much remarked upon—disapprovingly.)

In contrast to Schoenberg, who at about this time remarked in a notable essay that "on revient toujours," Stravinsky, in the course of a conversation about the Symphony in Three Movements with his friend and musical assistant, the composer Ingolf Dahl, said testily, "I never return—I only continue." If the symphony reminded some of its first listeners of *Le Sacre du printemps*—and that, however authentic, is a narrow band of the Stravinsky experience—it is, more essentially, an exploring, forward-looking piece. Tautly concentrated and quite short (twenty-two minutes or so), it nonetheless feels big, like a symphony. At the same time, Stravinsky achieves a sense of symphonic breadth and pace without making development of themes in the familiar sense the mainstay of his composing.

Like most of Stravinsky's music from *Le Sacre* on, the Symphony in Three Movements is made of blocks set unmitigated, unmodulated, side by side; here, in fact, is a connection with Stravinsky's past both more essential and more interesting than any surface similarities to *Le Sacre* or any other score. The first movement falls into three large divisions, roughly in the proportions 2:3:1. The first of these sections is in the big-band style; the second is more chamber-musical in character or, more precisely, like one of Bach's most elaborate *Brandenburg* movements; the third in the main reverts to the manner of the first, but, carrying over some elements of the second, functions as well as a synthesis of the opposing elements.

Within each section, Stravinsky moves abruptly from point to point. In the first minute, the arresting opening gesture for almost the full orchestra (there is not, in the literal sense, a tutti until the finale) is followed by a passage of stalking horn and trumpet calls against chugging clarinet chords, and that by a passage for strings and piano which is one of the bits Robert Craft said "might have been introduced practically unnoticed at the Copacabana between stretches of bossa nova." But along with these jolts, or underneath them, Stravinsky sets things that bind, connections established by nicely placed reminders of certain harmonies or melodic contours or sonorities. Even the tempi of the tutti and concertante middle sections, though they feel very different, share a common pulse.

Stravinsky stated that this first movement was designed originally as a work with an important solo piano part (perhaps, like the original plan for *Petrushka,* something just short of a concerto); the piano is indeed conspicuous in the finished score of the symphony, but Craft points out that "none of the early sketches contains any piano part at all." The second movement, we were all astonished to learn some years ago, began as Stravinsky's response to the suggestion by his Hollywood neighbor Franz Werfel that he write the score for the film based on Werfel's novel *The Song of Bernadette.* (Like the *Jane Eyre* scheme and all of Stravinsky's other movie projects, this one soon got derailed, and the producers of *Bernadette* used more congruously sweet music by Alfred Newman.) In this Andante, Stravinsky gives a prominent part to the harp, and it becomes the task of the finale to provide a piano-harp synthesis.

Stravinsky waited a long time to let out the information about the *Bernadette* project. In his program note for the premiere of the symphony he insisted that the work was absolute music, admitting, however, that one could find it touched "by this our arduous time of sharp and shifting events, of despair and hope, of continual torments, of tension, and, at last, cessation and relief." Two years later, he wrote a severe letter to Ingolf Dahl, saying that "if passages from the program notes are used to imply extra-musical connotations in my work, I have to disclaim any responsibility for such interpretations." But in 1963, in *Dialogues and a Diary,* he admitted specifically the influence of movies in the first and third movements, of a documentary on scorched-earth tactics in China in the former, of newsreel footage of goose-stepping soldiers in the latter. Moreover, the last part of the finale was associated in his mind with "the rise of the Allies after the overturning of the German war machine."

Whatever the inner and outer sources, Stravinsky gave the New York Philharmonic-Symphony and us a work of remarkable brilliance and power. The first movement rocks with fierce accent, pungent harmony, and sapidly clangorous sound. In the Andante, Stravinsky follows Beethoven's frequent example of offering something more of an intermezzo or a bridge than a fully worked movement—or perhaps arrived at this idea on his own or by some other route. The finale is reached, without a break, by way of a seven-measure Interlude that, with an amazing economy of means, sets the scene for the harmonies and textures to come. After the transparent sonorities of this second movement, just a bit too hard-edged for "delicate" to be the right word—Stravinsky returns to the massive tones of the first movement. One of the finale's mini-chapters is a fugue whose jagged intervals suddenly look ahead to the Stravinsky of the late 1950s and 1960s. Stravinsky, by the way, suggests the possibility that this fugue is in some way the continuation of the one started, then "abandoned . . . like a very hot potato," in the corresponding movement of the Symphony in C. The abundant physical thrust of the first movement returns, too, and the finale, as Stravinsky's "program" indicates, finishes in assertive triumph.

Piotr Ilyich Tchaikovsky

Piotr Ilyich Tchaikovsky was born on 7 May 1840 at Votkinsk in the district of Viatka, Russia (now in the Udmurt Republic), some 700 miles east-northeast of Moscow, and died in Saint Petersburg on 6 November 1893.

Symphony No. 4 in F minor, Opus 36

Andante sostenuto—Moderato con anima (in movimento di Valse)— Molto più mosso
Andantino in modo di canzone—Più mosso—Tempo I
Scherzo (Pizzicato ostinato): Allegro—Meno mosso—Tempo I
Finale: Allegro con fuoco—Andante—Tempo I

Begun in the winter of 1876-77, the Symphony No. 4 was substantially complete by the end of May 1877, although work on its orchestration was delayed until the autumn. The entire work was completed in San Remo on 7 January 1878. Tchaikovsky entrusted the score to Nikolai Rubinstein, who conducted the premiere on 22 February 1878 in Moscow.

Two flutes and piccolo, two oboes, two clarinets, two bassoons, four horns, two trumpets, three trombones, tuba, timpani, triangle, cymbals, bass drum, and strings.

"Our symphony progresses." The other half of "our" was Nadezhda Filaretovna von Meck, who had come into Tchaikovsky's life some eight months before, in December 1876. She was a wealthy woman, recently widowed, tough, given to organizing things and people. Her ambition and prodding had made her husband, a timid German engineer from Riga, into a Russian Empire Gould or Vanderbilt (though not so crooked). Nadezhda's accomplished piano playing was not nearly adequate as expression of her passion for music. She loved Tchaikovsky's music to the point of obsession and, using as bridge the pianist and conductor Nikolai Rubinstein and the young violinist Yosif Yosifovich Kotek, who was a former pupil of Tchaikovsky's and now a kind of musical household pet to Mme. von Meck, she made contact with her idol. Almost at once they found themselves embarked on a voluminous, exhaustive, intimate correspondence, in addition to which 500 rubles were moved every month from the vast Meck account into Tchaikovsky's fragile one, bringing him years of blessed financial security.

Somewhere in his diaries, Kafka calls coitus our punishment for the joy of closeness. Piotr Ilyich and Nadezhda Filaretovna would have understood, certainly with respect to their relationship. He knew the pleasures both of sex and of closeness, but never found one connection that gave him both. The pre-Tchaikovsky emotional-sexual history of the managerial, diligently child-bearing Mme. von Meck is obscure, though David Brown writes in his biography of the composer that "according to [Meck] family tradition," Karl von Meck's fatal heart attack was brought about by his daughter Alexandra's revealing to him that the four-year-old Ludmila was Nadezhda's child by his secretary.

Clearly, her feelings for Tchaikovsky and his music were on some level erotic, but if the story of her affair with her husband's secretary is true, it makes the more understandable her unwillingness to chance having that feeling transmuted into sexual reality. She insisted that they must never meet, and with that liberating condition in effect, their mutually nourishing friendship, so strange and so understandable, lasted nearly fourteen years. Being rich as well as neurotic, Mme. von Meck was doubly entitled to caprice, and in a maggoty moment she broke contact, seemingly without warning—at least with no warning Tchaikovsky understood. This is one of the too many remaining mysteries in the Tchaikovsky biography, but it seems that financial difficulties, her failing health, and her children's hostility to her connection with Tchaikovsky, both personal and financial, all played their part. By 1890, when that happened, Tchaikovsky no longer needed her money, but he never got over the hurt of the sudden abandonment.

Mme. von Meck had been the only person other than his younger brother Modest and his nephew Bob Davidov (in other words, the only person who was not also a male homosexual) to whom he could reveal himself—though not about sex, at least not explicitly. Her absent presence was crucially important during the first year of their friendship because it was then that he took the most foolish step of his life: he got married. Unease—unease rather than terror, as it has most often been represented— at the thought that his homosexuality might become public knowledge; probably a desire to please his eighty-one-year-old father, who was in love with the institution of marriage and passionate about the idea of family; his bride's naïveté and want of intelligence; and a large dose of recklessness and plain lack of good sense on his part, all contributed to this disaster. At any rate, Tchaikovsky succumbed to the advances of a former pupil of his at the Moscow Conservatory, Antonina Ivanovna Milyukova. He tried to be as candid with her about his homosexuality as the manners and the permissible language of 1877 allowed, but she seems to have had no idea what he was talking about. They married, he fled, and with the massive support of relatives and friends he got his life back on track. His brother Modest, with others following suit, began to spin a web of fiction and calumny about Antonina Ivanovna from which biographers only began to disentangle themselves and the truth more than a hundred years later.[1]

It was soon after Nadezhda Filaretovna's appearance in his life that Tchaikovsky began the Fourth Symphony; it was in the aftermath of the catastrophic marriage that he completed it. In a state of high excitement he worked simultaneously on *Eugene Onegin* and the symphony; upon finishing these, he wrote one of his finest albums of songs, one that includes *Don Juan's Serenade* and *Amid the Noise of the Ball.* He realized at once the significance of Mme. von Meck's entrance into his life and knew that he wanted to dedicate his new symphony to her. In his letters it is "our symphony," sometimes "your symphony."

From the letters we can glean a progress report:

> Just now I am absorbed in the symphony I began during the winter. I should like to dedicate it to you because I believe you would find in it an

---

[1] Tchaikovsky's friend Kashkin gave currency to what became a favorite legend, that, in despair over what he had done, the composer stood for hours in the river Moskva with the intention of, literally, catching his death of cold. By an odd irony, it was when Milyukova's pursuit of Tchaikovsky was under way that someone suggested he make an opera of Pushkin's *Eugene Onegin,* the story of a middle-aged bachelor who lives to regret his brusque rejection of the innocently passionate, unmasked declarations of a girl on the border of womanhood. Many years later but psychologically as blind as ever, Antonina Ivanovna Tchaikovskaya, as she then was, wrote that *Onegin* was Tchaikovsky's only good opera, "the only one warmed with love," because it was "their story." In 1970, Tchaikovsky's marriage became the subject of a grotesque Ken Russell movie, *The Music Lovers.* The ads proclaimed it as "the story of a homosexual who marries a nymphomaniac!"

echo of your most intimate thoughts and emotions. Just now, any other work would be a burden—work, I mean, that would demand a certain change of mood and thought. (13 May 1877)

Our symphony progresses. The first movement will give me a great deal of trouble with respect to orchestration. It is very long and complicated; at the same time I consider it the best movement. The three remaining movements are very simple, and it will be pleasant and easy to orchestrate them. (24 August 1877)

I am working hard on the orchestration of *our* symphony and am quite absorbed in the task. None of my earlier works for orchestra has given me so much trouble, but on none have I lavished such love and devotion. . . . Gradually I have fallen more and more under the spell of the work and now I can hardly tear myself away from it. (21 December 1877)

In my heart of hearts I feel sure it is the best thing I have done so far. (24 February 1878)[2]

At one point, Mme. von Meck asked Tchaikovsky what their symphony "was about." Tchaikovsky shilly-shallied, explaining (as composers have so often tried to explain) that the answer was to be found in the music itself and not in words about the music. Nonetheless, he did oblige at length with a "program" in which the opening fanfare is identified with "*Fate*, the decisive force which prevents our hopes of happiness from being realized, which watches jealously to see that our bliss and peace are not complete and unclouded, and which, like the sword of Damocles, is suspended over our heads and perpetually poisons our souls."

Tchaikovsky had a rather more illuminating exchange about the Fourth Symphony with his friend the composer Sergei Taneyev, who, in addition to deploring the pervasiveness of reminders of ballet music, wrote that the way the fanfare functioned made him suspect a secret scenario. Tchaikovsky replied:

Of course my symphony is program music, but it would be impossible to give the program in words.* It would only appear ludicrous and raise a smile. But ought this not always to be the case with a symphony, the most lyrical of musical forms? Ought it not to express all those things for which words cannot be found but which nevertheless arise in the heart and cry out for expression? Besides, I must tell you that in my simplicity I had imagined the plan of my symphony to be so obvious that everyone would under-

[2] Modest Tchaikovsky: *Life and Letters of Tchaikovsky*, Vol. 1 (London: John Lane/The Bodley Head, 1906).
* This after 800 of them to Mme. von Meck. —M.S.

stand its meaning, or at least its governing ideas, without a specific program.

   Please don't imagine that I want to swagger before you with profound
emotions and lofty ideas. Nowhere in the work have I made the least effort
to express a new thought. In reality my work is a reflection of Beethoven's
Fifth Symphony. I have not of course copied Beethoven's musical content,
only borrowed the central idea. What kind of program does this Fifth Symphony have, do you think? Not only does it have a program, it is so clear
that there cannot be the smallest difference of opinion as to its meaning.
Much the same lies at the root of my symphony, and if you have failed to
grasp that, it merely proves that I am no Beethoven—a point on which I
have no doubt anyway.[3]

   Hans Keller, in his searching account of Tchaikovsky's symphonies
(in Robert Simpson's *The Symphony*) is, so far as I know, the only critic to
have picked up on the musical as distinct from the programmatic implications of the parallel with the Beethoven Fifth, pointing out that Tchaikovsky's opening fanfare serves as a structural marker in much the same way
as Beethoven's famous motto. He suggests, furthermore, that the dimensions as well as the unusual form of the symphony made Tchaikovsky feel
the *musical* necessity of such a marker. To the end of his life Tchaikovsky
thought himself clumsy about form. Let us say that he could be painfully
academic and astoundingly adventurous, and that he could miscarry at
both extremes. His moments of great daring yielded some compelling successes: the tone poem *The Voyevoda*, with its powerfully compressed coda,
is a little known instance and the *Symphonie pathétique* a famous and much
loved one.

   The Fourth Symphony is also among the great adventures and the
great successes, and for reasons that are easier to hear than to grasp by
description. It all has to do with harmonic design, that is to say, with
gravitational pull. In short, Tchaikovsky goes to surprising keys at surprising times. To cite his most blatant heterodoxy: having emphatically set up
F minor as a center of gravity in the introduction and the keening start of
the Moderato, he declines to return to that key until this long movement
is almost nine-tenths over. That moment is marked by the fourth appearance of the "fate" fanfare, and it is more powerful for the extreme delay.[4]

---

[3] Ibid.
[4] When the Fourth Symphony was first played in Boston in 1890, Louis Elson, the critic of the
Daily Advertiser, remarked about the fanfare that it "sounds as if Schumann's *[Spring]* Symphony
had suddenly joined the army."

If this evasion represents a centrifugal element, Tchaikovsky provides a countering centripetal force by setting up a network of harmonic reference across the entire symphony. Again, to cite a single grand example, "recapitulation" normally means a return to the original key as well as a return to all the themes. Tchaikovsky recapitulates the themes all right, but as we have seen, he holds off bringing back the tonic until the coda, instead setting the recapitulation in D minor, a key hitherto untouched, not even hinted at. But the finale of the symphony is in F major, closely related to F minor by virtue of sharing the keynote, F, but equally close to that surprising D minor.[5]

The burden of Tchaikovsky's musical and extramusical arguments is in this large, brooding movement with its latent—and not so latent—waltz content. What follows is picturesque support. The Andantino is a melancholy song introduced by the oboe, that most melancholic of wind instruments. Its impassioned climax is a reminder of the grieving phrases that dominate the first movement.

In the Scherzo, Tchaikovsky was especially proud of his novel instrumental scheme: the perpetual pizzicato and the assignment of distinctive material to each group in the orchestra. He described it to Mrs. von Meck in detail, though his little joke of having the pizzicato theme suddenly annexed by the woodwind was the sort of musical finesse he did not care to discuss with her. He worried about how fast the pizzicato could be played, first telling Rubinstein to take the movement as fast as possible, then withdrawing from that idea. Once the symphony was in circulation, he was annoyed because it was always the "cute" scherzo that made the biggest hit.[6]

The principal tune of the Finale, also introduced with an odd harmonic obliqueness (in an unstable A minor after just eight bars of F-major flourish), is a folk song, *There Stood a Little Birch*. The "fate" fanfare intrudes once more, making a musical as well as a programmatic point, after which the symphony is free to rush to its emphatic conclusion. This irresistible Finale beats all records for the number of cymbal clashes per minute.

---

[5] Major and minor keys whose scales are made of the same notes and which use the same key signature are one another's "relative major" and "relative minor." F major and D minor are two such keys.

[6] The Fourth Symphony had mixed success in its early years. The one time it truly made an impact was when it was introduced in Saint Petersburg by Eduard Nápravník, a conductor famed for the structural intelligence underlying his interpretations. See also my essay on Tchaikovsky's Symphony No. 6.

Symphony No. 5 in E minor, Opus 64

> *Andante—Allegro con anima*
> *Andante cantabile, con alcuna licenza*
> *Valse: Allegro moderato*
> *Finale: Andante maestoso—Allegro vivace—Moderato assai*
>   *e molto maestoso*

Tchaikovsky composed his Symphony No. 5 between May and 26 August 1888; he conducted the premiere in Saint Petersburg on 17 November that year.

Three flutes (third doubling piccolo), two oboes, two clarinets, two bassoons, four horns, two trumpets, three trombones, tuba, timpani, and strings.

Even the Tchaikovsky Fifth was once new music, and controversial new music at that. The first extended commentary on it in English was written by William Foster Apthorp, who by day was on the Boston Symphony's payroll as its program annotator and at night reviewed its concerts for the *Boston Evening Transcript*. Apthorp was famous for his dislike of new music, no matter whether it came from Russia, France, or Germany, and *Baker's Biographical Dictionary of Musicians* notes that "his intemperate attacks on Tchaikovsky elicited protests from his readers." As the Boston Symphony's wordsmith, Apthorp had to pull in his horns. Introducing the Fifth Symphony, when the great Arthur Nikisch brought it to Boston in 1892, Apthorp wrote that

> Tchaikovsky is one of the leading composers, some think *the* leading composer, of the present Russian school. He is fond of emphasizing the peculiar character of Russian melody in his works, plans his compositions in general on a large scale, and delights in strong effects. He has been criticized for the occasional excessive harshness of his harmony, for now and then descending to the trivial and tawdry in his ornamental figuration, and also for a tendency to develop comparatively insignificant material to inordinate length. But, in spite of the prevailing wild savagery of his music, its originality and the genuineness of its fire and sentiment are not to be denied.[7]

[7] Boston Symphony Orchestra program book, 21–22 October 1892.

"The general style of the orchestration," Apthorp noted, "is essentially modern, and even ultra-modern." But wearing his *Evening Transcript* hat, he was less cautious:

> [The Fifth Symphony] is less untamed in spirit than the composer's B-flat minor [Piano] Concerto, less recklessly harsh in its polyphonic writing, less indicative of the composer's disposition to swear a theme's way through a stone wall. . . . In the Finale we have all the untamed fury of the Cossack, whetting itself for deeds of atrocity, against all the sterility of the Russian steppes. The furious peroration sounds like nothing so much as a horde of demons struggling in a torrent of brandy, the music growing drunker and drunker. Pandemonium, delirium tremens, raving, and above all, noise worse confounded![8]

Tchaikovsky's own feelings about the Fifth blew hot and cold, as they did about so many of his works: "I am dreadfully anxious to prove not only to others, but also to myself, that I am not yet *played out* as a composer. . . . The beginning was difficult; now, however, inspiration seems to have come. . . . I have to squeeze it from my dulled brain. . . . It seems to me that I have not blundered, that it has turned out well."

Tchaikovsky's Fourth had been the symphony of triumph over fate and was in that sense, admittedly, an imitation of the Beethoven Fifth. For Tchaikovsky's own Fifth we have nothing as explicitly revealing as the correspondence in which he set out the program of the Fourth for his patroness, Nadezhda von Meck. There is, however, a notebook page dated 15 April 1888, about a month before Tchaikovsky began work on his new symphony, where he outlines a scenario for the first movement: "Intr[oduction]. Complete resignation before Fate, or, which is the same, before the inscrut[able] predestination of Providence. Allegro. (1) Murmurs of doubt, complaints, reproaches against XXX. (2) Shall I throw myself in the embraces of *faith???* A wonderful program, if only it can be carried out."

This is not helpful. First of all, what is XXX? X occurs in Tchaikovsky's diaries, as does Z. Most writers have assumed and declared that these codes refer to Tchaikovsky's homosexuality; in context, however, this makes no sense. Far more persuasive is the interpretation of Alexander Poznansky, whose revealing and extremely important Tchaikovsky biography of 1991 suggests that X refers to the composer's gambling addiction and Z to "his misanthropic anger . . . an irritation connected with card playing or exacerbated by it, though not specifically stemming from it." Whether the "XXX" in Tchaikovsky's scenario for the Fifth Symphony is

---

[8] Boston *Evening Transcript*, 23 October 1893.

connected to the X (or the Z) of the diaries remains unclear; we cannot be sure what he had in mind. Poznansky proposes that "the crisis sparking the creation of the Fifth Symphony was that which Tchaikovsky had experienced . . . eight months earlier as witness to [his friend] Kondratyev's deathbed struggle."

In any event, to pursue the verbal plan as it appears in the notebook through the first movement as he finally composed it is fruitless. Clearly, though, the theme with which the clarinets in their lowest register begin the symphony has a function other than its musical one: it will recur as a catastrophic interruption of the second movement's love song, as an enervated ghost that approaches the languid dancers of the waltz, and—in a metamorphosis that is perhaps the symphony's least convincing musical and expressive gesture—in majestic and blazing E-major triumph.

Tchaikovsky's wonderful gift of melody, his delight in "strong effects" and his skill at bringing them off, his fire and sentiment—these need neither introduction nor advocacy.[9] A word, though, about the orchestra. Rimsky-Korsakov, discussing *Sheherazade* in his memoirs, congratulates himself on the brilliance he has been able to achieve with an orchestra no larger than Glinka's. Tchaikovsky, too, produces remarkable effect with remarkable economy. His orchestra is anything other than extravagant, but the power and vividness of its *fortissimo* is amazing.

And what delight there is in the delicate passages: the color of the low strings in the introduction (with those few perfectly calculated interventions of the second violins); the beautifully placed octaves of clarinet and bassoon when the Allegro begins its melancholy and graceful song; the growls into which that movement finally subsides (with the timpani roll as the top note in a chord of cellos, basses, and bassoon); the low strings again in the measures that introduce the second movement's famous horn solo; those great, swinging pizzicato chords that break the silence after the catastrophe; those faintly buzzing notes for stopped horns in the waltz; the enchantingly inventive filigree throughout the middle part of that movement (for Apthorp, "descending to the trivial and tawdry in his ornamental figuration"); those propulsive chuggings of cellos, basses, drums, and bassoons in the Finale; the tough brilliance of the woodwind lines and the firmness of their basses.

Of course Tchaikovsky had not written himself out. As soon as he returned from a journey to Prague, where the experience of conducting the Fifth produced the most depressed of all his reports on it ("there is something repulsive about it"), he began work on *The Sleeping Beauty;* within

---

[9] When Apthorp writes about the "peculiar [Russian] character" of Tchaikovsky's melodies, he must refer to the way they droop, which is not 1890s Boston at all.

another year his finest operatic score, *The Queen of Spades*, was on its way; and *The Nutcracker* and the *Pathétique* were yet to come.

Tchaikovsky begins the Fifth with a portentous introduction. The tempo is fairly slow, the colors (low clarinets and low strings) are dark. The theme, suggestive here of a funeral march, sticks easily in the memory. Let us call it the Fate theme. Its rhythm is distinctive enough to be recognizable by itself, and that will prove to be useful. The introduction gradually subsides, coming to a suspenseful halt.

When the main part of the first movement begins, the tempo is quicker and the theme is new; nonetheless, we hear a connection because the alternating chords of E minor and A minor in the first twelve measures are the very ones with which the Fate theme was harmonized.[10] Clarinet and bassoon play the theme, the one I called a "melancholy and graceful song" and which I am surprised to see Tchaikovsky's biographer John Warrack call a "jerky little tune." Its first note is always a surprise: any of us would have begun it with B-E, but Tchaikovsky gives us the more oblique C-E. That and its little internal syncopations give it a delightfully individual flavor.

Tchaikovsky boils this up to a *fortississimo* climax, then goes without break into a new, anguished theme for strings with characteristic little punctuation marks for the woodwinds. With these materials he builds a strong, highly energized movement, which, however, vanishes in utter darkness.

In 1939, Mack David, Mack Davis, and André Kostelanetz came out with a song called *Moon Love*. It had a great tune—by Tchaikovsky. It is the one you now hear the French horn play, better harmonized and with a better continuation.[11] Before it begins, low strings in dense, dark chords set mood, key, and pace. Unlike the cobblers of *Moon Love*, Tchaikovsky is under no obligation to round off the tune and finish it. With a slight speeding up, it devolves into a brief duet with the oboe, before the cellos take up the great melody, the violins expanding on what the oboe sang before. Flexibility is of the essence here: Tchaikovsky indicates "some freedom" (*alcuna licenza*) as part of his general direction for this movement, instructs the horn soloist to play "dolce con molto espressione," and in

---

[10] Tchaikovsky's tempo/character marking Allegro con anima is not a common one. Primarily it suggests "with spirit" or "with grace," but *anima* also connotes "sentiment."

[11] That same year, Tin Pan Alley writers also raided Tchaikovsky's *Romeo and Juliet* for *Our Love* and Ravel's *Pavane pour une infante défunte* for *The Lamp Is Low*. The year's original songs included *All the Things You Are*, *God Bless America*, *I Didn't Know What Time It Was*, *Over the Rainbow*, and *South of the Border*. *Tonight We Love*, from Tchaikovsky's Piano Concerto No. 1, came along two years later.

addition constantly modifies the tempo with "animando," "ritenuto," "sostenuto," "con moto," and the like.

When he has built some grand paragraphs out of the horn melody and its various continuations, Tchaikovsky speeds up the music still more (Moderato con anima), at which point the clarinet introduces an entirely new and wistful phrase, which is picked up and carried further by the bassoon and then the several string sections. The spinning out of this idea is brutally interrupted by the Fate theme. The music stops in shocked silence. The great pizzicato chords I mentioned earlier restore order, the violins take up the horn melody, which other instruments decorate richly. Once again, there is a great cresting—Tchaikovsky actually writes *ffff*—and once again the Fate theme intervenes. This time there is no real recovery: with a final appearance of what was originally the oboe's continuation of the horn melody, the movement sinks to an exhausted close. "Resignation before Fate"?

In place of a scherzo, Tchaikovsky gives us a graceful, somewhat melancholic waltz. Varied and inventive interludes separate the returns of the initial melody, and just before the end, the Fate theme ghosts softly over the stage.

The Finale begins with the Fate theme, but heard now in a quietly sonorous E major. (Conductors do not always care to remember that Tchaikovsky marked this page only *mezzo-forte*). This opening corresponds to the introduction of the first movement. This time, though, the increase in tempo is greater, and the new theme is possessed by an almost violent energy.[12] A highly charged sonata form movement unfolds. Toward the end of the recapitulation, Fate reappears, this time just as a rhythm. This leads to an exciting and suspenseful buildup, whose tensions are resolved when the Fate theme marches forward in its most triumphant form: in major, *fortissimo*, broad, majestic. The moment of suspense just before this grand arrival has turned out to be a famous audience trap. The grand B-major chords and the pause that follows them represent a colon, not a period, and people who haven't really been listening but *have* noticed that the music has stopped, are liable to a premature ejaculation of applause at this point. After the Fate theme has made its splendid entrance, the music moves forward into a headlong presto, broadening again for the rousing final pages.

---

[12]Tchaikovsky is precise about tempi in this work, indicating by means of metronome marks not only what speeds he wants, but, more important, what relationships he wants between the speeds of different sections. By taking the first movement's Allegro con anima too slowly and the Finale's Allegro vivace too fast, many conductors exaggerate the difference between the two movements.

Symphony No. 6 in B minor, Opus 74, *Pathétique*

> *Adagio—Allegro non troppo—Andante—Allegro vivo—Andante*
> *come prima—Andante mosso*
> *Allegro con grazia*
> *Allegro molto vivace*
> *Adagio lamentoso—Andante*

Tchaikovsky wrote this, his last symphony between February and the end of August 1893 and conducted the first performance in the Hall of Nobles, Saint Petersburg, on 28 October, nine days before his death. The second performance, under Eduard Nápravník, took place twenty days later in the same hall as part of a memorial concert. The work is dedicated to Tchaikovsky's nephew Vladimir (Bob) Davidov.

Three flutes (third doubling piccolo), two oboes, two clarinets, two bassoons, four horns, two trumpets, three trombones, tuba, timpani, cymbals, bass drum, tam-tam (ad lib.), and strings.

At its premiere, the *Pathétique* was not received with contemptuous silence, as was the First Piano Concerto by Tchaikovsky's detested Brahms, nor did it elicit anything like a *Sacre*-sized *scandale*; rather, the occasion was that always depressing event, a *succès d'estime*. Tchaikovsky himself put it this way in a letter to his publisher, Piotr Jurgenson: "It is very strange about this symphony. It was not exactly a failure, but it was received with some hesitation."

We can only guess at the reasons. It is nearly impossible now to imagine encountering the *Pathétique* for the first time and as a new piece, but if we can make that leap we might see how an Adagio finale with a *pppp* close on cellos and basses alone could have been puzzling and somehow "unfinal."[13] Another factor would have been a weakness in the presenta-

---

[13] How pieces end is a fascinating and large subject. As for quiet endings to big orchestral works, few before the *Pathétique* come to mind: Schubert's *Unfinished* (where it happens unintentionally), the Brahms Third, Rimsky-Korsakov's *Sheherazade*, and, in the area of subversive modern music, Strauss's *Don Juan* and *Death and Transfiguration*, neither of which had made its way to Russia by 1893. We do seem to require a clear signal of closure—that is why, in the absence of coffee and dessert, we get fortune cookies in Chinese restaurants—and a *Pathétique* ending may not yet have been established and recognized as such a signal.

tion. Tchaikovsky, though he lacked a performer's temperament, had become an efficient conductor by the end of his life; he was, however, always affected by an orchestra's mood, and the Saint Petersburg players' initial coolness to the new score depressed him and sapped his enthusiasm for the task. At the second performance, which was under the baton of the excellent Eduard Nápravník, the *Pathétique* made an exceedingly powerful impression.[14]

Between the two first performances of the *Pathétique* there was a difference beyond Nápravník's commanding presence on the podium: Tchaikovsky had died twelve days before, and that of course was something the audience could not stop thinking about as they bathed in what the English writer Martin Cooper called the "voluptuous gloom" of this all but posthumous symphony. Black drapery and a bust modeled after Tchaikovsky's death mask heightened the atmosphere.

Tchaikovsky had died of cholera. There was an epidemic in Saint Petersburg, or at least a scare, and he had drunk a glass of unboiled water, fallen ill, and died four days later. There is little concord in the various accounts of when and where Tchaikovsky made that fatal mistake.

In 1979, a Russian émigrée musicologist, Alexandra Orlova, published an article in the English journal *Music and Letters*, claiming that Tchaikovsky had committed suicide by poison on order from a "court of honor" consisting of several of his fellow alumni of the School of Jurisprudence, where Tchaikovsky had studied in the 1850s. They supposedly feared disgrace to their alma mater in consequence of the impending disclosure of a liaison between the composer and a young nobleman. The story gained wider circulation as Orlova published further articles; her thesis was also accepted by David Brown, author of the most extensive Tchaikovsky biography in English and of the Tchaikovsky entry in *The New Grove Dictionary of Music and Musicians*.

Brown implied that the cholera story was a fabrication by the two

---

[14] In the audience at Nápravník's concert at the Réunion des Nobles was the future composer of *Le Sacre du printemps*, then a boy of eleven. His father, Fyodor Stravinsky, was the most distinguished Russian bass before Chaliapin and a famous interpreter of many Tchaikovsky operatic roles who, a month before, had taken part in the fiftieth-anniversary performance of Glinka's *Ruslan and Ludmila*. More than sixty years later, Igor Stravinsky recalled the first intermission of *Ruslan*: "Suddenly my mother said to me, 'Igor, look, there is Tchaikovsky.' I looked and saw a man with white hair, large shoulders, and a corpulent back, and this image has remained on the retina of my memory all my life." Of Nápravník, Stravinsky wrote: "In spite of his austere conservatism, he was the type of conductor which even today I prefer to all others. Certainty and unending rigor in the exercise of his art, complete contempt for all affectation and showy effects in the presentation of a work; not the slightest concession to the public; and, added to that, iron discipline, mastery of the first order, an infallible ear and memory, and as a result, perfect clarity and objectivity in the rendering . . . what better can one imagine."

men most in the composer's confidence, his brother Modest and his nephew Vladimir Davidov, always called Bob or Bobyk. It is to Bob, a homosexual like his uncles, that the *Pathétique* is dedicated. Bob Davidov committed suicide in 1906, which contributed to suspicions that something in Modest's account of the composer's last days and death was not on the up-and-up. Moreover, Modest's nervousness about potential scandal makes him a sometimes undependable historian and editor of the family correspondence.

When the suicide theory was aired again in the February 1981 issue of *High Fidelity*, it drew a rebuttal in the August issue by three specialists in Slavic studies, the novelist and critic Nina Berberova, the musicologist Malcolm Brown, and Simon Karlinsky, a historian of Russian music and literature. In the Spring 1988 issue of *19th-Century Music*, Tchaikovsky's biographer Alexander Poznansky refuted Orlova still more conclusively. Her account rests on exceedingly shaky foundations with respect to information, interpretation, and the rules of evidence, and does not merit being taken seriously.[15] We are back with that old acquaintance from so many program notes, the glass of unboiled water.

At the premiere of the *Pathétique*, Rimsky-Korsakov asked Tchaikovsky "whether he had a program for this composition. He replied that there was one, of course, but that he did not wish to announce it." In February 1893, Tchaikovsky had written to Bob Davidov that he was working on his new symphony with such ardor that it had taken him only four days to write the sketch of the first movement and that the rest of the score was already clearly outlined in his head. The new piece, he added, would have a program,

> but a program of a kind that would remain an enigma to all—let them guess, but the symphony will just be called *Program Symphony (No. 6)*, *Symphonie à Programme (No. 6)*, *Eine Programm Symphonie (No. 6)*. This program is saturated with subjective feeling, and often . . . while composing it in my mind, I shed many tears. . . . Do not speak of this to anyone but Modest.[16]

The day after the premiere, Tchaikovsky decided that *Program Symphony* was silly as long as he did not intend to divulge the program. Modest suggested *Tragic*, but Piotr Ilyich was not persuaded. "Suddenly the word *patetichesky* came into my head," Modest writes. "I went back and—I re-

---

[15]Conductors who want to titillate their audiences when chatting to them at concerts and symphony orchestra marketing directors in search of hot advertising copy still find the suicide myth useful.

[16]Quoted in Alexander Poznansky, *Tchaikovsky: The Quest for the Inner Man* (New York: Schirmer, 1991).

member as if it were yesterday—I stood in the doorway and uttered the word. 'Excellent, Modya, bravo, *patetichesky!*,' and before my eyes he wrote on the score the title by which it has since been known." But Tchaikovsky changed his mind once again. The next day, 30 October, he asked his publisher—the score with *patetichesky* was already on the way—"to put on the title page what stands below: To Vladimir Lvovich Davidov—No. 6—Composed by P. T." He added, "I hope it is not too late."

Jurgenson, who knew that a good title never hurt sales, ignored the request and sent the work out into the world as *Symphonie pathétique*. This title, then, which had the composer convinced for twenty-four hours anyway, did not get his final blessing. It is, however, permanently glued to the symphony and merits a moment's consideration. *Patetichesky, pathétique, pathetisch, patetico,* and our own *pathetic* all come, by way of the Latin *patheticus,* from the Greek *patheticos* and ultimately from *pathos,* which means "suffering." The words do not, however, carry the same weight of meaning in these several languages. In English, we most often meet and use the word in what dictionaries still list as its secondary meaning of "distressing and inadequate," and its familiarity in that sense colors and trivializes our response to Modest's title. Tchaikovsky's biographer John Warrack emphasizes that "the Russian word . . . carries more feeling of 'passionate' and 'emotional' in it than the English 'pathetic,' and perhaps an overtone, which has largely vanished from our word, of . . . 'suffering.' "

Tchaikovsky had begun the year 1893 in some depression over the reception of *The Nutcracker* and his one-act opera *Iolanta,* produced as a double bill at the Maryinsky Theater in Saint Petersburg in December 1892, and disappointed because a symphony begun the previous year had refused to jell. He was also still pained by the sudden end his mysterious patroness and pen pal Nadezhda von Meck had put to their relationship two years before. On the other hand, the world sent signals of success—Corresponding Membership in the French Academy and an honorary doctorate from Cambridge (where the citation mentioned the *ardor fervidus* and *languor subtristis* in his music)—and there was the sweet pleasure of reaping greater success than Saint-Saëns at a concert they shared in London.

Above all, it was the not-yet *Pathétique* that gave him pleasure. There was other work that year, including the Eighteen Piano Pieces, Opus 72 ("I go on baking my musical blinis," he wrote to Bob Davidov), a set of songs, an arrangement for vocal quartet of Mozart's Piano Fantasy in C minor, and the conversion of the previous year's aborted symphony into the first movement of the Piano Concerto No. 3, a score that would remain unfinished; the "Program Symphony" was, however, the project that was most compelling to him.[17]

As always, he had moments of doubt; in August he told Bob that the orchestration failed to realize his dreams and that he expected the work to be met with "abuse or at least misunderstanding." But even in that letter he conceded that he was "well pleased" with the symphony's contents, and in general his correspondence for that year indicates that he was composing with confidence and delight. "I certainly regard it as easily the best—and especially the most 'sincere'—of all my works, and I love it as I have never before loved one of my musical off-spring," he told Bob. To the Grand Duke Constantine he wrote, "Without exaggeration, I have put my whole soul into this work." Even during the dispiriting rehearsals, he maintained that this was "the best thing I ever composed or ever shall compose."

In February he had revealed to Bob that in this work there would be "much that is novel with respect to form. . . . For instance, the finale will not be a big Allegro but an Adagio on a considerable scale." In 1892 he had scribbled a scenario for a symphony: "The ultimate essence of the plan . . . is LIFE. First movement—all impulsive passion, confidence, thirst for activity. Must be short. (Finale DEATH—result of collapse.) Second movement, love; third, disappointments; fourth ends dying away (also short)." Obviously he changed his mind about much of this. The first movement is not short, though the finale is (in spite of his talk to Bob about "an Adagio on a considerable scale"), and the actual second and third movements do not correspond to this outline either.[18]

Tchaikovsky begins with an extraordinary sound, that of a very low bassoon solo rising through the murk of double basses divided into two sections, with violas in their most sepulchral register adding their voices to the cadences. This and the beginning of the finale, which is at precisely the same tempo, are the symphony's slowest passages. When this Adagio emerges into quicker motion it does so, unlike at the corresponding places in the Fourth and Fifth symphonies, in order to continue the same musical thought. Tchaikovsky stirs this nervous theme to a climax and then lovingly prepares the entrance of one his most famous—and beautiful—melo-

---

[17]Something else on Tchaikovsky's mind was the plan for his next opera. He thought to turn to one of his favorite authors, George Eliot, specifically to *The Sad Fortunes of the Reverend Amos Barton*. For him, Tolstoy was Eliot's only rival among contemporary authors, and he read *The Mill on the Floss*, *Adam Bede*, *Silas Marner*, *Middlemarch*, and *Scenes of Clerical Life* over and over again.

[18]The proportions of the four movements are roughly 2:1:1:1, the last movement being very slightly longer than the middle two.

dies, an utterly personal transformation of one of his favorite pieces, Don José's Flower Aria in *Carmen*. He wants it played "tenderly, very songfully, and elastically" and reinforces that direction with a detailed blueprint for heating it up (literally that—he writes "incalzando"), holding it back, and returning to the principal tempo. (Tchaikovsky assumes a flexible performance style, but, as one would not infer from the giddy havoc most conductors visit upon his music, he has in mind precise tempo relationships that are both structurally and expressively motivated.) The melody is expansively presented; then it disappears, dwindling by degrees all the way down to *pppppp*.[19]

The development is a fierce and accelerating storm whose high point is dominated by a theme that comes from the Russian Orthodox Requiem. The recapitulation is folded into the last mutterings of this tempest and, since the nervous first theme has received much attention in the development, Tchaikovsky moves directly to the great melody, richly rescored. It is a powerfully original and effective plan, to follow an almost recklessly spacious exposition with a combined, and therefore compressed, development and recapitulation. This time the dying of the great melody leads to a solemn—and taut—coda in which a brass chorale is quietly intoned over tolling scales in plucked strings.

Tchaikovsky was a wonderful waltz composer—after his slightly older contemporary in Vienna the best of his time. He had put a real waltz into his Fifth Symphony; now he includes a curious and melancholic variant of one. His Eighteen Piano Pieces, Opus 72, written in the spring of 1893, include what he calls a *Valse à cinq temps*, a waltz in five beats. Here he gives us another such piece, done beautifully and with haunting grace. Each 5/4 measure is made up of two beats plus three, and you could turn the movement into a normal waltz by stretching the first beat of each measure to double its length.

How does this fit into the symphony's program? Probably not at all, except insofar as it contributes another sort of tristful climate. This atmosphere, however, vanishes with the arrival of the next movement, a brilliant scherzo, full of strange flashes and thunders, that unveils itself as a

---

[19] As Tchaikovsky sends the fragments of the melody downward, he has to switch from clarinet to bassoon when the line goes beyond the range of the former instrument. In most performances you will hear a bass clarinet instead of the bassoon, conductors figuring that consistency of timbre and the bass clarinet's greater ease at playing nearly inaudibly contribute more to the projection of Tchaikovsky's thought than piety to the letter. Hans Richter was the first conductor to make this change. The counterargument is that (a) a really first-class bassoonist can achieve the *pppppp* asked for, and (b) Tchaikovsky, a fastidious orchestral thinker, very likely relished the idea of ending as well as beginning the exposition with the same color, that of the bassoon.

fiery march. Here we become particularly aware of Tchaikovsky's mastery at achieving astonishing variety—and volume—with a most economically constituted orchestra.

Tchaikovsky's Fourth and Fifth symphonies are "fate" symphonies that end in triumph, the former because the artist finds salvation in embracing the simple life, the latter because he co-opts the "Fate" theme and turns it into a victory march. The march in the *Pathétique* offers no affirmation; it does serve to set off more bitterly the lament of the finale. The second and third movements form a double intermezzo between the movements that carry the real burden of the Tchaikovsky's *patetichesky* program, but it is an intermezzo of immense dramatic power.[20]

A great cry pierces the echo left by the last bang of the march. The melody is scored so that its successive notes come in alternation in first and second violins. (Like so many points in the orchestral repertory, this makes sense only when the orchestra is seated with the second violins opposite the firsts, not behind them.) A new melody—in major—sets out to console, but its repetitions become obsessive and threatening, leading to catastrophe. From its shards there rises the first, lamenting melody. The snarling of stopped horns and a single, soft stroke on the tam-tam are the tokens of disaster, the harbingers of defeat. The music, over a dying pulse, sinks back into that dark region where it had begun and moves beyond our hearing. Small wonder that it was a bewildering experience on 28 October 1893 and one that became only too frighteningly clear just three weeks later.

---

[20] Deryck Cooke was the first to point out that the design of the Mahler Ninth is modeled on that of the *Pathétique*. The two gloom-pleased composers first met in January 1888 when Tchaikovsky came to Leipzig to conduct the Gewandhaus Orchestra. At the Opera he saw the premiere of Mahler's reconstruction and completion of Weber's *Die drei Pintos* and also heard Mahler conduct *Don Giovanni*. Four years later, Tchaikovsky was supposed to conduct the German premiere of *Eugene Onegin* in Hamburg but turned the assignment over to Mahler, who had prepared the production. "The local conductor is by no means the usual sort of mediocrity," he wrote to Bob Davidov, "but a real genius dying to take the premiere." The following year he heard and liked Mahler's conducting of *Iolanthe*, also in Hamburg. The Tchaikovsky pieces that appeared most often in Mahler's programs were the *Pathétique* and the *Manfred* Symphony. See also my essay on the Mahler Ninth.

Michael Tippett

Michael Tippett

Michael Kemp Tippett, knighted by Queen Elizabeth II in 1966, was born in London on 2 January 1905.

The word that first comes to mind is _abundance._ Abundance of spirit, abundance of fantasy, abundance of images, abundance of risk, abundance of reference and allusion, out-and-out abundance of musical events, of notes. Behind this abundance lies the burning need to communicate, to address through music some of the problems most central to the human condition, questions about love and commitment, about justice, about the inescapability of evil and of humankind's darker impulses.

The key is in Tippett's vocal works, in particular the oratorios _A Child of Our Time_ (1941), _The Vision of St. Augustine_ (1965), and _The Mask of Time_ (1981), the operas _The Midsummer Marriage_ (1952), _King Priam_ (1961), and _The Knot Garden_ (1969), and the Symphony No. 3 (1972). His major instrumental works, the symphonies, concertos, string quartets, piano sonatas, and the _Fantasia Concertante on a Theme of Corelli_ are links between these works, but also commentaries on them, extensions, and often the proving grounds where Tippett readied himself for the successive stages of his great voyages.

When someone asks me which work provides the most inviting entrance into Michael Tippett's world, I usually suggest the magical Corelli _Fantasia,_ if possible in Tippett's own recording. He wrote it for the 1953 Edinburgh Festival in celebration of the Corelli centenary. You could think, to begin with, that you were listening to a rather Romantic performance of one of Corelli's Opus 6 concerti grossi, but you soon hear that there is something wild in the way the cadences break away. The ornamentation takes on a life of its own: observing this changing relationship of embellishment to substance is like watching a building disappear as its growth of ivy and gingerbread comes ever more assertively to life—an experience none of us has had but one we can all imagine. It is also like a journey from waking to dreams, a journey into the world of those mysterious, irrational, but so illuminating proportions and relationships that life affords us at no other times. Considered purely as music, this fantastical voyage is luxuriant, densely textured, generous, profuse, the destination of it all being a tautly made, thoroughly undreamy fugue based on a fugue by Bach whose subject is another theme by Corelli.

You have entered Tippett's world with its belief in the truth of what lies behind and beneath surfaces, in the power of quotation and allusion, in impulsively rich musical gesture, in the possibility of unexpected connections. Tippett's music is shot through with "foreign" voices naturalized: the blues, Goethe's *Wilhelm Meister,* Schubert's *Die liebe Farbe* (in an orchestration of surpassing beauty in *The Knot Garden*), the ecstatic syllables of glossolalia, the Beethoven Ninth, Wagner, Monteverdi, Martin Luther King's "I Have a Dream," Hermann Broch's *The Sleepwalkers,* the sounds of a spaceship, bits of his own music, are among the things that ghost across the scene.

In *A Child of Our Time,* which is a meditation on a Jewish boy's shooting of a Nazi official and the *Kristallnacht* that was staged in reprisal, Tippett uses African-American spirituals in a way that invites comparison with Bach's use of congregational hymns in his Passions. These spirituals are musical anchors which, in the openness of their words and tunes, make for dramatic contrast with the more "artful" verbal and musical language of the oratorio's main track. Their presence is also a loud statement of Tippett's belief in the legitimacy of all forms of language and expression.

It took Tippett some time to develop a technique that would allow him to articulate what he imagined. He began late as a composer, then in effect began again by destroying or withdrawing virtually everything he had written into his mid-thirties. His music was—and is—difficult to conduct, sing, and play, and so he was handicapped by often having his works introduced in performances that were, let us politely say, not representative. (I once sat next to him at such a performance of one of his string quartets and can still feel in my left arm the electrifying force of his wordlessly transmitted rage.) Critics were snide: the standard portrait was of a bumbling amateur. In the 1960s he began more reliably to find competent, sympathetic interpreters, Colin Davis being the prince among them, and at last it began in the most literal sense to be possible to hear his music.

Long overshadowed by his brilliant friend Benjamin Britten, Tippett moved from strength to strength at the very time that Britten began his gradual withdrawal from the world. This was also when Tippett's music was starting to make a powerful impact in America. Tippett was in his sixties when he first visited the United States, but his feeling for that country had long been vivid and, from the American point of view, perhaps just a little starry-eyed. The uninhibited pluralism of his music that had seemed so puzzling, not to say refractory and dismaying, to his critics at home seemed to make him a peculiarly American composer. He himself has said, "I've got something in me that likes the Ivesian thing." And Aaron Copland, the most American of American composers, once wrote: "It is no problem at all for an American to like and empathize with Michael Tippett. . . . I can remember remarking to myself, when I first met him, how very American his personality seemed."

There are four Tippett symphonies, not counting an unpublished one from 1933–34. Tippett began to make sketches for his Symphony No. 1 in 1943. Soon after, he was imprisoned as a conscientious objector, and during the nearly three months he spent in Wormwood Scrubs he continued the planning of the work in his head. He completed the score in 1945, and the first performance was given in November of that year by Malcolm Sargent and the Liverpool Philharmonic. In its radiance and exuberant energy, it anticipates Tippett's next major work, *The Midsummer Marriage*, that joyous modern-day *Magic Flute*. The Symphony No. 2 followed in 1956–57.

The Symphony No. 3, completed in 1972 and introduced that year by Colin Davis, is the biggest of the four. The question behind it is, how do we, in the second half of the twentieth century, respond to Schiller's ode *To Joy* and Beethoven's setting of it in his Ninth Symphony? He makes his purpose clear by quoting the dissonant fanfare that introduces that famous finale, and he gives his answer, skeptical, but compassionate and not devoid of hope and dream, in a series of blues for soprano solo. The words are his own. Rich as Tippett's Third is musically, it is in some ways very much anchored to its own moment in history. The Symphony No. 4, a commission from Chicago, was completed and introduced in 1977.

Symphony No. 2

> *Allegro vigoroso*
> *Adagio molto e tranquillo*
> *Presto veloce*
> *Allegro moderato*

Tippett had his first thoughts about the Symphony No. 2 in 1952 and completed the score on 13 November 1957. Sir Adrian Boult and the BBC

Symphony Orchestra gave the first performance on 5 February 1958 in London. The dedication is to John Minchinton, a gifted but failed conductor who had been close to the composer in the 1940s.

Two flutes (both doubling piccolo), two oboes, two clarinets, two bassoons, four horns, two trumpets, three trombones, tuba, timpani, cymbals, bass drum, snare drum, piano, celesta ad lib., and strings.

In his liner note for Colin Davis's recording of the Symphony No. 2, Tippett writes:

> About the time I was finishing *The Midsummer Marriage* I was sitting one day in a small studio of Radio Lugano, looking out over the sunlit lake, listening to tapes of Vivaldi. Some pounding cello and bass C's . . . suddenly threw me from Vivaldi's world into my own, and marked the exact moment of conception of the Second Symphony. Vivaldi's pounding C's took on a kind of archetypal quality as though to say: here is where we must begin. The Second Symphony does begin in that archetypal way, though the pounding C's are no longer Vivaldi's.[1]

The archetypal C's were put on hold while Tippett composed, among other works, the *Fantasia Concertante on a Theme of Corelli*, the Divertimento on *Sellinger's Round*, the Piano Concerto, and the Sonata for Four Horns. The while, the symphony germinated in his mind:

> I pondered and prepared [its] structure: a dramatic sonata allegro; a song-form slow movement; a mirror-form scherzo; a fantasia for a finale. I prefer to invent the work's form in as great a detail as I can before I invent any sounds whatever. But as the formal invention proceeds, textures, speeds, dynamics, become part of the formal process. So that one comes closer and closer to the sound itself until the moment when the dam breaks and the music of the opening bars spills out over the paper.[2]

Around the time the dam broke, the BBC offered Tippett a commission for a work to celebrate the tenth anniversary of the Third Programme. The symphony ought to have filled the bill perfectly; in the event, Tippett completed the score too late for the anniversary year, and the first performance turned into one of the unhappiest moments of his professional life.

The BBC Symphony's concertmaster, Paul Beard, was a leader in the

---

[1] Liner note to Argo ZRG535 (1967).
[2] Ibid.

autocratic tradition, no friend of new music, and quick to call things "un-playable." In this instance, he insisted on renotating all the passages in which Tippett had grouped notes across barlines according to their natural phrasing. Tippett pointed out to Sir Adrian Boult that Beard's emenda-tions, aside from distorting the rhythm and phrasing, would make the work harder to perform, not easier. For all his prestige, Boult felt unable to stand up to the concertmaster whom he himself had appointed while he was the BBC Symphony's music director, and told Tippett that if he refused Beard's changes, the performance would be canceled.

Wishing to avoid scandal, Tippett gave the go-ahead, but the perfor-mance did indeed break down about two minutes along. Boult turned to the audience and said, "Entirely my mistake, ladies and gentlemen." Many of the London critics had scores, were aware of what had happened, and blamed Beard and the orchestra, so that there was an unpleasant contro-versy after all. The flames were fanned by R. J. F. Howgill, Controller of Music at the BBC, who weighed in with a letter to *The Times*, stating that the orchestra's "comprehensive technique [was] equal to all reasonable demands," in sum, placing the blame on Tippett. The chapter "Interpreta-tion and its Discontents" in Tippett's autobiography, *Those Twentieth Cen-tury Blues*, should be required reading for all to whom conductors are heroes.

The symphony begins with the pounding C's in the piano and lower strings, and they remain as an inescapable presence for about three-quarters of a minute. (Even though Tippett himself speaks of "pounding," he marks the C's *forte*, not *fortissimo*, and wants them to be *sonoroso* and not a tone-less, brutal noise.) It sounds like the firm assertion of a tonic, but already in the second measure, the horns subvert this by entering forcefully with a phrase that strongly implies the dominant, G. It is a very Stravinskian idea and the first of several signals that Tippett had been listening attentively and with joy to Stravinsky's Symphony in C and Symphony in Three Movements.

The horn phrase also serves notice that in this harmonic language it is possible to build upon reiterated C's with matter other than C chords. When the violins, soon joined by trumpets, come in with vigorously forward-moving sixteenth-note figurations, it is clear that they have taken this hint from the horns. This, in fact, is double dissonance, for just as the implied harmonies of these violin figurations constantly contradict C, so do their cross-rhythms make dissonance against the steady 2/4 thrust of the bass. This treble is even forceful enough to drive the bass off its obsession with C. Overall, the effect is of a driving Beethoven allegro reconceived in a post-Stravinsky idiom.

Temper and sonority change suddenly when wind instruments and celesta start a completely different kind of music: *pianissimo,* densely polyphonic, fanciful, and free from any constraints of barlines and regular metric accent. The opening music returns, but set now upon repeated E's. The harmonies shift more rapidly in a development section, or, as Tippett calls it here, "argument." The last phase of this is a delightful conspiratorial music for violins and flute, closely related to the violin sixteenths at the beginning of the movement. This is enough to make the low strings and horns think they must be late for the recapitulation, with the result that they come crashing in with their pounding C's. The woodwind music is deliciously reorchestrated for just a few solo strings and harp; the harmonic placement, too, is distant and veiled.

What follows can be construed as a second "argument," which goes first to a wonderfully gentle music for *pianissimo* divided strings, then to a passage beginning with woodwinds and low strings in which Tippett openly declares his debt to Stravinsky. The sonority is so Stravinskian that it is as good as putting the master's name up in neon lights. With a bravura outing for the timpani to heat things up, this builds to one more return of the pounding C's. This time the arrival is celebrated with a cymbal crash, and one of the trumpets joins in the festivity. The ending is categorical and perfectly timed.

The meditative and atmospheric Adagio is an orchestral marvel. The first note of the trumpet solo with which it begins, *pianissimo* and *dolcissimo,* is delicately accented by soft flutter-tongued notes on the flute, some of its notes are doubled (colored more than weighted) by a barely audible clarinet, and the melody is shot through with flecks of harp and piano. Tippett stresses that harp and piano must be perfectly balanced: it is as though he wants you to hear not two separate and familiar instruments, but a newly invented one. The harp-piano combination is another of his salutes to Stravinsky, specifically to the Andante of the Symphony in Three Movements. Stravinsky has surely been the most imitated of twentieth-century composers, but I do not know a more productive and fresh *imitatio* than this!

Tippett's second idea in this Adagio is a gorgeously embellished, intricately polyphonic duet for cellos. The harp and piano continue to add their fountains of arpeggios. A trumpet fanfare, richly punctuated, introduces a spaciously lyric, ineffably tender melody for violins. The earlier ideas return, quite transformed in color: a trombone takes the trumpet theme in a darker variant, and the cello polyphony moves into the violins.

The coda is breathtakingly beautiful. We hear the trumpet fanfare again. Just as we expect, it leads to the spacious string melody, but this breaks off after a single measure. *Pianissimo* horns begin a new idea, but leave it after just three chords. There is a reminder of the fanfare and its punctuations. They keep revolving before us, these fragments, ever quieter and more mysterious. It is the horn quartet that has the last word in a patch of exquisite polyphony which is also an echo of the Sonata for Four Horns that Tippett had completed just before he began this symphony.

The scherzo is a continuous stream of short beats (two eighth-notes) and longer ones (three eighths) appearing in unpredictable succession. This rhythmic pattern is the constant factor in a movement whose variety of colors and textures is a delight. There is brilliant and rapid conversation for brass, virtuosic flights for solo strings, a fanfare whose biting sound is a preview of Tippett's opera *King Priam*, the work that follows the Symphony No. 2, and more glittering music for the harp-and-piano combination.[3] It is a movement that starts quietly, builds to a fierce climax, and winds down to end with two bassoons flying in opposite directions and a single pop of a trumpet.

Right away, the finale suggests that Tippett means somehow to return to the music with which the symphony began. We are back with the pounding music, not literally the same as in the first movement, but close enough for obvious identification. It is not immediately clear where Tippett intends to go with this. His original outline of the symphony calls for the finale to be a fantasia, and this is what he delivers: a movement consisting of four sections not related like exposition, "argument," recapitulation, and coda of a sonata movement, but more like separate essays in divergent tones though all on the same subject.

The first section is the introductory music with the thumping bass; as Tippett's amanuensis Meirion Bowen points out, it is balletic and Stravinskian. The second is a sequence of eleven variations over a short repeated bass that evolves from the volatile gestures of the introduction. Such variations over reiterated basses—passacaglias—are an important feature in Tippett's music, almost as much so as in Britten's and Shostakovich's. With Tippett and Britten, this comes from an early and lifelong passion for Purcell. Tippett's orchestral imagination is again operating at the highest level, perhaps most so in the final "ghost" variation with *pianissimo* snare drum, muted trumpets, and sotto voce tremolando violins and violas.

The variations themselves also form a bridge from the athletic introduction to the lyric third section. Here, over trills in the woodwinds and still with flashes of harp and piano, the violins begin a rapturous and very long melody in their highest register; as this continues, it is passed to the violas and cellos, supported by a horn and then a bassoon, and it ends deep in the bass, arriving on the low D-flat. Tuba, timpani, and piano

---

[3] The bravura violin solos provided another occasion for Paul Beard to make trouble at the first performance by slowing them down hugely.

take this note a half-step down to C, and suddenly we really are back to the symphony's opening music, though at this point it is still in the *piano* to *mezzo-forte* range. As in the Adagio, the coda is fascinatingly fragmented: Tippett calls it "five gestures of farewell." He keeps returning to his low C, but the sound is different each time, and so is the outcome. Finally, the orchestra settles on a C-based chord, while a single trumpet continues to recall bits of the flurries that sounded against the C's at the very beginning. Then the last remnants of agitation subside, and the trumpet descends—G-E-C—through a chord of C major. The quietly firm final chord, a glorious sound sustained through eight measures, includes D and A and C-sharp, all "alien" to C, but, as Tippett writes, "When the C's return at the end of the symphony, we feel satisfied and the work completed."

Symphony No. 4

> *Tempo 1: slow crotchet pulse (eighth = c. 100)*
> *Tempo 2: steady crotchet pulse (quarter = c. 60)*
> *Tempo 3: fast crotchet pulse (quarter = c. 90)*
> *[Crotchets are quarter-notes]*

The Symphony No. 4, commissioned by the Chicago Symphony Orchestra, was begun in 1976, completed on 18 April 1977, and first performed on 6 October that year by the Chicago Symphony, Sir Georg Solti conducting. The dedication is to Ian Kemp, author of *the* major study of Tippett's music.

Two flutes (both doubling piccolo), two oboes and English horn, two clarinets and bass clarinet, two bassoons and contrabassoon, six horns, three trumpets, three trombones, two tubas, timpani, xylophone, marimba, glockenspiel, vibraphone, snare drum, tenor drum, bass drum, tom-tom, suspended cymbal, clashed cymbals, maracas, claves, wood block, triangle, wind machine, harp, piano, and strings.

Tippett's first three symphonies are, to varying degrees, in the tradition of the four-movement classical symphony as defined and certainly exemplified by Beethoven. The Third, with its allusions to the *Ode to Joy*, can even be construed as being quite specifically a response to the Ninth Symphony. Tippett's Symphony No. 4 emerges from a different background. It consists of a thirty-minute single movement, though this is in several sections that correspond—somewhat—to the exposition and recapitulation of a sonata-form, with a slow movement, a scherzo, and some episodes of development coming in between. The ambition thus to combine single-movement and multi-movement form can be found in, for example, Schoenberg's Chamber Symphony No. 1, Sibelius's Symphony No. 7, and the Fourth Symphony of Franz Schmidt.

Tippett also connects to another tradition, that of the Romantic tone poem, and such works as Liszt's *Les Préludes*, Strauss's *Ein Heldenleben*, and Elgar's *Falstaff*. These are powerful musical structures as well as vivid evocations of non-musical matter, or to go a step further, one could say, as Tippett has, that "in the best of [such works], the 'programmatic' element is ultimately only an alibi enabling the composer to produce a concentrated outpouring of music within a continuous, often lengthy and elaborate musical design." John Harbison has said that his own particular interest is in "the tone poem without a plot." That would be one way of describing the Tippett Fourth: *Heldenleben* without battles and wives and retirement to the Swiss Alps, *Falstaff* without Justice Shallow's moonlit garden and stern young Henry V. *Les Préludes*, though one would never guess it from the music, undertakes to ponder the question of life as a series of preludes "to that great song whose first note is sounded by death." Here, perhaps surprisingly, we may find a connection, for Tippett has described his Fourth Symphony as a "birth-to-death" piece.

One other part of the pedigree of this work should be mentioned, and I quote Meirion Bowen's program note for the first performance of the Fourth Symphony:

> Back in the 1920s, Tippett was taken by friends to the Pitt-Rivers anthropological museum in Dorset. . . . Here he saw an early film of a foetus growing inside the womb of a rabbit (?), with the process speeded up so that, at a particular stage, the initial single-cell form shook like a jelly and became two, then again later it became four. This birth-image remained in his mind. It underlies some motifs in [the Fourth] Symphony, and bears especially upon the central climax. . . . The prominence given to the wind machine in the score also relates to this overall theme, with "gentle breathing" sounds indicated at the start, and the whole work dying away finally with this instrument sounding on its own.[4]

---

[4] Chicago Symphony Orchestra program book, 6-7 October 1977.
   As you can hear on the otherwise excellent Solti-Chicago recording, the wind machine was a raucous failure. The indication at its first entrance (measure 3) is "gently breathing," but if

As you can see at the head of this essay, Tippett uses three tempi, each a little faster than the preceding one. These do not, however, represent three separate or consecutive movements; rather, you can think of each of them as a container for a bundle of musical ideas, with all three tempi appearing in alternation—sometimes very quick alternation— throughout the symphony. The overall design can be represented this way:

I. Introduction—exposition of Tempi 1, 2, and 3
II. Repeat of exposition, but with new material added
III. Slow movement
IV. Development of I and II
V. Scherzo
VI. Recapitulation of I and II, but varied further
VII. Coda

And here is a road map showing the terrain in slightly more detail:

I—In the slow Tempo 1, horns add a softly dissonant pair of lines in contrary motion to a chord of A major in strings, piano, and harp. Woodwinds, percussion, and the "gently breathing" wind machine then complete the sound, after which there is a quick crescendo and a stop. This happens twice more, but never quite the same: there are virtually no literal repetitions in this symphony. When this pattern has been completed for the third time, the introduction is over.

In Tempo 2, brass instruments introduce two new ideas, a rapid, ascending trumpet and horn scale (with one kink in it) and a declamatory three-note phrase for the trombones. In his score, Tippett labels this "power."

In Tempo 3, strings play a quick, dance-like music in triplets; this is called "vigour." This moves directly into a section dominated by woodwinds, in captivatingly capricious 5/8 time, and called "lyric grace." A little later, trumpets and trombones enter with quick chattering music, which Tippett marks with the word "radiance." This culminates in a short, highly energized percussion barrage. This concludes the first exposition.

II—Back in Tempo 1, Tippett begins the second exposition. The harp adds a new passage that ascends in wide steps; the horn music itself is more elaborate than before, this time involving all six instruments in the sec-

---

someone were rasping like that next to you in bed, you'd nudge them and get them to turn over. In *Those Twentieth Century Blues*, Tippett describes subsequent experiments with breathing-sounds and notes that "only recently [c. 1990], in experiments with the latest 'sampling' techniques in the Greenwich Village studio of the rock music producer, Mike Thorne, have the potential variety and flexibility of the breathing efforts come to fruition. I don't blame conductors for regarding the breathing noises as of low priority in rehearsals: there are enough notes in the piece to be got right without holding everything up while the various electronic machines are made to operate properly."

tion. Tippett also varies this second exposition by bringing in Tempo 3 before Tempo 2. The new element in Tempo 3 is an eloquent melody for cellos and basses, each group being divided into two sections. As the melody rises in pitch, the upper strings take it over. This string music is also a bridge into the return of Tempo 2, with its rising scales and declamatory trombones. The trumpets, emphatically cheered on by the timpani, add a new melody. This second exposition is further elaborated by one more visit to Tempo 3. Marimba and bassoon make their presence known in a four-note figure which they repeat often and which leads to a new, wide-ranging melody for strings. Like the first exposition, this one culminates in a *brillante* climax; this one, however, is even more forceful than the first, both because it is given more space and is at a higher pitch.

III—Again the music returns to Tempo 1 with the horns and the harp that was added in section II, but all this is richly elaborated and expanded. Tippett also adds a quietly fervent song for the flute. We are now in the symphony's slow movement. Violas, cellos, and basses (with cellos on top) softly sing a "warm and tender" melody, which is decorated by elegantly swirling woodwind scales. The central matter of this section is a flowing oboe solo, exquisitely harmonized by violins with piano and percussion. Eventually, the English horn takes the melody from the oboe and carries it to its peaceful final cadence.

IV—Tempo 2 returns with an explosion of timpani and low strings, who bring back the original Tempo 2 theme (Tippett marks this "tough, strict"). The tempo remains constant, but in all other dimensions this section brings tremendous variety. Trills become particularly prominent and add a fierce motor energy of their own. Finally, wind instruments, dominated by brass, use the rising scales with the kink to drive toward another crest. The response to this onslaught is a long silence.

V—When the music resumes, it is as different as possible: Tippett marks it "light, 'flying'," and it is volatile, broken in texture, unpredictable even by the standards of this symphony. This is the scherzo. Briefly, ear and mind get some respite in an interlude of "steady state" music for horns; then the "flying" scherzando music resumes, more complex and varied than before. Eventually the violins recall the wide-ranging melody they played toward the end of the second exposition; now—with a marking of "athletic, 'flying' "—they use it to start a virtuoso fugue for all the strings. This leads to yet another return, at a still higher pitch, of the climax with the percussion barrage.

VI—Once again Tippett pits opposites against each other as, without break, he shifts from the almost violent physical energy of what we have just heard to the quiet horn and harp music of Tempo 1. This is the recapitulation, which begins by bringing all the ideas associated with Tempo

1: the horn lines, which start from a single note and open out like a fan; the harp arpeggios, and the flute song. Everything is more poetically orchestrated than before as well as more fancifully expansive. Themes and sonorities from other sections of the symphony reappear, most of them fleetingly, just enough to serve as reminders and to satisfy our hunger for return and closure.

VII—Tempo 1 comes back, but in rapid alternations with loud and brassy interventions in Tempo 3. Then the frenzy subsides, and in the solemn *pianissimo* brass chords of Tempo 1, Tippett pays explicit homage to one of his great musical loves, Stravinsky's Symphonies of Wind Instruments.[5] Everything becomes very still in this closing music, which Tippett marks "calm and tranquil." Long silences separate the phrases, and with one last, peaceful exhalation, the symphony arrives at its close.

[5] Ian Kemp reports in *Tippett—the Composer and His Music* that one of the works Tippett chose for a BBC "Desert Island Discs" program in 1968 was the Symphonies of Wind Instruments. Another was his own Symphony No. 2.

Ralph Vaughan Williams

Ralph Vaughan Williams was born at Down Ampney, Gloucestershire, England, on 12 October 1872 and died in London on 26 August 1958.

In *R.V.W.—A Biography of Ralph Vaughan Williams*, Ursula Vaughan Williams, the composer's widow, writes about her husband's name: "Ralph's grandfather, Sir Edward Vaughan Williams, seems to have been the first . . . to use the double-barrelled but unhyphenated name. . . . Though occasionally—at school or in the army—Ralph was called Williams it is not correct. Ralph's name was pronounced Rafe, any other pronunciation used to infuriate him." The Eighth was the first symphony that Vaughan Williams numbered himself. His first three symphonies went by their names. The next three he called simply Symphony in F minor, Symphony in D major, and Symphony in E minor, but beginning with the D major his publisher intervened and added numbers to the titles.

Vaughan Williams declared himself as a symphonist in 1910, the year of the first performance of *A Sea Symphony*. Nearly thirty years earlier, when he was nine years old, he had passed a University of Edinburgh correspondence course in music and begun piano and theory lessons with his aunt Sophy Wedgwood. (She was one of the pottery Wedgwoods; through marriage, the Wedgwoods were linked with the Darwins, who played an important part in Vaughan Williams's family history.) He had gone to Charterhouse, the Royal College of Music, and Trinity College, Cambridge, and studied with Max Bruch. Only recently he had taken some months off from composing, teaching, and conducting to sharpen his technique with lessons from Ravel, and it is a curious thing that the work of Vaughan Williams in which we most sense Ravel's presence is his most "English" symphony, No. 3, the *Pastoral*.

Vaughan Williams had joined the Folk-Song Society and begun to collect Norfolk songs, a critical step toward the finding of his own musical language and one that also cemented a life-long friendship and artistic alliance with Gustav Holst. The music of earlier English masters like Byrd and Purcell had become an important part of his life, and he had edited the latter's *Welcome Odes* for the Purcell Society. A busy and responsible musical citizen, he put considerable energy into elevating the standards of amateur choral singing, contributed articles on conducting and fugue to Grove's *Dictionary of Music and Musicians* (supplanted only in *The New Grove* of 1980), and edited *The English Hymnal* (1906).

His *Norfolk Rhapsodies* (1905–06) and Housman song cycle *On Wenlock Edge* (1908–09) had established Vaughan Williams as a composer. His most significant achievement so far was the Fantasia on a Theme of Thomas Tallis, introduced five weeks before *A Sea Symphony*. This, a happy by-product of his labors on *The English Hymnal*, was the first work in which he spoke with full confidence and resonance the language of his English heritage; here, indeed, was the great declaration of independence for the new English music.

A Sea Symphony, music as generous and grandiloquent as its Whitman texts, is more a cantata than a symphony in the ordinary sense. (The Mahler Eighth, of which the same can be said, had its first performance in Munich a month before *A Sea Symphony*, each composer being contentedly unaware of the other's enterprise.) Vaughan Williams's first purely orchestral symphony followed in 1914.[1] This was *A London Symphony*, a work of sweet affection and what I suppose was nostalgia even eighty years ago. A *Pastoral Symphony* (with wordless soprano soloist) followed eight years later, a span in which Vaughan Williams composed just one nearly-major piece, the enchanting Romance for violin and orchestra *The Lark Ascending*. The main fact of those years was of course the 1914 war. Vaughan Williams first joined the Special Constabulary and later became a member of an ambulance unit of the Royal Army Medical Corps. There was little time for music.

In his program note for A *Pastoral Symphony*, Vaughan Williams remarked that it was "almost entirely quiet and contemplative—there are few *fortissimos* and few *allegros*." This is still what most people think of as the essential Vaughan Williams: quiet, contemplative, with few *fortissimos* and few *allegros*. By the time his Fourth Symphony came along in 1935, the composer of the operas *Hugh the Drover* and *Sir John in Love* (the source of the popular Fantasia on "Greensleeves"), the first three symphonies, *On*

---

[1] Vaughan Williams's first two symphonies were both much revised; these dates are of the first performances of their first versions.

Wenlock Edge, the Tallis Fantasia, *The Lark Ascending,* and *Flos campi,* seemed fixed more firmly than ever as the dean of England's "pastoral school." The sometimes harshly dissonant Fourth Symphony brought a real shock. "I feel that I have at last become master of my material," Vaughan Williams wrote to his former student, the organist and conductor Bernard Naylor, "but it now seems too late to make any use of it." Happily he was wrong: twenty-three more years of work lay ahead.

When the "peaceful" and reassuringly "pastoral" Fifth Symphony came along in the middle of the war—and everyone at that premiere well knew the reason they were in the Albert Hall was that the Queen's Hall, home of the Proms since their inception, had been destroyed in an air raid— many heard it as a "taking back" of the Fourth. Or, as Vaughan William's biographer Michael Kennedy remarks, "It was assumed that the composer, at seventy-one, had his eye on heaven and was chanting the *Nunc dimittis.*"

No such thing. In 1947, Vaughan Williams completed his Sixth Symphony. Closing a chapter begun with the Fourth, it was a strong statement that the composer, seventy-five at the time of the first performance, had not put himself out to pasture. Kennedy writes: "No one [as of 1964] has yet had the courage to play all [the Fourth, Fifth, and Sixth symphonies] in one concert-programme, but it would be a revealing spiritual and musical experience."

Three more symphonies followed the Sixth. The *Sinfonia antartica* (1952—with soprano solo and women's chorus), was a powerful spin-off from the score Vaughan Williams had written in 1948 for the film *Scott of the Antarctic.* The Eighth (1955), an inventive work too little known and understood, has a slow movement which is Vaughan Williams's last and moving visit to the world of serene music for strings. The Ninth (1957) is both dark and comic, Romantic and quirky. The orchestra includes flugelhorns and saxophones, about which the composer noted that, except perhaps for one place in the scherzo, they are not expected "to behave like demented cats." His jocular program note for this anything other than unshadowed Ninth is red herring at its tastiest. The cycle of Vaughan Williams's symphonies does not culminate in completion but stops with one more exploratory step on a lifelong and unfinished journey.

The deaths of Elgar, Holst, and Delius, all within a few months in 1934, had left Vaughan Williams the senior figure among British composers, but the phrase "Grand Old Man of English Music," which was glued to his name more and more often, enraged him.[2] He had no intention of departing in peace, not then, not later. The morning he did not wake from sleep, he had planned to attend a recording session of his Ninth.

---

[2] Vaughan Williams had no interest in being "grand" anything; characteristically, he refused both a knighthood and appointment as Master of the King's Musick.

Symphony in F minor (No. 4)

> *Allegro*
> *Andante moderato*
> *Scherzo: Allegro molto*
> *Finale con epilogo fugato: Allegro molto—Con anima*

Vaughan Williams sketched this symphony in 1931–32. By 6 January 1932 he had made enough progress for Vally Lasker and Helen Bidder to play it through on two pianos at St. Paul's Girls' School in London, where Gustav Holst was music master. This reading resulted in some substantial changes. Vaughan Williams completed the score in 1934; however, Ursula Vaughan Williams notes that "with him the word 'completed' had an entirely fluid meaning for changes were made in details throughout the next thirty years." The first performance was given on 10 April 1935 by Adrian Boult and the BBC Symphony Orchestra. The dedication is to his friend, the composer Arnold Bax.

Three flutes (one optional, one doubling piccolo), three oboes (one optional) and English horn, two clarinets, bass clarinet (optional), two bassoons, contrabassoon (optional), four horns, two trumpets, three trombones, bass tuba, timpani, snare drum, triangle, cymbals, bass drum, and strings.

Except in its honesty and strength, the Fourth Symphony struck—in some instances, alarmed—its first listeners as a total departure for the sweet singer of pastoral and religious idylls. Some pages of the oratorio *Sancta Civitas* (1925) and *Job* (1930) had showed Vaughan Williams capable of momentary dissonance, but no previous composition had suggested that he had in him a work so fierce in temper, nor one in which dissonance—and I mean rhythmic conflict as much as harmonic—was of the essence so much of the time. "I don't know whether I like it," he said when he rehearsed it with the BBC Symphony in 1937, "but this is what I meant."

What else he meant, other than F minor, allegro (even allegro molto), and so on, we cannot say, though heaven knows the question has been discussed enough. At the time of the first performance, Hitler had been in power two years, had staged major bloodbaths, promulgated the first anti-Semitic laws, and taken back the Saar; Mussolini was flexing his muscles by threatening to annex Ethiopia. None of the first reviewers made any connection between the music and current events; on the other hand, several of Vaughan Williams's friends were quick to rush in with their interpretations, and the thought was soon voiced that the new symphony should be called *Europe 1935*. It had in fact been sketched and its ferocious style set several years earlier, in 1931–32, but a habit of reading this symphony as symbolic of political developments on the Continent and, later, as a prophecy of World War II long persisted.[3]

All this annoyed Vaughan Williams, just as he would be annoyed again after the war by some of the topical, political, and apocalyptic interpretations imposed on his Sixth Symphony. In December 1937, he wrote an illuminating reply to his old friend Bobby Longman, who had voiced reservations about the Fourth:

> I agree with you that all music must have *beauty*—the problem being what *is* beauty—so when you say you do not think my F mi. symph. beautiful my answer *must* be that I *do* think it beautiful—not that I did not *mean* it to be beautiful because it reflects unbeautiful times—because we know that beauty can come from unbeautiful things (e.g. King Lear, Rembrandt's School of Anatomy, Wagner's Niebelungs etc.)
>
> As a matter of fact
>
> (1) I am not at all sure that I like it myself *now*. All I know is that it is what I wanted to do *at the time*.
>
> (2) I wrote it not as a definite picture of anything external—e.g. the state of Europe—but simply because it occurred to me like this—I can't explain why—I don't think that sitting down and thinking about great things ever produces a great work of art (at least I hope not—because I never do so . . .)—a thing just comes out—or it doesn't—usually doesn't—I always live in hope, as all writers must. . . .[4]

Vaughan Williams does not mention to Longman the odd story he told on some other occasions, namely, that reading a detailed description in *The Times* of a new symphony performed at what with characteristic bluntness he called a "freak" festival, had given him the idea of composing just such a work himself. If indeed the *Times* article played a significant role in the genesis of the Fourth Symphony and the story of this sudden

[3] In the light of these "news of the world in review" interpretations of the Fourth Symphony, it is interesting to note that the first German performance (the second on the Continent) was conducted in Bochum in January 1937 by Leopold Reichwein, the most committed Nazi among the major figures in the German musical world. As early as September 1933, Reichwein published an inflammatory article on the role of Jews in German music, and such was his reputation that in January 1934, anticipating violent demonstrations pro and con, the police prohibited a concert he was to conduct in Vienna. Fearing trial, he committed suicide in April 1945, the day after Soviet troops entered Vienna, where he was then living.

[4] Quoted in Michael Kennedy, *The Works of Ralph Vaughan Williams* (Oxford: Oxford University Press, 1964).

breakfast-table inspiration was genuine, it must have awakened a creative impulse already dormant in him, one awaiting just such a prompting.

Ursula Vaughan Williams is more inclined toward an autobiographical reading. She writes about the symphony that

> . . . no one seems to have observed how . . . closely it is related to the character of the man who wrote it. The towering furies of which he was capable, his fire, pride and strength are all revealed and so are his imagination and lyricism. He was experimenting with purely musical ideas; no sea or city, no essence of the country was at the heart of this score and what emerged has something in common with one of Rembrandt's self portraits in middle age.[5]

The violinist Elizabeth Trevelyan, wife of the historian R. C. Trevelyan (a friend from Vaughan Williams's undergraduate days), heard something like that too: "I found your poisonous temper in the Scherzo, contrasted with that rollicking lovable opening of the Trio, *most* exciting."

Mrs. Vaughan Williams notes that this was her husband's "first work without Gustav [Holst] beside him all the way." The two had been close friends since 1895, but the composer of *The Planets* and *Savitri* died in May 1934, a little before the completion of the Fourth. Vaughan Williams did, however, have the support of Arnold Bax, himself an original and too-little-known symphonist, who suggested a useful cut, and of the teacher and scholar R. O. Morris (also his first wife's brother-in-law), who was helpful with countless details. Above all, he felt indebted to Adrian Boult for a superb first performance; the rehearsals had assured the composer that the orchestration in this new musical adventure really worked.[6]

In "A Musical Autobiography," Vaughan Williams states that he "never had any conscience about cribbing," citing as one of several examples the opening of the Fourth Symphony, "cribbed . . . deliberately from the finale of [Beethoven's] Ninth Symphony."[7] Specifically, the source is the fanfare with which that finale springs into terrifying life. Vaughan Williams begins with Beethoven's semitone clashes. The first sound is a brutal grinding, *fortissimo*, of D-flat in the violins, high woodwinds, and trumpets against C everywhere else. The D-flat is an appoggiatura that resolves to

---

[5] Ursula Vaughan Williams, *R. V. W.—A Biography of Ralph Vaughan Williams* (Oxford: Oxford University Press, 1964).

[6] Boult's deeply understanding recordings of the Vaughan Williams symphonies constitute one of the most splendid of phonographic monuments; just the same, the Vaughan Williams performance not to be missed is the composer's own of the Fourth Symphony in 1937 with Boult's orchestra, the BBC Symphony. It is unequaled in fire and fury.

[7] In Hubert Foss: *Ralph Vaughan Williams: A Study* (London: Harrap, 1950).

C, but only briefly, and always to be instantly succeeded by a new dissonance. This is the first element of the opening theme, which moves in a
broadly swinging duple meter.

Having grabbed our attention, Vaughan Williams immediately presents two musical ideas that will appear throughout the symphony. The
first, played by the high instruments, is a four-note phrase of narrow intervals, resembling but not exactly producing the famous BACH cipher. This
is what the composer calls "the tail-end" of the first theme.

Ex. 1

The other, played just moments later by woodwinds and pizzicato strings,
is also a four-note figure, but stalking vigorously upward through two
fourths and a third.

Ex. 2

What comes next is in complete contrast, an expansive bit of opera
for the violins; Vaughan Williams marks it appassionato sostenuto. It is
followed immediately by another theme for strings and horns. This, too, is
appassionato, but altogether different in character, confined to a narrow
range (like Ex. 1), and rhythmically restless. A return to the violent opening gestures initiates a brief development. After that, a recapitulation only
hints at the first theme, but the glorious opera aria is given its due. This
time it is sent down to the bass, the high instruments providing a new
countertheme. This boils up to an immense climax, after which the music
subsides into a coda which is as beautiful a passage as any Vaughan Williams ever composed. It is a transformation of the second appassionato
theme, now played in a mellow D-flat major. Muted violins add a barely
audible commentary, and it is with those gestures that the music sinks to
its close. It is a surprising and wonderful destination for music that started
in such rage.

Vaughan Williams said of the slow movement that, although he had composed it, he "didn't know how it should go, but [Adrian] did. . . . Adrian *created* the slow movement." It begins with wind music based on the climbing phrase (Ex. 2). Over a pizzicato bass—quiet but heavy, Vaughan Williams directs—the violins play a tender melody. This restrained and subtle song sets the tone for the movement. The oboe offers a new theme to which strings, clarinet, and bassoon add softly flowing counterpoints. Then it is the turn of the second violins, who start a theme that takes another view of the oboe's theme. This briefly rises to *fortissimo*, after which the flute closes this chapter with a cadence that describes a gentle descent through one octave.

The flute's cadence gives the strings and horns something new to think about. This is what happens throughout this miraculous Andante: every event gives birth to another, and this flow of inspired generation seems never to stop. Now, with the flute theme as a point of departure, the music is carried to a luminous climax. What follows is not so much recapitulation as a calm disassembling of the music into its components. It is as though the composer were saying, "Look, this is all it was." The effect is magical. This poetic fragmentation may remind you of Sibelius, whom Vaughan Williams revered as the greatest of living symphonists and to whom he would dedicate his own next symphony.

Molto tranquillo, the flute returns with its cadential phrase; this time it is spun out into a cadenza-like fall, against soft chords for muted trombones. The very end of the movement gave Vaughan Williams trouble. He sets a *pianississimo* F-major chord for muted strings underneath the flute's last dreamy spins around a phrase in F minor. (Such major-minor collisions, which can, like this one, be very gentle, occur a lot in this symphony.) The strings disappear, and the flute is left alone to complete its descent from A-flat. It goes to the keynote, F. Logical as this is, it never sounded right or convincing to Vaughan Williams. Eventually, in one of those many changes that Ursula Vaughan Williams mentions, he changed the F to E. It is not logical at all, and it is completely right, the ending of this fantasy on a strange nowhere.[8]

The dream is ruthlessly shattered by the Scherzo that Bessie Trevelyan said so accurately reflected the composer's "poisonous temper." Example 2 gets it going and is immediately followed by a nasty, snarling version of Ex. 1. Mad rhythms ensue, but there is room as well for an almost amiable, jig-like tune. The trio is a brassy fugato on a vigorous theme that is another derivative of Ex. 2. The Scherzo returns, and then Vaughan Williams cribs from Beethoven again. This time he leans on the analogous place in

---

[8]You can hear the original ending on the composer's own recording; all others have E.

the Fifth Symphony and, over relentlessly beating drums and beginning in mystery, he makes a suspenseful transition into the Finale.

As in Beethoven, the destination is daylight. There we get a robust big-band version of the flute's cadential theme in the slow movement. Vaughan Williams then gives us a wind melody full of semitones and thus based on Ex. 1; this comes with a raucous oom-pah accompaniment. The next event is a vigorous, slightly Hindemith-tinged march. All this happens in quick succession, and these ideas are pursued at high voltage. There is a moment of reflection—twelve measures, richly scored, of a quiet recalling by the strings of the end of the first movement—and then, using the semitone theme as motor, everything pushes toward the recapitulation.

Except perhaps in the tantrums of the Scherzo, we have probably forgotten about the Fourth Symphony's famous aggressiveness and anger. The fugued epilogue can remind us. To begin with, it is built chiefly on Ex. 1, but as it goes along, this is combined with the Finale's other themes. Suddenly the beginning of the fourth movement returns in its *fortissimo* big-band scoring. It is as though innocence had suddenly been restored. But this is illusory. The semitones of Ex. 1 come in to twist the harmony, and seconds later we are thrown back into the music of the symphony's opening bars, with their fearsome dissonances. F minor and F-sharp minor (semitones apart) collide bloodily in a series of convulsive chords. Silence. Then F's and C's—an incomplete chord of F minor—end the symphony with one triple-*forte* slam.

Symphony in D major (No. 5)

> *Preludio: Moderato*
> *Scherzo: Presto*
> *Romanza: Lento*
> *Finale: Moderato*

Vaughan Williams made the first sketches for this symphony in 1936, though some of the ideas had already taken shape in connection with his opera—or as he preferred, his Morality—*Pilgrim's Progress,* a work that occupied him off and on from 1909 to 1952. He began to concentrate on the symphony in 1938, but repeatedly interrupted himself for work on film scores and other projects to do with the war effort as well as for such pieces as the *Serenade to Music* and *Five Variants of "Dives and Lazarus."* He completed the symphony at the beginning of 1943. In 1951, he made some revisions, described by his biographer Michael Kennedy as "mainly modifications of dynamics, one change of harmony, corrections of misprints and several clarifications of texture—all directed to seeing that 'the tune comes through.' "

Parts of the first and second movements in preliminary versions were included as *Funeral March for the Old Order* and *Exits of the Ghosts of the Past* in the score Vaughan Williams contributed in July 1938 to *England's Pleasant Land*, a pageant organized by E. M. Forster for the Dorking and Leith Hill District Preservation Society in the cause, as Kennedy puts it, of "preservation of the countryside from 'bungaloid' growth." The music was played by the band of the Second Battalion of the Duke of Cornwall's Light Infantry. On 31 January 1943, Margery Cullen and Ivy Herbert gave a two-piano reading of the complete symphony from the composer's manuscript at Abinger Hall near Forster's Surrey home for, as Ursula Vaughan Williams recalled, "an audience of three or four." The first public performance was given at a Promenade Concert in the Royal Albert Hall on 24 June 1943 with the composer conducting the London Philharmonic. The original dedication reads, "Without permission and with the sincerest flattery to Jean Sibelius, whose great example is worthy of imitation." In the printed score this was shortened to "Dedicated without permission to Jean Sibelius." The eminent dedicatee first had an opportunity to hear the work on 22 November 1946, when Clarence Raybould conducted a performance in Helsinki.

Two flutes (second doubling piccolo), oboe, English horn, two clarinets, two bassoons, two horns, two trumpets, three trombones, timpani, and strings. Kennedy notes that Vaughan Williams "was adamant that he did not want the two horns to be doubled. He had temporarily authorized doubling but regretted it."

Although the opening of the Fifth Symphony, with its "floating" French horns, is a salute to the similar opening of the Sibelius Fifth, Vaughan Williams never imitated Sibelius as, for instance, William Walton did in his Symphony No. 1. What I take Vaughan Williams's dedication to mean is that for him, as for Sibelius, the symphony was *the* form in which a composer might express his deepest, most complex feelings and realize his richest and most evolved compositional plans. Furthermore, Vaughan Williams had little sympathy for Elgar's music and none for Mahler's ("a tolerable imitation of a composer"), and was composing at a time when the discovery of Nielsen and the recognition of Shostakovich were still in the future; Sibelius, therefore, was inevitably *the* great and inspiring model among his symphony-writing contemporaries.[9]

In 1952, the London County Council invited Vaughan Williams to choose a program of his own music for a concert to celebrate his eightieth birthday. He asked for *A Song of Thanksgiving*, the Fifth Symphony, *Flos Campi*, and *The Sons of Light*.[10] It was inevitable that he should have included a symphony, of which by then he had six to choose from. Why the Fifth? For such an occasion he would naturally have avoided the aggressive—or as one might now say, "confrontational"—Fourth. The Sixth, with its disturbing close, is also not a birthday party piece; besides, it had been getting plenty of attention since its first performance four years earlier. The Fifth, more reticent, less spectacular than its neighbors, is their equal as a profoundly personal utterance, and its association with the cherished *Pilgrim's Progress* must especially have commended it to its author.

Beyond that, I can imagine that even with all nine symphonies in hand, Vaughan Williams would have chosen the Fifth. From the perspective of forty years later, it seems more and more clearly to represent the summit of his achievement as a symphonist, if not indeed of his lifework as a whole. While it stands in extreme contrast to the Fourth, it is not a revocation of that unsettling piece. Rather, it is an absorption of certain aspects of it. The language and the temper are quite different, but the compositional concentration and richness of the Fifth extend the discoveries of the Fourth; also, it was the release of giving way to unbridled vehemence in the Fourth that made possible the profoundly different and, I believe, even greater emotional intensity of the Fifth.

Browsing in Kennedy's *The Works of Ralph Vaughan Williams*, I came across a sad letter the composer wrote in 1942 to a member of the ensemble that had just played his Double Trio for strings: "The piece sounded dull and muddy—you know, I've tried all my life for *clarity* and never achieved it—I always put too many ingredients into the pudding." In its most desperate moments the Fourth Symphony sounds as though Vaughan Williams had surrendered to what he conceived as his inability to achieve

[9] Vaughan Williams's one encounter with Mahler the conductor was overwhelming. At nineteen, after hearing him lead *Tristan*, he could not get to sleep at all that night, and all his life he thought of that evening at Covent Garden as a landmark experience.

[10] *A Song of Thanksgiving*, originally *Thanksgiving for Victory*, for soprano, speaker, chorus, and orchestra, was commissioned and recorded by the BBC in 1944 for broadcast on the day of victory. Most of the text comes from the Bible, some from Shakespeare and Kipling. *Flos campi* (Rose of Sharon, literally *Flower of the Meadow*), a suite for solo viola, wordless chorus, and small orchestra composed in 1925, is one of Vaughan Williams's most magical compositions. *Sons of Light*, composed in 1950, is a cantata for chorus and orchestra on texts by the young poet Ursula Wood, who became Ursula Vaughan Williams not quite four months after the composer's eightieth birthday.

clarity. In the Fifth, cleansed by the violence of the Fourth, he achieved it, and achieved it sublimely: clarity of sound and clarity of spirit.

None of Vaughan Williams's symphonies, not even the *Pastoral,* is more profoundly impregnated than the Fifth with the modal melodic and harmonic world of English folk song and Tudor church music. Also, as Hugh Ottaway pointed out in his perceptive discussion of the nine symphonies for the BBC Music Guides, nowhere else does Vaughan Williams make such powerful use of the contrast between the modes and modern— i.e. post-1650—tonality.

If the two French horns played the first six measures of the Fifth Symphony alone, this would give us an unambiguous D-major beginning, matching the D-major title of the symphony. But they don't. Before they start, cellos and basses have already laid down a floor of C-natural. This destabilizes the gentle horn call, sets it afloat. For the moment, we cannot tell where we are harmonically, and the lyric phrase with which the violins respond to each of the horn calls adds to the mystery. (Without the horns, we would hear what the violins and the low strings play as clear C major.) The low C, embellished by undulations, remains stubbornly present, as does its associated "C-ness." The same is true of the horns and their "D-ness," which is sometimes D minor rather than D major. This double harmonic ground persists for a while, and the slowness of harmonic change, together with the easy tempo and the gentle dynamics, at once creates the atmosphere of calm so characteristic of this symphony.

The harmony darkens as the C in the bass becomes the foundation of a passage in C minor. From this darkness there bursts a glorious light, a violin melody, tranquil yet aspiring, and in the warm sunlight of E major. Some of the churchgoers among you will recognize its first phrase as the "Alleluia!" refrain in *For all the Saints,* one of the four original hymns Vaughan Williams contributed to *The English Hymnal* in 1906—and one of the great English hymn tunes. This ecstatic phrase meant much to Vaughan Williams, for he evoked it in several of his works, among them his Whitman chorus *Toward the Unknown Region* and the exalted Five Mystical Songs on texts by George Herbert.

This is the kind of moment that could be an apotheosis, but less than two minutes into the symphony, that idea makes no sense. Soon, therefore, the brightness is shaded and the first chapter of this Preludio quietly comes to rest. Suddenly the music moves forward at double its original speed. Strings scurry in veiled *pianissimo* and as though at cross-purpose. Behind them, distant wind instruments utter anxious cries. This boils up to an agitated climax. When it subsides we are back with the opening music, the "D" horns over the elaborated "C" bass. This time it leads at once to a grand arrival at the "Alleluia!" in a key as yet untouched, and for full orchestra, *fortissimo* and *tutta forza*. Almost immediately, Vaughan Williams diverts the music to an equally affirmative and even brighter G major. But he is not ready for such a clear-cut close. The Preludio ends quietly, but with the harmonic tension unresolved. The horns, muted and *pianissimo*, reiterate their D-major call; below, still more softly, and continuing beyond the last horn notes, the cellos and violas play C and D together.

The beginning of the Scherzo is—or should be—scarcely audible, and the harmonies are still modal like those of so much of the Preludio. Vaughan Williams said he was "temperamentally allergic" to Beethoven; nonetheless, perhaps in a spirit of vengeful tease, Beethoven sometimes creeps into his music. (Vaughan Williams admitted that he had "cribbed" the theme of Satan's Dance of Triumph in *Job* from the scherzo of Beethoven's F-major Quartet, Opus 135, and the end of the *Sea Symphony's* Scherzo from the *Missa solemnis*.) The mood here suggests both the goblins, as E. M. Forster called them, of the Beethoven Fifth and the peasants in the *Pastoral* (LvB's, not RVW's). The feathery orchestration is a delight.

The Scherzo was a diversion: the Romanza brings us back to the symphony's main emotional line. Of the four movements, this one is most closely connected to *Pilgrim's Progress*. Vaughan Williams inscribed words from that beloved book into the manuscript at the head of this section, though they were not carried over into the printed score: "Upon this place stood a cross, and a little below a sepulchre. Then he said: 'He hath given me rest by his sorrow, and life by his death.'" What the English horn plays over rich but *ppp* string chords is in fact associated with those words in Vaughan Williams's Morality.

This poignant solo is the first of several musical characters we encounter in this stirring movement. The next is an elaborately scored string melody that begins like the first movement's "Alleluia!" and leads to a series of solo woodwind phrases, each of which takes off from wide-ranging arpeggios. The third is an anguished passage in a faster tempo, associated in *Pilgrim's Progress* with Pilgrim's words, "Save me, Lord, my burden is greater than I can bear." These musical ideas are discussed in alternation until they lead to a coda in which a single violin and a solo horn sing celestial variants of, respectively, the string and English-horn themes.

Now, resolution. The Romanza began in C but ended in A major, which puts us on the doorstep of D major. This is the key announced on the symphony's title page but very little in evidence so far—except in the always undermined horn calls of the first movement. Clearly, though, the passacaglia—a series of variations over a repeated bass—intends to be in D major. Now we understand that D major—clear, supported, unambiguous

D major—has not been just a label but an agenda, a goal. One way of describing the symphony's scenario is to say that it recapitulates in thirty-some minutes the evolution in the history of Western music from the church modes to major and minor keys.[11]

Vaughan Williams is anything but strict about his passacaglia design. The variations stride cheerfully along, but with no great concern for precise reiterations of the seven-measure bass. Also the countermelody that the violins contribute in the first variation—a distant relative of the great melodies in the finales of Beethoven's Ninth and Brahms's First symphonies—eventually becomes more prominent than the bass itself. The scoring is exceptionally lovely, especially the use of solo viola and solo cello to double full sections of strings at the unison or the octave. With a splendid sense of timing, Vaughan Williams brings back the D-major horn calls, now in blazing *fortissimo*. One more "Alleluia" sounds, this one from the hymn *All Creatures of Our God and King*. Its sounds of praise rise skyward. Then, in peaceful meditation of the countermelody, the music arrives at its destination: a luminous D-major close, hushed, beatific, with an ineffable sense of peace. Here, if anywhere in music, is transcendence.

Symphony in E minor (No. 6)

> *Allegro*
> *Moderato*
> *Scherzo: Allegro vivace*
> *Epilogue: Moderato*
> (To quote the composer: "Each of the first three [movements] has its tail attached to the head of its neighbor.")

Using some material he had sketched in 1943 for a movie score, Vaughan Williams began this symphony "about 1944"—this is his own cautious for-

---

[11] Carl Nielsen, Vaughan Williams's slightly older contemporary and fellow-symphonist par excellence comes to mind here, inasmuch as he made the conquest of a particular key the central task of each of his mature symphonies. Vaughan Williams hardly knew Nielsen's music, but a revelatory performance by Barbirolli of the Symphony No. 5 that he heard toward the end of his life gave him great pleasure. It is an interesting coincidence that Nielsen used a wordless solo soprano and baritone in his Symphony No. 3, the *Espansiva*, just as Vaughan Williams had used a wordless solo soprano in his Third Symphony, the *Pastoral*. I can imagine that the two men, not dissimilar in their mixture of simplicity, crustiness, and willingness to get their hands dirty, would have found each other distinctly *simpatico* had they ever met.

mulation—and completed it in 1947. On 14 July 1946, Michael Mullinar, who had been Vaughan Williams's student at the Royal College of Music, gave a piano reading for a small gathering at the composer's house in London, and on 5 June 1947 did the same thing for students and teachers at the RCM. On 16 December that year, Sir Adrian Boult and the BBC Symphony read through the work in the BBC studios at Maida Vale; the first public performance was given by the same musicians in the Royal Albert Hall, London, on 21 April 1948. At the beginning of 1950, Vaughan Williams revised the Scherzo, clarifying some of the orchestration as well as adding a new countertheme for brass in a couple of places. The new version did not have a formal unveiling, but Boult recorded it with the London Symphony on 15 February that year. Vaughan Williams dedicated the work to Michael Mullinar in gratitude for his early piano readthroughs.

Two flutes and piccolo, two oboes and English horn, two clarinets, tenor saxophone (doubling bass clarinet), two bassoons and contrabassoon, four horns, three trumpets (fourth trumpet ad lib.), three trombones, tuba, timpani, snare drum, bass drum, triangle, cymbals, xylophone, harp (doubled if possible), and strings.

Ending, as it does, in eleven or twelve minutes of chill, unbroken *pianissimo*, the Sixth Symphony hardly seems a piece designed for "success," yet the reception at the first performance was overwhelming, and it took only a little over two years for the work to achieve 100 performances. Vaughan Williams's pleasure at having, as he liked to say, "rung the bell" and "done the real thing" was offset by the annoyance of having people insistently impose their extramusical interpretations on this work. In the 1930s he had had a hard time persuading some people that the Fourth Symphony was not political and moral commentary about Hitler and Mussolini, and that it really should not be subtitled *Europe 1935*. In 1948, the year the Sixth Symphony came, Hiroshima was a recent memory, the Soviet Union had just cut off road and rail traffic between Berlin and the West, and nuclear war was coming to be an ever-present threat. But no, Vaughan Williams said, his bleak finale was *not* a depiction of a world flattened by The Bomb, and when Frank Howes, the music critic of *The Times,* referred to the Sixth as his "War Symphony" (with capital W), the composer was aroused to real fury.

But no question, the Sixth Symphony is a disturbing piece, full of anguish, and it begins with a cry. In defiance of its title, "Symphony in E minor," it begins resolutely in F minor. Vaughan Williams can of course ram an E in the bass under the A-flat which the orchestra reaches on the second beat, thus claiming that the A-flat is really G-sharp and that we are in E. This is in fact what he does, but it fails to settle the matter. As Vaughan Williams himself points out, the music "[rushes] down and up again through all the keys for which there is time in two bars"; in other words, the harmony is exceedingly restless and unsettled, and F minor remains an assertive presence. The mood, for the moment at least, is savage.

What Vaughan Williams calls "fussy" sixteenth-notes have been prominent from the beginning, and these continue while violins, woodwinds, and horn introduce an impassioned new melody. It is immediately repeated in the bass with the fussy sixteenths on top. When this agitation subsides, an oddly saucy accompaniment starts up, to which various woodwinds soon add a tune with a stammer. For a moment the sound gets to be quite Broadway, partly because the saxophone climbs into a high register where it is extremely prominent. There is one more theme to come, a spacious D-major tune that sounds quite like the old familiar Vaughan Williams. The saucy accompaniment continues right through this. Both melodies, the hesitant and the spacious, get some more play, after which there is a recapitulation—"just enough," says Vaughan Williams, "to show that this is a Symphony not a symphonic poem." The spacious tune makes one more appearance, tranquillo, with harp accompaniment, and also in E major, which serves to settle the accumulated harmonic tension, though there is continuing argument between E major and E minor. The close is quiet.

The final E in the cellos and basses hangs over into the first measure of the second movement. In 1943, Vaughan Williams wrote the music for a film called *The Flemish Farm*, which *Halliwell's Film Guide* describes as a "tolerable wartime flagwaver." Not all of Vaughan Williams's score made its way into the soundtrack, and he rescued two of the out-takes for the Sixth Symphony. This second movement's first theme, a slow and sinister march, is one of them. Because of its rhythm, the studio orchestra always referred to it as "two hot sausages."

Ex. 1

A drumroll and a fanfare introduce an unharmonized *pianissimo* passage for the strings, which builds, then recedes. Suddenly the trumpets and timpani begin to insist on the "sausages" rhythm of Ex. 1. When we first heard this, it was part of a theme; now it takes on a life of its own and is bent on destroying whatever thematic or other musical activity is going on.[12] It cows the orchestra into silence; trumpets and drums, again *pianissimo* after their domineering triple *forte*, appear to have the last word. The English horn muses for a moment on the unharmonized string theme, but under its last notes, the persistent, destructive rhythm, now in the sullen, dark colors of timpani, bass drum, and pizzicato low strings, reminds us that it is still there, that this nightmare could return.

The English horn's last long C-flat constitutes the bridge into the third movement. It is a sardonic Shostakovich scherzo, polyphonic in texture, and based on a theme that climbs by great leaps and bounds. High woodwinds contribute a more straightforward theme with running sixteenth-notes. The saxophone adds a sleazy tune by way of a trio, and here I must quote Vaughan Williams, who was clearly in a very good mood when he wrote his program note for the first performance:

> [The saxophone tune] is repeated loud by the full orchestra. (Constant Lambert tells us that the only thing to do with a folk tune is to play it soft and repeat it loud. This is not a folk tune but the same difficulty seems to crop up.)[13]
>
> When [this] episode is over, the woodwind experiment as to how the [first theme] will sound upside down but the brass are angry and insist on playing it the right way up, so for a bit the two go on together and to the delight of everyone including the composer the two versions fit, so there is nothing to do now but to continue, getting more excited till the [saxophone] tune comes back very loud and twice as slow.[14]

This time it is the bass clarinet which, descending through two octaves, builds the bridge into the Epilogue. Vaughan Williams describes this music as "[drifting] about contrapuntally with occasional whiffs of theme. . . ." The two sections of violins lead off, all muted. The firsts show a definite bias toward F minor, the seconds then providing something like

---

[12] Nielsen, whose music Vaughan Williams only got to know later, and then very slightly, does something similar—and much more ruthless—in his Symphony No. 5. There is a lot of temperamental affinity between these two composers.

[13] Constant Lambert (1905–51) was a superlatively gifted English composer, conductor, and writer who had studied with Vaughan Williams at the Royal College of Music. The quip Vaughan Williams alludes to comes from *Music Ho! A Study of Music in Decline* (1934), a recklessly polemic but brilliant book of criticism. Schoenberg and Stravinsky are left for dead in the alley; Sibelius is hailed as the great symphonist of his time. Schoenberg shared Lambert's view on the uselessness of folk song as symphonic material. —M.S.

[14] Kennedy, *The Works of Ralph Vaughan Williams.*

an E-major/minor corrective. After a time, flutes play the first violins' theme in longer notes so that it sounds rather like a cantus firmus or chorale. The muted brass sigh three times, and a solo cello, unmuted but of course still *pianissimo*, responds to their dejection with a new musical idea. The oboe is the instrument that feels most free to sing out expressively in melodies of wide compass. The sounds themselves become ghostly, with string tremolandos and bell-like harmonics on the harp.

After one last outburst—but of course a *pianissimo* outburst by the oboe—the strings take the symphony to its end. Vaughan Williams wrote that he "never had any conscience about cribbing," and I suspect in these last measures he was cribbing from Strauss's *Also sprach Zarathustra.* That work ends in a strange back-and-forth between high instruments playing chords of B major, and basses punctuating those chords with C's. Vaughan Williams settles into an uncertain seesawing between chords of E-flat major and E minor, which have G as a note in common. The last chord, which finally disappears into the distance, is E minor, that being the symphony's keynote (just as in *Zarathustra* C, which is the keynote there, has the last word), but the E-minor chord is in its most unstable distribution, with B in the bass, and so the effect is anything but definite. The conductor Andrew Davis, comparing this "unanswered question" close with the oscillations that usher Berg's *Wozzeck* into silence, has observed that the Sixth Symphony "should not end with a sense of rest. A performance that sounds final is not a good performance."

"It never seems to occur to people that a man might just want to write a piece of music," said an exceedingly irritated Vaughan Williams to Roy Douglas, the musician who helped him in his later years with the preparation and revising of scores. Once he hinted that Prospero's farewell in *The Tempest* might provide a clue to his intentions. Was he remembering Beethoven's possibly teasing advice to Schindler—"Read Shakespeare's *Tempest*"—in answer to a question about the meaning of the D-minor Piano Sonata, Opus 31, no. 2? It would be very like him. Then again, as the English critic Stephen Johnson has pointed, the harmonies here are the same as those in his 1951 setting for an *a cappella* chorus of Prospero's speech.

> Our revels now are ended. These our actors,
> As I foretold you, were all spirits, and
> Are melted into air, into thin air:
> And, like the baseless fabric of this vision,
> The cloud-capp'd towers, the gorgeous palaces,
> The solemn temples, the great globe itself,
> Yea, all which it inherit, shall dissolve,

And, like this insubstantial pageant faded,
Leave not a rack behind. We are such stuff
As dreams are made on; and our little life
Is rounded with a sleep.

Does it help? I don't know. The hushed music speaks so eloquently and so disturbingly on its own. But of course it never hurts to read eleven lines of Shakespeare.

William Walton

William Walton

William Turner Walton, knighted by King George VI in 1951, was born in Oldham, Lancashire, England, on 29 March 1902 and died at Forio d'Ischia, Italy, on 18 March 1983.

Symphony No. 1

Allegro assai
Presto, con malizia
Andante, con malinconia
Maestoso—Brioso ed ardentemente—Vivacissimo—Maestoso

On 18 October 1931, Walton played what is now the first theme of the slow movement (but in an allegro version) to his friends Hubert and Dora Foss, though at this time he did not yet know that it would find its home in his first symphony. In 1932, work on the symphony began in earnest, but the finale was not completed until 30 August 1935. The first three movements were introduced by the London Symphony on 3 December 1934, and the first performance of the complete work was given by the BBC Symphony on 6 November 1935. The Chicago Symphony gave the American premiere on 23 January 1936. All these performances were conducted by Sir Hamilton Harty. The dedication is to Baroness Imma Doernberg.

Two flutes (second doubling piccolo), two oboes, two clarinets, two bassoons, four horns, three trumpets, three trombones, tuba, timpani (two players), tam-tam, cymbals, snare drum, and strings.

Walton was thirty when he took on his first symphony. He was already an experienced and immensely successful composer as well as obviously a brilliant one. A string quartet, which has not survived in the repertory, Walton himself being one of its chief detractors, put his name on the map internationally when it was selected as one of three works to represent England at the first festival of the International Society for Contemporary Music at Salzburg in 1923. Still more significant was the first public hearing that same year by an audience part delighted and part scandalized of a more personal musical statement, *Façade*, the recitation to dazzlingly apt chamber-musical accompaniment of Edith Sitwell's crackling and nostalgic poems.

There followed the vigorous *Portsmouth Point* Overture (1925) after a print by the early nineteenth-century caricaturist Thomas Rowlandson;[1] a Sinfonia concertante for orchestra with piano obbligato (1927); the Viola Concerto (1929), still the finest example of the genre; and the uninhibited big-screen oratorio *Belshazzar's Feast* (1931), for which Osbert Sitwell had drawn a libretto from Psalms and the Book of Daniel. By the time Walton completed his Symphony No. 1, he had also taken his plunge into the activity that would eventually bring him his widest audience, the writing of movie scores. His first was *Escape Me Never*, an Elisabeth Bergner weepie; the most famous of his later ones were *Major Barbara* and Laurence Olivier's Shakespeare films, *As You Like It, Henry V, Hamlet*, and *Richard III*.

The Symphony No. 1 is the culmination of Walton's conquest of maturity. I wrote an earlier version of this note for a Boston Symphony performance by Colin Davis, who contended that, like Humperdinck and Britten, Walton was a one-work composer. Outside of the "one work," *Hansel and Gretel*, I don't know my Humperdinck well enough to argue the point, but I felt—and still believed—that Davis's contention is almost as untenable for Walton as it is for Britten.[2] At the same time, one can make a strong case that the Symphony No. 1 is at a level of compositional ambi-

[1] In 1921 Walton had written but subsequently destroyed a Pedagogic Overture *Doctor Syntax* named for a character who appears in many of Rowlandson's drawings.
[2] For Davis, Britten's "one work" is the opera *Peter Grimes*, of which he has made a magnificent recording. Davis and Walton might have found common ground in their shared dislike of Britten. Actually Walton's feelings about Britten, which contained some element of homophobia, blew hot and cold. In his biography of Walton, Michael Kennedy recounts that when Walton and Yehudi Menuhin went into a Lucerne music store and found a display promoting a forthcoming production of a Britten opera, Walton promptly turned the large photograph of his younger colleague face to the wall.

tion, concentration, and sheer human urgency and strength Walton would not reach again. The somber Cello Concerto (1956) is an impressive work, quite moving in its pessimism, but it comes nowhere near the Symphony No. 1 in intellectual and psychic energy. Other later works of masterly facture such as the Violin Concerto which Walton wrote for Heifetz in 1939 and his Chaucer opera *Troilus and Cressida* (1951) are not devoid of sentiment or charm, but their sugar content is high for many a digestive system.

Walton's father was a teacher of singing, and it was from him that William received his first instruction in music. At ten he entered Christ Church Cathedral School at Oxford and was sufficiently precocious to matriculate as an undergraduate at sixteen. This was not, however, the beginning of a distinguished academic career. Walton flunked out, or, as the English so much more nicely say, was sent down, but not before he had read many scores and formed some crucial friendships, particularly with literary people such as Ronald Firbank and the three Sitwells. As a musician he was essentially self-taught, though once in a while he went for advice to Busoni, to Ernest Ansermet, and specifically on conducting, to Eugene Goossens. And as Walton's first biographer, Frank Howes, put it, "the Oxford connexion was ratified many years later by the conferment of an honorary D.MUS. in 1942 and an honorary Studentship of Christ Church."

David Cox has aptly written that "Walton began like a seventh member of Les Six. The style was marked 'continental,' pointed with wit and satire, bursting with exuberance. Nothing folksy." But the Andante of the *Sinfonia concertante* introduces a new tone of voice, a new color and sentiment, and what was begun there is pursued and splendidly fulfilled in the Viola Concerto. Buoyed no doubt by the success of *Belshazzar's Feast* at the 1931 Leeds Festival, Walton felt ready to commit himself to an uncompromisingly grand and serious statement.

But it was one thing to have ideas, quite another to figure out how most effectively to make them part of a forty-two-minute symphonic argument. In the course of Walton's wrestling with the material, ideas wandered from one movement to another, changing tempo and character as they went. Moreover, Walton was neither the first composer nor the last who found himself awed at the prospect of The First Symphony. At any rate, progress was slow, but with the encouragement and the specific criticism and advice of the pianist Angus Morrison and of Hubert Foss, an excellent writer who worked for Walton's publisher, Oxford University Press, Walton persevered.[3]

Sir Hamilton Harty announced a March 1934 premiere of the work

---

[3] One of Foss's assignments at OUP was to prepare Tovey's writings for publication.

as part of his first season with the London Symphony, and Adrian Boult hoped to give the second performance with the BBC Symphony two months later. But Walton had to dash the hopes of both conductors. Work had ground to a halt. He was ill; furthermore, he had been depressed since being abandoned by his lover, Imma Doernberg, referred to as "Willie's Baroness" by most of Walton's acquaintances.[4] Reluctant to deal with the irritated members of the London Symphony in the face of a second postponement, Walton permitted Harty to give a partial premiere. (Accounts, including Walton's own, vary as to how willing or how pressured he was in agreeing to this arrangement.) It was a huge success, and with no objection from the composer, Malcolm Sargent gave two more performances of the unfinished work four months later.

Ironically, this success made it even more difficult for Walton to go ahead with the finale. Kennedy writes:

> He still [in April 1935] did not know what to do about the middle of the movement. According to Walton himself, he rang up [Constant] Lambert, who suggested a fugue. "But I don't know how to write one." "There are a couple of rather good pages on the subject in Grove's Dictionary." So he read the Grove entry and wrote the fugue. But using it still worried him, perhaps because Vaughan Williams had also resorted to a fugue in the finale of his Fourth Symphony, which had its first performance on 10 April 1935.[5]

Still, on 30 August, Walton left a message for Foss that the symphony was finished, and Harty was able to introduce it two months later. Critical response was divided at first as to whether the finale was an afterthought—somehow it had not been made clear earlier that the three-movement version was an unfinished symphony—or whether it was the strongest part of the work. The latter view came to prevail, and the Walton First was perceived by many as the finest English symphony—depending on how the perceivers felt about Vaughan Williams—since the two by Elgar.

To English musicians and the English audience in the early 1930s, it

---

[4] Imma Doernberg, daughter of Prince and Princess Alexander von Erbach-Schoenberg and widow of Baron Hans-Karl von Doernberg, lived with Walton from 1931 until the spring of 1933. Michael Kennedy reports in his biography of the composer that Tibor Csato, the Hungarian doctor for whom Doernberg left Walton, "later said [that] Walton had been impotent at this time." It is remarkable under the circumstances that when the Symphony No. 1 was finally completed Walton still dedicated it to Baroness Doernberg. He quickly began a new relationship with Viscountess Alice Wimborne, which continued until her death in 1948.

[5] Michael Kennedy: *Portrait of Walton* (Oxford: Oxford University Press, 1989). Constant Lambert, a dazzlingly gifted composer and conductor, was another member of the Sitwell circle and a close friend of Walton's. His razor-sharp reading of some of the poems of *Façade* on a recording with the composer conducting and Edith Sitwell as the other speaker is unsurpassed—to my ear, unapproached. —M.S.

was above all the work of Jean Sibelius that represented the ideal of con-temporary symphonic writing. The point was made with special force in Constant Lambert's *Music Ho! A Study of Music in Decline,* a widely read and much discussed book that came out in 1934. A musical acquaintance once challenged me to write about the Walton First without mentioning Sibelius. It is not to be done. As David Cox notes, Walton's early music is in every way far from Sibelius, but his move toward the grand and seri-ous statement had meant, among other things, a move toward the Finnish master. Sibelius's concept of symphony is insistently present here, as are some of the techniques through which he realized his ideas. For all that, Walton's Symphony No. 1 is a free, strong, individual utterance, as far beyond mere imitation as, say, the Brahms First is in its relationship to Beethoven. Not many would wish to call Walton one of the great twentieth-century composers, but the claim that his First Symphony is one of the great twentieth-century symphonies is not excessive.

Walton begins this way: to a *pianissimo* timpani roll on B-flat, four horns, still softer and entering one at a time, add more B-flats, an F, and a G. Meanwhile, also in ghostly triple *piano,* an oboe melody unfolds over this in uncannily slow motion, its initial D-flat identifying the key as B-flat minor. This melody and what proceeds from it is a wide-ranging affair; nonetheless, the harmony stubbornly stays anchored to B-flat. When that B-flat at last yields, it is to a G pedal of twelve measures, whose purpose is to prepare the appearance of the next of Walton's firm harmonic moorings, this time C.

I have described this in some detail because no one feature of Wal-ton's First Symphony is more characteristic than these massive pedals. Walton got them from Sibelius, but he extends them so remarkably that they can remind us of music he is unlikely to have known in 1932 and perhaps never knew, the organa of the twelfth-century masters of music at Notre Dame in Paris, compositions whose magnifying-glass basses move rarely, but always with a sense of cataclysm.[6] Walton's huge pedal-points achieve two things: by their very physicality they convey the sense of largeness for which he strives, and they provide strong anchors in the face of some intensely dissonant buffeting; at the same time, they themselves are responsible for some of the dissonance. Something that comes across powerfully and engagingly is Walton's joy in dissonance as a stimulant whose potency is far from exhausted. The ideas with which the first move-ment is built are tightly related to one another. The whole movement, with its expansive development and drastically compressed recapitulation, suggests the effect of a single intense, enraged climax.

[6] They might also send our minds forward to the 1970s and the music of Steve Reich.

In the scherzo, more rage and, as the tempo marking tells us, malice. Rhythmic patterns shift between the mercurial and the obsessive. We notice, as well, Walton's pleasure in virtuosity. From both players and conductor he demands the utmost in concentration and skill.

The melancholy Andante, which cost Walton more time than the first two movements together, is full of virtuoso writing in another, nonaggressive sense. The feeling at the beginning, for example, that the C-sharp pedal is both absolutely still and vibrantly alive is achieved by the most fastidious and subtle distribution of colors and accents across horns and much-divided strings, all muted. In this inconclusive, quietly pained music we hear further manifestations of Walton's preference for growth and variation as opposed to literal restatements.

As I have noted, the problem of the finale at first stymied Walton, as it had so many composers from Schubert on. But he conceived, in the end, a strong design in which a majestic music stands at the beginning and end, with three kinds of quicker, more nervously excitable activity accounting for most of the span: first, ardent writing in Walton's violent *Belshazzar* manner; then a fugue on a leaping, long, ten-measure subject; after that, something scherzando in faster, shorter bars. The two timpanists enter with a view to breaking this music up.[7] They succeed, and their challenge opens the way for the triumphal peroration.

---

[7]Walton did not know Nielsen's Fourth Symphony, *The Inextinguishable* (1916), with its pair of warring, mayhem-creating timpanists.